2nd Edition

SOCIOLOGY A2

for AQA

Stephen Moore   Dave Aiken   Steve Chapman

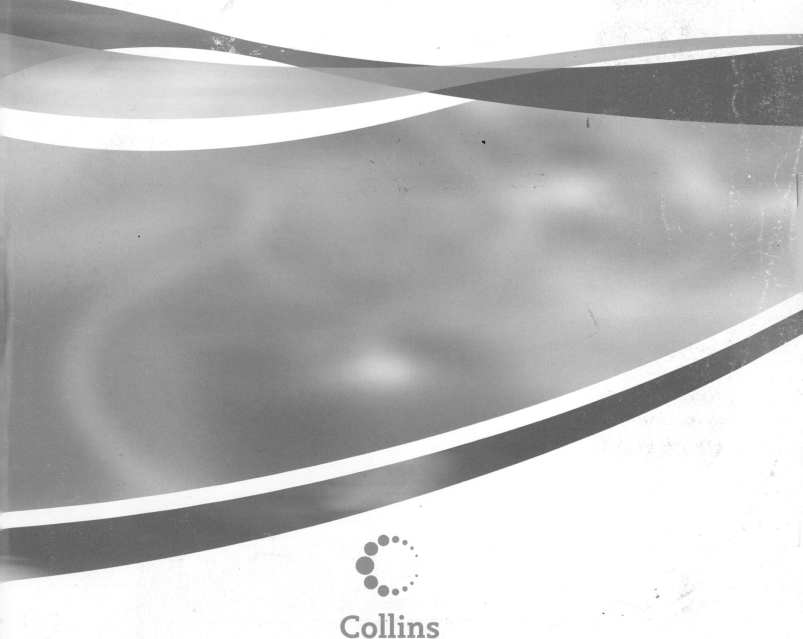

Collins

An imprint of HarperCollins*Publishers*

William Collins' dream of knowledge for all began with the publication of his first book in 1819. A self-educated mill worker, he not only enriched millions of lives, but also founded a flourishing publishing house. Today, staying true to this spirit, Collins books are packed with inspiration, innovation and practical expertise. They place you at the centre of a world of possibility and give you exactly what you need to explore it.

Collins. Do more.

Published by Collins
An imprint of HarperCollins*Publishers* Limited
77–85 Fulham Palace Road
Hammersmith
London W6 8JB

Browse the complete Collins catalogue
at **www.collinseducation.com**

© HarperCollinsPublishers Limited 2006

Reprint 10 9 8 7 6 5 4 3

ISBN 13 978 0 00 720064 1
ISBN 10 0 00 720064 1

British Cataloguing in Publication Data.
A cataloguing record for this publication is available from the British Library.

Commissioned by Thomas Allain-Chapman
Consultant editor Peter Langley
Project managed by Hugh Hillyard-Parker
Production by Sarah Robinson
Edited by Ros Connelly, Carol Schaessens
Cover design by Blue Pig Design
Internal design by Patricia Briggs
Typesetting by Hugh Hillyard-Parker
Figures typeset by Liz Gordon
Cartoons by Oxford Designers and Illustrators
Photo research by Suzanne Williams
Index by Indexing Specialists (UK) Ltd, Hove, UK
Printed and bound by Imago

Author dedications

Dave Aiken: As always, thanks especially to Maggie for her generosity of spirit, capacity for hiding resentment and seemingly limitless practical and emotional support and love. Thank you to the lovely Leo for reminding me that there is life beyond work. Thanks to the grown-up kids, Laurie and Amelia, for getting on with their own lives (congratulations to both for their excellent degree grades), to Steve Chapman and Pete Langley for their professional support, and to the Collins team for their patience.

In loving memory of Audrey Aiken (1930–2002)

Steve Chapman: For Fiona

CONTENTS

Sociology A2 for AQA

BILLIONS OF PEOPLE IN THE WORLD BELIEVE IN SOMETHING that has never been proved to exist. Many of these people base their lifestyles, values and morals on these beliefs. In fact, whole societies are sometimes structured around religious belief.

It's not surprising that sociologists take a strong interest in religion. They wonder about the role of religion in society: Why does it exist? What effects does it have? These issues make up the main parts of Topics 1 and 2.

People express their religious beliefs in many different ways. Some are members of huge faiths whose followers are spread across the world, while others express their spiritual beliefs in more personal ways – by consulting tarot cards or crystals, for example. Topic 3 focuses on organized religions and Topic 4 on the growth of what have become known as 'new religious movements'.

Religious belief and participation are not free from the divisions that cut across other aspects of social life. Topic 5 looks at gender and religion, including the role of women in religious organizations, feminism and religion, and explanations of women's high rates of religious participation and belief. The focus of Topic 6 is ethnicity and religion – in particular, the importance of religion in the lives of members of ethnic-minority groups in Britain.

In order to assess the extent to which religion has increased or declined in significance, it is important to clarify what precisely we mean by 'religion' and genuinely religious practice and belief. We also need to explore new trends that make comparisons with the past problematic. This is the focus of Topic 7.

Finally, Topic 8 asks whether religion is in decline in a world that seems to emphasize scientific explanations and rational ways of thinking. The evidence for and against secularization is considered and the difficulties of generalizing about this complex issue are acknowledged.

OCRspecification	topics	pages
Religious institutions		
Different theories of religion	Functionalist and Marxist theories are covered in Topic 1. Topic 2 focuses on a Weberian view. Feminist views are considered in Topic 5 and postmodern perspectives in Topics 3, 4 and 8	2–31 42–47
The role of religion as a conservative force and as an initiator of change	Covered in Topic 1 and, in particular, Topic 2	2–13
Cults, sects, denominations and churches and their relationship to religious activity	Covered in Topics 3 and 4	14–25
Explanations of the relationship between religious beliefs, religious organizations and social groups	Covered in Topics 5 and 6	26–37
Different definitions and explanations of the nature and extent of secularization	Covered in Topics 7 and 8	38–47

Religion as a conservative influence on society: functionalist & Marxist approaches

gettingyouthinking

Above left: A funeral

Above right: God can both explain poverty and offer hope of salvation from it.

Right: Members of a church meet for coffee in the vestry.

1 **What purpose does religion serve for the individuals in each picture?**

2 **What might happen to these individuals if religion suddenly ceased to exist?**

3 **Suggest some ways in which religion helps people in modern society cope with destabilizing influences in their lives.**

Sociologists who have studied the role of religion in society often tend to fall into one of two broad camps:

1 Those who see religion as a **conservative** force – 'Conservative' means keeping things the way they are. These sociologists see religion as a force for stability and order. They may well favour a functionalist (see Unit 4, p. 158) or a Marxist point of view (see Unit 4, p. 160).

2 Those who see religion as a force for social change – Supporters of this position point to the role of religion in encouraging societies to change. They may be influenced by the writings of Max Weber or by some neo-Marxist thinkers.

This first topic examines the first of these groups of thinkers.

Inhibiting change

Both functionalists and traditional Marxists adopt the view that religion inhibits change – that is, they identify a similar role for religion. However, functionalists tend to view this as a 'good' thing, while Marxists view it as a 'bad' thing.

Functionalist approaches

The key concern of functionalist writing on religion is the contribution that religion makes to the wellbeing of society – its contribution to social stability and value consensus. In his famous work, *The Elementary Forms of Religious Life*, Durkheim

(1912) relates religion to the overall structure of society. He based his work on a study of **totemism** among Australian aborigines. (A totem is an object, usually an animal or plant, which has deep symbolic significance.) He argued that totemism represents the most elementary form of religion.

The totem is believed to have divine properties that separate it from those animals or plants that may be eaten or harvested.

There are a number of ceremonies and rituals involved in worship of the totem which serve to bring the tribe together as a group and consequently to reaffirm their group identity.

Durkheim defined religion in terms of a distinction between the **sacred** (holy or spiritual) and the **profane** (unspiritual, non-religious, ordinary). Sacred people, objects and symbols are set apart from ordinary life, and access to them is usually forbidden or restricted in some way.

Why is the totem so sacred?

Durkheim suggests that the totem is sacred because it is symbolically representative of the group itself. It stands for the values of the community, who, by worshipping the totem, are effectively 'worshipping' their society.

Durkheim's distinction between the sacred and profane, is, in effect, the distinction between people and society. The relationship between god and humans (power and dependence) outlined in most religions is a reflection of the relationship between humans and society. It is not god who makes us behave, and punishes our misdemeanours, but society.

Durkheim argues that religion is rarely a matter of individual belief. Most religions involve collective worship, ceremony and rituals, during which group solidarity is affirmed or heightened. An individual is temporarily elevated from their normal profane existence to a higher level, in which they can recognize divine influences or gods. These divine influences are recognized as providing the moral guidance for the particular social group concerned. For Durkheim, however, gods are merely the expression of the influence over the individual of what he calls the '**collective conscience**' – the basic shared beliefs, values, traditions and norms that make the society work. The continual act of group worship and celebration through ritual and ceremony serves to forge group identity, creating cohesion and solidarity. God is actually a recognition that society is more important than the individual.

In maintaining social solidarity, religion acts as a conservative force; when it fails to perform this function, new ideas may emerge that effectively become the new religion. Thus, Durkheim regarded **nationalism** and **communism** as examples of the new religions of industrial society, taking over from Christianity, but performing the same essential functions. Durkheim and other functionalists are not saying that religion does not change – clearly its *form* does – but what remains unchanged is its *function*, and that, essentially, is to offer support for the status quo. Politics and its associated rituals, flag waving, parades and so on, are the new forms by which collective sentiments are symbolically expressed. Consequently, religion, in one form or another, is a necessary feature of any society.

The functions of religion in modern society

The key functions of religion can be summarized as follows.

Socialization

In modern societies, the major function of religion is to socialize society's members into a value consensus by investing values with a sacred quality. These values become 'moral codes' – beliefs that society agrees to hold in the highest regard and socialize children into. Consequently, such codes regulate our social behaviour – for example, the Ten Commandments (from the Old Testament) are a good example of a set of moral codes that have influenced both formal controls, such as the law (e.g. 'Thou shalt not kill/steal'), as well as informal controls, such as moral disapproval (e.g. 'Thou shalt not commit adultery').

Social integration and solidarity

Encouraging collective worship is regarded by functionalists as particularly important for the integration of society, since it enables members to express their shared values and strengthens group unity. By worshipping together, people develop a sense of commitment and belonging; individuals are united into a group with shared values, so that social solidarity is reinforced, deviant behaviour restrained and social change restricted. Also, religion and its associated rituals foster the development of the collective conscience or moral community, which helps people to understand the reality of social relations, communicate with others and establish obligations between people.

Civil religion

In modern societies, ritual and ceremony are common aspects of national loyalties. In the UK, street parades, swearing allegiance to Queen and country, and being part of a flag-waving crowd all remind us of our relationship to the nation.

This idea has been developed by some functionalist thinkers into the theory of '**civil religion**'. This refers to a situation where sacred qualities are attached to aspects of the society itself. Hence, religion in one form or another continues to be an essential feature of society. This is very evident in America where the concept of civil religion was first developed by Bellah (1970), himself American. America is effectively a nation of immigrants with a wide range of co-existing cultural and religious traditions. What does unite them, however, is their faith in 'Americanism'. While traditional religion binds individuals to their various communities, civil religion in America unites the nation. Although civil religion need not involve a connection with supernatural beliefs, according to Bellah, God and Americanism appear to go hand in hand. American coins remind their users 'In God we trust', and the phrase 'God bless America' is a common concluding remark to an important speech. Even the phrase 'President of the United States of America', Bellah argues, imbues the country's leader with an almost divine quality. The God that Americans are talking about, however, is not allied to a particular faith; he is, in a Durkheimian sense, the God of (or that is) America.

focus on civil religion

1 To what extent can the terms 'sacred' and 'profane' be applied to the situations above?

2 How can the situations in the photos be seen to:

(a) strengthen social solidarity?

(b) act as a conservative influence?

3 To what extent do you agree that the concept of civil religion is helpful in understanding religion today?

4 How might Marxists argue that, like religion, football rivalry diverts the attention of the working class from the real opposition, the ruling class?

Bellah, however, suggests that even civil religion is in decline, as people now rank personal gratification above obligation to others and there is, in his view, a deepening cynicism about established social institutions. However, the events of 11 September 2001 and their aftermath have undoubtedly led to a reaffirmation of Americanism and its associated symbolism.

Preventing anomie

Durkheim's main fear for modern industrial society was that individuals would become less integrated and their behaviour less regulated. Should this become widespread, **anomie** (a state of confusion and normlessness) could occur whereby society could not function because its members would not know how they should behave relative to one another.

Religious and civil ceremony prevents this happening by encouraging an awareness of common membership of an entity greater than, and supportive of, the individual. Some religious movements seem to have grown in times of social upheaval when anomie may have been occurring. For example, the industrial revolution in Britain was marked by a series of revivalist movements such as Methodism and Presbyterianism.

Coming to terms with life-changing events

Functionalist thinkers, such as Malinowski (1954) and Parsons (1965), see religion as functioning to relieve the stress and anxieties created by life crises such as birth, puberty, marriage and death. In other words, such events can undermine people's commitment to the wider society and therefore social order. Religion gives such events meaning, helping people come to terms with change. Most societies have evolved religious 'rites of passage' ceremonies in order to minimize this social disruption. For example, the death of a loved one can cause the bereaved to feel helpless and alone, unable to cope with life. However, the funeral ceremony allows people to adjust to their new situation. The group mourning also reaffirms the fact that the group outlives the passing of particular individuals and is there to support its members.

Criticisms of functionalism

● Church attendance is declining in most Western societies such as the UK. It is difficult to see how religion can be functioning to socialize the majority of society's members into morality and social integration, if only a minority of people regularly attend church.

● Some have argued that Durkheim's analysis is based on flawed evidence: he misunderstood both totemism and the behaviour of the aboriginal tribes themselves.

● Religion can have a negative effect on societies – it can be dysfunctional. Rather than binding people together, many of the world's conflicts have been caused by religion, e.g. in Northern Ireland and the Middle East.

● Much functionalist analysis is based upon the idea that a society has one religion, but many modern societies are multicultural, multifaith societies.

● The idea that religion can be seen as the worship of society depends on an assumption that worship is a collective act – people joining together to celebrate their god or gods. However, religious belief may be expressed individually (see Topic 3).

Durkheim did recognize that religion had a strong social control function, as the following quotation illustrates.

>> *Religion instructed the humble to be content with their situation, and, at the same time, it taught them that the social order is providential; that it is god himself who has determined each one's share, religion gave man a perception of a world beyond this earth where everything would be rectified; this prospect made inequalities seem less noticeable, it stopped men from feeling aggrieved.* >> (Durkheim 1912)

Marxists take this argument much further. They argue that religion, far from being an instrument of social solidarity, is an instrument of social control and exploitation.

Marxism and religion

The following quotations provide a summary of the classic Marxist position on religion.

>> *Religion is the sigh of the oppressed creature, the sentiment of a heartless world ... the soul of soulless conditions. It is the opium of the people.* >> (Marx 1844)

>> *Religion is a kind of spiritual gin in which the slaves of capital drown their human shape and their claims to any decent life.* >> (Lenin 1965)

Like Durkheim, Marx also argued that religion was a conservative force in society. However, he did not agree that this force was essentially positive and beneficial to society. Rather, Marx argues that the primary function of religion is to reproduce, maintain and justify class inequality. In other words, religion is an **ideological apparatus**, which serves to reflect ruling-class ideas and interests. Moreover, Marx describes religion as the 'opium of the people', because in his view it prevents the working classes from becoming aware of the true nature of their exploitation by the ruling class and doing anything about it. Instead, they see it all as 'God's will' and passively accept things as they are, remaining in a state of false consciousness. Religion acts as an opiate – a pacifying drug – in that it does not solve any problems people may have, but merely dulls the pain and, therefore, argued Marx, most religious movements originate in the oppressed classes.

However, as Engels pointed out:

>> *The history of early Christianity has notable points of resemblance with the modern working-class movement. Like the latter, Christianity was originally a movement of oppressed people: it first appeared as the religion of slaves and emancipated slaves, of poor people deprived of all rights, of peoples subjugated or dispersed by Rome. Both Christianity and the workers' socialism preach forthcoming salvation from bondage and misery; Christianity places this salvation in a life beyond, after death, in heaven; socialism places it in this world, in a transformation of society.* >> (Marx and Engels 1975)

Religion is seen by Marx as being ideological in three ways, as outlined below (Marx and Engels 1957).

1 Legitimating social inequality

Religion serves as a means of controlling the population by promoting the idea that the existing hierarchy is natural, god-given and, therefore, unchangeable. We can particularly see this during the **feudal period**, when it was widely believed that kings had a divine right to rule. During the 18th and 19th centuries, it was generally believed that God had created both rich and poor, as reflected in the hymn 'All Things Bright and Beautiful'. This stated (in what is now a little-used verse):

>> *The rich man in his castle,*
The poor man at his gate,
God made them, high or lowly,
And order'd their estate. >>

2 Disguising the true nature of exploitation

Religion explains economic and social inequalities in supernatural terms. In other words, the real causes (exploitation by the ruling class) are obscured and distorted by religion's insistence that inequality is the product of sin or a sign that people have been chosen by God.

3 Keeping the working classes passive and resigned to their fate

Some religions present suffering and poverty as a virtue to be accepted – and even welcomed – as normal. It is suggested that those who do not question their situation will be rewarded by a

synoptic link

crime and deviance

Religion has a contradictory relationship to crime and deviance. On the one hand, it can be seen as encouraging conformity, while on the other, it can provide justification for deviant subcultures to challenge the status quo. In the first case, 'official' religious organizations, such as churches, or civil religions, such as the monarchy, provide a sense of collective identity and belonging to a moral community with shared goals. Deviance is inhibited as the central values of the society are continually reaffirmed through religious or civil practice and ritual. In the second case, however, religion may be used to justify criminal activity, such as the bombing of abortion clinics or murdering innocent people as in the attack on the World Trade Center in New York on 11 September 2001 and in the London bombings of July 2005.

Furthermore, religious groups are often demonized by politicians and the mass media and some become the subject of moral panics. This has been the case with some fundamentalist groups and new religious movements both in Britain and the USA ((see p. 22).

place in heaven. Such ideas promote the idea that there is no point in changing society now. Instead, people should wait patiently for divine intervention. Religion offers hope and promises happiness in a future world. The appeal to a God is part of the illusion that things will change for the better. This prevents the working class from actually doing anything which challenges the ruling class directly.

Religion thus discourages people from attempting change, so the dominant groups can retain their power. Religion is used by the ruling class to justify their position. Church and ruling class are mutually reinforcing:

>> *The parson has ever gone hand in hand with the landlord.*>> Communist Manifesto (Marx 1848)

However, evidence for the traditional Marxist position is partial and tends to be of a documentary nature, looking at the nature of faith and the way in which the religion of the poor concentrates on the afterlife. Also, some traditional Marxists adopt the view that religion can bring about social change, a position also adopted by some neo-Marxists and discussed further in the next topic.

Evidence to support Marxist views of religion

● Halevy (1927) argued that the Methodist religion played a key role in preventing working-class revolution in 19th-century Britain. Most European nations apart from Britain experienced some type of proletarian attempt to bring about social change in this period. Halevy argued that working-class dissatisfaction with the establishment was, instead, expressed by deserting the Church of England, which was seen as the party of the **landed classes**. Methodism attracted significant numbers of working-class worshippers, and Halevy claims Methodism distracted the proletariat from their class grievances by encouraging them to see enlightenment in spirituality rather than revolution. In this sense, religion inhibited major social upheaval and, therefore, social change.

● Leach (1988) is critical of the Church of England because it recruits from what is essentially an upper-class base (80 per cent of bishops were educated at public school and Oxbridge). The Church is also extremely wealthy. Leach argues that as a result, the Church has lost contact with ordinary people. He suggests it should be doing more to tackle inequality, especially that found in the inner cities.

● Religion is used to support dominant groups in America. It has been suggested that modern Protestant **fundamentalist religions** in the USA support right-wing, conservative and anticommunist values. Fundamentalists often suggest that wealth and prosperity are a sign of God's favour, while poverty, illness and homosexuality are indicators of sin.

● Hook (1990) noted that the (then) Pope, John Paul II, had a very conservative stance on contraception, abortion, women priests and homosexuality (a stance shared by his successor, Benedict XVI). He points out that the Vatican's stance on contraception is causing problems in less developed areas of the world such as South America. Hook also suggests that the considerable wealth of the church could be doing more to tackle world poverty.

Criticisms of Marxism

Like functionalism, the Marxist theory of religion fails to consider **secularization**. Surely the ideological power of religion is undermined by the fact that fewer than 10 per cent of people attend church?

There are also some examples of religious movements that have brought about radical social change and helped remove ruling elites (see Topic 2). They demonstrate that religion can legitimate radical revolutionary ideas as well as ideologically conservative ones. Marx failed to recognize this. Neo-Marxists have recognized the way in which religion is sometimes used as the only means to oppose the ruling class. Recently in Britain, for example, churches have often provided safe havens for immigrant groups facing deportation by the government, enabling such groups to publicize their case further and to gain time and support.

KEY TERMS

Anomie – a state of confusion and normlessness.

Christian Right – fundamentalist and right-wing Christian groups, particularly powerful in the southern states of America.

Civil religion – events or activities that involve ritualistic patterns and generate the collective sentiments usually associated with established religions.

Collective conscience – beliefs, values and moral attitudes shared by members of a society that are essential to the social order.

Communism – political philosophy originated by Karl Marx that advocates common ownership of land and business.

Conservative – supporting things staying as they are.

Feudal period – medieval period when wealth in society was based on the ownership of land.

Fundamentalist religions – belief systems that argue the need to subscribe or return to traditional values and practices, usually involving the literal translation of, and belief in, a religious text.

Ideological apparatus – agencies (such as religion, education and the mass media) that transmit ruling-class ideology to persuade subordinate groups (e.g. the working class) that inequality is natural and normal, thereby ensuring their consent to it.

Landed classes – wealthy, land-owning aristocracy.

Nationalism – patriotic feelings towards a nation; belief that your nation is superior to others

Profane – ordinary, unreligious aspects of life.

Sacred – holy or spiritually significant.

Secularization – a process whereby religious beliefs and practices lose their social significance.

Totemism – a primitive religion involving the worship of certain objects seen to have a widespread influence over tribal life.

Check your understanding

1. What is the distinction between the sacred and the profane?

2. What is Durkheim's explanation of the true nature of the 'totem' and 'god'?

3. Identify and explain four functions of religion.

4. Explain, using examples, how civil religion performs similar functions to religion as it is usually understood.

5. How have functionalist ideas about religion been criticized?

6. How, according to Marxists, does religion benefit the capitalist class?

7. What evidence is there to support such views?

8. How, according to Engels, is socialism both similar to and different from early Christianity?

9. How can Marxist views on religion be criticized?

research idea

- Interview a sample of people who participate in different religions. Find out their views on the relationship between religion and society. Do they believe that religion should get involved with politics, or is it a purely private matter?

web.tasks

1. Go to the website of the *Guardian* newspaper at www.guardianunlimited.co.uk and, in the archive search section, key in the words 'government' and 'church'. What evidence can you find for the continuing influence of the church on politics in modern society?

2. Go to a search engine and type in the phrase 'Christian right + USA'. Investigate the extent to which they lend support for the Republican party (an American political party with conservative views).

exploring religion as a conservative influence

Item A

<< **Christian Right** groups, as the name implies, consist primarily of Christians, many of them fundamentalists; some have been known to claim that their political positions are, or ought to be, the views of all Christians. In reality, American Christians hold a wide variety of political views.

Many elements of the Christian Right sympathize with, support and sometimes influence the United States Republican Party. For example, such support is thought to have provided considerable backing for the campaign of US President George W. Bush.

Issues with which the Christian Right is (or is thought to be) primarily concerned with include:

- banning or heavily restricting abortion
- opposition to the gay rights movement and the upholding of what they consider to be 'traditional family values'
- support for the teaching of creationism (the Bible story of creation) in schools
- support for the presence of Christianity in the public sphere, such as the ending of government funding restrictions against religious charities and schools
- opposition to US court decisions widening the separation of church and state beyond historical tradition
- banning of books, music, television programmes, films, etc., that they view as indecent, especially pornography. >>

Source: www.nationmaster.com

1. (a) Identify and briefly explain **two ways** in which religion continues to have a significant role in modern society. (8 marks)

   (b) Using material from **Item A** and elsewhere, briefly examine the extent to which religion can be seen as a conservative force. (12 marks)

2. Assess the view that sociological arguments and evidence support Marxist views of the role of religion in contemporary society. (40 marks)

Religion as a force for social change: Weber and neo-Marxists

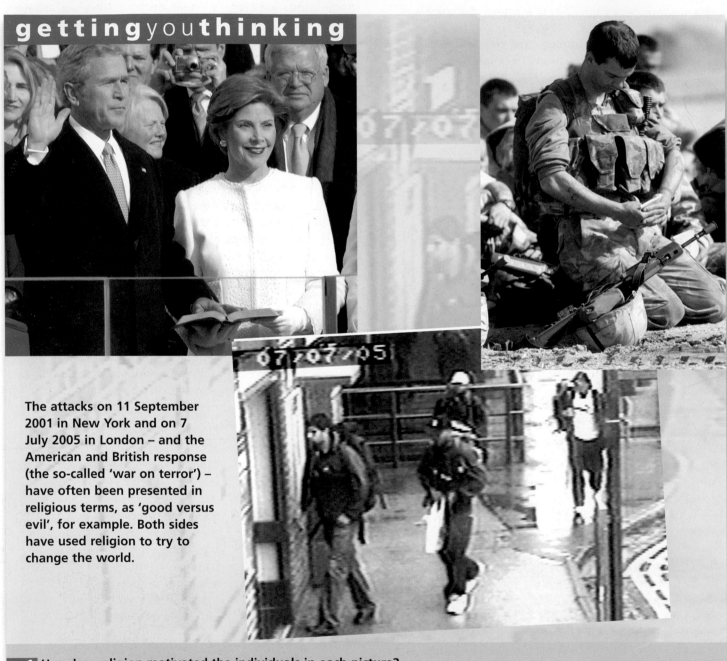

gettingyouthinking

The attacks on 11 September 2001 in New York and on 7 July 2005 in London – and the American and British response (the so-called 'war on terror') – have often been presented in religious terms, as 'good versus evil', for example. Both sides have used religion to try to change the world.

1 How has religion motivated the individuals in each picture?

2 How might their actions be viewed if religion did not exist?

3 To what extent do you think religion causes or justifies social change?

Both the functionalist and Marxist approaches covered in Topic 1 suggest that religion generally plays a conservative role in society – preventing change and supporting the existing social order. This topic looks at an alternative position – that it is possible for religion to change societies.

The role of theodicies

How do people make sense of a world full of suffering, unfairness, inequality and danger? Why are some people poor, while others are rich? Why are some healthy, while others die of cancer? Why do those we love always die? What will happen to me after I die? Why does God allow such terrible things to happen?

Many sociologists see religion as a means of providing answers to such fundamental questions and these answers are sometimes called '**theodicies**'. Berger (1967) uses the metaphor of a '**sacred canopy**' to refer to the different religious theodicies that enable people to make sense of, and come to terms with, the world. Some of these theodicies justify keeping things as they are – the **status quo** – while others encourage change.

Examples of religious theodicies

- In many Western religions, there is a belief that suffering in this life will bring rewards in the next.
- Hinduism suggests that living the 'right way' in this life will lead to a better future life on earth through **reincarnation**.
- Some theodicies include a belief in fate – people believe their lives are predestined and there is nothing they can do to change them. They may, however, devise ways to counter the bleakness of this perception. One way might be to be as successful as possible in order to highlight God's favour and thus reassure themselves of their ultimate place in heaven.
- Followers of some spiritual beliefs and practices such as the reading of **tarot cards** and **astrology** believe that life is fated or that certain things are meant to be.

Theodicy and social change

All these theodicies have social consequences. For example, Islamic fundamentalists in countries that have had **trade sanctions** imposed on them by Western countries that disapprove of their fundamentalism may gain strength from the sanctions and resulting material deprivations they suffer. One Islamic theodicy is the belief that suffering plays a role in gaining entry to heaven. Western sanctions, therefore, are seen as a means to divine salvation and so provide greater resolve.

Max Weber, in his famous work *The Protestant Ethic and the Spirit of Capitalism* (1958, originally 1905), identified one particular theodicy that may have helped to facilitate dramatic social change.

The Protestant ethic and the spirit of capitalism

Calvinists were a Protestant group who emerged in the 17th century and believed in **predestination**. According to them, your destiny or fate was fixed in advance – you were either damned or saved, and there was nothing you or any religious figure could do to improve your chances of going to heaven. There was also no way of knowing your fate. However, it was believed that any form of social activity was of religious significance; material success that arose from hard work and an **ascetic** life would demonstrate God's favour and, therefore, your ultimate destiny – a place in heaven.

Weber argued that these ideas helped initiate Western economic development through the industrial revolution and capitalism. Many of the early **entrepreneurs** were Calvinists. Their obsessive work ethic and self-discipline, inspired by a desire to serve God, meant that they reinvested, rather than spent, their profits. Such attitudes were ideal for the development of industrial capitalism.

synoptic link

stratification and differentiation

Weber used the concept of a theodicy of disprivilege to describe a situation whereby those who experience hardship and social disadvantage are able to endure such circumstances because they believe that they will be somehow compensated in their future lives or in the next life. Clearly, such a theodicy prevents social change as it is inclined to make individuals accept things as they are until salvation inevitably arrives. This may explain why the elderly are often more religious than the young. In the first instance, they often experience social deprivation and, second, ultimate salvation in the next life does not seem to be so far off! Similarly, women of all ages are more religious than men and are more likely than men to experience social deprivation.

Criticisms of Weber

- Some countries with large Calvinist populations, such as Norway and Sweden, did not industrialize. However, as Marshall (1982) points out, Weber did not claim that Calvinism *caused* capitalism – he only suggested that it was a major contributor to a climate of change. Calvinist beliefs had to be supplemented by a certain level of technology, a skilled and mobile workforce, and rational modes of law and bureaucracy.
- Some commentators have suggested that slavery, colonialism and piracy were more important than Calvinist beliefs in accumulating the capital required for industrialization.
- Marxists are also critical because, as Kautsky (1953) argues, capitalism predates Calvinism. He argues that early capitalists were attracted to Calvinism because it made their interests appear legitimate.

Neo-Marxist views on religion

Not all Marxists have followed the view that religion is purely 'the opium of the people' (see Topic 1, p. 5). Some have emphasized the revolutionary potential of religion. O'Toole (1984) has pointed out that:

<< Marxists have undoubtedly recognized the active role that may be played by religion in effecting revolutionary social change. >>

Writers who have tried to update the ideas of Marx to suit new developments in society are known as neo-Marxists. Some neo-Marxists have rejected the classic Marxist idea that all the cultural institutions in society such as the media, the law and religion are inevitably under the control of the ruling class. They argue that ruling-class domination is actually more effective if its members are not directly involved in these cultural institutions. This is because it will then appear that the media and so on are independent when, in fact, the economic power of the bourgeoisie means that whoever fills particular roles in these institutions, they are still under ruling-class control. Neo-Marxists call this apparent independence of cultural institutions **relative autonomy**.

The Italian neo-Marxist Antonio Gramsci (1971) wrote in the 1920s and 30s. Although he was aware at the time that the church was supporting ruling class interests, he did not believe this to be inevitable. He argued that religious beliefs and practices could develop that would support and guide challenges to the ruling class because the church, like other cultural institutions, was not directly under their control. Members of the working class could challenge the dominant class through the distribution of more radical ideas.

Otto Maduro (1982), also argued for the relative autonomy of religion, suggesting that in situations where there is no other outlet for grievances, such as in Latin America, the clergy can provide guidance for the oppressed in their struggle with dominant groups (see below).

Why do some religions encourage social change?

Most sociologists today do not believe that there is any simple one-directional relationship between religion and social change. Instead, they try to identify the particular factors that influence the role of religious beliefs and institutions in specific social contexts. MacGuire (1981) and Thompson (1986) argue that there are a number of factors that determine whether or not religion promotes change.

Beliefs

Religions that emphasize strong moral codes are more likely to produce members who will be critical of and challenge social injustice. The Reverend Martin Luther King and the Southern Baptist Church were at the forefront of the Black civil rights campaign in the 1960s. King's nonviolent demonstrations were important in dismantling segregation and bringing about political and social rights for Black people. Christianity was also a powerful opponent of apartheid in South Africa. Religious beliefs that focus on this world will have more potential to influence it than those that focus on spiritual and other-worldly matters. Christianity and Hinduism, therefore, have more revolutionary potential than, for example, Buddhism, which focuses on improvement of the self rather than society.

As the Focus on Research demonstrates (see right), religions with 'other worldly' beliefs are less likely to promote change than those with temporal or 'this worldly' beliefs.

Culture

Where religion is central to the culture of a society, then anyone wishing to change that society is more likely to use religion to help them bring about that change. In India, for example, Gandhi used the Hindu concept of *sarvodaya* (welfare for all) to attack British colonial rule, inspiring rural peasants and the urban poor to turn against the British.

Social location

Where a religious organization plays a major role in political or economic life, there is wide scope for it to influence social change. In situations where the clergy come from and remain in close contact with their communities, they are more able to mobilize them against negatively perceived outside influences. An Islamic revolution led by the Ayatollah Khomeini overthrew the Shah of Iran's pro-Western regime in 1979.

Internal organization

Religions with a strong centralized source of authority have more chance of affecting events. The Roman Catholic church was instrumental in bringing about the collapse of communism in Poland through its support of the opposition movement known as 'Solidarity'. This same authority can,

Gary Marx (1973)

Religion: opiate or inspiration?

Gary Marx studied the role of religious belief during the Black struggle for racial equality in the USA during the 1960s. In general, for Marx's nationwide sample of Black people, the effect of **religiosity** on attitudes to protest indicated that the greater the religious involvement, the less the militancy. However, this was not always the case. Marx found that the nature of religious belief affected its capacity to inhibit or promote change.

If Black people's religious beliefs were 'other-worldly' – stressing the powerlessness of humans and the promise of salvation in the world to come – then they provided little motivation to change society. In contrast those with 'this-worldly' (or temporal) beliefs – those that focused on the importance of this world – would be encouraged to try to change the world for the better glorification of God.

Marx concludes that until such time as religion loosens its hold, or comes to embody more of a temporal or 'this-worldly' orientation, it may be seen as an important factor inhibiting Black militancy overall.

Marx, G. (1973) 'Religion: opiate or inspiration of civil rights militancy among negroes?', in B. Beit-Hallahmi (ed.) *Research in Religious Behavior: Selected Readings*, Monterey, CA: Brooks/Cole

1 Why do you think that an 'other worldly orientation' appears to inhibit involvement in civil rights issues?

2 Why do you think that the religious conviction of figures in the civil rights movement such as Martin Luther King was so influential in increasing support for the civil rights movement?

however, have the opposite effect by restraining the actions of some parts of its organization. For example, the Pope has expelled some Latin American bishops for supporting liberation theology.

External organisation

In communist societies, and to some extent in Latin America however, the organisational support the church receives from outside the country is an important factor in its ability to resist the authorities and criticize existing social and political arrangements. A movement without a large external organisational structure is more susceptible to repression. Similarly, some would argue that religious organisations with a less obviously hierarchical structure are better equipped to frustrate state control as removal or imprisonment of their leadership makes little difference. Parkin (1972) argues that political leadership of the Black population in the southern states of the USA was frequently taken on by clergymen and that churches provided an organizational focus for the civil rights movement. However, as the Focus on Research shows (see left) the implications of religion for protest are often somewhat contradictory.

Religion and radical change

Revolutionary movements have deliberately used religion in an attempt to change society. In some Central and South American countries, such as Guatemala, Chile and El Salvador, where the police and military have been used to crush opposition, religion has become the only remaining outlet for dissent. This fusion of Christianity and Marxism is known as '**liberation theology**'. In the 1960s various radical groups and individuals emerged from within the Catholic Church in Latin America. They argued that it was a Christian duty to be involved in action leading to economic and political liberation. Catholics collaborated with Marxists in political and social action. In 1979 Catholic revolutionaries played a part in the overthrow of the Somoza regime in Nicaragua and the new government included a number of priests.

One other aspect of this discussion involves the reactionary nature of some religions – that is, their desire to turn the clock back to a time when society and its moral order were more in line with their religious ideals. Such religions are opposed to what they consider to be the undesirable state of modern society. Christian and Islamic fundamentalists illustrate the position well.

For Islamic fundamentalists, religion provides the basis for resistance to the process of Westernization. Iran and Afghanistan are obvious recent examples, but this is not a new phenomenon. In Egypt, the Moslem Brotherhood played an important part in the revolt that deposed King Farouk in 1952, Colonel Gaddafi, in Libya in 1969 led a revolution pledged to return to an Islamic way of life and

The Rev W.A. Criswell: an obituary

THE REV W.A. CRISWELL, former president of the Southern Baptist Convention has died at the age of 92. Christian fundamentalists have heaped praise on a man who spent 50 highly influential years insisting that the Bible is the unerring word of God and that its historical accuracy is beyond question.

Though this may seem a fringe attitude on this side of the Atlantic, Criswell led a denomination of some 16m people, ran four radio stations and established a seminary which has turned out hundreds of young graduates to spread the same message. He paid lip service to the constitutional separation of church and state, yet he and his followers worked untiringly to ensure that their conservative social agenda dominated the US political debate.

Based in Dallas, Texas, Criswell was part of the influential network surrounding the Bush family. The Rev Billy Graham, a White House adviser for 50 years, is a leading member of the First Baptist Church, which Criswell led; the elder George Bush regularly worshipped there, and his son made strenuous efforts to retain the backing of Criswell's adherents during his own presidential election campaign.

The relentless energy of this core conservative group – drawn from such disparate fields as the oil industry and the Christian right – led a Washington Post commentator to observe four weeks ago that 'for the first time since religious conservatives became a modern political movement, the president of the United States has become the movement's de facto leader' – a development for which Wallie Amos Criswell could claim much credit.

But Criswell's message, often delivered at enormous length, went back uncompromisingly to Genesis, where God created the world in six days and made man in his image. That led, quite naturally, to a repeated effort to encourage the teaching of creationism (the Bible story of creation) in American schools. It also brought such church rulings as its 1998 declaration that a woman's duty was to submit graciously unto her husband's leadership.

The Guardian, 15 Jan 2002

1 In what ways can the Rev W.A. Criswell be described as a fundamentalist?

2 How have Christian fundamentalists such as the Rev W.A. Criswell attempted to ensure that their views have influenced American politics?

3 To what extent do you think Christian fundamentalist groups, such as those described above, are an influence for social change or a conservative influence?

Islamic fundamentalists were involved in the assassination of President Sadat of Egypt in 1981. Christian fundamentalists in the USA have significantly influenced the policies of the Bush administration in relation to family life and social policy.

The nature and motivations of fundamentalist religious groups is explored further in the next topic.

web.tasks

1 Search the net for examples of liberation theology. Use a search engine such as Google and type in the following names:
  – **Archbishop Oscar Romero**
  – **Camilo Torres**
  – **Dom Helder Camara.**

2 Find the official websites of a range of religious organizations in Britain. Try to find their views on a range of political and moral issues. To what extent are they supporting or resisting change?

Check your understanding

1 What purpose do religious theodicies serve?

2 In your own words, explain one example of a religious theodicy.

3 What does Weber mean by the 'Protestant ethic'?

4 How did Weber suggest that the Protestant ethic contributed to the development of capitalism?

5 What criticisms have been made of Weber's work?

6 How can the idea of 'charisma' illustrate how religion can be an initiator of change?

7 According to neo-Marxists, how does the relative autonomy of cultural institutions such as religion benefit the ruling class?

8 What factors may determine whether religion has a radical influence?

9 How is fundamentalism related to both conservatism and change?

KEY TERMS

Ascetic – self-denying.

Astrology – the study of the positions and aspects of celestial bodies (stars, planets, moon) in the belief that they have an influence on the course of natural earthly events and human affairs.

Calvinists – a 17th-century Protestant sect based on the thinking of John Calvin.

Entrepreneurs – self-made, successful business people.

Liberation theology – a fusion of Christianity and Marxism that has been influential in Central and South America.

Predestination – belief that an individual's destiny is fixed before their birth.

Reincarnation – being reborn after death into another life.

Relative autonomy – the degree of freedom of state institutions such as religion from the direct control of the dominant class.

Religiosity – the importance of religion in a person's life.

Sacred canopy – an overarching set of religious ideas that serves to explain the meaning of life.

Status quo – current state of affairs.

Tarot readings – an occult practice that claims to predict the future through analysis of specific cards which are alleged to relate to the fate of the client.

Theodicies – religious ideas that explain fundamental questions about the nature of existence.

Trade sanctions – international boycott of the trade in key goods imposed on a country for its perceived wrongdoing.

research idea

- Interview (or conduct a focus group with) a small number of fellow students who attend religious events on a regular basis. Try to cover a range of religions. Ask them about their beliefs and their views about society.

  – Do they argue for social change or are they content with the way things are?

  – If they want change, what sort of changes are they looking for?

  – How do they think these might come about?

exploring religion as a force for social change

Item A

<< John Wesley, a leader of the great Methodist movement that preceded the expansion of English industry at the close of the 18th century, wrote:

'For religion must necessarily produce industry and frugality, and these cannot but produce riches. We must exhort all Christians to gain what they can and to save all they can; that is, in effect to grow rich.' (Quoted in Weber 1958)

These riches could not be spent on luxuries, fine clothes, lavish houses and frivolous entertainment, but in the glory of God. In effect, this meant being even more successful in terms of one's calling, which in practice meant reinvesting profits in the business.

The Protestants attacked time-wasting, laziness, idle gossip and more sleep than was necessary – six to eight hours a day at the most. They frowned on sexual pleasures; sexual intercourse should remain within marriage and then only for the procreation of children (a vegetable diet and cold baths were sometimes recommended to remove temptation). Sport and recreation were accepted only for improving fitness and health, and condemned if pursued for entertainment. The impulsive fun and enjoyment of the pub, dance hall, theatre and gaming house were prohibited to ascetic Protestants. In fact, anything that might divert or distract people from their calling was condemned. Living life in terms of these guidelines was an indication that the individual had not lost grace and favour in the sight of God. >>

Haralambos, M. and Holborn, M. (2004) *Sociology: Themes and Perspectives*, London: Collins

1 (a) Identify and explain two ways in which the Protestant ethic described in **Item A** may have aided the growth of capitalism. (8 marks)

(b) Using material from **Item A** and elsewhere, briefly examine the impact that religion may have upon people's everyday lives. (12 marks)

2 Analyse and evaluate the relationship between religion and social change. (40 marks)

Organized religion and religious activity

A Church of England congregation (left), a Jehovah's Witness (centre) and a mass wedding of 'Moonies' (right)

The pictures above shows members of various religious organizations.

1 How does each organization acquire its members?

2 To what extent does each claim to be the only true route to spiritual salvation?

3 How much influence does each organization have on its members? What type of influence is it?

Religious organizations

Religious organizations can be broadly grouped into four main types:

● churches
● sects
● denominations
● cults.

Churches and sects

Weber (1920) and Troeltsch (1931) were the first to distinguish between churches and sects. A church is a large, well-established religious body, such as the mainstream organizations that represent the major world religions – Christian churches (such as the Roman Catholic, Anglican and Eastern Orthodox churches), Judaism, Islam, Hinduism, and so on. However, the term 'church' is particularly associated with the Christian religion and today many prefer to call religions such as Islam and Hinduism 'faiths'. A sect is a smaller, less highly organized grouping of committed believers, usually setting itself up in protest at what a church has become – as Calvinists and Methodists did in preceding centuries (they are now considered to be denominations within the Christian Church – see below). In terms of membership, churches are far more important than sects. The former tend to have hundreds of thousands or even millions of members, whereas sect members usually number no more than a few hundred. Hence, the often widespread media attention given to sects is somewhat disproportionate.

Denominations

According to Becker (1950) a denomination is a sect that has 'cooled down' to become an institutionalized body rather than an active protest group. Niebuhr (1929) argues that sects that survive over a period of time become denominations because a **bureaucratic**, non-hierarchical structure becomes necessary once the **charismatic leader** dies. Hence, they rarely survive as sects for more than a generation. While they initially appear deviant, sects gradually evolve into denominations and are accepted as a mere offshoot of an established church. They no longer claim a **monopoly of truth**, and tend to be tolerant and open, requiring a fairly low level of commitment. However, Bryan Wilson (1966) rejects Niebuhr's view and suggests that some sects do survive for a long time without becoming denominations and continue to require a high level of commitment.

Cults

There is some disagreement among sociologists over how to classify a cult, but most agree that it is the least coherent form of religious organization. The focus of cults tends to be on individual experience, bringing like-minded individuals together. People do not formally join cults, rather they subscribe to particular theories or forms of behaviour. Scientology, for example, is claimed to have eight million members worldwide.

The terms 'sect' and 'cult' are often used interchangeably by the media to describe new forms of religious organization and there can be considerable **moral panic** about them, as we shall see in the next topic. Recently, sociologists such as Wallis (1984) have developed the terms 'new religious movement (NRM)' and 'New Age movement (NAM)' to describe these new forms of religion (see Topic 4).

Table 1.1 below summarizes the differences between churches, denominations, sects and cults.

Postmodernity and organized religion

For some sociologists, the advent of postmodern society (see Unit 4, p. 171) has resulted in:

- previously powerful religious organizations becoming less significant
- an increase in fundamentalist factions within all major world religions
- new types of religious movements and networks, and the development of the so-called 'spiritual shopper'.

Table 1.1 The differences between churches, denominations, sects and cults

This table illustrates key differences between types of religious organization. It is inevitably an over-simplification as religious organizations do not always fit neatly into these categories.

Feature	Churches	Denominations	Sects	Cults
Scope	National (or international); very large membership; inclusive	National (or international); large membership; inclusive	Local or national. Tend to start small but can become extremely large.	Local, national or international; inclusive; varies in size
Internal organization	Hierarchical; bureaucratic	Formal bureaucratic	Voluntary; tight-knit; informal	Voluntary; loose structure
Nature of leadership	Professional clergy with paid officials	Professional clergy; less bureaucratic; uses lay preachers	No professional clergy or bureaucratic structure; often charismatic leader	Individualistic; may be based on a common interest or provision of a service; inspirational leader
Life span	Over centuries	Often more than 100 years	Sometimes more than a generation; may evolve into a denomination	Often short-lived and dies with the leadership
Attitude to wider society	Recognizes the state and accepts society's norms and values. Often seen as the establishment view	Generally accepted but not part of formal structure; seen as a basis of non-conformist views	Critical of mainstream society; often reclusive with own norms and values	May be critical or accepting of society, but has a unique approach that offers more
Claims to truth	Monopoly view of the truth; strong use of ritual with little arousal of strong emotional response	No monopoly on truth; less ritual but clear emphasis on emotional fervour	Monopoly view of truth; aim to re-establish fundamental truths	No monopoly; borrows from a range of sources
Type of membership	Little formal commitment required; often by birth	Stronger commitment and rules, e.g. teetotalism or nongambling	Exceptional commitment	Membership flexible
Examples	Anglicanism, Roman Catholicism, Islam, Judaism, Hinduism, Sikhism	Baptists, Methodists, Pentecostalists	Mormons, Jehovah's Witnesses, Moonies, Branch Davidian, Salvation Army	Scientology, spiritualism, transcendental meditation, New Age ideas

Heelas *et al.* (2004)
The Kendal project

Kendal, a town of 28 000 people in the Lake District, has a church-attendance rate slightly above the national average, and is also something of a centre for alternative spirituality, offering the team from Lancaster University an ideal place to explore some of the key questions in current religious studies debates.

The researchers' book begins with the claim made by some commentators that traditional forms of religion appear to be declining, while new forms of alternative spirituality are growing.

The focus of the study was, therefore, on the two main types of sacred groupings:

- the 'congregational domain' (the various church congregations)
- the 'holistic milieu' (a range of activities involving the mind, body and spirit – such as yoga, tai chi, healing and self-discovery).

Between 2000 and 2002, questionnaires and interviews were conducted with members of each grouping – 26 congregations and 62 groups with a spiritual dimension, as well as a doorstep survey of over 100 households.

The researchers found that involvement in church and chapel – at 7.9 per cent of the population – still outweighs that in alternative spirituality, where only 1.6 per cent are estimated to be committed practitioners. However, alternative spirituality is catching up fast, as church congregations are in general decline (down from 11 per cent of the population in 1980) while the holistic milieu is growing. Furthermore, those churches that emphasized individuals 'in the living of their unique lives' were thriving, compared with those that subordinate all individuality to a higher good, e.g. 'the Almighty', which were contracting.

The writers see this as evidence of a 'spiritual revolution', whereby the forms of religion or spirituality that are doing best are those that help resource individuals in the living of their unique lives. These can be Christian or alternative. What people are seeking are forms of religiosity that make sense to them, rather than those which demand that they subordinate their personal truth to some higher authority. In other words, we are witnessing a **'subjectivization'** of the sacred.

While the study reaffirmed an overall decline in total numbers involved in sacred activities, the growth in the holistic milieu, primarily by women practitioners (80 per cent), seems to reflect the 'subjective turn of modern culture', whereby people see themselves more as unique individuals with hidden depths. This is part of a general process of perceiving individuals as consumers who can express their own individuality through what they buy, or buy into. The findings also suggest that the sociology of spirituality ought to take gender more seriously.

However, the age profile of the holistic milieu was very uneven, with 83 per cent who were over 40 and many who were ex-hippies who had maintained their affiliation with alternative spiritualities since the 1960s. Many in the holistic milieu also worked in people-centred, caring jobs, where personal wellbeing is a major concern. Given the relatively small number in such jobs and the other demographic and cultural factors, this would suggest that the rate of growth of the holistic milieu is likely to slow down. Nonetheless, on the basis of the Kendal research, the writers predict that holistic milieu activity will exceed church attendance within the next 20 to 30 years.

Adapted from Heelas, P., Woodhead, W., Seel, B., Tusting, K. and Szerszynski, B. (2004) *The Spiritual Revolution: Why religion Is giving way to spirituality*, Oxford: Blackwell

1 **What problems might the researchers have encountered when conducting a 'doorstep survey' about religious and spiritual belief and behaviour?**

2 **What do the researchers mean by:**

(a) 'spiritual revolution'?

(b) subjectivization?

According to Lyotard (1984), postmodern society is characterized by a loss of confidence in **meta-narratives** – the 'grand' explanations provided by religion, politics, science and even sociology. The 'truths' that these subjects and belief systems claim to be able to reveal have not been forthcoming. This has led to what Bauman (1992) calls a 'crisis of meaning'. Traditional religions, in particular, seem unable to deal with this crisis. Take, for example, the social conflicts caused in the name of religion and its inability to reconcile this with the claim to preach love rather than hate. Consequently, newer expressions of religiosity have become more individualistic and less socially divisive. This has enabled individuals to restore meaning to their lives without having to rely on religious institutions imposing their monopoly of truth. This can be seen in the decline of religious monopolies and the rise of NRMs and NAMs. Some established religions that remain have attempted to respond to these changes by watering down their content – according to Herberg (1960), they have undergone a process of internal secularization. Examples of this include the increased acceptance of divorce, homosexuality and the ordination of women in the Christian church, and the increasing popularity of Reform Judaism and Progressive Judaism.

Fundamentalism

Other established religions have encouraged a counterresponse to internal secularization and perceived moral decline by returning to the fundamentals, or basics, of their religious roots. Hence, there has been a rise in religious fundamentalism. Examples include Zionist groups in Israel, Islamic fundamentalists in Iran, Afghanistan and elsewhere, and the Christian Right in the USA. In the past 30 years, both Islamic and Christian fundamentalism have grown in strength, largely in response to the policies of modernizing governments and the shaping of national and international politics by **globalization**. The increasing influence of Western consumerism, for example, on less developed societies may be perceived as a threat to their faith and identity, thus provoking a defensive fundamentalist response. As Bauman puts it (1992), 'fundamentalist tendencies may articulate the experience of people on the receiving end of globalization'.

According to Holden (2002), fundamentalist movements, such as Jehovah's Witnesses, offer hope, direction and certainty in a world that seems increasingly insecure, confusing and morally lost.

Fundamentalism can sometimes lead to violence, especially where fundamentalists value their beliefs above tolerance of those who do not share them. In some cases, these beliefs can be so strong as to overcome any respect or compassion for others. They can sometimes even overcome the basic human values of preserving one's own life and the lives of others. The bombing of abortion clinics in the USA and the attacks on the Pentagon and World Trade Center Towers on 11 September 2001, and the suicide bomb attacks in Madrid (March 2004) and London (July 2005) are specific examples.

Table 1.2 Key features of fundamentalist groups

What fundamentalists do	Why they do it
They interpret 'infallible' sacred texts literally	They do this in order to counter what they see as the diluting influence of excessive intellectualism among more **liberal** organizations. They often use texts from scriptures selectively to support their arguments.
They reject **religious pluralism**	Tolerance of other religious ideas waters down personal faith and consequently fundamentalists have an 'us' and 'them' mentality.
Followers find a personal experience of God's presence	They define all areas of life as sacred, thus requiring a high level of engagement. For example, fundamentalist Christians are 'born again' to live the rest of their lives in a special relationship with Jesus.
They oppose secularization and modernity and are in favour of tradition	They believe that accommodation to the changing world undermines religious conviction and leads to moral corruption.
They tend to promote conservative beliefs including patriarchal ones	They argue that God intends humans to live in heterosexual societies dominated by men. In particular, they condemn abortion and detest lesbian and gay relationships.
They emerge in response to social inequality or a perceived social crisis	They attract members by offering solutions to desperate, worried or dejected people.
Paradoxically, they tend to make maximum use of modern technology	To compete on equal terms with those who threaten their very existence, the Christian Right, for example, use television (in their view the prime cause of moral decay) to preach the 'Word'. Use of the internet is now widespread by all fundamentalist groups.

Religion can have a direct impact on the stratification system of a society. In India, even today the caste system continues to affect the life chances of the lower castes. Across the Muslim world, response to the perceived **cultural imperialism** of Western countries (particularly the USA) is causing some Muslim countries to reconfigure themselves structurally along more traditional lines in attempting to restore Islam to its original purity and strength. A key idea is that Islam should respond to the Western challenge by affirming the identity of its own beliefs and practices. Such ideas sparked the revolution in Iran in 1979, which was initially fuelled by internal opposition to the modernizing Shah of Iran. He had tried to promote Western forms of modernization, such as land reform, extension of the vote to women, and the introduction of secular education. The Ayatollah Khomeini, who provided a radical reinterpretation of

Shi-'ite Islam (a minority, more orthodox faction), established a government organized according to traditional Islamic law. Religion, as specified in the Qu'ran, became the direct basis of all political and economic life. Men and women are now kept rigorously separated, women are obliged to cover their bodies and heads in public, practising homosexuals are sent to the firing squad and adulterers stoned to death.

Similar 'reconfiguration' has occurred in Afghanistan and Sudan, to name just two countries. All those supportive of perceived anti-Muslim sentiments or policies, as well as modernizing governments in countries with significant Muslim populations, are experiencing conflict and in some cases acts of terrorism, often (in the eyes of fundamentalists) as legitimate targets of *Jihad* or holy war.

Features of fundamentalist groups

Sociologists such as Caplan (1987), Hunter (1987), and Davie (1995) provide a useful summary of some of the key features of fundamentalist groups (see Table 1.2 on the previous page).

Individual choice and the postmodern world

The next topic explores the postmodernist view that society has encouraged the development of NRMs, as people assert their identity through individual consumption rather than group membership. The information explosion created by new

technologies has provided an opportunity for people to pick and choose from a vast array of alternatives in a virtual 'spiritual supermarket'. Those in developed countries where this choice is greatest, act as **'spiritual shoppers'**, picking those beliefs and practices that suit their current tastes and identity, but dropping them or substituting them for other products if those identities change.

However, postmodernists have been criticized for overstating the extent of individual choice. Critics, such as Bruce (2002), point to the continuing influence of group membership on identities, as evidenced by the ways in which factors such as class, gender and ethnicity continue to influence the spiritual life course. This is explored further in later topics, especially Topic 5 (gender) and Topic 6 (ethnicity).

researchidea

- Identify a small sample of students who participate in organized religious activity. Conduct semi-structured interviews with them, aiming to discover what appeals to them about that particular religious group. Do you find any differences between those who are involved in different kinds of religious organizations?

web.tasks

1 There are many sites that represent and discuss churches, sects and cults. Many are the websites of the groups themselves. Search for some websites of churches, sects and cults. Compare some organizations using some of the criteria in Table 1.1 on p. 15. What other differences and similarities can you identify?

2 Go to a search engine such as Google and type in the phrase 'Caste + modern India' How influential does caste still appear to be on Indian society?

Check your understanding

1. Briefly define 'church', 'denomination', 'sect' and 'cult', giving examples of each.

2. What evidence is given for the claim that previously dominant religious organizations have become less significant?

3. What does Herberg mean by the phrase 'internal secularization'?

4. In your own words, outline the key features of fundamentalism.

5. Give two possible reasons for the rising number of fundamentalist groups across the globe.

6. What do you understand by the term 'spiritual shopper'?

7. How does Bruce criticize the postmodern view of religion?

KEY TERMS

Bureaucratic – centralized form of organization run by official representatives.

Charismatic leader – leader who has a magnetic and powerful personality.

Cultural imperialism – the practice of the culture or language of one nation becoming dominant in another. It is usually the case that the former is a large, economically or militarily powerful nation and the latter is smaller and less affluent.

Globalization – a process whereby social and economic activity spans many nations with little regard for national borders.

Liberal – a concern with individual freedoms.

Monopoly of truth – a view that only the viewpoint of the holder can be accepted as true.

Moral panic – media-induced panic about the behaviour of particular groups.

Religious pluralism – where a variety of religions co-exist, all of which are considered to have equal validity.

Spiritual shoppers – a postmodern idea that people consume religion in much the same way as any other product.

Subjectivization – the increasing relevance of the self and personal experiences as a dominant feature of religion in late-modern society.

exploring the influence of organized religion

Item A

According to Gilles Kepel (1994) American fundamentalists are notable for their extraordinary skill in using the most up-to-date language and technology to disseminate their message. The electronic media have been centrally involved in changes affecting religion in the US since the 1960s. Billy Graham was the first to preach regularly across the airwaves amassing a large following. Other electronic preachers in the US include Oral Roberts, Jimmy Swaggart and Pat Robertson. 'The electronic church' – religious organizations that operate primarily through the media rather than local congregation meetings – has come into being. Through satellite communications, religious programmes can now be beamed across the world into developing countries as well as to other industrialized societies. Inspirational preachers use their star quality to convert non-believers, their charismatic qualities being projected to an audience of thousands or even millions of people. The electronic preaching of religion has become particularly prevalent in Latin America where North American programmes have inspired the growth of Pentecostal protestant movements in mostly Catholic countries such as Chile and Brazil.

Adapted from Giddens, A. (2001) *Sociology* (4th edn), Cambridge: Polity Press

1. (a) Identify and briefly explain two characteristics of religious fundamentalism. (8 marks)

   (b) Using material from **Item A** and elsewhere, briefly examine reasons for the growth of religious fundamentalism. (12 marks)

2. Assess the view that religion is becoming less centralized and more a matter of individual choice. (40 marks)

New religious and New Age movements

gettingyouthinking

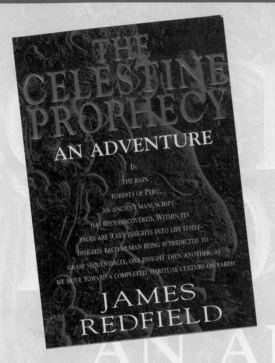

The Celestine Prophecy

The Celestine Prophecy by James Redfield fast became one of the top commercial publishing events of the1990s, hovering at the top of the *New York Times* best-seller list for several months. It has now been made into a major film. The fictional narrative centres around a search for ancient Mayan manuscripts known as the 'Nine Insights'. These insights purport to contain information and ancient wisdom about ultimate reality and man's place in it.

Essentially, according to the book, life's 'chance coincidences', strange occurrences that feel like they were meant to happen, are actually events, indicative of another plane of existence and following them will start you on your path to spiritual truth – a oneness of human spirit with the forces of the universe.

The success of the original book largely arose from the fact that many Celestine devotees believed the book's story to be true. The fact that Hollywood filmmakers believe that the potential interest is still sufficiently widespread to justify spending the millions of dollars involved in the making of a feature film would suggest that they, at least, believe that New religious beliefs have grown sufficiently to cross over into popular culture.

1 Have you ever experienced strange coincidences? Do you think that there may be something more to them than mere coincidence?

2 Do you think there is something beyond the physical world that traditional religions are unable to explain?

3 Do you believe that human beings have a spiritual aspect to their nature? Explain the reasoning behind your answer.

4 Which of the following would you be more interested in and why:

(a) an alternative religion or movement that promised you greater spiritual fulfilment?

(b) an alternative movement or religion that offered you the opportunity to be more financially and romantically successful?

If you answered 'yes' to any of questions 1 to 3 above, you are not alone. As the Kendal project showed (see Topic 3, p. 16), an increasing number of people are rejecting traditional religious explanations of spirituality as well as scientific accounts of the natural world. Some are even prepared to make life-changing commitments to realize their goal of spiritual fulfilment. This process of what some have called '**resacrilization**' has been accelerating since the 1960s.

Sociologists have adopted the concept 'new religious movements' (NRMs) as an overarching idea that embraces both cults and sects. The term was coined by Eileen Barker (1984) as a more neutral term than the highly negative meanings of the concepts 'cult' and 'sect' in popular culture. However, as Hadden and Bromley (1993) point out, the concepts of cult and sect do have precise meaning as used by sociologists (see Topic 3), and are free of prejudice. Nonetheless, it is true that this non-judgemental use of the word is not always understood as such by the general public. The term 'new religious movement' is value-free, but is not without its own problems. Most significantly, many NRMs are not new, and some are not even new to a particular culture.

The emergence of new religious movements (NRMs)

As we saw in the previous topic, membership of established 'mainstream' churches has dropped dramatically. However, affiliation with other religious organizations (including Pentecostal, Seventh-Day Adventists and Christian sects) has risen just as noticeably. It is estimated that there may now be as many as 25 000 new religious groups in Europe alone, over 12 000 of whose members reside in the UK (see the 'Focus on research' on the right).

Difficulties in measuring affiliation to NRMs in the UK

There are a number of difficulties in measuring affiliation to NRMs in the UK:

- Many of the organizations listed in the Focus on research, right, have a large number of followers who are not formally registered in any way. It is estimated that about 30 000 people have attended meditation courses run by Brahma Kumaris, for example.
- Some groups have disbanded their organizations but still have 'devotees' – an example is the Divine Light Mission, whose followers, once initiated with 'the Knowledge', continue to practise the techniques of meditation independently.
- Many organizations are based overseas and their supporters in the UK are not traceable.
- The commitment required varies enormously between organizations. While those who devote themselves full time to their movement are generally quite visible, part-time commitment is more difficult to identify.

Affiliation through practice and belief is much higher than formal membership for both traditional and new religions.

Classifying NRMs

Sociologists have attempted to classify such movements in terms of shared features. One way is to identify their affinities with traditional mainstream religions. For example, some may be linked to Hinduism (e.g. Hare Krishnas) and others to Buddhism (various Zen groups). Some NRMs, such as the Unification Church (Moonies), mix up a number of different theologies, while others have links with the Human Potential Movement, which advocates therapies such as transcendental meditation and Scientology to liberate human potential.

Wallis (1984) identifies three main kinds of NRM:

- world-affirming groups
- world-rejecting groups
- world-accommodating groups.

Peter Brierley
Membership of NRMs

Membership of new religious movements, UK 1980 to 2000

	1980	1990	2000
The Aetherius Society	100	500	700
Brahma Kumaris	700	900	1500
Chrisemma	–	5	50
Da free John	35	50	70
Crème	250	375	510
Eckankar	250	350	450
Elan Vital*	1200	1800	2400
Fellowship of Isis	150	250	300
Life training	–	250	350
Mahikari	–	220	280
Barry Long Foundation	–	400	–
Outlook seminar training	–	100	250
Pagan Federation	500	900	5000
The Raelian movement	100	100	100
Shinnyo-en UK	10	30	60
Sahaja Yoga	220	280	365
Solara	–	140	180
3HO	60	60	60
Hare Krishna	300	425	670
Others	50	575	1330
Total	3925	7710	14 625
% of UK population	0.007	0.014	0.028

* previously known as the Divine Light Mission

Compiled from: Brierley, P. (ed.) (2000) *Religious Trends 2000*, London: HarperCollins

1 Assess the reliability of the figures above.

2 Identify key patterns in the figures and suggest explanations for them.

World-affirming groups

These are usually individualistic and life-positive, and aim to release 'human potentials'. They tend to accept the world as it is, but involve techniques that enable the individual to participate more effectively and gain more from their worldly experience. They do not require a radical break with a conventional lifestyle, nor strongly restrict the behaviour of members. Research suggests that these are more common amongst middle-aged, middle-class groups – often in people who are disillusioned and disenchanted with material values and in search of new, more positive meanings. These groups generally lack a church, ritual worship or strong ethical systems. They are often more like 'therapy groups' than traditional religions. Two good examples of world-affirming groups are:

- *The Church of Scientology* founded by L. Ron Hubbard – Hubbard developed the philosophy of 'dianetics', which stresses the importance of 'unblocking the mind' and leading it to becoming 'clear'. His church spread throughout the world (from a base in California). Its business income is estimated at over £200 million per year through the courses members pay for, as well as through the sale of books.
- *Transcendental Meditation* (or TM) was brought to the West by the Hindu Mahareshi Mahesh Yogi in the early 1950s and was further popularized through the interest shown in it by the Beatles in the 1960s. Adherents build a personal **mantra**, which they then dwell upon for periods each day. Again, the focus is on a good world – not an evil one – and a way of 'finding oneself' through positive thinking.

World-rejecting groups

These organizations are usually sects, in so far as they are always highly critical of the outside world and demand significant commitment from their members. In some ways, they are quite like conventional religions in that they may require prayer and the study of key religious texts, and have strong ethical codes. They are exclusive, often share possessions and seek to relegate members' identities to that of the greater whole. They are often **millenarian** – expecting divine intervention to change the world. Examples include:

- The Unification Church (popularly known as the Moonies), founded in Korea by the Reverend Sun Myung Moon in 1954. The Unification Church rejects the mundane secular world as evil and has strong moral rules, such as no smoking and drinking.
- Members of Hare Krishna (Children of God, or ISKCON International Society for Krishna Consciousness) are distinguished by their shaved heads, pigtails and flowing gowns. Hare Krishna devotees repeat a mantra 16 times a day.

World-rejecting sects are the movements that have come under most public scrutiny in recent years, largely because of the public horror at the indoctrination that has even led to mass suicide. There is a growing list of extreme examples:

- the mass suicide of Jim Jones's People's Temple in Jonestown, Guyana in 1987
- the Aum Supreme Truth detonating poisonous gas canisters on a Tokyo underground train in 1995, leaving 12 dead and 5000 ill
- the suicidal death in 1997 of the 39 members of the Heaven's Gate cult in California.

The anticult movement

While most of these new religious forms have adopted strategies no different from those of other religions, they are commonly seen by the press and public as deviant – in particular, those that involve open sexuality (thus challenging conventional religious ethics). A small number of sects, for example, have recruited members by sending young female

synopticlink   crime and deviance

Sects, in particular, are often the subject of moral panics particularly as they tend to attract young people from middle-class backgrounds. The integrity of leaders is usually called into question and exaggerated accounts of either financial or sexual impropriety are common. The public reaction and that of the authorities is often amplified, sometimes leading to unanticipated consequences as the siege of the headquarters of the Branch Davidian sect in Waco, Texas, in 1993 illustrates. The sect predicted the end of the world and separated itself from the wider society. Its leader, David Koresh, was seen to be a charismatic 'God incarnate'. Membership involved whole families as well as people who had left their families to join. The wider societies' view was that Koresh had captured and indoctrinated people and was sexually abusing them. The group had also armed themselves in preparation for the 'end' and this became the excuse for police, military and FBI involvement. A 51-day stalemate between federal agents and members of the cult ended in a fiery tragedy after federal agents botched their assault on the sect's compound. About 80 Branch Davidians, including Koresh himself and at least 17 children, died when the compound burned to the ground in a suspicious blaze in September 1993. The FBI claim that the fire was a mass-suicide attempt by members of the sect whilst survivors claim that the FBI fired an incendiary device. Jurors in the criminal trial of surviving cult members were unable to determine who fired the first shot. Cult apologists and surviving members, many of whom still believe that Koresh will return, continue to criticise the Federal government both for its religious intolerance and for its selective application of gun controls in a state that generally defends the right to possess firearms.

members into the community to promise sexual favours to encourage converts. Others promote very open relationships, where members have many sexual partners within the group. Such sects are particular targets of the 'anticult' movement. (Note that the term 'cult' is misused in this context, 'sect' being more accurate.)

A number of individuals and agencies have attempted to raise public concern about what they feel are serious emotional, spiritual and physical abuses by some NRMs. Some parents of 'cult' members and disillusioned former members have become '**deprogrammers**'. For a fee (which in some cases in the US has exceeded $10 000), deprogrammers hold cult members against their will in order to make them abandon their religious faith. Sometimes, techniques such as physical and mental abuse, **sensory deprivation**, and sleep and food deprivation, are used. It is ironic that deprogramming involves the use of the very same practices that the 'cults' are accused of.

Signs of cultist behaviour

Robbins (1988) identifies the following signs of cultist behaviour:

- *Authoritarianism* – Control of the organization stems from an absolute leader or a small circle of elite commanders
- *Infallibility* – The chosen philosophy or **experiential panacea** is the only path to salvation, and all others are worthless. Anyone who questions or challenges what the cult offers is denied access or exiled.
- *Programming* – The belief in the infallibility of the cult's philosophy, experiential panacea and leader are derived from the abandonment of critical and rational thinking.
- *Shunning* – Members are encouraged to sever communications and relationships with friends and family members.
- *Secret doctrines* – Certain teachings are 'secret' and must never be revealed to the outside world.
- *Promised ones* – Members of the cult are encouraged to believe they were chosen, or made their choice to join the cult, because they are special or superior
- *Fire and brimstone* – Leaving the cult, or failing at one's endeavour to complete the requirements to achieve its panacea, will result in consequences greater than if one had never joined the cult in the first place.

Cult apologists

Cult apologists, such as Haddon and Long (1993), while not members themselves, both defend the right of such groups to exist and argue for more religious tolerance. They claim that:

- most cults are simply misunderstood minority 'religions'
- these movements only seem weird because people don't know enough about them and believe sensational media accounts
- anticult organizations and individuals misrepresent the beliefs and practices of such movements
- anticult organizations are intolerant of religious freedom.

World-accommodating groups

This final category of religious movement is more orthodox. They maintain some connections with mainstream religion, but place a high value on inner religious life. The Holy Spirit 'speaks' through the Neo-Pentecostalists, for example, giving them the gift of '**speaking in tongues**'. Such religions are usually dismayed at both the state of the world and the state of organized mainstream religions. They seek to establish older certainties and faith, while giving them a new vitality.

New Age movements (NAMs)

The term 'New Age' refers to a large number of religions and therapies that have become increasingly important since the 1970s. Many New Age movements can be classed as 'world affirming' (see above) as they focus on the achievement of individual potential.

Bruce (1996) suggests that these groups tend to take one of two forms:

- *Audience cults* involve little face-to-face interaction. Members of the 'audience' are unlikely to know each other. Contacts are maintained mostly through the mass media and the internet as well as occasional conferences. Both astrology and belief in UFOs are good examples of these. Audience cults feed a major market of 'self-help therapy' groups and books which regularly appear in best-seller lists.
- *Client cults* offer particular services to their followers. They have led to a proliferation of new 'therapists' (from astrological to colour therapists), establishing new relationships between a consumer and a seller. Amongst the practices involved are tarot readings, **crystals** and astrology. Many bookshops devote more to these sorts of books than to books on Christianity.

NAMs seem to appeal to all age groups, but more especially to women (see also Topic 5). Bruce (1995) suggests that those affiliated, however, already subscribe to what Heelas calls the '**cultic milieu**' (Heelas 1996) or '**holistic milieu**' (Heelas *et al.* 2004) – a mish-mash of belief in the power of spirituality, ecology and personal growth and a concern that science does not have all the answers. An annual celebration of New Age beliefs – the Festival for the Mind, Body and Spirit – takes place in London and Manchester.

The appeal of NRMs and NAMs

For sociologists, one of the most interesting questions is why people join or support NRMs.

Pragmatic motives

Motivations for affiliation with world-affirming groups can be very practical – financial success and a happier life, for example. These **pragmatic motives** are not the sort that many religious people would recognize and this is probably one of the main reasons why the religious nature of many NRMs is questioned.

Spiritual void

Since the decline in the importance of established religion, people seek alternative belief systems to explain the world and its difficulties. In addition, as postmodernists argue, there is also an increased cynicism about the ability of science to provide solutions to these problems. In the absence of either **grand narrative** (religion or science), people may seek to acquire a personal rationale. This can involve a process of 'spiritual shopping', trying out the various alternatives until they find a belief system that makes sense to them.

Marginality

Weber (1920/1963) pointed out how those marginalized by society may find status and/or a legitimizing explanation for their situation through a theodicy that offers ultimate salvation. This could explain the appeal of world-rejecting sects to some members of ethnic minorities or young social 'drop-outs'.

Relative deprivation

People may be attracted to an NRM because it offers something lacking in the social experience of the seeker – whether spiritual or emotional fulfilment. This could explain the appeal of NRMs to certain members of the middle class, who feel their lives lack spiritual meaning.

The appeal to the young of world-rejecting movements

Many young people are no longer children but lack adult commitments, such as having their own children. Being unattached is an outcome of the increasing gap between childhood and adulthood which, as Wallis (1984) has argued, has been further extended by the gradual lengthening of education and wider accessibility of higher education. It is to these unattached groups that world-rejecting movements appeal. They try to provide some certainty to a community of people who face similar problems and difficulties. What seems to be particularly appealing is the offer of radical and immediate solutions to social and personal problems.

Barker, in her famous study *The Making of a Moonie* (1984), found that most members of the Unification Church (the 'Moonies') came from happy and secure middle-class homes, with parents whose jobs involved some sort of commitment to public service, such as doctors, social workers or teachers. She argued that the sect offered a **surrogate** family in which members could find support and comfort beyond the family, while fulfilling their desire to serve a community, in the same way as their parents did in the wider society. High patterns of drop-out from NRMs suggest that the need they fulfil is temporary.

The appeal of world-affirming movements

World-affirming groups appeal to those who are likely to have finished education, are married, have children and a mortgage. There are two issues in the modern world that add to the appeal of world-affirming movements:

1 As Weber suggested, the modern world is one in which rationality dominates – that is, one in which magical, unpredictable and ecstatic experiences are uncommon.
2 There is tremendous pressure (e.g. through advertising) to become materially, emotionally and sexually successful.

According to Bird (1999), world-affirming sects simultaneously do three things that address these issues:

● They provide a spiritual component in an increasingly rationalized world.
● They provide techniques and knowledge to help people become wealthy, powerful and successful.
● They provide techniques and knowledge which allow people to work on themselves to bring about personal growth.

In some ways, there are common issues that motivate both the young and old. They both live in societies where there is great pressure to succeed and hence great fear of failure. Religious movements can provide both groups with a means to deal with the fear of failure by providing techniques that lead to personal success.

KEY TERMS

Crystals – belief in the healing power of semiprecious stones.

Cult apologists – non-cult members who are religiously tolerant and challenge the misinterpretation of cult practice common in the wider society.

Cultic or holistic milieu – a range of activities involving the mind, body and spirit, such as yoga, tai chi, healing and self-discovery.

Deprogrammers – individuals or groups who remove people from sects and resocialize them back into mainstream society.

Experiential panacea – cure-all, solution to life's ills.

Grand narrative – belief system, such as religion or science, that claims to explain the world.

Mantra – personal word or phrase given by a religious teacher (guru) which is used to free the mind of non-spiritual secular awareness and provide a focus for meditation.

millenarian – belief in a saviour.

Pragmatic motives – desire to acquire personally beneficial practical outcomes.

Resacrilization – renewed interest and belief in religion and therefore a religious revival.

Sensory deprivation – the deliberate reduction or removal of stimuli from one or more of the senses; simple devices such as blindfolds and earmuffs can cut off sight and hearing, while more complex devices can also cut off the sense of smell, touch, taste, thermoception (heat-sense), and 'gravity'.

Speaking in tongues – the power to speak in new (but often incomprehensible) languages – believed to be a gift from God.

Surrogate – replacement.

Check your understanding

1 Why are the numbers of those involved with NRMs probably much higher than membership figures suggest?

2 Briefly explain what Wallis means by the term 'world-affirming movements'. Give examples.

3 How does Bruce classify New Age movements?

4 What does Wallis mean by the term 'world-rejecting movements'? Give examples.

5 What is the response of mainstream society to world-rejecting movements?

6 What are world-accommodating movements? Give examples.

7 Identify and explain two examples of beliefs that predict fundamental world change.

8 Give three reasons for the appeal of NRMs/NAMs.

9 What is the relationship between age, social attachment and the appeal of NRMs?

research idea

● Conduct a survey or interview a sample of other students to discover the extent of New Age beliefs, such as reincarnation, among your peers. Try to assess their knowledge and experience of New Age phenomena such as tarot cards, crystal healing and astrology.

web.task

Go to the website of the Cult Information Centre at www.cultinformation.org.uk. Explore some of the organizations and incidents mentioned. Now go to the website of Inform at www.inform.ac/infmain.html). Compare the attitude to NRMs, cults and sects on each site. To what extent do you think their accounts of 'cults' are biased?

exploring new religious movements

Item A

The NAM 'is a miscellaneous collection of psychological and spiritual techniques that are rooted in Eastern mysticism, lack scientific evaluative data, and are promoted zealously by followers of diverse idealized leaders claiming transformative powers' (Langone 1993).

There are four main streams of thought within the NAM:

1 the 'transformational training' stream, represented by groups such as 'est' (Erhard Seminar Training) and Lifespring

2 the intellectual stream, represented by publications such as *The Tao of Physics*

3 the lifestyle stream, represented by publications such as *Whole Life Monthly* and organizations such as the Green Party

4 the occult stream, represented by astrology, tarot, palmistry, crystal power, and the like.

It is important to keep in mind that within this diversity, there is much disagreement. Many intellectual new agers, for example, ridicule believers in the occult stream of the new age.

The NAM is similar to traditional religions in that it subscribes to the existence of a supernatural realm, or at least something beyond 'atoms and the void'. But the NAM believer considers that spiritual knowledge and power can be achieved through the discovery of the proper techniques. These techniques may be silly, as in crystal power. But they may be very sophisticated, as in some forms of yoga. Its concepts have permeated our culture in a quiet, almost invisible way. For example, a Gallup survey of teenagers, several years ago, found that approximately one third of churchgoing Christian teenagers believed in reincarnation, a fundamental new age belief.

Professor Arthur Dole, University of Pennsylvania, *Cultic Studies Journal*, 7(1), 1990

1 (a) Identify and briefly explain two characteristics of the New Age Movement. (8 marks)

(b) Using material from **Item A** and elsewhere, show how 'New Age concepts have permeated (seeped into) our culture in a quiet, almost invisible way'. (12 marks)

2 Assess the view that cults and sects are only fringe organizations that are inevitably short-lived and of little influence in contemporary society. (40 marks)

Gender, feminism and religion

gettingyouthinking

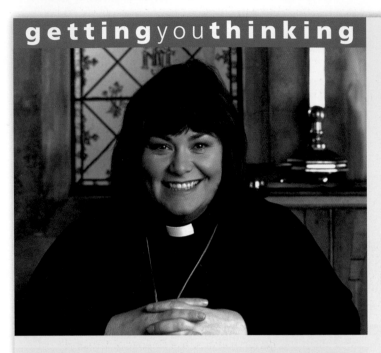

Gender and church attendance in the UK

Attendance	Britain		Northern Ireland	
(per cent)	*Men*	*Women*	*Men*	*Women*
Frequent	37	63	39	61
Regular	35	65	57	43
Rare	48	52	49	51

Source: *British Social Attitudes Survey* (1991) quoted in S. Bruce (1995)
Religion in Modern Britain, Oxford: Oxford University Press

1 Summarize the patterns of church attendance given in the table above.

2 Using both the table and the article above, identify reasons that can be given in support of the ordination of women.

3 Suggest reasons why women appear to be more religious than men.

Women as priests

It is now more than 10 years since the Church of England allowed women priests to be ordained. In fact, in 2004, the number of new female ordinands is, for the first time, equal to the number of male ordinands. The impact of a more feminized job market and positive representations of female priests in the media – in programmes such as The *Vicar of Dibley* (see left) and *A Seaside Parish* (which follows the work of Rev Christine Musser, an Anglican parish priest in Cornwall) – have been cited as contributory factors.

There is a lively debate in the Roman Catholic Church, however, over whether women should be allowed to be ordained as priests. In July 2004, seven women who were ordained by a rebel Austrian Bishop were excommunicated by the Pope.

Both sides of the debate are supported by groups of both men and women. Arguments for women priests include gospel evidence that Jesus was close to women and treated them as equals, and that there is some evidence that the early Church ordained women. For some, the ordination of women priests is about basic equality. Other people point out that many women have a more compassionate nature than men and so would be better suited to the role, especially given the fact that more women attend church than men.

Those opposed to women priests point out that Jesus was a man and that the person who represents him in the church should therefore also be a man. According to the organisation Women Against the Ordination of Women, the full acceptance of women is a **blasphemous** deviation from biblical truth. Also, they say that the Apostles were all men and that, while men and women may be equal before God, they are also different. Other opponents to women's ordination also point out that allowing women priests could cause an irreparable split in the church and so do more harm than good. Many Anglican male priests opposed to the ordination of women have, for example, defected to the Roman Catholic Church.

The decline of the goddess

Women have not always been subordinate to men where religion is concerned. In fact, until about 4000 years ago, the opposite appeared to be the case. Large numbers of **effigies** of naked, pregnant mother–goddess figures have been uncovered by archaeologists across Europe and Asia. In those prehistoric days, people worshipped the gods of nature, who were believed to provide sustenance to humans. They relied upon them for good weather, fertile land, abundant food to harvest, healthy offspring, and so on. The female sex was seen as being closer to nature, and as representing the mysteries of life and fertility. As Armstrong (1993) put it:

<< The Earth produced plants and nourished them in rather the same way as a woman gave birth to a child and fed it from her own body. The magical power of the Earth seemed vitally interconnected with the mysterious creativity of the female sex. >>

Armstrong argues that male aggression exhibited through the invasion of these prehistoric societies by more male-dominated cultures from the Northern hemisphere and the Middle East, needed a **patriarchal rationale** in order to justify such behaviour. Male gods became increasingly important, introducing a more aggressive spirituality. **Monotheism** – the belief in one God rather than many gods (**polytheism**) – was the final death knell for the goddess, as several major world religions came to adopt a single, male god.

Images of God in different religions

Although there is only one god in most contemporary religions (Hinduism being an exception), men and women tend to view that god differently. Davie (1994) showed that:

● women see God more as a god of love, comfort and forgiveness
● men see God more as a god of power and control.

An implicit recognition of the female connection with spirituality can also be seen in the Jewish religion, in which a person can only automatically be Jewish if their mother is. On the other hand, though, some Orthodox Jewish men include the following words in daily prayer:

<< Blessed art thou O Lord our God that I was not born a slave. Blessed art thou O Lord our God that I was not born a woman.>>

Christianity is also inherently patriarchal, with men made in 'the image and glory of God' and women made 'for the glory of man', as the following passage from the New Testament shows:

<<Wives be subject to your husbands, as to the Lord. For the husband is the head of the wife as Christ is the head of the church.>> (Ephesians 5:22–24)

There are many female characters in the biblical texts, and some are portrayed as acting charitably or bravely, but the primary roles are reserved for males. All the most significant Old Testament prophets, such as Isaiah and Moses, are male, while in the New Testament, all the apostles are men.

The most prominent females in the bible, Eve and Mary mother of Jesus, can be interpreted as reinforcing patriarchal ideas regarding, on the one hand, the dangers of female sexuality and, on the other, the virtues of motherhood. Similarly, the Qur'an, the sacred text of Islam, contends that 'men are in charge of women'. Even Buddhism (in which females appear as important figures in the teachings of some Buddhist orders) is dominated (like Christianity) by a patriarchal power structure, in which the feminine is mainly associated with the secular, powerless, profane and imperfect.

Sexuality and religion

Women's bodies and sexuality are also felt to be dangerous by many religions. Because women menstruate and give birth, they are considered to have a greater capacity to 'pollute' religious rituals. In addition, their presence may distract the men from their more important roles involving worship.

Bird (1999) points out that sexuality is an important issue in many religions. Roman Catholic priests are expected to be **celibate**, while (some interpretations of) Christianity and Islam (amongst others) are opposed to homosexuality.

Turner (1983) suggests that a disciplinary role with respect to sexuality is central to religion. Widespread importance is given to **asceticism**, a self-disciplined existence in which pleasure (especially physical pleasure) is repressed. This means that, in order to carry out priestly duties properly, there needs to be a degree of policing of the body – and the presence of women makes this more difficult.

Women in religious organizations

Patriarchal attitudes have meant that, until recently, women have been barred from serving as priests in many of the world's great religions and the more traditional factions continue to bar them. Islamic groups, Orthodox Jews and the Roman Catholic church continue to exclude women from the religious hierarchy.

Although women ministers have long been accepted in some sects and denominations, the Church of England persisted in formally supporting inequalities of gender until 1992, when its General Synod finally voted to allow the ordination of women. However, Anglican churches in other countries (such as Hong Kong, the USA, Canada and New Zealand) had moved to ordain women during the 1970s.

Simon and Nadell (1995) conducted research about women in religious organizations, drawing on evidence from in-depth interviews with 32 female rabbis and 27 female members of the Protestant clergy. They concluded that the women conduct themselves in totally different ways to the male members of their religious organizations. They asked the female rabbis whether they carried out their duties differently from male rabbis of the same age and training. Almost all of the women replied 'yes'. They described themselves as less formal, more approachable, more egalitarian, and more inclined to touch and hug. Seventeen out of the 27 female members of the Protestant clergy described themselves as less formal, more people oriented, more into pastoral care and less concerned about power struggles than the male clergy.

Feminism and religion

Many Christian feminists argue that there will never be gender equality in the church so long as notions of God continue to be associated with masculinity. Mary Daly (1973,1978) goes as far as to suggest that Christianity itself is a patriarchal myth. Although herself originally a Catholic, she argues that the Christian story eliminated other 'goddess' religions. She argues that Christianity is rooted in male 'sado-rituals' with its 'torture cross symbolism', and that it embodies women-hating.

Simone de Beauvoir in her pioneering feminist book, *The Second Sex* (1953), saw the role of religion in a similar way to Marx. However, she saw it as oppressive to women in particular. Religion is used by the oppressors (men) to control the oppressed group (women). It also serves as a way of compensating women for their second-class status. Like Marx's proletariat, religion gives women the false belief that they will be compensated for their suffering on earth by equality in heaven. She concludes:

≪ [Religion] gives her the guide, father, lover, divine guardian she longs for nostalgically; it feeds her daydreams; it fills her empty hours. But, above all, it confirms the social order, it justifies her resignation by giving hope of a better future in a sexless heaven. ≫

El Sadaawi (1980), a Muslim feminist, does not blame religion in itself for its oppressive influences on women, but blames the patriarchal domination of religion that came with the development of monotheistic religions. Such religions, she argues, 'drew inspiration and guidance from the patriarchal and class societies prevalent at the time'. Men wrote their scriptures, and the interpretation of them was almost exclusively male-orientated. This has, on many occasions, enabled men to use religion as an abuse of power. In the 14th century, for example, the Catholic Church declared that women who treated illnesses without special training could be executed as witches. Clearly, the traditional remedies administered by women were seen as as a threat to the authority of the emerging male-dominated medical profession.

Is religion necessarily patriarchal?

It should not be assumed that all religions are equally oppressive to women. In Roman Catholicism, for example, becoming a nun can be viewed as either oppressive or highly liberating. Holm and Bowker (1994) go as far as to suggest that religious organizations developed exclusively for women are the forerunners of the modern women's movement, in that they separate women from men (and therefore oppression) and they enhance women's sense of identity.

There have been some successful challenges to the patriarchal structure of organized religion. Gender-neutral language has been introduced in many hymns and prayers and the requirement in the Christian marriage ceremony for the bride to promise to obey her husband is now also optional.

Judaism has allowed women to become rabbis in its non-orthodox denominations since 1972, and even some Christian religions, particularly Quakerism, have never been oppressive to women. According to Kaur-Singh (1994), Sikh gurus pleaded the cause for the emancipation of Indian womanhood, fully supporting them in improving their condition in society.

Some writers highlight how there are signs of hope developing. Gross (1994) detects signs of a post-patriarchal Buddhism developing in the West that does not differentiate

focus on research

Helen Watson (1994)
The meaning of veiling

According to the Qu'ran, women should exercise religious modesty or *hijab* because their seductiveness might lead men astray. Many writers, including some Islamic feminists, have argued that this has been misinterpreted by men to mean that women must cover their bodies and faces in the presence of men who are not relatives, with the patriarchal motive of controlling women. Western commentators also are critical of the practice, seeing it as evidence of repression. As Julie Burchill (2001) writing in *The Guardian* commented, 'such women carry round with them a mobile prison'.

Watson (1994), however, demonstrated that the veil also has the potential to liberate. She interviewed three Muslim women who had alternative perspectives on the practice of veiling. Nadia, a second-generation British Asian woman studying medicine at university, chose to start wearing a veil at 16. She commented, 'It is liberating to have the freedom of movement to be able to communicate without being on show'. She found that far from being invisible it made her stand out as a Muslim and also helped her to avoid 'lecherous stares or worse' from men. The second woman, Maryam, was a middle-aged Algerian living in France. Upon moving to France she felt it more appropriate to wear a veil. She commented that 'it is difficult enough to live in a big foreign city without having the extra burden of being molested in the street because you are a woman'. The Islamic revolution in Iran had also made her more aware of the importance of Islam and she felt her conduct set a good example for the future generation. The third respondent, Fatima, was an older woman. She was less positive about veiling, seeing it as 'just a trend', but recognized that to turn against some of the less desirable Western values, e.g. the over-emphasis on women as sex objects, was a good thing. In her opinion veiling should be a matter of choice.

Adapted from Watson (1994)

1 **What criticisms could be made of Watson's research?**

2 **How does Watson's work serve as a caution to sociologists who interpret the practices of unfamiliar religions in simplistic terms?**

Linda Woodhead (2004) argues that the various periods of feminist writing have different emphases in their analysis of society and religion.

First-wave feminism was the feminist movement in the 19th century and early 20th century, primarily focused on gaining the right of women to vote.

Second-wave feminism originated in the 1960s and was mainly concerned with independence from men and greater political action to improve women's rights.

Third-wave feminism began in the early 1990s. Unlike second-wave feminism, which largely focused on the inclusion of women in traditionally male-dominated areas, it seeks to challenge and expand common definitions of gender and sexuality. It recognizes the impact of race, class and sexuality on the experience of both sexes. Third-wave feminists have been critical of earlier feminists for concentrating on Christianity and on the concept of patriarchy, which, they argue, is used as a blunt instrument made applicable to all women. The general assumption that all women involved in religion are in a state of false consciousness and so gain nothing from it has also been strongly criticized. Third-wave feminists have abandoned the 'sex war' stance and simple dichotomy between patriarchal male oppressors and innocent female victims and have shed light on the way in which both sexes may actually benefit from their involvement in religion.

Adapted from Fenn (2004)

roles for male and female members. Leila Badawi (1994) has noted aspects of Islam that are positive for women, such as being able to keep their own family name when they marry. In fact, most converts to Islam are female. Numerous writers have highlighted how veiling (the covering of the entire face and hair in the company of men outside the family), rather than being a submission to patriarchy, is in fact a means of ethnic and gender assertiveness. Leila Ahmed (1992) suggests that the veil is a means by which Muslim women can become involved in modern society, while maintaining a sense of modesty and correctness. As she puts it: '[Islamic dress] is a uniform of both transition and arrival, signalling entrance into and determination to move forward in modern society.'

Why are women more religious than men?

Whatever women's influence and status may have been in religious organizations, studies have consistently shown that women are more religious than men. Miller and Hoffmann (1995) report that women:

- are more likely to express a greater interest in religion
- have a stronger personal religious commitment
- attend church more often.

These patterns appear to hold true throughout life, irrespective of the kind of religious organization (cult, sect or church) or religious belief (astrology, magic, spirits, and so on).

One explanation for the more religious orientation of women is offered by Greeley (1992). He argues that before women acquire a partner and have children, their religiosity is not dissimilar to men's (although slightly more committed). But, 'once you start "taking care" of people, perhaps, you begin implicitly to assume greater responsibility for their "ultimate" welfare'. Greeley contends that women are more involved in caring than in practical responsibilities. Caring, it seems, tends to be associated with a more religious outlook.

Miller and Hoffmann (1995) identify two main explanations for such gender differences.

1 Differential socialization

Females are taught to be more submissive, passive, obedient and nurturing than males. These traits are compatible with religiosity, as such characteristics are highly esteemed by most religions. By the same token, men who internalize these norms tend to be more religious than men who do not.

2 Differential roles

Females have lower rates of participation in paid work and this, it is argued, gives women not only more time for church-related activities, but also a greater need for it as a source of personal identity and commitment. They also have higher rates of participation in child-rearing, which also increases religiosity because it coincides with a concern for family wellbeing.

Women and NRMs

Sects

Women tend to participate more in sects than men. Although it is difficult to estimate, Bruce (1995) has suggested that the ratio of female-to-male involvement is similar to that in established religion at about 2:1.

Women are more likely than men to experience poverty, and those who experience economic deprivation are more likely to join sects. As Thompson (1996) notes: 'They may not have the economic and social standing of others in society, but sect members have the promise of salvation and the knowledge that they are enlightened.'

Glock and Stark (1969) identify a number of different types of deprivation in addition to the economic, all of which are more likely to apply to women. They suggest that people who form or join sects may have experienced one or even a number of these.

- *Social deprivation* – This may stem from a lack of power, prestige and status. For example, if people experience a lack of satisfaction or status in employment, they may seek these goals via a religious sect. Those in unsatisfying lower-middle-class jobs (mainly occupied by women) may find satisfaction in the **evangelical goals** set by **conversionist** sects such as Jehovah's Witnesses or Mormons.
- *Organismic deprivation* – This is experienced by those who suffer physical and mental problems (again more likely among women than men). For example, people may turn to sects in the hope of being healed or as an alternative to drugs or alcohol.
- *Ethical deprivation* – People may perceive the world to be in moral decline and so retreat into an **introversionist sect** that separates itself from the world, such as Jim Jones' People's Temple. Again, women tend to be more morally conservative than men.

In the 19th century, many sects were initiated by women: Ellen White set up the Seventh Day Adventists, Mary Baker Eddy founded Christian Science, Ann Lee founded the Shakers, and the Fox sisters began the Spiritualist movement.

Cults

Cults involve a highly individual, privatized version of religious activity. This is mainly (although not exclusively) involved with promoting a notion of personal 'improvement'. Even where wider issues are addressed (such as social problems of crime, unemployment or the destruction of the environment), the solutions offered tend to be couched in personal terms (meditation, greater consciousness, etc.). This 'private sphere' of cult activity relates to traditional gender roles for women, which are based in the 'private' arena of the home. Women are also more inclined to see in themselves a need for self-improvement.

Women and NAMs

Historically, wherever nature is conceptualized, the role of women has been seen in terms of their 'essential femininity', that is, as being naturally different creatures to males – more attuned to the supposed natural rhythms of life. Thus, within the philosophies of New Age cults, women tend to be afforded a much higher status than men. This is one reason that may explain higher female involvement in NAMs, as many of them emphasize the 'natural', such as herbal and homeopathic remedies, aromatherapy and massage.

Women and fundamentalism

The resurgence of religious fundamentalism over the past decade has played a major role in attempting to reverse the trend of women's increasing autonomy and their pursuit of fulfilment beyond motherhood.

- In the USA, opposition to women controlling their fertility through abortion has sometimes ended in violence, with right-wing, religious fundamentalist pro-life groups adopting near terrorist tactics to close clinics down.
- Despite India's long history of reform and modernization, the rise of Hindu fundamentalism has made it difficult for governments there to intervene in family life or encourage greater freedom for women, despite their commitment to preventing the oppression of members of certain lower castes.
- Fundamentalist groups in Iran, Israel, Afghanistan and parts of the former Soviet Union similarly insist on ruthlessly conserving or reinstating of women's traditional positions.

Cohen and Kennedy (2000) suggest that 'the desire to restore fundamentalist religious values and social practices is associated with the fear that any real increase in women's freedom of choice and action will undermine the foundations of tradition, religion, morality and, it could be argued, male control'.

Women's traditional roles centre around child-rearing and the home. They are thus responsible for transmitting religious values from one generation to the next and upholding all that is most sacred in the lives of family members. Fundamentalism, both in the West (such as the Christian Right or the **Nation of Islam** in the USA) and elsewhere, has often emphasized the

Check your understanding

1 What evidence is there to show that women were not always subordinate to men in religion?

2 What caused men to dominate religion and religious practice?

3 What evidence for patriarchy is there in the world's major religions:
   (a) in terms of their scriptures?
   (b) in terms of roles in religious institutions?

4 Why, according to Bird, is sexuality such an important issue for many religions?

5 How do feminists view the role of religion?

6 What evidence is there to show that some religions are not necessarily patriarchal?

7 (a) What evidence is there for women's greater religiosity?
   (b) What explanations have been given for this?

8 What reasons are given for women's greater involvement in NRMs?

9 How has the resurgence of fundamentalism affected the role of women?

significance of protecting and defending women. The spin-off is that this re-empowers men by removing some of the **ambiguities** that have been associated with the modern world. But, as feminists assert, the apparent position of importance such women experience in upholding the faith, brings with it powerlessness and sometimes abuse at the hands of husbands and kinsmen.

However, not all women are unwilling victims of the return to traditional roles – as the work on Muslim women and veiling demonstrates. Research by Woodhead and Heelas (2000) shows how women converting to orthodox Judaism in the US are actually attracted by the status in the home that it provides them with. Such women can also be seen as seeking to remove the ambiguities of modernity, as they perceive them.

research idea

- Using an equal sample of males and females from amongst your peers, try to assess the extent of gender differences in religiosity. Focus on formal religious practice (e.g. church attendance), belief/non-belief in God, the nature of God (compassionate or powerful) and alternative beliefs, e.g. spirituality.

web.task

Search the web for 'the role of women in religion' using any search engine of your choice. Select an article on women in various religious organizations past and present and summarize it. Compare your reading with others in your class.

exploring gender, feminism and religion

Item A

Despite feminist criticisms of the prescriptive roles ascribed to women by many religions, significant numbers of women continue to be attracted to such religions. Davidman (1991) explored the reasons why culturally advantaged North American women were converting to Orthodox Judaism. Davidman's conclusion is that it is precisely because such religion maintains a clear distinction between the sexes that it becomes attractive to women who, in an increasingly dislocating world, value domesticity and their future role as wives and mothers. In contrast to the feminist goal of sexual liberation, careers and variation in family patterns, Orthodox Judaism offered clear gender norms, assistance in finding partners and explicit guidelines for family life. It legitimated their desires for the traditional identity of wives and mothers in nuclear families. Also, women are seen as central in the Jewish religious world and are given special status. In contrast to the liberal feminist goal of equality, such women seek the alternative of equity – the idea of equal but separate roles.

Adapted from Woodhead, L. and Heelas, P. (2000) *Religion in Modern Times: An Interpretive Anthology*, Oxford: Blackwell

1 (a) **Identify and briefly explain two reasons why the women described in Item A want to convert to Orthodox Judaism. (8 marks)**

(b) **Using material from Item A and elsewhere, briefly examine reasons for the greater religiosity of women relative to that of men. (12 marks)**

2 **Assess the view that religion, in general, has negative consequences for women. (40 marks)**

Religion and ethnicity

gettingyouthinking

Group	1970	1980	1990	2000	
Christian: Trinitarian* of whom:	9272	7529	6624	5917	mainly White ethnic majority
Anglican	2987	2180	1728	1654	
Catholic	2746	2455	2198	1768	
Free Churches	1629	1285	1299	1278	
Presbyterian	1751	1437	1214	989	
Orthodox	159	172	185	235	
Christian: Non-Trinitarian**	276	349	455	533	
Buddhist	10	15	30	50	mainly ethnic minority
Hindu	80	120	140	165	
Jewish	375	321	356	383	
Muslim	130	305	495	675	
Sikh	100	150	250	400	
Others	20	40	55	85	

Membership in the UK (thousands)

*Trinitarian churches are those that accept a view of God as the three eternal persons: God the Father, God the Son and God the Holy Spirit. These are the great majority of Christian churches.

**Non-Trinitarian churches accept a range of different views of God. These include sects such as: Christian Scientists, the Church of Scientology, Jehovah's Witnesses, Mormons (Church of Jesus Christ of Latter Day Saints), Spiritualists and the Unification Church (Moonies).

Adapted from Brierley, P. (ed.) *Religious Trends 2000*, London: HarperCollins

1 What is the overall trend in the membership of Trinitarian churches?

2 What do the figures tell us about ethnicity and religious practice?

3 In what ways does religion influence the way that you lead your life?

4 How important is it to you that children practise their faith or that they pass on their religious heritage to their children?

5 Does religion give you a personal motivation and strength that helps you to cope with the stresses and difficulties involved in society?

It is likely that most White members of your class will have had little to say about the role of religion in their lives. On the other hand, non-White students from different ethnic backgrounds may have said a great deal more. The statistics above show the continuing importance of religion in the lives of many minority groups in Britain. Why this is the case is much more difficult to explain and this is even harder when you take into account differences between first-generation immigrants and their children who were born in Britain.

The United Kingdom in the 21st century is a multifaith society. Everyone has the right to religious freedom. A wide variety of religious organizations and groups are permitted to conduct their **rites** and ceremonies, to promote their beliefs within the limits of the law, to own property and to run schools and a range of other charitable activities. For the first time in the UK since 1851, the 2001 Census included a question on religion. Although it was a voluntary question, over 92 per cent of people chose to answer it.

Religion and community solidarity

A study by the Policy Studies Institute (1997) found that 74 per cent of Muslim respondents said that religion was 'very important'. This compared with around 45 per cent for Hindus and Sikhs. In contrast, only 11 per cent of White people described themselves as belonging to the Church of England. Amongst Muslim men over the age of 35, four in five reported that they visit a mosque at least once every week.

There are various possible reasons why immigrants to Britain have placed a greater emphasis on religion than the long-established population:

● People had high levels of belief before migration and, as Weber (1920/1958) has suggested, being members of deprived groups, they tended to be more religious. Religion provides an explanation for disadvantage and possibly offers hope of salvation, if not elsewhere on earth then in the afterlife.

● Religion helps bond new communities – particularly when under threat. As Durkheim (1912/1961) has argued, it provides members with a sense of shared norms and values, symbolized through rituals that unite them as a distinctive social group.

However, religion has also become a basis for conflicts between cultures. The dominant culture often sees minority cultures in a negative light, as there is the feeling that newcomers to British society should **assimilate**. Ethnic-minority issues, such as arranged marriages, the refusal of Sikhs to wear motorcycle helmets and the growth in the number of religious temples and mosques (while many Christian churches have closed) suggest an unwillingness to assimilate and have created resentment from the host community. However, many second- and third-generation ethnic-minority Britons were born in the UK and their refusal to assimilate fully has led to a re-evaluation of what being British actually means.

In studying religion and ethnicity, it is clear that religions offer much more than just spiritual fulfilment. They have the power to reaffirm the ethnic identity of their adherents, albeit in uniquely different ways – as is clear from Table 1.3 on the following page.

focus on research

Home Office Citizenship Survey
Importance of religion in people's lives

This survey is the first to map the relevance of religion in the lives of people in England and Wales today. In a period of renewed interest in religion, it has provided much needed quantitative information about the importance of religion in shaping social attitudes and actions. Using data from over 15 000 interviews with people in England and Wales, this survey shows that:

● Almost four out of every five people expressed a religious affiliation. The largest number (74%) described themselves as Christians. Muslims, (2%) and Hindus (2%) were the largest of the remaining faith communities.

● Being affiliated to a faith community means different things to different groups. In particular members of minority religions tended to feel their beliefs were more fundamental to their sense of self-identity compared with many white Christians.

● The likelihood of religion being important to self-identity was greatest for people with the following characteristics:
  – Asian and Sikh, Hindu or Muslim; or black or mixed ethnicity and Christian
  – born in Africa, Indian Subcontinent or Middle East;
  – widowed or married
  – having a degree or diploma, A-Levels and or other unspecified overseas qualifications.

● Most respondents thought the government and employers were doing enough with regard to protecting religious rights and respecting religious customs. However, a sizeable minority of young people and women affiliated to Muslim and Sikh faith communities thought that the government was doing too little. A larger proportion of men than women were allowed to take time off work for religious purposes. The majority of respondents reported that their employers did not provide prayer facilities.

● For the most part, respondents with a religious affiliation lived in places with low to moderate levels of area deprivation; the exception were respondents affiliated to the Muslim faith community, who tended to live in areas with the highest levels of area deprivation.

Home Office Research, Development and Statistics Directorate, March 2004

1 Why do you think that members of minority groups feel religion to be more important to their sense of self identity than do White Christian-affiliated groups?

2 How might high levels of relative deprivation among members of Muslim communities affect their sense of identity and community solidarity?

Table 1.3 Differences in the significance of religion for first-generation Asian and African-Caribbean migrants to Britain

	African-Caribbean	Asian
Role of religion	Religion is used as a means of coping with the worries and the pressures of life through the joyful nature of prayer, as much through its immediacy and mood-affecting quality as its long-term contribution to personal development.	Asian groups tend to speak of control over selfish desires and of fulfilling one's responsibilities to others, especially family members. Prayer is seen in terms of duty, routine and the patterning of their lives.
Religion and family life	Used to develop trust, love, mutual responsibilities and the learning of right and wrong within the context of the family. African-Caribbeans express an individualistic or voluntaristic view of religion. Children should decide for themselves whether they maintain religious commitment into adulthood.	Used in a similar way, but Asians tend to adopt a collective or conformist approach. The expectation of parents is that their children will follow in adulthood the religion they have been brought up in; not to do so is to betray one's upbringing or to let one's family down.
Religion and social life	Little importance beyond fostering and maintaining a spiritual, moral and ethical outlook. The church offers opportunities to socialize and to organize social events in an otherwise privatized community of member families.	Muslims tend to see conformity to Islamic law and Islam as a comprehensive way of life, affecting attitudes to alcohol, food, dress and choice of marriage partner. The influence of religion is less extreme for most Sikhs and Hindus, but its importance for the first generation is still great.

Adapted from Modood, T., Beish0n, S. and Virdee, S. (1994) *Changing Ethnic Identities*, London: Policy Studies Institute

spotlighton

Muslims in Britain

Although early migrants saw themselves as temporary visitors, successive changes to immigration laws encouraged them to settle. The subsequent restructuring of manufacturing industries in the 1970s and the disappearance of many of the jobs in northern Britain for which South Asians had originally been recruited, encouraged a large number of them to become self-employed in the service sector. This was also affected by religious and cultural factors. A survey in the 1990s (Metcalf *et al.* 1996) found that two thirds of self-employed Pakistani people mentioned that being their own boss meant it was easier for them to perform their religious duties. Their strong religious faith gave them confidence to set up on their own despite a lack of formal qualifications and poor access to finance.

By the 1970s, Pakistanis and Bangladeshis no longer had the intention of 'returning home' and, as relatives joined them, they established a wide range of community organizations. They began at the same time to be more self-consciously Muslim and more observant in the practice of their faith. Factors affecting this strengthening of religious belief and practice included:

- the desire to build a sense of group identity and strength in a situation of material disadvantage, and in an alien and largely hostile surrounding culture
- the desire, now that communities contained both children, on the one hand, and elders on the other, to keep the generations together, and to transmit traditional values to children and young people
- the desire for inner spiritual resources to withstand the pressures of racism and **Islamophobia**, and the threat to South-Asian culture and customs posed by Western materialism and permissiveness.

The increased influence of Islam in the politics of Pakistan and Bangladesh in the 1970s, and the increased influence of oil-exporting countries in international affairs, most of which were Muslim, contributed to Muslim self-confidence and assertiveness within Britain. In addition, a sense of community strength grew through the 1980s from successful local campaigns to assert Muslim values and concerns – for example, for **halal food** to be served in schools and hospitals. The Rushdie affair in 1988 prompted demands by British Muslims for prosecution of the author of the book *The Satanic Verses* (Salman Rushdie) under British blasphemy laws. Though their demands were refused, this raised the profile of Muslims in Britain, especially when the Ayatollah Khomeini of Iran imposed a *fatwah* on Rushdie – a death sentence to be carried out by any Muslim, which lasted for 10 years. The Islamophobic aftermath following the bombing of the World Trade Center in 2001 and the London bombings of July 2005 also served to promote even greater assertiveness in defending both their community and Islam. One key consideration in discussing the experience of Muslims in particular, concerns their younger age profile compared with all other groups. Around 70 per cent of all British Muslims are under the age of 25.

Pentecostalism

Immigrants from the Caribbean have settled throughout Britain but are concentrated in inner-city areas. Many have established strong, culturally distinctive communities in urban areas such as Brixton in South London. However, while religious institutions are central to Asian communities, this is not necessarily the case where African-Caribbeans are concerned. Committed Christian African-Caribbeans often have a more individualist relationship to their religion, which means that the issue of identifying with a wider culture through religion, common with Asian religions, is less evident. African-Caribbean culture gives more choice about whether to be religious or not, and those that are see their involvement as one aspect of their lives rather than central to all aspects. Moreover, many African-Caribbeans are fully assimilated into British society and do not see the loss of religion as a threat to their identity. Indeed, like many White Britons, many do not give any significance to religion in their lives.

Many African-Caribbeans belong to racially mixed Christian denominations. However, the largest distinctively African-Caribbean churches consist of the Pentecostalist and the **charismatic** or **'house church'** **movements**. These churches have a distinctive style of worship with its roots in the Caribbean – Jamaica in particular. According to Hall (1985), when White Anglican missionaries met ex-slaves whose Jamaican folk religion included magical beliefs and behaviours, Christianity was assimilated into folk beliefs to form an 'Afro-Christianity'. Common features were **ecstatic trances**, night gatherings, processions led by a 'captain' to the sound of muffled drums. Afro-Christianity gave key biblical events high prominence and some struck a chord within the African heart. The story of Moses, for example, liberating the Israelites and leading them to the promised land, echoed a desire for many to return to Africa. (**Rastafarianism** has also picked up on this biblical theme.) Many African churches are characterized by the literal reading of the bible. They also maintain distinctively African folk traditions. 'Speaking in tongues' is believed to involve languages specifically given by God to improve communication with God, while divine healing is thought to prove God's power to redeem the people from sin.

Religion and ethnic identity

While there are significant differences in religiosity within the Asian and African-Caribbean communities, it is possible to make some initial generalizations about them. African-Caribbeans were mainly Christian on arrival in the UK, but were unable to access the existing religious institutions. However, Hindus, Sikhs and Muslims (for whom religion was part of their 'difference') had virtually no existing religious organizations and places of worship in Britain to join. From this flowed different experiences. On the one hand, the African-Caribbeans tried to join existing religious institutions and often had to come to terms with the racism displayed by the church and its congregations, a racism pervasive in British society at the time.

On the other hand, Asians had to make a collective effort to establish and practise their faith in a radically new social setting. As Modood *et al.* (1994) point out, for Asians their religion was intricately connected with their status as an ethnic group, but this was not the case for African-Caribbeans (see Table 1.3 opposite). Even for those who saw their Christianity as part of family tradition and culture, their religion was not significantly part of their sense of ethnic difference. Nonetheless, distinctively African-Caribbean forms of Christian spirituality in both the mainstream churches and in the Black-led churches have mushroomed in the past 20 years, as some African-Caribbeans have sought to establish their own churches and styles of worship.

The second generation

When examining the position of members of ethnic minorities born in Britain, Modood *et al.* (1994) found that there appears to be an overall decline in the importance of religion for all of the main ethnic groups and fewer said they observed the various rules and requirements. Even those who said that religion was important wished to interpret their religious traditions and scriptures flexibly. Also, fewer second-generation respondents regularly attended a place of religious worship. The least religiously committed were Sikhs. When asked how they saw themselves, virtually none of the second-generation Punjabis spontaneously said 'Sikh'. However, a decade earlier Beatrice Drury studied a much larger sample of 16- to 20-year-old Sikh girls and found that, if prompted, all saw their Sikh identity as fundamental (reported in Drury 1991).

Single-faith schools

Perhaps as a consequence of this decline in religious observance, many parents of ethnic-minority children want the option for their children of attending a faith school. In their view, such schools can be a positive influence on strength of religious commitment as well as in maintaining strong ethnic identities. Though these schools are currently relatively few in number (see Table 1.4), the government proposes to expand this aspect of educational provision. However, the events of September 11th, the continuing problems in Northern Ireland (in particular the events outside Holy Cross School in the Ardoyne) and the racial unrest that fuelled riots in Bradford and

Table 1.4 Voluntary aided schools 2000

Denomination	Number of Schools	
	Primary	Secondary
Church of England	4523	193
Roman Catholic	1752	356
Other Christian	47	27
Jewish	25	5
Muslim	4	3 (1 boys 2 girls)
Sikh	2	2 (girls)
Hindu	1	–
Total with a religious character	6354 (35%)	586 (13%)

Source: DfES (2000)

other English cities in 2001, all show ethnic fracture lines in our society. Opponents of faith schools see them as socially divisive, inhibiting understanding between communities and providing an easy target for racists.

Refer back to the table in 'Getting you thinking' (p. 32) and compare the proportion of different religious schools in Table 1.4 with the proportion of members of different religions. How fair is the current distribution of religious schools?

However, parents may be being overpessimistic in their perception of a loss of ethnic identity among their children. Johal (1998) has pointed out how in a country such as Britain, where religious pluralism is still a long way off, many British Asians have chosen to preserve and uphold the religious and cultural doctrines of their parents as a means of asserting a coherent and powerful identity and of resisting racism. As Johal puts it, 'holding on to these doctrines can provide a kind of **empowerment** through difference'. He also notes that many second- and third-generation Asians carefully manage their religious and cultural values. Issues such as choice of marriage partners, intra-ethnic marriage and diet 'often lead to the adoption of a position of selective cultural preference, a kind of juggling act in which young Asians move between one culture and another, depending on context and whether overt "Britishness" or pronounced "Asianness" is most appropriate'.

It certainly appears to be the case that Muslim women, often commented on for their apparent submissiveness and repression, have actually adapted well to the challenge of maintaining their cultural and religious identity, while at the same time becoming effective, well-integrated members of mainstream society. A number of studies such as that of Butler (1995) have explored this **cultural hybridity**. Recent research shows how veiling and the wearing of traditional dress may actually give Muslim girls greater freedom from patriarchal attitudes experienced by many White girls. (This was discussed further in Topic 5.)

Differences in styles of worship

While worship in Anglican churches is dominated by older people and women, and demands limited formal involvement of the congregation, Pentecostal church congregations comprise every age group and an equal balance of the sexes. There is a greater emphasis on religious experience than **religious dogma**, and worship is concerned with demonstrating publicly the joyous nature of religious conversion and the power of religion to heal people, both physically and mentally. Considerable involvement is required from worshippers in the form of dancing and 'call and response' between congregation and clergy.

Bird (1999) suggests that Pentecostalism has played a dual role for African-Caribbean people:

1 For some, it has enabled them to cope with and adjust to a racist and unjust society. It serves as an 'opium' for the people, as Marx has suggested.
2 For others, such as Pryce (1979), it encourages hard work, sexual morality, prudent management of finances and strong support of the family and community. In this sense, it reflects the Protestant ethic that Weber saw as essential in the development of capitalism (see Topic 1).

There are many other ethnic-minority religions, all of which can help to define and maintain a cultural identity, traditions and customs. Some provide direction and enable their members to cope in a racist and unjust society (e.g. Rastafarianism). Some religions or religious factions are antagonistic to society and the ambiguities of modernity. They offer solutions that may involve resistance and/or a return to fundamental principles felt to have been eroded through spiritual and moral decline. Such fundamentalism is discussed further in Topic 3.

KEY TERMS

Assimilate – blend in and integrate.

Charismatic movements – religious movements that believe that some individuals have gifts of the Holy Spirit such as the ability to speak in tongues and possess healing powers.

Cultural hybridity – to mix and match different cultural influences.

Ecstatic trances – an apparently hypnotic state where worshippers appear overwhelmed by their religious experience and unaware of the immediate physical world around them.

Empowerment – to be given greater power and recognition.

Halal food – food prepared and blessed according to Islamic law.

House church movement – a church body that doesn't assemble in an established church building but in the homes of its members. By their very nature, house churches tend to be smaller in size and counter-cultural in many ways, i.e. have a sect-like, world-rejecting quality. They exist all over the world.

Islamophobia – obsessive fear and hatred of Islam and Muslims.

Rastafarianism – Rastafarians (Rastas) worship Haile Selassie I (known as Ras [Prince] Tafari), former emperor of Ethiopia, considering him to have been the Messiah. Rastas believe that Black people are the Israelites reincarnated and have been persecuted by the White race in divine punishment for their sins. They will eventually be redeemed by exodus to Africa, their true home and heaven on earth.

Religious dogma – rules and regulations, commandments and formal requirements of a particular religion.

Rites – customary religious practices, e.g. baptism.

Check your understanding

1 Give two reasons why immigrants to the UK have placed a greater emphasis on religion than the indigenous population.

2 (a) How did the experience of Asian and African-Caribbean groups differ when they originally came to Britain?

   (b) How did this affect their sense of identity?

3 According to Modood, what changes have there been for second-generation Asians?

4 Identify arguments for and against the existence of religious schools?

5 Why have many second-generation Asians chosen to hold on to their religious identity?

6 Give examples of how recent world events have served to reaffirm religious commitment for many ethnic-minority groups.

7 What are the reasons for the growing popularity of Pentecostal churches?

8 What role does Pentecostalism play for African-Caribbean believers?

researchidea

• Interview a number of respondents from different religious backgrounds who wear religious artefacts such as Jewish headwear, the hijab or crucifixes.

  Try to determine how important they consider this right to display religious commitment to be. Are their motivations mainly cultural or religious?

web.task

Find the results of the The Home Office Citizenship Survey at www.homeoffice.gov.uk/rds/pdfs04/hors274.pdf

How was the survey carried out? Choose any one aspect of the findings and summarise them as a report for the rest of your class.

exploring ethnicity and religion

Item A

The most Christian parts of England and Wales were St Helens and Wigan, where 86.9 per cent of people were practising Christians. The least Christian were the multicultural areas of Tower Hamlets in London (38.6 per cent Christian) and Leicester (44.7 per cent). There are more than 1.5 million Muslims in England and Wales, with the largest concentrations in Tower Hamlets (36.4 per cent). Harrow in London (19.6 per cent of population) has the highest proportion of Hindus. Barnet in north London has the largest Jewish population (more than 46 000) while Westminster, home to London's Chinatown, has the most Buddhists (1.3 per cent). In Norwich, an unrivalled 27.8 per cent people said they had 'no religion'. An internet joke led to 390 000 claiming to be Jedi Knights – after *Star Wars*. They have been filed under 'no religion'.

Adapted from the 2001 Census HMSO

1 (a) Identify and briefly explain two reasons why inner-city areas have the highest proportion of non Christians. (8 marks)

   (b) Using material from Item A and elsewhere, briefly examine the impact of religion upon ethnic identity. (12 marks)

2 Critically examine the view that the religions of ethnic minorities have been more successful in maintaining membership and participation than those of established churches. (40 marks)

The problem of secularization

gettingyouthinking

Variation between groups

- According to the British Social Attitudes Survey (1998), only one-third of 18 to 24 year olds 'say they belong to a religion'. But the equivalent for those over 65 is just over three-quarters.
- 36% of frequent or regular church attenders are men, compared with 64% of women (see Topic 6).
- 16% of the middle classes attend church compared with 12% of the working class, yet of the non-attenders, more members of the middle class are non-believers.
- Minority-ethnic groups are generally more religious than Whites (see Topic 6).

1 Suggest reasons why these patterns exist.

2 What may the implications of these patterns be for the future religiosity of British society?

As the exercise above illustrates, patterns of religious commitment vary between groups. How much members of such groups affect others around them may influence the overall extent of religiosity that exists in a particular time or place. If certain ethnic groups are religious, but only constitute a small percentage of the population, it may be said that they have little impact on the society as a whole. But, if they are confined to a particular geographical region, then that area may appear to be highly religious and the impact of religion there strong. If women are more religious than men, they may have more influence on young children. Though the young are generally less religiously affiliated – that is, they tend not to be members of religious organizations – how can we know whether they express religious beliefs privately at home? Does the state of social inequality have a bearing upon religious commitment? For example, in periods of recession is religion more significant in providing a theodicy of disprivilege (see Topic 2)?

It is difficult to make conclusive statements about religious commitment. The complexity of operationalizing – defining and measuring – religious belief and religious activity has long haunted sociologists, particularly those concerned with judging whether or not religion is in decline in the modern world – the process known as secularization. This topic outlines some of the problems faced by sociologists in assessing this process, while Topic 8 looks at the actual evidence for and against secularization.

In order to judge whether secularization is or is not taking place, sociologists need to define and measure key concepts such as religion and religious belief, as well as secularization itself. This is by no means straightforward.

Defining secularization

Wilson (1966) provides the following 'classic' definition of secularization: 'the process whereby religious thinking, practices and institutions lose social significance'. This seems a general enough catch-all statement, and is one that has been widely adopted, but problems occur straight away. What exactly is 'religious thinking'? What is meant by 'significance'? How can you measure 'significance'?

A further problem arises from the approach or level of analysis adopted. Glasner (1977) identifies three levels of analysis in the study of secularization.

- *Interpersonal* – the extent to which religious beliefs do or do not guide individual behaviour and attitudes
- *Organizational* – the extent to which the church's importance in society is declining
- *Cultural* – the extent to which society is or is not influenced by religious ideas.

It is possible that secularization could occur at one level but not necessarily at others.

Like many other sociological concepts, the idea of secularization contains a number of difficulties and hidden assumptions. In addition, any account of the secularization process depends on the definition of religion adopted in the first place.

Brown (2001) suggests that participation has declined in the established churches mainly because of the changing role of women. When female church-attendance and participation were high, the same was true for both children and men. Women, with their domestic and maternal roles heavily emphasized in both secular and religious literature right down to about 1960, were the primary churchgoers, with children in tow and husbands – sometimes reluctantly – following suit.

stratification and differentiation

Brown further suggests that from the 1960s, feminism and the media presented women with other ways of understanding their identities, their sexuality and their lives generally than traditional Christian notions. 'British women secularized the construction of their identity, and the churches started to lose them (and their husbands and children).'

Defining religion

The problem with the debate about secularization is that writers use the same evidence to reach widely different conclusions. This is often because they are defining 'religion' in different ways. As Hanson (1997) points out, such definitional diversity leads to 'much misunderstanding and talking past one another'. Even before it starts, the debate can never be conclusive.

There are two main types of definition of religion: substantive and functional.

Substantive definitions of religion

These define a religious belief system as involving relations between the 'natural' and 'supernatural' spheres. This includes beliefs in God or gods, the afterlife, heaven, spirits, prophecy, and so on. Thus, religion is defined in terms of the structure and content of people's beliefs rather than what religion does for them.

Functional definitions of religion

Functional definitions characterize religion in terms of the functions it performs for individuals and society. These definitions are also called 'inclusive', because they include beliefs that have a religion-like influence but which theorists from the substantive camp would not include. For Marx, religion was the 'opium of the masses' and for Durkheim a form of 'social cement'. The same 'religious' functions may be now performed by television, going to a football match or civil ceremonies such as events involving the Royal Family. Using the functional definition, all these could be considered 'religious'.

The relationship between these two approaches to religion is clearly a problem. However, as Wilson (1982) has pointed out, those who define religion in substantive terms are more likely to support the **secularization thesis** because they can show that religious belief has declined as people accept other more rational explanations of the world. But those who see religion in functional terms are more likely to reject the secularization thesis. If the functions of religion are essential to the smooth running of society, they argue, even though religion may change, these functions still need to be fulfilled. What we call religion must simply remain in some form or another to fulfil them.

Measuring religious belief and practice

There is no clear definition of the boundaries of religious belief. Is a belief in fate or luck a religious belief? What about witches, ghosts or flying saucers? If they are, then an awful lot of people share such beliefs and may be termed 'religious', as Table 1.5 illustrates.

There are also problems in measuring religious commitment. In the UK, 33 per cent people say religion is very important personally (Pew Global Attitudes Project 2002). Does this mean, for example, that for a third of the population, religion has a significant impact upon behaviour? Furthermore, is such religiously influenced behaviour increasing or decreasing?

The validity of church-attendance statistics as an indicator of secularization

Many interpretivist sociologists suggest that church attendance statistics that appear to indicate religious decline should be treated with caution. Martin (1978) claims that relatively high attendance figures from the Victorian age may be a reflection of non-religious factors, such as the need to be seen by social

Table 1.5 The things people believe in

Responses to the question: *'Which, if any, of the things I'm going to read out do you believe in?'*

Percentage	Yes	No	Don't know
A soul/human spirit	67	24	9
Astrology	38	53	9
Ghosts	40	52	8
Telepathy	54	37	9
Guardian angels	31	61	8
Premonitions/ESP	64	29	7
Fortune-telling/tarot	18	75	7
Déjà-vu	66	30	4
Out-of-body experience	31	58	11
Reincarnation	24	64	12
Near-death experience	51	37	12
Psychics/mediums	28	63	9
Faith-healers	32	56	12
Dreams can predict the future	30	60	10

Source: MORI poll, Feb. 1998

superiors. Hamilton (2001) points out that the notion of an 'age of faith' in the past is an illusion partly created as a result of concentrating on the religious behaviour of the elite, about which we have more information than the vast majority of ordinary people. This may mean that the past was no more or less religious than the present. It often seems that the secularization thesis rests on the assumption that in the past there were 'fully religious societies'. It is against such societies that our 'godless' society is then compared. The idea of a more religious past remains, however, a potent belief. Williams (1956), in his study of Gosforth, showed consistently low levels of church attendance over some 400 years, yet each vicar believed it to be a recent phenomenon.

But does declining church attendance necessarily indicate a reduction in religiosity? People may still believe, but are too busy to attend, or see churches as inappropriate these days because they think that religion is a private matter. On the other hand, those who attend church may do so for reasons other than religion, to appear respectable or to make new friends or perhaps to get their child into a denominational school with a good academic reputation.

Also, different religious organizations demand varying degrees of commitment and religious intensity. The Church of England demands little from its members, whereas sects such as the Jehovah's Witnesses expect fairly intense activity and commitment. Whilst many people may say they are religious, the effect of that commitment on their lives and the society that they live in may vary immensely.

But is secularization best measured through church attendance anyway? Undoubtedly, there has been a decline in attendance, at least among Christians in Britain, but Britain is now a multicultural and multifaith society. To assume secularization on the basis of an analysis of the fortunes of Christianity is to dismiss the importance of other major world faiths supported in Britain. And at the global level, some social changes are enhancing the importance of religion. Many young Muslims have returned to Islam having been politicized by the widespread perception that Islam is under attack globally.

The reliability of church-attendance statistics as an indicator of secularization

Statistics about religious activity from the previous century are questionable because reliable data-collection practices were not in place. Contemporary statistics, too, may not be reliable because different religious organizations employ different counting methods. The Roman Catholic Church may underestimate the numbers in their congregation to reduce the capitation fees they have to pay, and the Anglican churches may overestimate to produce impressive totals, particularly to avoid church closure.

In terms of membership, the Roman Catholic Church counts those who have been baptized and confirmed, even though they may have taken no part in church life since their confirmation. The Church of Wales counts attendance at Easter Communion, whilst the Jewish religion documents the number of Jewish heads of households, regardless of their attendance.

focus on research
Shiner (1967)
Versions of secularization

Shiner (1967) identified six different versions of secularization used by sociologists:

- The decline of religion – where religious symbols, doctrines and institutions lose their social significance, e.g. Sunday shopping becoming more common.
- Conformity with the world – religious movements becoming focused on the goals of 'this world', such as money and personal fulfilment rather than the 'next'.
- **Disengagement** – where the church loses functions to other institutions and becomes less significant in moral and political terms, e.g. losing its role in education and counselling those experiencing personal suffering.
- Transposition of religious beliefs and institutions – where events that were previously regarded as the result of divine power become seen as human creations, e.g. the destruction caused by Hurricane Katrina (in August 2005) is blamed on global warming, rather than being interpreted as an act of God.
- **Desacrilization** of the world – scientific and rational explanations take precedence over religious faith, e.g. the acceptance of the 'big bang' theory of the origin of the universe.
- From sacred to secular society – religion moves from a central position in society and takes its place as one option in a marketplace of other possible philosophies.

Adapted from Watson (1994)

1 Do you consider any one of the above versions to be more significant than the others?

2 Can you think of any counter arguments to any of the secularization claims above?

Conclusion

Glock and Stark (1968) argue that not enough attention has been paid to the detail of defining religion and religiosity and that, because of this, the secularization thesis cannot be accurately tested. Indeed, the same empirical evidence can be used by different researchers to 'prove' both that secularization 'is' or 'is not' occurring. Martin has actually advocated the removal of the term 'secularization' from the sociological vocabulary, instead supporting the careful and detailed study of the ways in which the role of religion has changed at different times and different places.

However, despite the difficulties, a large body of sociological literature has emerged involving a debate between two groups of writers on opposite sides of the discussion who have sought to engage with the evidence on some level. This secularization debate is discussed in the next topic.

Check your understanding

1. Give two examples that show how a person's social identity may affect religiosity

2. According to the Mori poll of February 1998, which are the two things most believed in. Would you consider one more or less an example of religious belief than the other? If so why?

3. Give an example that illustrates a non-religious reason for attending church.

4. Give two examples of religious beliefs that fall within a substantive or exclusive definition of religion.

5. Give two examples of religious beliefs that fall within a functional or inclusive definition.

6. Which of these definitions of religion is more likely to support the idea of secularization and why?

7. What does Hanson mean when he says that definitional diversity leads to 'much misunderstanding and talking past one another'?

8. Which level of analysis of secularization do you consider to be the most significant and why?

9. What is the commonsense assumption about religiosity in the past? Why should such assumptions be challenged?

10. Why may contemporary statistics be unreliable?

11. Why do some sociologists consider that the secularization thesis cannot be tested?

KEY TERMS

Desacrilization – where sacred explanations give way to scientific rational explanations

Disengagement – where the religious institutions become less engaged in wider aspects of social life

Inclusive – all encompassing.

Secularization thesis – belief in the declining influence of religion in society.

research idea

- Conduct a survey to discover the extent of belief in a range of supernatural and spiritual phenomena among students at your school or college. To what extent do your results indicate widespread 'religious belief'? Would your conclusions be different if you used different criteria for measuring 'religious belief'?

web.task

Visit the websites of the National Secular Society at www.secularism.org.uk and the British Humanist Association at www.humanism.org.uk. What does each organization say about the problems they perceive religion causes for society?

exploring the problem of secularization

Item A

The question of secularization is further complicated by the fact that the phenomena of religious belief and practice are specific to the cultural context in which they occur. As Theodore Caplow argues, whilst religious belief and practice have declined in many European countries since World War II, no significant decline in religious belief or practice has occurred in the United States in the same period. If that were not complicated enough, there is also the question as to just what qualifies as religious belief and practice and how one measures this. Furthermore, there is the phenomenon today that, as Grace Davie puts it, people in Great Britain 'believe but they do not belong' to a particular Church. Other countries follow their own patterns of secularization with their own particular histories and forms of religious belief and practice that are better or worse described by the theory of secularization.

Adapted from Carroll, A. (2004) 'What is Secularization?', a paper given at the Scribani Conference Antwerp, September 2004, Round Table on Ethics and Faith, The Heythrop Institute for Religion, Ethics and Public Life

1. (a) Identify and briefly explain **two** social changes that would serve to indicate that society has become more secular. (8 marks)

   (b) Using material from **Item A** and elsewhere, briefly examine some of the difficulties sociologists face in establishing whether secularization is occurring. (12 marks)

2. Assess the view that secularization is so difficult to define that the concept is of little use to sociologists. (40 marks)

The secularization debate

gettingyouthinking

'Christianity will go. It will vanish and shrink. I needn't argue with that – I'm right and I will be proved right. We're more popular than Jesus now. I don't know which will go first – rock 'n' roll or Christianity.'

John Lennon (The Beatles), *London Evening Standard*, 4 March 1966

Right: the Swaminarayan Hindu Mandir (Temple), in Neasden, NW London, opened in 1995

1. **How do the photographs above challenge or support the view that religion in the contemporary UK is declining in significance?**
2. **What types of religion in Britain appear to be declining and which thriving?**
3. **Why do you think that John Lennon's comments caused international uproar, especially in the United States?**

Above: a former cinema in Woolwich, London, now being used as an evangelical church

Left: a former church now housing a carpet warehouse

What is the evidence for secularization?

Topic 7 explored some of the problems associated with the idea of secularization. This topic considers the evidence for and against this idea. One of the most influential supporters of the secularization thesis, Wilson (1966), defines secularization as 'the process whereby religious thinking, practices and institutions lose social significance'. He suggests that this is mainly reflected statistically in declining church attendance and membership, but he also argues that religion is losing influence over public life and affairs. Wilson mainly focuses on statistical evidence relating to religious institutions and their activity. Continue to bear in mind, however, that such statistics have questionable reliability and validity (see Topic 7).

Attendance

The strongest evidence for secularization in Britain comes from church-attendance statistics. According to the 1851 Census,

Table 1.6 Church membership in the UK 1900 to 2000				
Year	Members (000s)	Population (000s)	Members as % of population	% of population attending Sunday School
1900	8664	32 237	27	55
1920	9803	44 027	22	49
1940	10 017	47 769	21	36
1960	9918	52 709	19	24
1980	7529	56 353	13	9
2000	5862	59 122	10	4

Source: Brierley, P. (ed.) (2000)

approximately 40 per cent of the population attended church. By 1950, this had dropped to 20 per cent, and attendance was less than 7.5 per cent in 2000 (Brierley 1999). Sunday school attendance is also in decline (see Table 1.6).

Membership

Hamilton (2001) also points out that fewer people are church members (see Table 1.6).

Critics of the secularization thesis point to the growth of new churches and the fact that ethnic-minority churches have pretty much held their own. However, it is clear that the big organizations such as the Church of England and the Catholic church have declined badly, whereas those that have stayed stable or grown are the smaller ones (see Topic 6).

Age bias

Brierley also points out that the gross figures of decline hide a trend even more worrying for the future of Christianity in Britain: age bias. For each of his three English surveys (1979, 1989, 1999), he estimates the age profile of the various groups of denominations. With the exception of the Pentecostal churches, he notes that churchgoers are considerably older than non-churchgoers. This is the case even when the general ageing of the population is taken into account – see Table 1.7.

It would seem that fewer and fewer younger members are attending church – suggesting that, eventually, many congregations may die out altogether.

Table 1.7 Percentage of churchgoers aged over 65, 1979–99			
Church	1979	1989	1999
Anglican	19	22	29
Catholic	13	16	22
Methodist	25	30	38

Source: Brierley, P. (ed.) (2000)

Reduced moral influence

Church weddings now only make up approximately 40 per cent of marriages compared with about 75 per cent 30 years ago (Brierley 2001). This fact, together with the rising divorce rate, increase in cohabitation and the proportion of children born outside marriage, is seen as evidence that religion and its moral value system exert little influence today.

Lower status of clergy

As the number of clergy has fallen, their pay and status have declined. As Bruce (2001) states, the number of clergy is a useful indicator of the social power and popularity of religion. In 1900, there were over 45 000 clerics in Britain; this had declined to just over 34 000 in 2000, despite the fact that the population had almost doubled. In a patriarchal society, the very fact that women are now being ordained may in itself reduce the perceived status of the clergy.

Other aspects of secularization

Bryan Wilson (1966) and others – notably, Bruce (1996) and Wallis (1984) – cite evidence for secularization in addition to statistics. They argue that secularization is a development rooted in modernity and focus on three key processes: **rationalization**, disengagement and religious pluralism.

Rationalization

It is suggested that **rational** thinking in the form of science has replaced religious influence in our lives, because scientific progress has resulted in higher living standards. Moreover, science has produced convincing explanations for phenomena which were once the province of religion, such as how the world was created. Further, drawing on the work of Weber (who saw rationalization as being linked to the Christian tradition), Berger (1973) has suggested that Christianity has ultimately been its own gravedigger. Protestantism focused attention on this life, work and the pursuit of prosperity, rather than on the domain of God and the afterlife.

Disengagement

The disengagement, or separation, of the church from wider society is an important aspect of secularization. The Church is no longer involved in important areas of social life, such as politics. Moreover, Wilson argues, religious belief is no longer central to most people's value systems or personal goals. People are now more concerned with their material standard of living, rather than with spiritual welfare, and are more likely to take moral direction from the mass media than the church. Hamilton (2001) has suggested that churches themselves have secularized in an attempt to compromise with those who have rejected more traditional beliefs. For example, he argues the Church of England no longer supports ideas of the Virgin Birth, hell or even God as a real external force.

Religious pluralism

Bruce (1996) suggests that industrialization has fragmented society into a marketplace of religions. Wilson (1966) argues that, as a result, religion no longer acts as a unifying force in society. He points to the **ecumenical movement** as an attempt by institutionalized religion to reverse secularization because such unification only occurs when religious influence is weak. In particular, the growth in the number of sects, cults and NRMs has also been seen by Wilson as evidence of secularization. He argues that sects are 'the last outpost of religion in a secular society' and are a symptom of religion's decline. Competition between religions is seen to undermine their credibility as they compete for **'spiritual shoppers'**.

Religion in the USA: the Religious Economy Theory

However, the situation in the USA would seem to suggest that religious pluralism may, in fact, be responsible for the increasing appeal of religion there. In the USA, 40 per cent of the adult population regularly attend church. About 5 per cent of the US television audience regularly tune in to religious TV and 20 million watch some religious programming every week.

Warner (1993) puts the popularity of religion in the US down to the separation of religion from the influence of the state. The eighteenth-century American founders distinguished a series of principles of religious liberty, which included equality of faiths and separation of church and state. These principles encouraged religious pluralism.

In a pluralistic environment, the different religious traditions compete with each other for members. The result of competition is an expanding religious economy that results in more participants by expanding the base of participation rather than a struggle for the loyalty of a fixed number of participants. In cultures where one religious group has a monopoly, religious participation tends to decline. In the absence of competition, there is little incentive to expand one's market share.

In a competitive religious economy, some denominations/churches fare well, others fail to renew and lose ground. Even powerfully established religious traditions reach a point of stagnation; renewal is frequently achieved through groups breaking away from the established traditions, all vigorously competing with one another for new members who will support and justify their existence – they are well attended, because they work to attract customers, free from state interference.

Evidence against secularization in the UK

While established religion may appear to be in decline in Western countries such as Britain, the growth of their immigrant populations is causing an increase in religiosity. Islam is the fastest-growing religion in Britain and non-Trinitarian church membership has mushroomed.

However, in relation to the non-immigrant population, Grace Davie (1995) has characterized the situation in Britain as 'believing without belonging' – that is, people may admit to private religious beliefs but are less inclined to join religious groups or to attend religious services on a regular basis. In relation to church attendance, it could in fact be argued that this reflects 'belonging without believing'. That is, people may attend church for social or emotional reasons rather than religious commitment.

Vicarious religion

Davie compares the UK with other European countries such as those of Scandinavia. She suggests that religion is not practised overtly by the majority, but that most engage with religion on a **vicarious** level. In this sense, religion involves rituals and practices performed by an active minority on behalf of a much larger number, who (implicitly at least) not only understand, but also clearly approve of what the minority is doing.

Interruptions in 'normality'

One way to unravel what is happening is to observe societies when 'normal' ways of living are, for one reason or another, suspended and something far more expressive comes to the fore. Tragedy provides some examples. For example, in Sweden in 1994, the ferry, Estonia, sank with the loss of some 900 lives. Large numbers of Swedish people went to their churches, some to light candles and to mourn privately, but also to hear, articulated on their behalf (i.e. vicariously), both the sentiments of the people and the meaning of the tragedy for the country. Similarly, the death of Princess Diana in Paris in a car crash in 1997 drew large numbers of British people to church to make a similar sort of gesture. What is significant in both these examples is an awareness in the population as a whole that multiple and well-intentioned gestures of individual mourning are inadequate in themselves to mark the end of these particular lives; there is the additional need for public ritual or worship in the established church.

The Estonia and the Princess Diana examples are simply large-scale versions of what goes on in the life-cycles of ordinary people. People expect that they will have the right to the services of the church at critical moments in their lives such as birth, marriage and death. Churches must exist in order to meet such demands. So churches do not belong exclusively to those who use them regularly. European populations continue to see such churches as public utilities maintained for the common good.

Religious belief

Furthermore, despite very low levels of church attendance and membership, surveys show that there seems to be a survival of some religious belief. According to the 1998 British Social Attitudes survey, 21 per cent of those surveyed agreed to the statement 'I know God exists and I have no doubt about it', whereas only 10 per cent said that they did not believe in God at all. However, there may be a moral connotation attached to such surveys, such that people feel more inclined to answer 'yes', whether or not they actually believe in God.

Other criticisms of the secularization thesis

There is evidence that people prefer 'religious' explanations for random events such as the early death of loved ones. Many people still subscribe to the concept of 'luck' or 'fate', as evidenced by the growth of gambling opportunities such as the National Lottery and the relaxation of gambling laws.

There can be little doubt that religion plays less of a political role than it did in earlier centuries. However, national debates about issues such as the age of homosexual consent, the family, abortion and so on are given a moral dimension by the contribution of religious leaders. The media still shows a great interest in issues such as women priests, while religious programmes such as *Songs of Praise* still attract large audiences (7 to 8 million viewers). Some sociologists, notably Parsons (1965), have argued that disengagement is probably a good thing because it means that the churches can focus more effectively on their central role of providing moral goals for society to achieve.

According to Hamilton (2001), decline in religious practices may be part of a more general decline in organizational membership and increased privatization. For example, fewer people join trade unions or political parties. It may be that they still 'believe', but are more committed to spending their time with family or on individual priorities.

Thompson (1996) suggests that the influence of the new Christian evangelical churches is underestimated. In the absence of mass political campaigning, church-inspired campaigns have a high media profile, especially in the USA. Many New Right policies on abortion, media violence and single parents are, he argues, influenced by the evangelical churches.

Religious pluralism as religious revival?

The secularization cycle

Stark and Bainbridge (1985) argue that religion can never disappear nor seriously decline. They see religion as meeting the fundamental needs of individuals. We all seek compensations for what seems unattainable at any given time. The frustration a Marxist feels in an unjust capitalist society is compensated for by the promise of inevitable revolution; for a stressed Sociology student, the compensation may be the prospect of a university place and well-paid job. Stark and Bainbridge argue that sometimes individuals want rewards which are so great that the possibility of gaining them can only be contemplated alongside a belief in the supernatural – for instance, answers to our most fundamental questions, or a life after death. Only religion can answer these questions. The need for **religious compensators** is a constant whenever, wherever, and for whom, desired rewards are not obtainable.

Furthermore, the more religious organizations move away from the supernatural, the more people will turn to different organizations that continue to emphasize it. This might explain the relative success of traditional Orthodox and 'New' churches at holding on to their congregations, compared with the modernizing established churches, as well as the growth of NRMs, such as sects. Where the social conditions and the sect's

focus on research

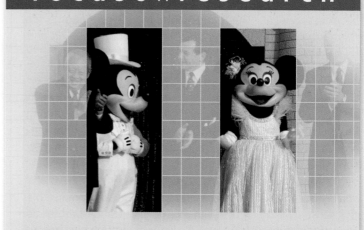

Lyon (2000)
Jesus in Disneyland

Lyon (2000) argues that the centrality of consumerism to postmodern life means that people choose what to believe in perhaps as readily as they choose what to wear. However, rather than declining, he sees traditional religious beliefs as merely relocating to the sphere of consumption. Furthermore, because many sources of identity, particularly work and nation, are becoming less significant, religion can become an important source of identity for individuals. However, in the postmodern world, people are less willing to accept an externally imposed narrative or story to put their lives in context and so they personalize the stories available to them from a much broader range of cultural sources. To support his arguments, he cites the example of a harvest day crusade held at Disneyland, California, where Christian evangelists and gospel singers preached and performed. Whereas this might once have been seen as an inappropriate, perhaps irreverent venue, religion here was being practised in a fantasy world, adapting, according to Lyon, to postmodernity and becoming part of it. People are therefore said to be seeking credible ways of expressing faith in contemporary modes outside the walls of conventional churches. Bruce (2002), however, sees this as evidence of secularization, rather than continuing religious vitality, as in his view, such arrangements have little impact upon the way people live their lives.

Adapted from Haralambos, M. and Holborn, M. (2005) *Sociology: Themes and Perspectives* (6th edn), London: Collins Education

1 **Explain how the harvest day crusade at Disneyland illustrates Lyon's argument.**

message match, the sect will grow into a major world religion – revitalising religious participation and completing the cycle by reversing secularization. This new religion will itself eventually become worldly and bureaucratic, restarting the cycle of secularization. From the Stark–Bainbridge perspective,

Mormonism is the latest in a long series of world religions arising from sects that flourish where conventional religion has become too weak. The Stark–Bainbridge interpretation is that there is a cyclical continuity of secularization, innovation and revival as a plurality of alternatives to traditional religion emerge, develop and themselves come to be replaced.

Religious pluralism as religious revival?

Studies by Greeley (1972) and Nelson (1986) argue that the growth of NRMs indicate that society is undergoing a religious revival. G.K. Nelson (1986) argues that, in the 1980s institutional religion lost contact with the spiritual needs of society because it had become too ritualized and predictable. In this sense, Nelson agrees with Wilson that established religion is undergoing secularization. The young, in particular, are 'turned-off' by such religion. However, Nelson argues that a religious revival is underway, and is being helped by the success of evangelical churches. These churches offer a more spontaneous religion, which is less reliant on ritual and consequently more attractive to the young.

But Bruce (1996) and Wallis (1984) point out that neither NRMs nor those churches that have increased their membership have recruited anywhere near the numbers of those lost from the established churches. Brierley (1999) estimates that the growth of non-Trinitarian churches of half a million members, amounts to about only one-sixth of those lost to the main churches.

The secularization myth? A global perspective

Many writers have pointed out that secularization has tended to be seen in terms of the decline of organized established churches in Western industrialized countries. However, if one looks at the world globally, then religion is as overwhelming and dominant a force as ever. As Berger (1997) comments, 'the world today with some exceptions is as furiously religious as it ever was and in some places more so than ever'. Religious revival among Christians in the USA, Jews in Israel and Muslims throughout the world has gone unexplained by proponents of the secularization thesis.

The postmodernist view

Postmodernists, too, see the development of New Age beliefs, what Heelas (2004) calls a '**holistic milieu**', as a rejection of science and modernity in the postmodern age. The true extent of New Age beliefs cannot be known, but the number of internet sites feeding such interests indicates that they are widespread. This new explosion of spirituality doesn't at first seem to detract from the secularization thesis because these private beliefs don't impact upon the way society runs. But, as postmodernists argue, consumption is the way society runs now, or is at least a very significant factor. So this is precisely where we should look to find openings for religious activity.

Secularization: an over-generalization?

As far as the UK is concerned, it is fairly obvious that profound changes are occurring in institutional religion. However, whether these changes can be described as secularization is difficult to ascertain. Religious participation through organized religion has declined, but the extent and nature of continuing belief still proves difficult to determine. Further, increased globalization has meant that **religio-political events** elsewhere have global significance and this is bound to have an impact upon religious influence in Britain. Bauman (1997) and Giddens (2001) for example, argue that religion is becoming more important in the late modern/postmodern world. According to Giddens:

>> *Religious symbols and practices are not only residues from the past: a revival of religious or more broadly spiritual concerns seems fairly widespread … not only has religion failed to disappear; we see all around us the creation of new forms of religious sensibility and spiritual endeavour.* >>

Check your understanding

1 What evidence on religious participation does Wilson give to support the secularization thesis?

2 What is the significance of the changing age profile for the future of religion in Britain?

3 What indicators are there of a reduced status of the clergy?

4 What, according to Wilson, is the significance of rationalization and disengagement for the secularization thesis?

5 How does Bruce argue that religious pluralism is evidence of secularization.

6 Why according to Stephen Warner is religious pluralism religion's 'saviour'?

7 How does Davie counter the view that religion in Britain is declining in significance?

8 What does Hamilton say about declining institutional affiliation?

9 What, according to Stark and Bainbridge, is the reason why religion can never disappear?

10 How do they explain the cycle of secularization, innovation and revival?

11 In what ways does a more global perspective demonstrate that secularization is a myth?

12 How do postmodernists view the secularization thesis?

KEY TERMS

Ecumenical movement – where churches come together in joint worship, each seeing the other as having something to offer.

Holistic milieu – a range of activities involving the mind, body and spirit, such as yoga, tai chi, healing and self-discovery.

Rational – based on reason, logic and science.

Rationalization – the use of reason and science to replace spiritual and religious thinking.

Religio-political events – instances of religion coming into conflict with governments which have national and sometimes international consequences.

Religious compensators – aspects of religion that provide temporary answers to fundamental queries about the nature of existence and satisfy universal needs.

Spiritual shoppers – a postmodern idea that people consume religion in much the same way as any other product.

Vicarious religion – religious practices of a socially approved of minority who symbolically represent the religious adherence of the majority.

research idea

- Interview your parents/grandparents and other older relatives to ascertain the level of belief and participation in religion, both past and present, in your family. Design a questionnaire measuring religious belief and practice to compare with your own age group. Collate the results for the whole class, and compare them.

web.task

Look at the website of the Keep Sunday Special Campaign at www.keepsundayspecial.net. Summarize the main objections Christian groups have to the secularization of Sunday.

Evaluate their arguments.

exploring the secularization debate

Item A

The death of religion was the conventional wisdom in the social sciences during most of the twentieth century; indeed, it has been regarded as the master model of sociological inquiry, where secularization was ranked with bureaucratization, rationalization, and urbanization as the key historical revolutions transforming medieval agrarian societies into modern industrial nations. As C. Wright Mills summarized this process: 'Once the world was filled with the sacred – in thought, practice, and institutional form. After the Reformation and the Renaissance, the forces of modernization swept across the globe and secularization, a resulting historical process, loosened the dominance of the sacred. In due course, the sacred shall disappear altogether except, possibly, in the private realm.'

During the past decade, however, this thesis of the slow and steady death of religion has come under growing criticism; indeed, secularization theory is currently experiencing the most sustained challenge in its long history.

Critics point to multiple indicators of religious health and vitality today, ranging from the continued popularity of churchgoing in the United States to the emergence of New Age spirituality in Western Europe, the growth in fundamentalist movements and religious parties in the Muslim world, the evangelical revival sweeping through Latin America, and the upsurge of ethno-religious conflict in international affairs.

C. Wright Mills (1959) *The Sociological Imagination*, Oxford: Oxford University Press., pp. 32–3

1 (a) Identify and briefly explain **two** ways in which religion has a less significant role in modern society. (8 marks)

(b) Using material from **Item A** and elsewhere, briefly examine the extent to which religion continues to have global significance. (12 marks)

2 'Claims that the United Kingdom is now a secular society are wrong. Both religious activity and religious belief are flourishing.'

To what extent do sociological arguments and evidence support this view? (40 marks)

WE ALL HAVE SOME EXPERIENCE OF POWER. Some of us wield it. Most of us are on the receiving end of it. However, it is not an easy concept to define because it takes so many different forms. Sociologists, therefore, take a keen interest in both the nature of power and its sources. This is the main focus of Topic 1.

You will have noticed that power is openly used by a variety of people, including your parents, your teachers, the police, your employers and the prime minister. You, too, probably have some power – you may be a prefect at school or a supervisor at work, but you also exercise more subtle and hidden forms of power as consumers and voters. Topic 2 looks at the distribution of power in society and asks whether it is evenly shared out or whether it is concentrated in the hands of a select few.

Whether you like it or not, the government plays a major role in your lives – the state defines and supervises all aspects of your existence from cradle to grave. Topic 3, therefore, investigates the function of the state and the central role that it plays in society.

Topic 4 is concerned with voting behaviour. Usually every four years or so, we the general public are called to vote, and our actions give politicians the mandate to put into action policies that directly affect our everyday lives. Sociologists are interested in exploring what issues inspire us to vote and why we are increasingly reluctant to cast our vote.

Many young people seem to be turned off by mainstream politicians and political parties. However, this does not mean that they are turned off by politics. Young people often get angry about a range of issues, such as debt in the developing world, animal experimentation, environmental degradation and human rights abuses. Topic 5 explores some of the reasons why these issues attract attention and what organizations exist to help people tackle them.

AQAspecification	topics	pages
Candidates should examine:		
Explanations of the nature and distribution of power	The nature of power is the focus of Topic 1, while the distribution of power is examined in Topic 2; Topic 5 is also relevant here	50–57 58–63 80–89
The role of the modern state	Covered in Topic 3	64–71
Different political ideologies and their relationship to political parties	Covered in Topic 4	72–79
The nature of, and changes in, different forms of political participation, including voting behaviour	Voting behaviour is covered in Topic 4, other forms of political participation in Topic 5	72–79 80–89
The role of political parties and movements, pressure/interest groups and the mass media in the political process.	The role of pressure and interest groups is the focus of Topic 5	80–89

UNIT **2**

Power and politics

Defining power

gettingyou**thinking**

All of the people shown above exercise some sort of power.

1 What type of power do you think they exercise?

2 How do these types of power differ from each other?

3 Rank these individuals in hierarchical order on the basis of how much power they exert over your life.

4 How might Madonna's success have equipped young females today with more power than their mothers?

The above exercise should have shown you that power can take several different forms and can be exercised in a number of direct and indirect ways. For example, you are unlikely to meet George Bush or Osama Bin Laden, but they still exercise considerable power over your life. For example, terrorism on the streets of Britain in 2005 is seen by some as a result of the policies of these two individuals. In 2005, the power of the police to stop and search you, and even use violence on you, considerably increased as a result of these terrorist attacks. Similarly, it can be argued that if you are a female, Madonna's success impacts directly on your capacity to exercise power. You exercise more power than your mother because Madonna's career over the years has contributed to an acceptance of a wide range of activities for women that were once considered deviant.

Max Weber and power

In the most general sense, power refers to any kind of influence exercised by individuals or groups on others. For example, Max Weber defined power as the chance or probability of an individual or group of people imposing their will on others despite resistance, i.e. where A has power over B to the extent that A can get B to do something that B would not otherwise do. This conception of power – the **zero-sum view of power** – implies that the exercise of power involves negative consequences for some individuals and groups because it involves repression, force and constraint. Weber believed that such power could be exercised in a range of social situations.

<< *Positions of power can emerge from social relations in a drawing room as well as in the market, from the rostrum of a lecture hall as well as the command post of a regiment, from an erotic or charitable relationship as well as from scholarly discussion or athletics.* >> (Lukes 1986)

Weber distinguished between two main types of power implied here – coercion and authority:

● Coercion is force, usually in the form of violence or military resources.
● Authority depends upon consent – that is, people believe that the power is **legitimate**.

---

f o c u s on . . .

Max Weber's types of authority

Weber argues that legitimacy can be derived from three sources.

● *Charisma* – Some individuals are able to direct the behaviour of others because they have exceptionally powerful personalities that inspire strong feelings of devotion and loyalty. These may be political leaders such as Adolf Hitler, religious leaders such as Gandhi or the Reverend Jim Jones (see Unit 1, p. 22) and sporting personalities such as José Mourinho or Sir Alex Ferguson. Note how some of your teachers may use their charisma to motivate you.
● *Tradition* – Power can be derived from historical precedent, such as that embodied in the succession of the Royal Family in the UK. Many people in the UK believe that the Queen has inherited the 'right' to rule and so consider themselves as loyal subjects.
● *Rational–legal* – Most authority in Britain, whether that of the prime minister, a police officer or a teacher, derives from formal rules which often take the form of laws. Such authority is thought to be impartially applied to everyone and enforced without bias. Consequently, people consent to obey this type of power, which is usually administered by a hierarchical **bureaucracy**. Morgan (1999) refers to this as 'the routinization of obedience'. The option of force still exists but it is used only as a final resort.

Some sociologists have highlighted other forms of power halfway between coercion and authority, e.g. influence (where people are persuaded to change their minds) and manipulation (where individuals are cynically deceived perhaps through control over education, knowledge, information and news).

Functionalism and power

Functionalists view power as a positive resource, characterized by consensus and legitimacy. Talcott Parsons (1963) argued that power results from the sharing of resources in order to achieve collective social and cultural goals. If A and B work together, they will both increase their power as well as benefit society. Power is therefore a functional resource working for the benefit of everybody and helping to maintain social order and strengthen social solidarity.

Parsons argued that if power is to be used to pursue collective goals effectively, it needs direction and organization. For this reason, members of society authorize some individuals via democratic elections (namely, politicians) to exercise power on their behalf. Parsons argues that if society is unhappy with the use of that power, members of society simply will not vote for them. In this way, power can never be monopolized and is always used to benefit the greater good. However, this view of power has been criticized as naive, as it fails to acknowledge that power can be accumulated in the hands of individuals with more interest in pursuing their own sectional interests than collective goals or common good.

Marxism and power

Marxists argue that power arises out of the social **relations of production** that characterize the economic system of production found in **capitalist societies** (see Unit 4 *Theory and methods*, p. 161). These social relations exist between two groups characterized by their access (or lack of access) to economic resources:

● the **bourgeoisie** or ruling class – a minority group who own and control the **means of production**, such as capital, land, factories, technology and raw materials
● the **proletariat** or working class – the majority group who have only their labour power, which they hire out to the bourgeoisie in return for a wage.

This class inequality is further deepened by the bourgeoisie's exploitation of the proletariat's labour power, in that the wealth of the dominant class is increased by the fact that the value of the goods produced by the worker always far exceeds the wage paid. This surplus value is pocketed by the bourgeoisie in the form of profit. Marxists argue, therefore, that inequalities in ownership and control – along with exploitation – lead to economic inequality, and this is the source of political and social power in society. In other words, power derives from class relationships.

Hegemony

Class domination and economic power are maintained through coercion (although this tends to be used as a last resort) and ideological **hegemony** (the control of ideas). Marxists argue that this latter concept is much more effective than force in controlling a proletariat which has the potential to be very disruptive if it decides that the organization of the capitalist infrastructure is unfair and unjust in how income and wealth are distributed. Hegemony or cultural dominance by the ruling class is needed in order to make sure that the working class regard bourgeois power as legitimate, and so reduce the potential for revolutionary protest.

According to Bocock (1986), hegemony occurs when the intellectual and moral ideas of the ruling class provide the dominant cultural outlook for the whole of society. Marxists such as Althusser (1971) argue that the bourgeoisie achieve this cultural dominance by using its economic power to define what counts as knowledge, ideas, art, education, news and so on. Social institutions such as the education system, the legal system, the political system, the mass media and religion, which Marxists see as making up the '**superstructure**' of capitalist society, play an important role in transmitting ruling-class ideology so that it is accepted by the mass of the population as 'normal' or 'natural'.

Westergaard (1996) argues that the result of hegemonic power is that workers fail to understand their own structural position correctly – that is, they fail to realize their true interests as exploited workers. This false class-consciousness means that they rarely realize their potential power for bringing about revolutionary change. The Frankfurt School of Marxism (see Unit 4, pp. 161–2) in a similar analysis argue that the working class has become 'ideologically incorporated' into capitalist society. Marcuse (1964) argued that this incorporation takes the form of encouraging 'one-dimensional thought': the general population is encouraged to indulge in uncritical and sterile forms of entertainment or mass culture that reduce their appetite for critical and creative thought and action that might challenge hegemonic power. Following on from Marcuse, White (2004) argues that Western culture today is dominated by a 'Middle Mind' – a mainstream consensus that is shaped by consumer culture that pleases everyone but moves, challenges or shocks no one. He notes:

<< When we accept the Middle Mind as our culture (or, worse yet, when we demand it as consumers), we are not merely being stupid or unsophisticated or "low brow". We are vigorously conspiring against ourselves. We murder our own capacity for critique and invention as if we were children saying, 'Can you do this for me?'. >>

According to Gramsci (1971), hegemony, and the resulting consent of the people, has enabled the ruling class to deal with any threats to its authority without having to use force. However, Gramsci argues that hegemony does not mean that subordinate classes will always lack power or that the power of the dominant class is absolute. He argues that power is potentially available to the subordinate classes if they become sufficiently class-conscious and politically organized to seize or

Sociology A2 for AQA

focus on...

Giddens and power

Leading sociologist Anthony Giddens (1968) is critical of functionalist analyses of power. He suggests that power is part of all social relations and interactions.

<< What slips away from sight almost completely in the Parsonian analysis is the very fact that power is always exercised over someone! Parsons virtually ignores, quite consciously and deliberately, the hierarchical character of power, and the divisions of interest which are frequently consequent upon it. However much it is true that power can rest upon 'agreement', it is also true that interests of power-holders and those subject to that power often clash. >>

<< All interaction involves the use of power because all interaction is concerned with the production and reproduction of structure, drawing upon rules and resources. Power relates to those resources which actors draw upon in interaction, in order to 'make a difference'. >>

Giddens, A. (1968) '"Power" in the recent writings of Talcott Parsons', *Sociology*, 2(3)

1 **Explain Giddens' criticism of Parsons in your own words.**

2 **Giddens argues that all interaction involves power. Explain how power might be involved in:**

a   **a group of friends talking**
b   **a family deciding which TV programmes to watch in the evening**
c   **a doctor–patient interaction**
d   **a parents' evening at school.**

to challenge the control of the means of production. Importantly, Gramsci argues that people in capitalist societies experience 'dual consciousness', i.e. their beliefs are only partly shaped by capitalist ideology because their beliefs are also influenced by their personal day-to-day experiences of society –

these sometimes contradict or challenge dominant ideology and so encourage some resistance and opposition to it. This 'resistance' might take an overtly political form (for instance, active campaigning or taking to the streets to oppose G8 talks) or a 'symbolic' form (such as setting out to challenge dominant institutions and beliefs through the use of 'shock', e.g. through fashion statements or simply substituting a hedonistic lifestyle for the 9 to 5 lifestyle demanded by capitalism).

Neo-Marxists such as Stuart Hall (Hall and Jefferson 1976) have developed **relational conceptions of power** – that is, they recognize that power is a process which involves **ideological struggle** between the capitalist class and groups such as working-class youth. The capitalist class is normally able to impose cultural hegemony and so obtain the consent of most of the people to rule. However, pockets of **symbolic resistance** among sections of the working class indicate that power is not a one-way process. Gilroy (1982a) suggests that working-class crime may well be political, a means by which subordinate groups can enjoy some power through hitting back at the symbols of capitalist power such as wealth and property. The work of the Birmingham Centre for Contemporary Cultural Studies similarly suggests that working-class deviant youth subcultures may be symbolically resisting hegemonic definitions of respectability by adopting forms of style and behaviour that set out to shock. For example, the Punk subculture of the late 1970s incorporated conformist symbols, such as the Queen and Union Jack, as well as deviant symbols, such as Nazi insignia, into its dress codes in a deliberately provocative way.

Criticisms of the Marxist theory of power

Michael Mann (1986) takes issue with the Marxist view that all power is rooted in class relationships. He argues that there are two broad types of power:

● distributional power – exercised by individuals
● collective power – exercised by social groups ranging in size from nation states to families.

Mann notes that power has a number of unique characteristics:

● It can be *extensive* – It can involve the ability to co-opt large numbers of people across huge distances to work together in common interest. For example, some Muslim people, regardless of their nationality or ethnic group, express loyalty first and foremost to their religion.
● It can be *intensive* – It can command extreme loyalty and dedication from followers. For example, the power wielded by some leaders of religious groups, most notably Jim Jones of The People's Temple, has resulted in mass suicide.
● It can be *authoritative* – It is organized around rules and commands which are largely regarded as legitimate. For example, your head teacher or principal has the power to exclude you from school or college.
● It can be *diffused* – It results from natural or spontaneous processes rather than an individual or group issuing commands or physically imposing themselves on a subordinate group. For example, a fall in consumer demand for a particular product might force a manufacturer out of business.

Mann agrees with Marxists that economics (or class) is an important source of power but, as the examples above illustrate, he acknowledges other sources of power:

● World religions often wield ideological power independently of the economic system.
● Military power, particularly in the developing world, may be separate from economic power, as seen in the number of economic elites who have been deposed by military coups.
● The state has political power, which may result from democratic elections in the case of politicians and **meritocracy** in the case of civil servants. Mann notes that political power is not always used in ways which benefit the economically dominant classes – for example, the minimum wage legislation brought in by the Labour Government in 1999 was opposed by big business interests.

synopticlink   stratification and differentiation

Functionalists, such as Davis and Moore (1955), see stratification and social inequality as a functional necessity in modern societies, because certain social positions, e.g. occupational roles, are more important than others. In order to attract those with the most talent, high rewards are attached to these positions. Those in the top positions often wield economic power in that they enjoy a superior standard of living. They often make decisions that affect the economic wellbeing of other members of society, e.g. where to locate a new business. They also exercise authority legitimated by both law and state bureaucracy, e.g. head teachers can suspend pupils. Functionalists argue that this power is generally used for the benefit of society and our consent for its use is an important contributor to social order.

Marxists, on the other hand, see social class inequalities as the natural outcome of the social organization of capitalism. The bourgeoisie control the means of production and exploit the labour power of the working class. The vast profits made by the bourgeoisie give them political power. Consequently, they can use coercion and repression, if they so wish, in order to protect their interests through control of agencies such as the police, the security services and the armed forces. However, Marxists note that in modern capitalist societies, the bourgeoisie are more likely to use cultural and ideological forms of power, through agencies such as education and the mass media, to persuade the subordinate class that society is organized in a just fashion.

focus on . . .

Hegemony and resistance

1 **Explain how the people in the two photos above could be seen to be symbolically resisting hegemony.**

Mann argues that it is rare that any one social group in a single society is able to dominate more than two sources of power, especially as power is increasingly globalized – power networks now extend across the world and consequently no single interest group is able to monopolize power.

Abercrombie *et al.* (1980) are dismissive of claims that a dominant ideology characterizes contemporary society. They put forward three key reasons:

● Capitalism today is characterized by conflicts between capitalist interests such as small businesses, finance capital, industrialists, multinational companies and state corporations. This conflict undermines the idea that the capitalist class is transmitting strong and unified ideological messages.

● The subordinate class often rejects the so-called dominant ideology – as can be seen in surveys of working-class people who recognize that we live in a class society characterized by inequality. Such workers may express resistance through strikes and membership of trade unions.

● The simple fact that workers have to work in order to preserve their standard of living leads to their cooperation and participation. People conform, not because of ideological hegemony but quite simply because they fear unemployment and poverty.

Poststructuralism and power

Michel Foucault

Foucault (1980) rejects the link between social structure and power. He suggests that power is an inescapable part of everyday life. In particular, power plays a major role in the construction of identity.

According to Foucault, there is a significant relationship between power, knowledge and language. He argued that there exist bodies of knowledge and language which he terms **'discourses'**. These dominate how society sees, describes and thinks about how we should live our lives, in terms of family, sexuality, discipline and punishment, health and illness, and so on. Our power to behave in certain ways – and the power of others to prevent us behaving in those ways – is dependent upon dominant discourses.

In illustration, Foucault showed how, during the 18th century, there was a shift away from coercive forms of power associated with physical punishment (e.g. execution) to what he calls **'disciplinary power'**. This type of power saw a move to identify and categorize 'normality' and 'deviance' in the form of discourses in the fields of criminality, sexual behaviour and illness. Bauman (1983) notes how this type of power is based on the construction and imposition of surveillance (watching for deviation from normality), routine and regulation. 'It wanted to impose one ubiquitous [i.e. universal] pattern of normality and eliminate everything and everybody which the pattern could not fit.'

Disciplinary power

Foucault's conception of disciplinary power, i.e. discourses that control everyday behaviour via surveillance and discipline, first developed in state institutions such as prisons and asylums. For example, Foucault notes that people were no longer simply punished for crimes – rather there was an attempt to judge why people had committed particular crimes, i.e. to categorize them into specific types. A range of expert professions emerged with the power to observe, judge and categorize people's behaviour in terms of 'normality' and 'deviance'. These included psychologists, psychiatrists and social workers. Foucault notes how, over the course of the 20th century, such surveillance and judgement has expanded into institutions such as schools and workplaces. For example, educational psychologists now attempt to explain a range of behaviours exhibited by children in the educational system, ranging from high achievement through to truancy. At the same time, people who choose not to work are dismissed by experts as 'inadequate' or as 'social problems'. Foucault is therefore suggesting that our identity as well as our behaviour patterns are the result of these powerful judgements or discourses about what should count as 'normal' or 'conformist' behaviour.

Bio-power

Foucult identified a second conception of power which he termed **'bio-power'**. Bio-power is concerned with controlling the body and how it is perceived by the general population.

Foucault sees bio-power as especially influential in structuring discourses on sexuality and in shaping attitudes and behaviour among the mass of the population towards different types of sexuality. He claims that, from the 19th century onwards, discourse on sexual behaviour rapidly became dominated by professionals working in the fields of psychiatry, medicine and social work. He argues that this discourse on sexual behaviour has power over all of us because it defines what is and what is not 'normal' and 'what is and what is not available for individuals to do, think, say and be' (Clegg 1989).

Foucault suggests that the dominant discourse favours heterosexuality at the expense of homosexuality and other alternative sexualities. This power to impose definitions of 'normality' has become part of institutionalized life and results in individuals being criticized, treated prejudicially and punished for being different – that is, for indulging in non-heterosexual behaviour or for holding attitudes that challenge the dominant heterosexual discourse. Moreover, Foucault argues that bio-power is extremely influential because it shapes our own sense of identity. We unconsciously internalize aspects of the discourse and engage in self-discipline. We avoid behaviour and attitudes that are likely to provoke even more surveillance and discipline from official agencies. For example, if we are attracted to people of the same sex, we may avoid forms of behaviour which other people interpret as 'homosexual' in order to avoid judgement and perhaps prejudice and discrimination. Foucault claimed that such self-discipline leads to 'docile bodies' – that is, people who conform and consequently do not threaten social order.

Power and resistance

Foucault does not see power as an entirely negative concept. He sees that it has a positive dimension too, as people generally enjoy the freedom to choose to resist such power. He argues that the knowledge on which power is based can be challenged. For example, there are signs that in the West, homosexuality is becoming more socially acceptable (and therefore, less deviant), as the medical and psychological knowledge used to justify the repressive treatment of homosexuals in the past is challenged. It can be argued that the weakening of the dominant medical and psychological discourse about homosexuality has resulted in less surveillance, discipline and punishment, as illustrated by the virtual decriminalization of such behaviour in the Western world (although negative social attitudes towards homosexuality in some sections of the population still illustrate the power of the previously dominant discourse).

Evaluating Foucault's work

Foucault's work has been criticized for not being empirical in a conventional research sense. He tended to support his arguments with selective historical examples rather than systematically gathered contemporary data. Moreover, his work tended to be overly descriptive at the expense of explanation – for example, it is not entirely clear why disciplinary power and bio-power evolved, nor who exercises these types of power. Foucault did argue that no one group dominates disciplinary power but it may be unrealistic to suggest that no one group benefits more than others from exercising this type of power. However, his work has value in that it convincingly explores the relationship between knowledge and power. His observation that the wielding of power produces resistance which may lead to positive change is an interesting contrast with those theories which define power in more absolute and repressive terms.

Gender and power

Westwood and postfeminism

Westwood (2002) notes that feminist thinkers who focused on the concept of patriarchy insisted that the key issue in gender relations was power. Feminism saw itself 'as fighting for a reversal of the status quo in which men were seen to be dominant'. However, Westwood argues that this type of approach was crude and alienated women, because it cast women as powerless subordinates, oppressed and exploited by patriarchal power.

synoptic link   crime and deviance

A number of theories of crime use the concept of power to explain why particular social groups turn to crime. If we examine white-collar and corporate crime, we can see that it is underrepresented in the official criminal statistics. Criminologists such as Stephen Box (1981) and Hazel Croall (2001) argue that such crime is likely to be committed by high-status individuals with the power to cover up these crimes so that they go undetected. Marxists go further and suggest that the capitalist class make laws in order to protect their own interests and socially control the working class. They also have the power to prevent the passing of laws that might threaten their interests or can influence the content of such laws so that they are weakly enforced.

Other criminologists have focused on how lack of power might lead to the committing of crime. For example, left realists note that White and Black working-class youths commit crime because they experience 'relative deprivation' (a lack of economic power compared with their White middle-class peers) and 'marginalization' (a lack of the political power to change their situation). Marxist theories of deviant youth cultures, influenced by the work of Gramsci, focus on how working-class and Black youth can transform acts of deviance into types of cultural power and use these symbolically to resist the power of the capitalist class.

Westwood argues for the development of 'postfeminism', in which sociologists use Foucault's work on discourse to show how women can take control of their lives and identities. She cites Rubin (1998), who argues that females can exercise power through a series of strategies focusing on the microprocesses of power. Women can use their bodies, intuition and control of gestures to gain power and to construct their identities. Westwood uses the example of Diana, Princess of Wales, to demonstrate how the microprocesses of power can be amplified through the media. Westwood concludes that Diana was able to exercise power subtly by presenting herself as a victim of both adultery and institutional power. She made herself highly visible through the media and used her role as the mother of the future king to ensure her voice was heard.

Westwood argues that the Diana story raises many of the issues seen in a Foucauldian reading of power relations. For example, Diana's struggle for power stemmed from her attempts to construct an identity or individuality that was at odds with a discourse that stated that she should be an obedient subject of the monarchy. Such a discourse led to attempts to discipline her and control her behaviour. In her case, this disciplinary power eventually failed because she was able to develop visibility and utilize aspects of the microprocesses of power (especially in the field of sexual politics) that monarchy and society could not ignore.

Criticisms of Westwood

Westwood may be guilty of exaggerating the degree of power that women have in patriarchal societies. It can be argued that women still do not enjoy equal power and status with men in fields such as work, wealth, income and politics. Moreover, Princess Diana's power to resist the will of the monarchy may have been the result of her social-class position as much as her gender. Her wealth and social position afforded her the celebrity status that allowed her access to the media in order to promote her version of reality. Diana may also be a unique example in that the mass of ordinary women are unable to use their 'bodies, intuition and gestures' to gain power or get themselves heard.

In fact, the work of Foucault can be used to criticize Westwood's postfeminist position that women can control their own identities. Feminist sociologists have pointed to the way in which dominant discourses about female bodies shape female identity and self-esteem in ways that reinforce female powerlessness. For example, as Bartkey (1992) notes, dominant discourses about femininity celebrate thinness and this results in a strong disciplinary power over women's bodies focusing on weight, shape and appearance. Women, in response, may practise self-discipline by engaging in dieting, slimming, exercise, surgery, and even anorexia and bulimia.

Check your understanding

1. **How does the 'zero-sum of power' model define power?**

2. **What is the difference between coercion and authority?**

3. **What type of power is exercised by the prime minister?**

4. **What is the function of power according to Parsons?**

5. **Where does political power originate according to Marxists?**

6. **What is the function of the superstructure in regard to power?**

7. **According to Gramsci, how is the consent of the people gained by the ruling class?**

8. **Suggest two ways in which subordinate groups can acquire power according to Marxists.**

9. **How does Foucault suggest the exercise of power has changed over time?**

10. **How does Westwood use the example of Princess Diana?**

web.task

Search the worldwide web for lists of powerful men and/or women in Britain. What is the basis of the power of those who make up these lists?

researchideas

1. Construct a spider chart with a box in the centre symbolizing yourself. Draw lines to other boxes containing the names of significant people in your life, e.g. friends, brothers and sisters, parents, other relatives, teachers, employers, workmates. Use a different colour pen to symbolize the type of power relationship you have with these people – for example, if the relationship is based on authority draw a red line, as you would from you to your teacher. Some of your relationships may be based on coercion, persuasion, influence, manipulation, even ideology – use different colour lines to symbolize these. You may have to add categories or adapt existing ones.

2. Ask a small sample of other people (try to include people of different ages, gender, ethnic and class backgrounds) to construct similar diagrams. Compare the diagrams. What similarities and differences do you find?

Bio-power – term used by Foucault to describe concern with controlling the body and its perception.

Bourgeoisie – Marxist term describing the ruling (or capitalist) class in capitalist society.

Bureaucracy – form of organization associated with modern societies, consisting of a hierarchy of formal positions, each with clear responsibilities.

Capitalist societies – where one social class owns the means of production, while another class does the work.

Disciplinary power – the power to identify and categorize what is 'normal' and what is 'deviant'.

Discourse – ways of talking and thinking that dominate how society sees, describes and thinks about how we should live our lives.

Hegemony – situation where the ideology of the dominant class becomes accepted as the shared culture of the whole of society.

Ideological struggle – cultural conflict between the capitalist and subordinate classes.

Legitimate – justified and accepted.

Means of production – Marxist term referring to the material forces that enable things be produced, e.g. capital, land, factories.

Meritocracy – a society in which people are rewarded on the basis of merit, i.e. intelligence and ability, usually via examinations and qualifications.

Proletariat – in Marxist terms, the working class, who hire out to the bourgeoisie in return for a wage

Relational conception of power – power seen as a process that involves ideological struggle between the capitalist class and subordinate groups.

Relations of production – Marxist term referring to the allocation of rules and responsibilities among those involved in production.

Superstructure – Marxist term used to describe the parts of society not concerned with economic production, such as the media, religion and education.

Symbolic resistance – rebellion which takes an indirect form.

Zero-sum view of power – idea that power involves one person or group gaining and another person or group losing.

exploring definitions of power

Item A

Power in its various guises serves to integrate and stabilize key areas of social life. We are all affected by institutional power, i.e. the relatively routine arrangements of power involved in, say, the bringing up of children within a family, the management of an office within a large company, or indeed the exercise of judgement by government officials over who is deserving of welfare and who is not. As can be gleaned from these few examples, the issue of power is not one restricted to dictators, British Prime Ministers or military commanders. Institutional power is usually experienced as something quite ordinary: it is often, for example, the kind of thing that you only really know about when you are on the receiving end of it. As a child, you may have complied with or rebelled against the discipline laid down by your parents or a teacher, or later in life found yourself following, perhaps against your will, the instructions given by a bureaucratic manager, a doctor or a police officer. In particular, you may have found yourself doing something you did not want to do. The experience of imposition, of not being entirely in control of your own actions, is a familiar, indeed ordinary, consequence of finding yourself on the receiving end of an act of power. In such circumstances, it may seem relatively clear as to who has the power and who does not. However, we can also experience institutional power in far more anonymous ways, where it is altogether unclear that anyone is directing or controlling things. Take, for example, closed circuit television – such surveillance gives the impression that your behaviour is subject to some form of scrutiny and control, but it is difficult to work out who is imposing this form of institutional power on us.

Adapted from Allen, J. (2000) 'Power: its institutional guises (and disguises)', in G. Hughes and R. Fergusson (eds) *Ordering Lives: Family, Work and Welfare*, London: The Open University/Routledge

1 (a) **Identify and briefly explain two ways in which power is legitimated in the UK.** (8 marks)

(b) **Using material from Item A and elsewhere, briefly examine some of the problems that sociologists face in exploring who has power in modern societies.** (12 marks)

2 **Assess the view that power helps to maintain social order and strengthen social solidarity.** (40 marks)

The distribution of power

gettingyouthinking

Read through the following fictional scenario and then answer the questions that follow.

Imagine you are attending a Public Inquiry into whether a new road should be built between the port of Grimsby and the A1. There are two proposed routes. Route A will cost £210 million and will run straight through the only known habitat in the north of England of the rare wide-mouthed frog. It will also involve the blasting of a tunnel through the Lincolnshire Wolds, an area of outstanding natural beauty. Route B will cost £160 million but will run through the greenbelt around the historic city of Lincoln, as well as involve great disruption to traffic in the area while a bypass is especially built to take traffic away from the city centre. Five groups will give evidence to the Inquiry.

A Lincoln Chamber of Commerce

We favour Route B. The motorway will bring extra business and trade to the city which is good for our members. Hauliers and builders will especially benefit. In particular, it will increase the tourist trade to the city. The motorway will affect the surrounding countryside but there is plenty of it to enjoy that will not be affected. (Report prepared by John Smith of Smith Road Haulage Ltd and Stephen Brook of Brook Building Quarries Ltd.)

B Department of the Environment, Food & Rural Affairs

We approve of Route B for cost reasons. It will also attract foreign investors to the area because of the fast road-links to London. It will increase the status of the area and attract commuters in from London who can take advantage of rail links from Lincoln. Employment opportunities will increase, leading to full employment and higher wages. However, the department is also content with Route A because the Ministry of Defence requires a fast road from the Grimsby area to facilitate the efficient movement of nuclear waste in and out of RAF Binbrook. (This information is highly confidential and should not be disclosed to the Inquiry.)

C Friends of the Earth

We oppose both routes on the grounds that wildlife and the countryside will suffer. We are particularly concerned about the survival of the wide-mouthed frog, which is in danger of extinction across the country. Both roads will be a blot on the landscape. Existing rail services can easily deal with the container traffic from the port of Grimsby.

D North Lincolnshire Ramblers' Association

We oppose both routes. We are concerned that the natural beauty of the area will be ruined. We are concerned about the danger to children from more traffic, especially in terms of accidents and pollution. There may be an influx of new people into the area. Some of these may be undesirables and bring crime to the area. The value of our properties may fall considerably.

E National Farmers' Union

We favour Route A. This route involves less damage to the environment compared with Route B. The danger to the wide-mouthed frog is over-estimated. It can be moved to another habitat. The land around Route B currently attracts about £200 million in EU subsidies – the NFU estimates that we would only receive about £70 million from the Ministry of Transport if the land is compulsorily purchased whereas our members would receive approximately £90 million for the less fertile land around Route A.

1 Look carefully at the five briefs. If you were representing these organizations, what information would you disclose to the Inquiry? What would you hold back and why?

2 What does this exercise tell you about the decision-making process?

The point of this exercise is to demonstrate that decision-making is not a straightforward process. You will have noticed that four of the groups have a vested interest in either one or both routes. Moreover, they probably made decisions not to divulge all of the information they had because it might have prejudiced the Inquiry against them. The Inquiry, then, is basing its conclusions on incomplete information. There are three groups who would benefit enormously whichever road is built. Only one group has nothing to hide. Ironically, this group, Friends of the Earth, is most likely to lose.

What this exercise tells us is that decision-making is not an open process. Rather there are hidden dimensions to it that we rarely see. It is important to examine the distribution of power if we want to gain insight into the decision-making process in modern societies.

Pluralism

Robert Dahl (1961) carried out an **empirical** study of decision-making in New Haven, USA surrounding three contentious issues. He employed a range of methods which he believed would precisely measure the exercise of power. These included:

- looking at changes in the socio-economic background of those who occupied influential political positions in the community
- measuring the nature and extent of the participation of particular socio-economic groups
- determining the influence of particular individuals
- randomly sampling community-based activists and voters
- analysing changing voting behaviour.

Dahl's research concluded that:

1 Power in modern societies is **diffused** and distributed among a variety of community elites who represent specific interests in fairly unique areas. No one group exerts influence in general.
2 Moreover, each group exercises **countervailing** power – that is, each serves as a check on the others thus preventing a monopoly of power.
3 Power is also **situational**, tied to specific issues. If one group does succeed in dominating one area of policy, it will fail to dominate others.
4 All elites are **accountable** because they rely on popular support and must constantly prove they are working in the public interest rather than in their own.

Dahl concludes, therefore, that societies are characterized by democratic **pluralism**. Power is open to all through political parties and pressure groups. No interest group or individual can have too much of it.

Elite pluralism

Grant (1999) is an elite pluralist, meaning that he accepts that power in the UK is in the hands of **elites** or leaders of pressure groups, political parties and government departments, rather than all members of society having equal access to power. He argues the following:

- Power is widely dispersed between a greater range of pressure groups than ever before.
- Most interest groups in the UK are now represented.
- There now exist multiple arenas in which these pressure groups can influence policy on behalf of their clients, such as Parliament, regional assemblies in Scotland and Wales, the European Union, the mass media and the courts.

As well as lobbying politicians, many of these pressure groups use direct action, such as demonstrations, blockades, advertising, boycotts of consumer goods, internet canvassing and sometimes even violence. Grant acknowledges that some groups have more influence than others, but argues that pressure-group politics is generally a just way of managing the democratic process.

Pluralism: the critique

Dahl was criticized by Newton (1969), who notes that about 50 to 60 per cent of the electorate fail to vote in US presidential elections. It is therefore not enough to assume that inclusion within a community is evidence of sharing in the power process. Newton suggests that Dahl overstates the 'indirect influence' that voters have over leaders for five reasons:

- Votes are often cast for packages of policies and personnel rather than leaders, and it is extremely difficult for a sociologist to work out what a vote actually stands for. Consider, for example, votes for the Labour Party in the 2005 election. Could the Labour leader, Tony Blair, regard these as support for the Iraq War? Some people voting Labour may have been against the war, but voted the way they did because Labour's other policies – on the economy, poverty, and so on – remained attractive or because they were not attracted to the policies of the other political parties.
- Indirect influence via the medium of voting assumes voters' interests are similar and that these are clearly communicated to politicians. Clearly, however, the motives of a stockbroker working in the City of London in voting for Labour are going to be different to those of a traditional trade unionist.
- It is also assumed that voters are represented by selfless politicians. There is a failure to recognize that power may be wielded in self-interest or on behalf of powerful groups that have little in common with the electorate.
- The needs of groups such as the poor, the unemployed, the young, single mothers and asylum seekers can be ignored because they lack the economic and cultural power to be heard.
- The power of elected officials may be severely constrained by permanent officials such as civil servants. Ambitious plans to bring about great social change may be slowed down or watered down because of advice and pressure from those responsible for the day-to-day implementation of such policy. The television comedy series *Yes, Minister* is both a realistic and humorous illustration of this process.

However, in his defence, Dahl did acknowledge that political apathy, alienation, indifference and lack of confidence among the poor and ethnic-minority sections of US society did create obstacles to effective participation in political life.

Second and third dimensions of power

Bachrach and Baratz (1970) note that Dahl only looked at what Lukes (1974) calls the 'first dimension of power' – decisions that can be seen and observed. Dahl neglected the second dimension of power – the ability to prevent issues from coming up for discussion at all. Power, then, is not just about winning situations but confining decision-making to 'safe' issues that do not threaten powerful interests. In short, power may be expressed through '**non-decision-making**'. Non-decision-making can work in three ways:

1   The powerful can ignore the demands of the less powerful. If these demands are put on the political agenda, they can effectively be undermined via fruitless discussion in endless committees and public inquiries.
2   Some issues may not be raised simply because opposition is anticipated. See Lukes' second dimension of power.
3   Dominant interests can **mobilize bias** in that they can shape the values, beliefs and opinions of the less powerful so that they support the interests of the powerful or, at the very least, do not challenge the decision-making process. See Lukes' third dimension of power.

Lukes takes this critique further by identifying a third dimension of power. He suggests some groups exercise power by deliberately manipulating or shaping the desires of less powerful social groups. However, he also acknowledges that powerful groups may pursue policies that they genuinely believe will benefit the whole community, but which in the long term actually benefit the interests of the powerful more than others. He argues, therefore, that we need to identify who benefits in the long term from particular decisions. For example, a couple may make a joint decision that the female will stay at home to raise the children, but the male may benefit in the long term from this decision in terms of career development, income, influence over decision-making, etc. Lukes argues that this third dimension of power is the most potent type of power because it is rarely questioned or challenged.

A study by Saunders (1979) of two policies in a rural community illustrates this point. The two policies were the preservation of the environment and the maintenance of low rates (a form of property tax). These would appear to be in everybody's interests, but the reality was different:

● Preserving the environment ensured that private housing was scarce and expensive, and council house-building was restricted. Farm labourers were forced into tied housing and therefore dependence upon their employers. No new industry was allowed to develop and this resulted in farmers being able to maintain the low wage levels paid to their employees.
● Low rates meant that little was spent on services that would benefit the poor, such as public transport, welfare and education provision.

Elite theory

Classical elite theory stresses that power is concentrated in the hands of an elite – a closed minority group. Pareto (1935) argued that concentration of power is an inevitable fact of life. In any society, power is exercised by the active few, who are supposedly better suited to such a role than the passive masses because they possess more cunning or intelligence, or because they have more organizational ability. Some elite theorists simply suggest that some elites are 'born to rule'.

Pareto saw power as a game of manipulation between two dominant elites who compete with each other for power:

● the foxes (who used cunning and guile) – e.g. politicians and diplomats
● the lions (who exercise power through force) – e.g. military dictators.

Pareto argued that all states are run by these elites and all forms of government are forms of elite rule. Political change is merely the replacement of one elite by another, as the elite in power becomes either decadent, i.e. soft and ineffective, or complacent, i.e. set in their ways. In fact, Pareto argues that history is simply a 'circulation of elites'.

Similarly, Mosca (1939) argued that the masses will always be powerless because they don't have the intellectual or moral qualities to organize and run their societies. He suggested that a minority were more cultured, rational, intellectual and morally superior compared with the masses and were more suited to rule over them. He argued that elections are merely mechanisms by which members of this elite have themselves elected by the masses. Mosca believed in government *for* the people, and dismissed the idea that government could ever be government *by* the people. Mannheim (1960) agreed, but went further, arguing that democracy could not work because the masses were 'irrational', i.e. incapable of rational decision-making. 'Cultured' and 'rational' elites, he claimed, were essential to maintain civilization.

focus on pluralism

Abercrombie and Warde (2000) argue that the pluralist view of power in Britain is undermined by four processes:

1   Many interests are not represented by pressure groups and political parties. For example, fewer than half the workforce is represented by trade unions. Sections of society such as the poor, single mothers, women in general, ethnic minorities and young people lack specific groups that represent their interests in the political arena.
2   Some interests (in particular finance capitalism and employers) are overrepresented in terms of powerful interest groups working on their behalf.
3   Many campaigning groups are undemocratically organized and dominated by self-perpetuating **oligarchies**.
4   There is evidence that key institutions in the UK are run by elites who share similar economic, social and educational backgrounds.

1 What is meant by the pluralist view of power?

Some critics have suggested that this is a very simplistic view of power and politics because real differences between governments are dismissed. Both socialism and democracy are seen to conceal elites. However, no criteria are provided by which we can measure the so-called superior qualities of elites. It is merely assumed that the masses are inferior and that the elite is superior.

C. Wright Mills: the power elite

The American sociologist C. Wright Mills (1956) regarded the USA as a society characterized by elite rule. He argued that three key elites monopolize power in modern societies like the USA:

- the economic or business elite, symbolized by the growth of giant corporations controlling the economy
- the political elite, which controls both political parties and federal and state governments
- the military elite.

Mills argued that the activities of each elite were interconnected to form a single ruling minority or 'power elite' dominating decision-making in the USA. The cohesiveness of this group is strengthened by their similarity of social background, i.e. White, male, Protestant, urban and sharing the same educational and social-class background. Moreover, there is interchange and overlap between these elites in that company directors sit on government advisory committees, retired generals chair business corporations, and so on. Such unity, argues Mills, means that power elites run Western societies in their own interests; the bulk of the population is manipulated by the elite through their control of education and, particularly, the newspaper and television news media.

Moore (2001, 2003) and Phillips (2004) have both documented the 'special relationship' between what Phillips calls the 'American dynasty' of the Bush family, the American political **establishment**, economic corporations such as Haliburton and Enron, military incursions in both Afghanistan and Iraq, and an uncritical mass media, especially symbolized by Fox-News. Both authors generally agree that the power elite dominates American politics today and the brand of 'crony

capitalism' that it attempts to impose on the rest of the world is alienating vast sections of the world's population, particularly in the Islamic world. Moore's film *Fahrenheit 9/11* is a particularly interesting critique of this power elite.

Marxism and the distribution of power

Marxists believe that elites constitute a ruling class whose major aim is the preservation of capitalist interests. Marxists argue that exploitation of the working class has led to the concentration of wealth in the hands of the few. For example, in the UK the wealthiest one per cent of the population own about 23 per cent of total wealth, and the wealthiest 10 per cent own 56 per cent of all wealth – mainly in the form of company shares (Inland Revenue 2004). This economic elite is united by common characteristics, such as inherited wealth and public school and Oxbridge connections. Marxists argue that the class structure is of central significance because those who own what Abercrombie and Warde (2000) call 'property for power' – the means of production such as **finance capital**, land, technology and factories – are able to exert power over everyone else.

Direct and indirect rule

Miliband (1970) argued that the capitalist class rules both directly and indirectly in the UK.

- Direct rule – The capitalist class rules directly by forming Conservative governments. Miliband argued that direct and open rule by the ruling class is common in history, as is their willingness to confront working-class dissent and protest.
- Indirect rule – The ruling class also rule indirectly by occupying powerful positions in the **civil service** and **judiciary**. The upper levels of the civil service (responsible for advice and policy) are mainly drawn from the same background as the economic elite. Like other members of this elite, their outlook tends to be conservative and suspicious of change.

s y n o p t i c link   c r i m e a n d d e v i a n c e

A number of criminologists have drawn attention to crime committed by elites. Slapper and Tombs (1999) define white-collar crime as that committed by the individually rich or powerful against the corporations or sectors in which they work. These people have access to unique forms of crime by virtue of the positions of power and influence they hold. Examples include:

- insider dealing – individuals illegally use their knowledge of an impending takeover of companies they are involved with to buy shares in those companies, which they then sell at a profit
- pension fund fraud – the businessman,

Robert Maxwell illegally 'borrowed' millions of pounds from the pension fund of the employees of Mirror Group Newspapers to prevent the collapse of his business empire

- fictitious trading and accounts – recently, both the Enron and WorldCom groups in the USA collapsed after their directors were found to have faked invoices and accounts
- bribery and corruption – members of the political elite, i.e. government ministers and members of Parliament, have been forced to resign and even been prosecuted after taking cash from businesses in return for asking questions in parliament.

Miliband argued that the groups that constitute the political elite (that is, members of the government, politicians in general, top civil servants and so on) and the economic elite share similar educational backgrounds in terms of public school and Oxbridge experience. They often have family connections and are members of the same London clubs. They are therefore similar enough to constitute a ruling class. Moreover, elite members often 'swap' roles. For example, top civil servants on retiring often take up directorships in business whilst prominent businessmen often appear on government committees.

Economic power and ideological power

Marxists also suggest that economic power results in ideological power. The ruling class exerts influence over the ideas transmitted through a range of social institutions. Miliband, for example, focused on the role of the media in promoting the view that the national interest is best served by capitalist interests. This can be seen in advertising campaigns that promote companies such as BP as symbolizing 'security, reliability and integrity'. Television programmes and tabloid newspapers reinforce capitalist values by encouraging people to see the way to fulfilment as being through the acquisition of material goods. Such ideological power leads to hegemony or cultural domination. People accept that the culture of capitalism (based on consumerism, materialism and individualism) is good for them and so consent to power being held by the capitalist class or its representatives, who are seen to manage the economy effectively and thus maintain their standard of living.

Divisions within the capitalist class

Miliband therefore argued that the ruling class rules but does not necessarily govern – instead it rules the government by the fact of common background and therefore class interest.

If we examine the statistical evidence in regard to social and educational backgrounds, it does seem to support Miliband's argument that those in elite occupations do share characteristics and there is considerable overlap between these groups. Scott (1991) refers to this overlap as 'the establishment' and claims it monopolizes the major positions of power and influence.

However, in criticism of this Marxist argument, other sociologists have pointed out that government economic policy has generally failed to benefit those groups who dominate capitalism. Some actually suggest that the economic elite is characterized by conflict and division. Scott points out that the interests of industrialists may be different from those of finance capital. He notes the existence of 'power blocs' within the capitalist class which form alliances to promote their interests. He notes how different power blocs dominate the political and economic decision-making process at different points in history in Britain. For example, **manufacturing capital** was dominant in the 1950s, while in the 1980s and 1990s, finance capital (i.e. the City) was dominant. It could be argued that power today is dominated by transnational companies and currency speculators, as economies become increasingly globalized. However, Marxists argue that it does not matter which power bloc dominates, the overlap between them guarantees that capitalist interests are generally promoted before the interests of the rest of society.

Poulantzas: power and the capitalist system

Poulantzas (1973) suggested that the common social background of the ruling class is less important than the nature of capitalism itself. It does not matter whether elite groups rule directly or indirectly because the ruling class will always benefit as long as capitalism exists. Most governments across the world, whether they are on the right or left of the political spectrum, accept that economic management of their economies involves the management of capitalism in such a way that they do not lose the confidence of international investors or The Stock Exchange. Moreover, legislation in favour of subordinate groups, such as pro-trade union or health and safety laws, benefit the capitalist class in the long term because it results in a healthy, fit and possibly more productive workforce.

Poulantzas argued that the capitalist class will always ultimately benefit unless the whole system is dismantled. The capitalist class does not have to interfere directly in decision-making – the fact that the decision-making process is happening within a capitalist framework will always benefit it.

Conclusion: pluralism or elitism?

The overall evidence seems to support the view that elites dominate decision-making in both Britain and the USA. There is no doubt that these elites share some elements of a common social background and culture. However, this is not the same as suggesting that these elites constitute a unified ruling class working to promote its own economic and political interests. At best, the evidence for this is speculative.

Check your understanding

1. What does Dahl mean when he says that power is diffused?

2. What does Lukes identify as the three dimensions of power?

3. What is the most potent type of power, according to Lukes?

4. Outline the contribution of 'foxes' and 'lions' to our understanding of power.

5. What is the power elite?

6. In what ways does a ruling class rule both directly and indirectly according to Miliband?

7. How does the term 'the establishment' assist an understanding of the distribution of power?

8. Why are the common social backgrounds of elites not that important, according to Poulantzas?

KEY TERMS

Accountable – those in power can be held responsible for their decisions and actions.

Civil service – paid officials who work in government.

Countervailing power – an alternative source of power that acts as a balance to the prevailing power source.

Diffused – spread widely.

Elite – small, closed, dominant group.

Empirical – based on first-hand research.

Establishment – informal network of the powerful, linked by shared social, economic and educational backgrounds.

Finance capital – financial investment institutions.

Judiciary – judges.

Manufacturing capital – businesses that make products.

Mobilization of bias – a situation where dominant interests control the way in which a political system operates in such a way that some issues are never actually discussed.

Non-decision-making – the power to prevent some issues from being discussed.

Oligarchy – control by a small elite.

Pluralism – the theory that power is shared amongst a range of different groups in society.

Situational – holders of power vary from issue to issue, no one individual or group is dominant.

exploring the distribution of power

Item A

Pluralists believe that elections, or the certainty that an election must come, mean that a governing party must always conduct itself in a way that will ultimately appeal to the majority of the electorate. There is evidence that widespread retrospective voting does occur: many voters do remember major features in the overall performance of an administration, and this acts as a check upon it. When the election comes, the government knows that, to win, it must have the backing of a 'majority of minorities'. However, there are three pieces of evidence that support the view that a ruling class exists in the UK. First, no elected government in Britain has sought to abolish the capitalist economy based on private ownership. No government has seriously tried to reorganize industry so that firms are managed by their workers, or extended welfare services so that they provide adequate provision for all the population from the cradle to the grave. Second, business interests are not merely one group amongst a number, but are the best organized and wealthiest of all groups and were able, as in the early 1970s, to mount extensive newspaper campaigns against nationalization. Third, the best organized social grouping within Britain is finance capital, popularly known as the City of London. British economic policy has been mainly devoted to protecting finance capital through keeping a strong value of the pound sterling enabling these institutions to invest abroad on a massive scale.

Adapted from Abercrombie, N. and Warde, A. (2000) *Contemporary British Society* (3rd edn) Cambridge: Polity Press, and O'Donnell, M. (1992) *A New Introduction to Sociology* (3rd edn), London: Nelson

1 (a) Identify and briefly explain two features of British politics according to pluralist theory. (8 marks)

(b) Using material from **Item A** and elsewhere, briefly examine some of the reasons why some sociologists argue that a ruling class exists in the UK. (12 marks)

2 Assess the view that power in modern capitalist societies is concentrated in the hands of a few. (40 marks)

The state

getting you thinking

1 What do you think the people in these images have in common?

2 What role do the people in these occupations play in your life?

3 Do you think the role they play is an important one?

4 Who pays for these people and institutions? How?

All the uniformed people pictured in these images are servants or employees of the state. The state serves the society of which you are a member, so all these state institutions play a crucial role in your life whether you realize it or not. The police protect you from crime, and help maintain law and order. The army exists to ensure you are defended if the country is invaded by a foreign army. Doctors and nurses are dedicated to keeping you alive and healthy. All of these things come courtesy of the state!

What is the state?

Abercrombie and Warde (2000) note that the state is made up of a combination of major social institutions that organize and regulate British society.

≪ *The state consists of that set of centralized and interdependent social institutions concerned with passing laws, implementing and administering those laws, and providing the legal machinery to enforce **compliance** with*

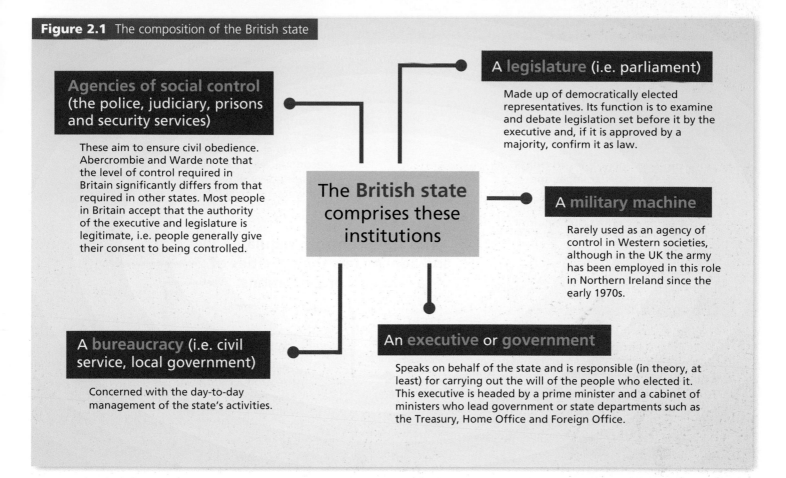

Figure 2.1 The composition of the British state

Agencies of social control (the police, judiciary, prisons and security services)

These aim to ensure civil obedience. Abercrombie and Warde note that the level of control required in Britain significantly differs from that required in other states. Most people in Britain accept that the authority of the executive and legislature is legitimate, i.e. people generally give their consent to being controlled.

A legislature (i.e. parliament)

Made up of democratically elected representatives. Its function is to examine and debate legislation set before it by the executive and, if it is approved by a majority, confirm it as law.

The British state comprises these institutions

A military machine

Rarely used as an agency of control in Western societies, although in the UK the army has been employed in this role in Northern Ireland since the early 1970s.

A bureaucracy (i.e. civil service, local government)

Concerned with the day-to-day management of the state's activities.

An executive or government

Speaks on behalf of the state and is responsible (in theory, at least) for carrying out the will of the people who elected it. This executive is headed by a prime minister and a cabinet of ministers who lead government or state departments such as the Treasury, Home Office and Foreign Office.

them. These institutions rest upon the state's monopoly of legitimate force within a given territory, which means that most of the time the laws of Britain are upheld. The powers of the state ultimately rest upon this threat of legitimate force.>>

A state, then, is a central authority that exercises legitimate control over a given territory. It can use political violence against either its own citizens or other states to enforce that control.

Abercrombie and Warde argue that the British state is characterized by six significant and far-reaching powers:

- It has an almost unlimited ability to make and enforce law, although final appeals can now be made to the European Courts.
- It is able to raise large sums of money via taxation.
- It employs about one-fifth of the UK's total labour force.
- It is a major landowner.
- It controls instruments of economic policy, especially control over currency exchange and interest rates.
- It regulates the quality of provision of both services and commodities on behalf of the general public. OFSTED, for example, inspects the quality of schools on behalf of the state.

We can add another power which has increased in recent years: surveillance and recording. Supporters of human rights have become very concerned at the state's ability to observe our behaviour via CCTV and at its accumulation of information about its citizens through birth, marriage and death registration

data, taxation and social security details, criminal records, and so on. Human-rights campaigners are concerned about the proposal, announced by the Labour government in 2003, that all citizens will be required to carry ID cards, linked to a National Identity Database. In 2002, the police announced that all genetic samples taken from citizens, whether guilty of a crime or not, would be kept on police file.

A brief history of the British state

The state as it is today is the result of a long historical process in which power has been effectively transferred from the monarchy to the people. The 19th century, in particular, saw the power of the House of Commons increase as the vote was extended to the middle classes. This led to the emergence of distinct political parties with distinct ideologies and high-profile leaders. Elections resulted in the party with the largest share of the vote forming the government and its leader becoming the prime minister. Nineteenth-century governments generally adhered to **laissez-faire** policies (meaning that they were generally reluctant to interfere in the daily social and economic lives of their citizens). Consequently, state policy involved minimal legislation.

During the 20th century, elections became even more important, as the vote was extended to all citizens aged 21 and

Figure 2.2 Organizations controlled, regulated and administered by the state

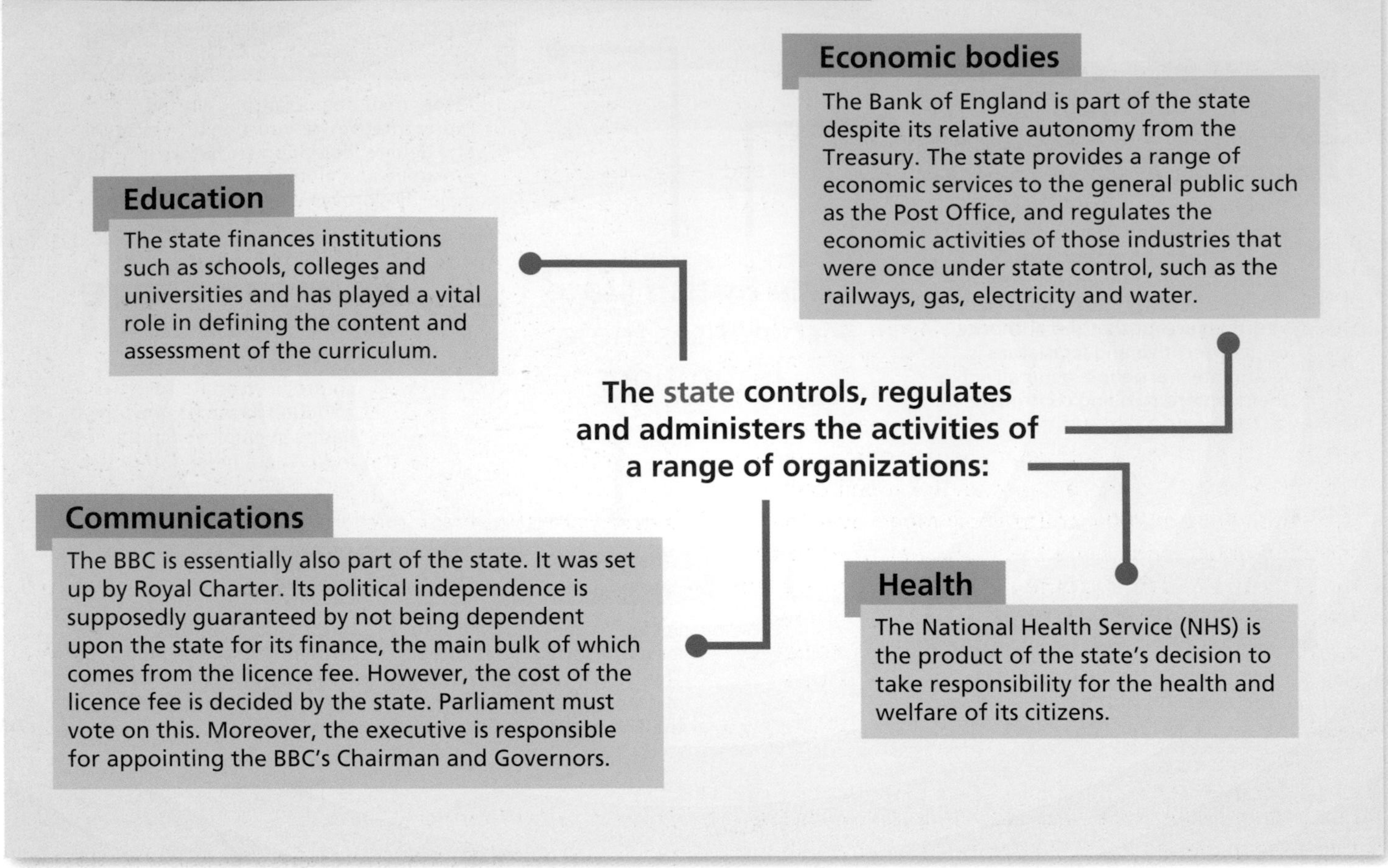

Economic bodies

The Bank of England is part of the state despite its relative autonomy from the Treasury. The state provides a range of economic services to the general public such as the Post Office, and regulates the economic activities of those industries that were once under state control, such as the railways, gas, electricity and water.

Education

The state finances institutions such as schools, colleges and universities and has played a vital role in defining the content and assessment of the curriculum.

The state controls, regulates and administers the activities of a range of organizations:

Communications

The BBC is essentially also part of the state. It was set up by Royal Charter. Its political independence is supposedly guaranteed by not being dependent upon the state for its finance, the main bulk of which comes from the licence fee. However, the cost of the licence fee is decided by the state. Parliament must vote on this. Moreover, the executive is responsible for appointing the BBC's Chairman and Governors.

Health

The National Health Service (NHS) is the product of the state's decision to take responsibility for the health and welfare of its citizens.

over in 1928. Political parties produced manifestos of their policies in order to attract voters and, once in power, governments saw it as the state's responsibility to manage the economy and look after the welfare of its citizens.

The post-1945 period saw a massive transformation in the size, range and power of the state. As Abercrombie and Warde (2000) observe:

<< *It has at its disposal enhanced powers of observing, recording and repressing the population (particularly through computer databases). It provides a wide range of services administered by large bureaucracies (both the civil service and local authorities). And it plans and acts on behalf of society as a whole, since, if matters were left to each individual, many would suffer unnecessary deprivation.* >>

For example, the Labour government of 1945–51 extended the role of the state in a number of extraordinary ways.

- It **nationalized** key industries such as the railways, mines, iron and steel.
- It set up the National Health Service (NHS).
- It extended state services in regard to social welfare and the alleviation of poverty.
- The 1944 Education Act extended state control over all aspects of education with the exception of the private sector.

Up to 1979, a consensus existed between the main political parties on welfare and economic policy. State management by both these parties when in government was remarkably similar. However, after Conservative leader Margaret Thatcher's election victory in 1979, there was a fracturing of this consensus, as the Conservative government committed itself to 'roll back' the frontiers of the state. Nationalized industries were **privatized**, public utilities and council housing were sold, taxation was lowered and there were attempts, albeit unsuccessful, to reduce the size of the welfare state.

The Labour government that came to power in 1997, after 18 years of Conservative government, has committed itself to a so-called '**third way**'. This is usually taken to mean the state taking **paternalistic** responsibility for the '**socially excluded**' while encouraging the general population to take responsibility for their own actions. The 'third way' also extends to the state taking responsibility for maintaining stable economic conditions, although, as we shall see later in this topic, global influences can undermine state actions in this area.

Theories of the modern state

Pluralist theories of the state

As we saw in Topic 2, pluralists like Robert Dahl (1961) argue that modern democratic societies are characterized by power being dispersed between a plurality of elite groups, as represented by political parties and pressure groups.

What should be defined as 'crime' has always been the subject of fierce debate and this is particularly the case when it comes to 'state crime'. When we watch James Bond assassinate an enemy of the British state, we tend not to think of this action as a 'crime' partly because of the fictional and entertainment context, but also because we interpret Bond's actions as justified in the context of the villain threatening our British way of life. However, there is evidence that employees of the British state have behaved in ways that could be interpreted as 'criminal'. For example, the British state has been alleged to have 'murdered' individuals through assassination and the so-called 'shoot-to-kill' policy in Northern Ireland. In 1988, the SAS killed three unarmed IRA members in Gibraltar, while in 2005, controversy raged over the shooting and killing of the Brazilian, Jean Charles de Menezes by the British police at Stockwell tube station. There is also evidence that the British state has used torture in Iraq, Northern Ireland and Kenya. However, criminologists note that the extent of state crime is

James Bond: state servant or criminal?

extremely difficult to measure because these acts are often carried out by the most secretive agencies of the state, and so are often invisible. Governments also have the power to cover up such activities by controlling the flow of information and even preventing the publication of information in the 'public interest'.

Although these elites share a basic consensus on social values and goals (e.g. they agree that violence is not a legitimate strategy), they are often in conflict with each other. The function of the state, according to pluralist theory, is to act as a neutral, independent referee or 'honest broker', whose role is to reconcile and accommodate competing interests. Aron (1967) saw the state as in the business of compromise. Resources such as power and capital are primarily in the hands of the state and its role is to distribute such resources to deserving causes on the basis of public or national interest. The state therefore regulates competing interest groups and operates to ensure that no one group gets its own way all of the time. Aron argued that the state and its servants, such as the civil service, are neutrally serving the needs of all by ensuring that all competing interest groups have some influence on government policy.

Marxist theories of the state

Marx and Engels (1848) described the state as a 'committee for managing the affairs of the whole bourgeoisie'. Marxists argue that while the state gives the illusion of serving the general will of the people, in reality it serves class interests. Althusser (1971) noted that agencies of the state are essentially ideological apparatuses that function to cultivate a picture of the state as being above any specific interest. However, the reality is that the state serves to reproduce, maintain and legitimate capitalism, ruling-class interests and therefore class inequality.

There are, however, variations in the Marxist approach, outlined below.

Instrumental Marxism

Miliband (1970) and other 'instrumental Marxists' see the state as an instrument controlled directly and indirectly by the ruling class. This view argues that the state is operated and controlled by those representing the interests of capitalism. Miliband argued that the view that the civil service and judiciary are neutral institutions is an ideological one aimed at disguising their true function – to protect the economic interests of the ruling class. Instrumental Marxists argue that political and economic elites are unified by social and educational background and therefore constitute a ruling class.

Structuralist Marxism

Structural Marxists such as Poulantzas (1973) argue that the social backgrounds of those who occupy key positions doesn't really matter. The state is shaped by the economic structure of capitalist society and therefore its actions will always reflect the class relations built into the structure of capitalism. The social relations of capitalism are characterized by class inequality, so the state will always reproduce such inequality unless capitalism is dismantled. However, Poulantzas argued that in order to fulfil its role unchallenged, the state needs to be **relatively autonomous** or free from the direct control of the ruling class. There are a number of reasons for this:

● The bourgeoisie have their own internal conflicts. The state must be free of interference from these in order to represent their interests as a whole.

● The state may need to make concessions to subordinate classes every now and then in order to prevent social disorder. These concessions may not benefit the ruling class in the short term, although they are likely to benefit their objective interests in the long term.

- The state can promote the ideology that it represents the national interest or consensus.

The work of Westergaard (1995) suggests that the state, even when managed by Labour governments, has done very little to challenge the inequality inherent in modern capitalist Britain. Economic inequalities in terms of the distribution of income and wealth continue to persist whilst health inequalities have actually widened in recent years. For example, the incomes of the richest 1 per cent have risen sharply since 1997, the wealthiest 10 per cent of the population now own 56 per cent of the UK's wealth, and the gap in life expectancy between the bottom fifth and the general population has widened by 7 to 8 years. From a Marxist perspective, these are indications that state social policy is generally benefiting the bourgeoisie. As Hastings (2005) notes:

<< *Until the 20th century, disease was no respecter of purses. The wife of a Victorian financial colossus was almost as vulnerable to the perils of childbirth as a maid in his household. The tombstones of the great reveal how many died before their natural spans were exhausted. Today, medical science can do many extraordinary things for people able to pay. There has never been a wider gulf between the remedies available to the rich and those on offer to most of the poor, even in societies with advanced public healthcare systems.* >>

Hegemonic Marxism

Hegemonic Marxists point out that the mass of the population consent to the state managing capitalism, despite the fact that it mainly benefits the ruling class rather than society in general. Gramsci (1971) argues that the ruling class are able to manage the state in such a way that hegemony – cultural and ideological domination – is achieved. People accept the moral and political leadership of high-status groups without question because the ruling class control the ideas and beliefs held by members of society, using state agencies and the mass media. However, Gramsci noted that the bourgeoisie was unable to exercise total control over the flow of ideas in any society. Sections of the working class, especially intellectuals amongst them, can gain access to ideas and beliefs that challenge hegemony, giving the proletariat some influence over the policies of the state, e.g. through trade-union and welfare-state legislation. However, Westergaard and others have suggested, using Lukes' concept of a third dimension of power (see Topic 2, p. 60), that in the long run such policies have generally benefited the bourgeoisie more than the proletariat.

Hall (Hall and Jefferson 1976) used the concept of hegemony in explaining Margaret Thatcher's victories in three general elections in 1979, 1983 and 1987. He argues that her management of the state was characterized by '**authoritarian populism**'. She was able to use the ideological apparatus of the media to portray herself as a strong, resolute and moral leader – the Iron Lady – and to convince the general public that

synoptic link   stratification and differentiation

The Marxist theory of social stratification sees capitalist society as characterized by an economic system in which a capitalist minority owns and controls the means of production, while appropriating the surplus value produced by the labour power of the proletariat. The economic system or infrastructure, therefore, produces a class system in which the ruling class exploits the working class. However, this class inequality is always under threat from the possibility that the subject class may object to this state of affairs and turn to revolutionary action in order to reverse it. Marxists argue that the capitalist class has developed a superstructure of social institutions whose function is to reproduce and legitimate the class inequality found in the infrastructure. The superstructure is made up of the state, i.e. its executive (the government), the civil service, the legislature (parliament), the judiciary and laws, agents of social control (such as the police, security services, the armed forces and the BBC) and institutions such as the educational system, the welfare-state and healthcare system, as well as social institutions not directly controlled by the state, such as religion and the mass media. The function of this superstructure is to transmit ruling-class ideology, i.e. capitalist values and

The BBC: part of the state's superstructure?

beliefs, in order to convince all members of society, but especially the working class, that the way capitalist society is economically and socially organised is natural and just. Marxists argue that the superstructure is so effective that it produces false class consciousness – members of the working-class are not aware that they are being exploited and oppressed and never become conscious of the conflict of interest between themselves and the bourgeoisie.

a good dose of strong economic medicine, whilst painful, was good for them. She convinced a substantial section of the nation that those who dissented from her vision were the 'enemy within' and threatened the security of the nation, the state and the family. Some Marxists have suggested that this analysis might be useful in explaining the election victory of Tony Blair in 2005, despite the extensive opposition to his decision to join in the invasion of Iraq in March 2003.

Evaluation of the Marxist view

Despite differences of interpretation, all three Marxist positions agree that the state serves the interests of the dominant class. However, as we saw in Topic 2, this is a difficult assertion to prove. We can see economic and social connections between the political elite and members of the economic elite, but this does not necessarily mean that they are using the mechanisms of the state to advance ruling-class interests.

Concepts such as 'ideology' and 'hegemony' are difficult to operationalize and to use as a means of measuring degrees of power. It is also unlikely that hegemony is experienced universally. Over the past 30 years, the state has consistently faced opposition in the form of urban riots by the powerless, strikes, new social movements and terrorism, and it has been forced to use coercion and force on a number of occasions.

The view that the British state is an instrument of the capitalist class can also be criticized because a great deal of economic policy has been unsuccessful. The state has been unable to prevent events such as stock market crashes, devaluation of sterling and the decline of heavy industry and manufacturing. If the state is an agent of the ruling class, its success is far from complete.

Jessop and the workfare state

Jessop (2002) rejects the theories of both Miliband and Poulantzas, although he accepts that capitalism has a powerful effect upon state activities and policies. He argues that the state is not an agent of capitalism. Rather, he argues that the state enjoys 'operational autonomy', meaning that it can operate in ways that can cause damage to capitalist interests, although it generally operates to make sure that capitalism behaves responsibly and for the general good of society. However, he does acknowledge that as a global system, capitalism exerts more influence than the state – it enjoys what he calls 'ecological dominance', in that capitalist investment secures mass employment which is good for society. Moreover, the profit-driven market approach now dominates most areas of social life, including even education and health.

Jessop notes that there has been a sea-change in state regulation of capitalism that itself has been shaped by the global expansion of capitalism. Up to the mid-1970s, state regulation was characterized by intervention in the economy aimed at securing full employment and low inflation, as well as by social democratic schemes of welfare-state provision. Jessop argues that this welfare-state regulation has been replaced by what he calls the 'workfare state', where the

state and private corporations work in partnership to ensure that British companies can compete healthily in the global marketplace. This cooperation between public and private has also expanded into the public sector, especially in health and education. Moreover, the workfare state encourages members of society to take more individual responsibility for their welfare and future. Jessop notes that, as a result, the state has lost some of its functions, but he argues that it still exerts great influence as a result of its willingness to be flexible in its response to globalization.

Criticisms of the modern state

- Abercrombie and Warde are critical of what they call the 'secret state'. They note that civil servants rarely appear in public to explain or justify their actions. Judges and senior police officers are generally not accountable for their decisions or actions. The security or intelligence services also largely operate outside the law.
- Some commentators have become concerned with the concentration of political power in the hands of the prime minister and a core of close advisers. Many of the latter are not elected officials or civil servants. Tony Blair was criticized for his presidential approach between 1997 and 2005 because the huge majority Labour enjoyed in parliament allegedly led to Labour MPs merely rubber-stamping executive decisions.
- New Right sociologists are still critical of what they term the '**nanny state**'. They see state policy as undermining personal responsibility and creating what they label as a '**dependency culture**'.
- State bureaucracy is seen by some as unnecessarily bulky and insensitive to the needs of ordinary people.
- The state is also accused of **institutional racism**. The immigration laws are the most obvious example, but sociological evidence indicates that institutional racism may be embedded in the everyday practices of the police, the judiciary, the prison service, the NHS – especially the mental-health sector – and in education.
- Feminist sociologists argue that the state is patriarchal. State agencies have until fairly recently been dominated by male personnel. State policy is also accused of being patriarchal, especially in the fields of family welfare and in its failure to get to serious grips with gender inequalities.

The future of the state

Recent research, for example by Abercrombie and Warde, suggests that the state and its power to act is under threat from a number of trends:

- *Regionalization* – as a result of increasing regional pressure, the Labour government has devolved some state powers to a Scottish Parliament, Welsh Assembly and Northern Ireland power-sharing assembly.

- *Europe* – the European Union (EU) has some legal authority over the British state especially in the fields of economic policy and trade. There are some concerns that this is eroding the power of ordinary people to take part in the democratic process because the agencies of the EU are not elected.
- *Internationalization* – British foreign policy is increasingly tied in with that of Europe or the USA. In the aftermath of the events of 11 September 2001, concerns were expressed that Britain had become a 'poodle' of the US administration.
- *Globalization* – It is argued by sociologists such as Held (2000) and Sklair (2004) that globalization threatens the very existence of the nation state for four reasons:

1 States find it almost impossible to control the international flow of money which can severely affect exchange rates and undermine economies. Some global currency speculators, such as George Soros, have the power to undermine state economic policy.

2 Transnational economic behaviour can severely disrupt economic policy by shifting investment and therefore employment between countries. It is argued that modern states, especially those in the developing world, are the puppets of global corporations. Such nation-states have to compete with each other for international investment and may even have to compromise some of their policies on taxation and welfare in order to attract it. For example, international organizations such as the International Monetary Fund (IMF) have insisted they will only give aid if countries agree to change their economic or welfare policies.

3 The global economy means that recession in one part of the world can undermine the economy in another part.

4 Global communications and the internet have made it difficult for states to regulate the flow of information across borders. There are concerns about transnational media influence, **cultural imperialism** and the use of the internet to encourage global dissidence and, especially, terrorism.

It is therefore argued that globalization challenges the traditional contexts in which states have operated, because they are less able to resist external events and forces. According to Held and McGrew (2002), there are very few states in the world today (UK included) that can make decisions without reference to other states or transnational interests in the form of economic corporations or international organizations such as the United Nations, European Union, NATO, World Bank, World Trade Organization or IMF. They argue that the modern state is undergoing transformation as its sovereignty is challenged and compromised by these global pressures.

Held and McGrew argue for new forms of cross-national institutions to assist the state in dealing with global challenges and conflicts in the fields of trade and currency, the environment, security and new forms of communication. They see a bright future in a more democratic EU and the transformation of the United Nations into a world parliament that would deal with global issues such as debt, AIDS, refugees, environmental pollution and famine.

KEY TERMS

Authoritarian populism – the view that strong leaders attract popular support.

Compliance – conformity.

Cultural imperialism – situation where one culture dominates and overrides other cultures. American culture is often accused of cultural imperialism.

Dependency culture – a way of life where people become incapable of independence and rely on the state to meet their needs.

Institutional racism – racism that is built into the routines and practices of an organisation.

Laissez-faire – to leave alone.

Nanny state – term used by the New Right to imply that the state acts as a 'nanny' to people by providing for their every need and not leaving them alone.

Nationalization – policy that involved governments taking important industries (e.g. coal) into state (public) ownership.

Paternalistic – fatherly, tending to be patronising.

Privatization – selling off previously nationalized industries to the private sector.

Relatively autonomous – term used by Marxists to show that the state can still represent capitalist interests even if it is not made up of capitalists.

Socially excluded – those members of the population who are not a part of mainstream society because of poverty and lack of opportunity.

Third way – political philosophy favoured by New Labour, a middle way between socialism and capitalism.

Check your understanding

1 What is the role of (a) the state executive and (b) the state legislature?

2 In what sense is the BBC a state institution?

3 Identify four ways in which the state was expanded between 1945 and 51?

4 What is the role of the state according to pluralist theory?

5 What are the key differences between Miliband and Poulantzas in regard to the role of the state?

6 Why is the neo-Marxist notion of 'rule by consent' problematical?

7 Why are Abercrombie and Warde critical of the state?

8 What problems has the state caused according to New Right sociologists?

9 Why is globalization a threat to the British state?

10 What effect has regionalization had on the British state?

exploring the state

Item A

Just about everywhere we turn in modern life we encounter the State. The State in some form is present when we post letters, use money to buy stamps, watch BBC television, travel abroad bearing passports, go to school or attend further or higher education. The State obliges birth, marriage and death to be registered. It takes a cut from every pound you earn. The roads you walk and drive on belong to the State. The State can declare you insane and institutionalize you. It can kick your door down at five in the morning and arrest you under the Prevention of Terrorism Act. It can conscript you and send you to fight in a foreign land. The State can remove all your belongings if you don't pay your taxes. Clearly, the State is a powerful and diverse organisation.

The agencies of the State are both highly secretive and powerful. Leading judges, who in theory are bound by the laws made by parliament, are actively engaged in making the law because they are continuously involved in interpreting existing laws. Likewise, the police are powerful because they have the scope to exercise discretion. Among the millions of law-breakers, the police decide who to stop on suspicion, and they do so in terms of a number of crude stereotypes of possible criminals. The security services also enjoy a very high degree of autonomy in their operations and operate largely outside the law. The elected parts of the State have little idea of the activities of the security services, or of the scale of their operations. On occasions, even the prime minister has not been made aware of the scale of operation of the secret security forces.

Adapted from Abercrombie, N. and Warde, A. (2000) *British Contemporary Society* (3rd edn), Cambridge: Polity Press; and Barnard, A. and Burgess, T. (1996) *Sociology Explained*, Cambridge: Cambridge University Press

1 (a) Identify and briefly explain two functions of the state. (8 marks)

  (b) Using material from Item A and elsewhere, briefly examine some of the reasons why critical sociologists believe that the state is both too powerful and secretive. (12 marks)

2 Assess the view that the state works in the interests of the powerful rather than the electorate. (40 marks)

Political parties and voting behaviour

gettingyouthinking

1 **Do you agree with Jessica Lever that most young people are more interested in voting for Big Brother contestants than for politicians. If so, why do you think this is the case?**

2 **Polls of young people suggest that the majority are interested in political issues. What sort of political issues is your peer group interested in and how do these relate to your support for, or apathy towards, conventional political parties?**

3 **Do you agree with Alex Folkes that the voting age should be lowered to 16? Explain your view.**

4 **What would motivate you to go out and vote for a political party?**

<< Are political parties doing enough to attract young people? That was the question raised yesterday when 17-year-old Jessica Lever wowed the Conservative Party conference with a speech urging the party to do more to capture the youth vote. The A-Level student from Hertfordshire told delegates she would be voting Conservative next year, but not enough of her contemporaries would unless the party went into schools and explained to students what they stood for. Most young people were more interested in voting for *Big Brother* contestants than for politicians – 'but it's up to the politicians to make politics matter,' she said.

Alex Folkes, campaign director of *Vote at 16*, said political parties needed to take a more coherent approach to getting young people involved in politics - and that included giving them the right to vote. 'We are encouraged by some aspects of what every party is doing, but it tends to be isolated examples of good practice rather than a sustained commitment.' And he added: 'We need to boost participation by young people in politics and while voting at 16 is not by any means the whole answer, it's a way to get people involved early in life. They are not only more likely to carry on voting, but also will see the issues of interest to them addressed by politicians.'>>

Adapted from www.politics.co.uk

Sociologists who study voting behaviour have tended to focus on the relationship between voting and social class. However, the last two general elections, in 2001 and 2005, have seen record low turnouts, particularly among young people, and this has prompted interest in other variables, such as age, in an attempt to explain the apathy and indifference that seems recently to have overcome the British voting public.

Political parties

Politics is the site of a struggle between belief systems represented by political parties. In Britain, this struggle has generally been between belief systems or ideologies associated with the 'left' at one extreme (with their emphasis on equality for all and social change) and the 'right' at the other extreme

(associated with **individualism**, **free enterprise** and respect for tradition). However, this is an over-simplified view because in the period post-1945 up to the 1970s, **consensus** rather than ideological struggle characterized British politics. In addition, traditional right and left ideologies, as represented by the Conservative and Labour parties respectively, have undergone a political 'make-over' in the last two decades.

The Conservative party

The **right-wing belief** system that characterizes this party is generally focused on preserving tradition and established institutions. Conservatives are particularly concerned with defending the concept of social hierarchy. They believe that inequality is a good thing because it motivates people to adopt **entrepreneurial skills** and work hard. However, Conservatives also believe that a role of government is to provide help for those who are unable to help themselves. This paternalistic streak in Conservative thought led to post-1945 Conservative governments committing themselves to the concept of the welfare state and the maintenance of full employment as an aspect of economic policy.

An ideological struggle amongst the right in the 1970s led to the emergence and dominance of a New Right ideology. This could clearly be seen in practice during the term of Margaret Thatcher's government (1979–90). This government preached minimal state intervention, the promotion of free enterprise and individual choice, and the determination to challenge the power of organizations such as the trade unions. However, after the removal of Margaret Thatcher as Conservative leader in 1990, the emphasis changed again. The Conservative ideology associated with the premiership of John Major (1990–97) shifted back in favour of paternalism. Under the party's next three leaders, William Hague, Ian Duncan Smith and Michael Howard, Conservative ideology became more **populist** by tapping into people's **nationalist** fears about Europe taking away British sovereignty and the impact of immigration on British identity.

The Labour party

The **left-wing belief** system has also undergone radical change since 1979. From 1945 to the 1970s, the Labour party was generally seen as the party of the working class and its ideology was predominantly socialist in principle. Nationalization of key industries such as coal, steel and the railways, the setting up of the welfare state, (especially the NHS) and the introduction of the comprehensive system in education can all be seen as socialist ideology (**socialism**) put into practice.

However, the party reacted to the election defeat of 1979 by embarking on a re-evaluation of its ideology and a revamp of its image. This resulted in Labour jettisoning many of the overtly socialist principles embodied in its constitution and describing itself as a party aiming to work for all sections of the community, rich and poor. Tony Blair's election to the Labour

leadership in 1994 saw a major shift to the centre in terms of ideology, as Labour politicians made statements about New Labour being a **social democratic** party rather than a socialist one. Labour presented itself as forging a 'third way' towards a common good, and being trustworthy and competent enough to look after the economy prudently.

Voting behaviour

The sociological study of voting behaviour is known as **psephology**. Generally speaking, studies of voting behaviour can be divided into three broad groups of theories dealing with the periods 1952 to 1979, 1979 to 1997 and 1997 onwards.

However, although sociological theories of voting behaviour tend to be focused on these specific time periods, there are common interrelated themes that have been recycled over and over again.

1952 to 1979

Early studies of voting behaviour saw a very strong statistical correlation between social class and voting behaviour. This is known as class or **partisan alignment**. Butler and Stokes (1971) studied voting behaviour between 1952 and 1962 and discovered that 67 per cent of their **objective** working-class sample (based on the Registrar-General's classification of occupations) voted for the Labour Party. They noted an even stronger relationship between **subjective class** (based on self-evaluation of respondents) and voting behaviour. They found that where subjective evaluation agreed with objective classification, 80 per cent of their sample voted Labour.

Studies of Conservative voters in this period reached similar conclusions: 75 to 80 per cent of the (objective) middle-class vote went to the Conservative Party. Some sociologists saw these figures as evidence of the institutionalization of class conflict, with the Labour Party and Conservative Party representing the natural interests of the working class and middle class respectively.

synopticlink

stratification and differentiation

Social class can be examined in both an objective and subjective sense. Objectively, sociologists, using occupational classifications such as the NS-SEC, can classify jobs into nine categories based on factors such as skill levels, salary, promotion prospects, control over their work, whether they exercise authority, etc. These can be further subdivided into a manual working class and a non-manual middle class.

Some sociologists have noted that although social class may be an objective state, subjective observations often have more meaning for people. The subjective feeling of being working class or middle class involves identifying with a cultural identity. For example, the

evidence suggests that manual workers traditionally saw trade union membership, a close-knit community and an extended kinship network as essential elements of their working-class identity. Political attitudes were also part of this subjective sense of class identity. Traditional working-class identity was bound up with a 'them-(the bosses)-versus-us' type attitude towards employment, along with socialist ambitions for social justice and equality of opportunity. The evidence, even in 2005, suggests that the majority of manual workers still see voting Labour as an important part of their identity, despite some decline in numbers.

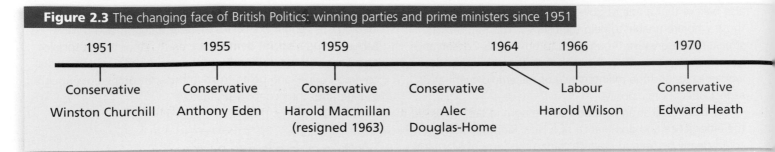

Figure 2.3 The changing face of British Politics: winning parties and prime ministers since 1951

1951	1955	1959	1964	1966	1970
Conservative	Conservative	Conservative	Conservative	Labour	Conservative
Winston Churchill	Anthony Eden	Harold Macmillan (resigned 1963)	Alec Douglas-Home	Harold Wilson	Edward Heath

Early explanations of voting behaviour focused on the existence of so-called 'deviant voters' – a third of the working class were voting Conservative whilst one-fifth of the middle class were voting Labour. These trends suggested that the relationship between social class and voting behaviour was not so clear cut. McKenzie and Silver's explanation (1968) focused on the working-class **deferential** voter who, they argued, accounted for half of the working-class Conservative vote. They noted that statistically this type of voter tended to be older, have a lower income, be female and reside in rural rather than urban areas. Moreover, attitude surveys of such voters suggested that they subscribed to a world view in which high-status individuals such as aristocratic landowners were seen as naturally superior and destined to rule.

Frank Parkin (1972) argued that the working class are exposed to two types of value systems or ideologies:

- First, the working class is constantly exposed to the dominant value system (DVS) which endorses existing inequalities through agencies such as the media and education system. Workers are particularly exposed to this value system in areas where no alternative value system exists and are therefore unable to resist it. Deferential voters, therefore, were those who had internalized the ideological messages of the DVS.
- However, many manual workers had access to a subordinate value system (SVS) generated at the level of working-class community. This value system was underpinned by a recognition of class inequality and hostility towards employers. Workers could see that there was a contradiction between what they were being told in institutions like education and what they experienced for themselves, and consequently voted Labour.

McKenzie and Silver argued that many working-class deviant voters were '**secular voters**'. These young, affluent factory workers, like consumers in a supermarket, rationally evaluated the policies of political parties and voted in terms of individual goals rather than class loyalty. Other theories also zoomed in on the idea of 'rational choice' being an alternative variable to class. Butler and Rose (1960), for example, linked the emergence of secular voting to '**embourgeoisement**' – the theory that the increased affluence of the working-class in the 1950s was leading them to identify with middle-class values. However, Goldthorpe and Lockwood's (1969) study of affluent workers in Luton found that the working class and middle class actually subscribed to very different value systems.

Goldthorpe and Lockwood further developed the idea of the working-class secular or consumer voter because they discovered very little deep-seated loyalty to the Labour Party among well-paid factory workers. This study was one of the first to note that **class alignment** as a factor in voting behaviour was beginning to waver among large sections of the working class. For example, Goldthorpe and Lockwood's sample voted for Labour not because they were working class but for '**instrumental**' reasons – as a means to an end, as a method of achieving material success.

1979 to 1997

Explanations focusing on working-class instrumentalism in voting became very popular among sociologists in the light of the Conservative election victories in 1979, 1983 and 1987. In particular, the 1983 result was Labour's worst defeat since 1931 in terms of total votes cast (28 per cent). What was evident was that the traditional working-class vote had deserted Labour – little more than half of the manual working class voted for them.

Ivor Crewe and class de-alignment

The work of Ivor Crewe (1984) produced the most extensive research on why a substantial proportion of the working class no longer naturally voted Labour. He identified long-term structural factors that, he claimed, had fundamentally changed the composition and character of the working class. For example, he argued that the proportion of traditional manual workers in the labour force had declined as older, primary industries, such as mining and shipbuilding, had been hit by recession. A consequence of this was a decline in working-class community as younger workers migrated to the south in search of work. Crewe concluded that the traditional working-class manual worker expressing unwavering support and loyalty to trade unions and Labour along class lines was a dying breed. Crewe referred to this trend as '**class de-alignment**'.

Crewe argued that the expansion of the service sector and high-technology manufacturing in the 1970s had led to the emergence of a well-paid and non-unionized 'new working-class', mainly living in the south, who owned their home (because of the Conservative policy of selling council houses). This group no longer automatically identified with the Labour party. Rather, it acted instrumentally and made rational choices aimed at maintaining its affluent lifestyle. Crewe referred to this as '**partisan de-alignment**'.

Crewe identified a number of short-term factors that shaped the instrumentalism of these voters. Margaret Thatcher's Conservative party successfully portrayed itself as the home-

1974	1979	1983	1987	1992	1997	2001	2005

Labour	Labour	Conservative	Conservative	Labour
Harold Wilson (resigned 1976)	James Callaghan	Margaret Thatcher (resigned 1990)	John Major	Tony Blair

owners' party of mortgage tax relief and council-house sales. The Conservatives' promises of tax cuts and reduced public spending (implying further tax cuts) appealed to the material interests of this instrumental working class. Crewe concluded that the Labour vote in the 1980s remained largely working class, but that the working class was no longer largely Labour. Moreover, class was no longer the main variable influencing people's voting habits.

Criticisms of Crewe

If we examine Crewe's work closely, we can see that he was not saying anything radically new. His analysis is essentially a synthesis of 1960s voting theory. His 'new working-class' is very similar in character to the affluent workers identified by Goldthorpe and Lockwood. Their voting behaviour is instrumentalist and very much based on the notion of 'voter as consumer' making rational choices on the basis of material interests rather than class loyalty. Crewe's theory came under sustained attack from a number of quarters:

- His methodology was regarded as rather suspect. Empirically he was rather vague in the use of the concept 'new working-class'. He distinguished between 'old' and 'new' working class on the basis of such variables as home ownership, trade-union membership and living in the south. It is not clear how these variables operationalize long-term shifts in voting behaviour.
- Butler and Kavanagh (1985) believed that Crewe had underestimated the effects of short-term influences, such as the wave of patriotic fervour that swept the country following the UK's victory over Argentina in the Falklands War in 1982. They point out that opinion polls showed that Margaret Thatcher was at her most unpopular in the polls prior to Argentina's invasion of the Falklands and the odds were against a Conservative victory. The tabloid media overwhelmingly threw its weight behind Margaret Thatcher because of the Falklands victory. She was portrayed as a resolute, decisive, no-nonsense war leader – the 'Iron Lady' – and Labour leaders were unfavourably compared with her. The Conservative government was able to paint itself as the party of authority while the Labour Party was portrayed as led by weak individuals who could not control in-fighting in their own party, never mind run the country.
- Labour came under sustained attack from the majority of newspapers throughout the 1980s and 1990s until the *Sun* newspaper switched to Tony Blair in 1996. The Glasgow University Media Group (1985) documented that the Labour party was constantly presented as a 'divided'

party dominated by '**left-wing loonies**', who allegedly threatened the national interest. The hegemonic Marxist, Stuart Hall (Hall and Jacques 1983), suggests that media coverage reflected the cultural dominance of the capitalist class which saw Margaret Thatcher as someone who would protect their interests. Media owners, such as Rupert Murdoch, were happy to sell her brand of 'authoritarian populism' in return for Conservative government support for their dominance of the British media industry.

- The major critique of Crewe's work came from the sociologists Gordon Marshall and Antony Heath. Marshall (1987) argued that Crewe had exaggerated both class and partisan de-alignment. His research suggested that classes had not withered away and that class identities continue to exert a powerful influence on electoral choice. Marshall's survey-based research indicates that manual workers, whether situated in the north or the south, still think in class terms. Marshall argued that Labour had failed to attract the working-class vote because it had shifted ideologically too far in the direction of the Conservative party. Cynicism and disillusionment had resulted in working voters switching their votes to the Liberal Democrats, or simply not voting at all.
- Heath (1991) looked at voting behaviour between 1964 and 1987 and also concluded that Crewe's class de-alignment theories were wrong. Heath and colleagues argued that the main reason Labour had lost four elections in a row between 1979 and 1992 was their record of poor political management during this period. They claim that there was very little change in voting behaviour or social and political attitudes between 1979 and 1992. However, Heath's team does acknowledge that there have been changes in class structure. For example, the changing shape of the class structure because of the decline in primary industries and manufacturing, and the expansion of the service sector, has decreased the Labour vote by 4.5 per cent and increased the Conservative vote by 3.8 per cent.

The 1997, 2001 and 2005 elections

The analysis of the 1997 election result – a Labour landslide – suggests that little has actually changed structurally. Most routine and skilled manual workers, council tenants and trade unionists voted Labour, whilst the **salariat** and the elderly voted Conservative. Most sociologists now agree that structural changes such as class and/or partisan de-alignment had little bearing on this result. Rather, sociologists have focused on the

Traditionally, the majority of working-class voters have voted Labour whilst the majority of middle-class voters have voted Conservative. In other words, the Labour party was seen as representing the collective interests of manual workers, whilst the Conservative party was seen as representing individualism and enterprise, supposedly middle-class characteristics. However, the Conservative party cannot win elections without attracting a significant number of working-class voters. Moreover, a significant section of the middle-class vote for the Labour party. These types of voters who do not vote in accordance with their class interests are known as 'deviant voters'. Sociologists have attempted to explain the working-class vote by suggesting that these types of voter are either

deferential, i.e. they see their social superiors as more suited to political leadership, or they are rational and individualistic consumers who see collective class loyalty as less important than voting for a party whose policies are going to improve their standard of living.

Another form of deviance that has increased in recent years is non-voting, particularly among 18 to 24 year olds. It is argued that this group is particularly switched off by traditional party politics and is more likely to be attracted to new social movements that focus on single issues and engage in more unconventional forms of direct action. Such movements, and the deviance in which some of them engage, may be an important source of social identity for young people.

changing political environment as the major explanation. The Conservatives were, quite simply, extremely unpopular after 17 years of continuous rule. The John Major government was interpreted by the electorate as hopelessly divided over issues such as Europe, as incompetent at economic management and tainted by corruption. On the other hand, the public now had greater confidence in Labour. People could see that the party had modernized, that the leadership had distanced themselves from the trade unions and that the internal dissent of the 1980s had largely gone. Most importantly, there was public confidence in the leadership of Tony Blair and Gordon Brown. This confidence in Labour's ability to govern seemed to be confirmed by Labour's victory in 2001 although there were concerns about the turn-out of 60 per cent which was the lowest since 1935. Voter apathy continued in 2005 when only 61 per cent of the electorate turned out to vote. This election saw a downturn in Labour's fortunes – the government only picked up 36 per cent of the vote and lost 47 seats, although it still commands a majority of over 60 seats.

Social-class alignments

On the basis of these three elections, we can make a number of sociological observations:

- There is some evidence that a large section of the electorate are still committed to fairly stable ideological convictions that reflect the key differences between working-class and middle-class voters, i.e. the working-class vote is largely loyal to the Labour party whilst the middle-class vote is generally Conservative. For example, in 2005, Labour attracted 45 per cent of the unskilled working-class vote and 43 per cent of the skilled working-class vote compared, with only 28 per cent and 32 per cent respectively for the Conservatives. On the other hand, the upper-middle-class vote mainly went to Conservative candidates. Class-based voting is therefore still important.
- This social-class or partisan alignment is not straightforward, however. Labour, above all other political parties, has

recognized this and has had the most success in repositioning itself as a political party occupying the middle ground. Labour politicians have been reluctant to play the 'class card', whilst Tony Blair has made statements such as 'we are all middle class now' to reflect Labour's commitment to society as a whole rather than to narrow sectional working-class interests. Labour has had particular success in attracting a lower-middle-class vote.

- Deviant voters are still central to electoral success. For example, in 2001, more lower-middle-class people voted Labour than Conservative, but Labour lost some support amongst the skilled and unskilled working class. In 2005, almost one third of the skilled working class voted Conservative.

Consumption cleavages

Despite these social-class differences in voting behaviour, some sociologists have argued that 'consumption cleavages' are more important than social class in shaping voting behaviour. For example, in the 2001 and 2005 elections, more home-owners voted Conservative, although those with mortgages were more likely to vote Labour, while more council tenants and trade unionists voted Labour. Labour's share of the trade unionist and council tenant vote actually fell between 1997 and 2005, although Labour still attracted 56 per cent of the council tenant vote compared with 16 per cent for the Conservatives. Critics of the concept of 'cleavages' suggest that many of consumption symbols used by these sociologists (such as owning or renting a home, or trade-union membership) are, in fact, indicators of social-class membership, and, therefore, we should not be surprised that the majority of home owners vote Conservative because these are likely to be members of the middle classes.

Regional differences

Regional differences also now seem to be an important variable in voting behaviour. The Labour vote is mainly found in urban areas, the North, Wales and Scotland, whilst the Conservative vote is largely rural and found mainly in the South. For example, in 1997 the Conservatives did not win a single seat in Wales and Scotland. Again, this may reflect the fact that rural areas and the South are likely to contain large clusters of middle-class voters, although the concept of the 'deferential working-class voter' may still be valid amongst those who work in the countryside.

Ethnicity

In terms of ethnicity, voting behaviour has undergone little change, in that Labour has always attracted over 70 per cent of the ethnic-minority vote. For example, in 2001, 84.8 per cent of African-Caribbeans and Asians voted Labour. However, the decision to take the UK into the war in Iraq has had some effect on the Muslim vote in some parts of the country; there were signs in the 2005 election that the Liberal Democrats and independent candidates benefited from Muslims either switching their votes or not turning out at all in protest. The most striking example of this was in Bethnal Green and Bow in East London, a constituency with a significantly large Muslim population, where the antiwar campaigner George Galloway defeated the sitting Labour MP.

Gender

In terms of gender, the evidence up to 2001 suggested that women were more likely than men to vote Conservative, although in 2005 this differences in voting behaviour had almost disappeared. In fact, the evidence suggested that young women with children were more likely to vote Labour in 2005 because they believed Labour had managed issues such as childcare, the health service and education effectively. There is some evidence that the voting preference of females depends on age, in that younger women were more likely to vote Labour whilst older women were more likely to vote Conservative.

Political literacy and tactical voting

There is a widespread feeling among political analysts that voters are more politically literate than in the past. They have more knowledge about the policies of parties and are now more able to make informed judgements about the past and potential future performances of political parties, especially with respect to economic policy and its effect on their standard of living. In 1997 and 2001, so-called middle-class 'deviant voters' used this political knowledge in constituencies where Labour was weak by voting tactically for Liberal Democrat candidates in order to prevent Conservative candidates winning those seats.

Voter apathy

There are signs too that voter apathy is becoming a problem, especially among young people. In 2001 and 2005, only 60 and 61 per cent of the electorate respectively voted, compared with 71 per cent in 1997 (see Figure 2.4). Some commentators argue that conventional two-party politics are a turn-off, particularly for the younger generation who see very little difference between the messages propagated by the two main parties. For example, in 2001, it is estimated that less than 40 per cent of 18- to 24-year-olds voted in the general election.

White, Bruce and Ritchie (2000)
Young people's politics

White, Bruce and Ritchie carried out a qualitative study using focus group interviews. They aimed to explore the alienation that young people feel towards politics in order to explain their perceived lack of interest in voting and to come up with ways in which to engage them with the political process. The study confirmed a low level of interest in mainstream politics. There were three interconnected reasons for this:

- Young people experienced a lack of knowledge and understanding of politics. Many saw it as 'dull', 'boring' and 'complex' and having little relevance to their everyday lives.
- They lacked faith in politicians, whom they regarded as deceitful and out of touch with the needs and concerns of young people.
- Even those who were politically literate felt there were few opportunities before the age of 18 to get involved with the political process. As a result, they did not actively seek information about politics because they believed they were excluded from this adult world.

White, C, Bruce, S. and Ritchie, J. (2000) *Young People's Politics: Political interest and engagement amongst 14- to 24-year-olds*, York: J Rowntree Foundation

1 Why might focus group interviews be more suited than questionnaires to this type of topic?

2 On the basis of the findings above, what strategies might be adopted to increase young people's interest in politics?

Some sociologists, particularly Wilkinson and Mulgan (1997), argue that young people now make up a politically disaffected or 'switched-off generation'. There is some evidence for this. Fahmy (2004) notes that young people, compared with older citizens, are less likely to attend party political rallies, to contact their MP or local councillor, to join a political party or put themselves up for public office. Many studies indicate that young people's political knowledge of both political philosophy and process is poor, whilst surveys indicate that young people are less willing to trust politicians. This last point is important because it suggests that young people are cynical about politics rather than apathetic. Surveys indicate that they believe that politicians and political parties are 'out of touch' with their needs and that their views are not taken seriously anyway. Furlong and Cartmel (1997) also note that the 'life tasks' that engage young people – such as passing exams, leaving home, going to university, getting the first job, establishing intimate relationships, etc. – may be more important than political participation.

Fahmy argues, however, that young people are increasingly motivated by single issues relating to protecting the environment, animal welfare, the developing world (e.g. the Make Poverty History campaign in 2005 was very popular in schools and colleges), and/or issues relating to **identity politics**, rather than the more conventional issues of defence,

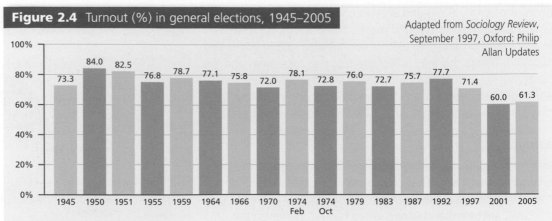

Figure 2.4 Turnout (%) in general elections, 1945–2005

Adapted from *Sociology Review*, September 1997, Oxford: Philip Allan Updates

health and education. Certainly, new social movements draw much of their support from the young (see Topic 5).

There is evidence that young people in particular reacted against the Iraq war in 2005. Labour attracted 42 per cent of the 18–24 age group and 42 per cent of the 25–34 age group, but lost 12 per cent of voters in these age brackets to the Liberal Democrats on the issues of Iraq and student tuition fees. However, there is some evidence that Labour lost seats in 2005 because those who voted Labour in 1997 and 2001 decided not to turn out, rather than through defections to the Conservatives or Liberal Democrats. There may be other reasons for this apathy, apart from the war in Iraq, such as possible disillusionment that Labour had not achieved more during its period in office or a perception that the result was a foregone conclusion, so there was no point in voting.

Check your understanding

1. How did the ideologies of the Conservative and Labour parties diverge after the post-war consensus was fragmented in the late 1970s?

2. What was the main influence on voting behaviour in the 1950s and 1960s according to Butler and Stokes?

3. Identify three characteristics of the deferential voter.

4. Outline Parkin's contribution to our understanding of voting behaviour.

5. In what ways was voting likened to shopping in a supermarket in the 1960s and 1970s?

6. In what ways does Crewe's 'new working class' differ from the traditional working class?

7. How do Butler and Kavanagh challenge Crewe's ideas?

8. How do Marshall and Heath view class and partisan de-alignment?

9. Identify three reasons why Labour won the 1997 general election.

10. What are the main variables influencing voting behaviour in 2001 and 2005?

researchidea

Invite your local MP or a representative from one of the main political parties into your school or college and grill them on how they intend to make politics more young-people friendly.

web.tasks

1. Use the election website of the Political Science department at Keele University to explore the 2005 general election:
www.psr.keele.ac.uk/area/uk/ge05.htm

2. To what extent are young people interested in politics? Analyse this issue using the resources at
www.politics.co.uk/issueoftheday/vote-at-16-parties-have-some-good-ideas-but-could-do-more-$3590183.htm

Class alignment – the idea that social class determines loyalty to political parties and therefore voting behaviour.

Class de-alignment – the view that the link between class and voting behaviour has been broken.

Consensus – agreement.

Consumption cleavage – social divisions based on people's ability to purchase desirable goods and services.

Deferential – the feeling that some people are naturally superior and should be looked up to.

Embourgeoisement – the view that the working class and middle class were converging in terms of lifestyle, attitude and voting behaviour.

Entrepreneurial skills – skills required to identify a market demand and then to set up and run a business to meet that demand.

Free enterprise – the idea that the market should determine the success or failure of business.

Identity politics – types of political action that focus on the extension of rights to groups which may be socially different from mainstream society.

Individualism – putting yourself and your family first.

Instrumental voter – a person who votes for a political party because they feel that party will make them better off.

Left-wing beliefs – in sympathy with socialism.

'Left-wing loonies' – abusive term used by tabloid press to describe some Labour councils in the 1980s.

Nationalist – belief that nation-state is the most important political unit.

Objective class – the categorization by government of people into a social-class category, traditionally based on occupation.

Partisan alignment – the sense of loyalty to a political party based on awareness of class membership.

Partisan de-alignment – the view that the working class no longer see themselves as naturally loyal to the Labour party.

Populist – attracting mass support, has popular appeal.

Psephology – the sociological study of voting behaviour.

Right-wing beliefs – in sympathy with conservatism.

Salariat – those who work in white-collar work who are paid a salary rather than a wage.

Secular voters – young affluent voters who rationally weigh up political policies in terms of how they will benefit their own standard of living and vote accordingly.

Social democratic – the view that social injustices should be addressed and that equal opportunities should be promoted.

Socialism – a set of ideas underpinned by belief in a more equal distribution of wealth, income and opportunities.

Subjective class – awareness of one's class position.

exploring voting behaviour

Item A

The rational-voter thesis is based on the idea that people have clear knowledge about specific party-political policies; judge the parties on these in an objective and informed way and then vote. The link is precise and calculating. However, the concept of the voter-consumer engaged in 'rational' voting is flawed in a number of respects. First, there may be no political party that represents an individual's views adequately in terms of its overall package of policies. For example, a voter may agree with the Conservative Party's stance on Europe but might disagree with its policies on the NHS. Second, the rationality thesis assumes that the media faithfully reflect the truth. However, the press in many European countries is highly partisan. Research by Golding, Deacon and Billig at the Communications Research Centre at Loughborough University suggests that campaigning in the 1997 general election was intensely 'presidential' (rather than issues-based) in style, with the two party leaders (John Major and Tony Blair) dominating the campaign and accounting for 43 per cent of all appearances by any candidate in the media. Finally, a large proportion of the electorate simply doesn't care about politics. There is no rational response to particular political messages because these are largely ignored.

Adapted from Brynin, M. (1998) 'Why do people support political parties?', *Sociology Review*, November, Oxford: Philip Allan Updates; and Williams, J. (1997) 'Research round-up, Election landslide', *Sociology Review*, September, Oxford: Philip Allan Updates

1 (a) **Identify and briefly explain two sociological reasons why people aged 18 to 24 years are less likely to vote. (8 marks)**

(b) **Using material from Item A and elsewhere, briefly examine some of the problems with the theory that voters are rational consumers. (12 marks)**

2 **Assess the view that long-term structural changes in the economy have led to fundamental changes in voting behaviour. (40 marks)**

Pressure groups and new social movements

gettingyouthinking

A strong rural force

The National Farmers' Union is the democratic organization representing farmers and growers in England and Wales. Its central objective is to promote the interests of those farming businesses producing high-quality food and drink products for customers and markets both at home and abroad.

The NFU takes a close interest in the whole range of rural affairs and works with politicians and officials – both in the UK and internationally – and other groups and organizations to advance rural interests.

Another key aspect of the NFU's work is encouraging a greater understanding of farming and rural life among school children and the wider public.

As well as representing its members' interests, the NFU provides a wide range of services to them including help with legal, planning and taxation matters, marketing and food promotion.

Mission statement

Greenpeace is an independent, campaigning organization that uses non-violent, creative confrontation to expose global environmental problems, and force solutions for a green and peaceful future. Greenpeace's goal is to ensure the ability of the Earth to nurture life in all its diversity.

Greenpeace does not solicit or accept funding from governments, corporations or political parties. Greenpeace neither seeks nor accepts donations that could compromise its independence, aims, objectives or integrity. Greenpeace relies on the voluntary donations of individual supporters, and on grant support from foundations. Greenpeace is committed to the principles of non-violence, political independence and internationalism. In exposing threats to the environment and in working to find solutions, Greenpeace has no permanent allies or enemies.

Animal liberation

The ultimate struggle. All too often animal liberation is seen, by those who do not understand, as a radical form of animal welfare. It's not about welfare, it's about freedom from oppression, it's about fighting abuses of power and it's about achieving a world in which individuals – irrespective of gender, race or species – are at liberty to be themselves. The state, the establishment and the multinationals seek to control our lives and imprison or kill us when we resist.

Compassion in World Farming

campaigns to end the factory farming of animals and long-distance transport, through hard-hitting political lobbying, investigations and high profile campaigns.

CIWF was started in 1967 by dairy farmer Peter Roberts. Peter and his wife Anna were becoming increasingly concerned with the animal welfare issues connected to the new systems of intensive factory farming that were becoming popular during the 1960s.

CIWF campaign through peaceful protest and lobbying and by raising awareness of the issue of farm animal welfare. We also produce fully referenced scientific reports. Our undercover teams provide vital evidence of the suffering of farm animals.

North West Hunt Saboteurs Association

18th February 2005 saw a day that many decent people had thought to believe may never come – the day that hunting with hounds was relegated to the history books.

The North West Hunt Saboteurs Association (NWHSA), is an organisation that is dedicated to the saving of the lives of hunted animals. Whilst the 18th February marked a very special day, it did not signal the end of that fight. There is still much work to do to ensure that the hunters do indeed desist with their sick pastime, make the switch to drag hunting, or face the consequences of breaking the law.

The ban is workable, can be enforced and bring an end to hunting as we know it. And this is where the continued role of hunt saboteurs comes in ... We do know that some blatant infringements of the law are taking place. And it's in cases such as these that hunt sabs are possibly best placed to gather evidence, as after all we are the people who have always been in the field with the hunts, know what constitutes illegal hunting and aren't afraid to get in amongst the action to get what is required. This of course doesn't mean that we won't intervene to save the life of the hunted animal – after all, that remains our sole aim as hunt saboteurs.

They seek to profit from the imprisonment or murder of those from the other species. They seek to own and control the land, the oceans and the skies which should be free to all. Animal Liberation is the struggle – indeed the war – against such tyranny in all its forms. We must fight this tyranny in all its forms. We must fight for the defenceless and the innocent. We must fight for a more compassionate world. We can, we must and we will win the ultimate struggle. When Animal Liberation is achieved, we shall all be free... free to enjoy the true liberty that has been denied us for far too long!

Examine the manifestos (statement of beliefs) of the five organizations on the previous page.

1 Allocate these organizations to the following categories:

A   Those that conform to mainstream political rules and work within the law to achieve their aims

B   Those that use both politically acceptable and unlawful means of drawing attention to their cause(s)

C   organizations that are generally in confrontation with the authorities.

Under each category, clearly state why the organization's beliefs and tactics may be acceptable or unacceptable forms of political action.

2 Are any of these organizations influential enough to shape their members' sense of personal identity?

You will have noticed that the organizations above occupy very different positions on a continuum of political protest. At one extreme are organizations such as the National Farmers' Union (NFU), which work within the existing political system to represent the interests of their members. The NFU is typical of what we call a '**pressure group**'. Two other organizations also operate within the conventional political world – Greenpeace and Compassion in World Farming (CIWF) – but reserve the right to work outside the democratic process in order to draw attention to particular causes. For example, CIWF uses undercover agents in factory-farming enterprises to gather evidence for animal cruelty. Both these organizations qualify as pressure groups, but they can also be classed as part of '**new social movements**', because membership usually involves a type of dedication to a cause which shapes the identity of the member. We can particularly see this in the case of social movement organizations and groups that lie *outside* the political mainstream. Membership of groups like the Hunt Saboteurs Society and especially the Animal Liberation Front (ALF) involve their members in actively opposing the democratic mainstream. Moreover, the fact of their membership tends to lie at the very heart of the identity of their members – in other words, an Animal Liberationist is likely to see membership of the ALF as a central defining component of their existence.

Pressure groups

Pressure groups are organized bodies that aim to put pressure on decision-makers such as government ministers, Members of Parliament, representatives in the European Union and local government. This pressure may take the form of mobilizing public opinion and/or lobbying behind the scenes in order to encourage policymakers either to make *no* change to existing policies and practices, or, more likely, to insist on reform and even radical innovation. Pressure groups seek to influence rather than to get elected.

Types of pressure group

It is generally accepted by sociologists that two broad types of pressure group exist.

- *Interest* or *sectional pressure groups* aim to protect the interests of their members or a section of society. This category would include the following:
  - trade unions representing workers
  - employer and trade associations, such as the Confederation of British Industry (CBI) and Institute of Directors
  - professional associations, such as the British Medical Association and the Law Society
  - even organizations such as the National Trust and Automobile Association.

  All of these protect the interests of particular social groups.

- *Promotional pressure groups* focus on specific issues or causes that members feel strongly about. Examples would include:
  - Greenpeace and Friends of the Earth, which aim to protect the environment
  - Oxfam, which aims to promote greater understanding and sensitivity towards issues such as poverty and debt in developing countries
  - Gingerbread which seeks to alleviate the problems and poverty of single-parent families.

However, this distinction is not watertight. For example, some interest pressure groups, such as trade unions, may also pursue causes that are in the wider public interest, such as the need for greater corporate responsibility in terms of health and safety. Professional associations such as the British Medical Association have drawn attention to the need to increase public spending to reduce health risks, such as specific types of cancer.

In addition, Morgan (1999) identifies the following types of pressure groups:

- Ad hoc or 'fire brigade' groups – formed to deal with specific new proposals, such as the building of a motorway. These are often disbanded once their aims and objectives are achieved.

- 'Idea' or think-tank groups – aiming to provide an ideological rationale or to carry out research for the aims and objectives of specific causes or issues. For example, the Fabian Society has provided the intellectual rigour that has underpinned socialism and the actions of trade unions, whilst the Adam Smith Institute has provided much of the New Right philosophy underpinning those organizations in favour of free-market government policies. Groups such as the Joseph Rowntree Foundation often provide the research and evidence in antipoverty campaigns.

- 'Political cause' groups – seeking to change the organization of the political system. For example, Charter 88 aimed to change the nature of democracy in the UK. It can be argued that the Human Rights Act in 2001 was a direct consequence of their campaign.
- 'Latent' groups – those which have not yet fully evolved in terms of organization, representation and influence. There are some social groups, such as the poor and minority ethnic groups, who experience a 'poverty of politics or protest' in that they have no formal organizations to speak out on their behalf. However, their 'representatives' may be consulted by the government or media, especially when moral panics develop around 'problems' perceived to be associated with such groups.

However, Morgan's typology is also by no means comprehensive or watertight. In recent years, we have seen the evolution of the 'celebrity' pressure group, with rock stars such as Sir Bob Geldof, Sting and Bono using their celebrity status to raise the public profile of issues such as famine, the degradation of the Amazonian jungle and debt in the developing world, in order to influence governments to change or modify their policies.

Insider and outsider status

Another useful way to look at pressure groups is to work out whether they have 'insider' or 'outsider' status when it comes to exercising power over the decision-making process.

Insider pressure groups

Pressure groups with insider status are often invited to send representatives to sit on official committees and to collaborate on government policy papers. Civil servants and ministers regularly consult with them. Such groups tend to use 'political brokers' or professional lobbyists who have inside knowledge of how the political process works and/or have official and non-official access to influential politicians and public servants. Such groups prefer to keep a low profile. This is not surprising because, as Duverger (1972) notes, some of these pressure groups, especially those representing the interests of capital, have 'unofficial power' – 'they actually have their own representatives in governments and **legislative bodies**, but the relationship between these individuals and the groups they represent remains secret and circumspect'.

Outsider pressure groups

Outsider groups, on the other hand, do not enjoy direct access to the corridors of power. Such groups attempt to put government under pressure by presenting their case to the mass media and generating public opinion in their favour. Their campaigns are likely to involve demonstrations, boycotts and media campaigns, writing to those with influence and occasionally giving evidence to government committees. Some pressure groups have gone further than this and either disobeyed the law or challenged the law through the courts.

Pressure groups and the distribution of power

Sociological theories of power have generally allocated pressure groups a central role in debates relating to the social distribution of power.

Pluralists see competition between pressure groups for the attention of policymakers as evidence of '**polyarchal democracy**'. In other words, modern democracies like the USA and Britain are seen as being characterized by many sources of power and influence. Pressure groups are seen as part of a diffused power network and are regarded as a force for democracy because they give ordinary people and minority groups an effective voice in the political process. It is suggested that pressure groups increase awareness of issues among the general public and that this prevents complacency among politicians. Moreover, pressure groups monitor government power in order to make sure that the state does not act in unjust or illegal ways. Such pressure may even result in changes in government policy. In this sense, pressure groups are a vehicle for social change which governments dare not ignore if they are to retain public support.

However, this view has been criticized for a number of reasons:

- **Neo-pluralists** suggest that pluralism exaggerates the openness of democratic societies. They argue instead that Britain is a '**deformed polyarchy**', meaning that some pressure groups, especially insider groups, have more influence than others because they are strategically better positioned to bargain with policymakers. Their control over scarce resources such as labour, skills, capital and expertise may mean that they always have insider status – they can use threats to withdraw these resources as a way of ensuring substantial influence over decision-making. It was believed that trade unions had such power until the late 1970s, whilst pressure groups representing capital may use their powerful influence over levels of financial investment to shape government economic policy.
- Marxists point out that the influence of some pressure groups may be disproportionate because of the nature of their membership. For example, some groups recruit exclusively from the more powerful and vocal sections of the community, such as the White middle class, and so exercise more power and influence than groups such as the elderly or ethnic minorities. Marxists also argue that powerful capitalist interests, such as finance capital and global corporations, dominate political decision-making and, therefore, competition between pressure groups. However, as we have already seen in Topic 2, it is relatively easy to identify these groups but generally impossible to prove the extent of their influence on the decision-making process. Moreover, analysis of economic government policy over the last 50 years indicates that these economic power blocs have not always benefited from such policy.
- Pressure groups are rarely democratic institutions themselves – members often have little say in the day-to-day running of such organizations.

- New Right analysts claim that the existence of pressure groups threatens to destabilize democracy. They argue that there are too many of them vying for political influence. Such **hyperpluralism** makes it increasingly difficult for governments to govern. For example, it is argued that in the 1970s, governments were weakened by competing demands (especially from trade unions), and this led to political stagnation and national decline.
- Recently, there has been concern about the disproportionate influence that global transnational corporations might be exercising over the domestic decision-making of national governments.

New social movements

Recent political sociology has moved away from the study of pressure groups to examine the emergence of new social movements (NSMs).

Hallsworth (1994) defines the term new social movement as:

<< the wide and diverse spectrum of new, non-institutional political movements which emerged or (as in the case of feminism) which re-emerged in Western liberal democratic societies during the 1960s and 1970s. More specifically, the term is used to refer to those movements which may be held to pose new challenges to the established cultural, economic and political orders of advanced (late-20th-century) capitalist society.>>

Storr (2002) notes that NSMs are a form of extra-parliamentary politics, i.e. they tend to operate outside of the formal institutions of parliament or government.

At this stage, it is useful to distinguish between new social movements and old social movements (OSMs). The term OSM is used to refer to older, more established political organizations, such as the socialist movement, or organizations representing working-class alliances, such as trade unions or employers' associations. OSMs mainly focus on bringing about economic change and tend to be class-based with formal and centralised organization.

In contrast, Diani (1992) argues that the key characteristics of a new social movement are:

- an informal network of interactions between activist groups, individuals or organizations
- a sense of collective identity
- a sense of opposition to or conflict with mainstream politics with regard to the need for social change.

Using Diani's definition, we can see that NSMs focus on broad issues such as environmentalism, animal rights, antiglobalization, anticapitalism, anarchism, human rights, gay rights, travellers' rights, etc. If we examine the NSM of environmentalism, we can see that it includes a wide diversity of groups and organizations, including pressure groups such as Greenpeace and Friends of the Earth, eco-warriors and anarchist groups such as Reclaim the Streets. The Reclaim the Streets group is also an excellent example of how interconnected NSMs are. The group was originally formed by a group of squatters in protest at the extension of the M11 in East London in the early 1990s, so it was originally an anti-road group. However, its activities have expanded to take in action in support of sacked Liverpool dock workers, organizing global carnivals 'against capital', as well as being heavily involved in antiglobalization protests in cities where the World Trade Organization hold

synopticlink

stratification and differentiation

It is useful when looking at the evidence for inequality in all its shapes and forms to consider the role of both old and new social movements.

OSMs such as socialism and trade unionism were very focused on social-class inequalities. They played a major role in the introduction of social policies that tackled poverty and class-based inequality in the UK, such as pensions, welfare benefits, the comprehensive education system and the National Health Service.

NSMs, on the other hand, are more likely to focus on single issues, such as human rights, animal rights, the environment and antiglobalization, as well as identity politics focused on women's rights, disability or sexuality – for example, gay rights have been promoted by groups such as Outrage and Stonewall. Interestingly, NSMs have tended to attract a very middle-class membership. Some sociologists suggest that NSMs are now more influential than OSMs because social class has declined as a source of identity in people's lives. However, survey evidence suggests that social class is still perceived by manual

Trade unionism: an example of an OSM

workers as the major cause of their low socioeconomic position. Groups representing the poorest groups continue to play a key role in encouraging the government to see the eradication of poverty as a priority.

meetings. Reclaim the Streets also protest using environmental actions such as 'guerilla gardening', whereby activists plant trees in unexpected places.

Some sociologists have suggested that some NSMs can be composed of ideas and informal networks, rather than specific organizations pursuing particular goals. A good example of this is feminism – it is difficult to identify a particular campaign group or set of influential women that works either defensively or offensively in the pursuit of a feminist or antipatriarchal agenda. Rather there exists a network of female academics who identify themselves as liberal, Marxist or radical feminists, pressure groups such as Gingerbread and the English Collective of Prostitutes, and voluntary groups such as Rape Crisis, that recognize a common theme – that most women in the UK share similar experiences in terms of how a patriarchal society views and treats them.

Types of NSM

Hallsworth argues that if we examine the ideological values underpinning the activities and philosophy of NSMs, we can see two broad types:

- defensive NSMs
- offensive NSMs.

Defensive NSMs

These are generally concerned with defending a natural or social environment seen as under threat from unregulated industrialization and/or capitalism, impersonal and insensitive forms of state bureaucracy and the development of **risk technology** such as nuclear power or genetically modified (GM) crops. Examples of such organizations include animal-rights groups such as the Animal Liberation Front, environmental groups such as Friends of the Earth and the antinuclear movement. Such groups call for an alternative world order built on forms of **sustainable development** in tune with the natural world, as well as social justice for all.

A variation on defensive NSMs is a form of association that Hetherington (1998) calls the '**bunde**', made up of vegetarian groups, free-festival goers, dance culture, squatters, travellers, and so on. This social network of groups has characteristics similar to defensive NSMs. They generally resist the global marketplace, are anticapitalist, and oppose the rituals and conventions that modern societies expect their members to subscribe to, such as settling down in one permanent place or abiding by social standards of hygiene. The bunde therefore create their own spaces, such as 'Teepee valley' in Wales, and gather in 'tribes' at key events and places, such as Stonehenge and Glastonbury, to celebrate symbolically their alternative lifestyles. The bunde can experience intense hostility from society. For example, the police have been accused of singling out traveller convoys for regular surveillance and harassment.

Offensive NSMs

These aim to defend or extend social rights to particular groups who are denied status, autonomy or identity, or are marginalized and repressed by the state. The concept of

difference, therefore, is central to these movements. Hallsworth argues that such NSMs are concerned with exposing institutional discrimination and advancing the social position of marginalized and excluded groups such as women, gay men and lesbians, minority ethnic groups, refugees and those denied human rights.

Whether defensive or offensive, NSMs are generally concerned with promoting and changing cultural values and with the construction of identity politics. People involved in NSMs see their involvement as a defining factor in their personal identity. NSMs provide their members with a value system which stresses 'the very qualities the dominant cultural order is held to deny' (Hallsworth 1994). This value system embodies:

- *active participation* – people genuinely feeling that they can help bring about change as opposed to feeling apathy and indifference towards formal politics
- *personal development* – wanting personal as opposed to material satisfaction
- *emotional openness* – wanting others to see and recognize their stance
- *collective responsibility* – feeling social solidarity with others.

The organization of NSMs

Often the organizational structure of NSM organizations is very different to that of other political organizations. OSMs are often characterized by high levels of bureaucracy, oligarchic control by elite groups, limited participation opportunities for ordinary members and employment of full-time officials. Hallsworth notes that the internal organization of NSM groups is often the diametric opposite of this. They are often characterized by low levels of bureaucracy, the encouragement of democratic participation at all levels of decision-making for all members and few, if any, full-time officials. Often such organizations are underpinned by local networks and economic self-help, both of which deliberately aim to distance their activities from traditional political institutions and decision-making. Mainstream politicians are mainly concerned with raising economic standards and improving standards of living. Those actively engaged with NSMs are more likely to be motivated by postmaterialist values – for example, they may wish to improve quality of life for animals and people, or encourage lifestyles that are more in harmony with the environment.

The social characteristics of the members of NSMs

Research into the social basis of support for NSMs suggests that members and activists are typically drawn from a restricted section of the wider community, specifically from the youth sector. Typical members of NSMs are aged 16 to 30 and tend to be middle class in origin; they are likely to be employed in the public and service sector of the economy (teaching, social work, and so on), or born to parents who work in this occupational sector. Other typical members are likely to be peripheral to (i.e. on the margins of) the labour market, such as students and the unemployed. However, Scott (1990) points out that it is difficult to make accurate generalizations about the membership of NSM groups. For example, many of the anti-veal export campaigners at Brightlingsea in Sussex in the late 1990s were middle aged or retired.

Cohen and Rai (2000) are critical of those sociologists who distinguish between OSMs and NSMs. They point out that organizations such as Amnesty International, Greenpeace and Oxfam are not that new, and have often used very traditional methods such as lobbying ministers, MPs and civil servants to pursue their interests. Moreover, it is too narrow to say that political parties and trade unions are mainly concerned with class politics or sectional economic interests. Political parties, particularly those of a socialist and liberal tendency, have been involved in identity politics, promoting and protecting the legal and social rights of women, minority ethnic groups, refugees, asylum seekers, and gay men and lesbians, as well as campaigning for human rights and democracy abroad. Both the Green and Liberal Democratic parties have long been involved in environmental campaigns.

Cohen and Rai do acknowledge that the nature of social movements has changed in two crucial respects:

- New media technology, particularly the internet and e-mail, have improved the ability of social movements to get their message across to much larger audiences than in the past. This has put greater pressure on politicians to bring about social change.
- Some social movements have taken advantage of this new media technology to globalize their message. For example, Greenpeace has members in over 150 countries.

NSMs and political action

The type of political action adopted by some NSMs deliberately differs from the activities of OSMs and pressure groups. The latter generally work within the existing framework of politics and their last resort is the threat of withdrawal of whatever resource they control – for example, labour or capital investment. Many NSMs tend to operate outside regular channels of political action and tend to focus on 'direct action'. This form of political action includes demonstrations, sit-ins, publicity stunts and other obstructive action. Much of this action is illegal, but it often involves fairly mild forms of mass civil disobedience, such as anti-roads protestors committing mass trespass in order to prevent bulldozers destroying natural habitats, the Reclaim the Streets movement disrupting traffic in the centre of London, and Greenpeace supporters destroying fields of GM crops. However, there have been instances of action involving more serious forms of illegal and criminal action – for example, damaging nuclear-weapons installations or military hardware, fire-bombing department stores that sell fur goods, breaking into animal-testing laboratories and attacking scientists with letter and car bombs.

Kate Burningham & Diana Thrush

The environmental concerns of disadvantaged groups

NSMs mainly attract a middle-class clientele, so how do disadvantaged people perceive environmentalism and organizations such as Greenpeace? This research carried out focus-group interviews with 89 members of disadvantaged groups in Glasgow, London, North Wales and the Peak District. It found that the poor are more interested in local issues, such as the rundown state of the areas they lived in, rather than national or global environmental concerns. This stemmed from real anxieties about meeting basic economic needs, which left little time for them to think or worry about wider or more abstract concerns. They gave priority to their most immediate problems, and so environmental concerns were viewed as too distant. They knew little about environmental organisations or eco-warriors beyond the media stereotypes, and generally perceived activists as too extreme. No one in the sample belonged to an environmental NSM, although this was put down to the lack of a local presence from such organizations rather than lack of interest. Finally, the sample expressed confusion about green consumerism, particularly about the merits of organic food and non-genetically modified foods. Most felt that buying environmentally friendly food was too expensive anyway.

Burningham, K. and Thrush, D. (2001) *Rainforests Are a Long Way from Here: The Environmental Concerns of Disadvantaged Groups*, York: Joseph Rowntree Foundation

1 **What problems of reliability and validity might arise in the use of focus-group interviewing?**

2 **Using evidence from the above study, explain why working-class people appear to be less interested than middle-class people in the goals of NSMs.**

The nature of politics

Many sociologists (e.g. Scott) argue that the emergence of NSMs in the 1960s indicates that the nature of political debate and action has undergone fundamental change. It is suggested that up to the 1960s, both political debate and action were dominated by political parties and pressure groups that sought either to protect or challenge the economic or material order. In other words, politics was dominated by class-based issues. However, the emergence of the women's movement and the civil-rights movement led to a recognition that wider social inequalities were of equal importance and resulted in a concern to protect, and even celebrate, the concept of 'social difference'. It was argued that affluence in Western societies meant than economic issues became subordinated to wider concerns about long-term survival, reflected in increased interest in social movements related to antinuclear technology, peace, the environment and global issues such as debt.

Theories of NSMs

The Marxist Habermas (1979) saw membership of NSMs as arising out of the nature of postcapitalism, in which the majority of people enjoy a good standard of living and are supposedly, therefore, less interested in material things. In such societies, priorities change – economic matters are of less importance than issues such as protecting human rights and democracy from an ever-encroaching state bureaucracy. NSMs, therefore, are a means by which democratic rights are protected and extended.

Touraine (1982), another Marxist, agrees, arguing that NSMs are a product of a postindustrial society that stresses the production and consumption of knowledge rather than materialism, consumerism and economic goals. The focus on knowledge has led to a critical evaluation of cultural values, especially among the young middle class, who have experienced greater periods of education. NSMs are therefore concerned with the promotion of alternative cultural values encouraging quality of life, concern for the environment and individual freedom of expression and identity. Touraine sees NSMs as at the heart of a realignment of political and cultural life. He suggests that they are in the process of replacing political parties as the major source of political identity.

Marcuse (1964) argued that NSMs are the direct result of the **alienation** caused by the capitalist mode of production and consumption. He suggested that capitalism produces a superficial **mass culture** in order to maximize its audience and profits. However, the emptiness of this culture has led some middle-class students whose education has given them critical insight, to reject materialism. NSMs, therefore, are a form of **counterculture** that encourages people to focus on unselfish needs, such as concern for other people or the environment.

synoptic link

A range of NSMs have engaged in forms of direct action involving criminal behaviour. These organizations claim that such behaviour is political, in that conventional political action has failed to bring about much needed social change. The Animal Liberation Front, in particular, has engaged in what some see as 'terrorism' – using car bombs against scientists who test drugs and cosmetics on animals, and firebombing laboratories that experiment on animals and department stores that sell fur products. The ALF justifies such law-breaking as necessary in order to prevent the 'murder of innocent animals'. Even more mainstream pressure groups, such as Greenpeace, have elected to use criminal action in order to gain mass-media attention for particular causes, e.g. Greenpeace members publicly destroyed a field of genetically modified maize in order to draw attention to the 'dangers' of such crops. The antiglobalization movement regularly confronts the police in its attempts to disrupt meetings of the World Bank and summits between leaders of the G8 nations. Elements of this movement see criminal damage to symbols of globalization, such as McDonalds outlets, as necessary political action. Sometimes such direct action can show anomalies in existing laws so that politicians will be motivated to change them. For example, Outrage

crime and deviance

Direct action

organized a mass gay kiss-in in Piccadilly in the late 1990s to demonstrate how the law discriminated against gay men and lesbians. These types of direct action are useful to illustrate the neo-Marxist idea that some crimes are deliberate and conscious acts aimed at overcoming injustices perpetrated by the current economic and political system.

Other writers believe that NSMs are the product of a search for identity rather than the product of common political ideology or shared economic interests. Alberto Melucci (1989) argues that the collective actions and political campaigns associated with NSMs are not organized in a formal sense. It is this informality or looseness that appeals to its membership. This belonging to a vast unorganized network is less about providing its members with a coherent and articulate political manifesto or ideology than about providing a sense of identity and lifestyle. In this sense, Melucci argues that NSMs are a cultural rather than political phenomenon. They appeal to the young in particular because they offer the opportunity to challenge the dominant rules, whilst offering an alternative set of identities that focus on fundamentally changing the nature of the society in both a spiritual and cultural way.

Melucci suggests that NSMs have made a significant cultural contribution to society because direct action, even if unsuccessful in conventional terms, reveals the existence of unequal power structures and makes people aware that these require challenging. In fact, Melucci argues 'that to resist is to win' – in other words, the mere fact of a protest action is a kind of success, because it is a challenge to existing power structures. Road protesters might fail to prevent a road being built, but, as Field (quoted in Storr 2002) notes:

<< *resistance to road building is not just about stopping one particular project. Every delay, every disruption, every extra one thousand pounds spent on police or security is a victory: money that is not available to spend elsewhere. 'Double the cost of one road and you have prevented another one being built' is an opinion often expressed by activists. In such an unequal struggle, to resist is to win.* >>

Postmodern accounts of NSMs

Postmodernists argue that the meta-narratives that were used to explain the world are in decline, as the modern world evolves into a postmodern world. Meta-narratives are the 'big theories' – science, religions and political philosophies (e.g. socialism, conservatism, nationalism, liberalism and social democracy). The search for truth, self-fulfilment and social progress through these meta-narratives has largely been abandoned as people have become disillusioned by the failure of these belief systems (as seen in the fall of communism) and/or the damage caused by them in terms of war, genocide, environmental destruction and pollution. The postmodern world is characterized by global media technology, which has led to knowledge becoming relative, i.e. it is accepted that all knowledge has some value. Moreover, in the postmodern world, knowledge is also an important source of power and personal identity. Access to the knowledge marketplace allows people a greater degree of choice about how they should consume knowledge in order to shape their personal identity. Postmodernists see NSMs as offering nuggets of relative knowledge that contribute important dimensions to personal identity. For example, people may partly define themselves by making statements that involve membership of causes such as

vegetarianism, the anti-globalization movement or the Make Poverty History campaign.

Crook et al. (1992) argue that in postmodern society, sociocultural divisions (e.g. differences in consumption and lifestyle) are more important than socioeconomic divisions (e.g. differences between social classes). Consequently, the traditional 'them-versus-us' conflict between employers and the working class has gone into decline and politics is now concerned with more universal moral issues. This has led to the emergence of new political organizations – NSMs that generally appeal to people's moral principles as well as their lifestyles. For example, we may be convinced by the moral arguments advanced by environmental organizations to consume in an ecologically responsible fashion and to dispose of our waste by recycling. Getting involved in NSM activities, therefore, is both a political statement and a lifestyle choice.

Commentators such as Ulrich Beck (1992) and Anthony Giddens (1991) note that in a postmodern world dominated by global media and communications, there is a growing sense of risk – people are increasingly aware of the dangers of the world we live in. In particular, there is a growing distrust of experts such as scientists, who are seen as being responsible for many of the world's problems. Giddens uses the concept of 'increasing **reflexivity**' to suggest that more and more people are reflecting on their place in the world and realizing that their existence and future survival increasingly depend on making sure that key political players, such as governments and global corporations, behave in a responsible fashion.

However, not all sociologists agree that we have entered a postmodern age. Meta-narratives still seem important. Religious meta-narratives, in particular, have re-emerged as important explanations of terrorism and suicide bombings in the UK. Crook and colleagues have been criticized for overstating the decline of social class, and for suggesting that sociocultural differences in consumption and lifestyle are not connected to socioeconomic differences. As Marxist critics have noted, the poor do not enjoy the same access to cultural consumption or NSMs as other sections of society.

Global social movements

There is evidence that NSMs are becoming increasingly globalized. Klein, in her book *No Logo* (2001), suggests that global capitalism, with its strategy of **global branding** and marketing, is responsible for the alienation fuelling an emerging global anticorporate movement. She identifies five aggressive branding and marketing strategies adopted by global corporations that have resulted in the superficial mass culture that has led to this alienation:

- *Logo inflation* – The wearing of logos such as the Nike swoosh or FCUK on clothing has become a universal phenomenon.
- *Sponsorship of cultural events* – Rock festivals are increasingly sponsored by global corporations. Even the visit of Pope John Paul II to the USA in the late 1990s was sponsored by Pepsi.
- *Sport branding and sponsorship* – Corporations such as Nike and Adidas have attempted to turn sport into a philosophy

of perfection by recruiting sports icons such as Michael Jordan and David Beckham to promote their products.

- *The branding of youth culture* – Youth trends such as snow-boarding, hip-hop and skate-boarding have been hijacked by corporations in order to make brands 'cool' and 'alternative'.
- *The branding of identity politics* – Some corporations, most notably Nike and Benetton, have identified their products with liberal issues that young people are likely to identify and sympathize with, e.g. antiracism.

Klein argues that young people are disillusioned with capitalism. This, she claims, is the result of their increasing realization that what counts as youth identity in modern society is often a product of corporate branding rather than individual choice. Moreover, people are beginning to understand that excessive branding has led to corporate censorship – the elimination and suppression of knowledge that does not support corporate interests – as well as the restriction of real choice, as two or three corporations dominate particular markets. The antiglobalization social movement has also drawn people's attention to how the activities of global corporations in the developing world sustain debt, subsistence wages and child labour. Consequently, people see governments of all political persuasions as colluding with global corporations or as ineffective in the face of corporate global power. Klein argues that what unites all these people as they join a loose network of antiglobalization groups and organizations is their desire for a citizen-centred alternative to the international rule of these global brands and to the power that global corporations have over their lives. Examples of this alternative in action include consumer boycotts of environmentally unfriendly goods and goods produced by child labour or regimes that regularly engage in human-rights abuse. The global anticorporate movement has also provided networks in which high-profile organizations such as Greenpeace and Oxfam have been able to collaborate and exert pressure on governments and transnational companies.

NSMs – the end of class politics?

There has undoubtedly been a huge surge of interest in NSMs in the past 30 years, but it is a mistake to conclude that this indicates the end of class politics. An examination of the distribution of power, studies of voting behaviour and the activities of pressure groups indicates that class and economic interests still underpin much of the political debate in Britain. It is also important not to exaggerate the degree of support that NSMs enjoy. Most people are aware of such movements but are not actively involved in them. However, conventional political parties and pressure groups can still learn a great deal from such movements, especially their ability to attract the educated, articulate and motivated young.

Check your understanding

1. What are the main differences between sectional and promotional pressure groups?
2. What is the difference between an 'insider' and an 'outsider' pressure group?
3. How do pluralists and neo-pluralists differ in their attitudes towards pressure groups?
4. Why are Marxists critical of pressure groups?
5. Identify three differences between old social movements and new social movements.
6. What are the main differences between defensive NSMs and offensive NSMs?
7. In what ways might membership of NSMs be related to anxieties about postindustrial society?
8. How do Marxists like Marcuse explain the emergence of NSMs?
9. How is the notion of 'increasing reflexivity' related to membership of new social movements?
10. What evidence is there that NSMs have become globalized?

research idea

Choose an issue, such as vivisection, testing drugs on animals or using animals in testing perfumes, and research one or more of the following:

1. The depth of feeling about the issue in your school or college. Find this out either by conducting a brief questionnaire or by asking people in your school or college to sign a petition asking for it to be banned.
2. The plans of conventional political parties with regard to the issue.
3. What pressure groups and/or social movements exist in regard to your issue and what tactics are they adopting to bring the issue to public attention?

web.task

www.resist.org.uk/ **is the coordinating site for most of the organizations that make up the anti-globalization social movement. Click on their website and go to the 'Links' page. This lists all the organizations/issues that are affiliated. Choose a sample of organizations and find out their aims and tactics.**

KEY TERMS

Alienation – an inability to identify with an institution or group to which you might belong.

Bunde – term used by Hetherington to describe a new form of association made up of vegetarian groups, free-festival goers, dance culture, travellers, and so on.

Counterculture – a culture that is in opposition to authority.

Deformed polyarchy – situation where some pressure groups have more influence than others because they are strategically better positioned to bargain with policymakers.

Global branding – attempts by global corporations to make their image and products recognizable worldwide.

Hyperpluralism – a situation where there are too many pressure groups competing for influence.

Legislative bodies – the state, parliament, the judiciary, i.e. agencies that have the power to make laws.

Lobbying – a means by which pressure groups and NSMs inform politicians and civil servants of their concerns and/or pass on information that will assist their cause; pressure groups often employ lobbyists to promote their cause in parliament.

Mass culture – a superficial entertainment culture propagated by the mass media that undermines people's capacity for critical thinking.

New social movements – loosely organized political movements that have emerged since the 1960s, based around particular issues.

Neo-pluralists – writers who have updated the idea of pluralism.

Polyarchal democracy – society in which many sources of power and influence exist.

Pressure group – organized body that aims to put pressure on decision-makers.

Reflexivity – the ability to reflect on your experiences.

Risk technology – technology that poses dangers to society, such as nuclear power.

Sustainable development – strategies for modernizing the developing world that result in a fairer distribution of wealth and resources.

exploring pressure groups and NSMs

Item A

It has been suggested that by the late 1960s people had become disillusioned with established political parties and this led to the growth of the NSMs and also of pressure groups. Coxall (1981) argues that the 1960s and 1970s witnessed an explosion of pressure group membership. He cites the examples of Shelter, which by 1969 had more than 220 affiliated branches, and the Child Poverty Action Group, which by 1970 had over 40. He argues, however, that despite this growth, they still mobilized only a minority of the population. In the 1980s, groups such as CND went into decline but others, notably those concerned with the environment and animal welfare, rose to take their place.

A good example of the latter group is the Animal Liberation Front (ALF). Some observers have noted that membership of the ALF is like membership of an extraordinary fundamentalist religion. Since its foundation in 1976, animal rights terrorists have targeted butchers' shops, science laboratories, fur farms, live exports, dog-breeding farms and high-street chemists. Most animal rights activists begin their career around the family kitchen table as young teenagers by refusing to eat meat, and then going on to become vegans – who reject the use of all animal products, such as milk, cheese or leather. This rejection is based not on taste but on the moral conviction that killing animals for human consumption is wrong. In their own minds, ALF members are possessed of a blinding religious truth: our society is built on the unnecessary killing of animals and they are morally bound to use all means, including violence, to stop the daily holocaust of animal lives.

Adapted from Kirby, M. (1995) *Investigating Political Sociology*, London: Collins Educational; and Toolis, K. (2001) *The Guardian*, Wednesday 7 November

1 (a) Identify and briefly explain two differences between old and new social movements. (8 marks)

(b) Using material from Item A and elsewhere, briefly examine some of the features unique to the belief systems and organization of new social movements. (12 marks)

2 Assess the view that the popularity of new social movements is an indicator that we are now living in a postmodern age. (40 marks)

IF WE EXAMINE A RANGE OF SOCIAL INDICATORS in the UK, such as income, standard of living, education and health, we can see that we enjoy a fairly affluent lifestyle, especially compared with many countries located in Africa and Asia. World sociology is concerned with explaining why these global inequalities exist. Topic 1 asks the question 'What is development'? In other words, what do we in the West take for granted in terms of our lifestyles that might be absent in the poorer parts of the world?

We often see distressing images from the developing world showing the effects of famine, war and disease. Some sociologists suggest that many of these countries' problems come about because they cling to traditional values and institutions, and fail to modernize along Western lines. Topic 2 examines the validity of this position.

Topic 3, on the other hand, examines the proposition that the poorer countries have failed to modernize because of the obstacles put in their path by Western nations. Indeed, some people argue that Western countries have accumulated their wealth at the expense of poorer countries. The validity of this argument is assessed by examining both historical and contemporary evidence.

A major concern of the 21st century so far has been the relationship between aid, debt and poverty. Both the general public and leaders of the Western world have expressed concern about the crippling debts owed by poorer countries to Western banks. Topic 4 examines the effect of debt on the development of poorer nations and looks at the strategies available to tackle this problem.

Population growth across the world has raised concerns about the ecological future of our planet. Rapid increases in population, especially in the developing world, has led to anxiety about pressures on both natural resources and the global environment. Topic 5 examines the evidence with regard to population and consumption.

Topic 6 examines the role of women in the developing world. Many feminist sociologists argue that patriarchy or male dominance is a global phenomenon. This topic examines the evidence in areas of work, power and family life to assess whether patriarchy takes the same sorts of forms as it does in the West.

The world is becoming a much smaller place. News is now almost instantaneous as global satellite media networks proliferate. Culture is becoming increasingly globalized as our lifestyles – in terms of food, clothing and leisure pursuits – are shaped by a diverse range of global influences. Topic 7, therefore, examines the phenomenon of globalization in order to assess its impact on our daily lives.

AQAspecification	topics	pages
Candidates should examine:		
Different definitions and explanations of development and underdevelopment	Definitions of development are examined in Topic 1; explanations are covered in Topics 2 and 3	92–101 102–117
The cultural, political and economic interrelationships between societies	These interrelationships are the focus of Topics 2, 3 and 8	102–117 148–155
The role of aid, trade and transnational corporations and international agencies in different strategies for development	The role of aid and international agencies is discussed in Topic 4; transnational corporations in Topics 2 and 8. Trade is part of the discussion of globalization in Topic 8.	102–109 118–125 148–155
Development in relation to urbanization, industrialization and the environment	Covered in Topic 7	140–147
Employment, education, health, demographic change and gender as aspects of development	Demographic change is the focus of Topic 5. Gender is examined in Topic 6	126–131 132–139

World sociology

Defining development

gettingyouthinking

Babies dying

Refugees

Poverty

Flies

The results of a survey indicating the images of Africa that were held by Year 9 pupils in a sample of London secondary schools

Bald children

Disease

Kids with pot bellies

Starvation

Drought

War

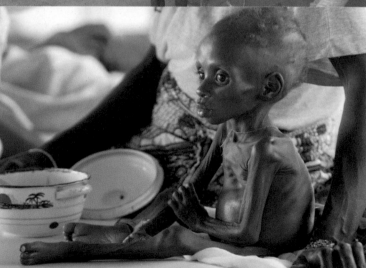

1 Look at each of the images of the children on this page in turn and explain what feelings each picture provokes in you. Suggest reasons for the predicament of each child. How would you go about improving their chances of survival into adulthood?

2 Examine the results of the survey into children's images of Africa. Do these images reflect the dominant images in your head? What other images might you add to this list? Where do people get such images from?

3 What does the cartoon tell us about our perception of problems in the developing world?

The simple but tragic fact: there are just too many people and not enough being grown to feed them all.

Surveys generally indicate that the sorts of images of children used opposite provoke two distinct sets of feelings among young people in the UK:

- Some feel compassion and pity, and perhaps an overwhelming need to help. If you felt this way, you probably constructed a detailed list of solutions that focused on how we in the West might help these children out of poverty. In this case, you are probably the type of person who gives generously to charities that target children in the developing world, such as Comic Relief.
- Many feel indifference. If this was true for you, the likelihood is that you have seen these types of images so many times now that you may have become immune to their emotional content. If so, you are experiencing what is known as 'compassion fatigue'. Such feelings are likely to be accompanied by nagging questions such as 'Why do we always need to put our hands in our pockets?' and 'Why don't these people sort themselves out?'

You are likely to find both these sets of feelings present in any group of young people, such as your own sociology class. Neither set is right or wrong. Both groups of people share similar characteristics in that they both have images of places like Africa that are similar to the ones held by the children in the survey opposite. Note how negative these images are. They are generally images of Africa starving, Africa overpopulated with too many babies, and Africa as victim of natural disasters, such as drought and volcanoes, or self-inflicted disasters, such as war. Such images are the product of **value-judgements** that we make about how people should live their lives. They are constructed relative to our own experience. Our standard of living in the UK generally ensures that most children in the UK survive healthily into adulthood. We should, therefore, not be too surprised that our ideas about how societies like these in Africa should change or develop are based on our own Western experiences. Moreover, some of us will quite naturally jump to the conclusion that their problems are created by their failure to adopt our way of life.

We should not underestimate the role of the mass media in constructing our perceptions of other parts of the world and the explanations and solutions available to their problems. Few of us have had actual experience of these parts of the world and consequently our perceptions are ultimately formed by the images we see in the media. Media analysis may be partial and selective, as the cartoon opposite indicates.

It is important to understand that our perception, together with media representations, of developing countries reflect a wider academic and political debate about how sociologists, politicians and aid agencies should define development. As we shall see, the dominant definitions of development that exist involve the same sorts of value-judgements that informed your reaction to the poverty and suffering of children in the developing world.

Affluence and destitution

World sociology is concerned with explaining the relationship between different countries and peoples of the world, and, in particular, the economic and social differences between them. World sociologists aim to explain why the nations of the world exist in a hierarchy of affluence which ranges from utter destitution to immense wealth (Harris 1989). For example, in 1997, the richest fifth of the world's population enjoyed an income 78 times as great as the poorest. Most of this wealth is concentrated in the industrialized world – North America, Western Europe, Japan and Australasia (see Fig. 3.1). Most of the destitution is concentrated in the less developed world – which consists mainly of most of Africa, South and Central America, the Indian subcontinent and most of East Asia. Evidence suggests that this wealth gap between the developed and developing world, despite the billions of pounds given in aid over the past 50 years, is actually getting wider.

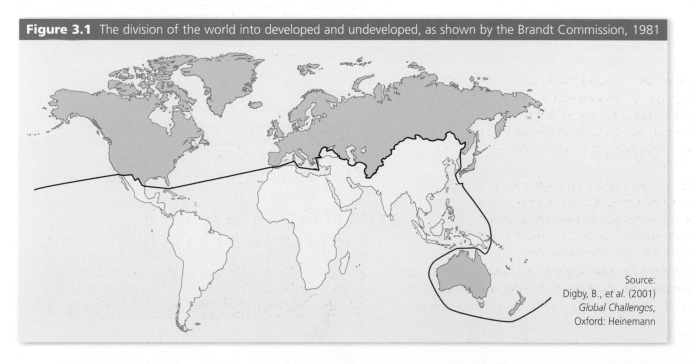

Figure 3.1 The division of the world into developed and undeveloped, as shown by the Brandt Commission, 1981

Source:
Digby, B., *et al.* (2001)
Global Challenges,
Oxford: Heinemann

The Commission for Africa was set up by the British Prime Minister Tony Blair in early 2004. It was composed of 17 individuals, 9 of whom were from Africa. Its aim was to identify solutions to the continent's most serious problems. Its report was published in 2005. Here is an extract from that report:

<< We live in a world where new medicines and medical techniques have eradicated many of the diseases and ailments which plagued the rich world. Yet in Africa, some four million children under the age of five die each year, two-thirds of them from illnesses which cost very little to treat. ... We live in a world where scientists can map the human genome and have developed the technology even to clone a human being. Yet in Africa we allow more than 250 000 women to die each year from complications in pregnancy or childbirth ... We live in a world where rich nations spend as much as the entire income of all the people in Africa subsidising the unnecessary production of unwanted food, while in Africa hunger is the key factor in more deaths than all the continent's infectious diseases put together. >> (pp.5–6)

This unit will generally distinguish between the rich and poor regions of the world by using the terms 'developed world' and 'developing world'. However, these terms are themselves not without problems because world sociologists are not in total agreement as to how development should be defined and, therefore, measured. Moreover, even within these two worlds there are enormous differences in terms of wealth, poverty, health, education, etc.

Development: the terminology problem

This topic area uses the terms 'developed' and 'developing' worlds but there are a confusing range of terms used by world sociologists and textbooks. Up to the 1990s, the terms 'First World' (i.e. the West), 'Second World' (i.e. communist countries) and 'Third World' (i.e. the developing world) were in common use but the collapse of **communism** has largely rendered such terms redundant. Some sociologists also objected to such terms because they imply superiority and inferiority between the developed and developing worlds. Other sociologists divided the world into 'North' (i.e. the industrialized world) and the 'South' (i.e. the developing world) after the Brandt Report (1981) on global inequality but if you look at a map you will see this is not geographically very accurate. It also implies that countries within these broad categories are very

much alike in their development features, which is not the case. The situation is therefore complicated by the diversity of economic and social progress found in the developing world today. This has prompted the use of the following terms, which acknowledge the hierarchical nature of the world today, i.e. global stratification.

- *More economically developed countries (MEDCs)* – i.e. the developed world of the West.
- *Newly industrialized countries (NICs)* – i.e. countries such as the Asian Tigers (Singapore, Hong Kong, Taiwan and South Korea), as well as China and Malaysia. These countries have rapidly industrialized in the past 40 years with the help of transnational investment and today have a large share of the global high-tech manufacturing market in computers and electronics, textiles (particularly sportswear) and plastics. Economic growth consequently has been positive, although it still does not compare with that experienced by the MEDCs. These countries still score low on some of the social indicators of development, such as life expectancy, general standards of living and existence of poverty.
- *Oil Producing and Exporting Countries (OPEC countries)* – These countries became wealthy in the 1970s as oil prices rose. Most are situated in the Middle East, e.g. Saudi Arabia and the United Arab Emirates, but they include Nigeria, Venezuela and Indonesia. Despite the experience of great economic growth, wealth and income tends to be concentrated in very few hands in these societies.
- *Former communist countries (FCCs)* – Countries that are struggling to convert their economies along capitalist lines, e.g. Poland, Romania, Lithuania. The economic progress of these societies has been generally poor, although their populations usually experience economic and social living standards that are superior to developing countries in the rest of the world.
- *Less economically developed countries (LEDCs)* – These are mainly dependent on agriculture and raw materials, although they have experienced some industrialization and fairly extensive **urbanization**. For example, in many South American nations, particularly Mexico, Brazil, Argentina and Chile, people enjoy a reasonable standard of living, especially in urban areas, but economic and social progress in these countries is impeded by massive debt and rural poverty. India and Pakistan have both developed nuclear power and weapons but mass rural poverty continues to impact negatively on mortality rates and life expectancy.
- *Least economically developed countries (LLEDCs)* – These are the poorest countries in the world, e.g. the Sub-Saharan African countries of Niger, Mali, Burkina Faso, Mauritania,

synopticlink **stratification** and **differentiation**

World sociology is essentially an examination of global stratification and the inequalities of wealth, income, health and education that stem from the fact that nations are ranked in a hierarchy of affluence and

destitution. Within both the developed and developing worlds, stratification systems based on status categories such as social class, gender, race/ethnicity, caste and tribe can clearly be seen.

have engaged
enriching them
These critics ar
be added to th

- the protect
  basic huma
  imprisonme
- the encour
  maintenan
  grounds sh
- the freedor
  repression,
  elections.

The six recomm
(2005) do add
developing wo
in People' (and
better healthc
environment a
equitable trade
highlights the
It argues that
bad governme
not open to sc
in the loss of r

However, th
Development
Commission re
institutions on
that the **indus**
possible route
that the real r
development I
to be dominat
developing soc
materials and
consumer mar

Sudan, Ethiopia and Somalia, which experienced famine in 2005. Bangladesh has experienced a number of natural disasters in the past decade. What most of the LLEDCs have in common is that, despite billions of dollars of aid, **absolute poverty** is the daily norm and social and economic conditions for the majority of their citizens have actually grown worse.

- *Socialist developing societies (SDCs)* – These countries, which include Cuba, Nicaragua and Vietnam, are either communist/socialist in political character or have experienced a socialist government for a significant period of time. Although they do not exhibit significant economic growth, they have made profound advances as far as social equity is concerned, and consequently have quite well-developed education and health systems. Life expectancy is good, infant morality and deaths of women in childbirth are low, and literacy rates are high.
- *Fourth World* – This term is used by feminists to describe all women because, regardless of whether they live in the rich developed world or the least developed world, it is argued that they are subjected to exploitation by men and are the victims of patriarchal inequality.
- *Fifth World* – A term used by the feminist, Gloria Steinem (1995), to describe the female part of the population used as cheap labour, particularly in the sweatshops of the least developed world.

These terms have now come into more general sociological use, but they are not entirely satisfactory, mainly because they give the impression that batches of countries experience economic and social problems in an **homogeneous** fashion. Although countries may share some characteristics in terms of lack of development, it is important to realise that there are often more differences than similarities between them. For example, people living in Mozambique in Africa and Honduras in Central America may both experience **subsistence poverty**, but in a quite different way, because of cultural differences and the specific locales in which they live. It is increasingly being recognized that countries have unique problems and needs that are the result of geographical, religious, ethnic, cultural, political, economic and social factors specific to them. These then interact with global economics and culture in ways that may differ qualitatively from other seemingly similar societies. This, of course, makes it difficult, if not impossible, to place such countries into off-the-peg categories.

Despite these difficulties of categorization, most sociologists working in the development field are largely (but not entirely) agreed on what economic and social factors need to be present to judge a society as lacking in development (see Table 3.1).

This list of features in Table 3.1 is by no means exhaustive – there are plenty of other negative social characteristics that could be added to the list, e.g. many developing nations have had some experience of war in the past 50 years. Moreover, it is also important to understand that this list is also **value-laden**, i.e. is constructed using Western value-judgements as to what is good and bad. For example, we tend to assume in the West that personal happiness, standard of living and

development are bound up with our economic conditions. However, not all societies or sociologists accept this as necessarily true, and therefore, they may object to the presence or absence of the factors above as indicating a lack of development. We shall return to this theme later.

Measuring development 1945–80

The period 1945 to 1980 saw the dominance of two overlapping approaches to development, especially with regard to how Western governments, multilateral agencies (such as the World Bank and International Monetary Fund) and **non-governmental organizations** (such as development charities like Oxfam) managed assistance to the developing world:

- development as economic wellbeing
- development as social wellbeing.

Table 3.1 The developing world: its distinguishing features
Developing countries, in contrast with the developed world, are likely to have the following features: - a colonial past - economies based on agriculture (especially the export of cash crops) and the extraction of raw materials, rather than manufacturing industry - low economic growth (e.g. a large proportion of income from exports is likely to be used to service foreign debt) - vast inequalities in ownership of and access to land - large sections of the population may be unemployed or underemployed - a subsistence standard of living – the World Bank estimates that 800 million people live in absolute poverty in the developing world, i.e. living on $1–$2 dollars or less a day. - a young and fertile population that is growing rapidly - high rates of child malnutrition - low life expectancy - high rates of infant mortality - death from preventable and treatable diseases, such as measles, due to a lack of basic medical provision, e.g. the number of doctors, hospitals and clinics per head of population is low - high levels of adult illiteracy - lack of access to free schooling - lack of basic infrastructure and services, including telecommunications, roads, electricity supply, clean water and sanitation - lack of civil and human rights - totalitarian and repressive governments - patriarchal forms of inequality.

tightened
1980s. Ma
commitme
policy mai
honoured
The Intern
developme
to save m
aimed at
developing
the wellbe

Miller

In 1990, tl
wellbeing
Millenniun

Goal 1: t

In 1990, n
developino
less than S
suffering f
by 2015. /
proportior
to 21 per
extreme p

Goal 2: t

In 2005, r
universal
children a
Only 85 p
developin
read and
literate in

Goal 3:
women

Progress t
employme
education
secondary
regions of
Saharan /
especially
men's in r

Goal 4:

Each year
i.e. 30 00
deaths ha
children a
and relati
40 years.

Imposing Western-style democracy

The notion that developing societies should adopt Western-style **democracy** is also a contentious aspect of development. The emphasis on it up to the 1990s was very much a product of the ideological conflict between the free West and the Soviet Bloc, i.e. the Cold War. Western models of development generally tend to assume that democratic forms of development are more suitable than communist or **socialist** models of development – which are often dismissed as extremist and dangerous. There is evidence that Western governments and agencies such as the World Bank and International Monetary Fund (IMF) distributed aid in the past on the condition that socialist/communist policies were jettisoned. In practice, this has meant that policies that have positive benefits for people in developing countries, such as collective farming cooperatives, land reform and welfare benefits, have been cut back or abandoned altogether because of the stringent political conditions attached to Western aid.

The experience of Cuba suggests that alternative socialist models of development can have positive benefits. Despite decades of enforced isolationism (the USA has imposed a trade embargo on Cuba that has made it extremely difficult for it to export its goods), Cuba has achieved literacy rates, infant-mortality rates and life expectancy comparable to those experienced in the West.

People-centred, local development

Korten (1995) argues that development strategies are too often in the hands of Western experts who fail to consult local people or take account of their local knowledge and skills. He argues that development needs to be more 'people-centred' and to focus on empowering local people to encourage them to take more responsibility for their community. Similarly, Amartya Sen (1987) argues that development needs to be about restoring or enhancing basic human capabilities and freedoms, giving people real choices and power over their daily situations.

A good example of this in recent years has been the success of 'microcredit'. This is the invention of Mohamed Yunus, a professor of economics at Dhaka University in Bangladesh who set up the Grameen Bank which lends money in tiny amounts to landless women. These extremely poor women have no collateral and so are unable to borrow money from conventional banks. Yunus' enterprise has had considerable success: it has over 2.3 million borrowers and lends $35 million every month to fund over 500 types of economic activity. Some 98 per cent of loans are repaid. Similar banks have been set up successfully in over 50 developing countries. Microcredit has resulted in self-sufficiency, i.e. dependence on people's own resourcefulness and skill rather than dependency on Western aid agencies.

Influence of globalization

It is argued by some sociologists that development as a concept needs to redefined in the context of globalization. It has been suggested that culturally, socially, politically and economically, national and regional boundaries are less important than ever.

As a result, we now have to consider definitions of development and 'consequently' the inter-relationship between the developed and developing world within the context of global economics, culture and communications. This theme will be examined in depth in Topic 8.

'Post-development' school

Critics of Western models of development such as Sachs (1992) and Esteva (1992), known as the 'post-development school', argue that development was always unjust, that it never worked and that it has now clearly failed. They suggest that development is a 'hoax' in that it was never designed to deal with humanitarian and environmental problems. Rather, it was simply a way of allowing the industrialized world, particularly the USA, to continue its dominance of the rest of the world. They point out that the poor have actually got poorer in the developing world despite 40 years of development. As Black (2002) concludes:

<< Instead of creating a more equal world, five decades of 'development' have produced a socioeconomic global apartheid: small archipelagos of wealth within and between nation-states, surrounded by impoverished humanity. >>

research idea

Conduct a survey that investigates the general public's images and understanding of the developing world. You should ask questions about:

1 the origin of their images
2 what they think are the causes of problems in the developing world
3 how they see the developing world solving its problems and
4 whether they see the West, and especially the UK, making a contribution in terms of causes and solutions.

What do your results tell you about which model of development the general public might subscribe to?

web.task

The United Nations website contains detailed reviews of the Millennium Development goals. In addition, the United Nations Development Programme website: www.undp.org is particularly good and contains an impressive range of information about development projects across hundreds of countries being carried out by United Nations agencies.

In contrast, Allen and Thomas (2001) acknowledge that development has not always succeeded but they challenge this post-development position. They point to the economic success of the Asian **tiger economies** and China. They also suggest that the evidence with regard to reductions in mortality and increases in literacy also support the view that development has, on balance, made a difference in the developing world.

So what is 'development'?

The lesson to be learned from this topic is that the concept of development is about social change. However, we have seen that defining what form that social change should take is not an easy, straightforward process. There are now a number of models of development impacting on global inequality today; the United Nations' Millennium model; the Africa Commission model; the Islamic model; the socialist/communist model; and the people-centred model. All have something to contribute to our understanding of global stratification. Moreover, what is now increasingly recognized by development agencies is that these models of development may have to be individually tailored in order to reflect each country's individual circumstances whilst acknowledging the impact of global influences.

Check your understanding

1. Identify five key differences in the living standards of the developed and developing world.

2. Identify two reasons why the terms 'First World' and 'Third World' are now thought to be obsolete.

3. Why can Western models of development be seen as ethnocentric?

4. Identify three negative consequences of Western forms of development for people in the developing world.

5. Why are economic indices of development seen as unsatisfactory as measures of development?

6. What are the main characteristics of 'basic needs' development?

7. In addition to the industrial–capitalist model of development, what three alternative types of development are identified in this topic?

exploring definitions of development

Item A

Absolute poverty describes a situation in which people are barely existing, where the next meal may literally be a matter of life or death as the cumulative effect of malnutrition and starvation enfeeble all, particularly children, whose weakness gives them the tragic distinction of having the highest mortality rate for any group anywhere in the world. Thus in these circumstances poverty takes on an 'absolute' status since there is nothing beyond or 'beneath' it except death. Many in the developing world are close to this very vulnerable position, relying on aid, food relief or their own meagre returns from squatter farming, scavenging on refuse tips, prostitution, street hawking and so on. For such people, statistics about relative GNPs can have no meaning or worth.

GNP for selected countries, 1992 and 2003

Country	Per capita GNP (US$) 1992	Per capita GNP (US$) 2003
Japan	28 220	33 520
USA	23 120	36 562
Brazil	2770	2825
Nigeria	320	314
The Gambia	390	269

Source: World Development Report, 1992 & 2003

Adapted from Webster, A. (1990) *Introduction to the Sociology of Development*, Basingstoke: Macmillan, p.16 and *World Development Report*, 1992 and 1997

1. (a) Identify and briefly explain some of the problems associated with development terms such as 'third world', 'North and South', and 'developing world'. (8 marks)

   (b) Using information from **Item A** and elsewhere, briefly examine the view that statistics measuring development as economic wellbeing 'have no meaning or worth'. (12 marks)

2. Evaluate the view that the influence of Western ideas on definitions of development has created more problems than solutions for developing nations. (40 marks)

Modernizing the world

gettingyouthinking

1 **Which image above do you associate with the developed world, and why?**

2 **Which image above symbolizes lack of development and why?**

3 **Some people argue that even if we could eradicate poverty tomorrow in the developing world, these countries would still fail to develop. What do you think is the basis of this argument?**

It is very likely that you associated the image showing science and technology with the developed world. This is not surprising as you are probably aware that your rather comfortable standard of living (compared with that experienced by 17 year olds in developing societies) is underpinned by scientific discovery and constantly evolving technology. You are probably also aware, having seen countless images in the media, that parts of the developing world lack our taken-for-granted access to such technical support. It is easy to attribute this to poverty, but there are those who believe that it has more to do with beliefs, values and attitudes. In other words, aspects of the culture of developing worlds (such as religious beliefs) will, they argue, always prevent progress. As we shall see, there are those who strongly believe that it is not enough to inject aid in the form of money into the developing world, but that physical and material development can only come about if attitudinal development occurs as well. However, as the industrialized world piles increasing pressure on the environment, having the 'right' attitudes can come at a terribly expensive price.

Modernization theory

After World War II (1939–45), it became clear that many countries in Africa, Asia, Latin America and the Caribbean were remaining poor despite exposure to capitalism and the rational and scientific ways of thinking that underpinned this economic system. This observation was coupled with a concern among the leaders of wealthier countries that widespread poverty, encouraged by the strong mass appeal of communism, could lead to social unrest across the world – particularly in the ex-colonies of the European powers that had recently acquired their political independence. Crucially, such political instability was seen by US politicians as likely to limit the growth of the United States economy in that communist ideology was anti-capitalist and likely to impede US trade interests. In response to these potential developments, American economists, sociologists and policymakers developed the theory of modernization.

In terms of its sociological input, the roots of modernization theory lie in the work of the classical 19th-century sociologists, Durkheim and Tonnies, who both argued that societies evolve through predictable stages towards **modernity**. Durkheim (1893/1960), for example, saw traditional societies organized around what he called 'mechanical solidarity' (i.e. the sharing of similar beliefs and occupational roles and a strong sense of community) evolving into more complex societies organized around 'organic solidarity' (i.e. beliefs are less likely to be shared, roles are more likely to be specialized and **individualism** has replaced community). Tonnies (1887/1957) saw traditional societies based on 'gemeinschaft' (i.e. traditional community values reinforced by kinship and religion) giving away to modern societies based on 'gesellschaft' (i.e. community has been replaced by more rational, selfish, impersonal and superficial relationships). Sociologists who developed the modernization theory adopted this idea that societies progress through **evolutionary** stages. For example, Huntington (1993), for example, describes modernization as an evolutionary process that brings about revolutionary change. In terms of international development, it is assumed that development should follow a similar evolutionary path as that taken by the industrialized nations of the developed world. Modernization theory made the 'beguiling promise: all nations, however poor, were able, with the implementation of the "correct" policies to achieve a modern standard of living by following exactly the same growth path as that pioneered by the Western nations' (McKay 2004, p. 50).

Modernization theory, therefore, can be seen to have two major aims.

- By focusing on the process of development, it attempts to explain why poorer countries have failed to develop. In particular, it has attempted to identify what economic and cultural conditions may be preventing a country from modernizing.
- It aimed to provide an explicitly non-communist solution to poverty in the developing world by suggesting that economic change (in the form of capitalism) and the introduction and encouragement of particular cultural values could play a key role in bringing about modernization.

Before we begin to examine the mechanics of modernization theory, it is important to understand the profound influence this theory has had (and is still having) on the relationship between the developed and developing worlds. No other sociological theory can claim to match its influence on global affairs – not even Marxism which, of course, has steadily declined in credibility since the collapse of the Soviet Bloc in the early 1990s. Much of Western, especially American, foreign-aid policy is underpinned by the principles of modernization theory.

The process of development

Walt Rostow (1971) suggested that development should be seen as an evolutionary process in which countries progress up a development ladder of five stages. This model of development allegedly follows the pattern of development that the developed countries experienced between the 18th and 20th centuries.

- *Stage 1* – Rostow argued that at the bottom of this evolutionary ladder are traditional societies whose economies are dominated by subsistence farming, i.e. they produce crops in order to survive rather than to make profits. Consequently, such societies have little wealth to invest and consequently have limited access to science, technology and industry. The LLEDCs are generally in this position today. Moreover, Rostow argued that in addition to these economic barriers to development, cultural barriers also exist in that people in traditional societies generally

subscribe to traditional values that impede modernization, e.g. religious values that stress **patriarchy** (thus preventing intelligent and skilled women from competing equally with men), **ascription** (being born into a particular position, role or trade, and consequently lacking the innovation to try new roles or ways of doing things), **particularism** (judging people and allocating them to tasks on the basis of **affective relationships** rather than what they are capable of or what they have achieved), fatalism (the view that things will never change, i.e. accepting one's lot) and **collectivism** (putting the social group before self-interest). Rostow saw traditional institutions such as the extended family, tribal systems, and religions as responsible for disseminating such values, and thus limiting the potential for social change.

- *Stage 2* – The second stage – the preconditions for take-off – is the stage in which Western values, practices and expertise can be introduced into the society to assist the take-off to modernization. This may take the form of science and technology to modernize agriculture, and infrastructure such as communications and transport systems, as well as the introduction of manufacturing industry. Investment by Western companies and aid from Western governments are, therefore, essential to this stage. These 'interventions' would produce economic growth and the investment required to act as the fuel for 'take-off'. As McKay notes; 'the image of take-off is particularly evocative, full of power and hope as the nation is able to launch itself into a bright new future'.

- *Stage 3* – This 'take-off' stage involves the society experiencing economic growth as these new modern practices become the norm. Profits are reinvested in new technology and infrastructure, and a new entrepreneurial and urbanized class emerges from the indigenous (native) population that is willing to take risks and invest in new industries. The country begins exporting manufactured goods to the developed world. This new wealth trickles down to the mass of the population as employment in these new industries grows and creates a demand for consumer goods as living standards rise.

- *Stage 4* – The fourth stage – the drive to maturity – involves continuing economic growth and reinvestment in both new technology and the infrastructure, i.e. particularly education, mass media and birth control. A modern, forward-thinking population takes advantage of the **meritocratic** opportunities available to them and, as a result, continues to benefit from ever-rising living standards. These economic benefits are reinforced through export earnings as the country strengthens its place in the international trade system.

- *Stage 5* – Finally, the society hits the ultimate stage of development – the age of high mass consumption or modernity – in which economic production and growth are at Western levels, and the majority of the population live in urban rather than rural areas, work in offices or in skilled factory jobs and enjoy a comfortable lifestyle organized around **conspicuous consumption**. Life expectancy is high and most citizens have access to a welfare state that includes healthcare and free education.

However, despite Rostow's influence on US foreign policy (he was a special adviser to the State department) and on how American aid was distributed to the developing world in the 1960s, major parts of the developing world, especially Africa and South Asia, remain desperately poor. Many of these societies have failed to progress beyond the traditional stage, despite huge injections of Western aid. Some modernization theorists have attempted to explain this persistent subsistence poverty by suggesting that cultural factors are more important than economic factors in explaining poverty in the developing world. It is argued that such countries have access to the capital and technology (via Western aid and expertise) needed to modernize but have failed to take advantage of these opportunities because of fundamental flaws in their cultural value systems.

Talcott Parsons (1964) argued that such societies are often dominated by traditional values that act as obstacles to development. People are committed to customs, rituals and practices based firmly on past experience and consequently they are often fatalistic about their future. Inkeles (1969) noted that such people are unwilling to adjust to modern ideas and practices, i.e. to entertain the notion of social change.

Parsons was particularly critical of the extended kinship systems found in many traditional societies. He argued that these hinder **geographical** and social **mobility**, which he claimed is essential if a society is to industrialize quickly and effectively. They also encourage traditional values and norms such as ascription, particularism and collectivism which undermine modernity by discouraging individual incentive, achievement and therefore, social change. Parsons argued that these societies needed to adopt the values that had propelled Western societies to such economic success such as **meritocracy** (i.e. rewarding effort, ability and skill on the basis of examinations and qualifications), **universalism** (applying the same standards to all members of society), individualism, competition and futureorientation (i.e. seeing the future as full of possibilities). Parsons argued that the adoption of these values would lead to the emergence of an 'entrepreneurial spirit' among sections of the population, which would generate economic growth. Moreover, he argued that such societies should be strongly encouraged to replace traditional institutions such as the extended family and political systems based on tribe, clan, caste or religion with nuclear families and

democratic political systems respectively. Parsons claimed that these traditional institutions stifled the individual initiative, free enterprise, geographical mobility and risk-taking necessary for societies to develop and modernize.

Modernization, interventionism and social engineering

Modernization theorists, then, see the West as playing a crucial role in assisting and guiding the development of poorer countries. A number of **interventionist** 'motors' of development emanating from the West are thought to be essential in bringing about the social organization and values necessary for development.

1 Rostow and others argued that traditional societies needed to encourage Western companies to invest in building factories and to train the local population in technical skills. Moreover, official aid programmes could supplement this process by paying for technical expertise and specialist equipment, as could borrowing from both the World Bank and the commercial banking sector. It was argued that the wages paid to the local labour force would '**trickle down**' and stimulate the economy of the developing nation by creating demand for manufactured goods.

2 Bert Hoselitz (1964) argued that the introduction of meritocratic education systems (paid for by official aid and borrowing) would speed up the spread of Western values such as universalism, individualism, competition and achievement measured by examinations and qualifications. These values are seen as essential to the production of an efficient, motivated, geographically mobile factory workforce. Similarly, Lerner (1958) argued that Western values could more effectively be transmitted to developing societies if the children of the political and economic elites of these countries were educated in Western schools, universities and military academies. It is suggested that these future leaders of the developing world could then disseminate Western values down to the mass of the population.

3 Inkeles (1969) argued that the mass media was a crucial agent in bringing about modernity because it rapidly diffused ideas about the need for geographically mobile,

synopticlink stratification and differentiation

Modernization theory is very influenced by the functionalist theory of stratification in terms of both its explanation of global stratification and its solution to global inequalities. Parsons argued that modern societies were characterized by open social-class systems underpinned by universal meritocratic education systems, entrepreneurial values and both geographical and social mobility, whilst developing societies were characterized by closed, feudal-like systems underpinned by traditional values such as ascription and religious superstitions.

Modernization theory argues that in order to develop, poorer countries need to modernize by adopting Western stratification systems that reward individualism and achievement measured by examinations and qualifications. Modernization theory, like functionalism, would argue that high rewards in the West are deserved because they reflect the more scientific measurement of achievement in contrast with unfair ascriptive practices found in the developing world.

nuclear-family units, family planning, secular beliefs and practices and the adoption of the democratic process – all essential components of modern development.

4 Hoselitz (1984) argued that urbanization should be encouraged in the developing world because:

– it is easier to spread Western ideas and values amongst a concentrated city population than a thinly dispersed rural population

– in the city, the individual is free from the obligations and constraints found in rural areas

– cities have a cultural effect on the rest of society. Malcolm Cross (1979) notes that 'the city is the key entry point for Western values and ideas to undeveloped societies; the city is the nucleus for the cultural penetration of the modernizing society'.

Modernization theory believed that these motors of development would produce a new capitalist entrepreneurial middle-class who believed in change, and who were willing to take risks and therefore drive progress forward. As Timmons Roberts and Hite (2000) note, 'in a traditional society the entrepreneur is a social deviant because he is doing something new and different; in a modern society change is routine, innovation is valued, and the entrepreneur esteemed'.

Some general criticisms of modernization theory

Ethnocentrism

Some commentators claim that modernization theory is ethnocentric in four ways:

● It implies that the traditional values and social institutions of the developing world have little value. Modernization theory clearly argues that Western forms of civilization are technically and morally superior and that the cultures of developing societies are deficient in important respects. Often such societies are defined as 'backward' if they insist on retaining some elements of traditional culture and belief and/or if they apply fundamentalist religious principles to the organization of their society.

This is certainly true of early modernization theorists such as Parsons but neo-modernization theory argues that capitalist culture can make use of traditions within societies in order to bring about modernization. Edwards (1992), for example, suggests that the economic success of the Asian tiger economies and China is due to a successful combination of the Chinese Confucian religion and Western rational thinking and practices. Religion in these societies has encouraged the emergence of a moral and authoritarian political leadership that demands sacrifice, obedience and hard work from its population in return for prosperity. This has paved the way for an acceptance of Western economic and cultural practices such as widespread respect for meritocratic education for both men and women, discipline and the acquisition of technical skills.

● It ignores the crisis of modernism in both the developed and developing worlds. In the developed world there are problems such as inequalities in the distribution of wealth, poverty, homelessness, high rates of crime, drug abuse and suicide. In the developing world poverty has not been eradicated and the resulting disillusion may lead to non-Western societies resisting modernization because they equate it with Western or American **cultural imperialism** or exploitation.

● It reflects Western propaganda and ideology. Rostow's book (1971) was subtitled 'a non-communist manifesto' and in it he actually described communism as a disease. Malcolm Cross points out that Inkeles' modern man is essentially an individualized version of the **American Dream**. Western models of development generally tend to assume that democratic forms of development are more suitable than communist or socialist models of development – which are often dismissed as extremist and dangerous. There is evidence that the US government in the period 1960 to 1980 supported oppressive right-wing elites (especially in Central and South America, and in Iran and the Philippines) that had questionable human-rights records simply because such elites took an anti-communist stance. As mentioned in Topic 1, there is evidence too that Western governments and agencies such as the World Bank and International Monetary Fund (IMF) have distributed aid on the condition that socialist/communist policies were jettisoned.

However, in defence of modernization theory, one could argue that it rightly celebrates American capitalism as a success. It may be mainly interested in opening up new markets for its products, but it also genuinely believes that capitalism can bring benefits to the developing world.

● Ethnocentric interpretations of development tend to exclude contributions from sociologists located in the developing world. Consequently, the notion that development needs to be **culture-specific** – i.e. that it needs to be adapted to the particular needs of particular societies, rather than being universally imposed in an homogeneous fashion – is neglected. Carmen (1996) argues that modernization is a 'Trojan horse' because acculturation, i.e. the taking over of indigenous cultures by Western culture, is 'at the heart of the development business'.

Modernization theory clearly sees development as a process initiated and implemented by outside forces. McKay (2004) suggests that this emphasis on the role of outside experts, the central role of aid and the stress on the introduction of Western values and institutions because it downgrades the role of local initiative and self-help. Carmen (1996) argues that such an approach is demeaning, dehumanizing and results in dangerous delusions because often the people of the developing world end up internalizing the myth that they are incapable and incompetent, and are themselves the problem. As Sankara (1988) notes, their minds end up being colonized with the notion that they should be dependent and should look to the West for direction. Galeano (1992) concludes 'they train you to be paralysed, then they sell you crutches'.

Questioning the benefits of education

It has been argued that education only benefits a small section of developing societies. There is evidence that educated elites monopolize top positions and restrict upward mobility, and engage in human-rights abuses in their desire to hold onto power. **Neo-liberals** such as Bauer are particularly critical of governing elites in the developing world who they argue undermine development by acting as a '**kleptocracy**', i.e. such elites are often self-seeking, interested only in lining their own pockets. They create vast inequalities in wealth through corruption and the siphoning-off of aid into their own bank accounts, Interestingly, the Africa Commission report (2005) has also addressed this issue by suggesting that poor governance and corruption in Africa is partly to blame for the state Africa finds itself in today.

Ecological limits

Modernization also has **ecological** limits. The existing process of modernization cannot be extended to all societies because of the limits of the planet. For example, for all nations to enjoy similar standards of living would involve a six-fold increase in global consumption and result in unsustainable pollution. There are already signs in some developing societies that modernization is leading to environmental degradation. As Esteva and Austin (1987) note:

> <<In Mexico, you must either be numb or very rich if you fail to notice that 'development' stinks. The damage to persons, the corruption of politics and the degradation of nature which until recently were only implicit in 'development' can now be seen, touched and smelled. >>

There is evidence that Western models of development create problems for the populations of developing societies. For example, indigenous peoples have been forcibly removed from their homelands, aggressive advertising and marketing have created **false** (and ultimately harmful) **needs** such as smoking cigarettes, grave environmental damage has been done to rainforests and child labour has been exploited – all in the name of progress towards the industrial–capitalist model of development. Marxist and post-development sociologists refer to this process as **underdevelopment** and suggest that development strategies are essentially aimed at maintaining exploitative practices such as ensuring cheap labour for transnational corporations and new markets for Western products. Development, therefore, may not be positive progress

if it means increasing social and economic divisions and inequalities within a country.

How societies develop

Cross (1979) argues that modernization theory assumes that all societies will advance in the same way through a fixed set of changes. However, this can be challenged in two main ways.

Diversity of societies

There is no reason to assume that traditional societies share the same features or that capitalism will mould societies in the same fashion. The evidence suggests that there exist a diversity of both traditional and capitalist societies. Modernization theory has been slow to understand that value systems and institutions tend to be culture-specific. For example, Ethiopia and Somalia are neighbouring countries, but their cultures are quite different from one another and they each require different development programmes.

Western domination

Traditional societies cannot develop in the same way as modern Western societies because they exist within a global economy dominated by Western interests. For example, it may not be in the industrialized world's interest to let poorer countries develop manufacturing industry that may compete with their own.

Marxist commentators have pointed out that developing nations cannot follow the same path as the developed world because the world has dramatically changed. The developing countries do not have an equal relationship with the rich and powerful developed economies. As McKay (2004) notes, the rules of global trade are rigged in favour of Western businesses and banks, and the governments of developed countries have the power to erect trade barriers, i.e. by imposing tariffs and quotas, to prevent developing countries competing with their own industries. In fact, Marxists such as Andre Gunder Frank (1971) have gone as far as insisting that the lack of development that we see in the developing world today is the direct result of the development of the West. This theme will be explored in more detail in Topic 3.

The postmodernist critique of modernization theory completely dismisses the assumption that the developing world is homogeneous and undifferentiated. They argue that the development path of a society and its choices in regards to

synopticlink   crime and deviance

Modernization theory strongly implies that developing nations subscribe to traditional values that are 'deviant' because they inhibit progress towards modernity. The dominance of modernization theory in development studies and practices has meant that development models

other than those based on Western lines, e.g. communist/socialist or Islamic, are often perceived as 'deviant' and consequently they are often dismissed as extremist or somehow backward. A good example of this is Rostow's reference to communism as a 'disease'.

development goals are historically conditioned and shaped by a web of power relations. Postmodernists see the process of development as a discourse shaped by disparities in power between the developed world and the developing world. This dominant discourse is **paternalistic** in that the developed world is treated 'as a child in great need of guidance' whilst the poor are seen as a problem to be solved by Western experts and aid. Postmodernists such as Escobar (1995) argue that the aim of development should be to escape from this trap and 'to reflect the real needs and goals' of the poor, although it is unclear how this should be achieved. Other postmodernist thinkers have focused on the modernist concept of 'progress' and suggested that this needs to be replaced with a greater sense of pessimism or an acknowledgement that the world and, therefore, development paths involve more risk than in the past.

The influence of modernization theory today

Despite these **empirical** and theoretical problems, modernization theory still exerts a considerable influence especially on the policies of organizations such as the United Nations, the World Bank and the International Monetary Fund which 'lead' and finance much of the world's development initiatives and programmes. This is because, despite all the criticisms thrown in the direction of modernization theory, industrial–capitalist democracies are regarded as generally successful societies because they have raised the standard of life of the majority of their citizens. Subsistence poverty has been almost totally eradicated in the developed world.

The 'people first' aid policies of non-governmental agencies (which aim to help the rural poor by helping them take control of agricultural projects through training and education) are still based on the quite distinct modernization principle of 'intervention'. As Burkey (1993) notes 'the poor are seldom able to initiate a self-reliant development process without outside stimulation. An external agent must therefore be the catalyst'. Critics of this modernization approach are keen to describe it as paternalistic but they very rarely offer alternatives that are not idealistic in their view of what the poor can achieve on their own.

Neo-liberal theories of development, dominant in the 1990s, were strongly influenced by aspects of modernization theory. This movement gained great confidence from the collapse of communism and reasserted many aspects of modernization theory. In particular, it portrayed development as involving a straightforward path towards modernity so long as developing societies recognized that traditional cultural systems (especially the system of obligations found in traditional kinship systems) impede the proper working of the free-market economy, which they claimed could deliver the benefits of development more effectively than economies that were centrally planned or characterized by government intervention. Neo-liberals argued that government interference in the economy should be kept to a minimum. This idea was particularly influential in the International Monetary Fund, which often lent money to

Inglehart and Baker (2000)
Modernization and cultural change

The assumption that cultural ideas can initiate economic growth is challenged by empirical evidence collected by Inglehart and Baker (2000) based on a study of 61 pre-industrial societies. They found that all the pre-industrial societies for which they had data placed a strong emphasis on: religion, male dominance in economic and political life, deference to parental authority and traditional gender roles, and the importance of family life. Such societies were also authoritarian, found cultural diversity threatening and were generally opposed to social change. Advanced industrial societies tended to have the opposite characteristics. However, Inglehart and Baker's data suggests that such cultural characteristics were the product of economic insecurity and low levels of material well-being rather than the cause of it. Culture therefore may be less important than differential access to scarce resources.

Inglehart, R. and Baker, W. (2000). Modernization, cultural change, and the persistence of traditional values. *American Sociological Review*, 65(1), February, pp. 19–21

1 **Explain how Inglehart and Baker reach the conclusion described in the final sentence above.**

developing countries in the 1990s on the condition that government spending, particularly on social projects such as health, education and welfare, be cut back.

However, some neo-liberals such as Bauer (1982) have taken this perspective into areas that challenge some of modernization theory's approaches to poverty reduction. For example, Bauer argues that foreign aid has not only encouraged the greed of the kleptocracy who have largely controlled its 'distribution' but it has also stifled the free market – for example, food aid, in particular, often brings down local prices and makes it difficult for local producers to get a fair price for their products. These ideas will be further explored in Topic 4.

The work of the neo-modernization theorist, Samuel Huntington (1993) has been very influential in recent years.

He strongly affirms the importance of culture as the primary variable for both development and the conflict generated by that development. He asserts that the world is divided into eight major 'cultural zones' based on cultural differences that have persisted for centuries. These zones were shaped by religious traditions that are still powerful today, despite the forces of modernization. The zones are Western Christianity, the Orthodox world, the Islamic world, and the Confucian, Japanese, Hindu, African, and Latin American zones.

Huntington sees future world confrontations and conflicts developing between these cultural zones. He suggests that the roots of this conflict lie in the exceptional values and institutions of the West that have brought it economic success and that are lacking in the rest of the world. Huntington argues that non-Western civilizations resent this success and what they see as the West's attempts to impose its version of modernity upon them through control of institutions like the United Nations and the World Bank. Huntington concludes that resistance to Western forms of modernization are now more likely to take the form of a return to fundamentalism in the Arab world and the sponsorship of international terrorism against Western interests and targets. Huntington's ideas seem particularly significant in the USA after the events of 11 September 2001.

American policy in Afghanistan and Iraq, and the 'war on terror' can be seen as a direct response to the conflict that Huntington identifies. 'Nation-building' in Iraq and Afghanistan focuses on a central aspect of modernization theory, i.e. the export of American values, particularly democracy, free trade and women's rights, in order to break the hold of what the Americans see as the tyrannical power of religion and tradition – which they view as the main cause of poverty, inequality and inhumanity in this part of the world. This view, of course, neglects the Islamic view that poverty and inequality are in fact caused by US economic and cultural imperialism, i.e. the very 'modernist' culture that the Americans are attempting to introduce in Iraq and Afghanistan.

The contribution of modernization theory

Early modernization theory can rightly be criticized for dismissing the culture of the developing world as irrelevant. However, it is often too easy and 'politically correct' to blame the problems of developing societies on colonialism, world trade, debt, global capitalism, etc. These factors are important, but modernization theory has probably been right (and certainly unpopular) in insisting that in order to reduce poverty, we need to understand culture or at least take it into account when assessing development progress. As we shall see, this once deeply unpopular view is again in fashion, as seen in some postmodernist accounts of development that suggest that culture is, and always has been, more important than economics in encouraging social change.

Sociology A2 for AQA

Check your understanding

1 **What are the two major aims of modernization theory?**

2 **What are the economic characteristics of traditional undeveloped societies according to Rostow?**

3 **Identify four cultural values or institutions that allegedly hold up development.**

4 **How are geographical mobility, kinship systems and modernization inter-connected?**

5 **What is the role of aid, debt and transnational investment in development?**

6 **How might education and urbanization help accelerate modernization?**

7 **What characteristics does Rostow's final stage of development have?**

8 **Explain what is meant by the two meanings of 'crisis of modernism' in terms of their critique of modernization theory.**

9 **Why is modernization theory criticized for being ideological?**

10 **How do Cross and Inglehart and Baker challenge modernization theory?**

11 **What influence does modernization theory have today?**

12 **Why is there conflict between the West and the Islamic world, according to Huntington?**

research idea

Think about your own experience of modern society. Using the knowledge obtained from this topic, make a list of development-friendly values, attitudes and agencies. Follow this up with a mini-survey of your friends and family to see how many of them subscribe to the traditional values (e.g. community, cooperation, particularism) that are so disapproved of by some modernization theorists.

web.task

Visit www.worldbank.org/ – the World Bank website – and using the search facility, look for policy statements or documents that focus on culture, poverty, population growth, education, etc. What aspects of World Bank policy endorse the view that it supports an industrial–capitalist or modernization model of development?

KEY TERMS

Affective relationships – relationships based on love.

American Dream – a set of ideas associated with the USA suggesting that if you work hard, you can be an economic success regardless of your social background.

Ascription – the occupying of jobs, authority within the family and political roles on the basis of inheritance or fixed characteristics such as gender and race.

Collectivism – the notion that members of the family/tribal unit put the interests of the group before self-interest.

Conspicuous consumption – consuming goods for status reasons, e.g. wearing designer labels.

Cultural imperialism – global dominance of American culture such as McDonalds and Disney.

Culture-specific – relevant to a particular culture.

Ecological – concerned with the environment.

Empirical – based on first-hand research.

Evolutionary – gradual change or progress that is the result of natural accumulation.

False needs – the outcome of intensive advertising that persuades people that a particular consumer item is vital to their social wellbeing despite it being potentially harmful in the long term.

Geographical mobility – being able to move around the country easily to meet economic demands for particular skills.

Individualism – the notion that individual self-interest should

come before the interests of the group.

Interventionist – believing in the need to take an active role to change a situation.

Kleptocracy – corrupt elites in the developing world who defraud their own people by pocketing aid, taking bribes, etc.

Meritocracy – system that rewards people on the basis of merit, i.e. intelligence, effort, ability, qualifications, and so on.

Modernity – the state of being modern or fully developed.

Neo-liberal – the view that the free market is the best way of organizing societies; against government intervention in society.

Particularism – loving someone or treating someone in a certain way on the basis of them being a member of your family regardless of their level of

achievement outside the family group.

Paternalistic – patronizing. Not believing others are capable on their own.

Patriarchy – system of male domination.

Trickle down – view that wealth will 'drip' down to benefit the less well-off.

Underdevelopment – term used to describe the process whereby capitalist countries have distorted and manipulated the progress of less-developed countries to their own advantage.

Universalism – the idea that occupational roles be allocated on the basis of universal norms such as achievement measured by examinations and qualifications.

exploring modernization theory

Item A

According to the modernization theorist, J.A. Kahl, 'modern man' experiences a relatively low degree of contact with extended family, a high level of individualism and contact with the mass media, and a pronounced interest in urban living. The 'modern man' is stimulated by the city and urban life – 'he sees it as open to influence by ordinary citizens like himself' and he sees society as a meritocracy. Modern man reads newspapers, listens to the radio and discusses civil affairs. Kahl concludes that the more modern one's men, the more likely a society

is to develop and modernize, i.e. to become like the United States.

Oliver Roy argues that Muslims who live in Western societies as well as those who live in Islamic societies are generally not traditionalists. Instead, they live with the values of the modern city. They are fascinated by the values of consumerism. They live in a world of movie theatres, cafes, jeans, video and sports, but they live precariously from menial jobs or remain unemployed in immigrant ghettos with the frustrations inherent in an unattainable consumerist world.

These people see themselves as the outcasts of a failed modernism and, for reasons to do with the cultural history of Islam, their exclusion from modernity takes a religious meaning. Militant resistance to modernity and what is perceived to be its source, i.e. the secular West, becomes the central component of Islamic identity.

Adapted from Cross, M. (1979) *Urbanization and Urban Growth in the Caribbean* quoted in M. O'Donnell (1983) *New Introductory Reader in Sociology*, London: Nelson Harrap, pp.242–3, and Hoogvelt, A. (2001) *Globalization and the Post-colonial World*, Basingstoke: Palgrave, pp.212–15

1 (a) Identify and briefly explain the five stages of Rostow's ladder of development. (8 marks)

(b) Using information from Item A and elsewhere, briefly examine the view that traditional attitudes and values need to be replaced with 'modern' cultural lifestyles. (12 marks)

2 Evaluate the strengths and weaknesses of modernization theory in explanations of why some societies have not made much progress in terms of development. (40 marks)

Underdevelopment and dependency

1 **What do you think the cartoon symbolizes about the relationship between the developed and developing worlds?**

The message from the cartoon is clear: the wealthy nations of the world got rich on the backs of the poorer nations, who are still being exploited today and keeping the West's 'lavish' life style going. This is essentially the message of the Marxist-based 'dependency theory'.

The Marxist economist-sociologist, Andre Gunder Frank provided the major critique of the principles underlying modernization theory. Frank (1971) argued that developing countries have found it difficult to sustain development along modernization lines (see Topic 2) – not because of their own deficiencies, but because the developed West has deliberately and systematically underdeveloped them in a variety of ways, leaving them today in a state of **dependency**. Hence, Frank's theory is known as dependency theory.

The world capitalist system

Frank argued that since the 16th century, there has existed a world capitalist system that is organized in a similar fashion to the unequal and exploitative economic or class relationships that make up capitalist societies. This world capitalist system is organized as an interlocking chain consisting of **metropolis** or **core nations** (i.e. the developed world) that benefit from the economic surplus of **satellite** or **peripheral countries** (i.e. the developing world). These peripheral countries 'have low wages, enforced by coercive regimes that undermine independent labour unions and social movements. The metropolis exploits

them for cheap labour, cheap minerals and fertile tropical soils' (p.12). This results in the accumulation of wealth in the developed world, and in stagnation and destitution in the developing world.

For dependency theory, then, underdevelopment in the periphery is the product of development in the centre, and vice versa. In turn, the elites of the developing world living in their own urban metropolis (i.e. cities) and sponsored by the core countries exploit those living in rural regions or the periphery of their own countries. Foster-Carter (1985) suggests that the ultimate satellite is a landless rural labourer, who has nothing and no one to exploit and is probably female.

The origins of dependency

Slavery

Frank argued that dependency and underdevelopment were established through slavery and **colonialism**, both of which helped kick-start Britain's industrial revolution. Over a 200-year period (1650 to 1850), the triangular slave trade (see Fig. 3.2) shipped approximately nine million Africans aged between 15 and 35 across the Atlantic to work as an exceptionally cheap form of labour on cotton, sugar and tobacco plantations in America and the West Indies, owned mainly by British settlers. This generated tremendous profits for both the British slave-traders and the plantation owners. Britain also enjoyed a virtual

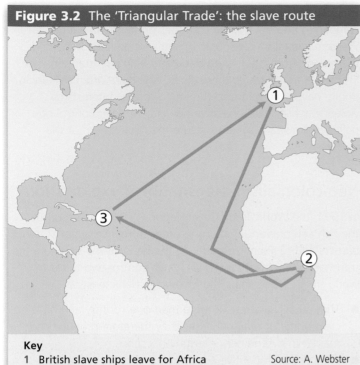

Figure 3.2 The 'Triangular Trade': the slave route

Key
1 British slave ships leave for Africa loaded with weapons and other goods for trading.
2 Goods are exchanged for slaves.
3 Slaves are exchanged for Caribbean produce and ships return to England.

Source: A. Webster (1990) *Introduction to the Sociology of Development*, Basingstoke: Macmillan

● Colonies were primarily exploited for their cheap food, raw materials and labour.
● The most fertile land was appropriated for growing cash crops for export to the West.
● New markets were created for the industrial world's manufactured goods.
● Local industries, especially manufacturing, that attempted to compete with those of the colonial powers, were either destroyed or undermined by cheap imported manufactured goods from the West.
● Divisions and conflicts were created or reinforced between indigenous peoples as the colonial powers sponsored some tribes and social groups, giving them wealth and power as a reward for acting as their agents of social control.
● Arbitrary borders were imposed on countries (especially in Africa), which are partially the cause of civil wars and refugee problems today.

Contemporary forms of dependency: neo-colonialism

Many colonies have achieved political independence today, but dependency theory argues that their exploitation continues via **neo-colonialism**. Frank (1971) noted that new forms of colonialism have appeared that are more subtle but equally destructive as slavery and colonialism.

Neo-colonial exploitation and world trade

World trade is one aspect of neo-colonialism. Despite political independence, the legacy of colonialism means that the economies of developing countries are still dependent upon the developed nations in a number of ways:

● Developing nations are still dependent for their export earnings upon a small number of cash crops or raw materials (see Table 3.3 on the next page). This overconcentration on **primary products** (often a single commodity) was the result of the way that colonial powers reorganized societies after conquest in order to produce one or two particular crops or materials required by their industries.

monopoly over raw materials such as cotton, tobacco and sugar, which benefited industrial expansion such as that found in the Lancashire/Yorkshire textile industry.

Colonialism

Colonialism locked much of Africa, Asia and Latin America even further into an exploitative relationship with the capitalist West. During the period 1650 to 1900, using their superior naval and military technology, European powers, with Britain at the fore, were able to conquer and colonize many parts of the world. As Harrison (1990) argues, this **imperial** expansion was to work the greatest transformation the human world has ever seen. The principal result of European rule was the creation of a global economy. Consequently, colonialism had a number of effects that benefited the world capitalist system.

Table 3.3 Examples of countries reliant on a limited range of agricultural produce in their exports, 1990

Country	Type of produce	Named produce as % of agricultural exports	All agricultural produce as % of merchandise exported
Réunion	Sugar	93.3	79.2
Cuba	Sugar	92.3	88.2
Uganda	Coffee	92.2	86.4
Ghana	Cocoa	85.8	41.2
Jamaica	Coffee	81.2	19.9
Swaziland	Sugar	78.3	38.1
Martinique	Bananas	66.4	60.8
Sri Lanka	Tea	66.2	39.0
Bangladesh	Jute	64.8	12.7
Ecuador	Bananas	60.0	28.7

Source: J. Chrispin and F. Jegede (2000) *Population, Resources and Development*, London: HarperCollins

- Overproduction of the primary products, or any fall in demand caused by variation in Western tastes and lifestyles, can have a severe negative effect upon their economies. This situation is made worse by the fact that their markets often consist of only a few metropolitan countries rather than many – with the main one usually being the colonial mother country.
- Western nations can limit the amount of goods, especially manufactured goods, imported from the developing world by imposing **tariffs** (a type of import tax that results in the goods becoming more expensive than home-produced goods) and quotas.
- Western inflation means that, over the past 30 years, the prices of manufactured goods produced by the West have risen rapidly whilst the prices of the primary products mainly produced by the developing world have actually fallen. Hayter (1981) notes that cash crops are 'false riches' because countries have to produce more and more of them to get the same amount of manufactured goods in return. In 1960, the earnings from 25 tons of natural rubber would buy four tractors, but today it is not enough to buy one. As Hayter notes 'in their desperate search for foreign exchange, underdeveloped countries produce more and more, thus setting up a vicious circle of overproduction and declining prices'.

The exploitation of this export-orientated primary production found in developing countries is often made easier by a class alliance between the agents of the developed world, i.e. the transnational companies and the local landed elite. The power and economic interests of the latter often derived from colonialism. As Hoogvelt (2001) notes, their 'economic interests became increasingly intertwined with those of the advanced capitalist states, and their cultural lifestyles and tastes were a faithful imitation of the same'. Cardoso (1972) points out that

these elites paved the way for the penetration of transnational companies into developing countries on favourable terms for Western capitalism (see Topic 8) and economically benefited themselves from the related trade and banking arrangements. In some extreme cases, these elites, which are often military in origin, have even removed threats to foreign interests by violence, while their repressive powers, i.e. their control of police and military, serve to assure the cooperation of the masses.

Neo-colonialism; transnational exploitation

In 1994, the World Trade Organization (WTO) was set up by the rich and powerful nations in order to reduce national trade barriers and to liberalize trade. At the heart of the WTO are the transnational companies (TNCs) which control two-thirds of world trade. These share the following characteristics.

- They usually operate in more than one country and have no clear home or national base. They therefore produce and market in a genuinely international sense.
- They seek competitive advantage and maximization of profits by constantly searching for the cheapest and most efficient production locations.
- They have geographical flexibility in that they can easily shift resources and operations across the world.
- They are responsible for three-quarters of world trade and about one-third of all global economic output.

If we look at a league table of the world's top 100 most important economic units, we will see that half are nation-states and half are TNCs. Approximately 130 nation-states (mainly in the developing world) have economies smaller than the top 50 TNCs. It is argued by neo-Marxists that TNCs exercise power without responsibility. Bakan (2004) refers to transnational corporations as 'institutional psychopaths', and notes that they are programmed to exploit and dehumanize people for profit. TNCs have been accused of acting immorally and illegally in their pursuit of profit in the following respects.

- Shell in Nigeria and RTZ in Angola have exploited natural resources with ruthlessness and indifference. Indigenous people have had their land forcibly seized and, despite international protests, have been removed at gunpoint from their homelands by local elites working on behalf of these TNCs.
- The sweatshop conditions of transnational factories in developing countries have been criticized, especially for use of child labour and exploitative rates of pay.
- TNCs have been responsible for ecological damage in countries like Nigeria.
- TNCs have refused to take responsibility for the welfare of local people killed or injured by their factories and plants. The explosion at Bhopal in India at the Union Carbide plant killed 2800 people and injured 28 000 people in 1984. The company has not paid a cent in compensation.
- TNCs have influenced tastes and consumption patterns in the developing world in negative ways. For example, Nestlé has been criticized for its aggressive marketing of baby-milk

Dependency theory is useful for illustrating the relativity of definitions of deviance in that Marxists argue that the capitalist countries of the West have made it rich in a deviant and criminal fashion by exploiting the developing world, both historically through slavery and colonialism (which often involved genocidal policies), and in the present day, by rigging terms of trade and, therefore, defrauding poorer countries, tying aid to conditions which benefit Western interests and condoning unethical

transnational activity. In particular, we can see that transnationals may have engaged in criminal and unethical behaviour by collaborating with local elites to seize the land of indigenous people illegally, particularly in Brazil and Nigeria; by neglecting the health and safety of their workers and local populations, e.g. the Union Carbide chemical plant disaster of 1984 in India; and the ethically suspect marketing campaigns of products detrimental to health, e.g. cigarettes and baby milk powder.

powder in areas without easy access to clean water. Other TNCs have been criticized for their marketing of high-tar cigarettes, and drugs and pesticides banned in the West for being dangerous to health.

- There is evidence that TNCs have interfered in the internal politics of developing countries and have even financed military coups against political leaders of developing countries they don't like. The military coup against the democratically elected socialist president of Chile, Salvador Allende in the early 1970s, was sponsored by American multinational companies unhappy at his nationalization of the copper industry.

Transnational exploitation of the resources and labour of developing societies, then, is seen by Dependency theorists as a crucial aspect of neo-colonial power.

Neo-colonialism, aid and debt

Dependency theory argues that official aid and the international debt crisis that has stemmed from borrowing money from Western governments and multilateral organizations such as the World Bank and IMF is the third major component of neo-colonialist exploitation. This will be examined in detail in Topic 4.

Solutions to dependency

Timmons Roberts and Hite (2000) argue that there are two sets of views when it comes to ideas for fixing these situations of dependency.

Breaking away from dependency

The first view argues that 'underdevelopment is not a phase but a permanent, inescapable position. In other words, the only way this situation of dependency can be escaped is to escape from the entire capitalist system' (p.13). Frank's theory of dependency suggests that the peripheral or satellite countries can never develop in a sustained way so long as they are stuck in what Paul Baran (1957) calls an 'imperialist' stage of capitalism and remain part of the world capitalist system. One solution is

'isolation' as in the example of China (although even that country is now adopting capitalist free-market principles and trading extensively with the West). Another solution is to 'break away' at a time when the core or 'metropolis' country is weak, as in times of war or recession. This may involve a socialist revolution in order to overthrow the local elite – as in Cuba in the early 1960s. However, Frank was pessimistic about this and believes that, sooner or later, the global capitalist economy will reassert its control through denying the rogue country access to free world trade, applying sanctions to countries that attempt to trade with it and through the threat of military force. This has been Cuba's experience for the past 40 years.

Associate or dependent development

The second view argues that despite dependency, there is some scope for what has been called 'associate development' or 'dependent development' through nationalist economic policies such as Import Substitution Industrialization (ISI). ISI involved industrialization aimed at producing consumer goods that would normally be imported from the developed world. ISI transformed the economies of South America, as Green illustrates (quoted in Hoogvelt (2001), p.243):

>> *By the early 1960s domestic industry supplied 95 per cent of Mexico's and 98 per cent of Brazil's consumer goods. From 1950 to 1980 Latin America's industrial output went up six times.* >>

However, ISI eventually failed for the following reasons:

- It neglected to address the issue of class and income distribution – that is, the existing elites controlled ISI and this led to further deepening of income and wealth inequalities in these societies.
- It was still dependent on the West for technical expertise, spare parts, oil, etc.
- The export-orientated form of industrialization adopted by the Asian tiger economies was seen as more successful.

Despite these difficulties in coming up with realistic solutions, Hoogvelt argues that the influence of dependency theory on the political ideologies of many developing countries in the 1960s and 1970s shouldn't be underestimated. She notes that political leaders, particularly in Africa, used the principles of

Elliot and Harvey (2000)
Jamaica's plantation economy

A case study of Jamaica carried out by Elliott and Harvey (2000) supports the work of Frank. They conclude that Jamaica's development problems will never be solved by policies that ignore the vast inequalities in power arising from Jamaica's political, social and economic history. They suggest that the root of Jamaica's contemporary problems lie in the creation of the plantation economy by the British, which resulted in vast inequalities in ownership of land that persist to this day. Today the Jamaican economy continues to serve the needs of the Jamaican ruling class rather than those of the masses.

Elliott, D.R. and Harvey, J.T. (2000) 'Jamaica: An Institutionalist perspective', *Journal of Economic Issues*, June, pp. 393–401

1 In what ways does Elliott and Harvey's study support the work of Frank?

measure the amount of investment put into the developing world and compare it with the amount of profit taken out. However, it is generally agreed that this is a crude and imprecise method that does not necessarily measure dependency, exploitation, and subordination. Similarly, it is unclear how and why Frank categorized particular societies as part of the 'metropolis' or as 'satellites'. Moreover, Frank paints the relationship between the metropolis and satellite as always negative, but some commentators have suggested this is oversimplistic, e.g. it could be argued that Canada and Taiwan are satellites of the USA because both are very dependent upon US trade. However, it is doubtful whether these relationships are exploitative. The health of the US economy depends on maintaining positive trade relationships with both countries. In other words, the interconnectedness of the global economy means that capitalist economies are often interdependent, i.e. the USA needs Canada and Taiwan as much as they need the USA.

Benefits to developing nations

Clearly, modernization theory would argue that Western aid and transnational corporations do bring benefits to developing nations. For example, the economic success of the Asian Tigers can be partly attributed to the role of Japanese aid and transnational investment. However, in reply, neo-Marxists point out that these societies are heavily in debt, while their industrial base is largely controlled by Japanese TNCs. Their economies have also demonstrated instability in recent years, as the Japanese economy has faltered and foreign investment has been withdrawn. In 1997, Thailand, Indonesia and South Korea had to accept Western rescue packages. Moreover, the economic success of these economies is founded on people working very long hours for very low wages. Economic growth may have been rapid but it has only benefited the top 10 per cent of these societies.

Role of homegrown elites

The issue of homegrown elites, however, is another aspect of exploitation not seriously addressed by dependency theory. Frank ignored the fact that Western exploitation of developing nations has often occurred with the connivance of the elites of the developing world. Such elites played a crucial role in slavery and colonialism whereas today many of them sit on the boards of the transnational companies that have invested in their countries and have taken financial advantage of the huge sums of money being injected into their countries via aid. As the Africa Commission (2005) notes, poor governance and corruption by this elite kleptocracy is partly responsible for the poor condition of many African countries today.

Creation of infrastructure

John Goldthorpe (1975) and other liberals have argued that colonialism had the positive benefits of providing developing countries with a basic infrastructure. Moreover, it provided people with wage-labour and made more efficient use of land. He also points out that those countries without colonies (such as Germany and Japan) have performed economically better

dependency theory to argue for development as liberation from Western exploitation. Political and social movements in Africa in this period consequently stressed nationalism, self-reliance and delinking as a means of countering neo-colonialism.

Criticisms of dependency theory

A number of criticisms have been made of dependency theory.

Defining 'dependency'

Frank's biggest problem was that he failed to be precise in his use of terms. 'Dependency' is extremely difficult to operationalize and, therefore, test or measure empirically. Some sociologists, such as Myrdal (1968), have attempted to

than those with empires, whilst countries such as Afghanistan and Ethiopia, which were never colonized, face severe problems of development because they lack the infrastructure provided by the colonial powers.

Different levels of exploitation

Timmons Roberts and Hite (2000) note that Frank's version of dependency theory fails to explain why there appear to be greater levels of exploitation over time or why there are significant differences among poorer countries. Later dependency theorists such as Gereffi (1994) and Evans (1979) have addressed these issues by noting that the influence of the core is not always homogeneous and that differences among elites in the periphery can explain different political regimes, economies and class relationships within the peripheral countries.

World systems theory

Some sociologists, notably Chase-Dunn (1975) and Gereffi (1994), argue that the overly descriptive nature of dependency theory means that it does not have much explanatory power. These sociologists subscribe instead to a variation on dependency theory called **world systems theory**, which was a response to criticisms of dependency theory. The founder of world systems theory was Wallerstein (1979). His theory has four underlying principles to it:

1 Individual countries or nation states are not an adequate unit of sociological analysis. Rather, we must look at the overall social system that transcends (and has done for centuries) national boundaries. Capitalism is responsible for creating the world order or Modern World System (MWS) because capital from its beginning has always ignored national borders in its search for profit. At the economic level, then, the MWS forms one unified system dominated by the logic of profit and the market.

2 Wallerstein builds upon dependency theory by suggesting that the MWS is characterized by an economic division of labour consisting of a structured set of relations between three types of capitalist zone: the core, semi-periphery and periphery (see Fig. 3.3). The 'core' or developed countries control world trade and monopolize the production of manufactured goods. The 'semi-peripheral' zone includes countries like Brazil and South Africa, which resemble the core countries in terms of their urban centres but also have extremes of rural poverty. Countries in the semi-periphery are often connected to the core because the latter contract work out to them. Finally, Wallerstein identifies the 'peripheral' countries (such as much of Africa), which are at the bottom of this world hierarchy. These countries provide the raw materials, e.g. cash crops to the core and semi-periphery and are the emerging markets in which the core countries market their manufactured goods.

3 Wallerstein argues that countries can be upwardly or downwardly mobile in the hierarchy of the MWS although most countries have not been able to move up. This obviously partially solves one of the weaknesses of

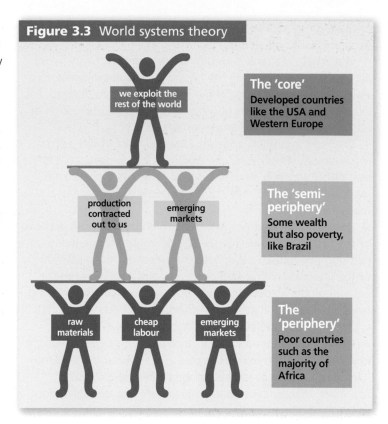

Figure 3.3 World systems theory

we exploit the rest of the world

The 'core'
Developed countries like the USA and Western Europe

production contracted out to us

emerging markets

The 'semi-periphery'
Some wealth but also poverty, like Brazil

raw materials

cheap labour

emerging markets

The 'periphery'
Poor countries such as the majority of Africa

dependency theory, i.e. the fact there is such tremendous economic variation in the developing world. It could be argued that the Asian Tiger economies have moved up into the semi-periphery. Some have argued that the UK may now be a semi-peripheral economic power rather than a core one. Wallerstein's model, therefore, is more flexible than Frank's because it allows us to look at the world system as a whole and to explain changes in the fortune of individual countries.

4 The processes by which surplus wealth is extracted from the periphery are those already described by dependency theory, i.e. historically through slavery and colonialism and contemporaneously through forms of neo-colonialism.

Wallerstein goes on to suggest that this MWS is constantly evolving in its search for profit. The signs of this are constant commodification (attaching a price to everything), **de-skilling**, proletarianization and mechanization. Wallerstein shows his Marxist roots by insisting this will lead to the **polarization** of class. It will supposedly generate so many dispossessed, excluded, marginal and poor people that in the long term the world economy will be located within a socialist world economy.

Evaluation of world systems theory

The main problem with world systems theory, as with Marxism generally, is that it is too economistic. It assumes that the economy is driving all other aspects of the system, i.e. politics, culture, and so on. Bergesen (1990) argues that it was military conquest and political manipulation of local peoples that imposed economic dependency on developing nations rather than the logic of capitalism. Wallerstein has also been accused of being vague about how challenges to the established capitalist order can be mounted and how the socialist world economy will come about.

Wallerstein is also criticized by modernization theory, which accuses him of neglecting the importance of internal factors, especially cultural factors, in the failure of LDCs to develop. For example, his critics point out that he ignores the corruption of LDC elites and their wasteful spending.

The most important criticism, however, is of Wallerstein's methodology. The theory, like Frank's, is highly abstract. It is also rather vague in its definitions of concepts such as 'core', 'peripheral', etc. and many of its propositions cannot be measured or tested.

However, despite these criticisms, Wallerstein's work was one of the first to acknowledge the 'globalization' of the world (although he himself never uses the word). He drew attention to the international division of labour which some see as the basis of global inequality. Lately, however, sociologists working from a globalization perspective have noted that relationships within the world system are far from one-way. Economic interdependence can also mean that problems in the developing world (such as financial crises caused by debt) may have profound ripple effects on the economies of core countries, thereby causing unemployment and destabilization of Western currencies. These themes will be explored further in Topic 8.

The contribution of dependency theory

Dependency theory, and particularly Frank, were probably at their most influential in the 1970s, and certainly were important in distracting attention away from the dominant modernization theory idea that lack of development was solely caused by the internal culture of developing nations. Frank was able to shift thinking away from the notion that developing societies were to blame for their situation. Instead, he focused on examining the role that Western societies played in bringing about the conditions in which developing societies found themselves after independence, along with the role of aid, trade and transnationals in maintaining global inequality. However, the fundamental weakness of dependency theory was that it offered no realistic solutions to global poverty. It was also hamstrung by the fact that capitalism as an economic system has brought tangible benefits to the world. The credibility of dependency theory was further undermined after the global collapse of the European Communist bloc in the 1990s and the apparent conversion of China to entrepreneurial capitalism in the last decade.

KEY TERMS

Colonialism – the take-over and exploitation of countries, usually by means of superior military force.

Commodification – applying an economic value to a range of human activities.

De-skilling – breaking down expensive complex occupational skills into routine and simple tasks.

Dependency – the state of being dependent on more powerful countries for investment, trade, aid, debt relief, charity, etc.

Imperial – empire-building.

Metropolis or **core nations** – terms used by Frank to describe the developed world.

Neo-colonialism – modern forms of exploitation of poorer societies by rich societies, which are usually dressed up as beneficial, e.g. aid, world trade and transnational investment.

Polarization – the Marxist idea that the experience of

workers will become so alienating that they will see the need for socialist revolution.

Primary products – crops and mineral extracts.

Proletarianization – the process by which professional, managerial and white-collar workers experience convergence with working-class conditions of work, service, etc.

Satellite or **peripheral countries** – terms used by Frank to describe the developing world. The terms indicate its dependence on the 'core' nations.

Tariffs – taxes on imports to protect a country's own industries.

World systems theory – explains development in terms of the ever-changing economic relationships between countries in the 'modern world system'.

Check your understanding

1. Define 'underdevelopment' and 'dependency'.

2. Outline Frank's theory of the world capitalist system.

3. Who is at the very bottom of this system according to Foster-Carter?

4. How did the triangular slave trade result in a super-accumulation of capital for Britain?

5. What advantages did colonialism have for Western capitalism?

6. How are the economies of the developing world locked into and dependent upon the developed nations today?

7. What role have some elites of developing countries played in the world capitalist system?

8. Apart from world trade, what two other forms of Western intervention are described as neo-colonialist today?

9. How does dependency theory criticize the modernization view that urbanization is a catalyst of positive change in the developing world?

10. What solutions does Frank offer for dependency?

11. How does the solution of dependent development differ from that offered by Frank?

12. Identify the similarities and differences between the theories of Frank and Wallerstein.

web.tasks

1 **Follow bananas and world trade generally on the net by accessing 'Unpeeling the Banana Trade', Fairtrade Foundation on their web page:** http//www.fairtrade.org.uk

See the Caribbean Banana Exporters Association side of the story on: http://www.cbea.org/

2 **Check out the websites for the following charities/pressure groups and note their comments on world trade.**

- **Traidcraft:** www.traidcraft.co.uk/ – **click on 'factsheets'**
- **Christian Aid:** www.christian-aid.org.uk
- www.maketradefair.com/
- **World Development Movement:** www.wdm.org.uk/ – **click on 'The Tricks of the Trade'**
- **Actionaid:** www.actionaid.org.uk

researchidea

Bananas are a really interesting topic to research if you want to understand the way that world trade is loaded in favour of the developed world. A 'trade war' broke out between Europe (which supports bananas produced by a confederation of Caribbean countries) and the USA (which supports bananas produced by American transnationals in Latin America) in 2003. Find out as much as you can about this. Your school or college Geography department may have copies of the following useful books: *Global Challenges* (Digby 2001) or *Population, Resources and Development* (Chrispin and Jegede 2000). Your research should focus on the following:

- the role of past colonial relations
- the role of TNCs
- tariffs
- trade blocs
- the role of the World Trade Organization
- the impact on both Caribbean and South American farmers.

exploring underdevelopment and dependency
Item A

Colonial powers laid the foundation of the present division of the world into industrial nations on the one hand, and hewers of wood and drawers of water on the other. They wiped out indigenous industry and forced the colonies to buy their manufactures. They undermined the self sufficiency of regions like Africa and transformed it into a source of raw materials for Western industry. Sometimes they forced locals to grow the desired crops. Sometimes they bought land or just seized it to set up their plantations, drafting in cheap labour to work them. In this way the colonial powers created the world economic order that still prevails today, of industrial centre and primary producing periphery, prosperous metropolis and poverty-stricken satellites. Apologists of empire – and there are some, even today – point to the benefits it often brought; education, science and technology, the rule of law, efficient administration and so on. However, despite this, almost all the imbalances that now cripple the economies, societies and politics of the developing world had their origins in colonialism.

Adapted from Harrison, P. (1990) *Inside the Third World: The Anatomy of Poverty* (2nd edn), Harmondsworth: Penguin

1 (a) Identify and briefly explain some of the features of the world capitalist system according to dependency theory. (8 marks)

(b) Using information from Item A and elsewhere, briefly examine the consequences of the historical exploitation of developing societies by Western countries. (12 marks)

2 Evaluate the view that the less developed world is deliberately and systematically kept in a state of underdevelopment by richer capitalist nations. (40 marks)

Aid and debt

gettingyouthinking

Sociology A2 for AQA

FACT

The total cost of providing debt relief for the 20 worst affected countries would amount to between £3.25 billion and £4.54 billion. This is roughly the equivalent to the cost of building EuroDisney.

FACT

The £16 billion Britain is spending on 232 Eurofighters would cancel the entire debt of South Asia and Sub-Saharan Africa.

FACT

Britons spend £5 billion a year on sweets and chocolate.

FACT

The £20 billion that Britons pocketed in 1997 in windfall payments from building societies would cancel the entire debt of the lowest income countries in the developing world.

Ali, the sieve-maker's daughter, Zenithou, has half a face, the rest has been eaten by a sickness called the Grazer or Noma which eats through the muscles, the tissues and bones. In Niger where they live, there is no war, famine or pestilence, but the Grazer is kept supplied with children by the starvation diets and a collapsing health system caused by pressure of international debt. In Niger, the poorest country in the world, they spend three times more money paying off foreign debt than on health and education. Debt means that they have no money to buy the antiseptic cream and mouthwash Zenithou needs to treat the Grazer. As a result, the World Health Organization estimates that 80 000 children will die from this very treatable disease in this region. Niger owes Britain £8 million. If we cancelled this debt, Niger could inoculate 750 000 children from measles, which kills nearly one in three children in Niger before they are 5 years old.

Adapted from 'Suffering from Plague – The Plague of Debt' by Maggie O' Kane, *The Guardian*, 11 May 1998

1 Look carefully at the facts accompanying each of the pictures above. What is your view of the morality of the spending decisions above? Do you believe that we should take a lead in helping developing nations out of debt or even in cancelling it altogether? Try and list your reasons for and against such actions.

2 In your opinion, do we have a moral obligation to help children like Zenithou? What should the UK do about the Niger debt? How would we feel if 80 000 British kids died because of measles?

Many people believe that debt is of one's own making and that interference, by assisting in any way or cancelling the debt, only encourages countries to become overdependent on Western help. However, in considering the questions on p. 118, you may have suggested that debt is not the fault of the debtors. You may have argued that the cause of the problem lies with the developed world (and especially the desire of Western banks to lend money in order to make profit) and the organization of world trade. The truth lies somewhere in between.

Whatever 'truth' we go with, the facts tell us that children like Zenithou are suffering early death because of debt. Imagine how people would feel if children regularly died in the UK because of debt to building societies and banks. And yet Zenithou and 80 000 other children, have done so indirectly because the Niger owes the UK money. This section explores some of these issues and looks at the interconnectedness of British aid, world trade, the debt of the developing countries and children's deaths.

Aid

'Aid' refers to any flow of resources from developed countries to the developing world, which may take the form of:

- a financial grant or material gift that does not have to be paid back
- a loan with interest.

Aid mainly involves the transfer of capital (i.e. money), but may also be made up of expertise (i.e. experts are sent and their wages are paid by the donor country), science and technology, medicines and contraceptives, weapons, and so on.

Types of aid

There are essentially five broad types of aid, outlined below.

Bilateral aid

Bilateral aid involves governments in the developed world giving aid to governments in the developing world. This is known as 'official development assistance' and in the UK is administered by a branch of the Foreign Office, i.e. the Department for International Development (DfID), formerly the Overseas Development Agency (ODA). Bilateral aid accounted for about 51 per cent of the DfID budget in 2000/01.

Multilateral aid

Multilateral aid involves the UK donating capital (46 per cent of the DfID budget in 2000/01) to agencies such as:

- the **World Bank** – This institution was set up after World War II by Western governments. Although all countries can join, US economic interests dominate its policy. It makes loans to member states at interest rates below those of commercial banks in order to finance **infrastructure** development projects such as power plants, hydroelectric dams and roads. It is also the world's largest funding source for agricultural development. The Bank's International

Table 3.4 Top five recipients of DfID aid in 2004/5

Rank	Country	Aid received (millions)
1	India	£259
2	Bangladesh	£128
3	Tanzania	£97
4	Sudan	£84
5	Afghanistan	£80

Source: Statistics on International Development (SID), DfID 2005

Development Association makes soft loans, i.e. with no or very low interest rates to the poorest countries.
- the International Monetary Fund (IMF).
- the European Union – The UK, along with other member states, contributes to a European aid fund which allocates grants rather than loans to developing countries. Food aid has also been an important aspect of EC aid.
- the United Nations – A small proportion of the UK's aid budget is allocated to UN agencies such as UNICEF (i.e. the UN's Children's educational fund).

Commercial banks

These lend money to developing countries at commercial rates of interest. In 2000/01, private flows from the UK to developing countries were estimated at £1.4 billion.

Non-governmental organizations (NGOs)

NGOs include charities such as Oxfam and Save the Children Fund, which aim to raise donations from the general public by raising awareness of problems in the developing world. NGO fundraising is usually matched by donations from the DfID. However, aid raised by NGOs is minute compared with bilateral and multilateral aid. The NGOs in the UK raise approximately £50 million annually (remember 50 per cent of this comes from the DfID), which is less than one tenth of DfID official aid. NGOs prefer to target the 'poorest of the poor' and so tend to work with voluntary groups, rather than the governments of developing countries, on small-scale aid projects such as **irrigation schemes** and well-boring, as well as rural health and education schemes.

Emergency aid

This is humanitarian relief that is raised in response to specific circumstances, such as natural disasters (e.g. the tsunami that devastated South East Asia in 2004), famine (e.g. in Ethiopia in 1985 and Niger in 2005), and war, with its resulting refugee problems (e.g. Darfur in Sudan in 2004/05).

The UK government's record on aid

In 1969, a UN commission recommended that 0.7 per cent of rich countries' GNP (i.e. less than 1 per cent!) should be given in aid. This excludes both loans and **military aid**. However, very few rich countries, including the UK, have managed to meet this target. For example, the UK official aid total in 2000/01 totalled £2.8 billion – this sounds a lot, but is only 0.32 per cent of Gross National Income (formerly GNP). Excluding emergency aid (i.e. responses to disasters, etc.), Sub-Saharan Africa received 54 per cent of all bilateral aid in 2000/01 whereas Asia only got 29 per cent.

Overall, aid flowing from the developed world to the developing world is growing. In 2005, US$78.6 billion was given in aid and this figure is projected to rise to above US$125 billion by 2010.

Modernization and aid

As we saw in Topic 2, according to modernization theory, official aid is a crucial component required for take-off into industrialization. This was a view shared by policymakers after World War II and especially the World Bank. As a result, aid was spent by the countries receiving it on importing Western technicians and experts to develop industry and modernize agriculture. Moreover, aid aimed to change cultural attitudes by setting up meritocratic education systems focused on literacy, and family-planning programmes targeted at freeing women from the powerlessness and dependency caused by the patriarchal family system.

These early aid strategies acknowledged that elites in the developing world would be the primary beneficiaries of aid, but it was argued that the poor would benefit in the long run as wealth 'trickled down' from the better off to the local economy and stimulated local production and markets. Indeed, this modernization approach did generate some early successes, as shown by the fact that the large quantities of aid distributed in the 1950s meant that global levels of infant mortality, life expectancy, literacy levels, etc., improved slowly but surely. In the 20 years following independence, many African nations experienced economic growth.

However, the aid bubble is generally perceived to have burst in the late 1970s. Both absolute poverty and relative poverty (i.e. the gap between rich and poor) in the developing world has actually increased in the past 30 years.

Diseases of poverty, such as tuberculosis and malaria, once thought to be under control, have returned with a vengeance and today are major killers of children in the developing world. Moreover, despite fantastic amounts of aid pouring in, countries such as Bangladesh have actually become poorer in the 1980s and 1990s. Such trends have led some sociologists and economists to talk about the 'poverty of aid' and 'the end of development'.

Dependency theory and aid

Neo-Marxists, in particular, argue that aid creates and sustains unequal relationships and, consequently, they have questioned the functions of official aid. They reject the view that the primary function of aid is to assist development. Rather, they suggest that it functions to bring about and sustain underdevelopment, and to benefit a Western monopoly of wealth, consumption and political power. Other critics have suggested that organizations

like the World Bank and IMF have adopted inappropriate and ineffective aid strategies that have primarily served the interests of the transnational corporations that dominate global capitalism. Theresa Hayter (1981) argues that official aid is a form of neo-colonialism because the development promoted by aid is aimed at reproducing, maintaining and legitimating the interests of the capitalist metropolis.

The political agenda of aid

The allocation of UK and US aid has often depended on whether the political ideology and practices of the developing country have met with Western approval. This was most obvious during the Cold War when the regimes of developing countries were rewarded with aid for aligning themselves with the capitalist world, whilst others were punished for adopting socialist policies or for being seen as too close to the Soviet Union. The effects of the famine in Ethiopia in 1985 (which led to Band Aid, Live Aid and Comic Relief) were probably worsened by the fact that, despite extensive warnings of potential famine by the UN, both the USA and UK refused aid on the grounds that Ethiopia had a Marxist government.

The focus on anticommunism can also be seen in the US military-aid programme. By the end of the 1950s, there was a 4:1 proportion of military to economic aid in terms of US spending. Much of this was sent to South and Central America, where it was used by right-wing governments to repress groups fighting for a more just social order. The result of such aid was often the creation of vast inequalities in wealth and land ownership between elites and the rural poor.

However, the fall of communism in the 1990s has not diluted the political character of both US and UK aid. There has merely been a shift in emphasis, as new political threats are identified. Developing countries are rewarded with aid today for supporting Western strategic interests, e.g. Kenya was rewarded with aid for providing US forces with port facilities during the Gulf War in 1991, while Turkey was denied massive US aid for refusing to let the USA lease air-bases during the same conflict. In 2005, developing nations are rewarded for assisting the USA's war against international Islamic terrorism. As George W. Bush stated in 2001: 'Over time it's going to be important for nations to know they will be held accountable for inactivity. You're either with us or against us in the fight against terror'. This policy will have negative economic implications for the poorest countries, who have little or no political, strategic or commercial advantages for the developed world.

The economic agenda of aid

Neo-Marxists argue that there is an economic motive at the heart of all official aid and that this is the expansion of global capitalism. Aid is aimed at opening up new markets for Western goods and services. The evidence strongly supports this argument because approximately 75 per cent of British aid is **tied**, i.e. the recipient country has to spend the grant or loan in the UK. Such aid stimulates the economy of the UK in the following ways:

- A substantial number of jobs in the UK depend on the orders placed by developing nations using official aid. Oxfam suggests that the UK aid programme often appears to be more concerned with supporting ailing or inefficient sectors of British industry than the poor of the developing world.
- The DfID can also control what the money is spent on, e.g. they may insist that the aid is spent on infrastructure or technology that the UK supplies. For example, British aid to India has resulted in the purchase of millions of pounds worth of helicopters and airport-surveillance equipment. Oxfam notes that such projects very rarely benefit the poor.
- There is evidence that the British government has given aid to countries such as Indonesia and Malaysia in return for securing weapons, aircraft and construction contracts for British industry. John Major, the British Prime Minister at the time, was upfront about British motives and said 'here is the British government backing British business in achieving orders abroad and maintaining billions of pounds of British exports in Malaysia'.
- Tied aid creates artificial markets because the developing country will need spare parts and technical expertise from the donor country for many years to come.
- Much of the money borrowed went to fund projects which have failed to generate the capital required to pay back both the loan and the interest on it. In the 1980s, this led to countries taking out further loans in order to repay the interest on the original loans. Capital that might have been invested in technology, healthcare, education and the eradication of absolute poverty, went straight back to the West in the form of loan repayments, e.g. it was estimated in 1993 that rich countries got back £3 in debt repayments for every £1 donated in aid.
- There is some evidence too that aid undermines indigenous markets – in particular, food aid may depress the prices of locally produced crops and throw local farmers out of business, consequently making the country even more dependent upon the West.

In 2001, the DfID, announced that it was bringing tied aid to an end. However, in 2002, the UK announced that Uganda was buying an air-traffic control system from British Aerospace using DfID grants. In 2005, the UK Development Secretary, Hilary Benn, pledged that the UK would no longer provide aid on the condition that countries adopt free market ideas. Both the World Bank and IMF both impose these conditions today on loans and debt relief. Benn has stated that the only conditions the UK will impose in the future will be transparency and tackling corruption, respect for human rights and helping the poor. However, research in 2005 shows that DfID aid is still dependent on the recipient country achieving between 40 and 50 benchmarks, many of which encourage the introduction of free market policies or international investment, before British aid is given – for example, Guyana has been told that it must privatize its water supplies if it is to receive DfID aid.

Yasmin Alibhai-Brown (2005) is critical of initiatives such as Live Aid, Live 8 and the Make Poverty History campaign because she argues these campaigns perpetuate the dependency culture created by colonialism, and encouraged by aid, debt and unfair

focus on . . .

Aid in Sierra Leone

Even before Sierra Leone's 11-year civil war was ended in February 2002, the aid advisers from Washington and London had arrived in the capital of Freetown with their prescriptions for development and tackling poverty. Their solution to the problems of the second poorest country in the world was to privatize virtually the entire country, including, most controversially, the national water utility. The World Bank and the IMF came up with a complex aid package with lots of strings. In the long term, privatization, including water and sanitation, was a core requirement. In November 2002, Britain signed a 10-year agreement with Ahmad Tejan Kabbah's government. The UK is Sierra Leone's largest bilateral development partner, with £104.5m in aid in three years. The UK is supporting the National Commission for Privatization which intends to privatize 24 public enterprises including shipping, roads, the airline, telecommunications, housing, the postal service, the national power authority and water. Department for International Development officials said that UK aid was conditional on 37 benchmarks this year. Privatization of water, through various forms of management contracts, is probably one of the most sensitive and disputed areas of development, dividing those who believe it is an economic good, and others who regard water provision as a human right.

Source: *The Guardian*, 24 September 2005

1 How does the extract above illustrate some of the problems of aid?

trade terms. She claims that Bob Geldof has 'infantilized' Africa by giving the impression that the continent is incapable of modernization without the help of White pop stars and politicians.

Dependency theory has also raised concerns about the 'aid business', which now employs hundreds of thousands of people worldwide. Hancock (1989) refers to the largely White and

- Women often lack **reproductive rights**. They do not have the power to decide whether to have children, when to have them and how many they should have. They are often prevented from making rational decisions about contraception and abortion. Men make all these decisions. Instead, women are strongly encouraged to see their role and status as tied up with being a mother and being dependent upon the male head of household. This lack of reproductive rights is one of the main causes of high maternal death rates in the developing world.
- Both the developed and developing world have experienced a feminization of poverty – 70 per cent of the 1.5 billion people living on $1 a day or less are women. Many are denied access to credit, land and inheritance.

- Foster-Carter (1985) notes that **purdah** is practised in many Islamic countries (in West and South Asia, and North Africa). This is the custom of making women wear clothing that covers them from head to toe. This often prevents them from playing an active role in social, economic and political life. As Foster-Carter 1985) notes, 'women's participation in public life ranges from limited to non-existent. Often, even to enter the public domain (e.g. walk in the street) requires varying degrees of veiling'. Most people are now familiar with how the hardline Islamic regime of the **Taliban** treated women in Afghanistan, but they are unaware that these rules about women's dress codes apply in varying degrees across a range of developing societies. There is evidence that females are more likely to be subjected to violence than men. In war, rape is often used as a weapon against the female population and women prisoners are often subjected to sexual slavery. In conflicts in Africa, for example, women and children make up the majority of civilian casualties as well as refugees.
- There is evidence that religious stress on the importance of male children is encouraging the **infanticide** of female babies in India and China.
- In Africa, it is estimated that 6000 girls every day are subject to genital cutting or female circumcision (removal of the clitoris) in order to enhance their future husband's enjoyment of sex.
- There is evidence that in rural India, between five and ten women a day die because of dowry-burning, where husbands kill wives so that they become free to marry again and attract a dowry.
- The emphasis on women marrying and becoming mothers means that cultures and families may not regard the education of female children as a priority.

tend to be used as the yardstick in terms of quality of life for women in developing countries. However, such views may be guilty of ethnocentrism and therefore of imposing Western values on such societies. For example, it is often assumed by Western feminists that aspects of patriarchy in developing countries are morally wrong, repressive, exploitative and barbaric. Development is often associated with bringing these cultural practices to an end. This, of course, assumes a moral superiority among Western feminists and simplistically dismisses such cultural behaviour as being the product of ignorance. However, some Muslim women argue that Islam values and empowers them. For example, the wearing of the **burkha** ensures that women control how men perceive their bodies.

Modernization theory

Modernization theory would argue that the low status of women in developing societies is another obstacle to development, for two reasons:

- Their potential contribution to the economy is not being fully realized.
- Their status as mothers contributes to overpopulation.

Boserup (1970) called for greater educational opportunities for adolescent girls in order to break the cycle of early childbearing. Modernization theorists believed that the creation of industrial jobs by multinational companies would encourage female economic independence from men. Moreover, family planning, health education and a sympathetic media transmitting Western values would reinforce female liberation and sexual equality, which (according to modernization theory) are essential components of the Western-industrial model of development.

The marginalization thesis

This perspective on development suggests that the introduction of capitalism in developing societies has led to women being increasingly excluded from economic life, restricted to the home and being forced to be dependent upon men. A number of observations can be made to support this thesis, which is similar in tone to dependency theory.

● Colonial powers and missionaries brought with them, and imposed upon indigenous peoples, traditional Western values about males and females, e.g. a woman's place is in the home. Abbott and Wallace (1997) note: 'Western notions of femininity and the family have been imposed upon other models of gender and rendered them "peculiar", "heathen", "unliberated" or "sexually exotic".' Colonialism probably introduced new forms of inequality which reaffirmed the ascribed roles encouraged by religion. As Leonard (1992) argues, the colonial powers introduced a 'money economy, based on wage labour and **cash crops**, into Africa and Asia. Men were absorbed into the cash economy while women were left with all the work associated with subsistence food production'. However, there is evidence that colonialism challenged some aspects of ascribed gender roles that were harmful to women, e.g. the British made female circumcision, infanticide, *suttee* (the burning of wives after the death of their husbands) and dowries illegal.

● Leonard notes that the emphasis on exporting cash crops in the developing world today has resulted in men rather than women being employed as agricultural labourers. Moreover, many men migrate to other regions in search of such work, leaving women to subsist without male help on the smaller and poorer plots of land not taken by elites or multinational companies for cash-crop production.

● The modernization view that men's wages will trickle down to women rarely occurs in practice. Moreover, Leonard notes that in Africa many men are unused to the status of being a wage-earner and they see their wage as their own money rather than as a means of supporting their families.

● Aid projects also marginalize women. Information collected from 46 African countries showed that only 3.4 per cent of trained government workers providing agricultural advice to people in rural areas were women. The introduction of modern agricultural technology is primarily aimed at male tasks and used almost exclusively by men.

● Leonard's review of official aid programmes concludes that aid is not gender-neutral. Rather, it comes with Western values attached – values that are often male-dominated and male-orientated. Aid workers bring with them the patriarchal prejudices about women and technology found in their own societies. For example, science and technology are considered masculine activities in the West because women are not supposed to understand technical matters. As a result, technical aid in terms of training and equipment tends to be aimed at men rather than women, despite the fact that women play a greater role in the production of food than men. Even irrigation systems are seen to be a male domain – men are trained to use pumps, wells and filtering systems despite the fact that women play the central role in supplying water to fulfil the household's needs. Moreover, aid planners tend to neglect other aspects of female work such as domestic tasks because they do not consider this 'real work' as it is unwaged or because they undervalue the role of women.

The exploitation thesis

This view is essentially a Marxist–feminist position. It suggests that modernization is about imposing an exploitative global system of capitalism on developing societies.

Many Western transnational companies (TNCs) have relocated their mass-production assembly lines producing electronic equipment, textiles, sports shoes, etc., to export-processing zones or centres (EPZs) mostly in developing countries. TNCs are attracted to these zones by governments offering benefits such as tax privileges, cheap labour, restrictions on the activities of trades unions and limited or non-existent health, safety and environmental regulations. The work exported to the EPZs is generally standardized and repetitive, calls for little technical knowledge and is labour-intensive. The majority of workers in these factories (90 per cent) are young women, who are employed because the TNCs regard

synoptic link   stratification and differentiation

The experience of women in developing countries can be linked to the concepts of patriarchy, subordination and exploitation focused on by feminist theories of gender stratification. Western feminists have identified a number of social areas in which women face inequality both in the West and the developing world, although they acknowledge that the experience of women in the developing world may be more extreme and potentially

devastating. However, female sociologists in the developing world have argued that patriarchy and men are not the only enemy of women in the poorer parts of the world – women's experience of poverty in the developing world has a great deal in common with that of men and may have more to do with nationality, ethnicity, religion, caste and social class than gender.

them as cheap, pliable and docile. The exploitation of these women takes several forms:

- Low pay – women workers in the EPZs are paid lower rates than male workers. Wages are often only about 10 per cent of those in developing societies and working hours are often 50 per cent higher. Consequently, women in the EPZs are producing more for less pay.
- Western owners do not invest a great deal in training female workforces. The work is generally regarded as unskilled

despite high skill levels being evident. However, because girls have already learned these skills in the home (e.g. sewing), the skill is downgraded.

- TNCs take advantage of what Elson and Pearson (1981) call 'women's material subordination as a gender', i.e. the fact that women will put up with lower wages or accept oppressive working conditions. They do this because either there is no alternative or the patriarchal conditions of their society mean the job is only temporary until they achieve the cultural goal of marriage and childbearing. As a result, TNCs are able to control their female workforces socially with little protest, e.g. sacking them when they become pregnant, minimizing toilet breaks, bullying by management.

Leonard (1992) and others conclude that TNCs aim to exploit female labour rather than provide women with training, fair pay and job security. However, in criticism, we have to acknowledge that the wages earned from such work are superior to the subsistence living eked out of rural existences. Also, it does allow some escape from the powerful forms of patriarchy found in the countryside such as arranged marriages. Such developments, alongside urban living and access to education, constitute major changes for women. Nonetheless, as Foster-Carter (1993) points out, such changes often bring with them new forms of exploitation 'in which the price of gaining some measure of autonomy and income of one's own is often submission to long hours, low wages and the advances of chauvinist male bosses'.

focus on research

Maria Mies (1986)
A Marxist–feminist perspective

Mies's research was conducted from a Marxist–feminist perspective. She argued on the basis of her findings that capitalism could not spread in the developing world without the subordination and exploitation of women. She found that women were employed in multinational factories in the developing world, particularly in the electronics, textile and garment industries, at lower wages and in poorer conditions compared with male workers. Often women's work was regarded by management as supplementing that of the male breadwinner and as a result, they were paid less on casual insecure contracts. Moreover, women workers were vulnerable to a range of hazards from allergy to dyes, exposure to carcinogenic chemicals and deterioration of eyesight due to close work. Those who suffered from such problems were often dismissed without compensation and were forced into the sex trade to survive.

Mies, M., (1986) *Patriarchy and Accumulation on a World Scale: Women in the International Division of Labour*, London: Zed Books

1 **Which aspects of Mies's work indicate that she is a Marxist feminist?**

Solutions to gender inequalities in the developing world

Marxist–feminist approaches

Marxist–feminists argue that socialism is committed to dismantling patriarchal regimes in the developing world. Molyneux's (1981) study of societies that were both Marxist–Leninist and Islamic found that such regimes were willing to challenge traditions such as child marriage and the veil, as well as being fully committed to maximizing women's education and job opportunities. However, there was little sign of change within the home. As Elwood (*New Internationalist* 1986) said of the old Soviet Union, 'women can fly to the moon but they still have to do the ironing when they get home again'.

Radical feminist approaches

The international feminist movement, too, has not always understood the nature of the developing world. The radical-feminist insistence that men were the enemy failed to address what women in developing nations saw as their main problem, i.e. uneven development and neo-colonial exploitation. Women's subordination only formed part of this. Feminists in these regions argued that their immediate task was to join with men to fight such exploitation and oppression. Moreover, women in the developed world have different priorities to those in developing nations. Whilst women in the developed world were campaigning against the trivialization of women in the media, women in the developing world were focusing on acquiring the reproductive rights that women in the West took for granted. Moreover, women in the developing world were physically at risk from male violence for even daring to campaign for such rights. In other words, it was recognized that nationality, social class, ethnicity and religious identity were just as important (and in some cases, more important) than gender as a source of inequality.

Postmodern feminist approaches

Hunt (2004b) notes that postmodernists have drawn attention to how the category of 'woman' has been constructed, and particularly how specific female groups in the developing world have been perceived by Western feminists. Mohanty (1997) is critical of the way Western feminists have presented women in the developing world as 'ignorant, poor, uneducated, tradition-bound, domestic, family-orientated, victimized, etc.' compared with Western feminists, who are seen as 'educated, modern, as having control over their own bodies and sexualities, and the freedom to make their own decisions' (p.80). Mohanty suggests such views of women in developing world smack of ethnocentric and colonial attitudes.

Cohen and Kennedy (2000) point to a form of **postmodern feminism** that appeared in the 1990s, made up of feminists from both the developed and developing worlds who share a more global agenda. It was generally agreed that the **globalization** of the world had led to common problems for women, such as:

- Sex tourism and prostitution – There has been a growth in the numbers of women and girls from the developing world being trafficked for forced sexual activities. The UN estimated that four million people were trafficked in 1998 – as Van der Gaag (2004) notes: 'Traffickers exploit women's desire to make a better life for themselves with promises of jobs as waitresses, dancers, models, maids and nannies. Once they arrive, their passports are taken away and they are forced to work as prostitutes. And even if they manage to escape, their families will often not have them back as they have been "dishonored".' (p.52)
- Environmental degradation – **Eco-feminists** such as Shiva (1989) argue that women are more inclined towards nature than men and therefore more protective of the natural world. About 60 to 70 per cent of the world's agricultural

workers are women and there are worrying signs that these women are more likely than men to be victims of environmental pollutants such as pesticides.
- Christian, Hindu and Islamic forms of religious fundamentalism have led to attempts to reverse the progress made by women in the past 50 years. Attempts have been made to restrict women's reproductive rights (e.g. by reversing abortion legislation) and to return women to the home.
- Economic globalization – TNCs tend not to recognize national differences any more when it comes to exploiting workforces. Women in both the developed and developing world are likely to be exploited in the search for profit.
- The international debt crisis – Feminist action groups have supported the 'breaking the chains' of debt movement because they appreciate that women and children in the developing world bear the brunt of debt in terms of less spending on health and education.

Inclusion of gender in development policy

Pearson (2001) notes that, since the mid-1990s, the major development agencies have responded positively to the critique that women's issues were neglected by development policy. Consequently, gender has been incorporated into the indices of development used by multilateral aid agencies such as the UK's Department for International Development, the World Bank and United Nations. For example, the Millennium Development goals include the promotion of gender equality, the empowerment of women and the improvement of maternal health. The Gender Empowerment Measure (GEM) indicates whether or not women play an active part in economic and political life across both the developed and developing world. All these agencies now check, as a matter of course, that gender is considered across a range of projects including civil engineering works and famine relief.

In particular, NGOs have championed a number of projects aimed at alleviating the feminization of poverty. For example, micro-credit schemes in countries such as India and Bangladesh make small amounts of credit available to the poor to cover subsistence needs, so that they can invest in livestock, equipment, fertilizer, etc. These schemes are seen to particularly empower women (who are often responsible for domestic production). For example, research by Kilby (2001) into 80 micro-credit schemes suggest that women who take part in these self-help schemes experience increased mobility, respect, dignity, assertiveness and support.

s y n o p t i c link   crime and deviance

A major global problem that has been developing over the last few years is sex-trafficking. It is estimated that at least 1,400 women a year are trafficked from abroad into the UK sex industry. Victims are often promised jobs in bar-work or nannying but on arrival in the UK, they have their passports confiscated by criminal gangs, are kept captive

and are forced to sell sex. The UK's response to victims of trafficking has been criticized because women who are released from this ordeal are usually deported as illegal immigrants and often end up being retrafficked or ostracized by their communities back home because they have sold sex.

There has also been a growing realization in development theory that the concentration on women in recent years has led to the neglect in understanding of men and masculinity. In the developed world, this has resulted in sociologists investigating a so-called '**crisis of masculinity**'. Researchers have begun to focus on examining how masculinity is constructed in the developing world in order to understand the nature of patriarchal gender-relations. However, it is important to acknowledge that all these changes in perspective with regard to gender are still in their infancy.

The future?

The prognosis for women in the developing world is, at best, mixed. On the plus side, the expansion of both education and family planning does constitute progress. Adamson (1986) argues that there is now a generation of women in the developing world who see education as the norm and not the exception. These women will demand more input into political and domestic decision-making. When they have daughters, they will pass down these modern attitudes and so positive change will continue to occur. Foster-Carter is a little more pessimistic. He notes the growing influence of fundamentalism, especially in India and some Islamic societies, such as Pakistan and Algeria. In some societies, industrial capitalism has led to women's social and material positions being worsened because women have been forced into peripheral areas of the global economy (i.e. into low-paid, low-skilled jobs that are not good for their health or into the sex industry).

Van der Gaag (2004) notes 'the advances women have made over the last 20 years cannot hide the fact that for millions of women life is still very grim. And now even the gains that have been made are under threat' (p. 11). Van der Gaag argues that there are signs of a growing backlash against women's rights in the 21st century. The rise of religious conservatism or fundamentalism has resulted in more legal and social restrictions being placed on women in 25 countries between the late 1990s and 2002, including the USA. She notes that beliefs and practices, e.g. genital mutilation, are being dredged up from the past by Islamic fundamentalists as an 'Islamic duty', despite the fact that they have nothing to do with Islam or the Qur'an. She notes that often Islamic fundamentalists see women's rights as the product of decadent Western thought and practices, and for that reason oppose such rights on the back of a general anti-Western feeling. Van der Gaag suggests that for some Muslim women, veiling has become 'part of a wider statement against the West'.

However, Van der Gaag notes that women are organizing themselves in the developing world to oppose patriarchal inequality – some 30 000 women attended the UN women's conference in Beijing in 1995. However, even in our own, so-called 'modern society', sexual equality is still some way off. In the USA, the re-emergence of 'family values' during George W. Bush's presidency has led to a backlash against abortion rights both in the USA and in the developing world. In 2001, Bush introduced a policy that disqualifies NGOs from receiving US aid if they provide legal abortion services in the developing world. Thus, $34 million was withheld from the UN Population Fund on the grounds that the programme supported abortion.

Hunt (2004b) argues that women's rights and issues need to be more firmly embedded in mainstream development policies. There are signs that this is happening as reflected in the Millennium development goals and their focus on gender. However, the dominance of neo-liberal policies in aid programmes and economic policy generally suggests that gender equality is viewed as a natural outcome of economic growth. Hunt points out that the gender inequality and patriarchy still apparent in the developed West suggest that this neo-liberal assumption may be overly optimistic.

Check your understanding

1 **Identify four aspects of patriarchal inequality experienced by women in the developing world.**

2 **What are reproductive rights and how do women in the developed and developing world differ in access to them?**

3 **What is the relationship between religion and patriarchy in the developing world?**

4 **Why might Western critiques of cultural and religious practices be ethnocentric?**

5 **What is the key to women's development according to Boserup?**

6 **What effect did colonialism have on the social status of women in the developing world?**

7 **Why is aid not gender-neutral?**

8 **What forms does exploitation of female labour by transnationals take in the developing world?**

9 **Why might exploitation of women by transnationals be acceptable for many women in the developing world?**

10 **Why has the international feminist movement not always understood the nature of the problems faced by women developing world?**

11 **What international problems are thought to be shared by women today?**

12 **What is the future of women in the developing world likely to be?**

research idea

- Find out how three of the major British aid agencies, e.g. Oxfam, Cafod, Christian Aid are specifically targeting women's development in the countries in which they are involved.

KEY TERMS

Burhka – long enveloping garment worn by Muslim women in public.

Cash crops – crops grown to sell rather than to use.

Crisis of masculinity – the notion that masculinity is under threat because of the rapidly changing nature of work and that this has undermined men's sense of their role and power in the world.

Eco-feminists – feminists who link the social position of women to environmental issues.

Globalization – the increasing interconnectedness and interdependency of the world.

Infanticide – the practice of killing unwanted children, usually female children, at birth.

Postmodern feminism – a branch of feminism that suggests that there is a diversity of female experience in the world and that no one feminist theory is capable of explaining the range of culture-specific patriarchal experiences that women have.

Purdah – Muslim custom of keeping women in seclusion by requiring them to wear clothing that shields them from public view.

Reproductive rights – rights relating to women's choice to have children and control their bodies.

web.tasks

1 **Visit the New Internationalist website – www.newint.org/ – and access the Magazine mega index and click on 'W'. This will give you access to all the articles on women in the developing world published by the magazine in the last ten years. Their search engine is also worth using because they monitor articles on women in the developing world produced by a host of other agencies such as Amnesty International.**

2 **Compare the treatment of women across the world at Human Rights Watch – www.hrw.org.**

exploring gender in the developing world

Item A

The received wisdom used to be that modernization benefits women as well as men, and that women in the developing world face the same problems as men: technological and institutional backwardness, poverty, illiteracy, malnutrition and ill health. However, this is a misconception: development projects that benefit one section of society (men) do not automatically benefit the other (women). They hurt rather than help women in the long term and impose increased burdens. The general drift of development projects, both in the technology they transmit and in the training they provide, benefit men and make women even more invisible than they were.

Adapted from Carmen, R. (2000) *Autonomous Development: Humanizing the Landscape: An Excursion into Radical Thinking and Practice,* London: Zed Books; and Digby, B., *et al.* (2001) *Global Challenges,* Oxford: Heinemann, p.200

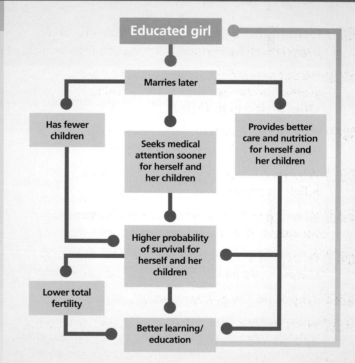

---

1 **(a)** Identify and briefly explain some of the disadvantages that women experience in developing societies. **(8 marks)**

(b) Using information from Item A and elsewhere, briefly examine the view that meritocratic education can free women from patriarchal constraints in the developing world. **(12 marks)**

2 Evaluate the view that the introduction of capitalism in developing societies has led to women being increasingly excluded from economic life and being dependent upon men. **(40 marks)**

Urbanization and environment

gettingyouthinking

1 **Compare the two cities using the photographs provided.**

We tend to equate modernity with living in cities. They are the hub of modern life and centres of consumption, with their shopping centres, cinemas, pubs, clubs and supermarkets. Moreover, cities like New York and London are symbols of Western affluence. It is no wonder that people in the developing world aspire to them. Nevertheless, there is a dark side to urban life – all Western cities contain pockets of poverty and miseries, such as crime, suicide and mental illness.

This topic explores the reality of city life in the developing world and why these problems are likely to be heightened for the urban citizens, of say, Mexico City, Beijing or São Paulo.

This unit also examines the related problem of environmental **degradation**. Most countries of the developing world aspire to the economic growth and wealth experienced by Western nations. However, the evidence suggests that if developing societies ever achieved the West's current level of economic and industrial development, this would put an intolerable strain on the world's resources and ecological stability. There is evidence, too, that present rates of consumption of the world's resources, most of which are consumed (and often wasted) by the urban citizens of Western cities, have contributed to a looming environmental crisis, of which global warming and climate change are likely consequences.

World sociology and urbanization

In 1900, the only country in the world that could be described as 'urban' was Great Britain. The 20th century, however, saw massive migration from the countryside to the towns and cities of both the developed and the developing world. Cohen and Kennedy (2000) note that there were approximately 185 million people living in the towns and cities of the poorer world in 1940. By 1975, this figure had increased to 770 million. Until the 1950s, most of the world's most populated cities were to be found in the developed world. This situation was reversed only 40 years later and now the most populated cities in the world are (in no particular order) Mexico City, São Paulo, Tokyo, Shanghai, New York, Kolkata (Calcutta), Mumbai (Bombay), Beijing, Los Angeles and Jakarta. Note that only two of these cities are in the developed world. Today, there are three times as many city dwellers in the developing world as there are in the developed world.

These trends have been partly caused by rapid population growth in the developing world (see Topic 5), but the 20th century also saw that population gravitating towards urban areas, through a combination of **push** and **pull factors** (see Table 3.7). The fact that urban dwellers in developing societies

Table 3.7 Push and pull influences on migration to cities in the developing world

Push (from rural areas)	Pull (to the cities)
Poverty	The availability of jobs especially in transnational factories and services
Displacement by new agricultural technology	The perception that greater number of waged jobs are available
Loss of land	Access to services such as education and health
Natural disasters, e.g. drought, flood, earthquakes	Perception that urban life offers greater opportunities in terms of living standards, i.e. bright lights and glamour
Disasters caused by poor governance, e.g. war, displaced refugees	Escape from traditional constraints of family, culture and religion
Changes in aspirations among younger people as they access modern media	The perception that urbanization = Westernization = sophistication

tend to be younger and consequently more fertile than city populations in the West also contributes to rising urban populations in the poorer countries. There were seven cities in 1950 with populations of over 5 million. It is estimated that this number will rise to 93 by 2025 and that 80 of these will be in the developing world. In fact, whilst urban growth in the poorer countries is growing quickly, it is actually falling in the developed world as people make the decision to move out of cities.

Urbanization and modernization theory

We saw in Topic 2 that modernization theorists such as Rostow and Hoselitz urge developing societies to adopt Western models of economic growth, as well as cultural beliefs, practices and institutions. Urbanization, i.e. the trend towards living in cities rather in rural villages, is regarded as a universally positive phenomenon by modernization theorists, because European societies underwent a period of sustained urbanization in the 19th century and developing societies are encouraged to follow the same development path.

On an economic level, cities are seen to help boost growth by giving industrialist–capitalists access to a massive concentrated pool of labour for their factories. The wages paid to city factory workers supposedly filter down to help develop other city services, such as housing, shops and infrastructure.

Very importantly, however, cities are seen to play a central role in promoting cultural change. Cross (1979), for instance, states that 'the city is the nucleus for the cultural penetration of the modernizing society', meaning that the large populations of cities ensure that modern norms and values spread rapidly. Hoselitz argues that cities are catalysts of modernization in that they loosen ties to traditional institutions and value systems by reducing dependency on community and extended kin. As a result, values such as ascription, fatalism and collectivism soon go into decline. The modern person living in the city learns very

quickly that the dominant urban values are individualism, achievement, **activism** and meritocracy. Consequently, city life sees the development of modernist values more conducive to progress and development. The result is an entrepreneurial population more prepared to take risks, more receptive to the possibility of geographical and social mobility, and willing to make investments in order to accumulate personal profit.

The critique of modernization theory

The picture of urbanization painted by modernization theory has turned out to be an overly-ideal one, when we consider the actual experience of urbanization in both the developed and developing worlds.

Rapidity of growth and social problems

First, urbanization in European and American cities was very gradual – it tended to take place over a period of 100 years – and was largely responsive to employment opportunities. However, the urbanization of developing societies has been much more rapid, and population growth has wildly exceeded the number of jobs available. Urban populations are, therefore, largely unemployed or underemployed, and this has created grave social problems as people struggle to survive.

The infrastructure of these cities, e.g. services such as housing, clean water, sanitation and policing, is generally unable to cope with the sheer weight of numbers and, as a result, '**shanty towns**' have developed with shelters constructed out of whatever materials can be found. The standard of living in these towns tends to be very poor and the sorts of classic problems associated with lack of development are very apparent, e.g. high child and maternal mortality, malnutrition, low life expectancy.

Moreover, a new set of modern urban problems appear, as people turn to illegal or unconventional means to raise their income, such as crime, especially gun crime, drug-dealing, prostitution or begging. Suicide and mental health problems, too, are becoming major problems in these new urban environments. Generally, then, the simple cause-and-effect model that modernization theory applies to urbanization (i.e. that people will be attracted to cities because of the pull factor of jobs) does not really apply to the developing world.

Dual-sector economy

The development of shanty town or *favelas* or *barrios* (as they are called in Central and South America) has led to the development of a dual-sector economy in many cities in the developing world. As Peace (2005) notes, in this situation, a minority of people are lucky enough to find work on reasonable pay in a tiny formal sector, consisting of legitimate, regulated and unionized employment, although this is often in the public sector rather than in productive work. Many other inhabitants, however, are forced to eke out a meagre living in a bloated informal sector, consisting of unregulated or illegal employment such as sweatshops. These are often exploitative (in terms of the wages paid) and dangerous (in terms of health and safety). The informal sector also includes subsistence forms of economy as the unemployed turn to begging in order to survive. These two sectors often overlap in that the informal sector may provide the formal sector with a cheap supply of labour.

Environmental problems

The urban haphazard sprawl associated with shanty towns can also create serious environmental problems. Often, these urban centres lack effective public transport, which means overreliance on cheap (and environmentally damaging) cars. Environmentalists note that Mexico city sprawls over 950 square miles (twice the size of Greater Manchester and far more dense) and its residents' three million automobiles emit a total of 12 000 tons of pollutants into the atmosphere every day.

Death of community

Modernization theory may be guilty of looking at Western development, and particularly, urbanization, through rose-coloured spectacles. It ignores the widely accepted view that city life in the West has killed the concept of community and that this, in turn, has led to serious social problems in urban areas in the developed world, including social isolation, alienation, crime and drug abuse.

Urbanization and dependency theory

The modernization support for urbanization as the focus for development planning and policy has been criticized by dependency theory. In contrast, dependency theory suggests that urbanization in the developing world is not acting as an effective force for development – rather, it is likely to sustain underdevelopment. Dependency theorists note that modernization theory based its view of urbanization on the European experience. However, European urbanization was a response to industrialization, when people migrated to towns and cities to take work in factories. In developing societies, people have migrated to cities leaving behind land which provided subsistence; however, factory jobs are not available in large numbers, because transnational investment tends to be in highly mechanized forms of production. Cohen and Kennedy (2000) note that the urban poor:

>> *have a wide variety of occupations and activities. Religious ascetics, the insane, the physically disabled, micro-traders (selling items like matches or nuts), touts for taxis or rickshaw-pullers, beggars, those seeking work, apprentices and their 'masters' – all these are part and parcel of the rich social landscape in the cities of the poor countries.* >> (p.147)

An urban underclass

These migrants to the city end up in the slums, and their existence is so poor that some Marxists argue that they constitute a class below that of the proletariat, i.e. a **lumpen-proletariat** or **underclass**. The hope of Marxists is that this group might demonstrate some revolutionary consciousness as they become aware that the urban elite – the successors of those put into power by colonial rule – own and control a disproportionate share of wealth and monopolize political power in the city. There has, in fact, been little sign of such dissent in these cities. However, local elites have been aware of this possibility and so the cities in the developing world have often been the focus of repressive social controls and human rights abuses, as these elites see the concentration of the poor and disprivileged as a threat to their power.

In the 1990s, the Chinese authorities became particularly concerned at the numbers of urban poor and, particularly, the migration from the countryside. They reacted to this perceived threat to social order by demolishing a Beijing shanty town containing over 100 000 people, by returning 190 000 migrants and beggars to their home provinces and imposing internal controls on the movements of workers.

The colonial legacy and neo-colonialism

Dependency theorists have argued that the developed world should take some responsibility for the rapid growth of cities in the developing world. It is argued that many of the large urban cities in poorer satellite countries were established under colonialism (such as Kolkata and Mumbai) and were used as the administrative centres for removing capital, raw materials and cash crops to the developed world. These cities tended to have a better infrastructure than the rest of the colony because the colonial administrators resided there, as did the homegrown elites sponsored by the West, who often were the bureaucracy of the colonial state. Shops and services largely developed in the colonial city in response to the wealth of the colonial administration and the bureaucratic elite. Roberts (1978) argues that the neo-colonial cities of the developing world are consequently characterized by historical inequalities:

>> *Modern skyscrapers, sumptuous shopping, office and banking facilities coexist with unpaved streets, squatter settlements and open sewerage ... the elegantly dressed are waylaid by beggars and street vendors; their shoes are shined and cars are guarded by urchins from slums.* >> (quoted by Cohen and Kennedy, p.266)

After independence, these cities remained the centre of these less-developed societies and were seen by the rural poor as symbols of opportunity and potential affluence, leading to mass migration from the countryside. Cohen and Kennedy note that 'the business districts and wealthy parts of these cities are often like islands surrounded by seas of poverty' (p.265).

Dependency theorists argue that cities in developing societies continue to act as staging-posts for neo-colonial exploitation of the labour, raw materials and cash crops of the developing world. Transnational corporations, in particular, act in similar

An examination of urbanization in the developing world reveals an extremely unequal distribution of life-chances paralleling that of our own developed world. The urban poor in the shanty town areas of cities in the developing world experience extreme inequalities in access to employment, income, education and healthcare, compared with the elites and foreign expatriates who often enjoy lifestyles comparable to those found in the West. However, it is important to acknowledge that the poor in Western cities are relatively better off, in that their poverty is not usually of the absolute subsistence kind. Note, too, that environmental degradation is caused by rich and poor alike, in that the wealthy in both the developed and developing worlds overconsume and waste natural resources, whilst the poor overuse the marginal resources to which they have access.

ways to the colonial powers, by establishing their operational headquarters and factories in urban areas. Dependency theorists argue that cities play a key role in ensuring that poorer countries remain in a state of underdevelopment because they monopolize any surplus capital that might be generated by exports or aid. Spare cash or aid investment tends to be largely spent on the social problems that beset the urban poor in order to avoid social unrest, e.g. feeding the urban poor who do not produce any food for themselves can be very expensive. It has also been spent on expensive vanity projects, such as airports, hotels and conference centres that enhance the look of the city, but only benefit local elites or tourists.

The global city

Cohen and Kennedy note that some cities are perceived to have the characteristics of 'global' or 'world' cities in that:

- they are based in rich industrial countries
- they are often the corporate headquarters of TNCs, stock exchanges, and major banks, insurance companies and pension funds
- they are interconnected as sites of global transport, especially air
- they are often political centres of power
- they are centres of communications, information, entertainment and news.

Global cities are integrated with one another on the basis of these characteristics. In fact, it can be argued that such cities have more in common with each other than they do with the provincial cities in their own country, e.g. London probably has more in common with New York and Hong Kong than it has with Leeds or Manchester.

According to Marxists, global cities are a symbol of the global capitalist economy and at the centre of the new international division of labour (see Topic 8).

Cohen and Kennedy note that such cities are international and **cosmopolitan** in that they attract international migrants made up of professional workers, entrepreneurs, and unskilled workers who are exploited for their cheap labour in various service industries. They are culturally cosmopolitan, too, in the diversity of languages spoken, the number of religions

practised, forms of dress, types of food served and the multicultural lifestyles on display. Suffice to say, no cities in the developing world are considered to have the characteristics that qualify them as global.

World sociology and the environment

In the last 25 years, there has been a rise in interest in the relationship between development and the environment. In particular, there is a growing awareness that environmental degradation cannot continue at its present rate without having major implications for the living standards of people in the developed and developing worlds alike. As Kingsbury *et al.* (2004) note:

>> *Our rush to achieve material development has been predicated on the capacity of the physical environment to support it. In some cases, the environment has been despoiled, and in others, it is simply running out of resources.* >> (p.266)

Ellwood (2001) agrees:

>> *The increasingly global economy is completely dependent on the larger economy of the planet Earth. And evidence is all around us that the planet's ecological health is in trouble.* >> (p.90)

There are concerns about how long current developmental processes can continue before local and global ecological systems collapse. Kingsbury points out that environmental degradation does not respect state boundaries and widespread environmental collapse is no longer a case of 'if', but of 'when and where'. Some areas of the world have very limited capacity and are more prone to degradation because of overuse. These areas tend to be in the very poorest parts of the world, such as Sub-Saharan Africa.

Environmental pressure points

A number of pressure points have been identified with regard to environmental degradation.

There have been some concerns about the relationship between transnational corporations (TNCs) and corrupt local elites in developing countries. TNCs may be attracted to investment in these countries because local elites are willing to turn a blind eye to practices that are either banned outright or strictly controlled in the West because of their implications for the health of workers and/or the general population. These practices involve:

- the use of pesticides banned because of their potential carcinogenic properties
- the exposure of workers to dangerous toxic chemicals or materials such as asbestos

- the unregulated emission of greenhouse gases and pollutants into the atmosphere.

There is evidence, too, that TNCs have failed to take responsibility for the consequences of environmental disasters. For example, in India, the US chemical multinational Union Carbide has still not paid any compensation to the families of the 10 000 killed and 20 000 disabled by the Bhopal disaster, while Shell has generally ignored international condemnation of its role in destroying the Nigerian delta environment and the displacement of the Ogoni tribe in its exploitation of gas and oil fields.

Population

This is covered in some detail by Topic 5, but it is worth briefly revisiting some points of interest here. Neo-Malthusians such as Ehrlich have argued that the earth's resources cannot sustain present levels of population growth. Moreover, the poverty experienced by the bulk of people in the developing world is thought to increase environmental degradation through more desperate use of resources. Neo-Malthusians have, therefore, recommended that population be controlled through state policies. China, India and Indonesia are examples of countries which have taken measures to curb fertility.

However, critics of neo-Malthusians suggest that the world does have the resources to cope with present population growth, but if the standard of living of the populations of the developing world was raised to the standard enjoyed by most people in the West, consumption of natural resources would become unsustainable. The irony here is that we can maintain present levels of natural resources if the poor in developing countries stay in a state of perpetual underdevelopment. There is another way we can sustain the environment and natural resources as well as raising the poor out of their poverty, but this is unpopular in the West because it involves reducing global consumption, and particularly, Western overconsumption and waste of the world's resources. For example, Rees (1996) estimates that about 10 to 14 acres of land are used to maintain the lifetime consumption of the average person in the West, but the total available productive land in the world, if shared out equally, would only come to 4.25 acres per person. The rich world is, therefore, consuming the resources of the poor.

Cohen and Kennedy note that 1.1 billion people in the world constitute a 'consuming class' and most of these live in the developed world.

≪ *The consuming class eats meat and processed/packaged foods, depends on numerous energy-intensive gadgets, lives in climate-controlled buildings supplied with abundant hot water and travels in private cars and jet aeroplanes. Mostly it consumes goods that are soon thrown away when*

fashions change. In sharp contrast, the 1.1 billion poorest global inhabitants mostly travel on foot, rely on local resources for shelter and possessions (stone, wood, mud, and so on), mainly eat root crops, beans, lentils and rice and frequently drink unsafe water. ≫ (p. 326)

Moreover, the 'throwaway economy' created by the consuming class produces vast amounts of waste – much of which is toxic or made of materials and wrapped in packaging that is not eco-friendly, i.e. it may inflict damage on the environment because it does not naturally break down.

Industrial and agribusiness development

There are worrying signs that industrial technology both in the West and in those countries relatively new to industrialization, has had – and is still having – profound effects on the global environment and climate. For example, carbon dioxide levels in the atmosphere continue to rise because of the burning of fossil fuels such as coal and oil in factories, cars, tankers and jet-planes. These fuels result in the emission of greenhouse gases. It is estimated that if China continues on its present path of economic growth, it will contribute 40 per cent of global carbon dioxide emissions by 2050. In addition to these gases, industry worldwide continues to poison rivers and lakes through the massive use of fertilizers and pesticides.

Species extinction

Ellwood notes that the global extinction crisis is accelerating, with dramatic declines in wildlife. Habitat loss is the major cause of the decline in numbers of many species. In the past 500 years, Ellwood notes that mankind has forced 816 species to extinction:

≪ *Scientists reckon the normal extinction rate is one species every four years. Today's die-off rate is estimated at 1000 to 10 000 times the natural rate.* ≫ (p.92)

Deforestation

Kingsbury argues that deforestation may be the world's most significant environmental problem, along with desertification.

Deforestation has a number of major implications because rainforests absorb carbon dioxide as well as producing the oxygen upon which all life depends. It is estimated that some of the world's major rainforests in areas such as Indonesia, Borneo and the Amazon Basin will be completed deforested within 30 years. At current rates of logging, Chile, which has one-third of the world's temperate rainforest, will be completely deforested by 2022.

This environmental destruction is often motivated by poverty and debt. Brazil cleared 12.5 per cent of rainforest in the Amazon Basin between 1978 and 1996 in an attempt to meet loan repayments to the World Bank and commercial banks in the West. The logging industry mainly exports the hard wood to Europe and the USA for furniture manufacture. Other types of wood is exported to meet the demand from Western culture for newspapers, magazines, etc. Such export earnings, therefore, help pay off Brazil's debts to the West. Ironically, recent IMF insistence that Brazil keep to repayment schedules has led to the cutting of funding for rainforest conservation. There is a human cost, too, as the indigenous Amazon tribes are forced off their land and in some cases, murdered by commercial loggers.

Desertification

It was estimated by Juara in 2000 that drought and desertification affected 1.2 billion people across 110 countries. Desertification is mainly the result of the overcultivation and overgrazing of poor-quality land by the poor, who are often forced to keep using unsustainable land in order to survive. The more fertile land in many developing countries is not usually owned or controlled by the poor and is used to grow cash crops for export, such as the cut flowers found in British supermarkets in the winter.

Desertification reduces the ability to produce food in some countries, which leads to famine. It has its greatest effect in Africa. Kingsbury points out that desertification is getting worse. In 1970, Africa was self-sufficient in food production, but by 1984, a quarter of Africa's population was being kept alive by food aid and imported grain because of desertification, soil erosion and drought.

Water pollution

Kingsbury notes that the pollution of the world's waterways, e.g. rivers, streams and lakes, for industrial and food purposes has reduced the amount of clean drinking water and seriously threatens the continuing existence of some animal and plant life. In particular, he argues that access to clean drinking water is probably the world's most immediate environmental problem because this has been seriously threatened by the waste products of industrialization, the increased use of pesticides, insecticides and chemical fertilizers, and population growth. Kingsbury estimates that a single person requires up to 20 litres of water a day for drinking, food preparation, sanitation and bathing. However, in 2001, more than a billion people did not have access to piped water or had less than this minimum amount. For example, in Pakistan in 2002, a large majority of the country's 135 million people did not have access to drinkable water.

Why does environmental degradation occur?

Economic necessity

Many of the poor in developing countries have no choice but to use and reuse environmental resources. In other words, this type of behaviour is a matter of economic necessity and survival. As Ellwood argues:

<< the desperately poor do not make good eco-citizens. Tribal peoples plunder the forest on which they depend for survival; animals are poached and slaughtered by impoverished African villagers for their valuable ivory or their body parts. >> (p. 95)

Greed

The desire to accumulate wealth, by local elites and international corporations, usually at the expense of others, results in the exploitation and selling-off of environmental resources. At the same time, cost-cutting in order to increase profits may lead to unscrupulous behaviour, such as the illegal dumping of toxic waste.

Western consumer demand

Most developing countries are dependent on relatively few raw materials or cash crops for a large part of their income and in order to pay off their debts. This may result either in overproduction or in the use of production techniques that pay little attention to the environmental costs, because the emphasis is on cutting costs.

Globalization

It is argued that export-led economic growth, i.e. cash-crop production for the world market, and the debt of the developing world have speeded up consumption of the world's natural resources. In particular, debt has kept prices of natural resources low because, in order to pay off their debts, developing countries have expanded their raw material and cash-crop exports. However this oversupply has led to falling prices as natural resources flood the market. Moreover, the emphasis on free markets in World Bank and IMF policy has led to cuts in environmental spending as these organizations insist that developing governments interfere less in their economies.

Sustainable and appropriate development strategies

In the 1980s, there was a move towards introducing more **sustainable** forms of development in order to protect the global environment in the long term. There was an increasing realization amongst agencies such as the World Bank that development had a global dimension and that it should be targeted at what Korten (1995) calls the 'the global threefold human crisis' of deepening poverty, social disintegration and environmental destruction. Development strategies in the 1980s, therefore, focused on ameliorating problems which might otherwise threaten chaos at a global level.

Sustainable development

In 1987, the World Commission on Environment and Development (WCED) concluded that economic development in both the West and the developing world should be compatible with greater responsibility for the global environment. The Commission advocated the policy of sustainable development. A central component of this idea was the acknowledgement that poverty in the developing countries might be a major cause of global environmental problems such as global warming. The Commission argued that the construction of a more equitable economic relationship between the developed and developing worlds would reduce the need for the developing world to overexploit their environments and thus slow down environmental destruction. Moreover, the WCED argued that rich countries should aim to reduce pollution and put clean air before higher living standards. In the 1990s, 178 UN member states agreed to pursue sustainable development. The United Nations, too, has adopted sustainable development as part of its Millennium Development goals.

Another consequence of sustainable development thinking has been the realization that big aid projects may actually cause a great damage to the social and natural environment. For example, in the 1960s and 1970s, $125 billion was spent on large dams in order to provide hydro-electric power, irrigation and anti-flooding systems. However, dams have generally failed to be cost-effective and have not generated the expected income that the countries involved need in order to pay off the debt accrued by their construction. Dams have had a terrible human cost, too, in terms of displacing local people – between 40 and 80 million people have been displaced by dam building, about 50 per cent of those in China and India.

However, sustainable development has been undermined by consumption and continual rises in living standards and expectations. As Kingsbury notes:

>> *Technological development has led many and perhaps most of the world's population to, if not expect, then at least to want more, of almost everything, as the developed world has and continues to do.* >> (p.287)

A good example of the negative effect this can have on the environment is the case of China, cheap fridges and chlorofluorocarbons (CFCs). It has long been recognized that CFCs deplete the ozone layer and in the West manufacturers of refrigerators, the main producer of CFCs, have converted to non-CFC fridges. However in China, rises in living standards have led to a demand for cheap fridges produced by Chinese manufacturers. Unfortunately, these happen to be CFC producing fridges. When the international community protested, China replied that its people could not afford CFC-free fridges and it was not willing to deny them the right to preserve their food.

In addition to China's non-cooperation, the USA (which accounts for 36 per cent of emissions) and Australia (the biggest polluter per capita in the world) have also failed to commit to reducing their emission of industrial pollutants such as carbon dioxide (i.e. greenhouse emissions); this has also seriously undermined the future success of this type of development.

Appropriate development

The concept of sustainable development has been supplemented by the concept of **appropriate development**. This suggests that 'small is beautiful', and that social and ecological outcomes should have precedence over GNP. Moreover, such development should be operated by people in their localities without the need for external expertise or capital, i.e. dependence on the West.

A good example of *inappropriate* development would be the provision of diesel-powered electric generators, which rely on both oil and spare parts from the developed world. A more appropriate example of development technology that is both sustainable and can be operated using only local expertise might be wind or solar power.

Check your understanding

1 What were the trends with regard to urbanization during the 20th century?

2 What are the implications of urban dwellers in the developing world being young and fertile?

3 Identify three push factors and three pull factors that attract the rural poor to cities in the developing world.

4 Why does modernization theory see cities as central to development?

5 Why does dependency theory argue that urbanization in the developing world contributes to underdevelopment?

6 What was the relationship between cities in the developing world and colonialism?

7 Identify four types of environmental degradation.

8 What is the relationship between population, consumption and environmental degradation?

9 Identify four reasons why environmental degradation has occurred.

10 Identify two development models which aim to challenge environmental degradation.

web.task

Visit **www.newint.org** and use the search facility to find articles on both urbanization and environmental degradation.

'Think global, act local'

Elkington (1999) notes that there is tension between economic development and environmental concerns 'with one side trying to force through new rules and standards, and the other trying to roll them back' (quoted in Kingsbury et al., p.289). Elkington argues that development should focus on a 'triple bottom line', i.e. economic prosperity, environmental quality and social justice.

The World Bank has recently argued along similar lines, stating that sustainable development should pay attention to five types of 'capital':

- *financial* – i.e. careful planning and money management
- *physical* – i.e. infrastructure
- *human* – i.e. health and education
- *social* – i.e. the quality of interactions
- *natural* – i.e. natural resources, such as water and climate.

The slogan 'think global, act local' is fast becoming the slogan of sustainable development. Elkington argues that if the world does not put environmental and social responsibility on a similar level to economic prosperity, we will run the very real risk of extinction.

KEY TERMS

Activism – the willingness to bring about social change by taking action.

Appropriate technology – small-scale technology that is pragmatic and not dependent on Western expertise or materials.

Cosmopolitan – modern and diverse.

Degradation – deterioration.

Lumpen-proletariat – see underclass.

Pull factors – the attractions of urbanization that draw people to the city.

Push factors – those influences, usually negative, that pressure people into leaving their normal environments.

Shanty towns – very poor 'towns' with almost no sanitation, facilities and proper housing that develop outside cities in some developing countries because people are drawn to the city but find there is nowhere to live or that they cannot afford anywhere.

Sustainable development – aid strategies that address the relationship between poverty and environmental destruction.

Underclass – the very poor, who experience subsistence poverty, especially in the cities of the developing world.

Urbanization – the growth of towns and cities as people migrate from the countryside.

exploring urbanization and environment

Item A

Faith in economic growth as the ultimate hope for human progress is widespread. Unfortunately reality shows otherwise. As Ayres argues:

<< There is every indication that human economic activity supported by perverse trade policies is well on the way to perturbing our natural environment more and faster than any known event in planetary history, save perhaps the large asteroid collision that may have killed off the dinosaurs. We may well be on the way to our own extinction.>>

Ayres may well be right when he accuses globalization of accelerating the process of global environmental decline. Export-led growth and debt in the developing world have combined to speed up the rapid consumption of the Earth's irreplaceable resources. The persistence of poverty has also spurred environmental decline. In Madagascar, one of the world's most devastated environments, an island once covered in lush forests has turned into a barren wasteland as local people slash-and-burn jungle plots to grow food. In a few short years the land turns to scrub-infested desert, and the people continue their cycle of cutting and burning. Less than a tenth of Madagascar is still tree-covered and the forest is vanishing at a rate of 500 000 acres a year. Poverty is the core of the problem: 70 per cent of the island's 14 million people live on a dollar a day.

Adapted from W. Ellwood (2001) *The No-Nonsense Guide to Globalization*, London: Verso, pp. 93–5

1 (a) Identify and briefly explain **two** of the problems associated with cities in the developing world. (8 marks)

(b) Using information from **Item A** and elsewhere, briefly examine the view that poverty is a major cause of global ecological damage. (12 marks)

2 Examine the view that urbanization, industrialization and globalization have contributed to major social and environmental problems in the developing world. (40 marks)

Globalization

gettingyouthinking

1 In what ways are the USA's domestic problems such as crime tied to global processes?

2 What two global processes led to Juan Paredes becoming a coca farmer?

3 How would you go about persuading Juan Paredes not to produce coca?

Americans consume more cocaine than any other industrialized country. Over 22 million say they have tried it, and between two and three million are addicted to it. In 1989, around 2500 Americans died from it. In 1990, one in five people arrested for any crime was hooked on cocaine or crack. Americans spend $110 000 million a year on drugs ($28 000 million on cocaine), more than double the profits of the USA's top 500 companies put together.

Juan Paredes worked as a tin-miner in Bolivia until the late 1980s. In the early 1980s, 79 per cent of his country's export earnings came from tin. However, technological advances in the West meant that large Western companies such as Coke, Pepsi and Heinz switched to substitutes such as aluminium. In October 1985, the worldwide price of tin set by speculators at the London Tin Exchange fell from £8000 to £4000 per ton, putting thousands of miners like Juan out of work. Juan turned to farming instead and managed to obtain the title to four hectares of land. Very soon, he was attracted to the growing of a crop that yielded up to four or five harvests a year, which had a seemingly limitless demand and which earned him far more than tin-mining ever did. That crop was coca. By 1991, Bolivia was the largest producer of the coca leaf in the world and the second ranked producer of refined cocaine.

Adapted from Cohen, R. and Kennedy, P. (2000) *Global Sociology*, Basingstoke: Palgrave; and Chrispin, J. and Jegede, F. (2000) *Population, Resources and Development*, London: HarperCollins

You will probably have realized from doing the above exercise that crime in the USA cannot be analysed in isolation from global processes. The problems faced by the USA in terms of drugs are very much related to economic globalization – especially the fact that countries like Bolivia and Colombia desperately need American dollars to pay their debts to Western banks. However, because their economies are tied up with a single crop or raw material, any fall in demand or price in the global market place is going to result in poverty in this part of the world. This means that poor farmers will be tempted to produce illegal crops in order to survive. The coca leaf therefore is a global crop in that it links the poorest in the poor countries together with the most desperate in the West.

Defining globalization

Cohen and Kennedy (2000) suggest that the function of sociologists today is to provide a 'sociology for one world', i.e. a global sociology that investigates and analyses the increasing interconnectedness and interdependency of the world.

Cochrane and Pain (2000) (in Held 2000) illustrate these ties that bind us together:

≪ *Drugs, crime, sex, disease, people, ideas, images, news, information, entertainment, pollution, goods and money now all travel the globe. They are crossing national boundaries and connecting the world on an unprecedented scale and with previously unimaginable speed. The lives of ordinary people everywhere in the world seem increasingly to be shaped by events, decisions and actions that take place far away from where they live and work.* >>

Steven (2004), too, notes that:

<< *Despite huge differences in distance, upbringing and social context, many of us now listen to the same music, read the same books and watch the same films and television. Youth in Soweto listen to LA rap; viewers in southern China's Guangdong province watch pirated tapes of Jackie Chan; Sri Lankan refugee kids in Toronto come home from school to settle down in front of Tamil movies rented from the local grocery store. Teenagers and their young siblings in almost every place on earth know Bart and Lisa Simpson. I can sit at my home computer downloading the latest communiqués from Mexico's indigenous Zapatista rebels and out of the corner of my eye watch the World Cup live from Korea on the TV in the next room.* >> (pp.16–17)

What Cochrane and Pain, and Steven are describing is 'globalization' – the emergence of a global economic and cultural system which, allegedly, is incorporating the people of the world into a single global society. Cohen and Kennedy argue that globalization needs to be understood as a 'a set of mutually reinforcing **transformations**' of the world. These include the following:

● *Changes in the concept of time and space* – Developments such as the mobile phone, satellite television and the internet mean that global communication is virtually instantaneous, whilst mass travel enables us through tourism to experience a greater range of other cultures.

● *Economic markets and production in different countries* are becoming interdependent because of the growth in international trade, the new international division of labour, the growing influence of transnational corporations and the global dominance of organizations like the World Trade Organization.

● *Increasing cultural interaction* through developments in mass media (especially television, films, music and the transmission of news and international sport). We can now encounter and consume new ideas and experiences from a wide range of cross-cultural sources in fields such as fashion, literature and food.

● *Increasingly shared problems* – These may be:
  1 Economic: We are becoming much more aware that the economic decisions we make about our lifestyle preferences and leisure pursuits can cause problems such as unemployment, debt and the loss of livelihoods for workers and peasants thousands of miles away. Similarly, the financial problems experienced by the Asian tiger economies in 1998/99 led to unemployment in the UK.
  2 Environmental: The Chernobyl nuclear disaster of 1986 demonstrated quite vividly that ecological disasters do not respect national boundaries – today, acres of land in the Lake District and Wales still experience high levels of radiation because of the fall-out from this accident thousands of miles away. Environment degradation is not only caused by Western industry and **consumption**, but also by unwitting damage caused by the poor in the developing world engaging in overcultivation and deforestation. The resulting global climate change has implications for everyone in the world.
  3 Other common problems include worldwide health problems such as AIDS, international drug-trafficking and the sort of international terrorism practised on 11 September 2001 in New York and 7 July 2005 in London.

Kennedy and Cohen conclude that these transformations have led to 'globalism', a new consciousness and understanding that the world is a single place. Giddens (1999) notes that most of us perceive ourselves as occupying a 'runaway world' characterized by common tastes and interests, change and uncertainty and a common fate.

However, as sociologists we also need to be cautious in our use of the term 'globalization' – as Wiseman indicates: 'Globalization is the most slippery buzzword of the late 20th century because it can have many meanings and be used in many ways' (quoted on p.12 of Held 2000). We can illustrate this by looking closely at the theoretical interpretations of the concept.

Theories of globalization

Cochrane and Pain (2000) note that three theoretical positions can be seen with regard to globalization:

1 **Globalists** believe that globalization is a fact that is having real consequences for the way that people and organizations operate across the world. They believe that nation-states and local cultures are being eroded by a homogeneous global culture and economy. However, globalists are not united on the consequences of such a process:
   – Hyperglobalists (sometimes called optimists or positive globalists) welcome such developments and suggest globalization will eventually produce tolerant and responsible world citizens.
   – Pessimistic globalists argue that globalization is a negative phenomenon because it is essentially a form of Western (and especially American) imperialism, peddling a superficial and homogeneous mass form of culture and consumption. Such a view focuses on the dangers of what has variously been called the '**McDonaldization**' or 'Coca-Colonization' of the world (see later in this topic).

2 **Traditionalists** do not believe that globalization is occurring. They argue that the phenomenon is a myth or, at best, exaggerated. They point out that capitalism has been an international phenomenon for hundreds of years. All we are experiencing at the moment is a continuation, or evolution, of capitalist production and trade.

3 **Transformationalists** occupy a middle ground between globalists and traditionalists. They agree that the impact of globalization has been exaggerated by globalists but argue that it is foolish to reject the concept out of hand. This

theoretical position argues that globalization should be understood as a complex set of interconnecting relationships through which power, for the most part, is exercised indirectly. They suggest that the process can be reversed, especially where it is negative or, at the very least, that it can be controlled.

Economic globalization

It is in the area of economic globalization that the debate between traditionalists and hyperglobalists can most obviously be seen. Thompson (2000) notes that the hyperglobalist position claims there has been a rapid and recent intensification of international trade and investment such that distinct national economies have dissolved into a global economy determined by world market-forces. This view has attracted two forms of criticism:

- Neo-Marxists accept that a strong globalization process has occurred, but condemn it as an extension of global capitalist exploitation.
- Traditionalists argue that the international economy has not gained dominance over national economic policies.

The new international division of labour (NIDL)

The neo-Marxist, Frobel, notes that from the 1970s onwards, we have seen substantial movement of industrial capital from the advanced industrialized world to the developing world (Frobel *et al.* 1980). This movement was due to rising labour costs and high levels of industrial conflict in the West, which had reduced the profitability of transnational corporations (TNCs). Many developing nations in the 1970s and 1980s set up export-processing zones (EPZs) or free trade zones (FTZs), in which transnational companies were encouraged to build factories producing goods for export to the West (see Fig. 3.4 opposite). There are now some 800 EPZs or FTZs in the world. Even socialist Cuba has got in on the act! Developments in manufacturing meant that labour could be fragmented into a range of unskilled tasks that could be done with minimal training, whilst computer-controlled technology enabled production to be automatically supervised. Klein (2000) notes that 'to lure the TNCs into their EPZs, the governments of poor countries offer tax breaks, lax health and safety regulations, a low minimum wage and the services of a military willing and able to crush labour unrest. Integration with the local culture and economy is kept to a bare minimum'.

This new international division of labour (NIDL) is thought by hyperglobalists to benefit world consumers by enhancing competition and thus keep the prices of goods reasonably low. However, traditionalists like Frobel see the NIDL as merely a new form of neo-colonial exploitation. In addition to exploiting peasants who grow cash crops for Western consumption, he argues that TNCs are now exploiting wage labourers (especially women) in factories throughout the world. Klein agrees and

notes that 'entire (developing) countries are being turned into industrial slums and low-wage labour ghettos'.

Pessimistic globalizers share these concerns. They point out that as TNCs relocate production in their search for lower costs and higher profits, so the prospects of employment in the West decline. Wages in the UK will need to be kept sufficiently low so that TNCs see investment in the UK as an attractive option. In the long term, EPZs benefit TNCs rather than developing countries because today there are over 70 countries competing to make their EPZ more financially attractive than that of their neighbour. Ellwood (2001) notes:

<< *Corporations have the upper hand, trading off one nation against another to see who can offer the most lucrative investment incentives. Tax holidays, interest-free loans, grants, training schemes, unhindered profit remittances and publicly-funded sewers, roads and utilities are among the mix of 'incentives' that companies now expect in return for opening up a new factory or office.* >> (p. 62)

World trade

Another important aspect of economic globalization is the General Agreement on Tariffs and Trade or GATT, which was a set of rules established in 1944 to govern global trade. GATT particularly aimed to reduce trade barriers and competition between nations. In 1994, the World Trade Organization (WTO) was set up to replace GATT. It has 137 member states. The WTO has taken over and extended the GATT agreements on trade in goods, as well as negotiating a new GATT – which covers services such as telecommunications, banking and investment, transport, education, health and the environment. The main impact of these economic rules has been the increase in the flow of global finance from $17.5 trillion in 1979 to over $3000 trillion in 2000.

Marxists and other global pessimists have criticized the free-trade agenda of the WTO. They claim that global trade rules are unfair and biased against developing countries as these countries are being pressured to open up their economies immediately to Western banks and transnationals, and to abandon tariffs (i.e. taxes) on imports from the West. Organizations such as the World Bank and IMF have tied aid and loans to developing countries to these free-trade conditions. However, under the GATTs, the developed countries are allowed to impose quotas restricting the import of manufactured goods from the developing world. It is argued that such imbalanced rules mean that the WTO is a rich man's club dominated by the developed industrial nations

Transnational corporations (TNCs)

As mentioned earlier, the activities of transnational corporations in the global economy have caused some concern. TNCs have taken advantage of the relaxation of trade rules brought about by GATT and the WTO, and as Ellwood (2001) notes, they 'have become the driving force behind economic globalization, wielding more power than many nation-states'. Today, 50 of the 100 largest economies in the world are run by multinationals

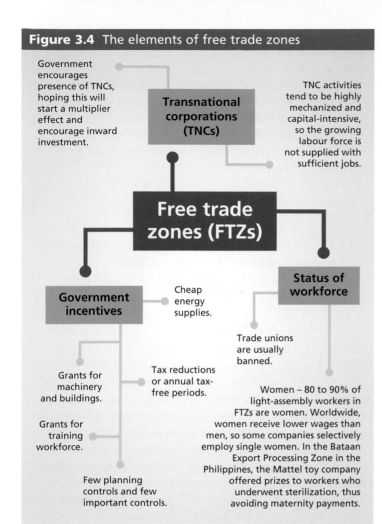

Figure 3.4 The elements of free trade zones

Government encourages presence of TNCs, hoping this will start a multiplier effect and encourage inward investment.

Transnational corporations (TNCs)

TNC activities tend to be highly mechanized and capital-intensive, so the growing labour force is not supplied with sufficient jobs.

Free trade zones (FTZs)

Government incentives

Cheap energy supplies.

Grants for machinery and buildings.

Tax reductions or annual tax-free periods.

Grants for training workforce.

Few planning controls and few important controls.

Status of workforce

Trade unions are usually banned.

Women – 80 to 90% of light-assembly workers in FTZs are women. Worldwide, women receive lower wages than men, so some companies selectively employ single women. In the Bataan Export Processing Zone in the Philippines, the Mattel toy company offered prizes to workers who underwent sterilization, thus avoiding maternity payments.

for example, the ten largest corporations in the telecommunications industry now control 86 per cent of the global market. Mergers have significant human effects in terms of job losses worldwide. Monopoly also has the effect of increasing both the economic and political power of large corporations over national and regional governments, especially those found in the developing world. In particular, there are concerns that transnationals, along with the World Bank and IMF, are pressurizing smaller, less economically powerful countries to open their economies up to private investment. One particularly worrying contemporary trend has been the attempt by US private healthcare companies to influence the WTO to encourage the privatization of healthcare in developing countries. Water is another resource which transnational companies have recently targeted for private investment.

Another concern about transnational behaviour has focused on the deregulation of global finance which, together with the revolution in microelectronics, i.e. computers, the internet and e-mail, has led to massive movements of money across the globe. In particular, it has resulted in transnational finance corporations engaging in currency speculation for profit. This has resulted in the destabilization of currencies both in the developed and developing worlds, and led to economic suffering for millions in terms of unemployment and loss of savings.

However, it would be a mistake to dismiss all transnational investment in the developing world as exploitative. Although there exist quite legitimate concerns about transnational abuse of power and unethical behaviour, these corporations can bring about positive change. As Ellwood notes:

<< *They are at the cutting edge of technological innovation and they can introduce new management and marketing strategies. It's also true that wages and working conditions are usually better in foreign subsidiaries of multinational firms than in local companies.*>> (pp. 61–2).

McDonaldization

George Ritzer (1993) argues that another aspect of economic globalization is McDonaldization, 'the process by which the principles of the fast food restaurant are coming to dominate more and more sectors of American society as well as the rest of the world'. Ritzer argues that McDonaldization has impacted upon economic production and consumption in four ways:

rather than countries, e.g. Mitsubishi is bigger than Saudi Arabia whilst General Motors is larger than Greece. The combined annual revenues of the biggest 200 corporations are greater than those of 182 nation-states or 80 per cent of the world's population. Moreover, it is estimated that a third of all trade within the global economy is business between branches of the same corporations. Why are these economic trends important? The answer lies in the fact that corporate decision-makers rarely consider the social, environmental and economic consequences of their actions for the people of the developing world.

The trend in transnational business is towards monopoly, and mergers between corporations occur frequently. Concentration is particularly taking place in banking and mass media. Today,

synopticlink
stratification and differentiation

Marxists argue that globalization is merely an extension of the capitalist stratification system. Exploitation of workers has been globalized in the setting up of a new international division of labour in which the labour power of proletariats in both the developed and developing world are exploited for their surplus value by

the agents of global capitalism – transnational companies. On the other hand, postmodernists see globalization as a positive phenomenon because it has created a new class of global consumers with a greater range of choices from which they can construct a hybridized global identity.

The process of globalization, with its focus on shrinking the world and transcending national barriers, may have brought us into contact with a new set of problems in terms of crime and deviance:

- Political deviance in the form of global Islamic terrorism (reacting to what is perceived as the 'moral and social depravity' of Western, particularly, American, cultural imperialism) has now directly targeted both the UK in 2005 and global forms of consumption dominated by Westerners, such as tourism.
- Social problems, such as drug abuse and the sexual exploitation of women, are increasing in the UK.

These trends may correspond to the increase in global traffic in both drugs and women. As seen earlier, there is some evidence that farmers in poorer countries turn to the production of drug crops as the price of more legitimate cash crops fall because of Western-dominated world trade agreements. Poorer countries may also be tempted into drug crop production because of their debt crisis.

- Some of the activities of Western-based transnational companies in poorer countries can also be criticized as being criminal and unethical. The lack of international laws that can police the activities of transnational companies allows such corporate crime to continue unpunished.

- *Efficiency* – Producing and consuming burgers is likened to an assembly-line experience
- *Calculability* – Achieving maximum quantity with minimum input
- *Predictability* – Standardization of product, service and environment
- *Control* – Tasks are de-skilled through technology.

Ritzer sees the process as essentially dehumanizing both for workers and consumers. Moreover, he suggests that it is essentially another form of US economic and cultural imperialism. Spybey (1998), however, rejects this argument and suggests that McDonalds is a true symbol of genuine globalization because the company accommodates local culture and customs wherever it sets up business. Spybey points out that true globalization is actually a combination of global and local influences – there is 'interpenetration' between the two. For example, burgers in McDonalds in India contain no meat because of local Hindu beliefs. In this sense, the global McDonalds has an effect upon the local (i.e. by setting up a fast-food outlet), but the local has an effect upon the global too.

The need for global controls

The activities of TNCs illustrate a lack of global control by national governments and agencies such as the United Nations. Quite simply, there is no international law in place to regulate the activities of such organizations, despite their blatant and consistent infringement of human rights. This lack of control is not unique to the activities of TNCs.

Globalization also results in opportunities for cross-border crime, which is thought to be worth $500 billion a year. International criminal activity includes people-trafficking, computer fraud, illegal arms-dealing, smuggling, violating patents and copyright agreements, and drug trafficking. The latter is particularly profitable. The world turnover in heroin went up 20 times between 1970 and 1990, whilst cocaine turnover went up 50 times. As described earlier, drug-

trafficking is truly a global phenomena as it is linked to the poverty of certain countries, which is a result of their position within the global capitalist system. The international trading system means that poor farmers in countries such as Bolivia, Nepal and Jamaica cannot survive on the income provided by legitimate cash crops and turn instead to the production of coca or poppies (from which heroin can be manufactured).

Globalization also increases the possibility of **white-collar crime** because of more open borders and international computer link-ups. Drug money is also often '**laundered**' through legitimate global banking operations.

Finally, violence is also taking on a global dimension as international drug gangs compete with each other for global dominance. Terrorism, too, has also moved beyond national boundaries. Osama Bin Laden's al-Qaeda group has recruited from a range of Arab, Asian and European nations. Moreover, the actions of al-Qaeda have become global actions in their choice of targets (i.e. US and UK embassies around the world, and the hotels, nightclubs and restaurants used by Western tourists), and in their use of media technology (e.g. passing on videos of atrocities to the Al-Jazeera television network, knowing that such images will be transmitted globally within hours on television and on the internet).

The globalization of culture

The global growth and spread of cultural goods (especially cinema, television, radio, advertising, music and the internet) in recent years has been phenomenal. McKay (2000) notes that the total number of television sets in the developing world has grown so rapidly that it has had a globalizing effect on people in the developing world.

Hyperglobalists see the global media as beneficial because it is primarily responsible for diffusing different cultural styles around the world and creating new global hybrid styles in fashion, music, consumption and lifestyle. It is argued that in the postmodern world such cultural diversity and **pluralism** will become the global norm.

Pessimistic globalists, in contrast, are concerned about the concentration of the world's media in the hands of a few powerful media corporations. Media conglomerates, mainly American (such as Disney, Microsoft, Time Warner and AOL) and Japanese (such as Sony) have achieved near monopolistic control of newspapers, film archives, news programmes, television and radio, advertising and satellites. It is suggested that media moghuls are able to influence business, international agencies and governments and consequently to threaten democracy and freedom of expression.

It is also argued that such media corporations are likely to **disseminate** primarily Western, especially American, forms of culture. For example, most films released by these organizations are produced in Hollywood and so are of a certain formulaic (predictable) type. There have been concerns that these Western forms of culture reflect a cultural imperialism that results in the marginalization of local culture. As Steven (2004) argues:

>> *For the past century, US political and economic influence has been aided immensely by US film and music. Where the marines, missionaries and bureaucrats failed, Charlie Chaplin, Mickey Mouse and The Beach Boys have succeeded effortlessly in attracting the world to the American way.*>>

Mass advertising of Western cultural icons like McDonalds and Coca-Cola has resulted in their logos becoming powerful symbols to people in the developing world (especially children) of the need to adopt Western consumer lifestyles in order to modernize. There is a fear that this may undermine and even destroy rich local cultures and identities. Some commentators refer to this as 'coca-colonization.'

However, transformationalists are critical of cultural-imperialist arguments for three reasons.

- These arguments make the mistake of suggesting that the flow of culture is one way only – from the West to the developed world. This focus fails to acknowledge how Western culture is enriched by inputs from other world cultures and religions.
- It assumes that people in the developing world are **consumer dopes**. In fact, their involvement in global culture may result in them accessing a wider range of choices.
- It underestimates the strength of local culture. As Cohen and Kennedy (2000) observe:

>> *On occasions, some inhabitants of Lagos or Kuala Lumpur may drink Coke, wear Levi 501 jeans and listen to Madonna records. But that does not mean they are about to abandon their customs, family and religious obligations or national identities wholesale even if they could afford to do so, which most cannot.*>> (p.243)

Responses to globalization

There are a number of social and collective responses to the phenomenon of globalization.

- Robertson (1992) notes that we select from the global only that which pleases us and then alter it so that it is adapted to our local culture or needs. He calls this 'glocalization'. Cohen and Kennedy refer to this as 'indigenization', i.e. the local 'captures' the global influence and turns it into an acceptable form compatible with local tastes. For example, the Indian film industry in the form of '**Bollywood**' combines contemporary Western ideas about entertainment with traditional Hindu myth, history and culture.
- We may mix global ingredients to produce new fused or hybrid inventions – some world music mixes Western dance beats with traditional styles from North Africa and Asia. Cohen and Kennedy call this 'creolization'.
- Global communication means that it is now difficult for people to avoid reflecting on world events or acknowledging that we live in a world characterized by 'risk'. This may result in a broadening of our identities, especially if we choose to champion a particular global cause related to issues such as the environment or debt relief. Such choices may be partly responsible for the rise of the antiglobalization movement, especially among young people.
- Our knowledge of the global may heighten our awareness of and loyalty to the local – our sense of Britishness may become stronger, for example.
- Some religious and ethnic groups may resist globalization because they interpret it as Western imperialism. For

Here, Señora Carter, is the statue of Simón Bolívar, who liberated Latin America from foreign domination ...

Source: Allen, T. and Thomas, A. (2001) *Poverty and Development in the 21st Century*, Oxford: Oxford University Press

example, Kingsbury *et al.* (2004) note that the idea of a 'global community' means that global norms are interpreted and enforced by a small number of states. The USA, in particular, has set itself up as a 'global policeman' protecting what it argues are global interests. However, some cultures may interpret the pursuit of such interests by the USA, as well as the economic and cultural dominance of US transnationals and brands, as an attack upon the 'purity' of their own cultural or religious beliefs. Such an interpretation is likely to be reinforced by the extreme poverty found in countries with large Muslim populations. There is some evidence that this rationale may underpin Islamic attitudes towards the West and the military actions of groups such as al-Qaeda.

Is globalization actually occurring?

The answer to the question in the heading depends on what theoretical position you decide to take. The problem with neo-Marxist and traditionalist views is that they tend to overfocus on economic globalization and neglect the globalization of culture. They also make the mistake of viewing globalization as a one-way process and as a form of cultural imperialism. They consequently tend to see globalization as leading inevitably to **dystopia**.

Pessimistic globalizers, such as Barber and Schulz (1995), fear that we are turning into a 'McWorld' in which cultures and consumption will be standardized. However, the limited evidence we have so far suggests that **hybridity** – cultural borrowing and mixing – rather than uniformity may be the outcome of global cultural change. Cohen and Kennedy optimistically state that globalization will lead to an extension in human rights, universal access to education and communications and multicultural understanding. However, we must remember that the phenomenon of globalization is fairly young and, as Cohen and Kennedy soberly note, 'globalization has so far done little to diminish the blight of poverty and wretchedness in which about half of the world's inhabitants is forced to live' (p.372). Kingsbury argues that until globalization challenges such poverty, it is likely that global conflict, especially between East and West, will be a fact for some time to come.

Check your understanding

1 What are the four transformations of the world that have led to globalization according to Cohen and Kennedy?

2 What is globalism?

3 What is the difference between a positive globalist and a pessimistic globalist?

4 What is meant by the phrase 'coca-colonization of the world'?

5 How does the 'new international division of labour' differ from previous forms of capitalist production?

6 Why are transnationals attracted to EPZs?

7 What is McDonaldization?

8 Identify four criticisms of TNC activity in the developing world?

9 Why are some sociologists anxious about the globalization of culture?

10 What is globalization?

11 Why might globalization be leading to greater awareness of the world's problems and a desire to change the world for the better among young people?

12 Why are some sociologists like Wiseman sceptical about the use of the term 'globalization'?

web.tasks

1 **Visit the Guardian website and research the arguments for and against globalization contained in the special report at www.guardian.co.uk/globalisation. This site contains over two dozen links to a range of excellent websites on globalization. Most of them are critical, such as:**

- **www.corpwatch.org – the website of Corporate Watch, which keeps an eye on the activities of transnational corporations**
- **www.mcspotlight.org/ – aims to track the activities of McDonalds and other transnationals**
- **www.nosweat.org.uk/ looks critically at those companies allegedly running sweatshops in the EPZs**
- **www.wdm.org – an educational and campaigning organization focusing on UK foreign policy, debt and globalization**
- **www.iatp.org – antiglobalization research focusing on sustainable development and world trade**
- **www.resist.org.uk/ is a site that co-ordinates the antiglobalization movement.**

2 **Finally, if you are cheesed off with the way that Harry Potter has been transformed into yet another global commercial brand, visit www.barrytrotter.com/ to read the latest instalment 'Harry Potter and the fight against global capitalism'.**

KEY TERMS

Bollywood – Indian film industry based in Bombay.

Consumer dopes – people who are easily manipulated into spending their money.

Consumption – consuming material and cultural goods and resources.

Disseminate – transmit, spread

Dystopia – a future characterized by disaster and negative events.

Globalists – those who believe that globalization is occurring.

Hybridity – new cultural forms resulting from a mixture of different cultural influences.

Laundered – process of transferring money gained illegally into respectable accounts.

McDonaldization – a term coined by Ritzer (1993) to describe the process by which the principles of the fast food restaurant are coming to dominate more and more sectors of American society as well as the rest of the world.

Pluralism – variety of groups.

Traditionalists – in terms of globalization, those who do not believe that globalization is occurring

Transformationalists – theorists who believe that the impact of globalization has been exaggerated by globalists but argue that it is foolish to reject the concept out of hand

Transformations – social changes.

White-collar crime – crime committed by the middle and upper classes in the context of corporate life.

research idea

In order to assess the influence of globalization in your own life, construct a questionnaire that operationalizes the concept of cultural globalization in terms of the use of:

- global brands and logos
- transnational services like McDonalds, Burger King and Starbucks
- clothing and trainers
- tastes in film, music and television programmes.

Contact schools abroad via e-mail and ask students to fill in your questionnaire.

exploring globalization

Item A

Globalization implies that the boundaries between nation-states become less significant in social life. One example of this can be seen in economic life, where world trade is increasingly dominated by transnational corporations and capital can be moved rapidly by investors from one country to another as the international financial markets are connected by computerized technology. Globalization can also be seen in culture where television programmes, films and books are made for an international market.

This cultural globalization can also be seen in the worldwide spread of tastes in food; for example, hamburgers, pizzas and curries, while identified as American, Italian or Indian, can be found in restaurants all over the world.

To many living outside Europe and North America, globalization looks like Westernization or even Americanization since the US is now the sole superpower, with a dominant economic, cultural and military position in the global order. Many of the most visible cultural expressions of globalization are American – Coca-Cola, McDonalds, etc. Globalization, some argue, destroys local cultures, widens world inequalities and worsens the lot of the impoverished. It creates a world of winners and losers, a few on the fast track to prosperity, the majority condemned to a life of misery and despair. Some argue that this is less of a global village and more like global pillage.

Adapted from Taylor, P. (1997) *Investigating Culture and Identity*, London: HarperCollins, p.128; and Lecture 1, 'Runaway World', one of the BBC Reith Lectures, BBC Radio 4 given by Anthony Giddens (1999)

1 (a) Identify and briefly explain some of the problems associated with transnational corporations. (8 marks)

(b) Using information from Item A and elsewhere, briefly examine the view that globalization increasingly looks like Westernization or even Americanization. (12 marks)

2 Examine the view that the concept of globalization has been exaggerated. (40 marks)

SOCIOLOGISTS' PASSION FOR UNDERSTANDING THE WORLD around them is one they share with many other people: writers, journalists, politicians and others have their opinions about the causes of, and remedies for, social problems, for example. However, what distinguishes sociologists from these other groups of people is, first, that they generate and use theory to explain society and, second, that they carry out research activities that provide the evidence for these theories. This unit, therefore, covers the very fundamentals of sociology as a subject. You will already have studied research methods and basic sociological theory at AS-level. This unit reviews much of the AS material, taking a deeper look at theoretical and methodological issues, while also covering significant areas of new ground.

The first two topics on sociological theories are divided into two main categories – modernist theories, and feminist, late-modern and postmodern theories. The rest of the topics consist of a detailed exploration of sociological research methods. Topic 3 asks whether sociology can claim (or even wishes to claim) that it is a science and the implications this debate has for the subject.

We follow this up in Topic 4 by exploring the use of quantitative methods in sociology – in particular the advantages and disadvantages of using surveys and statistical approaches. Topic 5 explores more interpretivist models of society, which seek to understand society by understanding how people think and act by observing them in their daily lives, and wherever possible joining in with them. These approaches are generally known as qualitative methods. Topic 6 then examines how both quantitative and qualitative researchers actually go about asking people questions – through questionnaires, interviews and focus groups.

Topic 7 explores newer methodological ideas associated with feminist writers and postmodernists.

Topic 8 considers the uses of existing material in sociological research – known as secondary data.

Topic 9 takes the whole issue of values and ethical behaviour in research and discusses just what we mean by value-freedom, how important it is for sociology and whether it is an outdated concept.

There is considerable debate at the moment in sociology as to its role: should it simply engage in theoretical and methodological debates, or should it actually suggest policies as a result of the research? This is the subject matter of the final topic, which explores the relationship between theory and practical policy.

AQAspecification	topics	pages
Candidates should examine the following areas, which are also studied at AS- level:		
The different quantitative and qualitative methods and sources of data, including questionnaires, interviews, observation techniques and experiments, and documents and official statistics	Quantitative methods and experiments are covered in Topic 4; qualitative approaches such as observation in Topic 5. Questionnaires and interviews are the subject of Topic 6; documents and official statistics are included in Topic 8	182–205 212–219
The distinctions between primary and secondary data and between quantitative and qualitative data	Topics 4, 5 and 6 cover primary data, Topic 8 secondary data. Quantitative methods are discussed in Topic 4, qualitative approaches in Topic 5	182–205 212–219
The relationship between positivism, interpretivism and sociological methods	Postivism is examined primarily in Topic 4, interpretivism in Topic 5	182–199
The theoretical, practical and ethical considerations influencing the choice of topic, choice of method(s) and the conduct of research	These issues are discussed throughout Topics 3 to 8	174–219
The nature of social facts and the strengths and limitations of different sources of data and methods of research	The nature of social facts is discussed in Topic 3. Evaluation of different methods and sources is included in Topics 4 to 8	174–181 182–219
Consensus, conflict, structural and social action theories	These modernist theories are the focus of Topic 1	158–165
In addition, candidates should examine:		
The concepts of modernity and post-modernity in relation to sociological theory	Topic 1 is concerned with modernist theories and concepts, Topic 2 with postmodernity	158–173
The nature of 'science' and the extent to which sociology may be regarded as scientific	Covered in Topic 3	174–181
The relationship between theory and methods	The focus of Topics 4, 5 and 7	182–99,206–12
Debates about subjectivity, objectivity and value freedom	Covered in Topic 9	220–225
The relationship between sociology and social policy	Covered in Topic 10	226–231

Modernist sociological theories

gettingyouthinking

Use your knowledge from your AS-level studies to match each of the sentences below with the sociological theories they are most closely associated with. Explain your decisions.

1 Society is like a human body – every part of it helps to keep society going.

2 The ruling class benefits in every way from the operation of society while the workers get far less than they deserve.

3 Britain is a patriarchal society. Men generally have more power and prestige than women across a range of social institutions.

4 People have an active role in shaping social life. People do not feel themselves to be the puppets of society.

5 Society has experienced such major upheavals that the old ways of explaining it just won't work any more. We are entering a new sort of society.

6 Social behaviour is determined and made predictable by the organization of society.

If you are not sure, the possible answers are given below (upside down). The actual answers to the questions are provided at the end of the topic on p. 165.

Social structure theory – functionalism – feminism – Marxism – social action theory or interactionism – postmodernism

During your AS-level Sociology studies, you will almost certainly have met most of the main sociological theories. The exercise above will have reminded you of some of these. In the first two topics of this unit, we will be drawing these ideas together and exploring them further.

This topic explores what are known as modernist theories. 'Modernism' or 'modernity' refers to a period of history in 19th- and 20th-century Western societies that was characterized by major technological, social and political advances. It was within this period and driven by these ideas of rational, progressive thought that sociology was born. The main modernist approaches are Marxism, functionalism and **social action theory** (**interactionism**), and these have dominated sociology for much of the subject's existence.

Modernist theories are divided into two main perspectives – structural approaches and social action approaches:

● *Structural approaches* attempt to provide a complete theory of society. They begin their analyses from the 'top', by looking first at society as a whole and then working down to the individual parts, and finally to individuals. There are

two main structural theories: Marxism or conflict theory (and its developments, neo-Marxism), and functionalism or consensus theory (and its developments, neo-functionalism). These theories may start from the same position, but they come to very different conclusions.

● *Social action theories* do not seek to provide complete explanations for society; instead they start by looking at how society is 'built up' from people interacting with each other. Quite how far 'up' they arrive is a matter of debate – though one version of social action theory, known as **labelling** theory, does seek to explain the construction of social rules.

Functionalism

Functionalism is closely associated with the work of Talcott Parsons. His work dominated US sociology and vied with Marxist-based approaches in Europe from the 1940s until the 1970s. Today, it still provides us with a useful and relatively simple framework for approaching the study of society.

Parsons' aim was to provide a theoretical framework that combined the ideas of Weber, who stressed the importance of understanding people's actions, and those of Durkheim, who emphasized the necessity of focusing on the structures of societies and how they function.

Parsons' starting point, taken from Durkheim, was the organic analogy – that is, he imagined society as similar to a living being that adapts to its environments and is made up of component parts, each performing some action that helps the living being to continue to exist. In the case of human beings, for example, our organs provide functions to keep us alive – for example, the heart pumps blood. It exists for that purpose and we would not have it if there was no need to pump blood. Other creatures have developed alternative methods of survival – for instance, reptiles do not have hearts as they do not pump blood around the body. Similarly, institutions exist, or don't, because of their functions for the maintenance of society.

Just as our bodies need to resolve certain basic needs in order to survive, so do societies. Parsons (1952) suggests that there are four needs (or **functional prerequisites**) that all societies have to overcome:

- *Adaptation* (the economic function) – Every society has to provide an adequate standard of life for the survival of its members. Human societies vary from hunters and gatherers to complex industrial societies.
- *Goal attainment* (the political function) – Societies must develop ways of making decisions. Human societies vary from dictatorships to democracies.
- *Integration* (social harmony) – Each institution in society develops in response to particular functions. There is no guarantee that the different institutions will not develop elements that may conflict. For example, in **capitalism** the economic inequalities may lead to possible resentment between groups. Specialist institutions therefore develop that seek to limit the potential conflict. These could include religion, notions of charity and voluntary organizations.
- *Latency* (individual beliefs and values) – The previous three functional prerequisites all deal with the structure of society. This final prerequisite deals instead with individuals and how they cope. Parsons divides latency into two areas:
  - *Pattern maintenance*: this refers to the problems faced by people when conflicting demands are made of them, such as being a member of a minority religious group and a member of a largely Christian-based society. In contemporary sociological terms, we would call this the issue of identity.
  - *Tension management*: if a society is going to continue to exist, then it needs to motivate people to continue to belong to society and not to leave or oppose it.

Pattern variables

For a society to exist, it must fulfil the functional prerequisites listed above. However, 'society' is a concept that does not exist in itself, but is rather a term for a collection of people. When Parsons says that a 'society' must resolve certain problems, what he actually means is that *people* must act in certain ways

that enable society to fulfil its needs and ensure its continuation. This is the role of culture, which emphasizes that members of society ought to act in particular ways and, in doing so, ensure that the functional prerequisites are met.

Parsons claims that in all societies there are five possible cultural choices of action. The different answers the cultures provide lead to different forms of social behaviour and thus different ways of responding to the functional prerequisites. It is within these five sets of options that all cultural differences in human societies can be found.

Parsons calls these cultural choices of action **pattern variables**. They are:

- *Affectivity or affective neutrality* – Societies can be characterized either by close interpersonal relationships between people, or by relationships where the majority of interactions are value-free. For example, a small rural society may well be based upon personal knowledge of others, whilst in a large, urban society people hardly know each other.
- *Specificity or diffuseness* – The relationships people have can be based on only one link or on many. We may know others simply as a teacher or a colleague, whereas in simpler societies, they may be cousin, healer, ceremonial leader and so on.
- *Universalism or particularism* – In contemporary societies, we believe that rules should apply equally to everyone (even if they don't), yet in many societies rules are not regarded as necessarily being applicable to all. Royalty, ethnic groups, religious leaders may all be able to behave differently.
- *Quality or performance* – This is linked to the previous pattern variable. Should people be treated according to their abilities or by their social position at birth?
- *Self-orientation or collectivity orientation* – Do societies stress the importance of individual lives and happiness or that of the group?

The answers that the culture of a society provides for these five pattern variables determines the way that people behave, which Parsons describes as social roles.

Criticisms within the functionalist approach

Robert Merton (1957) belonged to the same functionalist approach as Parsons. However, Merton was critical of some of Parsons' arguments and proposed two amendments to functionalist theory:

- Parsons assumed if an institution was functional for one part of society, then it was functional for all parts. But Merton points out that this ignored the fact that some institutions can be both **dysfunctional** (or harmful) for society, as well as functional. In particular, he cites the example of religion, which can both bring people together and drive them apart.
- Merton suggests that Parsons failed to realize the distinction between manifest (or intended) functions and latent (or unintended consequences) of these actions. Merton says that this makes any analysis of society much more complex than Parsons' simple model.

Merton (1938) famously applied functionalist theory to an understanding of crime and deviance. Merton argued that societies have agreed cultural goals and, linked to them, culturally approved means of achieving these goals. Normally, there is a balance between them and societies remain harmonious. However, under certain circumstances, these means and goals do not

mesh adequately together. He argued that the culture of the USA had developed too strong a stress on obtaining the culturally approved goal of financial success, but there were inadequate culturally approved means for a significant proportion of the population to do so. The result was a growth in crime and other forms of deviance.

focus on research

Pete Saunders (1996)

Do the best reach the top?

Functionalist theory suggests that society is formed as it is because that is functionally the best way of maintaining its existence. This includes inequalities in class and status. Many critics argue it is not true that the most gifted achieve the top positions, but that success has more to do with inheritance and parental support. Saunders wished to demonstrate that in fact the best do achieve. He used evidence from the *National Child Development Study*, a longitudinal study of 17 000 children born in 1958 to see what their chances of social mobility were. In 1991, he had access to information on 6800 individuals from the study in full-time employment and concluded that occupational status was closely related to ability and effort. His results, therefore, support the functionalist argument.

Saunders, P. (1996) *Unequal but Fair? A study of class barriers in Britain*, London: IEA

1 In what ways do Saunders' results 'support the functionalist argument'?

Criticisms outside the functionalist approach

Sharrock *et al.* (2003) argue that there are several main criticisms of functionalism, listed in the next column.

- Functionalism overemphasizes the level of agreement or consensus in society. Apart from the simplest of societies, people have different values and attitudes within the same society.
- Parsons suggests that society is rather like an organism, yet this is not true. Organisms actually exist as biological entities, have a natural form and a natural life cycle. Society, on the other hand, is a concept, consisting of the activities of possibly millions of people. There is no natural cycle or natural form.
- Functionalists have real problems explaining social change. If, as Parsons claims, institutions exist to fulfil social needs, then once these needs are fulfilled, there is no reason to change them. Unless, therefore, there are some external changes which impact on the four functional prerequisites, societies should never change in form.
- Parsons seems to ignore differences in power. Yet differences in power can have strong impacts upon the form that society takes and whose interests it reflects.
- Finally, as interactionists point out, human beings in the Parsonian model of society seem rather like puppets having their strings pulled by all-powerful societies via pattern variables. Interactionists, postmodernists and late-modernists all combine to argue that people are much more 'reflexive', making choices and constructing their lives.

Neo-functionalism

Other writers following in the functionalist tradition include Mouzelis (1995) and Alexander (1985). Both these writers argue strongly for the overall systemic approach provided by Parsons. They dispute criticisms of Parsons that suggest he is not interested in how people act, and argue that with some modification Parsonian theory can allow for people to be 'reflexive', making decisions for themselves. These modifications to the theory also help explain social change.

Marxism

The second major sociological perspective that, like functionalism, aims to create a total theory of society by linking individual motivations and wider structural context is the tradition that has developed from Marxism. Marxism derives from the 19th-century writings of Karl Marx (1867/1973), who sought to create a scientific explanation of societies. His starting point was that the economic system of any society largely determined the social structure. The owners of the economic structure are able to control that society, and construct values and social relationships that reflect their own interests. Other groups in society, being less powerful, generally accept these values and social relationships, even though they are not in their interests.

Marx began by suggesting that all history can be divided into five periods or epochs, which are distinguished by ever more complex economic arrangements. The history of all societies begins with what he entitled 'primitive **communism**' – simple societies, such as hunters and gatherers, where there is no concept of private property and everything is shared. From that point it passes through the ancient societies such as that of Asia and Rome, through feudalism until it reaches the crucial stage of capitalism. According to Marx, capitalism would inevitably give way to the final stage of history, that of communism.

The Marxist model

Marx developed a theoretical model to describe the development of societies through these epochs. In each of the five epochs there is a particular economic structure (the economic base or **means of production**), which, except in primitive communism, is always controlled by a ruling class. This ruling class then constructs a whole set of social relationships (the **relations of production**) that benefit them and allow them to exploit all others who do not share in the ownership of the means of production. According to Marxist economic theory, the means of production are always advancing, becoming more complex and capable of producing greater wealth – nothing can stop this onward march of technology. However, the values that the ruling group create to benefit themselves tend to move much more slowly. Within each epoch, at the beginning, the values of the ruling class help technology move forward, but over time, because the values do not move as fast, they begin to get in the way of the move forward of technology – in fact, they actually impede it. At this point, a new, challenging group arises with values and ideas that would help the means of production advance, and, after a degree of conflict, they gain control of society and begin to construct their own relations of production. A new epoch has started and the process begins again.

Applying the model to capitalism

Marx believed that contemporary society has reached the stage of capitalism. The majority of his work was about the state of capitalist society and the factors that would, in his opinion, lead on to a communist society.

Within capitalism, there is a ruling class, or 'bourgeoisie', that owns the industry and commerce. All other people who work for a wage, no matter how prestigious or well paid, are members of the working class or proletariat. The bourgeoisie construct relations of production to their own benefit, including concepts of private property, wage labour and the justification of wide inequalities of wealth. The majority of the population

accept the inequalities of the system because of the way that dominant institutions such as religion and education justify the prevailing economic and social situation. Marx describes them as suffering from '**false consciousness**'. However, there always is a degree of conflict between some groups in society who are aware of their exploitation and the bourgeoisie – Marx saw these people as being 'class conscious'. **Class consciousness** manifests itself in terms of strikes and political protest, all examples of **class conflict**.

Over time, capitalism will enter a period of crisis, caused by ever-increasing competition amongst industries, leading to fewer and fewer large employers – who are able to lower the wages on offer to such an extent that the majority of the population live in poverty. At such a point, with a tiny minority of very rich capitalists and a huge majority of relatively poor people, radical social change is inevitable. This change will usher in the final epoch of communism.

Criticisms of Marx

Marx's work has probably been subjected to more critical discussion and straight criticism that any other sociological theory. This is mainly because it is as much a political programme as a sociological theory. However, specific sociological criticisms of Marx's work include the following:

- The description of capitalism and its inevitable move towards a crisis has simply not occurred. Indeed, capitalism has grown stronger and, through globalization, has spread across the world.
- The polarization of people into a tiny rich minority and an extremely poor majority has also not occurred. There is huge inequality, but at the same time there has been a massive growth in the middle classes in society – the very group that Marx predicted would disappear.
- Capitalism changed significantly after Marx's death with the introduction of a wide range of health, pension, housing and welfare benefits, all of which were missing from Marx's analysis.

Neo-Marxism

The basic model of Marxist theory has provided the platform for an entire tradition of writing in sociology. His ideas have been taken up and developed by a wide range of sociologists, keen to show that the model, suitably amended, is still accurate. Neo-Marxists seek to overcome the criticisms listed above.

The extent of writings within the Marxist tradition is too great to cover in any detail, but three versions of neo-Marxism provide us with a fairly representative sample of developments.

The Frankfurt School

The Frankfurt School is associated with the works of three major neo-Marxists: Marcuse, Adorno and Horkheimer, all of whom were originally at Frankfurt University. In separate books, Marcuse (1964/1991), Adorno (1991) and Horkheimer (1974) criticized Marx for being an **economic determinist** – that is for believing society is mainly determined by the economic system.

They argued that people's ideas and motivations are far more important than Marx ever acknowledged. Their critique contained three important elements:

- *Instrumental reason* – According to Adorno, Marx failed to explore the motivations as to why people accepted capitalism and the consumer goods it offers. Adorno suggests that it was wrong of Marx to dismiss this as simply 'false consciousness'. So people work hard to have a career and earn money, but quite why their aim should be to do this is never explored. Thinking in capitalism is therefore rational in terms of achieving goals themselves as long as the actual reasons for having those goals are not thought about rationally.
- *Mass culture* – Marcuse argued that Marx had ignored the importance of the media in his analysis. Marcuse suggested that the media play a key part in helping to control the population by teaching people to accept their lot and to concentrate on trivial entertainment.
- *The oppression of personality* – The third element of their critique of Marx focused on the ways that individuals' personality and desires are controlled and directed to the benefit of capitalism. Before capitalism, there was no concept of 'the work ethic'; people did the work that was required and then stopped. Capitalism, and particularly industrial production, needed people who accepted going to work for the majority of their lives and having little leisure. In the early stages of capitalism, therefore, pleasure and desire as concepts were heavily disapproved of – hence the puritan values of Victorian England. But in later capitalism, when it was possible to make money out of desires (and in particular sex), the desires were emphasized. Sex is now used, for example, to sell a wide range of products. According to the Frankfurt School, therefore, even our wants and desires are manipulated by capitalism in its own interests.

Althusser and the concept of relative autonomy

One of the most sociologically influential neo-Marxist approaches was provided by Althusser (1969), who argued that Marx had overemphasized how much the economic system drove society. Althusser suggested that capitalist society was made up of three interlocking elements:

- the economic system – producing all material goods
- the political system – organizing society
- the ideological system – providing all ideas and beliefs.

According to Althusser, the economic system has ultimate control, but the political and ideological have significant degrees of independence or autonomy. In reality, this means that politics and culture develop and change in response to many different forces, not just economic ones. Althusser used the term **relative autonomy** to describe this degree of freedom of politics and values. This may not at first seem very important, but what it suggests is that society is much more complex and apparently contradictory than in traditional Marxist analysis. So, the march towards a communist state is not clear, but is confusing and erratic.

Althusser also used this argument in his analysis of politics and the state. For Marx, the role of politics was simply to represent the interests of the ruling class, but for Althusser, the state was composed of two elements:

- **repressive state apparatuses** – organizations such as the police and the army
- **ideological state apparatuses** – the more subtle organizations including education, the media and religious organizations.

Both sets of apparatuses ultimately work for the benefit of capitalism, but there is a huge variation in the way the perform this task, with some contradictions between them.

Althusser's work provided a huge leap forward in neo-Marxist thinking, as it moved away from a naive form of Marxism (rather similar to functionalism), which simply said that everything that existed did so to perform a task for capitalism. Instead, while recognizing this ultimate purpose, Althusser highlighted the massive contradictions and differences between the various institutions of society.

Harvey: a late-modernist approach to Marxism

Some of the most recent and interesting sociological theorizing within neo-Marxism comes from the contemporary work of Harvey (1990). Harvey is extremely unusual for a neo-Marxist in that he develops Marxism within a postmodernist framework. As we see in the next topic, postmodernism is a movement that sees a fragmentation of society and a move toward image and superficiality in culture. Harvey argues that this move to postmodernity has been the result of economic changes occurring in the 1970s leading to the move away from manufacturing to commerce, media and retail as the main employers. Coupled with the development of globalization, these changes have presented massive challenges to capitalism.

According to Harvey, capitalism has, however, been clever in its responses to these economic changes, developing new sources of profit through the creation of whole new areas of commerce – what he calls **flexible accumulation** – in particular, through the manipulation of identity, with developments in fashion, travel and new forms of music. Globalization, too, has been utilized to produce cheap goods, which are given added value by being marketed in the more affluent nations.

At the same time, Harvey points out that there have been many real changes that have affected capitalism quite drastically. For example:

- National governments are less powerful than ever before in modernity, and so change now lies at the global, rather than national, level.
- Real political discourse within the traditional frameworks of government and political parties has been replaced by image politics, where what *appears* to happen is more important than what *actually* happens.
- Social class as the dominant form of division between members of societies has been partly replaced by a range of divisions linked to gender, ethnicity, religion and even alternative political movements, such as the green movement.

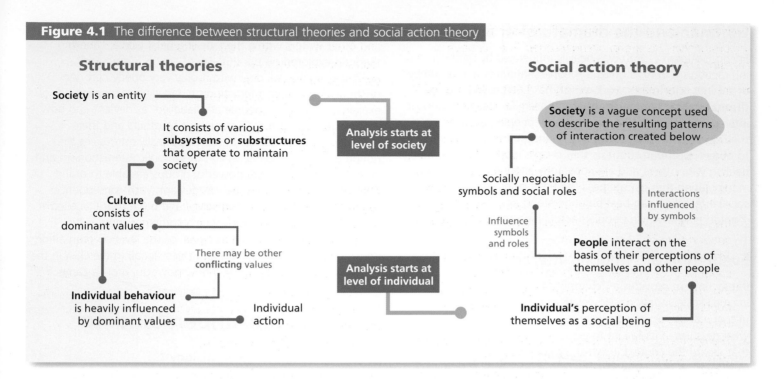

Figure 4.1 The difference between structural theories and social action theory

Structural theories

Society is an entity

It consists of various **subsystems** or **substructures** that operate to maintain society

Culture consists of dominant values

There may be other **conflicting** values

Individual behaviour is heavily influenced by dominant values

Individual action

Analysis starts at level of society

Analysis starts at level of individual

Social action theory

Society is a vague concept used to describe the resulting patterns of interaction created below

Socially negotiable symbols and social roles

Influence symbols and roles

Interactions influenced by symbols

People interact on the basis of their perceptions of themselves and other people

Individual's perception of themselves as a social being

Social action theories

According to social action theories, the way to understand society is not to start analysis at the top (analysing the structure of society, as Marxism and functionalism do), but to begin from the 'bottom' – analysing the way people interact with each other. Social action theorists do not set out to construct a grand theory along the lines of Marxism or functionalism, but are much more content to sketch out the rules of social interaction. These approaches (which are sometimes referred to as 'phenomenological approaches') explore the day-to-day, routine actions that most people perform. Interactionists (social action theorists/phenomenologists) set out to see how individuals actually *create* society through these routine actions.

Symbolic interactionism

Symbolic interactionism – the full name for interactionism – derives from the writings of Mead (1934) and then Blumer (1962) at the University of Chicago. Both Marxism and functionalism seemed to suggest that people were like marionettes controlled by the 'relations of production' or the 'pattern variables'. Instead, symbolic interactionism sees people as actively working at relationships, creating and responding to symbols and ideas. It is this dynamic that forms the basis of interactionists' studies.

The theory of symbolic interactionism has three core ideas: the symbol, the self, the interaction.

- *The symbol* – The world around us consists of millions of unique objects and people. Life would be impossible if we treated every separate thing as unique. Instead, we group things together into categories which we then classify. Usually, we then give each group a name (which is a symbol). Examples of symbols include 'trees', 'women', 'gay men', 'terrorists'. You will immediately see that the symbol

may evoke some feelings in us; they are not necessarily neutral terms. So, the world is composed of many symbols, all of which have some meaning for us and suggest a possible response or possible course of action. But the course of action we feel may be appropriate may not be shared by everybody.

- *The self* – In order for people to respond to and act upon the meanings that symbols have for them, they have to know who they are within this world of symbols and meaning. I cannot decide how I ought to behave until I know who I am and therefore what is appropriate for me to do in certain circumstances. This crucially involves us being able to see ourselves through the eyes of others. Blumer suggests that we develop this notion of the self in childhood and in particular in games playing. When engaging in a game with others, we learn various social roles and also learn how these interact with the roles of others. This brings us to the third element of interactionism, the importance of the interaction itself.

- *The interaction* – For sociology, the most important element of symbolic interactionism is actually the point at which the symbol and the self come together with others in an interaction. Each person in society must learn (again through games) to take the viewpoint of other people into account whenever they set out on any course of action. Only by having an idea of what the other person is thinking about the situation is it possible to interact with them. This is an extremely complex business – it involves reading the meaning of the situation correctly from the viewpoint of the other (What sort of person are they? How do they see me? What do they expect me to do?) and then responding in terms of how you see your own personality (Who am I? How do I want to behave?). There is clearly great scope for confusion, error and misunderstanding, so all people in an interaction must actively engage in constructing the situation, reading the rules and symbols correctly.

Goffman and the dramaturgical approach

Erving Goffman (1968) was heavily influenced by symbolic interactionism in his studies of people's interaction in a number of settings. Goffman's work, which has been called the **dramaturgical** approach, is based on similar ideas to symbolic interactionism in that he explores how people perceive themselves and then set out to present an image of themselves to others. Goffman suggests that people work out strategies in dealing with others and are constantly altering and manipulating these strategies. The basis of his ideas is that social interaction can best be understood as a form of loosely scripted play in which people ('actors') interpret their roles.

Evaluation of symbolic interactionism

Interactionism provides a rich insight into how people interact in small-scale situations. However, as a theory it is rather limited in scope and is as much psychological as sociological. Its main weakness lies in its failure to explore the wider social factors that create the context in which symbol, self and interaction all exist and the social implications of this. This means that it has no explanation of where the symbolic meanings originate from. It also completely fails to explore power differences between groups and individuals, and why these might occur.

web.task

Add to your notes and depth of knowledge on sociological theory by looking at sections of the following excellent website from Hewett School. Go to:
www.hewett.norfolk.sch.uk/CURRIC/soc/Theory1.htm

Some of these criticisms were answered by Becker (1963) and other writers within the labelling perspective. Labelling theory is explored on pp. 258–65 of Unit 5 (*Crime and deviance*), so we will deal with it only very briefly here. An offshoot of symbolic interactionism, labelling theory focuses on explaining why some people are 'labelled' as deviant and how this impacts on both their treatment by others and their perception of themselves. Becker specifically introduces the notion of power into his version of symbolic interactionism and demonstrates how more powerful groups are able to brand certain activities or individuals as deviant, with consequences that are likely to benefit themselves and harm those labelled deviant. One particular study which combines these is his analysis of the imposition and repeal of the laws on prohibition (making alcohol manufacture and sales illegal) in the USA in the early 20th century. He showed how powerful groups came

Check your understanding

1. What is the 'organic analogy'?
2. In your own words identify and briefly explain 'functional prerequisites'.
3. What are the 'means of production' and how do they relate to the 'relations of production'?
4. What does Harvey mean by 'flexible accumulation'?
5. Explain in your own words what the key difference is between social action theories and structural theories.
6. Explain any one criticism of interactionism.

KEY TERMS

Capitalism – term used originally by Marx to describe industrial society based on private ownership of property and businesses.

Class conflict – in Marxist analysis, the inevitable conflict arising between social classes based on their differing economic interests.

Class consciousness – in Marxist analysis, the awareness of belonging to a social class.

Communism – term used originally by Marx to describe societies where ownership of land, businesses and so on is shared and not privately owned.

Dramaturgical – refers to Goffman's version of interactionism, in which he sees people rather like actors in a play, with some of the script written and some ad-libbed.

Dysfunctional – in functionalist theory, activities or institutions which do not appear to benefit society.

Economic determinism – belief that the form of society is mainly determined by the economic system.

False consciousness – in Marxist analysis, the lack of awareness of being exploited.

Flexible accumulation – a term used by the neo-Marxist writer Harvey to explain how capitalism has continued to find new ways of profiting from people.

Functional prerequisites – in functionalist theory, societal needs.

Ideological state apparatuses – a term used by the neo-Marxist writer Althusser for those institutions which he claims exist to control the population

through manipulating values, such as the media.

Interactionism – shorthand term for symbolic interactionism.

Labelling – a theory developed from symbolic interactionism which was adapted for use in studies of deviance.

Means of production – in Marxist analysis, the economic structure of a society.

Modernism (modernity) – a period in history characterized by the belief that rational thought can be used to understand and explain the world.

Pattern variables – in functionalist theory, cultural choices as 'suggested' by the society.

Relations of production – in Marxist analysis, the social relationships in a society.

Relative autonomy – a term used by the neo-Marxist writer

Althusser to suggest that society is not determined as much as Marx suggested by the economic base.

Repressive state apparatuses – a term used by the neo-Marxist writer Althusser for those institutions which he claims exist to control the population through aggressive means, such as the police.

Social action theory – another name for symbolic interactionism; social action theories focus on how society is built up from people interacting with each other.

Symbolic interactionism – a theory associated with G.H. Mead that argues that people constantly work via symbols (language, writing, and so on) to construct society through the process of social interaction.

together, based on a mixture of genuine zeal and self-interest, to introduce the prohibition laws and he explores the consequences for society. It is, therefore, possible to apply symbolic interactionism to broader social situations and also to include power in the analysis.

Conclusion

In this topic, we have explored a variety of modernist theories, which provide two approaches to understanding society. The first is the structural approach utilized by Marxism and functionalism. This approach starts from the 'top' and works downwards and claims to provide a total theory of society. The second approach starts its analysis from the bottom and works upwards. This is the social action approach utilized by symbolic interactionism. Both approaches have strengths and weaknesses, which has led sociologists to take sides in a debate lasting more than 20 years. However, changes in society during the 1980s led many sociologists to be dissatisfied with both approaches. We move on to see the results of this dissatisfaction in the next topic.

research ideas

1 Conduct a small study of your own in which you explore the nature of symbolic interaction. How do people respond to symbols? Do they respond differently?

2 Choose a selection of 10 pictures and words. Ask a group of students what each picture or word means to them and what actions each one might suggest they do. You could include photos of almost anything, from an ashtray to a xylophone – the point is to explore what thoughts and actions everyday objects imply for people.

Answers to 'Getting you thinking'

1	Functionalism	4	Social action theory or interactionism
2	Marxism	5	Postmodernism
3	Feminism	6	Social structure theory

exploring modernist theories

Item A

The functionalist method sees any system as having needs or requirements. If the system is to survive, and to continue in more or less its current form, then these needs must be met in some way. The idea of need is quite simple. A human body needs food if it is to survive; it will die without this food. How then can functional analysis be used in the study of societies? The first step is to identify the needs of society. A society is assumed to be a relatively self-contained unit. As such it has many internal needs. These include the biological and psychological needs of its members and the needs to maintain boundaries and identity. However, many needs can only be met if the society draws on resources from the external environment, for example by producing food – the economic need. These theories see social systems as characterized by harmony and consensus. Marx's view, on the other hand, viewed conflict and division as normal features of all societies. Social systems develop over time as a result of contradictions that arise as a result of their economic systems.

Adapted from Fulcher, J. and Scott, J. (2003) *Sociology* (2nd edn), Oxford: Oxford University Press

Item B

The difference between society and nature is that nature is not man-made, but society is. While not made by any single person, society is created and recreated afresh, by participants in every encounter. It is indeed only made possible because every member of society is a practical social theorist who draws upon their knowledge and resources, normally in an unforced and routine way.

Giddens, A. (1993) *The New Rules of Sociological Methods*, London: Hutchinson

1 (a) Identify whether the approaches to sociology discussed in **Item A** are structural or social action theories. (2 marks)

   (b) Identify the **two** theories referred to in **Item A**. (4 marks)

   (c) Identify and briefly explain **two** of the societal needs identified in **Item A**. (4 marks)

   (d) With reference to **Item A** and elsewhere, briefly examine the reasons why some sociologists suggest that a structural perspective is the best way to understand society. (10 marks)

2 Assess the contribution of functionalism to an understanding of society. (40 marks)

Feminist, late-modern and postmodern sociological theories

gettingyouthinking

Kate Rainbow, the 31 year old owner of a communications company, says ... 'It's only now becoming obvious, but the market in accessorizing is huge _ Swarovski crystal covers for Blackberries, laptop bags, phone fascias and phone charms. The potential to customize phones and gadgets will grow immensely. People, women in particular, want to make their gadgets individual in some way. Lee agrees: 'Increasingly the lines between jewellery or accessory and gadget are being blurred. You can literally wear your phone or your digital camera around your neck on necklaces designed for that purpose.'

Extract from Polly Vernon 'She's gotta have it', *The Independent Technology Magazine*, Issue 1, 31 July 2005

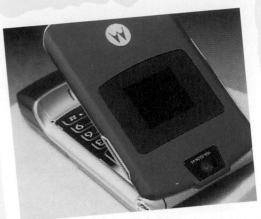

PRETTY IN PINK
The ultimate accessory for the swankiest fashionista, the Motorola Pink Razr oozes style and sophistication. Mirroring the design of the Motorola Razr, this limited-edition Pink Razr will be on every woman's wish list. Plus, its digital camera is ideal for capturing those festive moments, while its two-speaker sound system means you can party to your favourite Christmas tune.

Source: *Eve* magazine, December 2005 issue

1 **Look at the photograph and the text in the top right-hand corner. What do you think it and the main text below tell you about:**

(a) **women today**
(b) **modern technology?**

2 **Is this photograph illustrating fashion or technology? Explain your answer.**

3 **Does it matter if modern technology (mobile phones/MP3 players, etc.) is stylish or is what it looks like irrelevant?**

4 **Do you think that young people now live in a world transformed by technology?**

As we explored in Topic 1, sociology emerged during the period of modernity and the subject was shaped by the dominant ways of thinking of that time. Reflecting the natural sciences, sociology searched for a theoretical perspective that could explain how society was structured, how it functioned and how it changed over time. The theoretical approaches of Marxism and functionalism both claimed to do this, but by the 1970s, sociologists began to accept the fact that these major theoretical approaches simply failed to provide an adequate explanation for the existence of society. It was during this period that social action perspectives became popular, but for most sociologists these had limited value as they never claimed to provide the overarching theoretical frameworks that functionalism and Marxism had claimed. By the 1980s (and ten years earlier for feminists), sociologists were aware, through their studies of culture, gender, social class and the economy,

that enormous changes were taking place. The traditional 'modern' social characteristics of strong social classes, clear gender roles and party-based politics, all linked to an economic system based on industrial production, were no longer an accurate reflection of British (and most other Western) societies. Sociological theory was simply unable to explain these changes. It was in this vacuum that a new breed of theorizing emerged.

One group of writers believed that modernity had moved towards what is now commonly known as '**late modernity**' (or '**high modernity**' according to Giddens (1984)). A separate, much more radical group of theorists argued that society really had totally changed and had moved into a **postmodern** era – hence the term 'postmodernists'.

A third group of sociologists are feminists, who provide the bridge in sociological theorizing from structural and interactionist theories through to postmodern approaches.

Feminism

Gender roles and the issue of patriarchy are explored in a number of units in this book. Feminism as a social and political movement has been concerned to expose the inequalities that exist in the treatment of women in society. However, linked to this movement has been a development in theoretical approaches to explain the situation of women in society.

In many ways, feminism could be seen to be the battering ram that smashed down the closed doors of sociological thinking. Feminism initially emerged from a Marxist theoretical framework, but many feminist writers soon found this approach too constricting and moved beyond this towards more radical theories. Eventually, as we shall see later, feminism and one of its offshoots, 'queer theory', began to question some of the very basic concepts upon which sociology was built – in fact, the very notion of male and female came under attack.

Marxist feminism

The first writers in modern feminist sociology were heavily influenced by Marxist or critical sociological theories. **Marxist feminists** argued that the subordination of women to men was directly linked to their position within a capitalist society. Women benefited capitalism in two important ways:

- Women provided free domestic labour to capitalism. With the exclusion of women from paid employment in the early to mid-19th century, women remained at home to undertake 'housework'. By undertaking household tasks at no cost to the employers, women enabled men to work longer hours. By providing support, comfort and meals to the male, the workers were in a better state to work harder and more effectively.
- Women provided the means by which the next generation of workers (the children of the working class) were born and brought up – again, at no cost to the employers. Marxist feminists called this second function the '**reproduction of labour power**'.

Marxist feminists then simply adapted traditional Marxist theory to account for the situation of women. However, a number of criticisms of this approach emerged. One major criticism was that this approach was 'teleological', a way of saying that the starting point of the argument was also the conclusion. Marxist feminists believed that there had to be a reason why women were excluded from the workforce and then undertook domestic labour for men. The answer had to be (given Marxist theory) linked to it benefiting capitalism. They therefore looked for the benefits to capitalism of women working at home and came to the conclusions we have just seen. Walby (1986) points out, for example, that one could just as easily have argued that women staying at home harmed capitalism. If women were employed, they would provide competition to men for work and wages could be lowered, for example. Also, as we now know, increased income from employment for women actually increases profits for capitalism through the improved spending power of women.

Radical feminism

However, perhaps the most important criticism provided by **radical feminists** such as Millett (1970) and Firestone (1971) was that patriarchy was to be found in most societies and was not necessarily linked to capitalism. According to these writers, men and women form 'sex classes', which have very different interests and levels of power. Men are the dominant class and use their power to exploit women in any way possible, not just economically. In a famous phrase, Millett argued that the 'personal is political', by which she meant that men exploit women through and in their personal, particularly sexual, relationships. These radical feminists focused on the issues of male/female emotional relationships, their sexual activities and the routine use of violence by men against women. It was within this tradition that claims were made that 'all men are rapists' – meaning that heterosexual sexual relationships were based upon imbalances of power in which women were effectively coerced into seeing sexual intercourse within male terms. Also, as we shall see later, the radical feminists argued that same-sex relationships between women were defined as being deviant, rather than a normal alternative.

Dual systems approach

Delphy (1977) takes a slightly different approach, emphasizing, like the radical feminists, the key role of the family. Like Marxists, however, she argues that the household is an important and underrated place of work. Indeed, she refers to 'housework' as 'the domestic mode of production' and argues that the work performed by women is highly productive, and yet men dominate within the household as they have the economic power. Within the family, the views and wishes of men prevail. Some support for this position comes from studies of family poverty (Joseph Rowntree Foundation 1995) which indicate that even rates of poverty are much higher for women and children in families than for men, as men are more likely than women to spend money on themselves rather than the family.

Walby (1986) suggested that the radical-feminist and Marxist approaches could, in fact, be combined. In the **dual systems approach**, women were seen as being exploited by both capital and by men. There was, however, some degree of tension between these two systems, as we saw earlier in Walby's criticisms of the Marxist feminist approach. In the early 19th century, a series of laws were passed that restricted the hours and conditions of women (and children's) employment. These laws benefited the male workers, but disadvantaged the employers, as there were fewer people competing for work. They further benefited men by ensuring that women were dependent upon them as they had no wage. Overall, however, Walby sees capitalism and patriarchy running along together, to exploit women.

Criticisms of feminist theory

Feminist theory has not gone uncriticized. A huge amount of debate has been generated by the approaches just explored.

First, some feminist writers, notably radical feminists seem to suggest that patriarchy occurs everywhere, though in different forms. Other feminists, such as the Marxist feminists, argue instead that patriarchy is located within capitalism. Clearly, the two positions are contradictory. Furthermore, if patriarchy is universal, then this might suggest that there is some biological basis for it. This is because one of the key tests used by sociologists to prove some form of behaviour derives from 'the social' is that the behaviour either varies across societies or simply does not exist in some. However, where some behaviour is universal, then sociologists usually accept that this is biological in origin. So, if patriarchy exists across all societies, as radical feminists believe, then it could be argued that the basis lies in biology. This has led some feminist sociologists to argue that whilst women are in the stages of advanced pregnancy, childbirth and child-rearing, they are more likely to be dependent on men. Patriarchy can therefore be linked to reproduction. However, other writers, such as Walby, strongly reject this biological basis.

More recently, Delamont (2001) amongst others, has pointed out that feminist writers seem to assume that women share a common position of exploitation. She points out instead that there are many divisions between women on grounds of income and social class, ethnicity and religion.

A further development of this argument, which leads us into contemporary theory on gender and patriarchy, is that the categories 'male' and 'female' are closed and oppositional. That is the theoretical position of early feminism: that men and women are *essentially* different. However, Robert Connell (1995) has developed a rather different approach to this and suggests that the traditional notion of two sexes with one sex dominating another is too simple.

Masculinities

Once pointed out, it could seem strange that feminism spent little or no time exploring the notion of masculinity. Indeed, ideas about men in much feminist writing fail to question any of the stereotypes about men, their behaviour and attitudes. Connell has made this exploration the heart of his work on patriarchy and theory. He points out that most feminist theorizing on patriarchy has been based on exploring what *structures* constrain women. Feminist theory then debates whether it is 'the family' or 'the economic system', or possibly both together. Connell suggests that it is more useful to look at how people actually behave – what he calls their 'practices' (behaviour). Connell's work bears a resemblance to Giddens' theoretical approach, in that he sees the social world as consisting of how people behave. If they behave differently, then the supposed structures will no longer exist. The relevance to gender and patriarchy is that both men and women engage in practices that result in us believing in and actually having two sexes, male and female. The roles of women and the structure of patriarchy only exist within a framework of the practices of both men and women. Connell then sets out to disentangle what these practices are and how they maintain the roles of men and women.

According to Connell, society has a gender order: a hierarchy of different sorts of masculinities and femininities. At the top of the hierarchy is what he calls '**hegemonic masculinity**'. (The term 'hegemonic' refers to a dominant way of thinking and acting.) Heterosexuality is the foundation of hegemonic masculinity, but this also involves toughness, a degree of authority and the ability to unleash aggression. Idealized versions of this hegemonic masculinity as portrayed in the media often include sports and film stars. Most men cannot achieve this level of masculinity, but because it benefits men overall, they nevertheless support this ideal, engaging in what he calls '**complicit masculinity**'. There are other forms of 'subordinated masculinity', particularly that of 'homosexual masculinity', which is stigmatized and excluded by those who subscribe to hegemonic masculinity.

It is not just masculinity that is variable and hierarchical in form; a ladder of femininities exists too. Top of this ladder is 'emphasized femininity', which consists of 'sociability, compliance, desire for titillation and acceptance of marriage and child-rearing'.

The key point about Connell's work for feminism is that he brings a complexity to bear on the subject and an awareness that any analysis of gender has to realize that there are numerous different sorts of male and female behaviour. To speak about 'male' and 'female' as if they were two coherent and clearly distinguishable groups is mistaken. Instead, he emphasizes the importance of seeing a range of behaviours.

Late modernity and postmodernity

The distinction between late-modern and postmodern theory

Most students of sociology are understandably confused over the distinction sociologists make between late modernity (or 'high modernity') and postmodernity.

Perhaps the simplest way of dividing the two is that late modernity sees society as having changed and developed new aspects. The task of the late-modernist theory is to adapt more traditional theories of sociology.

Postmodern theorists argue that the whole 'sociological project' was part of a period of history – modernity – in which a particular way of viewing society developed that was closely related to a set of economic and social circumstances. We have now moved into a new set of economic and social circumstances based largely on communication and image, and therefore traditional sociological models have no value at all.

Late or high modernity

In the previous topic on modernism, we saw that the major split between theoretical approaches concerned which 'end' of human society sociologists emphasized. On one side of the argument were 'structural' theorists, such as Marx and Parsons, who, no matter what their differences, stressed that the only way to understand human behaviour was to locate it firmly within a dominant, controlling structural framework. Their theories suggested that people were manipulated by their cultures. On the other side, however, writers from the social action tradition, such as the interactionists, argued equally passionately that the only way to see society was as an abstract concept consisting of the interaction of individuals and groups. People were actively engaged in defining the world around them and then responding to these definitions.

By the 1980s, most sociologists began to tire of this argument and looked for ways out of it – there had to be a way to combine the two perspectives.

Giddens' structuration theory

The best known and currently highly influential attempt to resolve the argument can be found in the work of Giddens (1984). Giddens calls his theory **structuration theory**, which, as you can tell from the name, combines the concepts of structure and action.

Structure in Giddens' writings

The starting point for Giddens is that there is such a thing as structure, but only as a way to describe patterns of behaviour of people in society. Structure has no existence beyond this. He therefore rejects the traditional modernist notion of something 'out there' that determines how we behave.

<< Society only has form, and that form only has effects on people, in so far as structure is produced and reproduced in what people do. >> (Giddens and Pierson 1998)

The simple way that Giddens himself explains this is by using the example of a language. We all use a series of words and grammatical rules to communicate. We may not know all the words and we may not be aware of what the rules actually are – we just use them. The language therefore exists, but it only does so because we make it exist through our use of it. Giddens calls this 'situation'.

Bearing this in mind, structure consists of two key elements: *rules* and *resources*. Both of these combine to influence how we act:

● Rules are procedures we generally follow in everyday life. They can be formal or informal depending upon the situation and their perceived seriousness. Rules are not fixed

and may be changed over time. (Again, think of his analogy with language.)

● People have differing resources – by which he is referring to access to different levels of power. These resources consist of material resources (such as wealth and income), symbolic resources (such as personal or job-related prestige), biological resources (such as physical attractiveness) and cognitive resources (such as intelligence or skills).

The structure of society, then, consists of people following rules, but different people have different resources to deploy in order to use or amend these rules.

Agency and the duality of structure

If structure is actually only people (or '**agents**' as Giddens calls them) behaving in certain ways, then why is it important? Because, Giddens argues, people draw from society the shared stock of knowledge that they use to guide their actions (that is, 'the rules' above). People therefore make society, but in doing so give themselves the rules and structure to guide them in their actions. This intimate two-way relationship is described by Giddens as the '**duality of structure**'.

Ontological security

Ontology refers to the issues to do with the reality of the world. According to Giddens, humans have a need for a sense of security, provided by rules and resources. As he puts it, people wish to believe that the 'natural and social worlds are as they appear to be'. He describes this situation as '**ontological security**'.

The desire for security and the existence of shared understanding helps people engage in regular patterns of social life. This regularity then helps society to remain stable.

Reflexivity and transformative capacity

In seeking ontological security, people are clearly seeking stability. However, we know that people also seek to bring about social change. You may also recall from your study of functionalism (see Topic 1, p. 160) that there was a real problem with the theory in explaining social change. Giddens says that this change takes place because people are constantly monitoring their situation and their place in society, and assessing whether they match their idea of self-personality – this process is known as 'reflexive monitoring'. If people are

synoptic link   stratification and differentiation

Giddens suggests that in high modernity, social class, though still existing, has changed. He accepts that differences in power and resources exist, but he rejects the notion of social class as consisting of traditional cohesive groups (as suggested by Marxists) and argues that a much more complex pattern of stratification has replaced it. Social classes are no longer clearly hierarchical, but now overlap considerably. Social classes are also highly fragmented within themselves, with different groups existing within each class. Finally, people within classes are aware of the meaning and implication of their claims to belong to a class and are able to amend or change their self-image.

unhappy or have an ideal of what they want, then they will actively seek change. Unlike in the Marxist or functionalist view, people are not puppets controlled by others. By engaging in reflexivity, people have a '**transformative capacity**' to change society.

As a way of illustrating his theory, Giddens points to Willis' *Learning to Labour* (Willis 1977) as an example of structuration, where the young lads' choices of action and the wider structure of society interact to provide an outcome that reflects both. Willis studied a group of 12 working-class boys for 18 months at the end of their schooldays, and then briefly into their first employment. The 'lads' showed little interest in studying, as they knew that their future lay elsewhere in unskilled physical labour. At school, they passed their time by 'having a laff' in lessons and making fun of teachers and the harder-working pupils ('ear 'oles'). Their choice of behaviour in school guaranteed their school failure, thus ensuring that the future that they knew would come about for them actually did come about. When they later entered these unskilled jobs, the skills of 'having a laff' and passing time enabled them to cope with the work. To summarize, the boys made choices based on their awareness of the wider society and their place in it. It is possible that they could have made other choices, but did not do so. The interaction of their choices and the 'reality' of society resulted in the outcome they predicted.

Criticisms of Giddens

Although Giddens' work is very influential and has attracted much attention, Cuff *et al.* (1990) question how original his ideas actually are. They suggest that these are really just a collection of ideas drawn from a variety of sources. Much of Giddens' work, they suggest, goes little further than the work of some of the founders of sociology. Many would argue that Giddens is merely updating Weber. Despite Giddens claiming the originality of ideas such as 'transformative capacity', sociologists such as Craib (1992) suggest that similar ideas can also be found in Marx, who once wrote 'men make their own history albeit not in circumstances of their own choosing' or even in Parsons' concept of pattern variables. Cuff and colleagues also suggest that Giddens' theory has rarely been successfully applied, least of all by Giddens himself. Giddens has used the example of Willis' work, yet Willis himself was working from a Marxist perspective.

Beck and the sociology of risk

Another sociologist pushing forward the boundaries of sociology within the 'late modernity' framework is the German sociologist Ulrich Beck. Beck (1992/1999) argues that a central concern for all societies today is that of risk and this concept has permeated the everyday life of all of us. There are three elements to Beck's thesis: **risk society**, **reflexive modernization** and **individualization**.

Risk society

According to Beck, modernity introduced a range of 'risks' that no other historical period has ever had to face. Note that Beck uses the term 'risk' in a very specific way. Throughout history, societies have had to face a wide range of 'hazards', including famine, plague and natural disasters. However, these were always seen as beyond the control of people, being caused by such things as God or nature. Yet the risks faced by modern societies were considered to be solvable by human beings. The belief was that industrialization, public services, private insurance and a range of other supports would minimize the possibility of risk. Indeed, the very project of sociology began with a desire to control society and minimize social problems.

However, in late modernity (which Beck calls 'advanced or reflective modernization'), the risks are seen as spiralling away from human control. No longer can risks be adequately addressed to the same standards as they were in modernity. Problems such as global warming and nuclear disaster are potentially too complex for societies to deal with.

Reflexive modernization

Late modernity, in which people are reflexive (as outlined in the work of Giddens), leads to their questioning how these risks became uncontrollable – that is, they begin to question the political and technological assumptions of modernity. People begin to be aware of risk and how they as individuals are in danger. They also seek ways of minimizing risk in all spheres of their lives. Risk and risk avoidance become central to the culture of society. This helps explain the growth in control of young children by parents trying to minimize any possible risk to them from cars, paedophiles and the material they watch on television. At the level of politics, there is a huge demand for governments to seek to identify and control every possible risk.

Beck argues that although it is the global political and technological 'system' itself that is the cause of the risk, there has been little attempt to confront the problems at this level; rather, risk avoidance operates at the personal and lower political levels.

Individualization

Beck links the move towards individualization with the move away from 'tradition' as an organizing principle of society. In modern societies, most aspects of people's lives were taken for granted. Social position, family membership and gender roles, for example, were all regarded as 'given'. In late modernity, however, there has been the move towards individualization, whereby all of these are now more open to decision-making. So, the background is of risk and risk awareness, and the foreground is of people making individual choices regarding identity and lifestyle as they plan their lives.

Criticisms of Beck

Beck has been criticized by a number of writers. Turner (1994) argues that Beck's distinction between 'hazard' and 'risk' is dubious. People have always faced 'risk' and have always sought to minimize this in whatever ways were available at the time, such as religion or some other means that we might now consider of little value. Nevertheless, there was an awareness that something could be done to combat the 'hazard'.

A second criticism derives from Beck's argument that the response to risk was largely individual. Yet a range of political movements have been formed to combat global warming, eradicate poverty in Africa and stop the spread of HIV/AIDS. These are all political movements which are international in scope and which indicate that people do believe that it is possible to control the risks that Beck identifies. In July 2005, a G8 summit took place at which the richest countries in the world committed themselves to seek to resolve poverty in Africa and global warming. A series of rock concerts was also put on across the world to draw attention to the need for the G8 leaders to tackle these issues. However, in defence of Beck, his writings have been so influential that one could equally reply that it is his work that has led people to believe it is possible to challenge global threats.

Elliot (2002) argues that Beck's work fails to recognize differences in power. Beck has suggested that the risk is spread across all groups in society and that differences in power are relatively unimportant. Elliot disputes this, suggesting instead that rich and powerful groups are able to limit risk and to have greater influence on the context in which the risk occurs.

Postmodernism

Postmodernist approaches to sociology emerged in the 1980s, providing a powerful challenge to traditional 'modernist' theories that sought to create an all-encompassing theory to explain society.

Two key postmodernist writers are Baudrillard (1980, 1994) and Lyotard (1984). Although Baudrillard had originally been a Marxist academic and his early works supported a neo-Marxist perspective, he later attacked the 'grand theories' such as Marxism and functionalism. Lyotard and Baudrillard dismissed these as merely **meta-narratives**, or elaborate stories, that effectively gave comfort to people by helping them believe there was some rational, existing basis to society. According to the postmodernists, sociological theory, like science and most other academic subjects, was simply a set of stories or narratives belonging to a specific period in history – the period of modernity, whose root lie in the 18th-century historical movement known as the Enlightenment. This was the term used by those at the time for an academic movement which applied rational thought to solving scientific, economic, political and social questions. It is difficult for us today to accept that it was really not until then that academics began to believe that the natural and social worlds were governed by forces or laws that could be uncovered through scientific endeavour. The more the laws of economics and science could be uncovered, it was argued, the greater would be the progress in ridding the world of hunger, disease, war and all other problems.

The Enlightenment gave birth, in turn to modernity, the period of 19th- and 20th-century history characterized by significant technological, social and political advances in Western societies. It was within this period that sociology was born. All of the founders of sociology were very strongly influenced by the idea that societies were progressing from traditional or premodern societies through to modern ones based on science, technology and the industrial process. This belief in scientific and social progress based on the application of rational thought was taken for granted until the 1970s when the postmodernist movement began to emerge.

KEY TERMS

Agents – Giddens' term for people.

Complicit masculinity – the idea that, although most men cannot achieve an 'ideal-type' of hegemonic masculinity, they still support it, since subscribing to this model benefits them.

Dual systems approach – a feminist approach which combined elements of radical feminism and Marxist feminism.

Duality of structure – the notion that people both make society and are strongly influenced by it.

Hegemonic masculinity – a term used by Connell to describe a dominant idea of how men ought to behave.

High modernity – Giddens' term for late modernity.

Hyperreality – the idea that we live in a world that is increasingly perceived and experienced via the media.

Individualization – a decline in accepting socially approved roles and an increasing stress on personal choices.

Late modernity – a term to describe contemporary society, in which the traditional social groupings, economic organization and culture have all changed so profoundly that traditional sociological explanations no longer hold true.

Marxist feminism – feminist theorists who base their theory on an adapted version of Marxism.

Meta-narratives – a postmodernist term used to refer to the structural theories of Marxism and functionalism.

Ontological security – the idea that people want to believe there is some reality beyond them in society, giving them the psychological confidence to engage in interaction.

Postmodern – a different perspective on contemporary society that rejects modernism and its attempts to explain the world through overarching theories. Instead, it suggests that there is no single, shared reality and focuses attention on the significance of the media in helping to construct numerous realities.

Radical feminism – feminist theorists (and usually political activists) who see men and male behaviour as the main cause of women's position in society.

Reflexive modernization – the idea that risk avoidance becomes a major factor in social organization.

Reflexivity – Giddens' term for the ability to perceive yourself as others see you and to create your own identity.

Reproduction of labour power – term used by Marxist feminists to explain the role of women in helping capitalism to renew itself by producing new children and socializing them.

Risk society – Beck suggests that contemporary societies are best characterized as ones where people are aware that they face complex risks that are not open to individual control.

Sign-objects – Baudrillard's term for the notion that we buy items to express ourselves, not for their function.

Simulacrum (plural 'simulacra') – media images that have no basis in reality, but which people increasingly model their behaviour upon.

Structuration theory – the term used for Giddens' theory, which seeks to combine both structural and social action theories.

Transformative capacity – the ability of people to change society.

At their simplest, postmodern theories argue that there cannot be any overarching theoretical explanation of society. This is because society exists only as a reassuring 'narrative'. In order to understand society as it is today, we need to have a deep awareness of the role of the media in creating an image of society that we seek to live out.

Lyotard

Lyotard argues that economic expansion and growth, and the scientific knowledge upon which they are based, have no aim but to continue expanding. This expansion is outside the control of human beings as it is too complex and simply beyond our scope. In order to make sense of this, to give ourselves a sense of control over it and to justify the ever-expanding economic system, grand narratives have been developed. These are political and social theories and explanations that try to make sense of society, which in reality is out of control. Marxism and functionalism and all other sociological theories fall into this category. The role of sociology, therefore, has been to justify and explain, while the reality of life for most people has simply not accorded with the sociological explanations. Lyotard sees contemporary society not as described in sociological theories, but as one that consists of isolated individuals linked by few social bonds.

Baudrillard

Baudrillard is also a critic of contemporary society. Like Lyotard, he sees people as isolated and dehumanized. Lyotard was particularly interested in the notion of knowledge as serving to justify the narratives of postmodern society. He argued that knowledge was a commodity that was bought and sold, and this buying was usually undertaken by big business and government. The result was that what people know about the world (knowledge) was that filtered through business and government. Baudrillard was also interested in the way that knowledge and understanding of the world are created, but his main emphasis was on the media.

The death of the social

Baudrillard notes that, in contemporary societies, the mass of the population expresses a lack of interest in social solidarity and in politics. The hallmark of this postmodern society is the consumption of superficial culture, driven by marketing and advertising. People live isolated lives sharing common consumption of the media, through which they experience the world. According to Baudrillard this can best be described as the 'death of the social'.

Media and the experience of the world

The media play a central role in the death of the social. Baudrillard argues that people now have limited direct experience of the world and so rely on the media for the vast majority of their knowledge. As well as gaining their ideas of the world from the media, the bulk of the population are also influenced in how they behave by the same media. Rather than the media reflecting how people behave, Baudrillard argues that people increasingly reflect the media images of how people behave. Of course, at some point, the two move so close together that the media do start once again to mirror actual behaviour, as actual behaviour 'catches up' with the media images.

Sign-objects and the consumer society

In the 21st century, a significant proportion of Western societies are affluent. Members of those societies are able to consume a large number of commodities and enjoy a range of leisure activities. However, Baudrillard argues that this consumption moves people ever further away from social relationships and ever closer to relationships with their consumer lifestyles. Yet the importance of objects in our lives has little to do with their use to us, but much more to do with what meaning they have for us. We purchase items not just because they are functionally useful, but because they signify that we are successful or fashionable. Consumer goods and leisure activities are, in Baudrillard's terms, '**sign-objects**', as we are consuming the image they provide rather than the article or service itself.

Hyperreality and the simulacrum

Baudrillard argues that, in modern society, it is generally believed that real things or concepts exist and then are given names or 'signs'. Signs, therefore, reflect reality. In postmodern society, however, signs exist that have no reality but themselves. The media have constructed a world that exists simply because it exists – for example, take the term 'celebrity'. A celebrity is someone who is defined as a celebrity, they do not have to have done anything or have any particular talent. It is not clear how one becomes a celebrity nor how one stays a celebrity. Being a celebrity occurs as long as one is regarded as a celebrity. Where a signs exists without any underlying reality, Baudrillard terms it a '**simulacrum**'. He believes that the society in which we live is now increasingly based upon simulacra. The fact that so much of our lives are based upon signs that have no basis or reality has led Baudrillard to suggest that we now live in a world of '**hyperreality**' – a world of image.

Check your understanding

1 **Explain the differences between Marxist feminists and radical feminists.**

2 **What does Connell mean by 'hegemonic masculinity'?**

3 **Why is social structure like a language, according to Giddens?**

4 **What is the difference between late-modern and postmodern theory?**

5 **What is a 'risk society'?**

6 **Explain in your own words the term 'hyperreality'.**

Criticisms of postmodernism

Postmodernism has been very influential in sociology and can probably claim to have generated the huge growth in the academic subject of media studies. However, its success has been more in pointing to the failure of grand theories rather than in putting anything positive in its place. Of course, postmodernists in reply would argue that that is precisely their point! Baudrillard or Lyotard, though they reject any idea of value-free sociology, do appear to be more critics of society than sociological theorists. Their work is shot through with value-judgements about what is real and what is worthwhile – so their dismissal of contemporary media-based society is less a sociological statement than a political one. Postmodernists have also been criticized for their failure to accept that not everything is hyperreal. People do live in reality, and some people have much greater access to goods and services than others.

exploring feminist, late-modern & postmodern theories

Item A

In modern societies self-identity becomes an inescapable issue. Even those who would say that they have never given any thought to questions or anxieties about their own identity will inevitably have been compelled to make significant choices throughout their lives, from everyday questions about clothing, appearance and leisure to high-impact decisions about relationships, beliefs and occupations. Whilst earlier societies with a social order based firmly in tradition would provide individuals with (more or less) clearly defined roles, in post-traditional societies we have to work out our roles for ourselves.

The mass media is also likely to influence individuals' perceptions of their relationships. Whether in serious drama, or celebrity gossip, the need for 'good stories' would always support an emphasis on change in relationships. Since almost nobody on TV remains happily married for a lifetime – whether we're talking about fictional characters or real-life public figures – we inevitably receive a message that monogamous heterosexual stability is, at best, a rare 'ideal', which few can expect to achieve. We are encouraged to reflect on our relationships in magazines and self-help books (explicitly), and in movies, comedy and drama (implicitly). This knowledge is then 'reappropriated' by ordinary people, often lending support to non-traditional models of living. Information and ideas from the media do not merely *reflect* the social world, then, but contribute to its shape, and are central to modern reflexivity.

Adapted from Gauntlett, D. (2002) *Media, Gender and Identity*, London: Routledge

Item B

The aspect of Madonna that strikes one most is her use of image. Martin Amis has said: 'She is the self-sufficient postmodern phenomenon ... A masterpiece of controlled illusion.'

In many ways Madonna is a victim of her own image. She lives totally within the artificially constructed reality of the image. She has become one with her Image. But she is not alone in that. This is central, not just to Madonna, but also to our culture. Think of the tremendous developments of our technological age and the impact of the media that has come with it; image is dominating more and more of our lives. And increasingly we see the blurring of image and reality, the fusing of the public and private persona, the dissolving of the differences, so that everything becomes image, and reality disappears. In politics, style replaces substance, in commerce packaging and promotion replace quality, in society how you look replaces who you are, form replaces content, the outer presentation replaces the inner reality.

Adapted from the website of 'Facing the Challenge' (www.facingthechallenge.org/madonna.htm)

1 (a) Identify **two** examples of significant choices people now have to make about their lives (**Item A**). (2 marks)

(b) Identify the **two** theoretical approaches associated with **Items A and B**. (4 marks)

(c) Identify and briefly explain the terms 'self-identity' and 'reflexive' (**Item A**). (4 marks)

(d) With reference to **Items A and B** and and elsewhere, briefly examine how late-modern and postmodern approaches argue that the media can affect identity. (10 marks)

2 Assess the contribution of feminism to our understanding of society. (40 marks)

Sociology and science

I RECENTLY TOOK PART in the filming of a TV celebrity game show. I was leading the game, but growing increasingly itchy to escape, so when the cameras were off momentarily, I requested that my fellow contestants vote me off, so I could get out of there as fast as possible.

They complied graciously and I left the set, then settled into the back seat of the Mercedes they'd mercifully sent for me and relaxed into the overwhelming relief at having made my getaway.

However, I suddenly felt ashamed of myself. First, I'd lent my presence and energy to a strain of the culture I abhor and so had gone against my own principles. Secondly, this found me in the position of having to vote someone off, something I found extremely hard. Thirdly, I … should have overridden my intense restlessness for the sake of winning and stayed the course.

By the time I arrived home, I felt as if I'd prostituted myself. I noticed that with this came a fall in energy levels, a feeling of exhaustion and a drop in my immune system, which triggered the start of a cold. This got my healer's mind working on how to clear shame as quickly as possible when it arises, for while it serves to point out our weaknesses, once these have been noted and acknowledged with a view to self-correction, to indulge it further is merely to beat ourselves up, and hence cause weakness throughout the mind–body–soul complex. So, I started by having a shower to cleanse my soul. Then I did some t'ai chi to rebuild my strength. Then I took some Bach Flower remedy of crab apple, which addresses shame and feeling inwardly dirty. Finally, I forgave myself for being human, weak and fallible. In addition to this short shame-dissolving routine, as mentioned in a previous column, unresolved shame, according to the Taoist view, resides in your buttocks. Place a palm over each buttock and wobble your buttocks with gusto, as this releases the memories trapped there. If you go for it now, watch for possible shameful memories it may throw up. If any arise, breathe in deeply, as if wrapping the memories into a bundle inside the breath, exhale fully and see the bundle escape into the air and dissolve. Inhale again, say, 'I forgive myself all my transgressions now – by forgiving myself now, I ensure I will not repeat my mistakes', and carry on as you were – except now, hopefully feeling refreshed and renewed.

The Observer, Sunday 11 July 2004

The extract above is taken from a weekly column on alternative health in *The Observer*.

1 **What is your initial reaction to the advice given?**

2 **What reasons can you give for this reaction?**

3 **If you were suffering from a serious illness and you could choose between the treatment offered by your doctor or that from an alternative practitioner, such as those above, which would you choose. (No, you cannot have both!) Give reasons for your choice.**

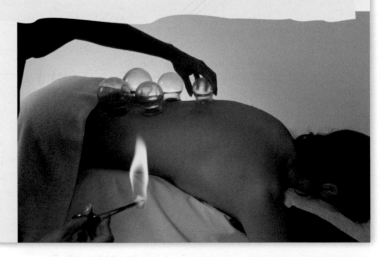

If you decided to choose conventional Western treatment, you may have done so because modern Western medicine is based on science, and scientific explanations dominate modern societies. Perhaps sociology, too, can provide scientific explanations of the social world.

But there may have been some doubt in your mind. Why should you trust a doctor? Who is to say that other ways of dealing with illness don't work? For sociology, equally, striving to become a 'science' may not be the best path.

Why sociology claims to be a 'social science'

For at least 100 years, sociologists have argued among themselves as to whether or not sociology is a science. For most students coming to the subject for the first time, this seems a fairly pointless debate – after all, who cares how you classify the subject, just get on with it!

But the issue was, and still is, very important. The existence of sociology as an academic subject was for a long time tied up with its acceptance as a science, because both funding and academic prestige are more likely to be gained when subjects are regarded as 'scientific'. This is largely based on the idea that scientific knowledge is superior to other forms of knowledge.

Sources of knowledge

As the introductory exercise showed, we trust some forms of knowledge more than others. However, in daily lives, people mix knowledge from different sources without thinking much about it. Wallace (1971) argues that, in all, there are four sources that we use to gain our knowledge about the world. These are as follows:

- *Authoritarian sources* derive from a person viewed as a source of true wisdom providing information for us. Because of our belief in this person's wisdom, we accept the explanation as true. This is similar to the way a young child will see their parents as the source of wisdom on most matters.
- *Mystical source* refer to somebody claiming an insight into the true nature of the world through some drug-fuelled or religious experience. Regular users of LSD and ecstasy claim that these drugs provide an insight into the real world beyond conventional barriers.
- *Logico-rational* sources of knowledge are based upon following the rules of logic – essentially, this is 'truth' that emerges from the work of philosophers.
- Finally, *scientific knowledge* rests upon generating ideas and hypotheses, and then rigorously testing them, through a variety of accepted methodologies.

According to Wallace, scientific knowledge is superior to other sources of knowing in its use of rigorous methods by which others can replicate or refute claims made. He suggests that this is not the case with the other three sources of knowledge. This means, then, that it is really the superior methodology of science that sets it apart from other sources of knowledge. Therefore, the effectiveness and accuracy of methods form the key to science. Any subject, such as sociology, which claims to be a science has therefore to pay great attention to the quality of the methods it uses.

Funding

Subjects receive funding for research from government departments, charities and commerce if they are seen to be 'scientific' and so more likely to produce reliable data that can be useful for these organizations. Subjects that are not seen as being 'scientific' (such as astrology, **parapsychology** and fortune-telling) are much less likely to receive the financial support of these organizations.

Prestige

The prestige of a subject is closely connected with its funding. For well over 200 years, according to Shapin (1995), the status of 'science' as the basis of knowledge, and of scientific

focus on research

Penelope Scott
Black people's health: ethnic status and research issues

A good example of the link between scientific status and receiving funding is given by Penelope Scott. Scott (1999) wanted to study the illness diabetes and its effect on British people of Caribbean descent. She planned to use qualitative interviews. Her attempts to obtain funding from the British Diabetic Association were initially turned down as the approach she used was not regarded as being sufficiently scientifically rigorous. Scott suggests that the perception of her research as lacking rigour occurred because the BDA was heavily influenced by a statistically based medical model of how research should be carried out. The more 'scientific' the approach she used – that is the more she used statistical models and followed the traditional 'positivistic' approach (see Topic 2) – the greater the likelihood of obtaining research funding.

Scott, P. (1999) 'Black people's health: ethnic status and research issues', in S. Hood, B. Mayall and S. Oliver (eds) *Critical Issues in Social Research*, Buckingham: Open University Press

1 Why might the method used by Scott be seen as 'unscientific'?

2 Suggest a method that might have been seen as more rigorous and scientific. Explain your answer.

methodology as the most effective way of researching, has been the pre-eminent method of understanding and studying the world. This reflects the dominance of modernist forms of thought (see Topics 1 and 2), which dominated all forms of thinking and social organization from the 18th century until recently – when it has been challenged by late-modern or postmodern ways of thinking and forms of social organization.

The result of sociology enjoying scientific prestige has been access to research funding, availability of the subject at A-level and university, and academic posts for people to teach it. According to Giddens (1976), much of the story of early sociology (indeed right up to the 1960s) was the promotion of sociology as a science by all the major sociologists, such as Weber, Durkheim, Merton and Parsons.

What is a science?

The modernist approach to science claims that it can be distinguished from other forms of knowledge by the way in which it goes about the process of understanding the world. This modernist approach stresses five key components that distinguish science from other forms of knowledge. Science is:

- empirical
- theoretical
- objective.
- testable
- cumulative

Empirical

By **empirical** we mean, in the strictest sense, 'knowable through our senses'. In practice, it means that the information can be counted or measured. The tradition comes from the philosopher Locke, who lived and wrote in the 17th century. He was arguing against metaphysical explanations of the world, which relied solely upon assuming that objects and powers existed beyond the 'physical realm'. Magic, some areas of religion and astrology are all metaphysical ways of explaining the world that cannot be proven (or disproved) and so cannot be empirical.

Testable

This leads us on to a crucial point about the importance of empirical knowledge – that it can be tested and revisited as many times as needed. This means that the knowledge gained is open to **verification** or **refutation** by others.

According to Karl Popper (1959), once knowledge is put forward for scrutiny, it should be possible to engage in the process of **falsification** – that is, that the empirical model can be tested with the aim of showing it to be false. Only if all tests have been applied and the knowledge still seems accurate, can scientists assume that it is the best existing explanation. .

Theoretical

Many students comment that good investigative journalism is the same as sociology in that it searches out 'the truth' behind events. This is not an accurate observation, however, because one of the main distinguishing features of sociology, like science, is that of theory construction. A theory seeks to uncover **causal** relationships between phenomena rather than simply describing these phenomena.

Cumulative

Scientific theory, it is claimed, builds on previous knowledge, so that there is an ever-growing, empirically testable body of such knowledge that moves us forward in our understanding of the world.

Objective

We discuss the question of objectivity in some detail in Topic 9, but the key issue here is that science blocks out personal prejudices and political views in its search for empirically testable propositions about the world.

The scientific tradition in sociology

As we have seen, traditionally, sociology has sought to be recognized as a science, and one school of sociology – the **positivist** one – has modelled its approach as closely as it can on the physical (or **natural**) **sciences**. The tradition began with the work of Comte and Quetelet, two founding fathers of sociology. They argued that philosophizing about the world was not enough. Statistics needed to be gathered so that cause and effect could be properly proven.

In a similar manner to the way physicists and biologists study the physical world, sociologists adopting the scientific approach seek to uncover general laws and relationships that they believe exist in the social world. Extreme examples of this approach include the work of Durkheim (1951) (for example, his study of suicide) see Unit 5, Topic 12), and also Karl Marx (1867/1973). Indeed, Marx's work was a lifelong attempt to show that there were laws of economics that would inevitably lead to a communist society.

Much later, the main sociological opposition to Marxist ideas came from Talcott Parsons and the **structural–functionalist school** he founded. Once again, Parsons (1951) was intent upon showing that society existed as a structure and that there were forces and social laws that existed independently of

synoptic link   stratification and differentiation

Karl Marx's theory of stratification was developed in the mid-19th century as part of his attempt to uncover the social laws that he believed controlled society. Marx fully subscribed to the idea that the scientific approach to studying society would eventually lead towards a full understanding of the dynamics of social processes. His analysis saw social classes as an inevitable outcome of industrialism and, equally inevitable, that class conflict would occur – with the final outcome being the collapse of the ruling class and the emergence of a communist society.

Although there are still some sociologists who subscribe to Marx's view of the inevitability of these social processes, most point to the move towards the fragmentation of social class and the growth of a more complex society based on consumption and identities formed on the basis of ethnicity, religion, gender, sexual orientation and income. The belief in the existence of scientific laws similar to the physical laws 'of nature' have very largely been discounted in sociology.

individuals. What is interesting, however, is that though Parsons and Marx were in total opposition, politically and theoretically, they both shared the belief that sociology is a science.

Throughout this and any other textbook of sociology, you will find endless examples of studies that are based on generalized statements about how humans will act in certain circumstances and what factors cause this. Explicitly or not, these approaches support the view of sociology as a science.

The work of Durkheim and Marx combined theory with a search for the evidence to support their ideas. However, another, parallel, approach, which was highly sympathetic to the vision of sociology as a science, was developed in the 19th century through the study of working-class life in Britain. This empirical work, which first emerged in the writings of Mayhew (1851) and Rowntree (1901), formed the basis of the British empirical tradition. (Here, information is gathered about various social phenomena, e.g. the lives of the poor, for its own sake, or to influence social policy.) However, the work never set out to be theoretical. This tradition has remained the most common form of sociological research funded by government and charities. These sorts of empirical studies cover issues such as educational success, crime rates, illegal drug use, and so on.

How do writers justify sociology as a science?

In order to understand this, we need to go back to the elements of science we looked at earlier.

Theoretical

Scientists who are dubious about sociology's claim to scientific status point out that natural objects are predictable because they simply react, whereas people have free will and are, therefore, not predictable. This makes a theoretical statement that involves making a general prediction (if X occurs, then Y will act in this way) impossible in sociology. However, although we cannot predict how individuals will act, we can predict how *groups in general* will act. For example, Durkheim claimed that there are clearly distinguishable patterns of suicide, with certain groups having distinctive rates over a number of years.

Empirical and testable

Natural scientists argue that in the physical world, there are phenomena that exist independently of the scientists, such as such as temperature and density. The scientist merely has to measure these phenomena. In contrast, they argue, society is created by people, and there are no phenomena 'out there' waiting to be measured.

For those sympathetic to the view that sociology is a science, this seems an unfair criticism. They argue that, although ultimately the creation of society, there are a wide range of phenomena that do exist separately from individuals, and that constrain and limit our behaviour (again, a possible answer to critics regarding free will). For example we are born into a society where a particular language exists and we have to conform to that language. It is in Durkheim's words a 'social fact' that exists independently and can be measured in an objective way. Theories can thus be tested to see whether they are true or false.

Cumulative

Again, like all sciences, sociological knowledge is cumulative. Sociologists have built up knowledge over time and accumulated a stock of knowledge about society. It is this cumulative information that forms the current-day sociology that you are studying.

Objective

A major criticism of sociology as a science is that if it deals with issues and concerns about which we all have strong feelings, then how is it possible for sociologists to be objective? Won't their values emerge in their choice of subject and their methods of study? This is a complex subject, so much so that we have devoted the whole of Topic 9 to it. However, positivist sociologists argue that it *is* possible to be value-free by adhering rigorously to the methodological process discussed below.

The methodological process in sociology

We saw earlier that there is a traditional process followed by physical scientists. Many of them argue that sociology is simply unable to follow this. We look at this in detail later in Topic 4, which deals with positivism, but critics have particularly concentrated on the difficulty of undertaking experiments in sociology. Sociologists have answered this by arguing that the sociological equivalent of an experiment is the **comparative method** (or multivariate analysis), as used by Weber to explain the emergence of capitalism in Britain and by Durkheim in his study of suicide (see Unit 5, Topic 12). The comparative method involves comparing societies to find out key differences that might explain different social phenomena.

Sociological criticisms of sociology as a science – and of science as a science!

So far, the dominant voices we have listened to in this topic have been those supporting the notion of sociology as a science. However, since the 1960s, especially with the growth of interactionist and later postmodern writings, there has been a range of criticisms from within sociology as to whether it can, or even should, claim to be a science.

Differences between the nature of society and the physical world

The first criticism comes from those who argue that the society is not comparable to the social world and to attempt to transfer the methods and ideas of the natural sciences is mistaken. This argument is less about methods and more about the reality of the world around us. Is there an objective world outside that exists independently of us, or is the world somehow 'constructed' through the ideas and activities of human beings? For Durkheim and all those who have followed his original ideas, the answer is clearly that there is a social structure that exists independently of our feelings and ideas. Therefore, the scientific approach can clearly be used. For many other sociologists, starting with Schutz (1972), there is no social world beyond our existence. Society only has an existence through the activities and beliefs of people and any attempt to study society has to recognize that we start from 'inside' the very thing we are trying to study. For Schutz, and many writers after him, the attempt to separate oneself from society and explore it as an outsider, is simply impossible. Schutz sees the role of sociology as being to explore the meanings that people construct – not to look for an external set of explanations.

Inappropriate scientific method

The second set of criticisms is based on the idea that scientific methods actually inhibit sociological research. Billig argues that this methodological straightjacket that scientific-oriented sociologists have imposed upon sociology actually gets in the way of scholarship (Billig *et al* 1998). Billig claims that historically, academics read widely across a range of texts and disciplines and then, based upon that, they presented new ideas and insights. Methodology was important, but more important was allowing people freedom to think of new ideas. According to Billig, contemporary sociology that attempts to be scientific actually limits itself within a narrow sphere of thinking and loses the point of the sociological enterprise. This argument reflects the earlier work of C.W. Mills (1959), who argued that the aim of theory and method is to enable what he calls the **sociological imagination** to be freed so that the sociologist can see 'underlying forms and tendencies of society' that others might miss. Being chained to a set of assumptions will block this 'imagination'.

Sociology as a social product of modernity

Bauman (2000) locates the desire to be seen as scientific within the broader context of the dominance of modernity and modernist thinking during the period of sociology's development. Bauman argues that science only held higher prestige because it reflected ways of thinking and social organizations that existed within the historical period known as modernity. Bauman further suggests that the key theme that all the original sociologists from Durkheim, Weber, Marx and even Parsons later in the middle of the 20th century struggled with was the question of *social order*. How was it that society, composed of millions of independently thinking individuals, did not collapse in chaos? This question was actually a central concern of modernity and so sociology was reflecting existing concerns and ideas (or 'paradigms' in Kuhn's terminology); it was not providing brand new insights at all.

Sociology ended up focusing on social class, 'race' and 'the family', thereby reflecting concerns, not innovating. Sociology was driven, therefore, not by some novel insights in to human behaviour, but by the desire to reflect wider social concerns.

But as late modernity/postmodernity has emerged, these structures and this 'doing remarkably similar things in similar circumstances' have weakened and are less important. Instead, people are much more self-aware in terms of image and self-seeking in terms of identities. The family, for example, is characterized by a range of alternative, more flexible and sexually diverse relationships. In late modernity, according to Bauman, the place of social science is therefore superfluous – and can be replaced by sociological thinking.

Is science a science?

Increasingly, natural science itself has come under fire for not matching the criteria of science discussed above. From the 1960s onwards, a number of sociologists began to put science itself 'under the microscope'. They found the traditional model of viewing science as a form of superior provider of knowledge was, to say the least, questionable. They suggest that if science itself does not actually fulfil the conditions of being a science, then why should sociology be so obsessed with it?

The paradigm critique

Kuhn (1962/1970) argues that one crucial element of science – that of cumulative progress – cannot be true. Kuhn argues instead that 'normal science' operates within a **paradigm** (or accepted framework of concepts regarding a particular area of knowledge). This framework includes assumptions regarding what is important, the correct procedures, and the right sort of questions to be asking. This paradigm dominates scientific thinking, and traps thought and investigation within it. Any attempt to step outside the accepted conventions is usually ignored and rejected.

Science changes in a series of scientific revolutions that create their own new paradigms, rather than through the accumulation of knowledge. Kuhn suggests that over time there is a gradual build-up of evidence that does not fit into the accepted paradigm and out of this unease emerges a distinctively new explanation that can accommodate the previous inconsistencies. A new paradigm is born and the process begins again. Kuhn calls this the 'process of scientific revolutions'.

Kuhn is himself not free from critics, however. Lakatos (1970), for example, has argued that Kuhn's idea of paradigms is too simplistic and only applies to the past, in relation to the abandonment of ideas regarding the earth being flat, or being the centre of the universe. Modern science is largely open and much more sophisticated in its thinking. Rarely in modern science have central ideas been abandoned.

Anti-methodology

Feyerabend (1975) argues that science has developed in an 'anarchic way' and the belief that there has been a gradual, coherent and cumulative advance in knowledge is completely wrong. Instead, he characterizes advances in science as chance, incoherence, sudden leaps forward and dead-ends. The false history that has been created is holding back scientists, as they seek to follow a false set of methodological procedures.

Experiments and open/closed systems

Sayer (1992) has pointed out that the model of the physical sciences presented to the public may be misleading. He argues that we need to distinguish between open and closed systems.

Sciences such as chemistry or physiology operate in closed systems, in which all **variables** can be controlled. This allows

The British Crime Survey is a yearly study of the crime levels in England and Wales. Each year, approximately 40 000 people are questioned about the crimes they believe have been committed against them. Government policy towards combating crime (particularly all the legislation on antisocial behaviour) is strongly influenced by the results of the study. The BCS is fully funded by the government and is regarded as the single most prestigious source of crime statistics. The study rigorously adheres to scientific values, using questionnaires that are devised by eminent criminological researchers who then can spend anything up to a year computing and analysing the findings. However, there are some significant problems:

- The BCS excludes the single largest group of victims of crime – those under 16 years of age.
- The ways in which the research measures fear of crime has been criticized for exaggerating actual levels of fear, partly by the way the questions are constructed, but also for the way the survey focuses on the fear.
- The BCS allows people to categorize criminal acts according to their own definitions – not the legal ones. The researchers then reclassify into types of crime according to their views of what the appropriate category is.

Critics therefore claim that this 'scientific study' then reflects the interests of the more powerful (older people), and their concerns (fear of crime), whilst excluding the views of the less powerful (people under 16). Finally, the actual classification of statistics are the construction of the sociologists who compute and analyse the findings, rather than those of the victims.

experiments to be carried out. However, other physical sciences such as meteorology and **seismology**, operate in open systems, in which the variables cannot be controlled. These sciences recognize unpredictability. Seismology cannot predict when earthquakes will occur, though it does understand the conditions leading to earthquakes. Meteorologists can explain the forces producing weather, but the actual weather itself is difficult to predict. So, certain sciences therefore do not necessarily follow the process which it is claimed is a hallmark of science.

From Sayer's viewpoint (known as **realism**) the social sciences are no different from many physical sciences. Their aim ought to be the uncovering of the relationship between the wider structures that determine the way we relate to other people in everyday life. For example, we can only understand the relationship between a student and teacher by referring to the education system, inequalities of power, the aim of education, and so on.

The feminist critique of science

Feminist sociologists, too, raise doubts on the status accorded to science. Their criticisms are based on three main concerns.

- According to Harding (1986), the (ontological) assumptions science has about society are based upon male perceptions and understandings. Mainstream knowledge is therefore really '**malestream**' knowledge. Women understand and experience the world in different ways from men and so male and female research is intrinsically different.

- Until recently, the majority of sociological studies were based on males – particularly in education, stratification and crime. Thus, as Hart (1994) says, until the 1990s we knew a lot about the lives of men and boys, but relatively little about women and girls.
- Research should not be neutral, but ought instead to be driven by the desire to change the world. Ramazanoglu (1992) has argued that the role of feminist sociology ought to be transforming gender relationships in such a way to bring about the equality of females with males. This underlying aim should therefore penetrate the subjects being studied and the methods used.

Modernity, postmodernity and science

Science and modernity have gone hand in hand, according to Rorty (1980), with the belief that rationality, truth, and science are all bound together, and that other ways of knowing the world are inferior.

Postmodernists challenge this view. For Rorty, scientists have simply replaced priests as the sources of truth. We want someone to be the experts and to make sense of the world for us. Science has taken on this role. Yet we now know that, despite the advances in science there may well be concepts and questions that it can never answer – questions about the origins of the universe, the concept of infinity, and so on.

Lyotard (1984) has also shown that the nature of language limits and channels science because if provides a framework to approach an understanding of the world. Language both opens up possibilities and closes down others since we think within language and are unable to conceive of something that is outside our linguistic framework. This is very similar to Bauman's critique of modernist sociology.

Science and values

We have noted before that sociology has problems in disentangling values from the research process. However, so, too, does science. Scientists do not work in an ideal world. Those who fund their research lead the direction of the work, and not all science necessarily benefits the world. Cigarettes are the result of 'science', yet are the biggest killer of adults in the more affluent societies. Pharmaceutical companies have produced numerous drugs that have been directly harmful to society, including heroin, thalidomide and barbiturates. Beck (1992) has pointed out that science has actually created new and serious risks for society – for example, pollution and global warming.

Sociology and science: the debate in a nutshell

Our discussion so far has suggested the following.

- Sociology has sought scientific status in order to obtain status and acceptance as an academic subject.
- Critics from the traditional sciences have argued that sociology does not meet the criteria of science both in terms of the components (theory, objectivity, etc.) and in terms of the process (**hypothesis**, experiment, etc.)
- One group of sociologists – who have been called positivistic sociologists – have rejected this criticism and have claimed that sociology can and does achieve the criteria to make it a social science.

- However, if we look critically at the nature of science itself, it would appear that the natural sciences also fail the criteria of being a science.
- Postmodernists argue that the whole debate itself is a reflection of outdated notions of a fixed, knowable world out there, waiting to be discovered. They argue instead that all knowledge is relative to the world of those who seek it, and that it is bounded by constraints of language and of culture.

So is sociology a science?

There is no simple answer to this question. According to writers such as Bhaskar (1986) and Sayer (1992), sociology can be as scientific as the natural sciences by adopting certain procedures. At the other extreme, postmodernists such as Rorty (1980) or Bauman (1978) would argue that the real question is why sociology would want to be seen as a science. They go on to say that the whole debate reflects the process of modernity – a period which we are now leaving.

Somewhere in the middle lie the bulk of sociologists who accept that there is a debate over the scientific nature of sociological study, but who get on with their research, attempting to make sense of society in the best and most honest way they can

web.task

Search for the websites of two pressure groups dealing with the issue of smoking: Ash (anti-smoking) and Forest (defending smokers' interests). Examine the research they refer to regarding cigarette smoking – are there crucial differences between them? It is worth noting that Forest receives about 90 per cent of its funding from the cigarette companies. What does this debate tell you about science, values and research.

Check your understanding

1. **Why has it been considered important that sociology should be classified as a 'science'?**

2. **What are the elements of a science?**

3. **What do we mean by 'falsification'?**

4. **What do we mean by the 'British empirical tradition'?**

5. **What was Kuhn's criticism of the cumulative element of science?**

6. **Explain the difference between closed and open systems of science.**

7. **Why is an understanding of modernity and post-modernity relevant to the debate on the nature of science?**

research ideas

1. Identify a range of behaviour and beliefs in phenomena that science cannot fully explain. You might think about religious and supernatural beliefs, fortune-telling, astrology, superstition and alternative therapies, for example.

2. Use interviews to discover the extent to which a sample of people believe in or have used these non-scientific approaches. What do your results tell us about trust in science today?

Causal relationship – a relationship between two factors in which one causes the other.

Comparative method – a method that involves comparing societies to find out key differences that might explain different social phenomena.

Empirical sociology – refers to sociologists who tend to conduct quantitative studies and tend not to theorize.

Falsification – the testing of an empirical model with the aim of showing it to be false.

Hypothesis – an initial plausible guess concerning the causal relationship between events.

Malestream – originally a feminist term implying criticism of traditional sociology for excluding women from the subject both as sociologists and as the subjects of research.

Natural sciences – see 'Physical sciences'.

Paradigm – a framework of thought that provides the way in which we approach and understand an issue.

Parapsychology – a disputed branch of psychology which studies a range of experiences such as mind-to-mind communication.

Physical sciences – the scientific study of the physical world. These include chemistry, physics, biology, botany, etc.

Positivists – those advocating an approach that supports the belief that the way to gain knowledge is by following the conventional scientific model.

Realism – the view that sociology should aim to uncover the relationship between the wider structures that determine the way we relate to other people in everyday life.

Refutation – showing something to be false.

Seismology – the study of earthquakes.

Sociological imagination – coined by C.W. Mills to suggest that as well as good methodology, sociologists should develop an open and questioning mind.

Structural-functionalist school – a version of society that starts by asking what function for a society a social phenomenon performs, e.g. 'What does the family do for society?' Associated with Talcott Parsons.

Variable – a social phenomenon that changes in response to another phenomenon.

Verification – showing something to be true.

exploring sociology and science

Item A

What Durkheim meant by this was that it was necessary to abandon all preconceived ideas and to study things as they really are. He held that all sciences must do this if they are to be objective and of any practical value. The transformation of alchemy into chemistry and astrology in astronomy occurred because the practitioners of the new sciences abandoned the common-sense preconceptions that they relied upon in their everyday lives. Instead they made direct observations of natural phenomena and constructed theories that could explain them. Sociology, Durkheim argued must move in the same direction…

Fulcher, J. and Scott, J. (2003) *Sociology* (2nd edn) Oxford: Oxford University Press

Item B

The history of science … does not just consist of facts and conclusions drawn from those facts. It also contains ideas, interpretations of facts, problems created by conflicting interpretations, mistakes and so on. On closer analysis we find that even science knows no 'bare facts' at all but that the 'facts' that enter our knowledge are already viewed in a certain way and are, therefore, socially created. This being the case, the history of science will be as complex, chaotic, full of mistakes and entertaining as the ideas it contains, and these ideas in turn will be as complex, chaotic, full of mistakes and entertaining as are the minds of those who invented them. Conversely, a little brainwashing will go a long way in making the history of science duller, simpler, more uniform, more objective and more easily accessible to treatment by strict unchangeable rules.

1 (a) **Identify the approach to sociology advocated by Durkheim (Item A). (2 marks)**

(b) **Identify two factors that are needed for practitioners to transform their subjects into sciences (Item A). (4 marks)**

(c) **Identify and briefly explain two problems with 'facts' identified in Item B. (6 marks)**

(d) **With reference to the Items and elsewhere, briefly examine the view that it is possible to study society objectively. (8 marks)**

2 **Evaluate the view that sociology can and should be seen as a science. (40 marks)**

Positivism and quantitative research methods

gettingyouthinking

Design a survey aimed at finding how happy young people are in Britain today.

1 Write down a detailed, step-by-step plan of what you are going to do.

2 How are you going to define and measure happiness?

3 To what extent do you think the results of your survey will give you an accurate picture of the distribution of happiness?

4 What problems are involved in trying to represent concepts such as 'happiness' in figures?

5 Do you think it is possible to measure feelings, beliefs or ideas?

We saw in the previous topic that there is considerable debate between sociologists over the scientific status of sociology. However, the fact is that in order to do their job, sociologists have to put this aside and get on with their research. Rather than splitting them into two completely irreconcilable camps, it is perhaps better to think of sociologists as being either more sympathetic to the use of traditional scientific methods (positivists) or more sceptical about whether this is the most useful way to proceed (**interpretive sociologists**).

The hypothetico-deductive method

Positivists believe that the scientific tradition is the approach that sociology must follow. Accordingly, they seek to follow the **hypothetico-deductive** research method: a series of steps providing what is regarded as the most scientific method of

finding information. By following these steps, the sociologist has the highest chance of generating accurate 'scientific' knowledge. These steps consist of the following:

- Background reading and personal experience – Through study and everyday observation the sociologist uncovers area of interest.
- Formation of a hypothesis – The sociologist formulates a causal link between two events.
- Devising the appropriate form of study to isolate the key variables – This is usually some form of questionnaire, interview or, less often, observation.
- Collecting the data – There are strict rules governing the way questionnaires and interviews are carried out to ensure **validity** and reliability.
- Analysing the data – Statistical models are often used here, such as 'tests of confidence', which allow the sociologist to demonstrate to others how likely their research sampling was to produce accurate results.

Definition 'Hypothetico-deductive'

Hypothetico

Refers to a hypothesis, which Punch (1998) defines as 'a predicted answer to a research question'. An example is the fact that people routinely think that there is more violent crime than there really is. A research question might be 'Why is this?' And the predicted answer (or hypothesis) might be that it is 'because the media focus on violent crime and exaggerate its extent'.

Deductive

Refers to the fact that the hypothesis is drawn from a broader framework of observation, possibly from an existing theory. Deductive refers to the process of working something out from the general to the particular.

- confirming, modifying or rejecting the hypothesis – this is done by searching for weaknesses as suggested by Popper (see Topic 3).
- theory formation or confirmation. However, no positivist claims their results are proved by their research, merely that they produce the best explanation until others can improve on it or possibly disprove it. Again, this derives from Popper's argument concerning falsification (see p. 176).

Most real research programmes are rather more complex and overlapping than the classic hypothetico-deductive approach – using some inductive features, for example. Nevertheless, it provides the model that positivistic sociologists seek to follow.

We shall look at an example of the hypothetico-deductive model later, but for the moment, in the next section we will examine some of the key **epistemological** issues it raises.

Theoretical approaches linked to positivism and quantitative research methods

The key question here is the nature of society. There are two extreme positions. At one extreme is the claim that society really exists 'out there' and it largely determines how we think and act. In this model people can arguably be portrayed as puppets of society. At the other pole is the argument that society only exists through the beliefs and activities of individuals interacting. This model of society sees people as creative actors making society.

Positivists generally support a theoretical model of society that is based on the idea that there is some form of structure that exists independently of individual views, perceptions or desires – sometimes known as the **structural model of society**. There are two main theoretical approaches that are most closely linked to positivism and both base their approaches on the idea of structure: structural functionalism and Marxism.

Structural functionalism

This derives from the work of Parsons (1952) and was heavily influenced by Durkheim and, to a lesser extent by Weber. Functionalism, you will recall, argues that institutions exist in society in the form they do because they contribute to the continuing functioning of society. Underpinning this theoretical model is the acceptance of a social structure that actively guides our actions and beliefs. The term used by Durkheim when referring to society was that there were **social facts** that existed whether or not the sociologist wanted it. In his classic study *Suicide: A study in Sociology* (1897/1952) (see Unit 5, p. 305), Durkheim believed that he had demonstrated through using statistics on suicide that clear patterns could be uncovered. The 'social facts' were the numbers and types of suicide.

Marxism

Marxist theory or 'dialectical materialism' was based on the belief that economic and social laws exist that govern human behaviour. Marx hoped that by uncovering these laws he would demonstrate that a communist society was the inevitable future. Although people's consciousness and actions play an important part, ultimately the laws are dominant. It is important to remember that although the original model of society devised by Marx was largely based on positivist ideas, most modern Marxist-inspired research is based on a mixture of quantitative and qualitative ideas.

Criticism

We mentioned earlier that there were two conceptions of the nature of society. We have just looked at the way positivism is largely linked to the structural model.

But this model of society has been strongly attacked by a range of other sociological perspectives, most notably those coming from a social constructionist perspective, such as symbolic interactionism. As mentioned in Topic 1, symbolic interactionism derives from the work of Blumer (1962), and is closely linked to labelling theory. Symbolic interactionism, labelling theory and ethnomethodology all stress the way that individuals work at making sense of the society around them. According to these approaches, then, society is created by the activities of people and not the other way around. Positivistic methods are, therefore, inappropriate, with their assumption of some objective reality. Instead (as we shall see in Topic 5), these social constructionist theories try to grasp the rules (if any) that guide people in their daily tasks of creating reality. This usually involves watching people and analysing their conversations and their activities. This takes us back to our earlier point regarding deductive and inductive reasoning. Whereas positivism generally uses a deductive framework, social constructionists start with an inductive one – building up from observations.

We will explore this approach in more detail in Topic 5, where we look at the methods most closely associated with the social constructionist approaches.

Quantitative research: the favoured method of positivists

Positivists believe that there is a social world 'out there', relatively independent of individuals, that can be uncovered by testing hypotheses through using rigorous research-collection techniques. They seek out valid **indicators** to represent the variables under study in order to study them in a reliable way.

This approach strongly favours using quantitative methods such as **surveys**, questionnaires and case studies.

Surveys

A social survey involves obtaining information in a standardized manner from a large number of people. This is done in order to maximize reliability and generalizability (See Topic 7). There are two main types of survey – longitudinal and cross-sectional.

Cross-sectional surveys

Cross-sectional surveys are often called 'snapshot' studies as they gather information at one particular time. These are the most common surveys which we are used to reading in newspapers and textbook and are often called 'opinion-polls'. This method is very useful for finding out information on a particular topic at one specific moment. If organized properly, these are quick to do, the results can be collated and analysed very quickly and findings are likely to be highly generalizable. However, there are two real difficulties with cross-sectional surveys:

- The indicators or questions chosen to measure a particular form of attitude must be accurate. If they are not, then the research will not be valid.
- The surveys provide information for one particular, static moment – they do not provide information over a period of time, so changes in views cannot be measured.

Longitudinal surveys

Longitudinal studies are surveys that take place over a period of time – sometimes years. The cross-sectional survey already mentioned is a very important method and is widely used by sociologists, in particular because of the very high reliability and generalizability of its findings. However, its weakness is that it provides information for one particular moment only. Changes in attitudes or behaviour over time are simply not measured by it, nor are longer term factors that might influence behaviour. So when quantitative sociologists are particularly interested in change they often switch to using a longitudinal survey. By following groups of people over a period of time, sociologists are able to plot the changes that they are looking for. However, longitudinal surveys suffer from some quite serious drawbacks. The biggest of these is the drop-out rate. Answering questions over time and being the object of study can lead to people getting bored or resentful. Separately from this, people move

Surveys Aims and weaknesses

Aims

- To uncover straightforward factual information about a particular group of people – for example, their voting intentions or their views on punishment of convicted offenders. This is because a survey allows information to be gathered from a large range and number of people.

- To uncover differences in beliefs, values and behaviour between people, but *only* when these are easily and clearly measured. If the beliefs and attitudes were complex or difficult to find unambiguous indicators for, then qualitative research may be more appropriate.

- To test a hypothesis, where it is necessary to gain more information to confirm or deny it.

Weakness

The *major weakness of all surveys* is that they cannot easily uncover complex views. This means that there is always an issue regarding the *validity* of quantitative research. Issues of indicators and the **operationalization** of concepts in general are crucial in the research design.

addresses, colleges and friendship groups, so tracking them becomes a complex and expensive task. For both these reasons, longitudinal surveys suffer from low retention.

This is also a problem because the survey will start to lack reliability and generalizability. Quite simply, this is because if the retention rate becomes too low then the views and behaviour of those who remain may well differ from the views of those who have left the survey.

Such surveys provide us with a clear, ongoing image of changes in attitudes and actions over time. The *British Household Panel Survey* is a longitudinal study that has studied over 10 000 British people of all ages, living in 5500 households. The interviewing started in 1991 and has continued every year since then. The information obtained covers a vast area including family change, household finances and patterns of health and caring. It is used by the government to help inform social policies.

Surveys and response rates

The validity and generalizability of all surveys are dependent on having high response rates. Response rates refer to the proportion of people approached in the survey who actually respond to the questionnaire or interview. The greater the proportion of people who return the questionnaires or agree to be interviewed, the greater the chance the survey has of being valid

Parker *et al.* (1998)

A longitudinal survey

The North-West Longitudinal Study involved following several hundred young people for five years between the ages of 14 and 18. The overall aim of this study was to assess how 'ordinary' young people, growing up in England in the 1990s, developed attitudes and behaviour in relation to the availability of illegal drugs, alongside other options such as alcohol and tobacco.

The main technique was a self-report questionnaire initially administered personally by the researchers (and then by post) to several hundred young people within eight state secondary schools in two, non-inner-city boroughs of metropolitan north-west England.

At the start of the research the sample was **representative** of those areas in terms of gender, class and ethnicity. However, attrition (losing participants) partly reduced this over time with the disproportionate loss of some 'working-class' participants and some from Asian and Muslim backgrounds.

A longitudinal study is able to address issues of validity and reliability far more extensively than one-off snapshot surveys, but in turn must also explain inconsistent reporting that occurs over the years. In general, the research provides a detailed account of how young people develop attitudes and behaviours through time.

Adapted from Parker, H., Aldrige, J. and Measham, F. (1998) *Illegal Leisure*, London: Routledge, pp. 48–9

1 How does this extract illustrate some of the advantages and disadvantages of longitudinal surveys?

Sampling in quantitative research

One of the main strengths of survey research is that it uses processes that ensure the people in the survey are representative of the whole population. When the people selected are representative, then the results of the survey are likely to be true for the population as a whole and therefore generalizable.

It is very difficult for sociologists to study large numbers of people as the costs of devising and carrying out the research is just too high. Instead, as we have seen throughout this book, sociologists tend to study a small but representative cross-section of the community. If this small sample truly mirrors the bigger population, then the results from studying this chosen group can be said to be true of the larger population too.

Quantitative surveys have two different methods of ensuring that their sample is representative and therefore the results are generalizable to the whole population. These two different methods are **probability** (or **random**) **sampling** and **quota sampling**. There are also other forms of sampling, snowball and theoretical, which are more commonly used in qualitative research. (These are discussed in Topic 5, p. 197.)

Probability or (random) sampling

Probability or random sampling is based on the same idea as any lottery or ticket draw. If names are chosen randomly, then each person has an equal chance of being selected. This means that those chosen are therefore likely to be a cross-section of the population. As we saw earlier, if the sample is representative, the results are likely to generalizable to the population as a whole.

The sampling frame

In order to make a random sample sociologists usually prefer to have a **sampling frame**, which is some form of list from which the sample can be drawn. British sociologists typically use Electoral Registers, (which are lists of people entitled to vote) or the Postcode Address File (which is the way that The Post Office links names and addresses to postcodes). However, for smaller studies sociologists could ask for permission to use the lists of students attending a school, or members of a club that keeps lists of names.

As Bryman (2004) points out, any piece of random sampling can only be as good as the sampling frame, so if this is inaccurate or incomplete then the sampling itself will not be accurate.

The different forms of random sampling

If the names are picked out entirely randomly, then this is known as 'simple random sampling'. However, when given a list of names, it is apparently quite difficult to pick in a truly random way, so very often a method is used whereby every 'nth' name (for example, every fifth or tenth name) on a list is chosen. This is known as **systematic (random) sampling.**

Stratified sampling is a further refinement of random sampling. Here, the population under study is divided according to known criteria (for example, it could be divided into 52 per cent women and 48 per cent men, to reflect the sex composition of the UK). Within these broad strata, people are then chosen at random. In reality, these strata can become quite detailed, with further divisions into age, social class, geographical location, ethnic group, religious affiliation, etc.

The final form of random sampling is known as **cluster sampling** and is used when the people the researcher wishes to interview (rather than use postal or e-mail questionnaires) are in a number of different locations. In order to cut costs and save time travelling to many different places, the sociologist simply chooses a number of locations at random and then individuals within these locations. This means that it is possible to generalize for the whole population of Britain by interviewing in a relatively few places. This approach has also been developed into the **multistage cluster sampling**, in which smaller clusters are randomly chosen within the larger cluster.

Random sampling is generally very easy to use and even if there is no sampling frame, it is possible to stop every 'nth' person in the street or college and ask them. It also has the enormous advantage that if certain statistical tests are used, then it is possible to say with a degree of statistical certainty how accurate the results are.

Problems with random sampling

There are a number of problems that can occur with random sampling. First, it is often difficult to obtain a sampling frame, particularly in the last few years since laws restricting access to information held on computers have been introduced

Where systematic sampling is undertaken, often by asking every 'nth' person in the street or wherever the appropriate location is, it can be extremely difficult for the researcher to maintain the necessary discipline to ask the correct person. If the person looks unpleasant or threatening, then researchers often skip that person and choose the next one! Also, factors such as the time of day or the weather can have an important influence on how representative the people in the street (or college) are. For example, stopping every tenth person in the high street of a town between 9 am and midday, usually results in a high proportion of retired and unemployed people. The sample is not representative and the results are therefore not generalizable.

Non-random (or non-probability) sampling

The main alternative to random sampling in quantitative sociological research is quota sampling.

Quota sampling

For research based on interviews, the main alternative to random sampling, which is commonly used by market research companies, is quota sampling. This can be used in any situation where the key social characteristics of the population under study are already known. For example, census information can give us a detailed picture of the UK population in terms of the proportion of people in each age group, income band, occupational group, geographical location, religious affiliation

and ethnicity. There is therefore no reason to try to seek a representative sample by random methods. All that has to be done is to select what the key characteristics are and then get the same proportion in the sample as in the main population. Each interviewer is then allocated a quota of people exhibiting the key characteristics. This guarantees that there is a representative coverage of the population.

The main reason for the popularity of quota sampling over random sampling is the very small number of people needed to build up an accurate picture of the whole population (as long as you know what key characteristics to look for). For example, the typical surveys of voting preferences in journals and newspapers use a quota sample of approximately 1200 to represent the entire British electorate.

However, quota sampling has a number of significant drawbacks, the first is that unless the researcher has the correct information on the proportion of people in each key category, then the method is useless. In this situation it is always better to use random sampling. The second drawback is that the statistical tests that can be used with random sampling to ensure that the results of the survey are accurate, cannot be used with quota sampling.

The most important drawback, though, is that quota sampling usually relies upon a researcher choosing people who fall into the quotas they have been given. Relying upon the interviewer's perception of who to interview can lead to all sorts of problems including the researcher making mistakes in deciding if people fit into the appropriate categories (for example, thinking people are younger than they are).

Experiments

An **experiment** is a form of research in which all the variables are closely controlled, so that the effect of changing one or more of the variables can be understood. Experiments are often used in the physical sciences, but are much less common in sociology. The reasons for their lack of use in sociology are that it is almost impossible to isolate a social event from the real world around it. This means that researchers cannot control all the variables, which is the essence of an experiment.

Furthermore, experiments usually involve manipulating people in ways that many people regard as immoral.

>> *When natural scientists carry out their research in laboratories, controlling variables is of crucial importance … Experimentation usually involves manipulating one* **independent variable** *and creating change in the* **dependent variable** *… What is important is that all other factors are held constant (or controlled) and are not allowed to contribute to any change which might occur.* >> (Moores 1998)

Finally, even if these two problems can be overcome, then what has been found to happen is the problem of the **experimenter effect**, where the awareness of being in an experiment affects the normal behaviour of the participants. Think of your own behaviour when you know you are being photographed, even if you are asked to 'look natural'!

Need and Evans (2001)
Secularization

An interesting study that illustrates the positivist approach and combines elements of both statistical analysis and comparative analysis is the work of Need and Evans (2001) on the factors affecting **secularization** (the decline in the importance of religion in society – see Unit 1, Topics 7 and 8).

Background
Sociologists in Britain have, until recently, believed that the growth in secularization (that is, the decline in organized religion) was a direct result of modernization, with its emphasis on rationality and science. However, there has never been a way to actually prove this. But recent changes in the political structures in Eastern Europe provide the chance to study the issue as, in 1990, most communist states abandoned their version of communism and adopted democracy. Part of the new, democratic constitutions allows freedom of worship, where previously there had always been state repression of religion.

Hypotheses
If modernization was the main reason for the decline in religion then younger people, who had not experienced communist repression at the time of first awareness of religious/moral issues, would have lower rates of religious attendance and higher levels of secularization.

On the other hand, if repression had been a more important factor and modernization was not the key, then older people would have lower levels of religious attendance and lower levels of secularization. This is because, once communism fell, they would have been able to attend church again without fear.

So, Need and Evans wanted to find out which was the more important influence on secularization: repression of the church or modernization.

Variables and indicators

Variables	Indicators of religiosity
● repression/ religiosity	● church attendance
● age/religiosity	● church membership

Indicator for repression and modernization
● age

Appropriate form of study
An international comparison was undertaken, using national sample surveys of ten post-communist societies. The sampling frame were electoral registers, from which people were selected randomly by computer.

Issues of reliability and validity
The surveys were designed in collaboration with the ten countries involved. Extensive cross-comparison of questions by multilingual researchers took place to ensure that the questions meant exactly the same in each country. A pilot study of 50 to 100 interviews were conducted to assess the reliability and validity of questions.

Open/closed systems
Need and Evans recognized that they could not simply isolate their variables from wider factors. They also therefore took into account different ethnic compositions of the societies and different religious traditions. They overcame the problem by using surveys from ten countries – five countries with Orthodox traditions and five with Catholic traditions.

Data collection
The people chosen from each country were then contacted by letter and subsequently interviewed – about 2000 in each country, with a 90% response rate.

Theory modification
The conclusions were not clear cut but, overall, the study found that older people were more likely to go to church and be religious than younger ones. This conclusion supported the modernization thesis and undermined the repression hypothesis. However, it did seem that religious traditions were significant and that countries with Catholic traditions were more likely to see higher attendance by younger people. Overall, the modernization theory was supported, although the study concluded that it does need to take into account the importance of the religious tradition of any particular country.

1 **Explain the ways in which Need and Evans' study is an example of positivist research.**

Howell and Frost (1989) conducted a sociological experiment to see which of the three forms of authority identified by Weber (charismatic, traditional and legal-rational – see Unit 2, p. 51) were most effective in getting tasks done. They found 144 student volunteers and divided them into groups. Each group was given tasks to perform, led by actresses who used different authority methods to undertake the tasks. They concluded that charismatic leadership was the most effective form of authority.

One form of experimental method which has been used more often by sociologists is the **field experiment**, where a version of an experiment is undertaken in the community. Garfinkel (1967) used this method to research ethnomethodology. He asked his students to behave 'inappropriately' at home, by refusing to take for granted anything that people said and questioning them on what they really meant.

Case studies

A **case study** is a detailed study of one particular group or organization. Instead of searching out a wide range of people via sampling, the researcher focuses on one group. The resulting studies are usually extremely detailed and provide a depth of information not normally available. However, there is always the problem that this intense scrutiny may miss wider issues by its very concentration. Case studies are used widely by both quantitative and qualitative researchers. McKee and Bell (1985), for example, studied a small community to explore the impact of high rates of unemployment on family relationships.

The main problem with case studies is that there is never any proof that the particular group chosen to be studied is typical of the population as a whole, therefore it may not be possible to generalize from the findings to other groups.

web.tasks

1 Go to www.mori.co.uk (the website of MORI, a polling organization). Look through a selection of survey results and and assess the methods of data collection used.

2 The UK government uses positivistic approaches to uncover information about the population. To find out how much information can be obtained, go to: www.statistics.gov.uk/

Click on the 'neighbourhood' heading on the top of the page. Fill in your postcode and explore. The site provides you with detailed information about your area.

KEY TERMS

Case study – a highly detailed study of one or two social situations or groups.

Cluster sampling – the researcher selects a series of different places and then chooses a sample at random within the cluster of people within these areas.

Cross-sectional survey – a survey conducted at one time with no attempt to follow up the people surveyed over a longer time.

Dependent variable – a social phenomenon that changes in response to changes in another phenomenon.

Epistemological – relating to theories of knowledge.

Experiment – a highly controlled situation where the researchers try to isolate the influence of each variable. Rarely used in sociology.

Experimenter effect – unreliability of data arising as a result of people responding to what they perceive to be the expectations of the researchers.

Field experiment – an experiment undertaken in the community or in real life, rather than in a controlled environment.

Hypothetico-deductive model – the research process associated with the physical sciences and used by positivists in sociology.

Independent variable – the phenomenon that causes the dependent variable to change.

Indicator – a measurable social phenomenon that stands for an unmeasurable concept, e.g using church attendance to measure religious belief.

Interpretive sociologists – those whose approach to sociology and research emphasizes understanding society by exploring the way people see society, rather than following traditional scientific analysis.

Longitudinal survey – a survey that is carried out over a considerable number of years on the same group of people.

Multistage cluster sampling – where subsamples are taken.

Operationalize – to put into practice.

Probability sampling – see Random sampling.

Quota sampling – where a representative sample of the population is chosen using known characteristics of the population.

Random sampling – where a representative sample of the population is chosen by entirely random methods.

Representative – a sample is representative if it is an accurate cross-section of the whole population being studied. This allows the researcher to generalize the results for the whole population.

Sampling frame – a list used as the source for a random sample.

Secularization – decrease in the importance of organized religion.

Social fact – a term used by Durkheim to claim that certain objective 'facts' exist in society that are not influenced by individuals. Examples include the existence of marriage, divorce, work, etc.

Stratified sampling – where the population under study is divided according to known criteria such as sex and age in order to make the sample more representative.

Structural model of society – theories based on the idea that society has some 'structure' over and above the interactions of people.

Survey – a large-scale piece of quantitative research aiming to make general statements about a particular population.

Systematic sampling – where every nth name (for example, every tenth name) on a list is chosen.

Validity – the need to show that what research sets out to measure really is that which it measures.

Check your understanding

1 Explain briefly in your own words the six stages of the hypothetico-deductive model.

2 What is the difference between 'deductive' and 'inductive' reasoning?

3 What model of society is positivism based upon?

4 Identify two types of random sampling – give one example of when each would be useful.

5 What is 'quota' sampling? What is the main advantage of this method?

6 Give one reason why sociologists tend not to use experiments.

7 What is a case study?

research ideas

1 Using the positivist criteria, conduct a small study using what you have learnt from this topic to find out what changes students would like to see in your school/college.

2 Carry out a small piece of research into the notion of 'happiness' or another abstract quality.

● Separately, ask a small selection of students in your school or college to define what they mean by 'happy' or 'sexy' or 'attractive' (or any other abstract term you wish).

● Choose three different definitions and then conduct three parallel surveys, asking people on a scale of 1 to 5 how happy or sexy or attractive they think they are.

● Compare and reflect on the result. What problems might your research throw up for positivist research?

exploring positivism & quantitative research methods

Item A

Positivism therefore assumed a passive human subject to laws. The social world was determined. There were causes of events. Research would uncover these laws by producing indicators of those events and relating them through statistical analysis. In sociology, positivism could ignore the meaning of events for those involved and concentrate on the relationship between behaviour and social positions

defined by categories such as age, class and sex.

The assumption of positivistic sociologists was that all human beings are subject to social laws of some kind. However, laboratory experiment was impossible in Sociology, because people cannot be controlled like physical matter, and because there are moral issues involved in experimenting on then. As a result naturally occurring

experiments had to suffice, particularly comparisons or tracing changes over time. Data was collected, used to establish relationships such as social class and attainment or criminality and urban conditions. Control was imposed through statistical analysis of the relationship between these variables.

Adapted from Shipman, M. (1997) *The Limitations of Social Research* (4th edn), Harlow: Longman

Item B

Despite being widely used and widely respected in the natural sciences, experiments are rarely used in sociology. Some of the reasons for this are ethical, others may be

practical. However some of the techniques of experiments are used in sociology and psychology, though sociologists are unable to have the complete control of variables

achieved by scientists. They will always face the problem of wanting to study people in society itself rather than in the false situation of a laboratory.

1 (a) Identify one assumption of positivistic sociologists referred to in **Item A**. (2 marks)

   (b) Identify **two** factors that limit the use of experiments in sociology (**Item B**). (4 marks)

   (c) Identify and briefly explain **two** types of 'variables' referred to in **Item B**. (4 marks)

   (d) With reference to **Item A** and elsewhere, briefly examine the reasons why experiments are rarely used in sociology. (10 marks)

2 Assess the view that positivistic methods are inappropriate for understanding society. (40 marks)

Interpretive sociology and qualitative methods

getting you thinking

Madonna uses secret nightclub 'focus groups' to pick songs for new album
By Chris Hastings, Arts Correspondent

They have been used to sell everything from washing powder to New Labour. But now it seems that even Madonna has woken up to the power of focus groups. The most successful female artist in chart history has chosen songs for her next album after secretly trying them out on nightclubbers.

The tunes, with her distinctive vocals removed, were played in clubs from Liverpool to Ibiza throughout June. The reaction of the crowds were filmed and used by the 47-year-old mother of two to determine the final track listing for Confessions On A Dancefloor, her 10th studio album.

Stuart Price, 28, the DJ and producer revealed rock music's first flirtation with market research in an interview for the singer's official website. "Whenever I was DJ-ing I'd take dub or instrumental versions out with me and test them at the club that night," he said. "I had my camera with me and the next day I'd tell Madonna, 'This is what a thousand people in Liverpool look like dancing to our song'."

He added: "You can work on a song for 12 hours but I guarantee you'll know within just 10 seconds of putting it on at a club whether it works or not. So these songs were tested on unwitting subjects throughout Europe."

Daily Telegraph, 13 September 2005

1 Do you think that music artists ought to do the music they believe in or what they think the audience wants?

2 Do you think this sort of market research is going to help Madonna? Explain your reasons.

3 Advertisers use focus groups to decide how to promote goods and services. Why do you think this is the case?

4 If you were promoting Madonna's music, what would you think is the best way to understand people's needs and motivations?

The 'natural' focus groups described above may provide Madonna with some interesting and useful evidence, but positivists (see previous topic) would be critical of the unscientific nature of this research. Methods in sociology reflect sociologists' theoretical assumptions. As you have seen throughout your course, the various theories start from very different beliefs about the nature of society.

Essentially, there are two ways to start analysing society. One is to begin by looking at society and how it influences people. To take this starting point reflects the belief that there really is a society 'out there' that is influencing our behaviour and directs us into routine patterns of action.

A second way of starting an analysis is to begin by looking at the individual, and then work one's way up to the social level. In starting here, the researcher is seeing individual perceptions and ideas as the building blocks of any larger social analysis.

It would be nice if the ideas of those who start at the bottom and work up and those who start at the top and work down met 'in the middle', but, sadly, this is not so. Indeed, the different starting points lead to quite different explanations of what society is like and how it operates.

In the last topic we looked at the methods used by those who start at the top. These positivistic methods are all based (explicitly in the case of functionalism and Marxism, and implicitly in the case of most quantitative research) on the idea that a society exists in such a way that it can be counted and gauged. In this topic we are going to look at the methodology of those who believe that analyses ought to start at the bottom – that is, with theories that stress how people perceive the world and interact with one another. These theories include interactionism (and labelling theory, which is a version of it) and there is also an overlap with postmodernism. These various approaches are typically referred to as interpretive or **phenomenological** approaches.

Recently there has been a move to try to integrate the two levels of theory, most notably in the work of Giddens (1991), but as we said earlier, so far sociologists have found it very difficult to find methods to combine the levels.

Theory and interpretive research

Bryman (2004) has argued that if there is one distinction to be made regarding the different aims of positivist and interpretive research, it is that while positivist research sets out to explain human behaviour through *analysing* the forces that act upon it, then interpretive sociology sets out to understand varieties of human behaviour by being able to *empathize* with it.

Weber and *verstehen*

The division between analysis and empathy can be traced back at least as far as Durkheim and Weber. As we have seen in earlier topics, Durkheim's attitude was that society could be treated as a 'thing' that existed beyond the individual and could be explored in a similar way to the physical sciences. For Weber, however, society was very different from an inanimate object. It consisted of thinking, purposeful people who acted as a result of a variety of influences, which could not be understood except by looking through the eyes of the individual actors. Weber used the term '**verstehen**' (similar to the English word 'empathy') to describe the sociological process that looking through the eyes of the individuals involved. In fact, Weber (1947) actually defined sociology as a 'science which attempts the interpretive understanding of social action in order to arrive at causal explanations'.

Symbolic interactionism and labelling theory

As mentioned in earlier topics, symbolic interactionism derives from the writings of Mead, Cooley and Thomas, all at the University of Chicago in the 1950s. This theoretical approach informed and developed alongside labelling theory. In the 1960s, Blumer further developed these ideas and gave the name symbolic interactionism to the approach. According to Blumer, societies do not have an existence independent of people's understanding of it. Social objects, events and situations are all interpreted by people in various socially learned ways and then people respond to them in terms of these learned **meanings**. Labelling theory, which is associated with Lemert (1967) and Becker (1963), shares this belief in the importance of symbols (which they call labels), but largely focuses on situations where one group or individual is able to impose its definition of the situation on others – usually with negative consequences for the people being labelled.

Symbolic interactionism and labelling theory tend to use qualitative methods, rejecting the positivist approaches.

Structuration theory

More recently, Giddens has argued in his structuration theory (1984) that there is a form of structure that exists beyond the control of individuals and which does constrain human action. However, Giddens argues that these structures only exist in so far as people make them exist. So, families exist only as long as people choose to stay within the particular set of relationships that define a family. Research, according to Giddens, must therefore understand the motivations and actions of individuals, before it can see how structures can 'exist'.

A good example of the difference between objective facts and perception of facts is Foster's (1995) ethnographic study of a housing estate (consisting mainly of blocks of flats) in East London. Objectively, the estate had a high crime-rate – at least according to official statistics. However, residents did not perceive the estate to be particularly threatening. Of particular significance was the existence of 'informal social control'. People expected a certain level of crime, but felt moderately secure because the levels were contained by informal controls and by a supportive network. Neighbours looked after each other and they believed that if any trouble should occur, they could rely upon each other for support. Furthermore, because of the degree of intimacy and social interaction on the estate,

synopticlink   **crime** and **deviance**

Participant observation is closely associated with the use of the labelling perspective to study deviance. Howard Becker (1963) conducted a famous participant observational study, using the labelling perspective, in which he investigated the way in which people began to use cannabis and how it gradually became part of their self identity. Becker argues that people who smoke cannabis regularly are not necessarily physically addicted or have some physical or even mental needs to use the drug, but instead incorporate the use of their drug into their lifestyle and identity. Their use and understanding of the drug therefore is very different from the view of those who do not smoke cannabis and disapprove of it. By seeing the use of cannabis through the eyes of the users, Becker provided a very different perspective from the dominant approaches of the time which sought to find the differences between drug users and non-users. However, Becker also clearly has sympathy and liking for the musicians he studied and worked with, therefore although the research was a breakthrough in understanding the process by which people learn to use drugs, rather than becoming 'addicted', it also demonstrates the dangers of participant observation of becoming too close to the people being studied.

The differences between **qualitative** and **quantitative** methods

Bryman (2004) suggests that the differences between qualitative and quantitative methods include:

- *Numbers versus words* – Qualitative methods tend use describe social life in words, whilst quantitative research uses far more numbers to paint the sociological picture.
- *Point of view of researcher versus point of view of participants* – In quantitative research the researcher is the one who decides what questions to ask and how to classify the responses. However, in qualitative research, the researcher starts from the point of view of the participants – and writes up what they say, no matter how confusing or contradictory.
- *Researcher is distant versus researcher is close* – In quantitative research, the sociologist usually stays 'outside' and is uninvolved with the participants. All the sociologist wants is to distribute and collect the questionnaires or interview results, which are then analysed. In qualitative research, the sociologist is heavily involved with the people being researched, as they attempt to understand what is going on.
- *Theories tested versus theories emerge* – In quantitative research, the sociologist usually has a hypothesis that he or she wishes to test and this forms the basis for the research. In qualitative research however, the theory may well emerge from the actual process of research. This is known as '**grounded theory**'.
- *Structured versus unstructured* – Quantitative research is usually very well structured as the information needs to be gained in a way that is reliable. Qualitative research, on the other hand, is usually far less structured and is more flexible and open. Incidentally, this does not mean that it is less well organized.
- *Hard reliable data versus rich, deep data* – Quantitative research almost always aims at being **generalizable** and thus is designed to be statistically correct. So a survey should provide information about the population as a whole. Qualitative research places much greater emphasis on a detailed understanding of the particular group being studied.

Interpretive approaches and method

Interpretive researchers largely reject the use of quantitative methods (that is, statistical surveys and other positivist approaches) and prefer instead **qualitative research**. Qualitative research methods refer to any approach in sociology that sets out to uncover the meaning of social action rather than measure it through statistics.

Interpretive researchers prefer qualitative methods for the following reasons.

Meaning

As we have just noted, qualitative research allows sociologists to search for the meaning for participants of events, situations and actions in which they are involved. This reflects the belief of interpretive approaches that only by understanding how individuals build up their patterns of interaction can a full understanding of society be presented.

Context

Interpretive research usually studies small-scale groups and specific situations. This allows the researcher to preserve the individuality of each of these in their analyses (in contrast with positivistic research which is based on large samples). Interpretive-based research provides the researcher with an understanding of the events, actions and meanings as they are influenced by specific circumstances. It is only within the contexts that action makes sense.

Unanticipated phenomena and influences

Positivistic research tends to fall into a format whereby researchers look for evidence to back up a hypothesis and then amend or reject it. In other words, positivistic researchers tend to anticipate certain outcomes – research does not start in a vacuum, but is based on a fairly clear idea of what should happen if variables react as expected. In qualitative research, the researcher does not necessarily have to have a clear idea of what they are looking for (see 'grounded theory', in the panel on the left) – researchers often start with an interest in a particular area and absolutely no idea of where it might lead. Without the 'blinkers' of the hypothetico-deductive model, researchers are much more open to the unexpected, and to fresh ideas.

Process

Positivistic forms of research are generally interested in outcomes (what happens if), however qualitative research is more interested in the process (what is happening). This reflects a belief by positivists that they are looking for patterns that can be generalized across society – they are not interested necessarily in the details of the actual processes that lead to the outcome. Interpretive sociologists, on the other hand, will be interested in the actual dynamics of the situation – the process.

most people knew who the offenders were, and felt that this knowledge allowed them some degree of protection, because they could keep an eye on the troublemakers.

Official statistics portrayed this estate as having major problems – yet ethnographic research showed that the estate actually provided a secure environment in which most people were happy.

Types of qualitative research methods

Qualitative research covers a wide range of methods, but the most common are: observational research (**ethnography**), focus groups and qualitative interviewing (qualitative researchers sometimes use secondary sources too). In this topic we will concentrate on just observational research and focus groups, leaving the interviewing and secondary sources to be discussed in the next two topics.

> **A note on ethnography:** We will be using the term *ethnography* quite often in this topic and it can be quite confusing. Ethnography is a general term commonly used by sociologists for participant observation or observation plus in-depth interviewing. So it is best to think of ethnography as a useful term for sociologists immersing themselves in the lives of the people under study, generally joining in as much social activity as possible, so that they can gain an in-depth understanding of the lives of a particular group.

Ethnographic research

Any sociologist undertaking this form of research has quite a number of decisions to make about what is the best form of observational research for their purposes.

The key decisions facing the researcher are:

- the extent of involvement with the group under study
- the amount of information that the sociologist gives the group about their research.

The following two examples illustrate the differences between the methods.

Extent of involvement with the group under study

Sociologists can choose the extent of their participation in a group from one extreme of simply being an external observer with no contact with the group whatsoever – this is known as **non-participant observation**, through to the other extreme of complete immersion in the group – in fact, actually becoming a full group member – known as **participant observation**. Of course, in reality, observational research usually falls somewhere in between.

In deciding the extent of their involvement in the group, the researcher has to decide what they wish to obtain from their research and weigh up the advantages and disadvantages of the role they adopt. Usually, qualitative researchers ask themselves three questions:

1. *What is possible?* – Is it actually possible to become a member of the group and be accepted? Differences in age, social class background, gender, lifestyle and education can all have an impact on this.
2. *What is ethically correct?* – Is it acceptable to join a group that is possibly engaging in harmful activities. What harm will come to them by the sociologist's actions? There is also an ethical dimension to the decision. It is one thing to observe a group engaging in immoral or illegitimate activity; it is quite another actually to be involved.
3. *What method will produce the most valid results? Will becoming a full member of the group actually improve the quality of the research?* – The more the researcher becomes involved with the group, the greater their chances of really getting in-depth information. The sociologist is able to see the situation through the eyes of the group being studied and so will be able to emphasize with the group.

On the other hand, by not getting too involved with the group being studied, the sociologist can avoid getting their personal feelings mixed up with their research perceptions and are much less likely to influence the group in any way (which would ruin the research).

Amount of information the sociologist gives

The sociologist has the choice to be completely honest about the role they are playing – this is known as **overt observation**, or the sociologist can tell the participants nothing and pretend to be a full member of the group – this is known as **covert observation**.

Once again, the sociologist will make the choice by balancing the three elements:

1. *What is possible?* – Is it actually possible to get away with being a member of the group? Will they find out and the cover be blown. For example, even if the sociologist is young looking and can get accepted by a youth group, how is it possible to hide their job and background?
2. *What is ethically correct?* – Is it acceptable to pretend to be a member of a group without letting them know what is really happening ? The ethical guidelines that most sociologists follow insist that informed consent is always obtained. What harm will come to them by the sociologists actions?
3. *What method will produce the most valid results?* – If by pretending to be a member of a group, the researcher is able to enter groups normally closed to researchers and is able to obtain information that results in greater sociological knowledge, then there is a strong argument for using this form of observation.

By balancing these three issues, in terms of the overt/covert and participant/non-participant decisions, the researcher can then decide exactly what form of observational research role they will use.

Gold (1958) has suggested that the result of making these decisions can lead to the researcher taking one of four roles:

- *Complete participant* – A fully functioning member of the group, acting in a covert (hidden) role.
- *Participant as observer* – The researcher joins in as a participant, but is overt (open) about their role.
- *Observer as participant* – The researcher is mainly there to interview and observe.

- *Complete observer* – The researcher simply observes what is going on around them, making no attempt to interview or discuss.

The process of participant observation

Making contact and gaining entry to the group

Participant observational research by its very nature is interested in groups about whom it is difficult to gain information by survey methods. In the majority of cases, it involves studying groups who are marginal to society in some way, very often engaging in deviant behaviour. Most sociologists are not already members of such groups!

The first problem is to make contact and then find some way to gain entry to the group. Most researchers use a contact or gatekeeper who opens the door for them. In Bourgois' study of East Harlem in the 1990s, it was a local part-time crack dealer, Primo who befriended him. However, not all groups studied are deviant, and many researchers simply ask their colleagues if they can study them (see 'Convenience sampling' on p. 197), or get a job, or perhaps join a society where they can observe people.

Lee Monaghan, for example, undertook a number of studies involving participant observation. The first one was about the culture of body builders and their use of drugs. Monaghan (1999) joined a gym and used his hobby as a body builder to study those who attended the gym. In a later study (2005) he used these contacts to get a job as a doorman in a club, where he undertook a further participant observational study on this form of employment.

Acceptance by the group

Gaining access and being introduced to a group does not necessarily mean that the group will accept the researcher as a member or observer. The next stage is to work out how one is going to be accepted. This has two elements: role and relationships

Role refers to the decision of whether to be covert or overt. Most sociologists take a fairly pragmatic view of what role to take, in the sense that they will adopt the role that gives them the greatest chance of getting the research material they want. The factors limiting that will be relationship issues, which we explore next and ethical issues (see p. 196) about how much harm the researcher may cause by acting covertly.

Relationships refer to the similarities and differences between the researcher and the group being studied. Age, ethnicity, gender, religion and social class are amongst the wide range of factors that influence the possibility of the researcher getting close to the people being studied and being able to empathize with them.

Recording the activities of the group

Once settled into a group, one of the biggest problems faced by the researcher in participant observation is how to record information. This is particularly problematic for researchers engaged in covert observation. There are a number of answers to the problem of how to keep a **field diary**.

Participant observation

Ethnographers usually live in the communities they study and they establish long-term, close relationships with the people they write about. In other words, in order to collect 'accurate data', ethnographers become intimately involved with the people we study …
I spent hundreds of nights on the street and in crackhouses observing dealers and addicts. I regularly tape-recorded their conversations and life histories. Perhaps more important, I also visited their families, attended parties and intimate reunions. I interviewed and in many cases befriended, the spouses, lovers, siblings, mothers, grandmothers of the crack dealers featured in these pages.

Adapted from Bourgois, P. (2003) *In Search of Respect* (2nd edn), Cambridge: Cambridge University Press

Non-participant observation

Daniel Kelly, Susie Pearce and Anne Mulhall studied the experiences of young people with cancer in a London hospital. Their research combined in-depth interviews with observation.

'Non-participant observation was used to capture a wide-angled view of the unit and to reveal issues that the participants were asked to expand upon during the interviews. Observations took place on eight different days for three hours each day'

Kelly, D., Pearce, S. and Mulhall, P. (2004) 'Being in the same boat: ethnographic insights into an adolescent cancer unit', *International Journal of Nursing Studies*, 41(8), pp. 847–57

The first is simply to remember as much as possible and then to write this up as soon after the events as possible. This has the enormous advantage of allowing the researcher to pay full attention to what is going on at the time, rather than being distracted by writing notes. Indeed, in covert observation, this is probably the only possible method. But the big problem is that the researcher is bound to forget things, and of course, it may be the things they forget that are the more important.

The second method is to make notes wherever possible as the action is unfolding. This leads to great accuracy, but is almost guaranteed to disrupt normal social interaction, as one person in a group making copious notes of what is going on rather stands out! In Ditton's (1977) study of workplace 'fiddles', he used to go to the toilets to write up his research, using the toilet paper for his notes!

Getting at the truth: influencing the group/getting influenced by the group

In observational research, it is hard to remain objective. Close contact with the group under study means that the sociologist's feelings almost always slip into their field diaries and research notes at some time. The closer to the group the researcher gets, the more likely it is that bias of some sort will creep in. So

Bourgois (2003) became close friends with some of the crack dealers in his study, for example: 'I interviewed and in many cases befriended, the spouses, lovers, siblings, mothers, grandmothers … of the crack dealers featured in these pages.'

Not only can the activities of the group influence the researcher positively or negatively, but the researcher can also influence the group. If the group is small and perhaps less educated than the sociologist, then the researcher's ideas might influence the group – thereby ruining the research. In his classic study of youths in Liverpool, Howard Parker actually gave them legal advice when they were caught by the police for stealing from cars (Parker et al. 1998).

Leaving the group

Everyone engaging in participant observation or ethnographic research must, at some time, leave the group. There are two issues here. The first is when to leave? Glaser and Strauss

Participant observation Advantages and disadvantages

Advantages

- **Experience** — Participant observation allows the researcher to fully join the group and see things through the eyes (and actions) of the people in the group.

- **Generating new ideas** — Often this can lead to completely new insights and generate new theoretical ideas. Also good for validity.

- **Getting the truth** — One of the problems with questionnaires, and to a lesser extent with interviews, is that the respondent can lie. Participant observation prevents this because the researcher can see the person's actual behaviour. This leads to high levels of validity.

- **Digging deep** — Participant observation can create a close bond between the researcher and the group under study, and individuals in the group may be prepared to confide in the researcher. Excellent for validity.

- **Dynamic** — Participant observation takes place over a period of time and allows an understanding of how changes in attitudes and behaviour take place. Again can raise level of validity.

- **Reaching into difficult areas** — Participant observation is normally used to obtain research information on hard-to-reach groups, such as drug users and young offenders.

- Scores very high for validity.

Disadvantages

- **Bias** — The main problem lies with bias, as the (participant) observer can be drawn into the group and start to see things through their eyes. Loses objectivity and therefore validity.

- **Influence of the researcher** — The presence of the researcher may make the group act less naturally as they are aware of being studied, unless the researcher is operating covertly.

- **Ethics** — How far should the researcher allow themselves to be drawn into the activities of the group – particularly if these activities are immoral or illegal?

- **Proof** — There is no way of knowing whether the findings of participant observation are actually true or not, since there is no possibility of replicating the research. In other words the results may lack **reliability**.

- **Too specific** — Participant observation is usually used to study small groups of people who are not typical of the wider population. It is therefore difficult to claim that the findings can be generalized across the population as a whole.

- **Studying the powerless** — Most (participant) observational studies are concerned with the least powerful groups in society. What about the powerful and their activities?

- Scores very low for reliability and generalizability

(see 'Theoretical sampling', opposite) argue that the correct time to get out of an ethnographic study is when new information does no more than confirm what the sociologist has already found out. They use the term 'theoretical saturation' to describe this situation.

The second issue is actually how to leave. This can be a very difficult thing. If the researcher likes the group and gets on well with the group being studied, then it might be very emotional to leave and may upset both group members and the researcher. On the other hand, if the researcher is engaged in deviant behaviour, it may actually be very dangerous to leave and so a strategy must be developed. In one classic study which studied a violent Glasgow youth gang, 'James Patrick' the researcher used a false name to infiltrate the gang, knowing that if they found him after he left, they would get their revenge. Indeed, to this day his real name is not widely known.

Of course, some people never quite leave. Philippe Bourgois (2003) admits to regularly going back to East Harlem in New York and has kept in touch with his principle gatekeeper (the person who gets the sociologist into the group in the first place and keeps the researcher linked in) – Primo. Interestingly, Primo was heavily influenced by Bourgois and turned from a crack user and part-time dealer into a small time businessman who gave up alcohol and drugs.

Causing harm: The ethical dimension of ethnographic studies

Possibly of all forms of research, apart from experiments, participant observation carries the most difficult ethical dilemmas. At virtually any stage in the proceedings, participant observation (particularly covert) can lead to harm to the researcher, to the participants or to the public.

But even if no harm comes to others, there is still the controversial issue that anyone undertaking covert participant observation does not get the consent of the people who they are studying. This contradicts one of the bases of all modern research, that those being studied give their informed consent. Holdaway (1982) for example was a police officer studying his colleagues without their knowledge. He knew that he was leaving the police force to work at a university once his research was completed. When the research, which was critical of his colleagues was published, some were angry as they felt that he had taken advantage of them

Sociologists therefore have to be very careful about what they do, and this can lead to many moral dilemmas. This is the last part of the introduction to Bourgois' (2002) study of East Harlem (New York) where he studied crack dealers and users.

<< *Finally, I want to thank my family. I will always be grateful to Charo Chacon-Mendez for coming with me to El Barrio, where we married at the very beginning of the research project. Her help was invaluable. I apologize for imposing so much anxiety on her when I regularly stayed out all night on the street and in crackhouses for so many years. I hope that it is not one of the reasons why we are no longer together. If it is, I regret it profoundly.* >>

Focus groups

A second very common form of qualitative research method is the focus group. A focus group consists of a relatively small number of people, usually less than 12, who are requested to discuss a specific topic. Focus groups ideally are representative of a particular **population** and are obtained through the most appropriate sampling techniques. (These can include both traditional qualitative or quantitative sampling methods.)

Focus groups give researchers an opportunity to hear an issue being discussed, with people able to discuss and challenge each other's views. Compared with the rather static interview method, focus groups are much more dynamic, with people demonstrating the thought process involved in how they came to their views. In the actual discussions, issues emerge that researchers may never have thought of and so those groups are often innovative. Finally, the focus group members have the power to concentrate more on issues they consider important than on the researcher's priorities. See the panel below for a summary of advantages and limitations of focus groups.

Focus groups Advantages and limitations

Advantages

- Allows researcher to understand *why* people hold certain opinions

- People can modify and change views, so demonstrating how strongly held their views are.

- Because it is a discussion the focus group will prioritize issues it thinks are more important. This may be different from the researcher's ideas.

- Focus groups are dynamic, with people probing each other's views and defending their own views.

- Focus groups study group views and interactions.

Limitations

- Researchers have limited control over what happens. The group discussion can veer off into irrelevant (for the researcher) areas.

- Membership of focus groups needs to be carefully run to ensure real discussion, and 'louder' people who dominate discussion need to be controlled.

- Focus groups generate a huge amount of material which is not clearly structured, this means that analysing the material is very difficult.

Sampling in qualitative research

There are three main types of sampling associated with qualitative research.

Convenience sampling

This refers to any group used for research that is easily available to the researcher. Convenience sampling is very commonly used in ethnography because problems of entry and acceptance by the group being studied are kept to a minimum. Typically convenience sampling is used for research into occupational groups such as nurses, teachers and students.

Though this is widely used, it can have serious drawbacks. Engaging in covert research can make a person feel like a spy. As seen earlier, where colleagues know and accept the researcher, any results that are critical of them may lead to problems between the researcher and colleagues after the research is over.

Snowball sampling

This is used in all forms of qualitative research – but is most common in studying deviant groups. This method involves finding one person initially who agrees to act as gatekeeper and then through them building up an ever bigger network of contacts. The main problem with this form of sampling is that the sample tends to be restricted to one group who have contacts. This may result in a very partial picture of social interaction.

>> *A snowball sample of men and women was built up by making contacts through various institutions such as luncheon clubs, local history groups and other social networks. Many were recommended to us by someone who had already participated, and we were able to interview some members of the same family.* >> (Hood and Joyce 1999)

Theoretical sampling

Theoretical sampling is different from the other types of sampling in that it is closely associated with a particular methodology known as grounded theory. In this approach, instead of starting off with a hypothesis and setting out to prove/disprove it, the researcher chooses an area of interest, begins the research and hopes that ideas will emerge from the process. Glaser and Strauss (1967) developed this approach based on the idea that the source of data collection would have to change as new ideas emerged in the research. At each stage of the research, Glaser and Strauss decided what next group or secondary source was needed to further their research and concentrated their efforts on finding this. When they had reached theoretical saturation (no new ideas are emerging) then it was time to finish.

>> *... but after ten interviews I gradually realized that I needed more interviewees of certain types. For example, initially I found I had only interviewed families with harmonious relationships and so I asked if they could find me families with problems.* >> (Darlington and Scott 2002)

Criticisms of research methods used in interpretive sociology

Positivist sociologists have not been shy in criticizing the methods used by qualitative researchers in the following ways.

Values

Positivists argue that although a value-free sociology may not be possible, there are reasonable limits to observe. Qualitative research is shot through with issues related to value bias, and it is almost impossible to untangle the personal biases of the researcher with the research 'insights' generated. The approach taken by feminists such as Mies (see Unit 3, p. 136), which commits itself to a particular value approach, is seen as going beyond the acceptable limit. However the very opposite can occur too. In Lee-Treweek's (2000) study of carers in homes for the elderly, she found that she increasingly disliked the 'carers' she was studying. Their attitudes to the old people so angered her that it was difficult to continue her study in value-neutral position as she wished.

Transferability

Qualitative research is often small scale and specific to a particular group. Positivists claim that it is difficult to transfer the results of research in one specific situation to others – that is, there are problems with **transferability**.

Generalizability

Generalizability follows from transferability. To what extent can general statements be made from highly localized and specific studies that aim to uncover the meaning of the interaction of a group in a specific situation?

Interpretive approaches to sociology have generated a range of sophisticated methods that can justifiably claim to provide extremely useful insights into the nature of social action. Interpretive approaches seek, above all else, to understand how people perceive the world about them and how this influences their actions – and the consequences of these actions for both themselves and others. The nature of the questions asked by these approaches therefore leads interpretive sociologists to use qualitative methods, rather than qualitative ones. Whether qualitative approaches are 'better' or 'worse' than qualitative approaches is like asking whether in theory, structural approaches are 'better' or 'worse' than interpretive approaches. There is no simple answer, except to say that each approach asks different questions that need to be studied in different ways.

Lack of transparency

According to Bryman and Burgess (1994), the qualitative methods associated with interpretive sociology are often unclear in how they reach their conclusions, resting heavily upon the intuition and understanding of the researcher. The reader of the research has to take it on trust that the perception of the situation as described by the interpretive researcher is accurate.

Triangulation and multistrategy research

In order to be clear about the different research strategies used by sociologists, we have made very clear distinctions between quantitative and qualitative research. In real life research, however, things are rather more complicated. While one group of sociologists are largely in favour of using quantitative methods wherever possible and other sociologists are largely in favour of using qualitative methods, both groups will dip into the 'other side's' methods if they think it will be useful.

So, quantitative researchers may well back up their work by including some observation or some in-depth, unstructured interviewing, whilst qualitative researchers may well engage in some structured interviewing or draw upon secondary sources in order to strengthen their research. This use of multiple methods is generally known as **triangulation** (though, strictly speaking it is really multistrategy research).

The term 'triangulation' originally referred to the use of different indicators in quantitative research as ways of measuring social phenomena. The aim was to overcome the problem of loss of validity where a faulty indicator was used. However, over time the term has come to mean the use of multiple methods in a particular piece of research, with the aim of improving its validity, reliability and generalizability.

KEY TERMS

Covert observation – where the sociologist does not admit to being a researcher.

Ethnography – term used to describe the work of anthropologists who study simple, small-scale societies by living with the people and observing their daily lives. The term has been used by sociologists to describe modern-day observational studies.

Field diary – a detailed record of events, conversations and thoughts kept by participant observers, written up as often as possible.

Generalizability – the ability to apply accurately the findings of research into one group to other groups.

Grounded theory – an approach to theory construction in which theory is generated during research.

Meaning – the word used by Blumer to describe the sense people make of a particular situation.

Non-participant observation – where the sociologist simply observes the group but does not seek to join in their activities.

Overt observation – where the sociologist is open about the research role.

Participant observational studies – where the sociologist joins a group of people and studies their behaviour.

Phenomenological approaches – approaches such as interactionism which stress how people perceive the world and interact with one another.

Population – the entire group the sociologist is focusing on.

Qualitative research – a general term for approaches to research that are less interested in collecting statistical data, and more interested in observing and interpreting the ways in which people behave.

Reliability – refers to the need for research to be strictly comparable. (Not a great problem with questionnaires and structured/closed question interviews.) This can pose a real problem in observational research, because of the very specific nature of the groups under study.

Transferability – the ability to transfer the results of research in one specific situation to others.

Triangulation (multistrategy research) – a term often used to describe the use of multiple methods (qualitative and quantitative) in research.

Verstehen – term first used by Weber in sociology, to suggest that the role of sociology is to understand partly by seeing through the eyes of those who are being studied. Similar to 'empathy' in English.

Check your understanding

1. What two ways are there for starting an analysis of society? What terms do sociologists use for these approaches?

2. Explain the meaning of *verstehen* in your own words. Why is it different from Durkheim's approach to sociology?

3. Identify and explain three reasons why interpretive sociologists prefer the use of qualitative methods in research.

4. What advantages does observational research have over quantitative methods?

5. Suggest two examples of research where it would be possible to justify covert observation.

6. Identify two advantages and two disadvantages of focus groups in research.

7. Why do interpretivist-based approaches have a difficulty with generalizability, according to positivist critics?

web.tasks

1. Go to the Joseph Rowntree website at **www.jrf.org.uk**. Select a summary of one piece of research. Why do you think the researchers used the particular methods they did?

2. Increasingly, sociologists are conducting ethnographic research on the internet. Go to the chat room, The Student Room at **www.thestudentroom.co.uk/** and explore the informal rules of conduct that govern the interaction.

researchideas

1 Design a research strategy using positivist ideas to discover why some young people are attracted to 'clubbing'. Now, design an alternative piece of research using interpretive ideas. How is the research different? How could each piece of research be criticized?

2 If there is a school or college canteen, spend half an hour observing the way that different people interact. You could choose to compare males and females, or couples versus groups of friends. How do people behave if they are sitting alone?

Next (and with the permission of the tutor) undertake a participant observational study of another class you attend (or perhaps your workplace).

Back in class, compare notes on your observations. What did you observe, if anything? What issues arise when doing this sort of research?

Incidentally, if you have studied people in some detail or engaged in participant observation (for example with your group of friends), then you should ask them for their permission to discuss their behaviour in class and you should certainly promise not to use their names in discussion.

exploring interpretive sociology and qualitative methods

Item A

<< Firstly, the social world is one which has been given meaning by its constituent actors. Therefore to explore this world, it is necessary to draw upon the concepts that actors themselves use. Consider the difference between the work of a virologist and a sociologist. Viruses do not speak and do not constitute their own behaviour. However, a sociologist who wishes to explore why gay men have unsafe sex must explore what gay men ... themselves understand by terms like unsafe, protection and sex.>>

Adapted from Bonnell, C. (1999) 'Gay men: drowning (and swimming) by numbers', in Hood, S., Mayall, B. and Oliver, S. (eds) *Critical Issues in Social Research,* Buckingham: Open University Press

Item B

Hobbs conducted a famous study of minor criminals and policing in East London. In this study Hobbs needed to spend large amounts of time in pubs, in the company of the criminals. Hobbs comments that 'I often had to remind myself that I was not in a pub to enjoy myself, but to conduct an academic inquiry and repeatedly woke up the following morning with an incredible hangover, facing the dilemma of whether to bring it up or write it up'.

Hobbs enjoyed the company of the police officers but he also disapproved of many of the things they did. He sometimes faced a moral dilemma in that he allowed things to happen that normally he might consider objecting to.

Hobbs, D. (1988) *Doing the Business: Entrepreneurship, the Working Class and Detectives in the East End of London,* Oxford: Oxford University Press

1 (a) Identify the approach to sociology advocated by the author of **Item A**. (2 marks)

   (b) Identify two factors that distinguish the work of a sociologist and a virologist (**Item A**) (4 marks)

   (c) Identify and briefly explain two problems faced by sociologists undertaking ethnographic research (**Item B**) (4 marks)

   (d) With reference to the Items and elsewhere, briefly examine the view that it is impossible to generalize from interpretive research. (10 marks)

2 Sociologists should always consider the meaning and interpretations that people have of the events in their lives.'

   Assess the effect this belief would have on sociological research methods. (40 marks)

Postmodern and feminist methodologies

gettingyouthinking

1 Compare the photos of people in London in 1950 and today. What differences can you see?

2 What other major social changes affecting contemporary life can you identify?

3 Suggest some explanations for these changes?

4 Briefly think about the major theories of Marxism and functionalism – do you think they are relevant for an understanding of recent social changes?

One of the most exciting developments in sociology over the past 20 years has been the emergence of postmodernism. In many ways this is rather strange, as apparently one of the key messages of postmodernism is that it rejects the very project of understanding society – the aim of sociology itself!

However, some sociologists have enthusiastically taken on board some of its messages and have incorporated them into what they see as a consequently revitalized and radical sociology.

In this topic, we look at the impact of postmodernism on research methods and explore how, by influencing methods, postmodernism has also led sociology into studying new areas previously considered outside its domain.

Postmodernism and the rejection of positivism

Postmodernists such as Bauman (1990), Lyotard (1984) and Baudrillard (1998), argue that the coherent 'picture' of the social and physical worlds drawn by modernists, is no more 'true' or 'real' than the picture previously painted by the

religions that dominated thought processes before modernity. Postmodernists see a fragmented, discontinuous world in which the desire for order has led people to impose a framework which ignores those things that do not fit neatly into the classifications and theories that have been constructed.

This idea of artificial structures imposed on a fragmented world has also been applied to sociology itself. Postmodernists argue that the nature of sociological theorizing is rooted in this false idea of structure and order. Not only this, but the methods used by sociologists are also a reflection of the mistaken belief in an organized, structured social world out there.

The postmodern critique of sociological methods has three strands: **relativity,** knowledge as control, and **narrative** and **discourse**.

Relativity

As you know, the assumption underlying positivism is that there is an objective, world 'out there' waiting to be uncovered by research. Postmodernists dispute this. They see, instead, many different, competing 'worlds' that exist only in particular contexts and at particular times. There is, quite simply, no objective reality waiting to be discovered. The objective, scientific analysis based upon a scrupulous following of the rules does not produce knowledge about the world – it simply produces another relative version of society . According to Sarap (1993), Lyotard argues that knowledge is only deemed to be true if it is accepted by those who are regarded as the appropriate people to decide upon its worth.

Knowledge as control

Scientists and other professionals and academics are not objective intellectuals engaged in a struggle to find the truth. According to Foucault (1963/1975), they, like any other group in society, are engaged in a struggle to have their concept of knowledge (as opposed to other, competing ones) accepted as reality. The reason for engaging in this struggle is that whoever has control over what is regarded as knowledge, and how to obtain it, gains considerable power in society. Scientists and professionals are therefore not disinterested and objective, but key players in a power struggle. A particularly good example of this can be found in medical knowledge. Despite the fact that about 20% of people in hospital actually contract another illness or are medically harmed in some way by the very 'healing process', doctors have gained control over the task of healing and of defining what is or is not a healthy body. Other ways of dealing with health have been labelled as 'complementary medicine' or 'alternative therapies', and denied equal status on the grounds that they are not scientifically rigorous.

Narrative and discourse

We have seen that, according to postmodernists, sociologists are yet another group seeking to impose their form of knowledge on society, which they do by claiming expert knowledge based on sociology as a form of science.

The outcome of sociological research is the production of explanations or theories that explain social phenomena. Postmodernists call these explanations 'narratives'. The implication is that they are no more than stories, giving a partial account.

Where sociologists have provided large-scale 'grand-theory', which claims to provide a full and complete explanation for human behaviour (e.g. functionalism), the term used by postmodernists is 'meta-narrative'. The reason for the dismissal of these theories is simply that there is no world out there waiting to be explained. All explanation is partial and grounded in the context of people's lives and experiences.

Linked to narrative is the concept of discourse. Discourse can be seen as the framework of language within which discussions about issues occur. Discourse therefore limits and locates discussion.

Postmodernist research

Postmodernism has also been a positive force in three main ways relevant to research.

- It has introduced new methods and approaches to research.

- It has introduced different topics to study.
- It has encouraged people to speak for themselves, thereby allowing their narratives to stand without necessarily interpreting them.

Deconstruction: a new method

Postmodernism argues that all knowledge is relative and that some knowledge is more powerful than others. So, postmodernist writers such as Baudrillard (1998) argue that these 'narratives' about what we consider to be knowledge crucially affect how we act. But they do not influence us in the way that Marxists or functionalists would argue, rather they interact with people to create new and fragmentary patterns of thought and behaviour that alter according to place, time, and an unknowable range of other factors. The task of postmodernists is to try to uncover the linkages and possible patterns that underlie these narratives.

Foucault suggests this process of **deconstruction** is like the activities of an archaeologist in that the sociologist carefully digs down layer after layer to explore the construction of narratives. The postmodern researcher is, however, not concerned to give the 'truth' but to look instead at how particular narratives emerge at different times and in different contexts. Furthermore, they are not seeking to make claims for anything beyond the particular area studied.

One particular area to which deconstruction is applied is the subject of sociology itself, so traditional concepts are taken apart and looked at in new ways.

Transgression: new areas of study

The second innovation that postmodernism brought to research was that of topic areas. Traditionally, sociologists have divided the subject matter of society into various categories and classifications – so we study religion, work, social divisions, crime, and so on. If there is no world out there, and if sociology is just one narrative amongst many others (with no claim of superiority) then we also need to look critically at the sociological enterprise itself. Why do we have these divisions? They don't actually exist and we don't divide ourselves into separate chapters as we live our lives!

Postmodernists suggest that we should **transgress** classification boundaries and think in new ways. Take criminology, for example. Traditionally this studies people who commit crime. But the category 'crime' covers a massive range of actions, which sociologically have little in common. Crimes are just what some people have managed to have declared illegal, no more, no less. A different way of looking at the area is to study why people do harm to others – irrespective of what form that takes. Immediately, torture by the state, low wages, child labour and a million other forms of harmful activity enter the area of study – thus transgressing traditional boundaries.

Furthermore, if all areas of knowledge are equally relative, then how do we know what is more important or relevant than anything else? This has liberated sociologists to study issues such as the body, sexuality, eating, and time – all areas which traditionally have been seen as marginal to sociology.

Recently, postmodern methods have entered the study of crime. In particular, Ferrell (1999) has suggested that crime is increasingly 'framed' by the media, in such a way that although the majority of people will not actually experience serious crime, their perceptions of crime and its impact is derived via media images. Ferrell calls this 'cultural criminology'. Ferrell has also extended this to explore the way that crime is increasingly being defined by the media, so that certain cultural forms are criminalized. He gives the examples of media campaigns against 'performers, producers, distributors and retailers of rap and gangsta rap music'.

Examples of postmodern research

The first thing to say is that, in terms of traditional ideas of research, there are not that many clear examples of postmodern research. Rather, postmodern ideas have percolated throughout sociology, enriching the subject by, on the one hand, providing us with a new way of looking at traditional problems, and, on the other, by giving us new subjects to explore.

Reanalysing sociological concepts

Foucault and knowledge

In *The Birth of the Clinic*, Foucault reanalyses texts that describe the emergence of the medical profession. Instead of accepting their ideas, he uses them to illustrate the way that new forms of thinking emerged with the development of medicine. The new forms of thinking or discourses then moved out into the wider society as the predominant way of thinking. As this scientific, rational thought came to dominate, it also ensured the importance of doctors and other professionals. Foucault's analysis challenged the traditional functionalist, Weberian and Marxist ideas of power and knowledge. Postmodernist research can thus involve a critical deconstruction of existing sociological concepts.

Youth culture

The study of youth culture has been dominated by critical sociologists who have seen it as a form of resistance by young people. The search by these sociologists has been to find the meaning of youth culture and to explain what is the significance of the clothes and music in it.

Postmodernists, such as Redhead (1993) have challenged this view and argued that youth culture has 'no meaning' as such but is simply a complex and ever-changing mixture of influences – ranging from resistance, through constructions of what looking good means, to the manipulation of media companies, overlaid with genuine innovation. According to Redhead, to seek the meaning of it all is completely mistaken.

Redhead uses secondary data in his work but also uses the writing of young sociology students, drawing upon their current experiences of clubbing.

New areas of study

Tourism

Urry (1990) has examined tourist attractions and argued that certain places have been constructed so that they are seen and experienced as places of leisure and tourism – rather than for any other characteristics. When people visit, they do so through a 'tourist **gaze**'. This tourist gaze may screen out certain unwanted characteristics and focus solely on the socially constructed tourist image. The Lake District becomes more than a mountainous (and rainy!) place, and instead becomes a place of tranquillity, poetry and beauty. Walkers go there not just to walk, but to experience these additional elements. Spain becomes a place for clubbing, sunshine and beaches, or possibly a retirement dream, rather than a modern, industrialized country with a full range of social problems.

Food

Baudrillard (1998) has looked at the idea of food, arguing that in affluent Western societies most people do not eat to satisfy hunger, rather eating carries with it numerous symbols. We are almost literally what we consume. In a world where the fixed structures of class, sexual identity and ethnicity have been challenged and become more fluid, consumption then becomes one way of defining who we are. Where we eat and what we eat makes statements about us, in much the same way as our clothes do. For example, eating small amounts of food, in fashionable, expensive restaurants clearly indicates our success and aspirations.

Feminism and methods

Feminist theory and methods are linked in this book to the postmodern movement, mainly because they have contributed importantly to the current fragmentation of sociology. Feminism and postmodernism have provided the most powerful intellectual critiques of traditional sociology and opened up massive new areas for study, as well as new methods to use.

Traditional theoretical and methodological approaches (Marxism, functionalism and even interpretive approaches) assumed that sexual identities, including the role of women, were of no sociological interest. This resulted in females and the female perspective simply being ignored. However, by the 1960s and increasingly in the 1970s some writers, such as Firestone (1972) and Millett (1970), suggested that knowledge (and methods) are linked to gender. Men and women have different experiences and different starting points from which they construct their knowledge. So, all knowledge is related to gender. Incidentally, this argument has also been extended to different forms of knowledge based on 'ethnicity', religion, disability and sexual identity. Studies of society are then actually studies of male society.

This resulted in a rapid growth of feminist theory, which sought to understand gender relations. We discuss feminist theory in some detail in Topic 2, and also later in Topic 9, but for now the important point is that this emergence of feminist theory was paralleled with the development of different feminist methods of research.

Harding (1987) has suggested that there are three key elements of this feminist methodology, as follows.

Women's experiences: a new resource

Harding argues that most research has been devised and conducted by male sociologists and that this has resulted in a concentration on issues of interest to males. Women have different interests and perspectives, which open up new areas for sociological investigation. For example she asks 'Why do men find child care and housework so distasteful?'

New purposes of social science: for women

Harding suggests the purpose of feminist sociological research ought to be to improve the position of women. Traditional social science has been concerned to 'pacify, control and exploit' women, but feminist research is committed and open about its own commitment – unlike the value-free model that has been used as a cover to control women. This commitment is known as 'feminist **standpoint**'.

Locating the researcher in the same critical plane as the subjects

This third element of feminist research aims to bridge the gap between female researchers and female subjects of research. Harding argues that the feminist researcher must examine all her 'assumptions, beliefs and behaviours' and make these clear to both the subjects of research and to the people who read the research. Not only this, but the 'class, race and gender' of the researcher must also be clearly stated. In doing so, the feminist researcher does not appear 'as an invisible, anonymous voice of authority, but as a real, historical individual with concrete, specific desires and interests'. Maynard has added that feminist research should include the perspective of the women being studied, so that research is seen as a joint activity, rather than one in which the sociologist is an expert who studies powerless subjects (Maynard and Purvis 1994).

These ideas have led to in-depth interviewing/discussion and participant observation being particularly favoured in feminist research.

Harding also addresses two other key points which concern feminists – the relative truth of male and female sociologists' accounts of the world and the question of whether men can ever undertake feminist research. The first question revolves around the problem faced by feminist sociologists that they can sometimes arrive at completely different accounts of society from male sociologists. So, who is right? Both? Or only one? Or neither? Harding's reply is quite simple – women are more able to understand society than men and therefore their accounts are to be preferred. The second question concerning

men conducting feminist research is one where Harding gives a possibly surprising answer. She believes men can do feminist research – particularly because there are areas, to do with male sexuality and male friendships, where they have greater potential for insight compared with females. However, they would have to follow the three key elements of feminist research mentioned above.

Focus groups

Feminist sociologists routinely use focus groups for their research. Wilkinson (1999) argues that this method fits the ethos of feminism in three ways. First, focus group research is less artificial than other methods because it emphasizes group interaction which is a normal part of social life. As women are able to discuss issues in the company of other women, they are more likely to divulge their true 'lived experiences' than in more artificial interviewing situations. Second, feminist research is concerned to minimize differences in power and status that can occur in research situations, where the more powerful sociological researcher may dominate the interaction. Focus groups tend to even out the power, by giving a group of women the chance to take control over the discussion. Finally, Madriz (2000) has further suggested that where focus groups consist of 'marginalized' women such as 'lower-socioeconomic-class women of colour' then the focus group gives them the sense of solidarity to make sense of their 'experience of vulnerability and subjugation'.

Feminist ethnography

Reinharz (1992) suggests that the most effective way to study women is to use ethnographic methods. She argues that these allow the full documentation of women's lives, especially those aspects that are regarded by males as unimportant (such as domestic tasks). Further, she suggests that ethnography allows researchers to see activities from the viewpoint of women, rather than from the traditional male sociological angle. Finally, Reinharz argues that feminist ethnographic research is less exploitative of the women being studied than traditional male ethnography. For example, Skeggs (2001) points that in her ethnographic research (see Focus on research on the next page), she was seeking to 'emphasize the words, voices and lives of the women', which fits well with the argument of feminist researchers for standpoint feminism.

Qualitative interviewing

Feminist sociologists have adopted the in-depth interview as their most used tool of research, according to Bryman (2004). Oakley (1981) argues that traditional structured interviewing is exploitative, offering the interviewee nothing in exchange for their information and reflects a power imbalance between researcher and interviewee, with the researcher deciding what is worth talking about. Therefore feminist unstructured/in-depth interviewing emphasizes that the two women involved are engaged in a discussion based on equality, in which the interviewee is equal in power with the interviewer and has

Bev Skeggs (1997)
Formations of class and gender

Beverley Skeggs studied 83 White, working-class young women over a period of 12 years using ethnographic measures, involving participant observation and in-depth interviews. The research began with the women enrolling on a health and social care course at a college in the North-West of England and Skeggs followed them through the rest of their education, their employment and their family lives. According to Skeggs, her work was feminist in that she was politically committed to providing a means for 'marginalized' women to express themselves. Furthermore, she wished to show how the young women's perceptions of the society they encountered influenced their actual behaviour. Skeggs argues that she did not exploit the women for her own career benefits, but that her research gave her 'subjects' a sense of self-worth and that she 'provided a mouthpiece against injustice, particularly with regard to disclosures of violence, child abuse and sexual harassment'.

Skeggs, B (1997) *Formations of Class and Gender*, London: Sage Publications

1 In what ways can Skeggs' research be described as feminist?

equal right to decide on the direction of the discussion. In her own research interviews on the transition into motherhood, Oakley was asked questions on a range of issues by the respondents and felt that by replying and even advising the women, she was fulfilling the criteria of feminist research methods.

However, feminist writers have had some problems in that their interpretation of women's responses to their questions do not necessarily square with the respondent's. For example, Millen (1997) interviewed 32 British female scientists about their work. However, her approach, based on feminist ideas was largely rejected by the respondents. Millen comments:

<< From my external, academically privileged position vantage point, it is clear that sexism pervades these

professions. However, the women did not generally see their careers and interactions with male scientists in terms of gendered social relations. There is therefore a tension between their characterization of their experience and my interpretation of it. >>

Discussion on feminist methods

This strong approach to the uniqueness and superiority of feminist research has not gone unchallenged. Mary Maynard, herself a feminist sociologist, disagrees with Harding's arguments. She suggests that the strong position taken by Harding belongs to an early era of feminism when there was a need to stake out its territory and stamp its mark upon sociology (Maynard and Purvis 1994). She also argues that no matter what central themes there are to feminist research, in the end if it is not rigorous and compelling in its accuracy, then it cannot claim to be sociological research.

She argues that the continuing stress on listening to women's experiences particularly through in-depth interviews has become political correctness and other forms of research are being prevented. This is taken up by Oakley (1998) who, although strongly associated with the use of qualitative interviewing methods, argues that the use of qualitative research methods in feminist studies reflected a desire by feminists to distance their work from the traditional scientific/positivist approaches, which were much favoured by the male sociology 'establishment'. According to Oakley that time has now passed and it is important for feminist researchers to use quantitative as well as qualitative methods in their research. This will allow them access to the prestige,

Check your understanding

1 Give two examples of meta-narratives in sociology.

2 Why does the postmodernist stress on the relativity of knowledge imply criticism of positivism?

3 Explain in your own words what is meant by 'discourse'. Give an example.

4 How do postmodernists view experts and professionals?

5 What do postmodernists do when they deconstruct a concept or theory?

6 Give one example of:
  (a) a traditional subject looked at in a new way by postmodernists, and
  (b) a new subject brought into the domain of sociology by postmodernists.

7 What are the three key elements of feminist methodology, according to Harding?

8 Give one criticism of Harding's approach.

funding and influence on government policy currently enjoyed by those following more positivistic methods. Interestingly, Oakley was one of the first feminist writers to argue for the use of in-depth, qualitative interviews, as we saw earlier, and clearly she feels that the wheel has turned too far and the total rejection of quantitative methods is harming feminist research.

web.task

Search the web for tourist information and images about a particular place. What impression of the place do they create?
To what extent do the images and information about the places reflect Urry's idea of the 'tourist gaze'?

exploring postmodern and feminist methodologies

Item A

In this study, undertaken from a feminist perspective, the researchers set out to explore the young women's views and experiences of violence. The researchers based much of their methodology on feminist principles. They were open to the subjects about their own feelings, background and belief and sought to answer any questions asked in an honest a way as possible. Furthermore, they sought to eliminate power and status differences between themselves and the young girls. The researchers claim that they accepted that the research had to be led by where the subjects wanted it to go, so it became fully participatory. The researchers eschewed quantitative methods and used a variety of qualitative approaches including in-depth conversations/interviews and simply 'hanging around' with the young women. In fact, Burman *et al.* describe their work as largely 'ethnographic'.

Burman, M.J., Batchelor, S.A. and Brown, J.A. (2001) 'Researching girls and violence: facing the dilemmas of fieldwork', *British Journal of Criminology*, 41, pp. 443–59

Item B

Frank comments on a research study into cancer where she herself was interviewed. She states how disrespected she felt when she read the research reports of an interview concerning her illness. Bits of her story were made to reappear as instances validating whatever point the social scientist was making in that particular chapter. In particular her pain and suffering were omitted by the researcher.

In sociological research, she argues, there is no space for the individual suffering felt by the patient, what appears instead is narrative which is part of a sociological discourse which the sociologists understand between themselves. Not fitting this pattern, 'suffering' is rejected and censored.

Adapted from Frank, A.W. (2001) 'Can we research suffering?', *Qualitative Health Research*, 11(3), pp. 353–62

1 (a) Identify the approach to sociology advocated by **Item A**. (2 marks)

   (b) Identify two concerns of the patient concerning the sociological research that included her own experiences **(Item B)**. (4 marks)

   (c) Identify and briefly explain two factors that distinguish the work of feminist sociologists from traditional methods **(Item A)**. (4 marks)

   (d) With reference to the Items and elsewhere, briefly examine the view that interpretive research should be value-free. (10 marks)

2 'Postmodernism is less concerned with researching reality than in declaring that reality is dead.'

   Evaluate the influence of postmodernism on sociological research. (40 marks)

Questionnaires and interviews in research

Source: The Times, 29 August 2005

gettingyouthinking

Which Austen heroine are you?

1 You identify most with:

a Sleeping Beauty
b Cinderella
c Beauty and the Beast
d The wicked queen (in Snow White)
e Tinkerbell
f The Little Mermaid

2 Your favourite movie star is:

a Dark, French and sexily brooding
b George Clooney
c Colin Farrell
d Matthew McConaughey
e Viggo Mortensen
f Harrison ford

...

10 What do you drink?

a What have you got?
b Champagne
c White wine/spritzers
d The latest trendy cocktail
e Red wine, vodka, and/or brandy
f You don't really drink much.

11 You flirt:

a With anyone who'll flirt back – gender immaterial
b With any good-looking man who crosses your path
c With men you like, but it's more mutual teasing and quick-witted banter than sexual innuendo
d Discreetly. It may feel to you like flirting, but your friends would never call you a flirt
e Yes, but you're uncomfortable if the conversation gets too sexually provocative
f Not really. It's rare that you meet someone you really connect with.

12 You dress:

a Down – jeans, sweaters, trainers
b Classy but sexy – you like to be noticed
c Attractive, but not flashy
d In the latest trends, and you like to show skin – low-rise jeans and a belly-button piercing
e Feminine – skirts, pretty tops, kitten heels
f To express your personality.

Scoring

Q1	a 2	b 1	c 3	d 4	e 5	f 6
Q2	a 4	b 3	c 5	d 2	e 6	f 1
Q10	a 5	b 4	c 2	d 3	e 6	f 1
Q11	a 4	b 5	c 3	d 1	e 2	f 6
Q12	a 1	b 4	c 3	d 5	e 2	f 6

41–51 You are Elizabeth (Pride and Prejudice) – outgoing, funny and direct. You want a serious relationship, but it's essential for you to find someone you can have fun with or teach to have fun. Your best matches are: Mr Darcy, Henry Tilney, Captain Wentworth ...

64–71 You are Lydia (Pride and Prejudice) – flirty, wild and thoughtless. You're not ready for a serious relationship – what you need is a series of fun flings, and any of these wild boys will do nicely – Henry Crawford, Willoughby, Mr Wickham ...

1 This is part of a 15-question quiz about personality types published in *The Times*. The questionnaire and answers are good fun – but if we were serious in asking questions about personality types, what sorts of questions might you ask?

The most common form of research in social science is based on simply asking questions and noting down the answers. Questions, either in questionnaires or interviews, are used in both qualitative and quantitative research equally. In this topic, we will explore the issues linked to the use of questionnaires and interviews and their relationship to particular methodological and theoretical approaches in sociology.

But not all sociologists agree that asking questions is adequate:

<< *Interviews and questionnaires allow access to what people say, but not to what they do. The only way to find out what 'actually happens' in a given situation is through observation.*>> (Darlington and Scott 2002)

The relationship of questionnaires and interviews to qualitative and quantitative research

Quantitative approaches

Quantitative approaches commonly use one of the following:

● *Questionnaires* – written questions which respondents are requested to complete by themselves. To emphasize this and distinguish them from **structured interviews** (see below), quantitative-style questionnaires are often referred to as 'self-completion questionnaires'. This style of questionnaires are likely to contain a majority of **closed questions**, i.e. questions with a very specific answer or with a given set of answers provided from which the respondent must choose.

- *Structured interviews* – a series of questions read out directly by the researcher to the respondent. No variation or explanation are allowed. There is the possibility of using scripted **prompts**. These are best viewed as oral questionnaires.

Qualitative approaches

Qualitative researchers usually use **semistructured** or **unstructured** interviews. These use a series of questions as a starting point for the in-depth exploration of an issue. Qualitative researchers also use similar discussion techniques in group interviews (more than one person interviewed at the same time) or in focus groups (where a topic is introduced by the researcher and then the group take the discussion where they wish).

Self-completion questionnaires: a quantitative method

Questionnaires are used by sociologists when they are looking for specific information on a topic (often to support a hypothesis). They are extremely useful in surveys, as they can reach a large number of people, since the printed questions can be handed out, mailed out, or put on the internet. Even though they are distributed to a large number of widely dispersed group of people, they are still very easy to administer and can

be very quick to get organized and distributed. They provide clear information, which can be converted into statistical data, through the use of coding.

In terms of the sorts of questions asked, most questionnaires generally use closed, rather than **open**, questions, as without a researcher present, people may become confused if the questions are complex. Questionnaires are also particularly useful when it comes to asking embarrassing questions where having an interviewer present may make the respondent feel uncomfortable.

Reliability

Questionnaires are highly standardized, so clearly everyone receives the same questions in the same format. This should make them highly reliable. However, it is never possible to know if everyone interprets the questions in the same way, so the questionnaires are not strictly the same.

Generalizability and representativeness

Questionnaires are widely used in survey work and, if the sampling has been correct, then the questionnaire should produce questions that are generalizable to the whole population. However, postal or internet questionnaires need not necessarily be answered by the person they were sent to. Anyone in the household or with access to a computer could complete the questionnaire. This throws some doubt on representativeness and generalizability.

The second main problem with all self-completion questionnaires is the low **response rate**. Unfortunately, many people cannot be bothered to reply to questionnaires – unless there is some benefit to them, such as the chance to win a prize. This is a serious drawback of questionnaires in research. A low response rate (that is when only a small proportion of people asked actually reply) makes a survey useless, as you do not know if the small number of replies is representative of all who were sent the questionnaire. Those who reply might have strong opinions on an issue, whereas the majority of people may have much less firm convictions – without an adequate number of replies, you will never know. This often occurs when questions are asked about moral issues such as experiments on animals, or abortion/termination. This is a crucial issue, which impacts on the generalizability of any research using self-completion questionnaires.

Validity

Questionnaires can have high validity if they are well designed and seek out answers to relatively simple issues. However, there are a number of problems that they have to overcome to ensure these high levels of validity. People who reply to the questionnaire may interpret the questions in different way from that which the researcher originally intended. So their replies might actually mean something different from what the researcher believes they mean. Even more problematic than this is the danger of people deliberately lying or evading the truth. There is little that the researcher can do, apart from putting in 'check questions' – which are questions that ask for the same information, but are phrased differently. However, without an interviewer present the researcher can never really know if the answers are true. Parker *et al.* (1998) used questionnaires to find out what sorts of drugs young people were using over a period of time. Later in follow-up interviews, one respondent said:

<< *The first time we had this questionnaire, I thought it was a bit of a laugh. That's my memory of it. I can't remember if I answered it truthfully or not. … It had a list of drugs and some of them I'd never heard of, and just the names just cracked me up.*>>

Designing a good questionnaire

When constructing a questionnaire, the sociologist has to ensure:

● *that the indicators are correct* – so that it asks the right questions, which unearth exactly the information wanted – in sociological terms, 'the concepts have been well operationalized'
● *that there is clarity* – the questions are asked in a short, clear and simple manner that can be understood by the people completing the questionnaire
● *that it is concise* – that it is as short as possible, since people usually cannot be bothered to spend a long time completing questionnaires
● *that it is unbiased* – the respondent is not led to a particular viewpoint or answer.

Collating and analysing self-completion questionnaires

As these are usually closed questionnaires, sociologists use a system known as 'coding'. This consists of allocating each answer a particular number and then putting all the answers into a type of spreadsheet. This spreadsheet can then be interrogated for information. All the different answers to the questions can be summarized and compared one against the other. Sociologists have numerous statistical software packages for this.

Questions about sex

A survey by the US National Opinion Research Center (Laumann *et al.* 1995) consisted of detailed questions about sexual behaviour using a sample of just under 3500 people and consisted of a mixture of questionnaires, telephone and face-to-face interviews. In order to make sure that they had a very high response rate, they were prepared to pay some people up to $100 to encourage them to reply to the questions. The sociologist Lewontin heavily criticized the study. His suggests that in both the questionnaires and interviews people simply lie. In particular, male respondents were either engaged in wishful thinking or were lying to themselves. He points out, for example, that the total number of sexual partners claimed by the males added up to 75% more than claimed by female respondents – he suggests that the numbers should more or less add up to the same totals. Furthermore, he expressed surprise that 45% of males aged between 80 and 84 were still regularly engaging in sexual activity. So, is it ever possible to get the truth about truly personal issues by asking people questions – whether through questionnaires or interviews?

1 **How does the extract above illustrate some of the problems involved in using questioning as a method of data collection?**

Structured interviews: a quantitative approach

Qualitative researchers use highly structured interviews, with the interviewer simply reading out questions from a prepared questionnaire. Effectively, they are oral questionnaires in which the researcher writes down the answers. (Hence the use of the term 'self-completion questionnaire' to distinguish it from the highly structured interview.)

Structured interviews are often used in conjunction with quota sampling (see Topic 4), as researchers often have to go out in the streets to seek people who fall into the categories

allocated to them. Once the person is identified, then the researcher will proceed with the structured interview.

The aim of the structured interview is to increase the reliability of questionnaires and the interviewer's role is deliberately restricted to reading out the questions and recording the answers. In limiting the role of the interviewer to the minimum, the possibility of **interviewer bias** is minimized and the possibility of reliability is maximized.

The advantages and disadvantages of structured versus unstructured interviewing are fully discussed in the next section.

Interviews: a mainly qualitative approach

Sociologists generally use interviews if the subject of enquiry is complex, and a self-completion questionnaire would not allow the researcher to explore the issues adequately.

Types of interviews

As we have seen, interviews fall between two extremes: structured and unstructured.

- At their most structured, they can be very tightly organized, with the interviewer simply reading out questions from a prepared questionnaire.
- At the other extreme, interviews can be highly unstructured – more like a conversation, where the interviewer simply has a basic area for discussion and asks any questions that seem relevant.
- In between is the semi-structured interview, where the interviewer has a series of set questions, but may also explore various avenues that emerge by **probing** the respondent for more information.

There are a three further types of specialist unstructured interviews sometimes used by sociologists:

- *Oral history interviews* – Respondents are asked about specific events that have happened in their lifetimes, but not necessarily to them. These interviews are almost always used to link up with other secondary sources.
- *Life history interviews* – These are a second form of unstructured interview in which people are asked to recount their lives. Like oral history interviews, this method is almost always linked to secondary sources.
- *Group interviews* – Interviews are usually conducted on a one-to-one basis, but there are occasions when group interviews are useful and these have similar issues in terms of reliability and validity to focus groups (see Topic 5). Group interviews are commonly used where the researcher wants to explore the dynamics of the group, believing that a 'truer' picture emerges when the group is all together, creating a 'group dynamic'. An example of this is Mairtin Mac an Ghaill's *The Making of Men: Masculinities, Sexualities and Schooling* (1994), in which a group of gay students discuss their experiences of school.

Reliability

Interviews always involve some degree of interaction between researcher and respondent. As in every interaction there is a range of interpersonal dynamics at work. Differences in age, ethnicity, social class, education and gender, amongst many other things, will impact on the interview. The less structured the interview the greater the impact of these factors. Reliability levels are, therefore, much lower than questionnaires and are directly related to the degree of structure of the interview. According to May (2001), the greater the structure, the higher the reliability – as the greater the chance of these variables being excluded and of the different interviews being comparable. However, Brenner *et al.* (1985) argue that 'any misunderstandings on the part of the interviewer and interviewee can be checked immediately in a way that is just not possible when questionnaires are being completed'. So, they believe that reliability is actually greater.

Representativeness and generalizability

Interviews are much more likely to be used in qualitative research, mainly because they allow for greater depth and exploration of ideas and emotions. Qualitative research tends to be more interested in achieving validity than representativeness. There is no reason why interviews should be any less generalizable than questionnaires, but as they are more likely to be used in non-representative studies, interviews have a reputation for being less generalizable. However, there is a much higher response rate with interviews than with questionnaires, as the process is more personal and it is often more difficult to refuse a researcher who approaches politely.

Validity

Interviews, particularly unstructured ones, have high levels of validity. The point of an unstructured interview is to uncover meaning and untangle complex views. Interviewing also has a significant advantage over self-completion questionnaires in that the interviewer is present and can often see if the respondent is lying or not. However, there are some problems ensuring that validity is high in interviewing.

We saw earlier that every interview is a social interaction with issues of class, gender, ethnicity and so on impacting on

---

s y n o p t i c l i n k **stratification** and **differentiation**

Social class has two elements, an objective one which reflects differences in employment, income and wealth, and a subjective one which consists of how people perceive their positions in the class structure. Much of the information on earnings and wealth can be obtained from secondary sources, but the subjective attitudes have been studied using questionnaires and interviews. There have been numerous such studies including the study of white-collar workers by Roberts *et al.* (1977)

and Devine's updating of the affluent worker research (1992). Devine conducted in-depth interviews with 30 male manual workers employed in the Vauxhall factory at Luton and their wives. Her research indicated that considerable changes had taken place since the original 'affluent worker' studies. Devine rejects the idea of a new working class and suggests, instead, that many more traditional working-class values have survived.

the relationship between the two people. Not only does this make each interview slightly different, it also means that validity can be affected. In particular, this can lead to the specific issue of interviewer bias – the extent to which the relationship between interviewer and respondent can change the respondents' answers to questions. There is a whole range of possibilities from respondents wishing to please the interviewer at one extreme to seeking to mislead them at other.

In fact, there is no reason why people should tell the truth to researchers, and this is particularly true when a sensitive issue is being researched. When questioned about sexual activities or numbers of friends, for example, people may well exaggerate in order to impress the interviewer. This can influence the **validity** of the research project. So it is rare now for interviews to be used for personal or embarrassing issues, with sociologists preferring self-report questionnaires.

It is easy for researchers, unknowingly, to slip their values into the research. Usually this happens in questionnaires as a result of the language used. In interviews there is a much wider possible range of influences to bias the research – as well as the language, there is the body language or facial expression of the researcher, or even their class, gender or ethnic background. In particular, interviewers should avoid leading questions.

Loaded words and phrases can also generate bias, i.e. the researchers use particular forms of language that either indicate a viewpoint or may generate a particular positive or negative response. For example, 'termination of pregnancy' (a positive view) or 'abortion' (a negative view); 'gay' or 'homosexual'.

The advantages of interviewing

- Interviewers can pick up non-verbal cues from interviewees.
- The interviewer can see whether the respondent might be lying, by seeing the situation through their own eyes.
- There is a higher response rate than with questionnaires.
- Interviews take place where interviewees feel comfortable.
- The more structured the interview, the higher the chance of replicating it and therefore of high reliability.
- The less structured the interview, the higher the validity as meaning can be explored.

Ethical issues in interviews

There can be significant ethical issues when using interviews in research as the interviewer can gain considerable information about the interviewee – some of which is potentially embarrassing for the interviewee. Trust needs to be established very early on and the person being interviewed has to have a reassurance that the information will be confidential. Any information that is published will be done in such a way that the interviewee remains anonymous.

Dorothy Scott studied child abuse in a children's home (Darlington and Scott 2002).

>> *Confidentiality also proved to be difficult as I became increasingly aware of the the difficulty of presenting findings of research based on an intensive analysis of cases without using illustrations which might be recognizable to the staff or the clients.* >> (p.38)

Collating and analysing interview data

Interviews are usually recorded and then this recording is then **transcribed** (written up) into notes. This is an extremely time-consuming activity. For example, Tizard and Hughes (1991) recorded interviews with students to find out how they went about learning – and every one hour of interview took 17 hours to transcribe and check. However researchers still prefer to do this, as taking notes at the time of the interview usually disrupts the flow, disrupting the atmosphere. The transcription is then studied for key themes. Increasingly, sociologists use special software that can be set up to look for key words or phrases and will then collate these into categories. By recording and transcribing interviews, sociologists have got independent evidence to support their claims and which they can also provide to other researchers should they wish to replicate the research. This is very important for qualitative sociologists, who are often criticized by quantitative researchers for their failure to provide independent evidence.

Check your understanding

1 Identify and explain three of the key issues in asking questions.

2 What do we mean when we talk about loaded questions and leading questions? Illustrate your answer with an example of each and show how the problem could be overcome by writing a 'correct' example of the same questions.

3 Why are 'response rates' so important?

4 When is it better to use questionnaires rather than interviews?

5 When would it be more appropriate to use 'unstructured interviews?

6 Give any two advantages of structured interviews compared with unstructured ones.

7 What do we mean by 'transcribing'?

research ideas

Your aim is to find out about a sample of young people's experience of schooling. Draft a closed questionnaire to collect this data. Collect and analyse the data quantitatively. Then draft guide questions for an unstructured interview to find out about the same issue. Conduct two or three of these interviews, either taping or making notes of the responses.

Compare the two sorts of data. What differences are there? Why do those differences occur? Which method do you think was most effective for that particular purpose? Why?

KEY TERMS

Closed questions – questions that require a very specific reply, such as 'yes' or 'no'.

Interviewer bias – the influence of the interviewer (e.g. their age, 'race', gender) on the way the respondent replies.

Open questions – questions that allow the respondent to express themselves fully.

Probes – tactics by which the interviewer can encourage the interviewee to expand on an answer, e.g. by asking them directly to expand or simply remaining silent as if expecting more detail from the respondent.

Prompts – possible answers to a question.

Response rate – the proportion of the questionnaires that are returned (could also refer to the number of people who agree to be interviewed).

Semistructured interview – where the interviewer has a series of set questions, but may also explore avenues that emerge by probing the respondent for more information.

Structured interview – where the questions are delivered in a particular order and no explanation or elaboration of the questions is allowed by the interviewer.

Transcribing – the process of writing up interviews that have been recorded.

Unstructured interview – where the interviewer is allowed to explain and elaborate on questions.

Validity – refers to the problem of ensuring that the questions actually measure what the researcher intends them to.

exploring questionnaires and interviews in research

Item A

Wellings *et al.* (1994) wished to study sexual behaviour in Britain, but were well aware that there might be some degree of embarrassment and that people might not be too keen to disclose very personal information to researchers they did not know. They were also concerned over the sort of language to use – clinical language or slang? Would it be better to let people complete questionnaires by themselves or should they be interviewed? Would respondents be convinced that their answers really were going to be confidential? After a small pilot survey, they decided to conduct the research face to face. This would allow the researchers to put people at their ease.

A combination of self-completed questionnaire and interview was chosen. The interview dealt with less personal issues such as family background, early sexual experiences and sex education.

Wellings, K., Field, J. and Wadsworth, J. (1994) *Sexual Behaviour in Britain: the National Survey of Sexual Attitudes and Lifestyles*, Harmondsworth: Penguin

Item B

<<We set out to compare how crime has been perceived by ordinary working class people at different periods over the last 60 years. We therefore decided to gather testimony from three generations of people. Fifty-four full-length tape-recorded interviews were completed (with 34 men and 20 women). Informants were drawn from various parts of the London Borough of Tower Hamlets. We aimed to find people who could provide testimony which would allow experiences, memories and interpretations of the past. There were obvious problems in interpreting and comparing testimonies about life in the East End over the last 50 years. We recognized that the recalling of images of the past would be affected by a number of factors: selective amnesia, telescoping of events, reinterpretation in the light of previous experiences, suppression of unpleasant memories or exaggeration of one's own involvement. We certainly came across informants who talked of the 'good old days' recounting stories of bed-bug infestation and chronic overcrowding while still insisting that 'life was better then'.>>

Hood, R and Joyce, K. (1999) 'Three generations: oral testimonies on crime and social change in London's East End', *British Journal of Criminology*, 39(1)

---

1 (a) Briefly explain what is meant by 'self-completed questionnaire' (**Item A**). (2 marks)

(b) Identify **two** problems of using interviews to study the issue of how people have perceived crime over a period of 60 years. (4 marks)

(c) Briefly explain **one** reason it was felt necessary to interview people over three generations to understand the changing perceptions of crime (**Item B**). (4 marks)

(d) Using material from the **Items** and elsewhere, briefly explain some of the problems experienced by sociologists in collecting primary data about sensitive issues. (10 marks)

2 Assess the usefulness of in-depth interviewing as a research method for sociologists. (40 marks)

TOPIC 8

Secondary data

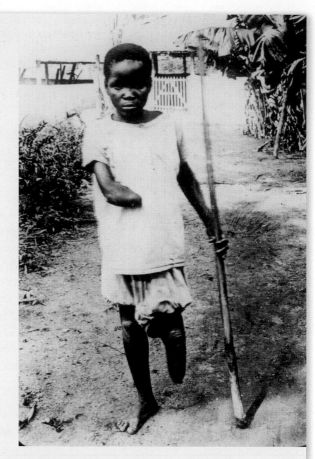

getting you thinking

The photo on the right was taken in the early part of the 20th century and used to illustrate an article in the magazine *History Today*. The article explores the way in which European colonialists exploited Africans around this period and, in particular, the way that Belgian colonialists would chop limbs off children if they failed to collect enough rubber. Below is the list of sources quoted by the writer that he used for his article.

Joseph Conrad (1995) Heart of Darkness (edited by D.D.R.A. Goonetilleke), Broadway Literary Texts 1

Frederick Karl and Laurence Davies, The Collected Letters of Joseph Conrad, Cambridge University Press

Marvin Swartz (1971) The Union of Democratic Control in British Politics During the First World War, Oxford: Clarendon Press

Wm. Roger Louis The Triumph of the Congo Reform Movement 1905–1908, Boston University Papers on Africa

Roger Anstey (1971) 'The Congo Rubber Atrocities – A case study', African Historical Studies, Vol. IV, 1

Source: Angus Mitchell (1998) 'New Light on the *Heart of Darkness*', *History Today*, December 1999, pp. 20–21

1 List the variety of sources used by the author (for example, are there any academic articles or novels?).

2 Why do you think that he used this range of material?

3 If you wanted to study a topic which happened in 1904, what would you do?

4 Can you think of any problems that might result from using the range of sources mentioned above?

In this topic we explore the way that sociologists can make use of material collected by other people for whatever reason. Because these resources are 'second-hand', when the sociologist comes to examine it, this data is known as **secondary data**. However, it is important to remember that it has equal status amongst sociologists with **primary data**, and can be just as difficult to collect and interpret as primary sources. Both qualitative and quantitative researchers make use of secondary sources for a variety of reasons, which we will explore in this topic.

Types of secondary data

A huge range of material can be considered as secondary data. Bryman (2004) suggests the following categories.

- *Life (personal) documents* – These include diaries, letters, e-mails, photographs and video recordings. They may be written down, or in visual or aural (i.e. can be heard) form.
- *Official documents* – These derive from the state and include official statistics, government and local authority reports, minutes of government meetings and of Parliament, and the whole range of officially sanctioned publications available.
- *Other documents that derive from organizational sources* – By this, Bryman means the publications of profit-making companies, charities and any other form of organization that produces some form of formal output.
- *The contents of the mass media* – This is a whole area of study by itself. The mass media refers to all organizations producing information and entertainment for a public audience. This includes radio, television, the internet, newspapers and magazines and novels.

- *Previous sociological research* – This covers all previously published sociological research and datasets.

Webb *et al.* (1981) also argue for the use of **trace measures** – these are the physical changes produced by human action, such as the number of lager cans left around a building after a group of young people go home after hanging around for the evening.

The advantages to sociologists of using secondary sources

Rather than starting afresh, all sociological research begins with a **literature search**, or review, which consists of finding and reading all relevant previous sociological research on the particular topic under investigation.

If the information required already exists, though perhaps in a different form, the researcher does not have to repeat the original research. Alternatively, the researcher may use the original data to reexamine previously published data or studies in order to interpret them in a new theoretical light.

Often, sociologists want to look back in history for information but there is no one able to provide a life or oral history. In these cases, the sociologist must use secondary sources, such as **official documents** and letters.

Sometimes, it is impossible for the researcher actually to visit or talk to the group directly. This could be for financial reasons, or because the group may be geographically too distant or scattered. More commonly, the sociologist thinks that studying the group directly would be too obtrusive (see below). This is where trace measures are often used.

Sociologists studying crime and deviance are often faced with situations where direct studies of the group might be considered unethical – a good example is research on children where it may not be possible to get informed consent. Although some sociologists are prepared to engage in participant observational methods, for example, that can involve them in illegal or immoral activities, other sociologists prefer to study these activities by the use of secondary data.

Finally, and overlapping with the previous point, there are groups engaged in activities that they do not want sociologists to study, because they may be illegal, deviant or immoral. For sociologists studying these groups, one of the few ways to gain information is to access any secondary data available.

Disadvantages of using secondary sources

All secondary sources (except trace sources) are created for a reason; this could well create **bias** and distortion. Government statistics are often neutral, but they are also often constructed in such a way as to throw a positive light on events or statistics. At worst, they can be simple propaganda. Private organizations such as companies, are concerned to produce a positive image of themselves. They will, therefore, only

produce information that promotes this image. This applies equally to charities and any other form of organization. **Life documents**, such as a diary, give a very one-sided view of what happened and are almost always bound to be sympathetic to the writer.

Historical sources contain the possibility of bias, which we have already noted for other secondary sources, but there is the even greater problem, according to May (2001), of their being influenced by particular historical events or cultural ways of thinking that the sociologist may not be aware of.

Finally, as we have seen throughout the book, the work of sociologists may contain errors and biases.

Assessing the quality of secondary data

Scott (1990) suggests that there are four criteria to use when judging the usefulness of secondary data to the researcher. These are:

- *Authenticity* – Is the origin of the data known and does the evidence contained there seem genuine?
- *Credibility* – Are the data free from error and distortion?
- *Representativeness* – Is the evidence shown by the data typical of its kind?
- *Meaning* – Is the evidence clear and comprehensive?

We will use these to guide us through the usefulness of each type of secondary sources.

Approaches to secondary data

Sociologists take different approaches towards analysing and using secondary data. There are four main approaches, outlined below.

Extraction

Extraction simply involves taking statistics or research examples from the original texts. It is commonly used when sociologists examine previous sociological sources and data bases.

Content analysis

In **content analysis**, documents and other sources are examined in great detail to see what themes run through them. There are two ways of doing this:

- Qualitative content analysis stresses exploring the meaning and looking for examples to illustrate the themes. This method is particularly commonly used in studies of the mass media.
- On the other hand, quantitative analysis will almost certainly use computer programs, which will count the number of times certain words (which are regarded as indicators of themes) or themes are used.

Semiotics

Semiotics is the study of signs. A sign is something that stands for something other than itself. For example, a Mohican haircut may indicate a rebellious attitude or a St George's Cross painted on a face signifies support for an England sports team Semiotics is often used in the study of youth culture, and is apparent in the work of both Marxist cultural studies writers and of postmodernist writers. Both these groups seek to analyse the meaning of the particular clothes, music and 'argot' used by young people. Similarly, sociologists interested in semiotics try to uncover the hidden meaning within the secondary data. It is particularly used in the study of life documents, especially photos and in music.

Hermeneutics

The term **hermeneutics** is used for the approach which seeks to analyse the secondary sources from the perspective of the person or organization originally compiling the data. So a hermeneutic analysis will look carefully at the political, social and economic context of the secondary data. Again, this is particularly commonly used in life documents and less commonly in organizational sources.

Life documents

Life documents include virtually all written, aural and visual material that derives from people's personal lives, including diaries, letters, e-mails, photographs and video recordings.

Traditionally, the material used by sociologists was written, but increasingly, there has been a growth in visual material such as photographs and home videos.

Life documents can give sociologists a detailed and very personal look into people's lives; as a way of seeing events through their eyes, it is an unrivalled method. They are also particularly useful when there is no other way to get hold of information, for example if the events have happened a long time ago and there is no one to interview. However, the writers may have distorted views of what happened, or they may well be justifying or glorifying themselves in their accounts.

Plummer (2000) suggested that the main forms of life documents include diaries, letters, photographs, film and what he calls '**miscellanea**', which consist of anything else reflecting one's life. We will examine each of these in turn.

Diaries

The key thing about diaries is that they chronicle events as they happen, rather than being filtered by memory or later events, as is the case with autobiographies. Diaries are also very detailed as they cover events day by day. This daily writing is also useful as if gives the sociologist a real idea of the exact timing of when things happen.

However, diaries cannot be relied upon for 'the truth', as people are not objective about their own lives. Instead they filter what happens around them according to their own biases

and perceptions. It is also important to remember why the diaries were being written, as many politicians and journalists have published diaries that were specifically written for later publication (for example, the diaries of the politician Tony Benn). This would suggest that the contents will be biased to ensure that they come to be perceived by the reader in a positive fashion.

Letters

The most famous example of the use of letters in sociology is Thomas and Znaniecki's *Polish Peasant* (1918). This is a study of the correspondence of recent immigrants to the United States with their families back in Poland. Thomas and Znaniecki placed an advert in the Chicago newspaper offering to pay for each letter handed to them, and received hundreds of letters. The letters gave them insights to the ordinary lives of immigrants and the issues that concerned them in their new lives in the USA. It also told them about the changes that occurred in family life and relationships as a result of the movement. The letters were divided into various categories by Thomas and Znaniecki, so there were:

- ceremonial letters, which marked formal occasions such as marriages, deaths and birthdays
- informal letters about everyday life
- sentimental letters about love and how family members were missed
- letters asking for and sending money and financial advice.

However, letters are always written with some purpose in mind and to convey a particular image of a person. For example, in Thomas and Znaniecki's work, the immigrant letter writers wanted to demonstrate to the people left in Poland what a success they had made with their lives, and so this 'filter' had to be taken into account when reading the letters.

Visual images

Millions of photographs and images are produced every year by families as the most common form of documenting their lives. Photographs have a very long history in sociology and in the early days of sociology in America, almost all research was illustrated with photographs. More recently, some sociologists have used photographs to 'capture' images of people's lives as a form of ethnographic study. Jackson (1978) used mainly photographs to explore the lives of prisoners and Harper (1978) photographed the lives of homeless people. These two sociologists argued that using image rather than text provides a powerful insight into people's lives.

Sutton (1992), however, is very critical of the use of photographs in sociological research. He points out that photographs are almost always taken when groups or families are engaged in holiday or festive occasions and that the photographs are also constructed to reflect a happy image ('Say cheese!'). He conducted a study of visits to Disneyland and concluded that these happy images reinforced the pleasant memories that families had of their visits, helping to forget the more negative experiences. Sutton therefore suggests that to use photographs (and videos) in research has serious drawbacks. However, as Plummer (2000) points out, photographs of events are not restricted to family holidays and occasions, and there is a wide variety of photographic images available which are not necessarily biased.

Miscellanea

Plummer uses this category to include the huge variety of other personal 'documents' that sociologists have used. For example, Schwartz and Jacobs (1979) studied people's suicide notes to try to understand the thoughts and emotion of people in their last hours before death.

However, the same point has to be made regarding miscellania as for all other life documents. The documents were produced for an effect; they do not necessarily represent the truth or even what people really thought. Taking the example of suicide notes, Schwartz and Jacobs point out that they were often intended to make other people feel guilty and to punish them. They were, therefore, written for an audience and may not necessarily tell their true feelings.

Official publications

Statistics compiled by governments and reputable research organizations are routinely used by sociologists. Governments have entire departments devoted to the production of statistics. In the UK, the Office for National Statistics produces these and collates them from other departments. These statistics provide far greater scale and detail than sociologists can generally

achieve and offer a source of information that is readily available, comprehensive and cheap to access.

Usually, the government will produce these statistics over a number of years – for example, the government statistical publication *Social Trends* has been published for over 35 years. This makes it is possible to make comparisons at various points in time.

Although these official statistics have many advantages, there are also some problems facing researchers using them. The statistics are collected for administrative reasons and the classifications used may omit crucial information or might classify groupings or activities in a way that is inappropriate for the researcher. So a researcher might be interested in the link between religion and income, but the official statistics may be collated on the grounds of ethnic origin or gender and average income.

Official statistics may also be affected by political considerations, as government will always seek to present the statistics in a positive light as possible. They may also reflect a complex process of interaction and negotiation – as is the case with crime statistics – and may well need to be the focus of investigation themselves!

Reports and government inquiries

The Civil Service and other linked organizations will often produce official reports that investigate important problems or social issues. However, although they draw together much information on these issues, they are constrained by their 'remit', which states the limits of their investigations. The government and other powerful bodies are therefore able to

s y n o p t i c l i n k   **stratification** and **differentiation**

The extent of social mobility in Britain has been a long-standing area of interest for sociologists. As long ago as 1949, the first study was conducted by David Glass (1954), who concluded that there was very limited movement upwards into the higher social classes. This study then heavily influenced the work of Goldthorpe and his colleagues in 1972, when they read the earlier Glass work and decided to amend both the way that social mobility was measured and how to define social classes (Goldthorpe 1980). Despite the research being very different (and much more sophisticated), the research was heavily influenced by the study of Glass's research and of its weaknesses. Goldthorpe's work found higher rates of social mobility, though there were high levels of self-recruitment into social classes.

Goldthorpe's work was criticized for not including women, so he then accessed a separate study (The 1983 British Election Survey) which contained useful information on women and social class, and incorporated this into the research (Goldthorpe 1983). Anthony Heath was also critical of Goldthorpe's work. He analysed

material available from the General Household Survey in order to criticize Goldthorpe (Heath and Payne 1999).

Goldthorpe's research results still dominated sociological thinking into the beginning of the 1990s. It motivated both the Essex social mobility study, which used much of Goldthorpe's framework (e.g. his social class classification), and, separately, Savage and Egerton (1997), who decided that they would use the data archives from The National Child Development Study (which initially had been created to study the health of children), a longitudinal study, starting in 1958 which had followed young children as they grew up.

Finally, in 2001, Roberts used data from both the Oxford Mobility Study by Goldthorpe, and Savage and Egerton's work in order to compare them and explore the contrasting results for a clear explanation of social class mobility (Roberts 2001).

Sociological research thus builds up gradually, with different researchers using previous work as secondary data and other researchers contrasting that with original research and also research based upon other datasets.

...e discussion of issues that they do not want to become the centre of public attention. For example, McKie et al. (2004) examined official government policy documents on health improvements for families in Britain. They used a particular perspective in their analysis, in that they explored exactly what benefits there would be for women as opposed to other family members. They conclude that there were significant gender inequalities in the official documents, with assumptions about the role of women being to care for other family members.

Documents from other sources

An enormous range of documents is produced by non-governmental organizations (NGOs) – that is, private companies, charities and other social groups. These include annual reports, press releases, advertisements and a range of statistical information about the company's aims and achievements. Increasingly, these are brought into the public domain via the internet.

However, sociologists are even more wary of taking NGOs' materials than they are of taking government ones. Most companies – and even non-profit-making organizations – have a vested interest in ensuring that their public image is positive. It is, therefore, extremely unlikely that negative information will be published by a company about itself. The complexity of using formal information produced by NGOs is illustrated by Forster's (1994) study of career-development opportunities in a large, multinational corporation. The more detail that Forster went into, the more contradictory the information he received:

<< One of the clearest themes to emerge was the apparently incompatible interpretations of the same events and processes amongst the three subgroups within the company – senior executives, HQ personnel and regional personnel managers. These documents were not produced deliberately to distort or obscure events or processes being described, but their effect was precisely to do this. >> (p. 160)

The mass media

The mass media produce an overwhelming amount of information each day, which not only reflects the concerns and values of society but also helps to shape these values. The mass media thus provide fertile ground for sociological researchers.

Content analysis is used by sociologists order to discover how particular issues are presented. They can do this in two ways:

- Using quantitative techniques, researchers simply count the number of times a particular activity or term appears in the media being analysed. This helps to prove a particular hypothesis, e.g. regarding the numbers of people from minority-ethnic backgrounds appearing on television. A slightly more sophisticated version of this might be to construct a content analysis grid, where two or more

themes can be linked, e.g. the number of times that newspapers run stories that link people from minority-ethnic backgrounds with negative events.

- In a similar way to the second form of quantitative analysis, researchers may use a qualitative form of content analysis to draw out general themes from the newspapers, film or television. They will, for example, seek to establish not just whether there is a negative association between ethnicity and social problems, but what forms any such association might take.

Quantitative approaches are useful because they provide clear, unambiguous statistics on the number of times topics appear in the press or are broadcast. They can also clearly state the criteria they use for the selection of themes. They are also replicable, because other sociologists can return to the original sources and check their accuracy. However, qualitative approaches have the strength of being able to explore the meaning of the theme or item being researched. Just having the number of times that an item is mentioned in the media does not give a true image of what is being discussed or the importance of the discussion. So, qualitative analyses tend to be more valid but less reliable.

Content analysis is very widely used in sociology, because it is simple and relatively cheap to access mass-media material and analyse it. Furthermore, there are no problems in finding a representative sample, as it is possible to obtain a wide variety of newspapers or television programmes. Importantly, it is an unobtrusive method of research – recording a television programme and then analysing it for its content themes does not impact in any way on the making of the programme.

However, Macdonald and Tipton (1993) suggest there is considerable risk of bias and distortion, for two main reasons:

- There are errors of various kinds, most importantly errors of fact, as the standards of journalists are not as high as academics.
- There is distortion of the facts – Newspapers and television programmes have various preferences as to what can be considered news and what 'angle' to approach the news from. The influences include journalistic values, proprietor's values and, perhaps most important in a competitive market, the audience at which the journalists perceive themselves to be aiming the news.

Furthermore, as Cohen (2002) points out, there is no single correct way to 'read' a newspaper's or television programme's hidden meanings. Each sociologist will approach the interpretation of the contents from their own perspective. Therefore, both reliability and validity are low in content-analysis studies.

One final further difficulty sociologists have in content analysis is actually knowing how the viewers or readers interpret the media output. We know from Morley's research (1980) that people approach and understand television programmes from very different perspectives. Sociologists cannot assume that the interpretation they have – even as a group of researchers agreeing on the content's meaning – will be the same as that of the viewer.

Sociological research and data archives

There are a number of **data archives** in Britain where the results of large research studies are stored. These can be accessed and the information reused by other researchers. Many of these can be found at The Data Archive (www.data-archive.ac.uk), based at the University of Essex. This holds over 4000 datasets from government, academic researchers and opinion poll organizations.

The huge advantage of these datasets is that they provide ready-made material, but the information that the researchers were originally seeking may not be the same as what is needed by the researcher using them as secondary data. If the researcher is not careful, it is possible to be led astray by the focus of the original research.

Although we have categorized data sets as purely sociological research, it is worth knowing that some are wholly or part-funded by the government. However, as they tend to collect information that is sociological in character rather than politically sensitive, most sociologists classify government-sponsored datasets as sociological research.

Perhaps the best-known data set is the Census, a survey of all people and households in the country, which takes place every ten years (the last Census was 2001, the next is 2011). All households in Britain are required to complete this by law. It is intended to be the most complete picture of Britain available. In recent years, there has been some concern that not everyone completes the Census – in particular, certain minority-ethnic groups, refugees and asylum seekers, and transient populations such as the homeless and travellers. It may, therefore, under-represent certain categories of the population.

Other well-known data sets include the longitudinal British Household Panel Survey and the General Household Survey which collects information on:

- household and family information
- housing patterns
- ownership of consumer items
- employment
- education
- health services usage
- income
- demographic changes
- smoking and drinking.

Previous sociological research studies

Previous studies as a starting point

Whenever sociologists undertake a study, the first thing they do is to carry out a literature search – that is, go to the library or the internet and look up every available piece of sociological research on the topic of interest. They can then see the ways in which the topic has been researched before, the conclusions reached and the theoretical issues thrown up. Armed with this information, the researcher can then construct the new research study to explore a different 'angle' on the problem or simply avoid the mistakes made earlier.

focus on research

Grimshaw *et al.* (2004)
Media image, community impact

Researchers very often include analysis of secondary data in research of any kind (for example, there will almost always be a literature review of previously published sociological work). Conversely, research using secondary data will almost always include other forms of research. The following is an example of multiple methods used to understand the relationship between racism and the media.

In 2003, Roger Grimshaw, Kate Smart, Kirsteen Tait and Beth Crosland (2004) carried out a research project which aimed to find out the impact of news reporting on levels of racist attitudes and activity against refugees and asylum seekers in London. They used the following methods:

- analysis of press coverage over a two-month period in a 'representative' sample of the national and London press
- focus groups with participants from London boroughs with high levels of refugees and asylum seekers to explore the impact of the media
- interviews with local refugee groups and local authority officials
- interviews with the editors of national and local newspapers
- a literature search of material on the relationship between the press and racism.

They concluded that there was unbalanced and inaccurate reporting of refugee and asylum-seeker issues and that this did have an impact on feelings towards these groups.

Grimshaw, R., Smart, K., Tait, K. and Crosland, B. (2004) *Media Image, Community Impact*, London: ICAR Kings College

1 **Suggest reasons why the researchers used each of these methods.**

2 **Suggest reasons why the researchers used so many methods in combination.**

Reinterpreting previous studies

Often, sociologists do not want to carry out a new research project, but prefer instead to examine previous research in great detail in order to find a new interpretation of the original research results. So the secondary data (that is, the original piece of sociological research) provide all the information that is needed. Sometimes, sociologists might conduct a **meta-analysis**. This is a formal term for the process of looking at the whole range of research on a topic and seeking to identify and draw together common findings.

A good example of how previous sociological work was used as secondary data is provided by Goodwin and O'Connor's (2005) reexamination of a little-known sociological study undertaken in the early 1960s on the lives of young people as they left school and entered work. They compared this with the transition from school to work today. The early work provided them with a detailed and rich database from which they could form hypotheses and make comparisons with contemporary research.

Sometimes, however, there are methodological errors in published research, as well as possible bias in the research findings. There have been many examples of research that has formed the basis for succeeding work and that only many years later has been found to be faulty. A famous piece of anthropological research which was used for 40 years before it was found to be centrally flawed was Mead's *Coming of Age in Samoa* (1945). Mead made a number of mistakes in her interpretation of the behaviour of the people she was studying, but as no one knew this, many later studies used her (incorrect) findings in their work.

Trace measures

One of the problems faced by all sociological researchers is the degree to which their presence and activities actually changes the natural behaviour of the participants. This problem is well recognized in participant observation and experimentation, but also exists to a lesser degree in survey work.

Webb has argued that sociology should use 'unobtrusive measures' in research wherever this is possible, so that this problem is eliminated (Webb *et al.* 1966). He points out that when people interact, they will often leave behind them some physical sign of their activities, the trace measures referred to earlier. According to Webb, there are two types of trace measures:

- *Erosion measures, which refers to things missing* – The most famous example of erosion measures (and the origin of the term) was the fact that the tiles around a particular exhibit in the Chicago Museum of Science and Industry which showed real chicks hatching out from their eggs, had to be replaced every six weeks because they became worn out by the sheer numbers of people visiting this exhibit. However, the rest of the museum only needed its tiles replacing after some years.
- *Accretion measures, which refers to things being added* – They were used by Rathje and Murphy (2002) in their study of rubbish thrown out by households, but they have also been used in studying graffiti in Belfast (to indicate 'ownership' of particular areas) and litter patterns (to demonstrate public use of space).

Check your understanding

1. What are secondary data?

2. What do we mean by the term 'hermeneutics? Give one other example of ways of approaching the study of documents.

3. Why do sociologists use secondary sources?

4. What are the disadvantages of using secondary sources?

5. What are the advantages and disadvantages of using official statistics and other government documents?

6. What are the advantages and disadvantages of using qualitative secondary data, such as diaries?

7. Give two examples of data archives. How can these be used by sociologists?

8. How can sociologists use trace measures in research?

research ideas

- You can conduct a simple trace measure experiment. Go around your house/garden and look at the objects lying around (anything from a photograph or a scratch in some wood to a CD) and think about the memories that these bring up. Think about the changes in you and your family since these first appeared, and what your feelings are.

web.task

Read more details about the research mentioned in the Focus on research on p. 217. Go to www.icar.org.uk and then to the publications link and choose 'Media Image, Community Impact'.

KEY TERMS

Bias – where the material reflects a particular viewpoint to the exclusion of others; this may give a false impression of what happened and is a particular problem for secondary sources.

Content analysis – exploring the contents of the various media in order to find out how a particular issue is presented.

Data archives – where statistical information is stored.

Extraction – taking statistics or research examples from the original texts.

Hermeneutics – the approach that seeks to understand the mindset of the person writing the original data, by exploring the context in which the document was first created.

Life (personal) documents – personal data in written, visual or aural form, including diaries, letters, e-mails, photographs and video recordings.

Literature search/review – the process whereby a researcher finds as much published material as possible on the subject of interest, usually

done through library catalogues or the internet.

Meta-analysis – studying a range of research on a particular topic in order to identify common findings.

Miscellanea – a term used by Plummer (2000) to refer to a range of life documents other than letters and diaries.

Official documents – publications produced by the government.

Primary data – Data collected by the sociologist themselves.

Secondary data – data already collected by someone else for their own purposes.

Semiotics – the study of the meaning of signs; data are examined for symbolic meaning and reinterpreted in this light.

Trace measures – physical changes as a result of human actions.

exploring secondary data

Item A

Burkitt (2005) wished to explore the way that people respond to particular events and how the government seeks to direct the population's thinking. He chose two major events: the peace demonstrations against the Iraq war in 2003 and the aftermath of the Madrid train bombings of 2004. Burkett undertook a qualitative content analysis of the coverage of these events in three major British newspapers *The Times, The Guardian* and *The Observer*. He looked at the manner in which the newspapers explored the issues and the sympathy they showed to the anti-war views expressed by protestors in both London and Madrid. Burkitt argued that the government has real difficulty in controlling the population when particularly strong emotions emerge amongst the mass of ordinary people, but otherwise the government can channel beliefs and views largely to reflect its opinions.

Burkitt, I. (2005) 'Powerful emotions: power, government and opposition in the "War on Terror"', *Sociology*, 39(4), pp. 679–95

Item B

Seale's (2002) study involves a detailed analysis of newspaper and magazine reports on the different ways that men and women overcome the problem of being faced by a diagnosis of cancer. The researcher analysed in detail the articles and uncovered a number of themes which centre around their heroism in facing up to this life-threatening situation. However, the media reports placed different interpretations upon the response of males and females; women transformed their lifestyles and attitudes to overcome cancer, while the men's approach was seen as depending upon their 'character'.

Seale, C. (2002) 'Cancer heroics: a study of news reports with particular reference to gender', *Sociology*, 36(1), pp. 107–26

1 (a) Identify the research method used in **Items A and B**. (2 marks)

   (b) Identify **two** reasons why the sample selected in **Item B** may not be representative of the British media (**Item B**). (4 marks)

   (c) Identify and briefly explain **two** criticisms that might be made of qualitative analysis of media sources (**Items A and B**). (6 marks)

   (d) With reference to **Item A** and elsewhere, briefly examine the view that official documents are a reliable source of data for sociologists. (8 marks)

2 Assess the usefulness of personal documents in sociological research. (40 marks)

Values and ethics

gettingyouthinking

1 Do you agree that we should continue to experiment on animals?

2 Imagine you have been given an opportunity to study scientists working in a lab who actually perform the 'experiments' on the animals.

(a) What would you like to find out?

(b) What would the first three questions of your questionnaire be?

(c) Do you think that you could conduct a series of interviews with the scientists without letting your views come across?

One of the most bitterly contested concepts in sociology has been over the question of the place of personal and political values in theory and research. Three distinct positions can be identified on this issue.

1 On one end of the debate are those sociologists who argue that if sociology wants to make any claim to scientific status then it has to be free of personal and political biases. This is known as **value-freedom** or **objectivity**.

2 A second position is that, ideally, our personal values should not intrude into our sociological studies, but that in practice it is simply impossible to keep them out – sociology as **value-laden**.

3 At the other extreme from value-freedom are those who argue that anyone doing sociology must surely use their studies to improve the condition of those most oppressed in society. Sociology is therefore more of a tool that helps bring about social change than just an academic subject studying society – **committed** sociology.

Value-free sociology

As we saw in Topics 3 and 4, there is a significant current of opinion in sociology (deriving from Emile Durkheim) that argues that we should seek to copy the methodology of the physical sciences such as biology or chemistry. One of the key ideas that these sociologists, or **positivists**, have taken from the physical sciences is that of the importance of objectivity in research.

As discussed earlier, positivists argue that the nature of sociological research is no different from that of the physical sciences – both branches of science (the physical and the social) study a series of phenomena, that exist totally independently of the scientists, and which can be measured and classified. On the basis of this, theories can be constructed and tested.

The 'social facts' positivists refer to are the statistics obtained by surveys and possibly from official publications. Properly constructed, they claim, these should be a perfect reflection of the subject under study. The evidence to show that surveys are objective and accurate exists in the accuracy of opinion polls on a range of subjects including voting and general elections; market research; extent of drug use and even sexual behaviour.

According to O'Connell Davidson and Layder (1994), personal biases and political opinions of researchers are irrelevant as long as the research is well designed and there is no attempt to distort or alter the findings. Finally, to ensure that no biases have inadvertently intruded, there is the check coming from publication of the research findings, which will include a discussion of methods used. The publication will be read and possibly criticized by other researchers.

Sociology as value-laden

This second school of thought believe that whether it is desirable or not, sociology cannot be value-free and it is a mistake to see it as such. They further claim that sociologists arguing that sociology is value-free are actually doing a disservice to the subject and identify a number of issues as evidence in support of their position.

Historical context

Gouldner (1968) has pointed out that the argument for a value-free sociology is partially based in a particular historical context. Weber has traditionally been associated with the idea that personal and political values should be excluded from research. Yet Gouldner claims that Weber was writing at a time when the Prussian (now German) government was making a strong attack on intellectual freedom. According to Gouldner, Weber was merely trying to prevent the government from interfering in sociology by claiming it was value-free. So, Weber was simply protecting sociology by this strategy.

Paying for research

Sociological research has to be financed and those who pay for the research usually have a reason why they want it done. Sociologists working for British government departments for instance, usually have to sign an agreement that if the department does not like the ideas or findings, then it has the right to prevent publication.

In *Market Killing*, Philo and Miller (2000) have argued that, increasingly, all sciences are having their critical researchers silenced through a combination of targeted funding by those who only want research undertaken into the topics of benefit to them and by the intrusion of commercial consultancies into research. This means that scientists benefit financially from certain outcomes and lose out if other outcomes are uncovered. They also point out that scientists allow their findings to be manipulated by public-relations companies, operating for the benefit of the funders – even when the findings do not necessarily support the funder's claims.

Career trajectories

As Gouldner (1968) pointed out, all sociologists have personal ambitions and career goals. They want to publish, get promoted, become renowned in their field. These desires can intrude either knowingly or subconsciously into their research activities. According to Kuhn (1962/1970), this involves accepting the dominant 'paradigms' at any particular time within sociology.

Personal beliefs and interests

Sociologists are no different from other people, in that they hold a set of values and moral beliefs. They might set out to eliminate these as best they can, but, ultimately, all our thoughts and actions are based on a particular set of values

and it is impossible to escape from these. The best that can be done is to attempt to make these values clear to both ourselves and to the readers of the research.

Similarly, sociologists find certain areas of study 'interesting'. Why are they drawn to these areas in the first place? Often they reflect personal issues and a desire to explore something important to them. This makes it more difficult to extricate personal values from the research process itself. An example of this is the work of Ken Plummer (2000), who has published widely on sexual issues and is a sociologist associated with 'queer theory'. He makes it plain that his own sexual preference encouraged him to become interested in gay issues:

>> *So, in a sense, I was actually exploring my own life side by side with exploring sociological theory. And I suppose that has shaped the way I think about these things today.* >>

Similarly, feminist writers are drawn to subjects of particular interest to women, indeed Harding (1986) accuses male sociologists of being biased in their choice of subject matter, and in their selection of 'facts'.

The domain of sociology

Today, sociology does have academic status and has been accepted as a 'social science'. As a subject it has developed a range of accepted ways of exploring the world, of sensible questions to be asked and reasonable research methods. It has joined other subjects in rejecting other non-orthodox approaches that claim to provide knowledge. For example, Collins and Pinch (1998) studied parapsychology and found that other social scientists believed that parapsychology was simply fantasy, therefore any research conducted by parapsychologists was dismissed out of hand. Any positive outcomes were simply regarded as the result of poor experimental methods or quite simply fraudulent.

Quite why social scientists simply reject alternative, non-orthodox approaches can be explained by postmodernism and by the work of Foucault outlined below. A good contemporary example is discussed by Mark J. Smith, who points to the great difficulty that environmental or 'green' sociology has had in getting its concerns over the environment accepted by the sociological 'establishment' – so that green concerns are seen as peripheral to the subject.

The postmodern critique

Postmodernists such as Lyotard (1984) and Baudrillard (1988) argue that the whole process of sociological and scientific thinking is itself based on a series of values about the nature of society. As we saw in our discussion of the growth of scientific thinking (Topic 3), science itself is a product of modernist thought.

Postmodernists dispute the assertion that rational thinking based upon verifiable evidence is superior to any other approach to understanding the world. They argue that, in fact, scientific thinking is just one of many possible ways of approaching an understanding of the world and that it is not inherently better – nor does it provide any superior 'truths'.

are other distinctive concerns that go beyond the value-freedom debate.

Whatever the view of the researcher regarding the importance of values in research, no sociologist would wish the actual procedure of research to harm those being studied or to produce a piece of research that was not as 'true' to the facts uncovered as possible. Ethical procedure is so important to sociologists that the British Sociological Association – the official body of sociology in Britain – has actually issued a guide to ethics that all researchers are expected to follow. Punch (1994) has summarized the main ethical concerns of sociology as follows:

- *Harm* – Any research undertaken must not cause any harm either directly or indirectly to those being studied (although a further question arises: what should a researcher do if the people under study are going to harm someone else?).
- *Consent* – Any person or group being studied, wherever possible, should give their consent to being the subject of research. This usually involves an honest explanation of the research being undertaken and the future use of the material obtained.
- *Deception* – The researcher should, wherever possible, be clear about their role to those being studied.
- *Privacy and confidentiality of data* – The information obtained should not breach the privacy of the person being studied, and nothing should be published that the person regards as confidential. Research therefore should not provide the real name or address of a person being studied.

Dealing with ethical issues

These ethical concerns may seem necessary but following them can pose great difficulties for sociologists engaged in certain research methods such as **covert participant observation**. Difficulties also arise in certain areas of research – for example, amongst young people, those engaged in criminal or deviant activities and those with learning difficulties or suffering from mental illness.

An example of both of these fine lines between acting ethically and crossing the boundary can be found in Hobbs' study of East End criminals and the CID (1988) – see Topic 5. Hobbs engaged in an ethnographic study of East End villains and local CID officers. During his study he found out about many illegal activities committed by both villains and police officers, including acts of violence. Hobbs decided not to pass any information from one group to the other, and despite knowing about criminal activities he decided that the most 'ethical' thing to do was not to interfere in any way.

Hobbs also mixed a covert style of research with the police with an overt one. Overtly, he was conducting research through interviews, but covertly he befriended a number of police officers and carefully studied them in their social lives without telling them what he was doing. Hobbs' work can be questioned for its rather dubious ethics in terms of condoning law-breaking behaviour (which was sometimes serious) and in researching the detectives informally without their consent. However, in doing both these activities, he produced a more vibrant and possibly more accurate piece of research than if he had adhered to the 'correct procedures'.

Check your understanding

1. **What is meant by 'positivism'?**

2. **How do positivistic sociologists think the problem of values can be overcome?**

3. **How can the funding for research influence its content, according to Philo and Miller?**

4. **Compare the views of Becker and Gouldner on values in sociology.**

5. **Why do postmodernists see it as impossible to even try to overcome the issue of values?**

6. **What do we mean by 'committed sociology'? Give two examples.**

7. **Identify and explain three ethical issues faced by sociologists.**

KEY TERMS

Committed – where an approach is open in its support of one particular approach, usually used with reference to Marxist sociologists, feminist sociologists and those wishing to confront racism and discrimination against people with disabilities.

Covert participant observation – when the researcher joins a group as a full member, and studies them, but does not tell them that he or she is a researcher.

Ethics – refers to issues of moral choices.

Hierarchical – some people are regarded as more important than others.

Left realism – a approach to social problems, which argues that is it better to cooperate with the authorities to solve social problems, even if fundamental social change is not brought about.

Malestream – originally a feminist term implying criticism of traditional sociology for excluding women from the subject both as sociologists and as the subjects of research.

Objectivity – the exclusion of values from research.

Positivism – an approach to sociological research which aims to use the rigour and methods of the physical sciences.

Value-freedom – the exclusion of values from research.

Value-laden – the belief that, whether or not it is desirable, sociology cannot be value-free and it is a mistake to see it as such.

web.tasks

1 Go to the MORI website at www.mori.co.uk. This contains a wide range of opinion surveys. Take a few examples of their surveys. Check who is sponsoring the research and see if you can identify any evidence of the intrusion of values, for example in the motives for the research and in the sorts of questions asked.

2 The British Sociological Association website lists all ethical issues that sociologists should consider when they undertake research. There is a summary by Punch in the main text, but it is worth exploring the original. Go to www.britsoc.co.uk and then click on 'Equality and Ethics'. On this page choose 'Statement of Ethical Practice'; finally go through each of the headings on this page.

Based on what you find there, what would you have to do if you wished to interview 14-year-old students in a local comprehensive to find out their views on drug use?

research idea

- Design two questionnaires aiming to discover young women's views of feminism. The first must discover that feminism is still important and relevant to young women, the second that it has gone too far and young women do not support it.

  What different questions could you use to get these different results? Could you interpret answers in different ways?

exploring values and ethics

Item A

<<Patriarchal knowledge is based on the premise that the experience of only half the human population needs to be taken into account and the resulting version can be imposed on the other half.>>

Spender, D. (1985) *For the Record: The Meaning and Making of Feminist Knowledge*, London: Women's Press.

Item B

<<There are therefore numerous points at which bias and the intrusion of values can occur. Values can materialize at any point during the course of research. The researcher may develop an affection or sympathy, which was not necessarily present at the outset of an investigation, for the people being studied. It is quite common, for example, for researchers working within a qualitative research strategy, and in particular when they use participant observation of very intensive interviewing, to develop a close affinity with the people they study to the extent that they find it difficult to disentangle their stance as social scientists from their subjects' perspective. This possibility may be exacerbated by the tendency that Becker identified for sociologists in particular to be very sympathetic to underdog groups.>>

Bryman, A. (2004) *Social Research Methods* (2nd edn), Oxford: Oxford University Press

1 (a) Identify the approach to sociology advocated by the author of **Item A**. (2 marks)

   (b) Identify two ways in which a sociologist's values can affect qualitative research (**Item B**). (4 marks)

   (c) Identify and briefly explain two criticisms of traditional sociology made by feminists. (4 marks)

   (d) With reference to the Items and elsewhere, briefly examine the way in which ethical issues may affect a sociologist's approach to their research. (10 marks)

2 'Values must inevitably enter research in many ways.' Explain and discuss this view. (40 marks)

TOPIC 10

Sociology and social policy

gettingyouthinking

Multiple sclerosis sufferer Colin Davis is arrested outside Britain's first cannabis café in Stockport, Great Manchester.

1 There has been much discussion about the legalization or decriminalization of cannabis. Explain your own view on this issue.

2 Why do you think that the government has not legalized its possession and use as yet?

3 Do you think that if sociological and medical researchers got together to provide the facts, this would change the mind of the government and the public? Explain the reasons for your view.

Sociology is first and foremost an academic subject that sets out to explore the way in which society operates and how it influences our lives – and for many sociologists, that is all they are interested in. For others, particularly those working in universities and research centres, sociological research is undertaken wholly or partly to inform and influence government **social policy**. This is particularly the case where the government or a pressure group provides the funding for the research.

The information obtained in research can have quite significant effects on social policy. In fact, so important has this applied branch of sociology become that there has recently been a considerable growth in the academic subject known as social policy, which only concerns itself with studying and influencing how governments respond to social problems.

Applying sociology: the positive view

According to Giddens (2001), there are four practical benefits of studying sociology:

- understanding social situations
- awareness of cultural differences
- assessment of the effects of policies
- increase in self-knowledge.

These form a useful framework for understanding the relationship between sociology and policy.

Understanding social situations

The most obvious outcome of sociology is that it allows us to understand the world around us, providing us with knowledge and insights. This understanding can take two forms:

- factual – provides us with the 'facts', which allow us to form a judgement or develop a theory
- theoretical – provides people with an explanation as to why something is happening.

Understanding society and poverty

An example of the way factual and theoretical understanding of social situations can influence social policy is the sociological study of poverty.

Factually

By the late 1960s politicians believed that they had eliminated poverty. The welfare state had been in existence for almost twenty years and everyone was guaranteed a minimum income, some form of housing and free healthcare; the issue of poverty gradually lost its political importance. However, a series of reports by Townsend (1979) and later by Mack and Lansley (1985) in the 1980s and 1990s showed that poverty remained a huge but hidden problem in Britain, with over 11 million people living in poverty. This research work continues, most notably at the Joseph Rowntree Foundation, where there is a continuous monitoring of the issue of poverty amongst other things.

This research has not only demonstrated the extent of poverty, but also the specific groups at risk of poverty – for example, women and children emerged as the poorest groups. This implied that policies to combat poverty had to look after women and children before anyone else.

Theoretically

The facts on poverty, however, can only be understood in relation to theory. Sociologists uncovered the extent of poverty by devising more sophisticated ways of measuring it. In particular, they brought in a 'relative deprivation' model of poverty (Townsend 1979), proving that poverty can only be understood in terms of what people normally expect to have in a society – even if this was well above the levels of destitution. This new way of defining poverty thereby allowed a whole new insight into the nature of poverty in advanced, affluent societies. Furthermore, sociologists were able to put forward a range of explanations for poverty based on their research, which identified a range of possible explanations for poverty. The result of these researches indirectly led to policies such as the Minimum Wage, which guaranteed a minimum hourly pay level, and the current system of Tax Credits, which provide additional help for people on low pay

More recently, Room (1995) suggested that seeing poverty as lack of money was too narrow a concept and so the more widely used term 'social exclusion' was introduced. This suggests that 'poor' people experience a much greater range of problems, which effectively cut them off from the wider society. Once again, a theoretical concept pushed forward our understanding of the nature of a social problem. Policy responses to this include targeting healthcare initiatives at the poorest and providing support for single mothers bringing up children alone, through the Home Start programme, as well as a range of other activities to draw those 'on the margins' back into society.

Awareness of cultural differences

A second important practical benefit, according to Giddens, is the way in which sociology can help people to see others' viewpoint, looking beyond the boundaries of their particular group. Lack of awareness of the activities and beliefs of other groups can lead to prejudice and discrimination. The information that sociology provides therefore allows us to respond to others' views in an informed and relevant way.

An outcome of this is the way that the recent governments have tackled discrimination in the areas of disability and race.

Disability

Disabled people often face very significant discrimination as a result of a stereotyping of their potential. They experience particularly high levels of unemployment, are discriminated against in many areas of social life and are much more likely than the majority of the population to be living in poverty. For example, they are seven times more likely to be unemployed than the average, and over 50% of families with a disabled male adult were living in poverty. This discrimination both ruins the lives of the people involved and at a political level, costs the government over £100 billion each year in state benefits.

Apart from having a higher chance of living in poverty, disabled people also have to cope with the stigma attached to disability, with people reacting to them in a patronizing or negative manner. Over time, sociological studies have built up a picture of the social and economic exclusion suffered by disabled people and this has led them to set up groups such as the Disability Alliance, Disablement Income Group and the British Council of Disabled People to demand better treatment. On the other side, their work and the work of sociologists has led to a greater public awareness and sympathy, resulting in the 1995 Disability Discrimination Act, which was followed by the Disability Rights Commission Act in 1999. Just as importantly, there has been a gradual shift in public opinion towards acknowledging the rights of disabled people.

Race

Opinion polls over the past 30 years have shown a consistent decline in expressed racism on the part of the majority population. The reasons for this are complex, but certainly one of the contributing factors has been the growth in understanding of the variety of cultures in Britain, and the problems that minority-ethnic groups face. Early sociological studies tended to emphasize the issues causing conflict, but increasingly, sociologists and others have demonstrated the variety and positive nature of the contribution of minority-ethnic groups to British life. 'White' people are more informed and aware of the variety of ethnic groups and are less likely to stereotype them as happened in the past. This awareness, plus the acceptance of a **plural** Britain, has led to the introduction of Race Equality legislation (1976 and 2000) to enforce equality.

Assessment of the effects of policies

Once politicians have recognized that a particular social problem exists, they are then able to develop policies to combat it. If sociological knowledge is used in doing this then the policies adopted may be those that appear to be most effective in combating the problem. However, it is actually extremely difficult to judge just how effective a policy has actually been, and this leads us to another use of sociology – that of evaluating the effects of a particular policy initiative.

Today, virtually all government initiatives are evidence-based – that is, when the government provides funding for new social projects, it requires evidence from the people actually running the programme to provide clear evidence that there is some benefit coming from that particular programme. Sociology is the key subject in providing this sort of research into the relevance and effectiveness of policy initiatives.

A good example of evaluation has been the way in which cost–benefit analyses of healthcare have been introduced in the NHS. Much of this work was pioneered by the University of York, where analyses were conducted to find out just how

effective certain medical procedures were in terms of better quality of life for patients and cost to the NHS. The government has developed this form of analysis to pharmaceuticals, and introduced a National Institute for Clinical Excellence which started in 1999 and which dictates what drugs and procedures the NHS is prepared to provide.

Increase in self-knowledge

For many sociologists this is the single most important aim of the subject. Sociology allows people to reflect upon their own experiences of life and in doing so 'liberates' them. Self-knowledge allows people to challenge images of themselves (perhaps currently stereotyped in the media) and to initiate policies that are more sympathetic to them. This is closely linked to Giddens' notion of reflexivity (see Topic 2).

Certain groups such as those with disabilities, minority-ethnic groups and the feminist and gay movements have all benefited greatly from this aspect of sociology. Sociological research has demonstrated the extent of discrimination against all these groups and this knowledge has empowered them because they are able to show the results to the government and demand action. The result of this has been a wide range of anti-discrimination laws. The publication of research has also allowed groups who have traditionally been discriminated against to become aware of their own shared identities and to take a pride in them. For example, sexual practices surveys showed that sexual activity between same-sex partners was not as infrequent as traditionally believed and opinion polls demonstrated that there was support for equal rights for gay people. This helped the gay community to have the courage to demand equal rights and to feel able to assert their own identities rather than having to hide their sexuality.

Sociology and social policy: critical views

The relationship between social policy and sociology has, however, been criticized by a number of writers. In particular, it

synopticlink

stratification and differentiation

Feminism and social policy

Feminists take different positions on the relationship between sociology and social policy. Radical and socialist feminists criticize liberal feminists for their research and close ties with government. Liberal feminists have been content to point out the way in which society discriminates against women in terms of employment, state benefits and within the family. Their aim has been to introduce anti-discrimination legislation and to change the attitudes of men to women. They would argue that they have largely succeeded in this. However,

radical and socialist feminists argue that this misses the point – the current patriarchal society is actually based on the exploitation of women and only by dismantling it and bringing about fundamental change can women achieve any form of liberation.

<< *Women appear in a sociology predicated on the universe occupied by men ... its methods, conceptual schemes and theories have been based on and built up within the male social universe.*>> (Smith 1973, p. 44)

A good example of the critical position in sociology is the debate between **realist** criminologists and critical criminologists (see Unit 5 Topics ? and ?). Realist criminologists, such as Lea and Young (1993), argue that sociological surveys indicate that the people who really suffer from crime are the poor and the powerless. It is therefore the duty of the government to introduce policies to prevent crime occurring against these groups, and to improve the quality of their lives. They should do this by better policing, better social conditions and by tackling the social and economic marginalization of the young males who commit most street crime.

Critical criminologists reject this, saying that the approach deals with the symptoms of crime, not the causes. For writers such as Scraton (and Chadwick 1982), it is a mistake to focus on the street crime committed by young men. These people engage in crime precisely because they are marginalized and brutalized by the

capitalist system. Critical criminologists argue that realism ignores the very real damage committed by corporations. For them, realists have been caught up in the very system, that should itself be attacked.

sees sociology as having been 'colonized' (i e taken over) by governments and thus its radical potential as having been tamed.

Critical sociology

For those belonging to the **critical sociology** tradition based on Marxism, the fault with much of sociology is that it has become too closely linked with the capitalist system – which to them is the main cause of the social problems and discrimination. Therefore sociology is not fulfilling its role as being a provider of knowledge that could liberate people, but actually serving the interests of powerful groups who could then impose their wishes in even more sophisticated ways.

Postmodernists and policy

Postmodernists such as Bauman (1990) take a position that is radically different from more traditional sociological approaches. They argue that sociology has no contribution to make to policy. Rational, scientific approaches to sociology using surveys or qualitative studies have often been used by government to introduce policies. But postmodernists claim that this is a waste of time; the existence of an orderly and manageable society 'out there' that we can understand and then manipulate is a comforting illusion. They would argue therefore that there can be no link between sociology and social policies. For postmodernists the role of sociology is simply to allow people to seek out an understanding of their personal lives within a social context.

>> *Deeply immersed in our daily routines, though, we hardly ever pause to think about the meaning of what we have*

gone through; even less often have we the opportunity to compare our private experience with the fate of others, to see the social in the individual, the general in the particular; this is precisely what sociologists can do for us. We would expect them to show us how our individual biographies intertwine with the history we share with fellow human beings. >> (Bauman 1990)

Politics and social policy

The assumption underlying much of traditional **empirical sociology** is that if research shows up social problems, then governments will respond by seeking to solve the problems on the basis of the evidence. However, this is not necessarily true for four key reasons.

- Governments act only when there are groups powerful enough to have their views taken into account by politicians. Gay people are now seen as a potential source of votes and as a group who occupy important positions across society. On the other hand, some of the poorest groups in society have little access to power, and may well be ignored by government.
- Governments are limited by financial constraints. To eliminate poverty amongst retired people would be simple – raise the state pension by a significant amount. Yet governments regard this as simply too expensive.
- Some policies will meet too much opposition from entrenched groups. The 'roads lobby', pharmaceutical and cigarette companies have all been very effective in protecting their interests despite evidence to show that many of their practices are harmful.

- Governments rarely engage in radical or long-term changes. In a democracy, governments operate within fairly short timetables based on election periods and are more concerned with popularity at the time of an election than introducing longer-term changes. They also are reluctant to commit themselves to very dramatic social change that could lead to upheaval – preferring to operate within the status quo.

So, although sociology can uncover the extent of social problems – and also suggest the causes – transferring this into policy does not necessarily happen.

We can see from the discussion above that there is no agreement amongst sociologists about whether sociology ought to be applied or not. For many sociologists the whole point of the subject is to use the knowledge to improve the quality of life for the majority of the population – however, these then split into two warring factions. One group argues that it is best to influence government policy to bring about reforms, whilst the other group argues that the insights sociology provides should help us to replace the current political and social system. Finally, there are those who argue that the point of sociology is that it is an academic subject and has no need to make any claim beyond its ability to throw light upon the nature of society and its relationship to the lives of individuals.

focus on research

Putnam (1995)
Social capital

Governments may only act on sociological research when these ideas fit into their ideological viewpoint and may ignore others. Blackshaw and Long (2005) provide an example of this in their research into the adoption of the concept of 'social capital'.

Putnam (1995) introduced the concept of 'social capital', which means the extent to which people are able to use social networks of friends and relatives. Putnam argues that this has declined in the USA and Britain, and that this has resulted in many social problems – particularly the crime that plagues large housing estates. The answer is to rebuild social capital through the employment of community workers and by giving grants to religious organizations to engage in voluntary work. This argument fitted perfectly with New Labour's approach to social problems and has been enthusiastically taken up by the government. However, according to Blackshaw and Long, strong criticism of the approach, which has suggested that social capital is not the answer for social problems, has simply been ignored, for the very same reason.

Putnam, R.D. (1995) 'Bowling alone: America's declining social capital', *Journal of Democracy*, 6(1), pp. 65–8

1 **How does the popularity of the term 'social capital' illustrate the point that 'Governments may only act on social research when these ideas fit into their ideological viewpoint ...'?**

Check your understanding

1 **Identify Giddens' four links between sociology and policy.**

2 **Give an example from the text which shows how sociology has influenced policy.**

3 **How can an awareness of disability issues influence policy?**

4 **Explain what evidence-based policymaking is.**

5 **Explain what is meant by sociology having been 'colonized' by government.**

6 **How do postmodernists view the relationship between sociology and policy?**

7 **If sociologists provide the 'facts' why don't governments always base their policies upon these facts?**

research idea

- Conduct a survey among sociology students at your school or college to discover which social issues they feel most strongly about.

  Have these issues been covered during your course? Are they included in the specifications of your examining board? To what extent has your study of sociology been relevant to the values and experiences of students?

KEY TERMS

Critical sociology – a term used for sociology influenced by Marxism.

Destitution – lacking the minimum resources necessary for food, clothing and housing.

Plural – refers to the fact that British society is now composed of a number of different cultures.

Realist sociology – a term used for sociologists, broadly sympathetic to the left, who wish to influence government policy – particularly in the area of crime.

Social policy – has two meanings. It can refer to government policy to solve social problems or the academic subject of studying social problems.

web.tasks

1 **Choose any one of the following government websites: the Home Office, NHS, Department for Education and Skills, Work and Pensions. Look up the sorts of research being undertaken. What is the aim of research? Do you think that the criticisms of radical sociologists that sociology is 'colonized' are justified?**

2 **Go to the website of the Joseph Rowntree Foundation at www.jrf.org.uk/. On the opening page, click on 'Read more about what we do'. Check through the research that sociology (or, more accurately, that branch of sociology – social policy) engages in.**

exploring sociology and social policy

Item A

<<Perhaps the most fruitful distinction with which the sociological imagination works is between the 'personal troubles of milieu'* and the 'public issues of social structure'. This distinction is an essential tool of the sociological imagination …

In these terms, consider unemployment. When, in a city of 100 000, only one man is unemployed, that is his personal trouble, and for its relief we properly look to the character of the man, his skills and his immediate opportunities. But when, in a nation of 50 million employees, 15 million men are unemployed, that is an issue and we may not hope to find its solution within the range of opportunities open to any one individual. >>

(NB: this was written in the late 1950s when it was normal to make what we would now regard as sexist assumptions.)

Wright Mills, C. (1959) *The Sociological Imagination*, Oxford: Oxford University Press

* *the particular social situation a person is in.*

Item B

<<Our role [as sociologists] is not first and foremost to be received as useful problem-solvers, but as problem raisers … but equipped with our special training in scientific methods and theory, it is our obligation as well as pleasure to penetrate these problems … we will probably [as it is] have to keep a constant fight going against being absorbed, tamed, and made responsible, and thereby completely socialized into society. >>

Christie, N. (1971) 'Scandinavian criminology faces the 1970s', in N. Christie et al. (1971) *Scandinavian Studies in Criminology*, London: Tavistock

1 (a) Explain briefly what is meant by 'social structure' (**Item A**). (2 marks)

(b) Identify and briefly explain the difference between 'personal troubles' and 'public issues' (**Item A**). (4 marks)

(c) Identify and briefly explain the distinction made by Christie between sociologists as 'problem solvers' and 'problem raisers' in **Item B**. (4 marks)

(d) With reference to the **Items** and elsewhere, briefly examine the view that sociological research benefits society. (10 marks)

2 Evaluate the view that sociological arguments and research findings generally have little influence on the policies of governments. (40 marks)

THIS UNIT BEGINS by exploring a simple, but quite frightening idea – that everyone is essentially self-seeking and that we are all quite capable of breaking the law. The only reason why we do not is that early in our lives we learn a variety of values and beliefs that prevent us breaking the law. The idea is frightening because it presents society as a very fragile thing with the potential to collapse at any time if social control fails. If the first topic illustrates the significance of learning how to behave, then the second one discusses the more formal mechanisms of control and punishment that exist.

Topic 3 explores what are often called 'strain' theories. It examines the way that people strive to make a success of their lives, but if various hurdles are put in their way by society, then they may turn to crime or deviance. Strain theories suggest that these hurdles (as we have called them) are placed unintentionally by society, but a much harsher version of this same idea is proposed by Marxists – the focus of Topic 4 – who argue that the powerful in society set out to block off the chances of the majority of the population, and so crime arises from this unfairness. An alternative to Marxism emerged in the form of labelling theory (Topic 5), which explores how certain groups come to define particular activities as being deviant and the consequences for those who engage in these deviant activities.

At this point we pause to draw breath, in Topic 6, by exploring the patterns of crime and how we measure these, before moving on to slightly more applied sociological theories. In Topic 7 we look at the way that acts of crime can be linked to specific places. Topic 8 explores the ways that gender is related to crime. As well as looking at the explanations put forward for low levels of female crime, we also examine the growth in interest in the notion of 'masculinity' – this has become a particularly important concept in recent years in understanding youth offending.

One of the key issues that Marxism (and to some extent labelling theory) raised was the way in which the crimes of the powerful tend to be ignored. We return to these issues in Topic 9, where we explore white-collar and corporate crimes to see why they occur and what explanations there are for the criminal justice system's relative lack of interest in this area.

Topic 10 takes us into a very controversial area, the relationship – if any – between ethnicity and crime. In this topic, we try to clarify the facts and provide explanations drawn from our earlier theoretical studies for these facts.

Topic 11 brings us bang up to date with the latest criminological ideas. The impact of postmodernism has been powerful in criminology and, above all else, there has been an attack on the idea that one can explain offending in rational, logical terms. Postmodernists have turned to emotions and impulse in their search for an explanation, and we examine these exciting ideas here.

The final topic deals with the notion of suicide and uses this as a way of illustrating the key debates in sociology in terms of both theories and methods.

AQA specification	topics	pages
Candidates should examine:		
Different explanations of crime, deviance, social order and social control	This covers a huge range of issues and stretches across Topics 1 to 5 and 7 to 11	234–265 274–303
The relationship between deviance, power and social control	This relationship is covered in Topics 1 and 2. It also relates to debates about class (Topics 4 and 10), ethnicity (9) and gender (8), as well as labelling (5) and left realist (11) theories	234–245 252–265 280–303
Different explanations of the social distribution of crime and deviance by age, social class, ethnicity, gender and locality	The statistical patterns are examined in Topic 6. Explanations of these patterns are to be found in the following topics: age (3 and 11), class (4 and 10), ethnicity (9 and 10), gender (8) and locality (7)	266–273 246–257 274–303
The social construction of, and societal reactions to, crime and deviance, including the role of the mass media	These issues are covered mainly in the context of a discussion of labelling theory (Topic 5)	258–265
The sociological issues arising from the study of suicide.	Covered in Topic 12	304–309

UNIT 5

Crime and deviance

Deviance and control theories

getting**you**thinking

The 'Social Responsibility' Quiz

1 You see someone chucking a used McDonald's burger carton on the pavement. Do you:

   a tell them to pick it up?

   b ignore it?

   c pick it up yourself and put it in the nearest bin?

2 You pass a homeless person begging in the street. Do you:

   a give them some money (at least to the value of 20p)?

   b pretend you haven't seen them?

   c tell them to 'get a job'?

   d say to them that you won't give them money, but you will buy/give them a cup of coffee and a sandwich if they want it?

3 A particular student is always being made fun of by other students in your year. Do you:

   a join in bullying them?

   b feel sorry for the person, but do nothing?

   c confront the bullies?

   d tell a tutor or person in authority?

4 You see a purse on the dance floor of a club. You pick it up and it contains just under £50. Do you:

   a hand it in to the manager of the club?

   b take the money?

   c leave the purse and the money on the floor?

Scoring				
Q1	a 5	b 1	c 2	
Q2	a 2	b 1	c 0	d 5
Q3	a 0	b 1	c 5	d 3
Q4	a 5	b 0	c 1	

Results

7 or less: You are a horrible person, aren't you! Change to Business Studies immediately!

8–12: You are someone who cares about other people – shame you don't actually do anything about it!

13–19: Caring, helpful and, perhaps, a little bit smug!

20: Very impressive, but a bit dangerous. Learn to keep your mouth shut and not to confront people, if you wish to live to an old age.

1 Why do you think people don't commit more crimes and deviant acts?

2 Do you think people are 'naturally' greedy and selfish, or do you believe that they are essentially generous and good? Explain why.

3 What do you think would happen if we had fewer police and fewer laws? Would chaos be the result or would people control themselves?

Before we begin to look at why some people commit criminal and deviant acts, it is useful to turn the question on its head and ask ourselves why most people actually conform. Some members of society may have been socialized to possess a strong sense of responsibility for fellow members of society. Others may not have the same sense of social responsibility, but have been effectively controlled by society so that their behaviour stays within certain limits. These processes of socialization and social control are central to an understanding of conformity and deviance. The first two topics in this unit consider these issues. This topic begins by considering the view that deviance can actually have a positive effect on society. It then moves on to look at the role of the family and the wider community in controlling behaviour.

Functionalist approaches to crime

Durkheim

For Durkheim, crime and deviance were central to any understanding of how society functions. He identified two different sides of crime and deviance for the functioning of society:

- a positive side that helped society change and remain dynamic
- a negative side that saw too much crime leading to social disruption.

Positive aspects of crime

According to Durkheim (1982, originally 1895), crime – or at least a certain, limited amount of crime – was necessary for any society.

He argued that the basis of society was a set of shared values that guide our actions, which he called the **collective conscience**. The collective conscience provides a framework with boundaries, which distinguishes between actions that are acceptable and those that are not. The problem for any society is that these boundaries are unclear, and also that they change over time. It is in clarifying the boundaries and the changes that a limited amount of crime has its place. Specifically, Durkheim discussed three elements of this positive aspect:

- *Reaffirming the boundaries* – Every time a person breaks a law and is taken to court, the resulting court ceremony and the publicity in the newspapers, publicly reaffirms the existing values. This is particularly clear in societies where public punishments take place – for example, where a murderer is taken out to be executed in public or an adulterer is stoned to death.
- *Changing values* – Every so often when a person is taken to court and charged with a crime, a degree of sympathy occurs for the person prosecuted. The resulting public outcry signals a change in values and, in time, this can lead to a change in law in order to reflect changing values. An example of this is the change in attitude towards cannabis use.

<!-- focus on box --></!-->

Definitions of crime and deviance

The American sociologist Marshall B. Clinard (1974) suggested that the term '**deviance**' should be reserved for behaviour that is so disapproved of that the community finds it impossible to tolerate. Not all sociologists would accept this definition, but it does describe the area usually covered by studies of deviance. In terms of Clinard's definition, crime and delinquency are the most obvious forms of deviance. **Crime** refers to those activities that break the law of the land and are subject to official punishment; **delinquency** refers to acts that are criminal, or are considered antisocial, which are committed by young people. Social scientists who study crime are often referred to as **criminologists**.

However, many deviant acts that are disapproved of are not defined as criminal. For example, alcoholism and attempted suicide are not illegal in Britain today. Some criminal acts are not even typically seen as deviant. Sometimes, outdated laws are left on the statute books even though people have long since stopped enforcing them. For example, under British law it is technically illegal to make or eat mince pies on Christmas Day and to shout 'taxi' to hail a cab. Deviance is also relative: there is no absolute way of defining a deviant act. Deviance can only be defined in relation to a particular standard, and no standards are fixed or absolute. As such, what is regarded as deviant varies from time to time and place to place. An act considered deviant today may be defined as normal in the future. An act defined as deviant in one society may be seen as perfectly normal in another. Put another way, deviance is culturally determined, and cultures change over time and vary between societies.

Adapted from Haralambos, M and Holborn, M. (2004) *Sociology: Themes and Perspectives*, London: Collins Education

1 Give an example of each of the following:

A an act generally disapproved of, but not criminal
B a criminal act often not seen as deviant
C an act likely to be considered deviant in one culture, but not in another
D an act that used to be seen as deviant but is not today.

Yvonne Jewkes (2005) carried out a content analysis of British newspapers in order to find out how they reported the activities of inmates in British prisons. Jewkes suggests that there are various 'frames' through which prisoners are viewed. These are: celebrity prisoners, pampered prisoners, sexual relations in prison, lax security and, finally, assaults on prisoners. Of these five frames or themes, four of them involve giving the impression that prisoners lead easy lives in a relatively pleasant environment and only the fifth covers negative aspects of prison life. Jewkes argues that the majority of

newspaper readers 'are looking for both confirmation of their existing views – which tend to be punitive – and for further opportunity to be shocked and outraged.' In order to get people to read their articles, therefore, the newspapers will reinforce these views. Jewkes's research is interesting as it partially supports Durkheim's argument that the law-abiding draw together in moral outrage at crime and this helps social cohesion. The newspapers in her study help maintain high levels of moral outrage.

- *Social cohesion* – Durkheim points out that when particularly horrific crimes have been committed, the entire community draws together in shared outrage, and the sense of belonging to a community is thereby strengthened. This was noticeable, for example, in the USA following the September 2001 attacks on the World Trade Center.

The negative aspects of crime: anomie

While a certain, limited amount of crime may perform positive functions for society, according to Durkheim, too much crime has negative consequences. Perhaps his most famous concept was that of '**anomie**', which has been widely used and adapted in sociology. According to Durkheim, society is based on people sharing common values (the collective conscience), which form the basis for actions. However, in periods of great social change or stress, the collective conscience may be weakened. In this situation, people may be freed from the social control imposed by the collective conscience and may start to look after their own selfish interests rather than adhering to social values. Durkheim called this situation anomie. Where a collapse of the collective conscience has occurred and anomie exists, crime rates rocket. Only by reimposing collective values can the situation be brought back under control.

Durkheim's concept of anomie was later developed and adapted by Merton, who suggested Durkheim's original idea was too vague. Merton (1938) argued that anomie was a situation where the socially approved goals of society were not available to a substantial proportion of the population if they followed socially approved means of obtaining these goals. According to Merton, people turned to crime and deviance in this situation. Turn to Topic 3, p. 247 for more details on Merton's theory.

Hirschi: bonds of attachment

Hirschi (1969) was also heavily influenced by Durkheim's ideas. Durkheim's concept of anomie suggests that if people are not 'controlled' by shared social values, then they look after their own short-term interests without concern for others. This led Hirschi to turn around the normal sociologist's question of 'Why

do people commit crime?' to another, equally intriguing one: 'Why *don't* people commit crime?'

By asking this question, Hirschi focuses sociologists' attention on what forces hold people's behaviour in check, rather than what propels them into crime. Hirschi argued that criminal activity occurs when people's attachment to society is weakened in some way. This attachment depends upon the strength of the **social bonds** that hold people to society.

According to Hirschi, there are four crucial bonds that bind us together:

- *Attachment* – To what extent do we care about other people's opinions and wishes?
- *Commitment* – This refers to the personal investments that each of us makes in our lives. What have we got to lose if we commit a crime?
- *Involvement* – How busy are we? Is there time and space for law-breaking and deviant behaviour?
- *Belief* – How strong is a person's sense that they should obey the rules of society?

The greater a person's attachment to society, the lower their level of crime.

The family and crime

Probably the most important agency that socializes us – and therefore provides the values that either strengthen or weaken the bonds Hirschi refers to (or the 'collective conscience' of Durkheim) – is the family.

Cambridge Study in Delinquent Development

The most famous study of the family is a piece of **longitudinal research** by Farrington and West (1990) in which 411 'working-class' males born in 1953 were studied until their late 30s. The study found the following:

- *Extent of offending* – By the age of 25, one-third of them were recorded offenders.
- *Concentration of offending* – Less than 6 per cent of the total sample accounted for over 50 per cent of all convictions.

The research demonstrated that there were consistent **correlations** between family traits and offending. In particular, offenders were more likely to come from homes with poor parenting – especially when the fathers themselves had criminal convictions. Furthermore, offenders were also more likely to come from poorer and single-parent families.

Family and morality

For some writers, the research of Farrington and West underlined their belief that the family was the key to understanding the causes of crime. Writers such as Dennis (1993) argue that the correlation between crime and certain family characteristics is a reflection of a much wider change in society. In particular, the traditional three-generation family structure had provided stability and a place in which moral values and a sense of community belonging had been passed on. However, since the 1960s, a series of changes in the family has weakened the **external patterns of social control** based on families and communities (where community members felt able to restrain extreme behaviour or young offenders) and also undermined the **internalized forms of social control** that had traditionally occurred through family socialization. The specific changes that Dennis blames are:

- *The changing role of women in the family* – The increasingly dominant role of the mother in the household has led to the marginalization of the father.
- *Increase in fathers leaving their families* – Dennis argues that there has been a decrease in the moral condemnation shown towards men who leave their families. The result of these two factors is that young males do not have role models on which to base their behaviour, and do not face the discipline at home that a father might provide.
- *Cohabitation* – The growth of cohabitation has undermined the belief that a partnership is for life, as is supposed to occur in marriage. This weakens the general moral 'fabric' of society and demonstrates that values and commitments are not fixed and permanent, but flexible. This, in turn, weakens the idea of strong central values which form the basis of society, and strengthens the view that morals are relative and negotiable – even moral stands on issues such as crime.

However, Scraton (2002) rejects Dennis's argument. He accuses Dennis of mixing up a moral argument, reflecting his own views, with a sociological one supported by evidence.

Communities and crime

The family may be the most important agency providing socialization to young people, but the family exists within a particular community. Farrington and West's research not only pointed to the importance of the family, but also to the social network in which the family is located.

The underclass

The close relationship between family, community and offending was taken up by the American writer Charles Murray (1990). He argued that over the previous 30 years, there had been an increase in what he termed 'the **underclass**'. By this, Murray refers to a clearly distinguishable group of young people who:

- have no desire for formal paid employment, preferring to live off benefits and the illegal economy
- have a range of short-term sexual liaisons
- routinely have children born outside serious relationships, so that fathers do not regard their offspring as their responsibility.

The children of these people are brought up with little or no concern for the values of the society in general. The result is that there is now a generation of young people who do not share the values of the wider society and who are much more likely to commit crime. Poorer communities are being destroyed by the underclass, who are driving out the law-abiding majority, and thus the members of the underclass are becoming ever more isolated and confirmed in their behaviour. Dennis and Murray's writings link very closely with the work of the right realists (see Topic 11, p. 299).

Etzioni: crime and communitarianism

One of the most influential writers in the USA is Amitai Etzioni, who has developed a theoretical and political argument known as **communitarianism**. For Etzioni (1993), changes in modern society have pushed decision-making further and further away from local communities. The conclusion of this process has been for people to lose interest in controlling their community. They regard themselves as powerless and this simply reinforces their acceptance that it is not their job to control others, but the role of the police and the state. Etzioni argues forcefully that social control can only be reconstituted when we take back control and engage in direct action in a variety of ways to control local offenders and to provide support for those in need locally. However, Moore and Scourfield (2005) have suggested that this can just lead to legitimizing the actions of vigilante groups and also to the free rein of prejudice when dealing with deviant groups.

Social capital

Putnam (2000) developed the concept of **social capital** to explain how communities can prevent or facilitate crime. His ideas link closely to those of Wilson and Etzioni. Social capital refers to the extent to which a person has a network of social contacts made up of friends and family in a particular area. According to Putnam, there has been a huge decline in communities and community organizations over the last 20 years. The cultural stress on individualism, the rise of television and social mobility have all contributed to a fragmentation of social groups. He argues that communities with low levels of social capital are more likely to have higher rates of crime and antisocial behaviour.

Portes (1998), on the other hand, criticizes the idea of social capital and other approaches that stress the importance of community, arguing that communities for some usually mean exclusion for others. A whole range of problems, ranging from racism to gang conflicts, can result from an integrated community. There is further discussion of the relationship between particular localities and crime in Topic 7.

Crime and control: a Marxist perspective

Marxists have mixed views on the argument that families and communities can cause crime through a collapse of social control. On the one hand, writers such as Scraton (1997) argue that crime is an indication of class conflict and that as most social control benefits capitalism, the decline of control might be bad for capitalism, but good for radical social change. On the other hand, left realists such as Matthews and Young (1992) see the decline of community controls and the resulting increase in crime and antisocial behaviour as directly harmful for the working class.

Box (1983) has suggested another way of looking at social control and crime. He agrees with the more right-wing writers in that it is release from social control that propels people into committing crime. However, his starting point is not that people are basically bad, but that capitalist society controls and exploits workers for its own ends – or, rather, for the benefit of the ruling class. When people are released in some way from direct control, then they are much more likely to commit crime because they see the unfairness of the system. Box argues there are five elements that can weaken the bonds of capitalist society and propel individuals into committing crime:

1 *Secrecy* – If people are able to get away with a crime, especially by not having it noticed in the first place, then they are more likely to attempt to commit crime. According to Box, this is one key factor that helps explain why white-collar crime (such as fraud) takes place. The majority of white-collar crime simply goes undiscovered.
2 *Skills* – Most people are simply unable to commit serious crime. Minor offending and antisocial behaviour generally occurs on the spur of the moment. Serious crime, however, requires planning and knowledge, plus the skill to carry it out.
3 *Supply* – Even knowledge and skill are not enough by themselves. The potential offender must also be able to obtain the equipment and support to be able to carry out most serious crimes. For example, a burglar needs a 'fence' to whom to sell his (burglary is an overwhelmingly male activity!) stolen goods.
4 *Symbolic support* – All offenders must have some justification for their activities. An excellent example of this are the techniques of neutralization suggested by Matza (Sykes and Matza 1962) (see Topic 3).
5 *Social support* – Coupled with the idea of symbolic support is the need for others who share similar values to support and confirm the values that justify crime. (Social support is another way of describing a subculture – see Topic 3.)

Box is suggesting therefore that control theory can be applied from a left-wing perspective and is not necessarily conservative in its approach. For Marxists, social control operates for the benefit of the ruling class and once this is weakened, it is possible that people will turn to crime to express their disillusionment with capitalism. **Critical criminologists** still take this position and argue that criminals are engaging in a form of political act in their crimes; if they were made more aware of the circumstances that propelled them into crime, they might well act in a more politically conventional way.

Conclusion

Control theories all share the belief that crime is the result of the restraints imposed by society being weakened. The overall approach is a very conservative one which stresses that if it were not for the family or local community then people would resort to their natural greedy and unpleasant selves. The underlying message of the approach is that the decline in the traditional family is potentially very dangerous for society.

The only, rather maverick, exception to this argument is Box's version of critical criminology which agrees that crime results from the weakening of social control – but sees social control as a bad thing, operating for the benefit of the ruling class.

KEY TERMS

Anomie – term, first used by Durkheim, to describe a breakdown of social expectations and behaviour. Later used differently by Merton to explain reactions to situations where socially approved goals were impossible for the majority of the population to reach by legitimate means.

Collective conscience – a term used by Durkheim to describe the core, shared values of society.

Communitarianism – approach linked with Etzioni, which claims that social problems should be sorted out by local people rather that by central government or their agencies (e.g. the police).

Correlation – a statistical relationship between two or more social events.

Crime – activities that break the law of the land and are subject to official punishment

Criminologists – social scientists who study crime

Critical criminology – work of criminologists influenced by Marxist thinking.

Delinquency – criminal or antisocial acts committed by young people

External patterns of social control – social control imposed by people on potential or actual offenders.

Internalized patterns of social control – social control that the person imposes upon themselves via their conscience, which is, in turn, largely the result of their upbringing.

Longitudinal research – sociological research method involving studying a group over a long period of time.

Social bond – in control theories, the forms of social control preventing people acting in a deviant way.

Social capital – the extent of social networks.

Underclass – term used by Charles Murray to describe a distinctive 'class' of people whose lifestyle involves seeking to take what they can from the state and living a life involving petty crime and sexual gratification.

Check your understanding

1. Give two examples of the positive aspects of crime according to Durkheim.

2. Explain how crime could be negative for society.

3. Explain the terms: 'attachment', 'commitment', 'involvement' 'investment' and 'belief'. Use an example of your own to illustrate each term.

4. What correlations did Farrington find between the family and criminal behaviour?

5. What is the 'broken windows' thesis?

6. According to communitarian theory, how could crime be stopped?

7. What five elements can weaken the bonds of society, according to Box?

8. What theoretical approach influences Box's writing? How?

research idea

- Conduct your own social-responsibility survey, as described in the 'Getting you thinking' at the start of this topic (on p. 234). Compare your findings with the ideas in this topic.

web.task

Your local authority will have a Community Safety Partnership detailing the activities your area is engaging in to tackle crime.
Visit it and see what initiatives are being carried out. You can find the address at www.homeoffice.gov.uk/crime/ (in bottom right hand corner). A typical example of a Community Safety Partnership site is www.safercambs.org/ . Try that first for ideas if you wish.

exploring deviance and control theories

Item A

For those on the right politically, the family is the key institution in generating law-abiding behaviour. Here discipline is learnt, impulse curbed, respect instilled and the grounding of civilized behaviour laid down in childhood to inform the adult throughout the future trials of life. But for those on the left, the focus on the family is seen as a 'red herring'. Thus it is argued that the type of family is irrelevant to the causes of crime and delinquency. Instead, the causes lie in the wider forms of social injustice, such as economic deprivation and racism.

Adapted from Young, J. (1999) *The Exclusive Society*, London: Sage

(a) Identify and briefly explain **two** problems in using a longitudinal study to discover the causes of crime. (8 marks)

This part of the question includes assessment of your understanding of the connections between Crime and Deviance and sociological methods.

(b) Using material from **Item A** and elsewhere, examine some of the ways in which sociologists have linked their explanations of crime to **one or more** of the following areas: families and households; health; mass media. (12 marks)

This part of the question includes assessment of your understanding of the connections between Crime and Deviance and other substantive topic(s) you have studied.

(c) Assess the view that crime is functional, inevitable and normal. (40 marks)

This part of the question includes assessment of your understanding of the connections between Crime and Deviance and sociological theory.

Policing, punishment and control

gettingyouthinking

1 How does each of the photographs illustrate an example of the way people are controlled?

2 What different types of control are being used?

3 Who is responsible for the control?

Social control

Societies can only exist if there is a degree of order and predictability, otherwise there would simply be chaos. This order is unlikely to arise spontaneously and so societies (or the more powerful members of society) develop methods to control those who fail to stick to the rules. They do so by a mixture of:

● **informal social control** based upon a range of **sanctions** such as negative comments, looks and exclusion

● **formal social control** based upon organizations that exist solely or partly to enforce 'order'.

The exact mixture between informal and formal control mechanisms used depends upon the type of society. For example, smaller and less complex groups with strongly shared values might rely more upon informal methods, whilst large, complex and multicultural societies generally have to use specific organizations.

Approaches to understanding social control

Sociologists agree that all societies need to impose control on their members, in order to ensure predictability of behaviour and stability. Beyond this, however, there is considerable dispute as to who benefits from this control and about how to explain the form that state control takes.

● Functionalist writers see the criminal justice system as operating to look after the interests of society as a whole. Without control and punishment, society would collapse into a state of anomie.

- At the other extreme, Marxist writers argue that the criminal justice system operates for the benefit of the ruling class. The law and the police are the agents of the ruling class and exist to eliminate opposition.
- Foucault (1977) put the issue of social control at the centre of his writings, and argued that any society is a battleground between competing interests. A key to gaining power is to control what is considered to be knowledge, and the methods of gaining knowledge. Those who succeed in having their definition of knowledge accepted gain power, and in turn will use it to enforce their view of the world. The criminal justice system and, particularly, the forms of punishment used play a crucial role in this by imposing the values of the powerful.

Changes in social control

Stan Cohen (1985) has suggested a number of key themes in the changing nature of the formal control in Western societies.

Penetration

Historically, societies had fairly simple forms of control – with the state passing a law which was then haphazardly enforced by whatever authorities existed at the time. However, Cohen argues that increasingly the law is expected to penetrate right through society, and that conformity and control are part of the job that schools, the media and even private companies are supposed to engage in.

Size and density

Cohen points out the sheer scale of the control apparatuses in modern society, with literally millions of people working for the state and other organizations involved in imposing control – and over a period of time, millions having that control imposed upon them. For example, approximately one-third of all males under 30 have been arrested for a criminal offence. Cohen points out that the range of control agencies is increasing and as they do so, they 'process' ever larger numbers of people.

Identity and visibility

Cohen argues that control and punishment used to be public and obvious, but more recently there has been a growth in subtle forms of control and punishment. Closed-circuit TV (CCTV), tagging, legally enforceable drug routines for the 'mentally-ill' and curfews are all part of an ever-growing and invisible net of control. He also notes that the state has handed over part of its monopoly of controlling people to private organizations. So there has been a growth in private security companies, doorstaff at nightclubs and even private prisons.

Feeley and Simon: actuarialism

Feeley and Simon (1992) have suggested another element of contemporary social control, which they term **actuarialism**. The term derives from the insurance industry, where the people who work out the chances of a particular event happening (and therefore the price to charge for insurance) are known as actuaries (see Topic 11, p. 300) for further material on actuarial approaches). Feeley and Simon argue that in contemporary society, the stress of social control has changed from controlling deviant behaviour, to controlling potentially deviant people. Therefore, agencies of social control work out just who is likely to pose the greatest risk of deviance and then act against them. The police patrol working-class and ethnic-minority areas, whilst the private security companies police the shopping developments, monitor people who enter and exclude the potential troublemakers – defined as the poor, the young and the homeless.

They extend Cohen's argument that other agencies as well as the state are involved in social control and argue that there is a process of **privatization** of social control agencies, with increasingly large amounts of surveillance and control of the population by for-profit companies.

Finally, Feeley and Simon argue that there has been a growth in new, more subtle forms of social control which they call **disciplining**, where people are helped in a non-coercive way to do what the organization wants. For example, Disney controls tens of thousands of people each day in its parks in subtle ways, but this still results in people behaving as Disney wishes.

Davis: Control of space

Davis, in the very influential book *City of Quartz* (1990), studied Los Angeles and pointed out that there is an increasing division between the affluent, living in segregated and (privately) protected areas, and the areas lived in by the poorer majority. The role of the police is to contain the poor, segregating them in their ghettos.

Punishment

A key component of social control is punishment. This has therefore been an area of interest to sociologists, as it helps us to resolve in whose interests social control operates and also to tell us about the extent and nature of formal social control.

Durkheim

As discussed in Topic 1, Durkheim (1960) believed that societies could only exist if the members shared certain common, core values, which he called the collective conscience. These common values dictate acceptable behaviour. However, many other values exist too which have rather less general acceptance (ranging from ones generally accepted to those that are openly in dispute). Thus a system of law exists that places a boundary line, clearly marking where actions go beyond the boundary of acceptance into behaviour generally regarded as so deviant as to be illegal.

According to Durkheim, when people act against societal values, then generally a system of informal control operates to coerce them back into conformity. However, if their behaviour crosses the boundary into illegal behaviour, then the formal system of punishment is generally used. Durkheim argued that both the basis and the form of punishment changes over time. In less complex, **mechanistic societies**, punishment is based on **retribution** – by which savage penalties are imposed upon the wrongdoer in order to demonstrate society's abhorrence at the breaking of the commonly shared values. The punishment will be both public and physical in nature – so people are executed, mutilated and branded.

As societies develop and become more complex (**organic societies**), then the punishment shifts away from public punishment to imprisonment, and the aim of the punishment is more to force the person to make amends for their wrongdoing. He called this '**restitutive** law'.

Marxist approaches

Early Marxist writers such as Rusche and Kircheimer (1939) agree with the general Marxist argument that laws reflect the interests of the ruling class. However, they go further and argue that the forms of punishment also reflect their interests. As these interests change, so do the forms of punishment. Rusche and Kircheimer claim, for example, that slavery was an early form of punishment because of the need for manual labour, and that in feudalism the state used physical punishment as there was slightly less need for labour, but the peasants still needed to be repressed. With the arrival of capitalism, the prisons served the useful purposes of, first, training workers in the disciplines of long hours of meaningless work (for example, the treadmill) in poor conditions, and, second, of mopping up the unemployed.

To support this argument, they pointed out that in times of high unemployment the prison population expands and then contracts in periods of high employment.

Foucault

Foucault's claims (1977) that punishment has changed over time – from being physical and public to **internalized** and intense – echo the work of Durkheim. In pre-industrial societies, offenders were seen as having offended against God or the rulers and were savagely punished for this. Punishment was conducted in public in order to warn others. However, over time – as crime came to be seen as deviance from accepted codes of behaviour – the aim of punishment was to bring the person back into society and under control. This is achieved by having 'experts' whose job it is to make sure that the person fully internalizes the need to conform. The punishment has shifted then from the body to the mind of the offender.

The police

The main agency responsible for the enforcement of social control is the police force. They are the arm of the state whose role it is to maintain public order and to enforce the law. There are two main positions in understanding the relationship of the police to society: the consensual approach and conflict policing.

Hough and Roberts (2004)
Perceptions of youth crime

Mike Hough and Julian Roberts conducted research on the public's attitudes to youth offending and the punishment of young people. They inserted additional questions into the Office of National Statistics Omnibus Survey (the ONS is a government department) which takes place every month (on a variety of subjects). Researchers have to buy a block of questions and Hough and Roberts bought a block of 30 questions. Government trained interviewers then conducted interviews with 1692 people aged over 16. The block of questions took about 15 minutes to complete. The response rate was 67 per cent.

Hough and Roberts found that people have negative perceptions about youth and the youth justice system. People believe that **offending rates** are higher than they are in reality and than young people are unlikely to be punished.

Hough, M. and Roberts J.V (2004) *Youth Crime and Youth Justice Public Opinion in England and Wales*, Oxford: Blackwell

1 **Suggest reasons why respondents believed that offending rates are higher than they really are.**

The consensual approach

A consensual approach sees the police as having a close relationship with the local area being policed, and the role of the police force being to represent the interests of the majority of law-abiding people, defending them against the minority of offenders. Police officers are drawn from the community and reflect its characteristics. Individual offenders are caught as a result of complaints made by the community.

Policing and forms of social control have been examined closely by neo-Marxist sociologists, who are interested in finding out the ways that capitalist society controls the proletariat. Althusser (1971) argues that the police are part of the 'state apparatus' that seeks to control the population by repressive methods. However, he also argues that there are other agencies involved in social control that perform the same task, but using a more positive approach; these include education, religion and the media. Therefore, rather than seeing the police as being a distinctive control group, they should be seen as part of a broad spread of 'repressive state apparatuses'.

In a similar manner, Hall *et al.* (1978) argue that most people provide little trouble to capitalism as they are sucked into it through employment, mortgages and consumption. The role of the police is to deal with those on the margins of society – young people, ethnic minorities, street-life people and such like – who pose a threat because they are not bonded into capitalism.

Conflict policing

This model of policing has been suggested by Scraton (1985), who argues that the police can best be seen as an occupying force, imposed upon working-class and ethnic-minority communities. Police officers largely patrol working-class and ethnic-minority areas where they impose the law and order that reflects the interests of the more powerful groups. Lea and Young (1984) describe this as **'military-style' policing**, which is characterized by the use of large numbers of police officers patrolling an area in vehicles, using advanced technology for intelligence gathering.

According to Reiner (1997), those who are stopped and searched, or questioned in the street, arrested, detained in the police station, charged and prosecuted, are disproportionately young men who are unemployed or casually employed, and from discriminated-against minority ethnic groups. The police themselves recognize that their main business involves such groups, and their mental social maps delineate them by a variety of derogatory epithets: 'assholes', 'pukes', 'scum', 'slag', 'prigs'.

Discretion, policing and the law

As we have noted, it is the job of the police to enforce the law. However, there are so many laws that could be applied in so many different circumstances that police officers need to use their **discretion** in deciding exactly which laws to apply and in what circumstances. Sociologists have been particularly interested in studying the nature of such discretion, and in seeing the implications for different groups in society. Discretion can also provide evidence to support one or other of the (consensual or conflict) styles of policing we have just discussed.

Reiner (1992) has suggested three ways of explaining the basis of police discretion: individualistic, cultural and structural.

Individualistic

The explanation for police discretion is that a particular police officer has specific concerns and interests and thus interprets and applies the law according to them. Colman and Gorman (1982) found some evidence for this in their study of police officers in inner London. In particular, they noted individual racist police officers who would apply the law more harshly on certain ethnic minorities.

Cultural

New recruits enter a world that has a highly developed culture – evolved from the particular type of job that police officers must do. Police officers are overwhelmingly White and male. They work long hours in each other's company and are largely isolated from the public. The result of this is the development of a very specific occupational culture – sometimes referred to as a **'canteen culture'**. According to Skolnick (1966) this has three main components – and we can add a fourth suggested by Graef (1989): that of masculinity.

- *Suspiciousness* – As part of their job, police officers spend much of their time dealing with people who may have committed a criminal offence. As part of their training, therefore, they are taught to discriminate between 'decent people' and 'potential trouble-makers'. According to Reiner (1992), they categorize and stereotype certain people as 'police property'. This involves regarding young males, and particularly youths from ethnic minorities, as potential troublemakers.
- *Internal solidarity and social isolation* – We have just noted how police officers spend large amounts of time in the company of their peers, isolated from the public. They also rely upon each other in terms of support in times of physical threat and when denying accusations from the public.
- *Conservatism* – Those who join the police in the first place are rarely politically radical, and while the actual job of policing emphasizes a non-political attitude – police officers must uphold the law – it also upholds traditional values and the very nature of the state. Added to the factors of social isolation and the majority recruitment from White males, this generates a strong sense of conservative values.
- *Masculinity* – The majority of police officers are male and drawn from the working class. The culture of police officers very much reflects traditional working-class values of heavy drinking, physical prowess and heterosexuality. Racial stereotyping is also heavily emphasized and linked with assuming the role of a police officer.

There have been numerous studies of the police from both quantitative and qualitative perspectives. It has been relatively easy to get hold of statistics showing the rates of arrest of criminals, or the numbers of stops and searches of people in the streets. However, these sorts of studies have rarely given an insight into how the police actually operate on a day-to-day basis. In order to do this, sociologists have generally resorted to using some form of participant observation. But the culture of police officers – the 'canteen culture' – is a closed one, so that anybody from outside the force trying to study police officers is usually forced into using covert participant observation. Two famous studies are by Holloway and Hobbs: in both, the researchers felt that the only way to uncover the reality of policing was not to declare their research interests openly. In fact, when Holloway undertook his research, he was a serving policeman.

sociological methods

Canteen culture

The result of their work was a detailed insight into the lives of police officers. However, although the research makes great reading, it is never possible to say for certain that the research is accurate or generalizable, as covert participant observational research is almost impossible to replicate.

Structural

A third approach, derived from Marxist theory, stresses that the very definition of law is biased in favour of the powerful groups in society and against the working class. Therefore, any upholding of the law involves upholding the values of capitalist society. Police officers' definition of crime in terms of street crimes and burglary (as opposed to white-collar or corporate crime and their repression of the working class) derives from their role as agents of control of a capitalist society. Their internal values simply reflect the job they have been given to do.

Evidence for this view can be found in Tarling's study (1988) which showed that over 65 per cent of police resources are devoted to the uniformed patrolling of public space – particularly poorer neighbourhoods and central city areas. The result is that, as Morgan found out, about 55 per cent of prisoners in police custody were unemployed, and of the rest, 30 per cent were in manual, working-class jobs. Most detainees were young, with 60 per cent being under 25, and 87 per cent of all of those arrested being male. Finally, over 12 per cent

were from African or African-Caribbean backgrounds – despite these groups forming less than 3 per cent of the population.

Topic 10 looks in more detail at the police in relation to ethnic-minority groups.

Having looked at the issue of social control, Topics 3 to 5 examine alternative sociological theories of the causes of crime and deviance. Later in the unit, Topic 11 explores realist and postmodern approaches to crime and deviance, which often focus on the issue of social control.

web.task

Search the following sites about the death penalty and attitudes to it. Can sociology throw any light on the debate?

- www.amnesty.org.uk/action/camp/dp/index.shtml
- www.deathpenaltyinfo.org/

KEY TERMS

Actuarialism – refers to the division of people into potentially deviant groups and controlling them on this basis.

Canteen culture – a term which refers to the occupational culture developed by the police.

Disciplining – the process of control through non-coercive methods.

Discretion – the fact that the police have to use their judgement about when to use the force of the law.

Formal social control – official, organized ways of enforcing conformity.

Informal social control – routine, cultural ways of enforcing conformity.

Internalize – when people come to accept, and possibly believe, some value or rule.

Mechanistic societies – technologically and socially simple societies, as identified by Durkheim, in which people are culturally very similar.

Military model of policing – policing which is imposed upon the population.

Offending rates – statistics referring to how many crimes are committed, and by which groups of people.

Organic societies – culturally and technologically complex societies, as identified by Durkheim, in which people are culturally different from each other.

Privatization – giving control from the state to private companies.

Restitutive – a model of law based upon trying to repair the damage done to society.

Retributive – a model of law based upon revenge.

Sanctions – measures taken to control a person or group.

Check your understanding

1 What three key changes in social control did Cohen identify?

2 What factors influence the way punishment has changed, according to Durkheim?

3 What explanation do Marxists provide for the development of prisons?

4 Identify and explain the two models of policing that have been identified.

5 Identify the components of the police occupational culture.

6 Why is an understanding of police discretion important?

research ideas

1 CCTV cameras are an extremely popular means of social control. How many of these are in your town centre?

Identify a couple of roads which are covered by CCTV and then ask a small sample of the people in that street if they are aware of the cameras. What are their views? Is Cohen's view true that there is an ever-growing web of hidden control?

2 Arrange to interview a local police officer about how they use their discretion. Are sociological explanations justified by the answers?

exploring policing, punishment and control

Item A

Police discretion is inevitable and sometimes desirable, given the nature and circumstances of everyday police work: the need to make choices at every level about priorities, the need to interpret general legal rules in specific enforcement situations, and so on. However, the problem is that police discretion is often exercised in discriminatory ways. The social functions and focus of police work remain remarkably stable over time, as some social groups were and still are more likely to be subject to police attention than others. A series of biases, involving not only the stereotypes used by the occupational culture, but also elements of policing routines and practices, produce patterns of bias on lines of class, gender and ethnicity. The occupational culture may also have resulted in discrimination against Black police officers and female officers.

Adapted from Carrabine, E., Iganski, P., Lee, M., Plummer, K. and South, N. (2004) *Criminology*, London: Routledge, pp. 278–9

(a) Using material from **Item A** and elsewhere, identify and briefly explain **two** problems in using interviews with police officers to find out about police discretion. (8 marks)

This part of the question includes assessment of your understanding of the connections between Crime and Deviance and sociological methods.

(b) Examine some of the ways in which the concept of social control is relevant to the study of **one or more** of the following areas: families and households; health; mass media; education; wealth, poverty and welfare; work and leisure; religion; power and politics; world sociology. (12 marks)

This part of the question includes assessment of your understanding of the connections between Crime and Deviance and other substantive topic(s) you have studied.

(c) Assess the usefulness of Marxist approaches to social control. (40 marks)

This part of the question includes assessment of your understanding of the connections between Crime and Deviance and sociological theory.

Strain and subcultural theories

1 What do you think of the people in the photos: are they having a good time or just acting stupidly – or both?

2 In your opinion, why do some young males start fights?

3 Who do you think are more important in influencing your day-to-day behaviour, your family or your friends?

4 If your friends wanted you to do something that you considered acceptable behaviour, but your parents expressly forbade it, what would you do?

You may well feel that your friends exert a considerable influence on your life. Sometimes, groups of friends develop norms and values that are unconventional and may encourage deviant acts. **Subcultural theories** share the common belief that people who commit crime usually share different values from the mass of law-abiding members of society. However, crime-committing people do not live in complete opposition to mainstream values, rather they have 'amended' certain values so that this justifies criminal behaviour – hence the term 'subculture'.

Strain is a term that is used to refer to explanations of criminal behaviour that argue that crime is the result of certain groups of people being placed in a position where they are unable, for whatever reason, to conform to the values and beliefs of society. Many sociologists use the term interchangeably with 'subculture'. Although, strictly speaking, they are not the same thing (for example, Merton is a 'strain' theorist and does not really discuss subculture), we have put them together here because of the degree of overlap between the two approaches.

The origins of subculture

Subcultural theories derive from two different schools of sociology – and if you think carefully about each of the later approaches we discuss, you will probably be able to tell which school of thought they derive from.

Appreciative sociology

The first parent-school is that of the University of Chicago, which developed in the early part of the 20th century in response to the dramatic social change that was taking place in US cities at that time. Chicago sociologists were determined to appreciate the wide variety of different cultures and lifestyles in Chicago that existed as a result of the huge influx of migrants arriving from all over Europe and southern USA. Chicago sociologists pioneered the use of participant observation in their research. They simply wanted to observe and note down the sheer variety and dynamism of urban life. Integral to this was

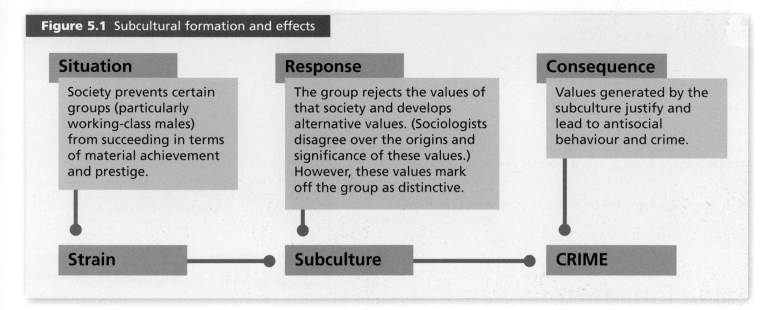

Figure 5.1 Subcultural formation and effects

Situation

Society prevents certain groups (particularly working-class males) from succeeding in terms of material achievement and prestige.

Response

The group rejects the values of that society and develops alternative values. (Sociologists disagree over the origins and significance of these values.) However, these values mark off the group as distinctive.

Consequence

Values generated by the subculture justify and lead to antisocial behaviour and crime.

Strain → **Subculture** → **CRIME**

the study of deviant groups, with Frederic Thrasher's *The Gang* (1927) and Whyte's *Street Corner Society* (1943) demonstrating that deviant groups in society had clear norms and values of their own that justified their different behaviour.

Strain theory

In the 1930s, Robert Merton (1938), tried to locate deviance within a functionalist framework. For Merton, crime and deviance were evidence of a poor fit (or a strain) between the socially accepted goals of society and the socially approved means of obtaining those desired goals. The resulting strain led to deviance.

Merton argued that all societies set their members certain goals and, at the same time, provide socially approved ways of achieving these goals. Merton was aware that not everyone shared the same goals; he pointed out that in a stratified society the goals were linked to a person's position in the social structure. Those lower down had restricted goals. The system worked well as long as there was a reasonable chance that a majority of people were able to achieve their goals. However, if the majority of the population were unable to achieve the socially set goals, then they became disenchanted with society and sought out alternative (often deviant) ways of behaving. Merton used Durkheim's term anomie, to describe this situation.

The following different forms of behaviour then could be understood as a strain between goals and means:

- *Conformity* – The individual continues to adhere to both goals and means, despite the limited likelihood of success.
- *Innovation* – The person accepts the goals of society but uses different ways to achieve those goals. Criminal behaviour is included in this response.
- *Ritualism* – The means are used by the individual, but sight of the actual goal is lost, e.g. the bureaucrat or the police officer blindly enforcing the letter of the law without looking at the nature of justice.
- *Retreatism* – The individual rejects both goals and means. The person dependent upon drugs or alcohol is included in this form of behaviour.

- *Rebellion* – Both the socially sanctioned goals and means are rejected and different ones substituted. This is the political activist or the religious fundamentalist.

Criticism of Merton

Merton has been criticized by Valier (2001) amongst others for his stress on the existence of common goals in society. Valier argues that there are, in fact, a variety of goals that people strive to attain at any one time.

Illegitimate opportunity structure

The idea of strain between goals and means had a very significant impact on the writings of Cloward and Ohlin (1960), who owed much to the ideas of Merton.

They argued that Merton had failed to appreciate that there was a parallel opportunity structure to the legal one, called the **illegitimate opportunity structure**. By this they meant that for some subcultures in society a regular illegal career was available, with recognized illegal means of obtaining society's goals. A good example of this is given in Dick Hobbs' book *Bad Business* (1998). Hobbs interviewed successful professional criminals and demonstrated how it is possible to have a career in crime, given the right connections and 'qualities'.

According to Cloward and Ohlin, the illegal opportunity structure had three possible adaptations or subcultures:

- *Criminal* – There is a thriving local criminal subculture, with successful role models. Young offenders can 'work their way up the ladder' in the criminal hierarchy.
- *Conflict* – There is no local criminal subculture to provide a career opportunity. Groups brought up in this sort of environment are likely to turn to violence, usually against other similar groups. Cloward and Ohlin give the example of violent gang 'warfare'.

Retreatist – This tends to be a more individual response and occurs where the individual has no opportunity or ability to engage in either of the other two subcultures. The result is a retreat into alcohol or drugs.

Evaluation of Cloward and Ohlin

This explanation is useful and, as Hobbs' work shows, for some people there really is a criminal opportunity structure. But the approach shares some of the weaknesses of Merton's original theory:

● It is difficult to accept that such a neat distinction into three clear categories occurs in real life.
● There is no discussion whatsoever about female deviancy.

Status frustration

Writing in the mid 1950s, Albert Cohen (1955) drew upon both Merton's ideas of strain and also on the **ethnographic** ideas of the Chicago school of sociology. Cohen was particularly interested in the fact that much offending behaviour was not economically motivated, but simply done for the thrill of the act. (This is as true today as it was in the 1950s, for vandalism typically accounts for about 18 per cent of current crime recorded by the British Crime Survey.)

According to Cohen, 'lower-class' boys strove to emulate middle-class values and aspirations, but lacked the means to attain success. This led to **status frustration** – that is, a sense of personal failure and inadequacy. The result was that they rejected those very values and patterns of 'acceptable' behaviour that they could not be successful within. He suggests that school is the key area for the playing out of this drama. Lower-class children are much more likely to fail and consequently feel humiliated. In an attempt to gain status, they 'invert' traditional middle-class values – behaving badly and engaging in a variety of antisocial behaviours.

Criticisms of Albert Cohen

● There is no discussion of females. His research is solely about males.
● The young 'delinquents' need to be brilliant sociologists to work out what are middle-class values and then invert them!
● Cohen fails to prove that school really is the key place where success and failure are demonstrated.

Focal concerns

In the late 1950s, Walter Miller developed a rather different approach to explaining the values of crime when he suggested that deviancy was linked to the culture of lower-class males. Miller (1962) suggested that working-class males have six '**focal concerns**' that are likely to lead to delinquency:

● *Smartness* – A person should both look good and also be witty with a 'sharp repartee'.

focus on research

Philippe Bourgois (2002)
In search of respect

≪ *I want to place drug dealers and street level criminals into their rightful positions with the mainstream of US society. They are not 'exotic others' operating in an irrational netherworld. On the contrary, they are 'made in America'. Highly motivated, ambitious inner-city youths have been attracted to the rapidly expanding, multi-billion dollar drug economy precisely because they believe ... [in] the American Dream.*

In fact, in their pursuit of success, they are even following the minute details of the classical yankee model for upward mobility. They are aggressively pursuing careers as private entrepreneurs: they take risks, work hard and pray for good luck. ≫

Bourgois, P. (2002) *In Search of Respect* (2nd edn), Cambridge: Cambridge University Press

1 **How does Bourgois' quotation above illustrate both the ideas of Merton, and of Cloward and Ohlin?**

● *Trouble* – 'I don't go looking for trouble, but ...'.
● *Excitement* – It is important to search out thrills (see Katz, Topic 8, p. 283).
● *Toughness* – Being physically stronger than others is good. It's also important to be able to demonstrate this.
● *Autonomy* – It is important not to be pushed around by others.
● *Fate* – Individuals have little chance to overcome the wider fate that awaits them.

According to Miller, then, young lower-class males are pushed towards crime by the implicit values of their subculture.

Evaluation of Miller

Miller provides little evidence to show that these are specifically lower-class values. Indeed, as Box (1981) pointed out, they could equally apply to males right across the class structure.

Subcultural theories are almost always based upon using observational methods. A famous example of participant observation is Howard Parker's book *View from the Boys* (1992). Parker studied a group of young males in Liverpool who stole car radios to fund their lifestyle, which involved cannabis use, heavy drinking and fighting. Parker joined in some of these activities and admits that he got so involved that he actually kept watch while they stole the radios. Towards the end of his study, when the 'Boys' were being prosecuted for their activities, they turned to him for support and advice. There are moral issues here about how far sociologists should get involved with those they are studying, but also methodological issues about the extent of bias in such studies.

Applying subcultural theory: the British experience

The studies we have looked at so far have mainly been American ones. However, subcultural studies were being undertaken in Britain too – though with a variety of results. Howard Parker (1974) successfully applied Miller's focal concerns in his study of working-class 'lads' in inner-city Liverpool (although, as we have already noted, he could probably have applied these equally successfully to rugby-playing students at Liverpool University).

On the other hand, studies by David Downes (1966) of young working-class males in London could find no evidence of distinctive values. Instead, Downes suggested that young working-class males were 'dissociated' from mainstream values, by which he meant that they were concerned more about leisure than their long-term future or employment, and were more likely to engage in petty crime. So, in the UK, evidence of distinctive subcultures has been fairly difficult to obtain.

Subterranean values

One consistent criticism of subcultural theories was that there was little evidence to demonstrate a distinct set of antisocial values. Even if there were subcultures, were they a response to middle-class values or to a distinctive set of working-class values? Matza put these criticisms together to make a strong attack upon subcultural theory (Sykes and Matza 1962). Matza argued that there were no distinctive subcultural values, rather that all groups in society used a shared set of **subterranean**

values. The key thing was that most of the time, most people control these deviant desires. They only rarely emerge – for example, at the annual office party, or the holiday in Agia Napa. But when they do emerge, we use **techniques of neutralization** to provide justification for our deviant actions (see Fig. 5.2). As we said earlier, the difference between a persistent offender and a law-abiding citizen is simply how often and in what circumstances the subterranean values emerge and are then justified by the techniques of neutralization.

Matza's critique of subculture is quite devastating. He is saying that all of us share deviant, 'subcultural values', and that it is not true that there are distinctive groups with their own values, different from the rest of us.

Subculture: the paradox of inclusion

In his book *On the Edge*, Carl Nightingale (1993) studied young Black youth in an inner-city area of Philadelphia. For Nightingale, subculture emerges from a desire to be part of the mainstream US culture – that is, subculture emerges from being rejected and marginalized by the mainstream society. Nightingale notes the way that Black children avidly consume US culture by watching television with its emphasis on consumerism and the success of violence – yet at the same time they are excluded economically, racially and politically from participating in that mainstream US culture. The response is to overcompensate by identifying themselves with the wider culture by acquiring articles with high-status trade names or

Denial of responsibility – The offender denies that it was their fault: 'it wasn't me, it was the alcohol/drugs'.

Denial of victim – The offender claims that in this particular case the victim was in the wrong – for example in a rape case where the woman was dressed in a way that 'led him on'.

Denial of injury – The offender claims that the victim was not really hurt or harmed by the crime. Often used to justify theft from a company as opposed to stealing from individuals.

Figure 5.2 Matza: techniques of neutralization

Condemnation of condemners – The offender feels a sense of unfairness of being picked on for something others have done and not been punished for.

Appeal to higher loyalties – The offender claims that the rule or law had to be ignored because more important issues were at stake. The offender was, for example, 'standing up for his family/community/race'.

Subculture as a concept is not solely related to crime and deviance; it is widely used throughout sociology to explain just why particular groups behave in ways that are different from the rest of society. These applications of the idea of subcultural theory are also often shot through with value judgements on the part of sociologists. In schools, for example, numerous sociologists, notably Willis, have uncovered antischool subcultures where the students oppose the values of the school and get pleasure from being disruptive. In Willis' study there seems a degree of admiration for the lads.

Murray has used the term in a much broader and more negative sense to claim the existence of an 'underclass' of people who prefer to live off state benefits and petty crime. The females are likely to have early pregnancies and are single parents, while the males will father a number of children by different partners, but are unlikely to support their children financially. Murray's arguments are strongly contested by other sociologists however. Whereas, Murray writes disapprovingly about the underclass, Stacey writes supportively about the development of gay and lesbian families. Stacey identifies a new subculture emerging of gays and lesbians rejecting the dominant values regarding the importance of heterosexuals as the only people able to have a family with children.

logos. Once again, drawing upon Merton's ideas, the subculture reflects the belief that it is not so much how these high-status goods are obtained rather the fact of possessing them. In the USA, these are often obtained through violence, expressed in violent gangs and high crime rates.

Similarly, Philip Bourgois' study of El Barrio (2002), looks at the lives of drug dealers and criminals in this deprived area of New York and finds that they, too, believe in the American Dream of financial success. The values of their 'subculture' are really little different from mainstream values, the only difference being that they deal drugs in order to get the money to pursue an all-American lifestyle.

So, both Nightingale's and Bourgois' versions of subculture take us back to the strain theory of Merton, and Cloward and Ohlin, emphasizing that the desire to be included leads to the actions that ensure that they are excluded from society.

Contemporary alternatives to subculture

Postmodernism

Most of the approaches we have looked at here, as well as the Marxist subcultural approaches described in Topic 4, seek to explain deviant behaviour by looking for some rational reason why the subculture might have developed. Recent postmodern approaches reject this explanation for behaviour. Katz (1988), for example, argues that crime is seductive – young males get drawn into it, not because of any process of rejection but because it is thrilling. In a similar manner, Lyng (1990) argues that young males like taking risks and engaging in 'edgework' as he puts it. By edgework, he means going right to the edge of acceptable behaviour and flirting with danger.

Neo-Tribes

Maffesoli (1996) introduced a postmodernist innovation in understanding subcultures with his argument for the existence of neo-tribes. Maffesoli was unhappy with the idea that the idea of subculture had been transformed from a concept based on values more into one of a group sharing a set of values. He suggested that it was much better to think of subcultures in terms of 'fluidity, occasional gatherings and dispersal'. Neo-tribes then referred more to states of mind and lifestyles that were very flexible, open and changing. Deviant values are less important than a stress on consumption, suitably fashionable behaviour and individual identity that can change rapidly.

Masculinity

Subcultural theory is overwhelmingly male subcultural theory. The assumptions underlying the vast bulk of the writings we have looked at within this tradition have been discussing masculine behaviour. However, as Collison (1996) points out, they may well have missed the significance of this. In order to explain male offending behaviour, it is important to explain the nature of being male in our society and the links masculinity itself has to crime. The work of Connell (1995) is particularly interesting here in that he sees the existence of a hegemonic masculinity which males both conspire with and aspire to.

Check your understanding

1 **What is meant by 'appreciative sociology'?**

2 **How does Merton use the idea of anomie to explain deviance?**

3 **How, according to A. Cohen, does school failure lead to the formation of subcultures?**

4 **How does the idea of 'techniques of neutralization' undermine some subcultural arguments?**

5 **What do we mean by the 'paradox of inclusion'?**

6 **Why is the idea of 'masculinity' relevant to understanding criminal behaviour?**

The emphasis of this hegemonic masculinity is very similar in values to Miller's early work on 'lower-class values'. However, Winlow (2004) argues that the values are best seen within the context of a changing economic social structure. Winlow suggests that the traditional (working-class) male values fitted physical work undertaken by men in industrial settings. These have now gone and the values are inappropriate for contemporary employment. He suggests too that the problem may be even greater for those young men excluded completely from employment.

web.task

Go to the Home Office Website. At
www.homeoffice.gov.uk/rds/pdfs/hors209.pdf
you will find the Research Study 209 on Findings from the 1998/99 Youth Lifestyles Leisure Survey. Look at pp. 34–35 on family and friends and offending. Does this provide any evidence to support or undermine subcultural theory?

KEY TERMS

Edgework – derives from Lyng. Refers to activities of young males which provide them with thrills, derived from the real possibility of physical or emotional harm (e.g. stealing and racing cars; drug abuse).

Ethnographic – form of observational research, in which researcher lives amongst, and describes activities of, particular group being studied.

Focal concerns – term used by Miller to describe key values.

Illegitimate opportunity structure – an alternative, illegal way of life that certain groups in society have access to.

Status frustration – according to Cohen, this occurs when young men feel that they are looked down upon by society.

Strain – term used by Merton and other functionalists to describe a lack of balance and adjustment in society.

Subculture – a distinctive set of values that provides an alternative to those of the mainstream culture.

Subcultural theories – explanations of crime and deviance focusing on the idea that those who deviate hold different values to the majority.

Techniques of neutralization – justifications for our deviant actions.

exploring strain and subcultural theories

Item A

<<We did not say that participant observation is the best method for gathering data for all sociological problems under all circumstances. We did not say this and, in fact, we fully subscribe to his view 'that different kinds of information about people and society are gathered most fully and economically in different ways, and that the problem under investigation properly dictates the methods of investigation'. We did say, and now reiterate, that participant observation gives us the most complete information about social events and can thus be used as a yardstick to suggest what kinds of data escape us when we use other methods. This means simply, that, if we see an event occur, see the events preceding and following it, and talk to various participants about it, we have more information than if we only have the description which one or more persons give us through questionnaires or interviews. We intended to refer only to specific and limited events which are observable, not to large and complex events.>>

Source: Becker, H. and Geer, B. (1969) 'Participant observation and Interviewing: a rejoinder', in G. McCall and J.L. Simmons (eds) *Issues in Participant Observation*, New York: Addison-Wesley

(a) Briefly explain what is meant by the term 'criminal underclass' using material from **one or more** of the following areas: families and households; health; mass media; education; wealth, poverty and welfare; work and leisure. (8 marks)

This part of the question includes assessment of your understanding of the connections between Crime and Deviance and other substantive topic(s) you have studied.

(b) Using material from Item A and elsewhere, examine some of the advantages and disadvantages of using covert participant observation methods to study subcultures. (12 marks)

This part of the question includes assessment of your understanding of the connections between Crime and Deviance and sociological methods.

(c) Examine the similarities and differences between subcultural theory and strain theory as explanations for deviant behaviour. (40 marks)

This part of the question includes assessment of your understanding of the connections between Crime and Deviance and sociological theory.

Critical criminologies

getting you thinking

In the 1990s, Russia moved from a communist-based economy to a capitalist one. Part of this process was to create a stock exchange where people could buy and sell shares in companies. Experts from Harvard University advised them and were, according to this article, accused of illegally obtaining up to $34m by using this knowledge.

'Harvard University and one of its star economists will pay almost $30m to settle civil charges* brought by the US government. It is alleged that the professor illegally made a personal fortune from work in the 1990s helping Russia privatize hundreds of companies. Andrei Shleifer was found guilty by a federal judge last year of inappropriately investing in the same financial markets he was responsible for creating in Russia.

In 2000 the government filed a suit against Harvard for up to $102. If the case had gone to court, Harvard would have been liable for up to $34m and Mr Shleifer could have owed three times that figure.'

Griffiths, K. (2005) 'Harvard to pay $30m to settle with US government', *The Independent*, 5 August, p. 58

*Civil actions in court consist of private disputes in which one side asks for financial compensation from the other side. Criminal actions are where people are charged with criminal offences and can be punished, including being sent to prison.

1 What are your immediate reactions to the newspaper article – surprise, anger, shrug of shoulders? Do you think that having to pay back a proportion of the money 'obtained' was an adequate punishment?

2 Do you think that the police and criminal justice system treat people equally? What reasons can you suggest for your answer?

3 Look at the photo of the children working in a factory in south-east Asia – they work up to 12 hours a day and earn a very low wage. It is legal. Do you think it is wrong? Do you think it should be made illegal (as it is in Britain)?

4 On what basis do you think that something should be made a crime?

5 Using your own ideas, can you find any examples of activities that you think ought to be crimes, but are not? Can you suggest why they are not crimes?

The activity above should have alerted you to the possibility that laws, and the way they are applied, may favour certain groups – in most cases the rich and powerful. This is the starting point for Marxist and neo-Marxist approaches – often referred to as critical criminology.

The traditional Marxist approach

Karl Marx himself wrote very little about crime, but a Marxist theory of crime was first developed by Bonger as early as 1916 and then developed by writers such as Chambliss (1975). The overall background to this approach was based on the Marxist analysis of society, which argues that society is best understood by examining the process whereby the majority of the population are exploited by the owners and controllers of commerce and industry. Marxists argue that this simple, fundamental fact of exploitation provides the key to unlock the explanations for the workings of society.

The key elements of the Marxist or critical criminological approach include:

- the basis of criminal law
- the dominant **hegemony** of the ruling class
- law enforcement
- individual motivation
- crime and control.

The basis of the criminal law

The starting point for Marxist analysis is that all laws are essentially for the benefit of the ruling class, and that criminal law reflects their interests. For example, concern with the laws of property ownership largely benefit those with significant amounts of property. For those who are poor, there is little to steal. Personal violence is dangerous, and the ruling class wish to control the right to use violence in society through their agents – the police and the army. Criminal law therefore operates to protect the rich and powerful.

Law creation and the dominant hegemony

In capitalist societies, the ruling class impose their values – that is, values that are beneficial to themselves – upon the mass of the population. They do this through a number of agencies, such as the education system, religion and the mass media. (This concept of ruling-class values being imposed upon the population is commonly known as 'hegemony'.)

This dominant set of values forms the framework on which laws are based in a democracy. However, we have just seen that, according to Marxists, the set of values is actually 'forced' on the people. Thus, what they believe they are agreeing to as a result of their own beliefs is, in reality, in the interests of the ruling class.

Law enforcement

Despite the fact that the law-making process reflects the interests of the ruling class, many of these laws could provide benefits for the majority of the population if they were applied fairly. However, even the interpretation and enforcement of the law is biased in favour of the ruling class, so that the police and the judicial system will arrest and punish the working class, but tend not to enforce the law against the ruling class.

Individual motivation

Marxist theory also provides an explanation for the individual motivation underlying crime. Bonger (1916), the very first Marxist writer on crime, pointed this out. He argued that capitalism is based upon competition, selfishness and greed, and this formed people's attitudes to life. Therefore, crime was a perfectly normal outcome of these values, which stressed looking after oneself at the expense of others. However, Bonger also said that in many cases, poor people were driven to crime by their desperate conditions

Crime and control

As we saw earlier, the ruling class in capitalism constantly seeks to divert the attention of the vast majority of the population away from an understanding of the true causes of their situation, and to impose their values through the mass media, religious organizations and the education system. These institutions provide alternative accounts of reality justifying the capitalist system as the natural and best economic system. Crime plays a significant part in supporting the ideology of capitalism, as it diverts attention away from the exploitative nature of capitalism and focuses attention instead on the evil and frightening nature of certain criminal groups in society, from whom we are only protected by the police. This justifies heavy policing of working-class areas, 'stop and searches' by the police of young people, and the arrests of any sections of the population who oppose capitalism.

An example of the traditional Marxist approach

William Chambliss' study of British vagrancy laws provides an illustration of the ways in which laws may be directly related to the interests of the ruling class. The first English vagrancy laws appeared in 1349, one year after the outbreak of the Black Death plague that was to kill more than one-third of the country's entire population. One result of the catastrophe was to decimate the labour force, so that those who were left could ask for high wages – and many people did this, moving from village to village in search of high pay. To combat this, the vagrancy laws were introduced, requiring every able-bodied man on the road to accept work at a low, fixed wage. The law was strictly enforced and did produce a supply of low-paid labour to help the workforce shortage. For almost 200 years the laws remained unchanged, but in 1530, changes were introduced which altered the emphasis of the laws to protect the concerns of an increasingly powerful merchant class from the many highway robbers who were preying on the traffic of goods along major highways. The vagrancy laws were amended so that they could be used to punish anyone on the road without a job, who was presumed to be a highwayman.

In both cases, the law was introduced and imposed in such a way as to benefit the ruling class – whilst apparently being concerned with stopping vagrants from travelling around England.

Criticisms of the traditional Marxist approach

1 The victims of crime are simply ignored in this analysis. The harm done by offenders is not taken into account. This is particularly important, as the victims are usually drawn from the less well-off sections of the population.

2 The explanation for law creation and enforcement tends to be one dimensional, in that all laws are seen as the outcome of the interests of the ruling class – no allowance is made for the complexity of influences on law-making behaviour.

The New Criminology

Partly as a result of these criticisms of what was a fairly crude Marxist explanation of crime, and partly as a result of the influence of interactionism (see Topic 5), Taylor, Walton and Young attempted to produce a fully social theory of deviance in *The New Criminology* (1973). This became an extremely influential book – possibly because it was a fairly successful fusing of Marxism and interactionism, the two most prominent theories of that time.

The new criminologists argued that in order to understand why a particular crime took place, it was no use just looking at the individual's motivation (e.g. alcohol or jealousy) and obvious influences (e.g. family background), which is what traditional positivist sociology might do. A Marxist perspective must be taken which looks at the wider capitalist society that helps generate the circumstances of the crime and police response to it. It is also important to use interactionist ideas to see how the behaviour of victim, offender, media and criminal justice system all interact to influence how the situation develops.

Ideology and the New Criminology

A further element of the New Criminology was that apart from the actual analysis that is suggested, it also argued that any sociology of crime and deviance had to be critical of the established capitalist order. This meant that instead of accepting the capitalist definition of crime and seeking to explain this, its role ought to be to uncover and explain the crimes of the rich. There was no attempt to be unbiased, rather the approach looked critically at the role of the police, the media and the criminal justice system in general – pointing out how they serve the needs of the ruling class.

Part of this critical approach to crime and criminal justice was to look in a fresh way at the ordinary criminal, who should best be seen as someone who is angry at capitalism and mistakenly expresses this anger through crime, rather than politics.

As we shall see in Topic 11, this later led to debates between '**left realists**', who seek to work within the current system, and those who remained true to the ideas of critical criminology.

A good example of critical criminology is the work of Stuart Hall *et al.* (1978) in *Policing the Crisis: The State and Law and Order*. In the 1970s, London witnessed a growth in 'muggings', i.e. assault and robbery of people in the streets. The media focused on this crime and a wave of publicity forced the problem to the top of the political and policing agenda. Although Hall did not exactly follow the model put forward in *The New Criminology*, the general critical criminological framework was used – see Table 5.1 below.

What a fully social theory of deviance must cover, according to Taylor *et al.* (1973)	Application of these ideas in Hall *et al.* (1978)
The wider origins of the deviant act	The 1970s was a period of considerable social crisis in Britain, the result of an international downturn in capitalist economies.
The immediate origins of the deviant act	This turmoil was shown in a number of inner-city riots, conflict in Northern Ireland and a high level of strikes. The government was searching for a group that could be scapegoated, to draw attention onto them and away from the crisis.
The actual act	Mugging – which according to the police was more likely to be carried out by those from African-Caribbean backgrounds.
The immediate origins of social reaction	Media outrage at the extent of muggings, linked to racism amongst the Metropolitan Police.
The wider origins of social reaction	The need to find scapegoats and the ease with which young men from African-Caribbean backgrounds could be blamed.
The outcome of social reaction on the deviants' further action	A sense of injustice amongst ethnic minorities and a loss of confidence by ethnic minority communities in the criminal justice system.
The nature of the deviant process as a whole	The real causes of crime were not addressed and were effectively hidden by the criminal justice system.

Table 5.1 The new criminology

Criticisms of the New Criminology

Traditional Marxists such as Hirst (1975) argued that the New Criminology strayed too far from the Marxist tradition. Others, such as Rock (1988), who were concerned directly in combating crime, argued that it gave far too romantic a view of criminals (in later writings, Young echoed this criticism and suggested it was one of the reasons for his development of left realism – see Topic 11). Feminist criminologists, such as Pat Carlen (1988), pointed out that there was absolutely no specific discussion of the power of patriarchy in the analysis, which simply continued the omission of women from criminological discussion.

Methodologically, it has always been extremely difficult to apply this perspective, as it is so complicated. In fact, no sociologist has actually managed to use this approach and so it remains more as an interesting model than an approach which guides research.

Marxist subcultural theory

A second strand of thought that developed from Marxism, was a specific explanation for the existence of subcultures amongst the working class. According to The Centre for Contemporary Cultural Studies (a group of writers at Birmingham University), capitalism maintains control over the majority of the population in two ways:

- ideological dominance through the media
- economic pressures – people want to keep their jobs and pay their mortgages.

Only those groups on the margins of society are not 'locked in' by ideology and finance, and thus are able to provide some form of resistance to capitalism. The single largest group offering this resistance is working-class youth.

According to Brake (1980) amongst others, this resistance is expressed through working-class youth subcultures. The clothes they wear and the language they use show their disdain of capitalism and their awareness of their position in it. Brake argues that this resistance, however, is best seen as '**magical**'. By magical, he means that it is a form of illusion that appears to solve their problems, but in reality does no such thing.

Figure 5.3 A subcultural analysis of skinheads

Skinheads: a 'magical' attempt to rediscover the working-class community

'Skinheads' football violence reflected a concern with their territory – linked to the redevelopment of traditional working-class communities in London in the '60s.'

'Skinheads' clothes were closely linked to the style of a traditional manual worker.'

Based on Cohen, P. (1972)
Knuckle Sandwich: Growing up in the working-class city,
Harmondsworth: Penguin

According to him, each generation of working-class youth face similar problems (dead-end jobs, unemployment, and so on), but in different circumstances – that is, society changes constantly so that every generation experiences a very different world, with the one constant being that the majority will be exploited by the ruling class.

Each generation expresses its resistance through different choice of clothes, argot (slang and patterns of speech), music, and so on. But each will eventually be trapped like their parents before them.

Criticism of the Marxist subcultural approach

Methodological Problems

Stan Cohen (1980) pointed out that these writers were simply biased in their analysis. They wanted to prove that working-class youth cultures were an attack on capitalism, and therefore

synopticlink

Paul Willis's *Learning to Labour* (1977) is a study of working-class boys in a secondary school. They realize early on the sorts of jobs they are going to get and reject the school and its concerns. They develop their own subculture, which Willis calls 'the lads'. This subculture is based on 'having a laff' and on rejecting school rules, teachers and work. However, their very rejection of school ensures that they are going to fail – thus making their belief come true – but, of course, they have been instrumental in their own failure.

education

made sure that they fixed the evidence to find this. He pointed out, for example, that there were many different ways to interpret the subcultural style of the groups, and that the interpretation that the Marxist writers had imposed was just one of many possibilities. The researches using this method knew what they wanted (signs of subcultural resistance) when they started looking at youth culture and so they extracted what they wanted to prove their theory and ignored what did not fit it.

Theoretical Problems

Blackman (1995) points out that the stress on the working-class basis of subcultural resistance ignores the huge variation of subcultures based on variations in sexual identity, locality, age, 'intellectual capacity' and a range of other social factors. Thornton (1995) argues that there is simply no 'real' social-class basis to youth subcultures at all; these are, in fact, creations of the media.

An overview of Marxist or critical criminological approaches

Critical criminology has provided a very powerful counterbalance to explanations of crime and deviance that focus on the individual, their family or the community in which they live. Critical criminology has forced sociologists to explore the wider social, economic and political factors which shape society. Perhaps most of all, they point out that crimes can only happen when people break the law, but that the law itself reflects differences in power between groups. Powerful groups, they claim, can ensure that the law, and the enforcement of the law, reflects their interests.

However, Marxism as a significant theoretical perspective in sociology has been on the wane for a number of years. The questions it raises remain as important, but the answers provided by critical criminologists have been less influential in the subject.

focus on research

Brake (1985)
Comparing youth subcultures

Brake undertook a comparative study of youth culture across the USA, Canada and Great Britain from the 1930s. Brake argues that all the variations in youth cultures across these countries can be traced back to young people's responses to particular social, economic and political events over the period. According to Brake, subcultures provide young people with both a collective and, within that, an individual identity. The actual basis of youth subculture, he argues, is one of resolving the specific social problems that young people face at any particular time. Brake suggests that the dominant influence on the form of youth culture varies according to social class, ethnicity or gender, depending upon how the young people experience their particular problems.

In order to gather material for his study, Brake undertook secondary analysis of the published research by other sociologists within each country on youth subcultures, and also reinterpreted some of his own earlier work. Brake supplemented this with reading and exploring non-sociological descriptions of youth activities over the period.

One major criticism of Brake's work is that he began with the theoretical idea that youth culture was a collective response to resolving young people's problems and then sought out support for this position. It is reasonable to argue that Brake was, therefore, selective in his choice of material.

Brake, M. (1985) *Comparative Youth Culture: The sociology of youth cultures and youth subcultures in America, Britain and Canada*, London: Routledge

1 What do we mean by a 'comparative approach'?

2 What did Brake use to obtain the evidence for his theoretical approach?

3 What problems are there with this approach?

web.tasks

1 **Look up the website** www.socialistparty.org.uk

To what extent do you think the Marxist analysis contained in it accurately explains today's problems?

2 **Using the worldwide web, look up newspaper reports and background information about any recent terrorist or criminal event. See if you can apply the 'New Criminology' framework of Taylor, Walton and Young to interpret the event.**

Check your understanding

1. How does the ruling class impose their values on others?

2. According to Marxists, how neutral is the law?

3. What is Bonger's explanation of individual motivation for crime?

4. How does Chambliss's research on vagrancy support a Marxist view of crime?

5. In what ways does the New Criminology utilize both Marxism and interactionism?

6. Why is it convenient for capitalism to find scapegoats?

7. How do Marxists explain the development of working-class subcultures?'

8. How do working-class subcultures resist capitalism?

9. In what way is their resistance 'magical'?

10. How have different Marxist approaches to crime and deviance been criticized?

research idea

- Choose any one contemporary subcultural style. What are the favoured clothes, argot, style of music and other distinguishing features (e.g. skateboard)? What explanations can you offer for the origins of these? Interview members of the group to find the meaning they give to their dress, language, and so on.

exploring critical criminologies

Item A

The criminal law is thus not a reflection of custom, but a set of rules laid down by the state in the interests of the ruling class, and resulting from the conflicts arising in class-structured societies; criminal behaviour is, then, the inevitable expression of class conflict resulting from the the exploitative nature of economic relations.

Criminality is simply not something that people have or don't have; crime is not something some people do and others don't. Crime is a matter of who can pin the label on whom, and underlying this socio-political process is the structure of social relations determined by capitalism.

Adapted from: Chambliss, W. (1975) 'Towards a Political Economy of Crime', *Theory and Society*, Vol. 2 (abridged)

(a) Identify and briefly explain **two** criticisms of the Marxist subcultural approach to deviance. (8 marks)

This part of the question includes assessment of your understanding of the connections between Crime and Deviance and sociological methods.

(b) Examine ways in which powerful groups are able to define what is and is not deviant. In your answer, use material from **at least two** of the following areas: families and households; health; mass media; education; wealth, work and leisure; religion; power and politics; world sociology. (12 marks)

This part of the question includes assessment of your understanding of the connections between Crime and Deviance and other substantive topic(s) you have studied.

(c) Using material from **Item A** and elsewhere, assess the usefulness of Marxist approaches to an understanding of crime and deviance. (40 marks)

This part of the question includes assessment of your understanding of the connections between Crime and Deviance and sociological theory.

Labelling theory

gettingyouthinking

1 **Are any of the people in these photos committing a crime?**

2 **Is their behaviour deviant? If so, which?**

3 **Will everybody agree about which behaviours are deviant? Why might there be different views?**

4 **What does this exercise tell us about deviance?**

Understanding deviance: reaction not cause

Most approaches to understanding crime and deviance (with the exception of Marxist approaches) accept that there is a difference between those who offend and those who do not. On the basis of this assumption, they then search for the key factors that lead the person to offend.

However, since the early 1950s, one group of sociologists influenced by **symbolic interactionism** have questioned this approach. They argue that this approach makes a mistake in its fundamental assumption that lawbreakers are somehow

different from the law-abiding. Labelling theory suggests instead that most people commit deviant and criminal acts, but only some people are caught and stigmatized for it. So, if most people commit deviant acts of some kind, it is pointless trying to search for the differences between deviants and non-deviants – instead the stress should be upon understanding the reaction to and definition of deviance rather than on the causes of the initial act. As Howard Becker (1963) puts it:

>> *Deviancy is not a quality of the act a person commits but rather a consequence of the application by others of rules and sanctions to an 'offender'. Deviant behaviour is behaviour that people so label.* >>

This is a radically different way of exploring crime; in fact, it extends beyond crime and helps us to understand any deviant or **stigmatized** behaviour. Labelling theory has gradually been adopted and incorporated into many other sociological approaches – for example, Taylor, Walton and Young (1973) have used it in their updating of Marxist criminology, while postmodernist approaches also owe much to it.

The best-known exponent of 'labelling theory' is Howard Becker. In the book *The Outsiders*, Becker gives a very clear and simple illustration of the labelling argument, drawing upon an anthropological study by Malinowski (1948/1982) of a traditional culture on a Pacific Island.

Malinowski describes how a youth killed himself because he had been publicly accused of **incest**. When Malinowski had first inquired about the case, the islanders expressed their horror and disgust. But, on further investigation, it turned out that incest was not uncommon on the island, nor was it really frowned upon provided those involved were discreet. However, if an incestuous affair became too obvious and public, the islanders reacted with abuse, the offenders were ostracized and often driven to suicide.

Becker, therefore, argues the following:

1   Just because someone breaks a rule, it does not necessarily follow that others will define it as deviant.
2   Someone has to enforce the rules or, at least, draw attention to them – these people usually have a vested interest in the issue. (In the example of the incestuous islanders, the rule was enforced by the rejected ex-lover of the girl involved in incest.)
3   If the person is successfully labelled, then consequences follow. (Once publicly labelled as deviant, the offender in Malinowski's example was faced with limited choices, one of which was suicide.)

Responding to and enforcing rules

Most sociological theories take for granted that once a person has committed a deviant or criminal act, then the response will be uniform. This is not true. People respond differently to deviance or rule-breaking. In the early 1960s, when gay people were more likely to be stigmatized than now, John Kitsuse (1962) interviewed 75 heterosexual students to elicit their responses to (presumed) sexual advances from people of the same sex. What he found was a very wide range of responses from complete tolerance to bizarre and extreme hatred. One told how he had 'known' that a man he was talking to in a bar was homosexual because he had wanted to talk about psychology! The point of Kitsuse's work is that there was no agreed definition of what constituted a homosexual 'advance' – it was open to negotiation.

In Britain today, British Crime Survey statistics show that young Black males are more likely to be stopped for questioning and searching than any other group. This is a result of the police officers' belief that this particular social group is more likely to offend than any other; for this reason, they are the subjects of 'routine suspicion'.

Criticism

Akers (1967) criticized labelling theorists for presenting deviants as perfectly normal people who are no different from anyone else until someone comes along and slaps a label on them. Akers argues that there must be some reason why the label is applied to certain groups/individuals and not others. As long as labelling fails to explain this, then it is an incomplete theory.

synoptic link   sociological theory

Labelling theory and symbolic interactionism provide similar analyses of individual behaviour. Symbolic interactionism argues that the social world consists of 'symbols' that have a culturally defined meaning to people and suggest appropriate ways of acting. These symbols are not fixed and may change over time. Every time two or more people interact with each other, they amend their behaviour on the basis of how they interpret the behaviour of the other people. A second element of symbolic interactionism is the way that people develop images of themselves and how they should 'present' themselves to other people, which is known as the 'self'.

The ideas of labelling theory are very similar, with some changes in language, so instead of symbol, the word 'label' is used. Instead of using the term 'the self', the term 'master status' is used.

There is one great difference between symbolic interactionism and the form of labelling developed by

Howard Becker

such writers as Becker: symbolic interactionism is not interested in power differences, whereas labelling theory focuses on the way that differences in power can lead to some people imposing labels on others (and the consequences of this).

The consequences of rule enforcement

As we have just seen, being labelled as a deviant and having laws enforced against you is the result of a number of different factors. However, once labelled as a deviant, various consequences occur for the individual.

The clearest example of this is provided by Edwin Lemert, who distinguished between '**primary**' and '**secondary**' **deviance** (Lemert 1972). Primary deviance is rule-breaking, which is of little importance in itself, while secondary deviance is the consequence of the responses of others, which is significant.

To illustrate this, Lemert studied the coastal **Inuits** of Canada, who had a long-rooted problem of chronic stuttering or stammering. Lemert suggested that the problem was 'caused' by the great importance attached to ceremonial speech-making. Failure to speak well was a great humiliation. Children with the slightest speech difficulty were so conscious of their parents' desire to have well-speaking children that they became overanxious about their own abilities. It was this very anxiety, according to Lemert, that led to chronic stuttering. In this example, chronic stuttering (secondary deviance) is a response to parents' reaction to initial minor speech defects (primary deviance).

The person labelled as 'deviant' will eventually come to see themselves as being bad (or mad). Becker used the term '**master status**' to describe this process. He points out that once a label has successfully been applied to a person, then all other qualities become unimportant – they are responded to solely in terms of this master status.

Rejecting labels: negotiability

The process of being labelled is, however, open to 'negotiation', in that some groups or individuals are able to reject the label. An example of this is Reiss's (1961) study of young male prostitutes. Although they had sex with other men, they regarded what they did as work and maintained an image of themselves as being 'straight'.

Deviant career

These ideas of master status and negotiability led Becker to devise the idea of a '**deviant career**'. He meant by this all the processes that are involved in a label being applied (or not) and then the person taking on (or not) the self-image of the deviant.

Figure 5.4 The process of labelling

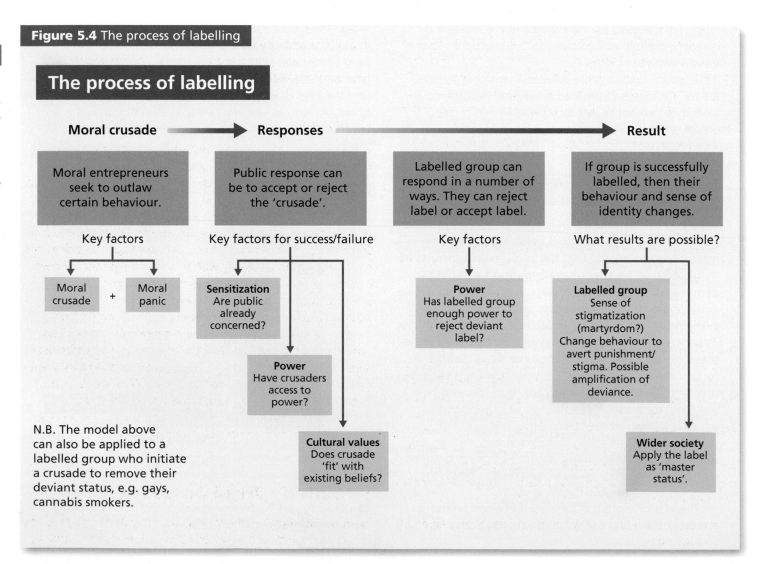

Labelling theory has been widely used in other areas apart from crime, as it is an approach which helps understand a contentious issue from the view of the person in the less powerful position. An excellent example of the significance of labelling is provided in Glaser and Strauss' study of dying (1965). In most cases, people do not die suddenly, but instead take weeks, perhaps even years in dying. They found that there were certain accepted ways of behaving which people labelled as dying were suppose to conform to. A dying person should:

>> *maintain relative composure and cheerfulness ... at the very least should face death with dignity ... they should continue to be a good family member and be 'nice' to other patients ... if possible they should avoid distressing or embarrassing staff members ...* >>

Patients who do not die properly are coaxed, coached and scolded in order to make them conform to the correct pattern of behaviour.

Creating rules

Once labelling theorists began the process of looking at how social life was open to negotiation and that rule enforcement was no different than other social activities, then attention shifted to the creation of rules and laws. Why were they made? Traditionally, sociologists had taken either a Marxist perspective (that they were made in the interests of the ruling class) or a functionalist/pluralist perspective (which argued that laws in a democracy reflected the views of the majority of the population). Becker (1963) doubted both these accounts and argued instead that:

>> *Rules are the products of someone's initiative and we can think of the people who exhibit such enterprises as '**moral entrepreneurs**'.* >>

So, labelling theorists argue that laws are a reflection of the activities of people (moral entrepreneurs) who actively seek to create and enforce laws. The reasons for this are either that the new laws benefit the activists directly, or these activists believe that the laws are truly to the benefit of society.

Becker's most famous example is his study of the outlawing of cannabis use in the USA in 1937. Cannabis had been widely used in the southern states of the USA. Its outlawing was the result of a successful campaign waged by the Federal Bureau of Narcotics which, after the repeal of the prohibition laws (that had banned alcohol), saw cannabis as a growing menace in society. Through a press campaign and lobbying of senior politicians, the Bureau was successful in outlawing the growing and use of the drug. However, Becker points out that the campaign was only successful because it 'plugged in' to values commonly held in the USA which included:

1 the belief that people ought to be in control of their actions and decisions

2 that pleasure for its own sake was wrong
3 that drugs were seen as addictive and, as such, 'enslaved' people.

The term Becker used to describe the campaign was of a '**moral crusade**', and it is this terminology (along with the concept of moral entrepreneurs) which sociologists use to describe movements to pass laws.

Criticisms

The idea that there are those who seek to pass laws or to impose rules upon others has been accepted by most sociologists. However, Marxist writers in particular have pointed out that there is a wider framework within which this is placed. Are all laws just the product of a particular group of moral entrepreneurs? If so, then what are the conditions under which some groups succeed and others fail? Labelling theory does not really answer this issue very well; in fact, labelling theory does not have a coherent theory of power, as it argues that more powerful groups are able to impose their 'definition of the situation' on others, yet does not explain why some groups have more power than others and are more able to get laws passed and enforced that are beneficial to them. In defence of labelling theory, Becker (1970) does suggest in a famous article ('Whose side are we on?') that there are differences in power and that it is the role of the sociologist to side with the underdog. (We explore this in more detail below.) However, no overall theory of differences in power is given.

Labelling and values

We have just mentioned a famous article by Becker, in which he argues that labelling theory has a clear value position – that is, it speaks up for the powerless and the underdog. Labelling theorists claim to provide a voice for those who are labelled as deviant and 'outsiders'.

However, Liazos (1972) criticizes labelling theorists for simply exploring marginally deviant activities, as by doing so, they are reinforcing the idea of pimps, prostitutes and mentally ill people as being deviant. Even by claiming to speak for the underdog, labelling theorists hardly present any challenge to the status quo.

Gouldner (1968) also criticizes labelling theorists for their failure to provide any real challenge to the status quo. He argued that all they did in their studies was to criticize doctors, psychiatrists and police officers for their role in labelling – and they failed ever to look beyond this at more powerful groups who benefit from this focus on marginal groups. Gouldner is putting forward a Marxist argument, by claiming that labelling theorists draw attention away from the 'real crime'.

Crime, labelling and the media

Labelling theory alerts us to the way in which the whole area of crime depends upon social constructions of reality – law creation, law enforcement and the identities of rule breakers are all thrown into question. The media play a key role in all three

of these processes, as most people's perceptions of crime are actually created – or at least informed – by the media.

Labelling theory has contributed two particularly important concepts to our understanding of the relationship between the media and crime:

- deviancy amplification
- moral panics.

Deviancy amplification

The term '**deviancy amplification**' was coined by the British sociologist Leslie Wilkins to show how the response to deviance, by agencies such as police and media, can actually generate an increase in deviance. According to Wilkins (1964), when acts are defined as deviant, the deviants become stigmatized and cut off from mainstream society. They become aware that they are regarded as deviants and, as a result of this awareness, they begin to develop their own subculture. This leads to more intense pressure on them and further isolation, which further confirms and strengthens them in their deviance.

Jock Young (1971) used this concept in his study of drug use in North London. He showed that increased police activity led to drug use being 'driven underground'. This had the effect of isolating users into a drug subculture, with 'a distinctive style of dress, lack of workaday sense of time, money, rationality and

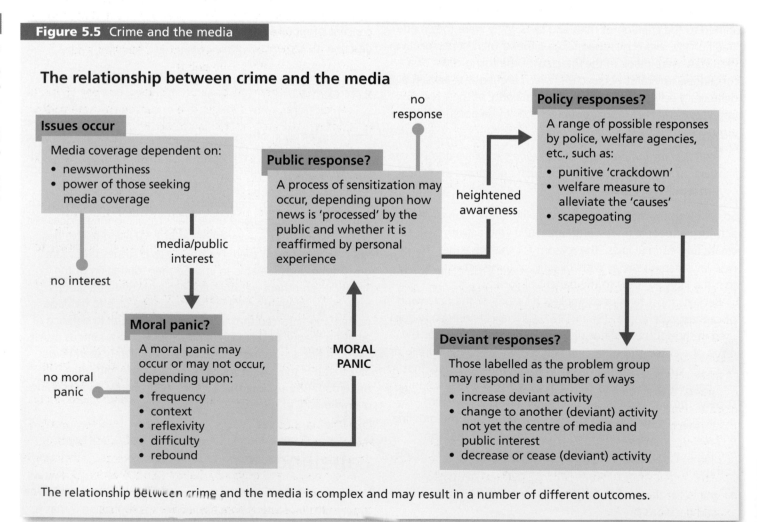

Figure 5.5 Crime and the media

The relationship between crime and the media

The relationship between crime and the media is complex and may result in a number of different outcomes.

Teachers claim to treat all pupils alike, but every child in the classroom knows the teacher's favourites and every class knows its reputation with the teachers. These pupils' awareness of their place in the eyes of teachers can affect their behaviour. This is commonsense knowledge in the classroom, but it is also how labelling theory is played out in the educational system.

Rosenthal and Jacobson's (1968) study, which involved telling teachers that some students were especially gifted – even though, unknown to the teachers, the pupils had been chosen entirely at random – resulted in the teachers having raised expectations of those pupils. As a result of this, the academic attainment of those pupils improved.

Mac An Ghaill's (1998, 1992) work on race and achievement also found that the students in his study believed that teachers have expectations of (sixth-form) students based on 'racial' labelling. Black students believed that teachers had higher expectations of, and aspirations for, Asian and White students.

Labelling in the classroom

rewards', thus making re-entry to regular employment increasingly difficult – which, of course, made it difficult for them to afford the drugs. The scarcity of drugs drove the price up and this drew in professional criminals who regarded it as worthwhile entering the illicit drug business; criminal rings developed and the competition between them led to violence. It also led to the use of dangerous substitutes and adulterants in drugs by suppliers, interested only in maximizing profits, thus creating a situation where users no longer knew the strength of drugs and were consequently more likely to overdose. The process described here caused wide public concern which spurred the police to intensify their clampdown even further, which only served to accelerate the spiral of this 'amplification' process.

Moral panics

The idea of **moral panics** both overlaps with and complements the concept of deviancy amplification. The term was first used in Britain by Stan Cohen in a classic study (1972) of two youth subcultures of the 1960s – 'mods' and 'rockers'. Cohen showed how the media, for lack of other stories, built up these two groups into **folk devils**. The effect of the media coverage was to make the young people categorize themselves as either mods or rockers. This actually helped to create the violence that took place between them, which also confirmed them as troublemakers in the eyes of the public.

The concept of moral panic and the role of the media in helping to create them, has been widely used in sociology since Cohen's original British work – though perhaps the best adaptation of this is the study by Hall and colleagues of 'mugging' (see Topic 4).

Moral panics: an outdated idea?

McRobbie and Thornton (1995) argue that 'moral panics', as described by Cohen in the 1960s, are outdated and have to be seen in the context of the development of the media and the growing sophistication of the audiences. McRobbie and Thornton make the following points:

- *Frequency* – There has been an increasing number of 'moral panics' – they are no longer rare or particularly noteworthy.
- *Context* – Whereas moral panics would scapegoat a group and create 'folk devils' in the 1960s, today there is no single, unambiguous response to a panic as there are many different viewpoints and values in society.
- *Reflexivity* – As moral panics as a concept are so well known, many groups try to create them for their own benefit. However, the same knowledge means that the media know this and do not necessarily wish uncritically to start a moral panic over an issue.
- *Difficulty* – Moral panics are much more unlikely to start in society because it is far less clear today what is unambiguously 'bad'. Society is too fragmented and culturally pluralistic.
- *Rebound* – People are more wary about starting moral panics as there is the possibility of it rebounding on them. So politicians who start a campaign about family values or drugs have to be very careful about their own backgrounds.

Labelling has been very important in helping to understand the role of the media. However, if what McRobbie and Thornton say is true, then by their very success, sociological concepts such as moral panic have gradually filtered into the wider society, so that journalists and politicians are now aware of them and use them in their decisions about what actions to take.

focusonresearch

Heckert and Best (1997)

The stigmatization of red hair

Heckert and Best conducted a study into the impact of having ginger hair. For some years there has been a negative image promoted about ginger-haired people and the researchers argued that people with ginger hair are negatively labelled and are treated as deviants. They interviewed 20 ginger-haired people in all, nine males and eleven females, using open questions. They found that ginger-haired people were viewed as having all or some of the following characteristics – hot tempered, clownish, weird, wild (women) or wimpy (men). They were typically treated more negatively in childhood and as a result had low levels of self-esteem. Interestingly, both researchers were ginger-haired!

Heckert, D.N. and Best, A. (1997) 'Ugly Duckling to Swan: Labeling Theory and the Stigmatization of Red Hair', *Symbolic Interaction*, 20(4), pp. 365–84

1 How might the researchers' own ginger hair have influenced respondents?

2 Evaluate the reliability and representativeness of this research.

KEY TERMS

Deviancy amplification – when the action of the rule enforcers or media in response to deviance brings about an increase in the deviance.

Deviant career – the various stages that a person passes through on their way to being seen as, and seeing themselves as, deviant.

Folk devils – groups associated with moral panics who are seen as troublemakers by the media.

Incest – sex between close members of a family (other than man and wife).

Inuits – previously known as 'eskimos'.

Master status – when people are looked at by others solely on the basis of one type of act (good or bad) which they have committed; all other aspects of that person are ignored.

Moral crusade – the process of creating or enforcing a rule.

Moral entrepreneur – person or group which tries to create or enforce a rule.

Moral panic – outrage stirred up by the media about a particular group or issue.

Primary deviance – the act of breaking a rule.

Secondary deviance – the response to rule breaking, which usually has greater social consequences than initial rule-breaking.

Stigmatized – labelled in a negative way.

Symbolic interactionism – a theory derived from social psychology which argues that people exist in a social world based on symbols that people interpret and respond to. Labelling theorists tend to substitute the term 'label' for 'symbol'.

Check your understanding

1 Instead of looking at the cause of crime, what does labelling theory focus on?

2 What theoretical approach does labelling theory derive from? How?

3 Explain and give one example of what labelling theorists mean when they say that the response to law-breaking is variable.

4 Explain the importance of the term 'master status' in understanding deviance.

5 In what way does the labelling approach to the introduction of laws differ from the Marxist approach?

6 How has labelling theory been criticized?

7 Explain the importance of the idea of 'deviancy amplification'.

8 What criticisms have been made of the term 'moral panic'?

research idea

- Conduct a survey to discover young people's perceptions of the elderly. Do their views represent particular labels and stereotypes?

  Then interview a small number of elderly people. Are they aware of stereotypes and labels? How do they feel about these labels? Do they affect them?

  Be sensitive in your interviewing technique, following the usual ethical guidelines.

web.tasks

1 Becker studied the way in which cannabis was made illegal (see above). Search the worldwide web for information about the campaign to make cannabis legal (or at least 'decriminalized') in Britain. Are there any parallels, in your opinion?

2 Search the worldwide web for newspaper and other information about any moral panic of your choice (e.g. concern over film violence, drugs such as ecstasy, underage sex). To what extent can you identify the key features of a moral panic, such as media exaggeration, the creation of 'folk devils', the activities of moral entrepreneurs, and so on?

exploring labelling theory

Item A

Labelling theory – with its rejection of so-called positivistic criminology – was closely allied to the development of the sociology of deviance. This sociology not only changed the theoretical base for the study of criminals, but also brought in its wake a dramatic restructuring of empirical concerns. Sociologists turned their interests to the world of expressive deviance; to the twilight marginal worlds of tramps, alcoholics, strippers, dwarfs, prostitutes, drug addicts, nudists; to taxi-drivers, the blind, the dying, the physically ill, the handicapped and even to a motley array of problems of everyday life. It opened up the field of inquiry so that it was possible to discuss a range of areas hitherto neglected – thereby enabling the foundations for a formal theory of deviance and a method for understanding the routine and the regular through the eyes of the powerless.

Adapted from Carrabine, E., Iganski, P. , Lee, M., Plummer, K. and South, N. (2004) Criminology: A Sociological Introduction, London: Routledge, p. 74

(a) Identify and briefly explain two ways in which deviance may be related to **one or more** of the following areas: education; health; mass media. (8 marks)

This part of the question includes assessment of your understanding of the connections between Crime and Deviance and other substantive topic(s) you have studied.

(b) Using material from **Item A** and elsewhere, examine some of the ways in which labelling theory contributes to a sociological understanding of deviance. (12 marks)

This part of the question includes assessment of your understanding of the connections between Crime and Deviance and sociological theory.

(c) Assess the usefulness of participant observation in understanding deviance. (40 marks)

This part of the question includes assessment of your understanding of the connections between Crime and Deviance and sociological methods.

Patterns of crime

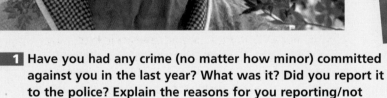

1 Have you had any crime (no matter how minor) committed against you in the last year? What was it? Did you report it to the police? Explain the reasons for you reporting/not reporting it.

2 Which of the three people in the photographs is most likely to be the victim of an attack at night on the streets? Explain the reasons for your answer.*

3 Which car is more likely to be stolen: a smart new BMW or a 15-year-old Vauxhall Astra? Explain your answer.*

4 Is bullying a crime? Please explain the reasons for your answer.*

5 At school/college, how does the institution deal with bullying, cannabis use and 'minor' thefts? What implications does this have for official statistics?

Answers to these questions are given on p. 273.

Our commonsense ideas about crime do not always match the picture revealed by statistics. Many of us believe that crime is something committed by the less wealthy against the more wealthy and more vulnerable sections of the community. This view may well have influenced your answers to the questions above. However, police figures indicate that poorer areas have higher crime rates than wealthy areas, that young men are more likely to be the victims of crime than old ladies, and that battered Ford Fiestas are more likely to be stolen than the latest executive BMW. But are these figures accurate, and how can we use statistics about crime to help us understand why some people commit crimes?

In order to understand why people commit crime, we need first to find out who commits crime and what sorts of crimes are committed. Sociologists use three different ways to build up this picture of crime. Each method provides us with particular information, but also has a number of weaknesses that need to be identified if our picture is to be accurate. The three methods of collecting information are:

● police-recorded statistics
● victim surveys
● self-report studies.

Police-recorded statistics

Police-recorded statistics are drawn from the records kept by the police and other official agencies, and are published every six months by the **Home Office**.

The **official statistics** are particularly useful in that they have been collected since 1857 and so provide us with an excellent historical overview of changing trends over time. They also give us a completely accurate view of the way that the criminal justice system processes offenders through arrests, trials, punishments, and so on.

Police-recorded statistics as social constructions

Police-recorded statistics are **social constructions** – they cannot be taken simply at their face value because they only show crimes that are reported to and recorded by the police. When we dig a little deeper, a lot of hidden issues are uncovered.

Reporting crime

Police-recorded statistics are based on the information that the criminal justice agencies collect. But crimes cannot be recorded by them if they are not reported in the first place, and the simple fact is that a high proportion of 'crimes' are not reported to the police at all. According to the **British Crime Survey** (Home Office 1998), we know that individuals are less likely to report a 'crime' to the police if they regard it as:

- too trivial to bother the police with
- a private matter between friends and family – in this case they will seek redress directly (get revenge themselves) – or one where they wish no harm to come to the offender
- too embarrassing (e.g. male rape).

Other reasons for non-reporting of crimes are that:

- the victim may not be in a position to give information (e.g. a child suffering abuse)
- they may fear reprisals.

On the other hand, people are more likely to report a crime if:

- they see some benefit to themselves (e.g. an insurance claim)
- they have faith in the police ability to achieve a positive result.

Recording of crimes

When people do actively report an offence to the police, you would think that these statistics at least would enter the official reports. Yet in any one year, approximately 57 per cent of all crimes reported to the police fail to appear in the official statistics. Figure 5.6 on the next page shows the proportion of the crimes committed that are reported to the police and the proportion recorded by the police.

The role of the police

Clearly the police are filtering the information supplied to them by the public, according to factors that are important to them. These factors have been identified as follows:

British Crime Survey

The British Crime Survey (BCS) was first introduced in 1982, heavily influenced by a similar type of survey which had been undertaken in the USA since 1972 (funded by the US Department of Justice). Originally, the UK studies were every two years, but since 2000, they have been carried out every year. The sample size is enormous, with almost 40 000 people being interviewed. The idea behind the study is that by asking people directly what crimes have been committed against them, the problems of crime reporting and police recording are avoided. Supporters of the survey suggest that it is more 'valid' than the police statistics.

The sampling technique is based on (a) all households in England and Wales and then (b) anyone over 16 living in these households. The households are selected using the Postcode Address File, developed by the Post Office to recognize all households in Britain. Interviews last 50 minutes and each person is asked if they have been the victim of a list of selected crimes. There is then a smaller 'sweep' (a subsample), who are asked to answer questions on a selected (sometimes sensitive) issues directly into a laptop computer.

Is the BCS more accurate than the police-recorded statistics? The answer provided by Maguire (2002) is that the BCS is neither better nor worse, but simply provides an alternative, overall picture of crime which helps fill in some gaps in the police-recorded statistics.

1 What steps does the BCS take to maximize the representativeness of the survey?

2 Can you identify any groups who may still be left out of the survey?

3 Why do you think respondents in the smaller subsample are asked to input their answers directly into a laptop computer?

Figure 5.6 Reporting and recording of crime

Proportions of BCS estimate of all crime reported to the police and recorded by them (comparable subset of crimes), year to September 2004

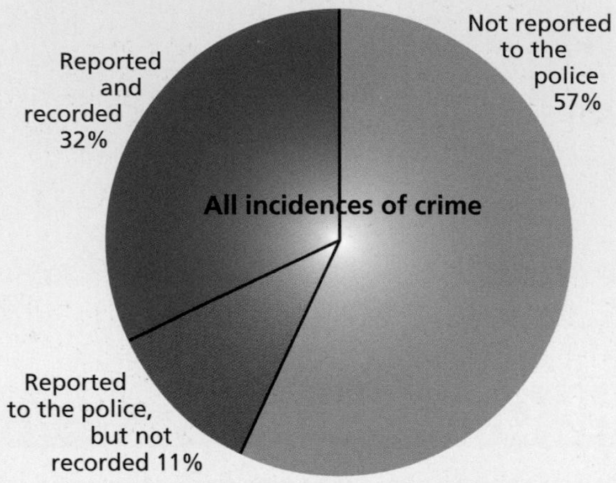

- Reported and recorded 32%
- Not reported to the police 57%
- Reported to the police, but not recorded 11%
- All incidences of crime

Source: Nicholas, S. *et al.* (2005) *Crime in England and Wales 2004/5*, Home Office Statistical Bulletin

- *Seriousness* – They may regard the offence as too trivial or simply not a criminal matter.
- *Social status* – More worryingly, they may view the social status of the person reporting the matter as not high enough to regard the issue as worth pursuing.
- *Classifying* – When a person makes a complaint, police crimes officers must decide what category of offence it is. How they classify the offence will determine its seriousness. So, the police officer's opinion determines the category and seriousness of crime (from assault, to aggravated assault for example).
- *Discretion* – Only about 10 per cent of offences are actually uncovered by the police. However, the chances of being arrested for an offence increase markedly depending upon the 'demeanour' of the person being challenged by a police officer (that is, their appearance, attitude and manner). Anderson *et al.* (1994) show that youths who cooperate and are polite to police officers are less likely to be arrested than those regarded as disrespectful.
- *Promotion* – Police officers, like everyone else, have concerns about career and promotion. This involves relationships trying to impress senior officers. However, at work they also need to get on with other colleagues, who do not like officers who are too keen (as this makes more work for everyone). Arrests reflect a balance between comradeship and a desire for promotion (Collinson 1995).

The role of the courts

Official statistics of crimes committed and punished also reflect the decisions and sentences of the courts. However, these statistics, too, are a reflection of social processes.

British courts work on the assumption that many people will plead guilty – and about 75 per cent of all those charged actually do so. This is often the result of an informal and largely unspoken agreement whereby the defence will try to get the charges with the lightest possible punishment put forward by the prosecution. (In the USA, this bargaining is far more open than in Britain, and is known as **plea-bargaining**.) The result is an overwhelming majority of pleas of guilty, yet these pleas are for less serious crimes than might 'really' have been committed. The statistics will reflect this downgrading of seriousness.

The role of the government

What is considered to be a crime changes over time, as a result of governments changing the law in response to cultural changes and the influence of powerful groups. Any exploration of crime over a period is therefore fraught with difficulty, because any rise or fall in the levels of crime may reflect changes in the law as much as actual changes in crime. A good example of this is the way that attitudes to cannabis use have shifted – while there has been an increase in the numbers of people possessing and using cannabis (both of which are a crime), the number of arrests for its possession has actually declined, as the police respond to public opinion. The police statistics might make it look as if cannabis use is actually declining, when it is not.

Victim surveys

A second way of estimating the extent and patterns of crime is by using **victimization** (or **victim**) **surveys**. In these, a sample of the population, either locally or nationally, are asked which offences have been committed against them over a certain period of time.

Strengths of victim surveys

This approach overcomes the fact that a significant proportion of offences are never recorded by the police. It also gives an excellent picture of the extent and patterns of victimization – something completely missing from official accounts. The best known victimization study is the British Crime Survey which is now collected every year and has been in operation since 1982 (see Focus on research, p. 267).

Weaknesses of victim surveys

- The problem of basing statistics on victims' memories is that recollections are often faulty or biased.
- The categorization of the crimes that has been committed against them is left to the person filling in the questionnaire – this leads to considerable inaccuracy in the categories.
- Victim surveys also omit a range of crimes, such as fraud and corporate crime, and any crime where the victim is unaware of or unable to report a crime.
- Despite victim surveys being anonymous, people appear to underreport sexual offences.

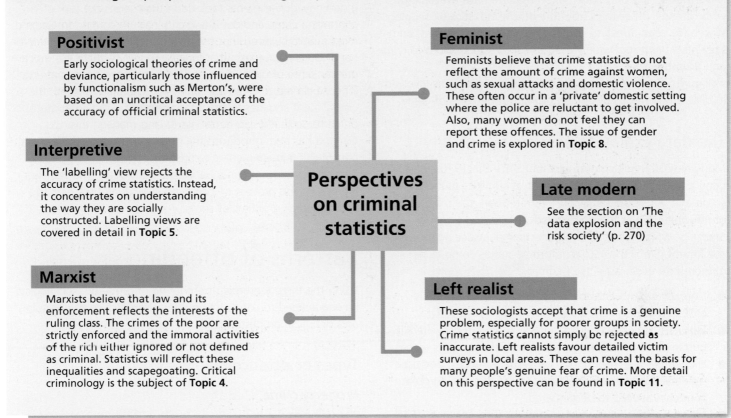

Different sociological perspectives take a range of positions on the usefulness of criminal statistics.

Positivist

Early sociological theories of crime and deviance, particularly those influenced by functionalism such as Merton's, were based on an uncritical acceptance of the accuracy of official criminal statistics.

Interpretive

The 'labelling' view rejects the accuracy of crime statistics. Instead, it concentrates on understanding the way they are socially constructed. Labelling views are covered in detail in **Topic 5**.

Marxist

Marxists believe that law and its enforcement reflects the interests of the ruling class. The crimes of the poor are strictly enforced and the immoral activities of the rich either ignored or not defined as criminal. Statistics will reflect these inequalities and scapegoating. Critical criminology is the subject of **Topic 4**.

Perspectives on criminal statistics

Feminist

Feminists believe that crime statistics do not reflect the amount of crime against women, such as sexual attacks and domestic violence. These often occur in a 'private' domestic setting where the police are reluctant to get involved. Also, many women do not feel they can report these offences. The issue of gender and crime is explored in **Topic 8**.

Late modern

See the section on 'The data explosion and the risk society' (p. 270)

Left realist

These sociologists accept that crime is a genuine problem, especially for poorer groups in society. Crime statistics cannot simply be rejected as inaccurate. Left realists favour detailed victim surveys in local areas. These can reveal the basis for many people's genuine fear of crime. More detail on this perspective can be found in **Topic 11**.

● The BCS itself suffers from the problem of not collecting information from those under 16, although this is not necessarily a problem of victim surveys as such. The British Youth Lifestyles Survey (2000), for example, was carried out specifically to obtain detailed information on crimes against younger people.

Local victim surveys

The BCS is a typical cross-sectional survey, and as such may contain some errors – certainly, it does not provide detailed information about particular places. This has led to a number of detailed studies of crime focusing on particular areas. These provide specific information about local problems.

The most famous of these surveys were the **Islington Crime Surveys** (Harper et al. 1986 and Jones et al. 1995). These showed that the BCS under-reported the higher levels of victimization of minority ethnic groups and domestic violence.

The media and sensitization

Victim surveys are dependent upon people being aware that they are victims. This may seem obvious, but in fact this depends very much on the 'victim' perceiving what happens to them as being a crime. The media play a key role in this as they provide illustrations of 'crimes' and generally heighten sensitivity towards certain forms of behaviour. This is known as

sensitizing the public towards (certain types of) activity that can be seen as a crime worth reporting. A positive example of this has been the change in portrayal of domestic violence from a family matter to being a criminal activity.

Self-report studies

The third method for collecting data is that of **self-report studies**. These are surveys in which a selected group or cross-section of the population are asked what offences they have committed. Self-report studies are extremely useful as they reveal much about the kind of offenders who are not caught or processed by the police. In particular, it is possible to find out about the ages, gender, social class and even location of 'hidden offenders'. It is also the most useful way to find out about victimless crimes such as illegal drug use.

Weaknesses of self-report studies

● The problem of validity – The biggest problem is that respondents may lie or exaggerate, and even if they do not deliberately seek to mislead, they may simply be mistaken.
● The problem of representativeness – Because it is easy to study them, most self-report surveys are on young people and students. There are no such surveys on professional criminals or drug traffickers, for example!

- The problem of relevance – Because of the problem of representativeness, the majority of the crimes uncovered tend to be trivial.

Nevertheless, the only information that we have available of who offends, other than from the official statistics of people who have been arrested, comes from self-report studies, and they have been very widely used to explore such issues as crime and drug use.

Figure 5.7 summarises the processes and problems involved in different methods of finding out about patterns of crime.

The data explosion and the risk society

Maguire (2002) has pointed out that since the 1970s there has been a huge increase in the amount of statistics gathered on crime and 'antisocial behaviour'. Before then, the main source of information was the government publication *Criminal Statistics*, which relied solely upon criminal justice agencies for the figures. Since the 1970s, information has come to be gathered on wider aspects of crime:

- Unreported and unrecorded offences – Information is collected through the BCS.
- Specialist subcategories of crime – There are now literally hundreds of crime categories that official statistics record.
- Hidden crime – Information on sexual offences, domestic violence, white-collar crime and, most recently, corporate crime has started to be gathered.
- Victim perspectives – Possibly the most recent innovation has been the collection of information from the victims of crime.

Garland (2001) suggests that it is not just an expansion of knowledge for its own sake that has driven the explosion of statistical information. He suggests instead that the answer can be found within the concerns of late modernity. During modernity, governments took upon themselves the task of controlling crime and punishing criminals. According to Garland, most people believed that the government had crime control in hand. Garland suggests that in late modernity, there is a much greater sense of uncertainty and risk, and governments are no longer believed to catch and punish all criminals. Instead, the government engages in **risk management** – it gathers statistics on crime so that it can better assess and manage this risk. Garland has also introduced the notion of '**responsibilization**' – part of risk management is to push responsibility for avoiding becoming victims of crime back onto individuals. The statistics are part of this process of informing individuals how best to avoid becoming victims of crime.

Patterns of offending

Using the three methods of gathering information, sociologists have managed to construct an interesting picture of offending and victimization patterns.

Types of offences

Property crime

According to the British Crime Survey, 62 per cent of crime in 2000 was accounted for by some form of property theft, with burglary and vehicle theft forming the bulk of these.

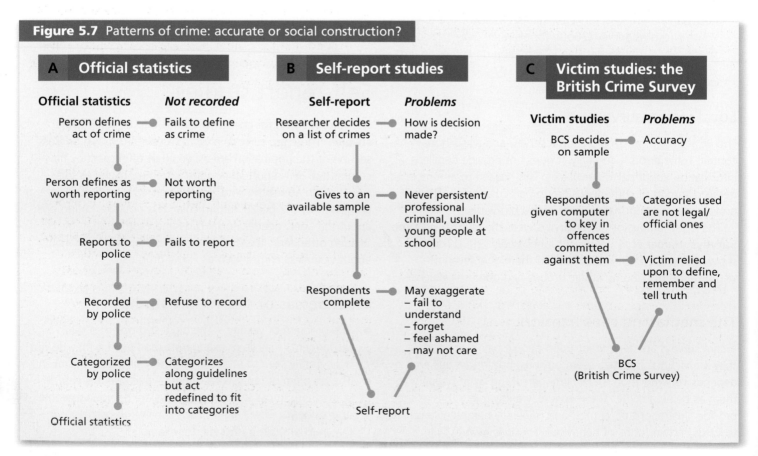

Figure 5.7 Patterns of crime: accurate or social construction?

Violent crime

All forms of violence account for approximately 20 per cent of BCS-reported crime, but the huge majority of these acts of violence – about 68 per cent – consisted only of very minor physical hurt (at most slight bruising). In fact, only about 5 per cent of violent crimes reported involved more than trivial injury.

Types of victims

Victims of violence

Young males, who form the majority of the unemployed or low-waged, have a particularly high chance of being victims. Interestingly, in about 88 per cent of cases of violence, the victim and perpetrator know each other.

Victims of property crime

Victims of property crime are most likely to be low-income households living in poorer areas (see Fig. 5.8).

Repeat victimization

Victim surveys demonstrate not only that some people are more likely than others to be victims in the first place, but that a proportion of the victims are likely to be targeted more than once (**repeat victimization**).

Twenty per cent of all households burgled experienced repeat burglaries and one tiny group has a disproportionately high chance of being victimized: 0.4 per cent of householders accounted for 22 per cent of all burglaries.

The statistics suggest that crime does not happen to everyone – it targets the poorer and less powerful groups in society more than the affluent. They also tell us that violent crime tends to happen between people who know each other, even live together.

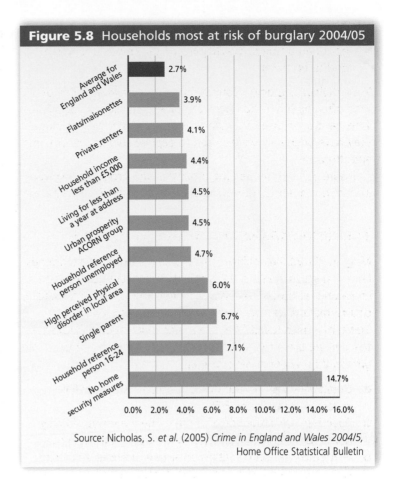

Figure 5.8 Households most at risk of burglary 2004/05

Source: Nicholas, S. *et al.* (2005) *Crime in England and Wales 2004/5*, Home Office Statistical Bulletin

Types of offenders

According to both official statistics and self-report studies, offenders are most likely to be young and male. The peak age of offending for males is about 18, and for females about 14 (see Fig. 5.9 on the following page).

The next four topics attempt to explain why some of the patterns identified here exist. They focus on crime and locality, gender, class and ethnicity respectively.

synopticlink   sociological methods

Newspapers and television news programmes bombard us with the latest government statistics on a huge range of issues, including crime, health, immigration, earnings, inflation … the list goes on. Typically, politicians from different parties are then interviewed and each places a different interpretation on what the statistics really mean: crime has risen or fallen; the number of patients treated by the NHS has increased or decreased, and so on. Sociologists, too, have their view on what official statistics mean, but their interest generally lies in how these statistics are constructed. Crime statistics depend largely upon people bothering to report a crime to the police and then the police recording that complaint as a crime. Even the alternative British Crime Survey statistics depend upon people considering an action worth marking down as a crime.

At the other extreme of social life – religion – the traditional measures of religiosity, such as church attendance and declared belief in God, depend upon why people go to church. If they do so for social reasons (to make friends, because their parents expect them to), then does it 'really' count? When people say they 'believe in God', what exactly do they mean by this?

Even factual statistics are subject to the critical gaze of sociologists. Wealth statistics are gathered from Income Tax information. If this is inaccurate, so are the official statistics. Yet, we know that the richest people have numerous mechanisms to avoid tax on their income and wealth.

All statistics are socially constructed and sociologists therefore bear this in mind whenever they need to use them.

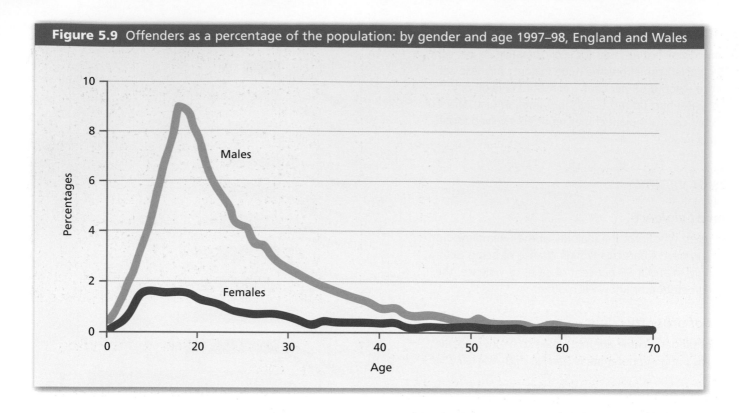

Figure 5.9 Offenders as a percentage of the population: by gender and age 1997–98, England and Wales

KEY TERMS

British Crime Survey – annual victimization survey carried out by the Home Office.

Home Office – government department responsible for criminal justice matters.

Islington Crime Surveys – famous local victimization studies focusing on one area of North London.

Official statistics – statistics released by government agencies.

Plea-bargaining – where there is an informal (sometimes unspoken) agreement that if an accused person pleads guilty to a lesser crime than that of which he or she is accused, the prosecution will agree.

Repeat victimization – where people are victims of the same crime more than once.

Responsibilization – Garland suggests this is the shift towards blaming people for becoming victims of crime, by suggesting they have not taken adequate precautions.

Risk management – the process whereby governments stop trying to prevent all crime and instead see it as their job to limit the risk of crime for the population.

Self-report studies – where people are asked to note down the crimes they have committed over a particular period.

Sensitizing – refers to the extent of disorder or minor criminal activity that people will accept.

Social construction – in this case, refers to the fact that statistics represent the activities of the people constructing the statistics rather than some objective reality.

Victimization (or victim) surveys – where people are asked what crimes have happened to them over a particular period.

Check your understanding

1 Explain why official statistics give a completely accurate picture of the workings of the criminal justice system.

2 Explain why official statistics do not give an accurate picture of the number and types of crimes committed.

3 Why might official statistics give a more accurate picture of the amount of car theft than the amount of domestic violence?

4 How might a person's 'demeanour' affect their likelihood of arrest?

5 Explain why so many people plead guilty in court.

6 Do reductions in arrests for possession of cannabis reflect a decrease in the use of the drug? Explain your answer.

7 Suggest three crimes that you think people might be willing to admit to being victims of when questioned in a victimization study.

8 Why might some people exaggerate the amount of crime that they have committed in a self-report study?

9 Suggest two reasons why young males might make up the majority of victims of violence.

10 Explain why repeat victimization may occur.

research ideas

1. The table below is based on a national sample of people aged 16 and over, who were asked to indicate what the greatest problem in their area was.

	Very/fairly big problem (%)	Very/fairly common (%)
Teenagers hanging around	32	51
Rubbish and litter	31	42
Vandalism	32	34
Drug use/dealing	33	31
Run-down homes	13	15
Noisy neighbours	9	14
Abandoned cars	13	14
Racial attacks	7	5
People sleeping rough	4	3

Conduct a small pilot survey of 14 to 16 year olds using the categories in the table. Do your results reflect the results here? Why do you think there may be differences?.

2. Carry out interviews with a small sample of people of different ages and genders to discover the factors that influence public reporting of crime. Does it depend on seriousness, whether the crime has a victim or other factors? Does likelihood of reporting correlate with variables such as age or gender?

web.task

Find the site of the Home Office at www.homeoffice.gov.uk

Go to the section on Research Development Statistics. Try to find figures about the amount and type of crime using official statistics, self-report studies and victim studies. What similarities and differences can you find? Try to explain the patterns you find.

Answers to Getting you thinking (p. 266)

2. The young man is more likely to be a victim of an attack.
3. The older car is more likely to be stolen.
4. Yes, generally, bullying is a crime as it involves threats and/or actual violence.

exploring crime statistics

Item A

The predominant focus on recorded crime is at best partial and at worst hopelessly ideological. Since the British Crime Survey started to be produced in the early 1980s, it has been clear that police-recorded crime figures provide a far from accurate picture of crime levels. Moreover, a whole range of crimes, from white-collar fraud and business crime to environmental crimes and state crimes, rarely if ever figure in police-recorded crime statistics.

Adapted from Carrabine, E. *et al.* (2004) *Criminology: A Sociological Introduction*, London: Routledge

(a) Identify and briefly explain **two** advantages of using official statistics to measure crime. (8 marks)

This part of the question includes assessment of your understanding of the connections between Crime and Deviance and sociological methods.

(b) Briefly examine the view that deviance can best be explained by reference to an individual's social background. In your answer use material from **at least two** of the following areas: families and households; health; mass media; education; wealth, poverty and welfare; work and leisure; religion; power and politics; world sociology. (12 marks)

This part of the question includes assessment of your understanding of the connections between Crime and Deviance and other substantive topic(s) you have studied.

(c) Assess the view that interactionist explanations of crime and deviance fail to consider the reality of crime as measured in official statistics. (40 marks)

This part of the question includes assessment of your understanding of the connections between Crime and Deviance and sociological theory.

Environmental approaches: the criminology of place and time

gettingyou**thinking**

1. **Look at the two photos above. Which one do you think has the higher rate of crime? What reasons can you give for your answer?**

2. **What different sorts of crimes might take place in the city during the day and during the night? What reasons can you give for your answer?**

3. **When you are walking home in the evening, do you feel more concerned than during the day? Are there any precautions you take if you are walking alone at night? What are they?**

4. **If you see a group of young males standing ahead of you on the street, do you alter your behaviour or route in any way? Give reasons for your answer.**

This topic explores the relationship of crime to places and times. This link is hardly an original idea – since the earliest recorded history, people have been warned against going to dangerous places, particularly at night-time. But sociologists have taken this basic idea and explored the links between where people live, work and have their leisure, and crime patterns.

We examine the explanation under two groupings:

● those concerned with locating offenders
● those concerned with exploring the location of offences.

Explaining offenders

Chicago sociology

The pattern

In the late-19th and early-20th centuries, one of the fastest growing cities in the USA was Chicago. The city also possessed one of the new university departments of sociology, and two of its researchers, Shaw and McKay (1931) began plotting the location of the addresses of those who committed crimes in the city. The results showed that, if they divided the city into **concentric zones**, each of the five zones they identified had different levels of offenders, with zone two (which was nearest the city centre) showing the highest rates.

This was interesting in itself, but they also found that because of rapid social change, the population living in zone two was changing regularly, so that although the various zones maintained their different levels of offenders over time, they were different offenders. This meant that there was something about the zones, rather than individuals who lived there, that was linked to crime rates.

The explanation: social disorganization

Shaw and McKay suggested that as each successive wave of immigrants arrived in the city, they were moved into the cheapest and least desirable zones – that is, the **zone of transition**. Over time, some were successful and they moved out to the more affluent suburbs, while the less successful remained. The places of those who had moved on were taken by newer immigrants, and so the process started again.

This pattern of high population turnover created a state of **social disorganization**, where the informal mechanisms of social control that normally hold people back from criminal behaviour were weak or absent.

Cultural transmission

In their later writings, Shaw and McKay (1942) altered the meaning of 'social disorganization' to refer to a distinct set of values that provided an alternative to those of the mainstream society. This amended approach came to be known as **cultural transmission** theory. They argued that amongst some groups in the most socially disorganized and poorest zones of the city, crime became culturally acceptable, and was passed on from one generation to the next as part of the normal socialization pattern. Successful criminals provide role models for the next generation by demonstrating both the normality of criminal behaviour and that a criminal career was possible.

Differential association

One criticism of Shaw and McKay and other members of the Chicago School of Criminology was that their theories were too vague and difficult to prove.

In response, Sutherland and Cressey (1966) introduced the concept of **differential association**. This states that someone is likely to become criminal 'if they receive an excess of definitions favourable to violation of law over definitions unfavourable to violation of law'. This simply means that if people interact with others who support lawbreaking, then they are likely to do so themselves.

Further tightening his approach in order to avoid criticisms of vagueness, Sutherland suggested that these definitions vary in frequency, duration, priority, and intensity:

- *frequency* – the number of times the definitions occur
- *duration* – over what length of time
- *priority* – e.g. at what stage in life (childhood socialization is more important than other periods)
- *intensity* – the status of the person making the definition (e.g. family member rather than a stranger).

Housing policies

Most British research failed to reproduce the clear pattern of concentric circles that the Chicago School had identified. Crime rates certainly varied by areas, but in more complex patterns.

One early study by Morris in 1957 found no evidence that people in areas of high delinquency held a coherent set of values that was any different from that of mainstream society.

Morris suggested that a key factor in the concentration of delinquents in certain areas was linked to the local council's housing policies. For example, in his study of Croydon, the local council's policy of housing problem-families together meant that these areas became, almost by definition, high-crime areas.

The impact of local-authority housing decisions was clarified much later by the work of Baldwin and Bottoms (1976), who compared two similar local-authority housing estates, separated by a dual carriageway. One of the estates 'Gardenia' had a 300 per cent higher number of offenders and a 350 per cent higher level of crimes than the other 'Stonewall'. The difference according to him was the result of a process that he named '**tipping**'.

Tipping

Most estates consist of a mixture of people from different backgrounds and with different forms of behaviour. Informal social control imposed by the majority of residents limits the offending behaviour of the antisocial minority. However, if for whatever reason (such as local-authority housing policies), the antisocial minority grow in number, their behaviour drives away some of the law-abiding families. Those who wish to enter the estate tend to be relatives of the antisocial families and this leads to a speed up in the law-abiding residents leaving. The estate has 'tipped' and becomes increasingly regarded as a problem estate.

synoptic link

Newspapers set out to produce colourful stories about people and places that the people who buy the papers want to read about. Journalists go to great lengths to uncover the names and addresses of deviants, publishing these in 'the public good'. The outcome is that both guilty and innocent people have been hounded out of their homes and neighbourhoods. Media campaigns which highlight negative aspects of a particular housing development will mean that people will be frightened to move into the area and those already living there may well feel even more fearful.

Sociologists, too, are interested in deviants and areas with social problems, but they are committed by their code of ethics to minimize the negative impact of their

sociological methods

studies on people and areas they research. Before any research programme, the sociologist has to obtain ethical approval from the university. Most important, they must demonstrate that no harm will occur to the people being studied. This is why virtually all studies since the 1980s use pseudonyms for individuals in the study, and alters the names of the schools, organizations and neighbourhoods where the research has taken place, so that no one will be able to trace the participants. In the study by Baldwin and Bottoms above, for example, the names 'Gardenia' and 'Stonewall' were used, while Stephen Ball, in his study of a comprehensive school, talks about 'Beachside Comprehensive'.

Those who are able to flee, do so. In Baldwin and Bottom's analysis, Gardenia had tipped, whilst Stonewall had not.

Disorder

W.G. Skogan (1990) in the USA has fleshed out this idea of tipping. He suggests that social control breaks down when, for example, there is a combination of physical deterioration in local buildings and parks, and an increase in social disorder in the form of public alcohol and drug use. This leads to a situation of disorder, which has three consequences:

- It undermines the mechanisms of informal social control and leads people to withdraw, thus undermining the bonds between people.
- It generates worries about neighbourhood safety, so that people avoid going out at night, thus making it easier for street crime to be committed.
- It causes law-abiding people who can afford it to move out of the area, and leads to a decrease in property values and the growth of housing to let.

Social capital

Social disorganization explains crime and deviance by a lack of common, shared values, although there is relatively little evidence to support this. However, more recently, there has been a shift back to understanding the role of values. In Topic 1, p. 237, we explored Putnam's concept of social capital, in which he argues that there has been a decline in the extent to which people are linked into family and friendship networks. The result is that individuals feel more alone and less confident about engaging in community activity. According to Putnam, this results in a weak community unable to impose social control on those who engage in offending.

In the USA, William Julius Wilson (1996) has adapted a version of this approach to explain the high levels of offending in deprived neighbourhoods. He argues that there is a high level of social interaction between people, so that it is not true that people are isolated. There are, however, low levels of social control. Wilson suggests that this comes from a sense of powerlessness and a lack of integration into the wider society. People in deprived areas do interact, but not in a way that provides social controls or positive social models for young people, as the adults themselves feel isolated from the broader society.

A study by Sampson *et al.* (1997) of inner-city Chicago provides support for Wilson's model. They found considerable social interaction between people, but little *community* organization as such – which they call '**collective efficacy**'. Areas with higher levels of collective efficacy had lower rates of crime than those without, no matter how much personal social interaction occurred.

Explaining offences

So far we have been exploring theories that look at where offenders live and why they have higher levels of offending. However, other approaches have looked at where offences take place and why they occur in these places and not others.

This distinction has been highlighted in Wilkstrom's (1991) study of crime patterns in Stockholm. This is particularly important as it demonstrates that the types and extent of offences vary across neighbourhoods. At its simplest, city centres, poorer districts and affluent areas adjacent to poorer districts have higher rates of crime. Within this, crimes of violence are more likely in the poorer districts, while burglary was more likely in the affluent areas adjacent to poorer districts. This observation shifted environmental theories towards explanations of these different patterns of offences.

Cognitive maps

P.J. and P.L. Brantingham (1991) argue that we all hold **cognitive maps** of the towns and cities where we live, so some parts of our local town are familiar to us and other parts much less known. In particular, we know the routes from our homes to where we study or work, and where we go for entertainment. According to the Brantinghams, offenders are most likely to commit offences where opportunities (e.g. houses to burgle) link with 'cognitively known' areas, and conversely that places that are less 'cognitively known' are less likely to be burgled (see Fig. 5.10). This provides an explanation for the patterns of crime we noted earlier, such as for burglary.

synoptic link

families and households and power and politics

The move towards late-modernity and the linked stress on the importance of the individual as opposed to the family or community, have had a significant impact on a wide variety of social issues. Some sociologists suggest that decline of informal social control by the family and community has helped contribute to the increase in offending rates. Others have pointed to the way that the decline of traditional working-class communities has impacted on voting patterns. The Labour Party, which once could rely on the solid support of equally solid working-class inner-city communities, is now aware that voting is based on a much wider range of issues, of which the interests of the individual are important. The claimed decline in community not only reflects the increase in divorce rates, but also contributes to increased levels of divorce and marital instability in that the pressures placed on couples to remain together have declined significantly. However, if the decline in community has occurred for the majority White population, for many ethnic groups the sense of community has not shown similar levels of decline.

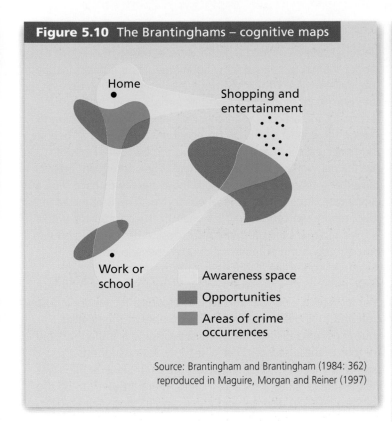

Figure 5.10 The Brantinghams – cognitive maps

Home

Shopping and entertainment

Work or school

Awareness space

Opportunities

Areas of crime occurrences

Source: Brantingham and Brantingham (1984: 362)
reproduced in Maguire, Morgan and Reiner (1997)

Opportunity theory

If crimes are most likely to be committed in areas that offenders know, then the next question must be why, within these areas, are some properties or people chosen and others are not? Clarke (1995) seeks to explain this with **opportunity theory**. Opportunity consists of two elements:

● how *attractive* the target is – for example, how much can be gained by committing a crime against this particular place or person and, if it is property, how easy it is to carry away and to sell afterwards

● how *accessible* the target is – for example, how easy it is to commit the crime.

Routine activities

These ideas of cognitive maps and opportunity were further developed by Cohen and Felson (1979) in their concept of **routine activities**. They argue that crimes are more likely to occur where the day-to-day activities of victims and offenders are likely to coincide, and where there is little in the way of formal or informal control to prevent an offence taking place. Cohen and Felson have introduced two new issues into the discussion with their definition:

1 Crimes are likely to occur where there is no 'capable guardian', such as a police officer, neighbours or informal social control engendered by a sense of community.

2 It is not just place that is important, but also time. For example, the person who is more likely to be 'mugged' is the person returning from work, walking along a quiet street, in the evening. We will explore this issue of time later.

Bernasco and Nieuwbeerta (2005)
How burglars choose their targets

Bernasco and Nieuwbeerta conducted a detailed study of burglary patterns in The Hague, in the Netherlands. They obtained information on 548 residential burglaries and from 290 (arrested) burglars across the city over a period of one year. They concluded that there were some very clear patterns of burglary. The affluence of the neighbourhood was not very important; instead, homes were more likely to be broken into if they were relatively near to where the offender lived and if there was perceived to be limited 'guardianship', meaning people keeping an eye on the property. Other factors were the high rate of burglary in areas of the city where there were mixed ethnic groups and a high proportion of single-parent families. Bernasco and Nieuwbeerta did not find any evidence for concentric zones where crimes were more likely.

Bernasco, W. and Nieuwbeerta, P. (2005) 'How do residential burglars select target areas? A new approach to the analysis of criminal location choice', *British Journal of Criminology*, 45(3)

1 To what extent do the methods used by the authors provide a representative picture of burglary?

2 Summarize the factors that appeared to make some houses vulnerable to burglary.

The privatization of public space

Sociologists have always been aware of the distinction between **private space** (where anyone can go) and **public space** (where entry is controlled by the owner), and its importance for the levels and types of offending. For example, as long ago as the 1960s, Stinchcombe (1963) used the term 'the institution of privacy' to illustrate how policing tended to be against deviant activities carried out in public, with much less stress placed on violence and abuse in the home.

However, in recent years, the issue of private and public space has re-emerged as an important debate for sociologists, as changes have taken place in the nature of urban life.

Shearing and Stenning (1983) pointed to the growth of shopping centres and leisure complexes, which are both public, in that they are spaces where (most) people are welcomed, and private, in that they are privately owned and the owners have the power to exclude those they define as undesirable. In housing, too, there has been the growth of gated communities – housing estates where only residents and guests are allowed.

Shearing and Stenning argue that the owners of these private 'public' spaces have taken over the responsibility for policing them – using CCTV and security guards – and this has led to the **privatization of public space**. The police have been increasingly confined to the more peripheral areas of the city and to the poorer (particularly 'problem') housing estates. The exclusion of undesirable groups (young people, known offenders, beggars) from these private 'public' areas, has simply displaced crime to the less affluent public areas.

Time: the nocturnal economy

Earlier, we noted the implication in Cohen and Felson's routine activities theory, that time is a crucial and neglected element in understanding crime. If different places have varying levels of crime and different styles of control, then so do different times. The busy city centre, filled with families shopping during the day, becomes the location for the young seeking pleasure at night. The same location, therefore, changes its meaning and possibilities with the closing of the shops and the coming of the darkness.

An interesting example of the significance of time is what Hobbs et al. (2000) call the '**nocturnal economy**'. They point out that in the last 15 years, there has been a huge growth in pubs and clubs, as Britain's younger people have increasingly embraced the leisure society. This involves, in Britain at least, going out at the weekend to clubs and pubs to consume alcohol (and possibly also drugs) and to enjoy oneself. In 2000, for example, there were over 200 million club admissions to the value of £2.5 billion. This means that there are huge numbers of young people who come together within a very narrow time-band in order to engage in the search for pleasure. Almost three-quarters of all violent incidents in urban areas occur during the weekend between 9pm and 3am, usually by and between groups of young males fuelled by drink and/or drugs.

Interestingly, as we saw before regarding the privatization of public space, at night-time too, there are relatively few police officers available, so that a medium-sized town might have 15 000 night-time 'revellers' with only 12 police officers on duty. The bulk of the 'policing' is performed by private security companies employed by the pubs and clubs. The high rates of violent crime occurring within this framework of time and space illustrate perfectly the three elements referred to by Cohen and Felson: offenders, targets, and lack of guardians.

The nocturnal economy and the global economy

Taylor (1999) has added a global perspective to discussions about the nocturnal economy and crime. His argument is that the development of the nocturnal economy is bound up with the process of globalization and its impact upon the British economy, in particular the impact on inner cities. According to Taylor, the impact of the global economy on Britain has been a huge decrease in manufacturing and the associated loss of traditional working-class employment. The consequent effects have been that many traditionally industrial towns have seen a significant decline in their local economies. This is reflected in a decline in town centres and the manufacturing districts, with shops and manufacturing premises closing down, and also in an increase in the numbers of people unemployed or in irregular work. Clearly, different cities have been affected differently, so that the North-East of England has been hit far harder than the South. However, in all cities, the leisure industry referred to above has taken over a number of the derelict buildings for clubs and bars, whilst providing a limited number of jobs in these services and in security. Taylor suggests that where the levels of unemployment have remained highest (yet the leisure facilities are still provided), there are likely to be the highest levels of disorder and crime, and in those cities where the unemployment has not risen, there is less crime – or at least a slower growth in crime.

Check your understanding

1. Shaw and McKay suggested two explanations for the behaviour of the people in the zones they identified. What are these explanations?

2. Explain, in your own words, what is meant by the term 'tipping'.

3. According to the Brantinghams, where are offences most likely to take place?

4. What information do 'cognitive maps' and 'routine activities theory' tell us about where and who are more likely to be targeted by offenders?

5. Briefly explain how the privatization of public space 'displaces' crime.

6. Why is the crime rate likely to rise during the hours of 9pm and 3am?

KEY TERMS

Cognitive maps – a personal map of a town based on an individual's daily activities.

Collective efficacy – the ability of a community to achieve their aims (which usually include limiting crime).

Concentric zones – widening circles.

Cultural transmission – values are passed on from one generation to the next.

Differential association – the theory that deviant behaviour is learned from, and justified by, family and friends.

Nocturnal economy – refers to the way that a leisure industry has developed at night, which provides the location of many offences.

Opportunity theory – crime occurs when there is an opportunity; stop the opportunity and crime is less likely to occur.

Privatization of public space – the way that public areas are increasingly being owned and controlled by companies, who police it in such a way as to exclude undesirables.

Routine activities – the normal activities of daily life provide the cognitive maps and opportunities for crime.

Social disorganization – a city area that does not have a shared culture.

Tipping – the process by which an area moves from being predominantly law-abiding to predominantly accepting antisocial behaviour.

Zone of transition – the cheapest, least desirable zones of the city, into which immigrants are moved.

exploring environmental approaches

Item A

The official crime rate is significantly higher in urban areas than in rural areas. Large urban areas provide greater opportunities for crime, for example more and larger shops, cars and business premises. There is also a greater police presence in urban areas, so more crime is likely to be detected. Different policing methods mean that the police are more likely to take formal action, such as arresting and prosecuting people, in urban areas. In the large cities, life is more impersonal and people do not know each other so well. Strangers are likely to go unrecognized and potential criminals are less likely to offend within a small rural community where everyone knows everyone else. Finally, social deprivation and other social problems are likely to be at their worst in the inner cities.

Adapted from Browne, K. (2005) *An Introduction to Sociology* (3rd edn), Cambridge: Polity Press.

(a) Identify and briefly explain **two** ways in which sociologists have suggested that social problems in the inner cities can lead to crime and deviance. In your answer you should use material from **at least one** of the following areas: families and households; health; mass media; education; wealth, poverty and welfare; work and leisure. (8 marks)

This part of the question includes assessment of your understanding of the connections between Crime and Deviance and other substantive topic(s) you have studied.

(b) Using material from **Item A** and elsewhere, examine some of the problems of using official statistics to study the extent of crime in urban and rural areas. (12 marks)

This part of the question includes assessment of your understanding of the connections between Crime and Deviance and sociological methods.

(c) Assess the usefulness of environmental approaches in explaining the causes and extent of deviance in society. (40 marks)

This part of the question includes assessment of your understanding of the connections between Crime and Deviance and sociological theory.

Gender issues and offending

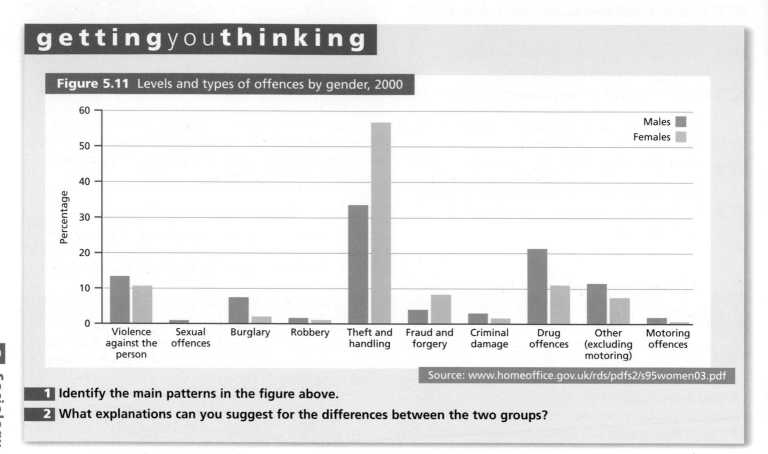

Figure 5.11 Levels and types of offences by gender, 2000

Source: www.homeoffice.gov.uk/rds/pdfs2/s95women03.pdf

1 Identify the main patterns in the figure above.

2 What explanations can you suggest for the differences between the two groups?

In this topic we want to explore the relationship that gender has to offending. Official records show an overwhelming predominance of males compared with females committing crime. Self-report studies, too, show a noticeable, if less marked, difference between the offending levels of males and females. Given this, there has to be something in the different construction of femininity and masculinity that can help us to explain these differences. In this topic, we will try to unravel some of the strands of explanation offered.

Before we do so, however, we need to explain why, surprisingly perhaps, there has been relatively little research that explicitly sets out to explain the links between gender and offending. It seems that most sociologists have started off with the assumption that males commit more crime, and have then moved on to explore why it is that only some males commit crime. Explanations offered by sociologists have, therefore, concentrated mainly on comparing offending males with non-offending males, without explaining why males are more likely to offend in the first instance.

The topic falls into two main areas of discussion:

● the issue of women and crime
● male gender roles and crime.

First, we ask why women have been ignored in the sociology of crime and delinquency, before turning to examine the explanations for lower rates of female offending. In the second part of the topic, we turn things on their head and ask what lessons the exploration of gender roles might have for male offending. The answers we arrive at may be rather surprising, for it seems that the opening-up of criminology by feminists provides us with clues as to why males have such high rates of offending. Indeed, so significant are these insights that much contemporary criminology is heavily influenced by them (see Topic 11 for more detail).

Invisible female offenders

Anyone studying the sociology of crime and deviance will notice after a while that it is mainly about male offending. In fact, it would not be unfair to call it the sociology of male crime and deviancy. Although it is true that the majority of offenders are male – comprising about 80 per cent of all official statistics on offenders – it is surprising that 20 per cent of all offenders are simply ignored.

Frances Heidensohn (1989) has criticized the male dominance of the subject (known as **malestream** criminology) and has suggested that there are four reasons why it is so:

- *Male dominance of offenders* – As the majority of offenders are male, for many sociologists it was therefore most appropriate to study them, rather than the minority of female offenders.
- *Male domination of sociology* – Although the majority of sociology students are women, it has always been the case that the majority of academics have been male. According to Heidensohn, sociological topics of investigation reflect a male view and male interests.
- *Vicarious identification* – This follows from the previous point. Men study what interests them, and, applied to crime, this is most often the lives of the marginal and the exciting, i.e. **vicarious identification**.
- *Sociological theorizing* – Male sociologists constructed their theories without ever thinking about how they could be applied to females. Most traditional theories are 'gender blind'; in effect, that means they ignore the specific viewpoint of women.

Explaining female crime: women's roles

Most theories that explain crime, as we saw earlier, implicitly accept that males are more likely than females to commit crime. In the process, criminologists have omitted to explain what it is that makes males more likely than females to commit crime. There have, however, been a number of exceptions to this and we explore these approaches in this section. Three major approaches to explaining the relationship between women and offending are:

- biological explanations
- sex-role theory
- changing role or 'liberationist' perspective.

Biological explanations

This approach has been used by different writers to explain why the overwhelming bulk of women do not offend and conversely why a small minority do. It starts from the belief that women are innately different from men, with a natural desire to be caring and nurturing – both of which tend not to be values that support crime. 'Normal' women are therefore less likely to commit crime. On the other hand, some women writers such as Dalton (1964) have claimed that hormonal or menstrual factors can influence a minority of women to commit crime in certain circumstances.

Sex-role theory

Sex-role theory argues that women are less likely to commit crime than men because there are core elements of the female

role that limit their ability and opportunity to do so. There are a number of different versions of this theory, all of which can fit quite comfortably together.

Socialization

According to this approach, girls are socialized differently to boys. The values that girls are brought up to hold are those that simply do not lead to crime. Talcott Parsons (1937) argues for instance, that as most child-rearing is carried out by mothers, girls have a clear role model to follow that emphasizes caring and support. Evidence to support this differential socialization was provided by Farrington and Painter (2004) in their longitudinal study of female offenders. They uncovered different patterns of socialization between offenders and non-offenders. In particular, they found that female offenders were much more likely to have had harsh or erratic parenting, and to have had little support or praise from their parents for their achievements at school and in their community.

Social control

Females are less likely to commit crime because of the closer levels of supervision that they are subjected to at home in childhood. This control carries on throughout life, with the role of women being more constrained that that of males. Heidensohn (1996), for example, says:

> ≪ An examination of female criminality and unofficial deviance suggests that we need to move away from studying infractions and look at conformity instead, because the most striking thing about female behaviour is how notably conformist to social mores women are. ≫

Heidensohn points to the wide range of informal sanctions to discourage women from straying from 'proper' behaviour, including gossip, ill repute and the comments of male companions. Hagan (1987) studied child-raising patterns in Canada and argued that there was significantly greater informal control of daughters' activities in families compared to sons.

Marginalization

In order to commit crime, a person needs to have the opportunity to do so. The narrower range of roles that women are allowed to have consequently limits their opportunities to commit crime, as they are more confined by their socialization and social control than men.

The result of these three influences on the lives of females, is to deflect them away from offending and towards conformity.

The changing role or 'liberationist' perspective

So far in this topic we have characterized female sex-roles as being more passive and less aggressive than those of males. However, a number of writers including Adler (1975) have suggested that the increasing rates of female crime are linked to their freedom from the traditional forms of social control, discussed above, and their acceptance into more 'masculine' roles. More recently, Denscombe (2001) has argued that changing female roles over the last ten years mean that increasingly, females are as likely as males to engage in risk-taking behaviour. In his research into self-images of 15 to 16 year olds in the East Midlands, in which he undertook in-depth interviews as well as focus groups, he found that females were rapidly adopting what had traditionally been male attitudes. This included such things as 'looking hard', 'being in control' and being someone who can cope with risk-taking. This provides theoretical support for the fact that female crime levels are rising much more quickly than male ones, not just in terms of numbers but also in terms of seriousness of crimes committed.

Westwood (1999) develops similar ideas when she argues that identities are constantly being reconstructed and reframed. The concept of a fixed female identity has limited our understanding of crime, and so we need to understand how women are reconfiguring their identity in a more confident, forceful way, and the possible link to the growth of female crime. However, Heidensohn (2002) disputes this argument, citing evidence from a number of other studies which show that convicted offenders tend to score highly on psychological tests of 'femininity', indicating, according to her, that they have not taken on male roles.

Transgression: A postmodernist critique

The various explanations of female crime put forward were not popular with feminist sociologists as they felt that they were not really adequate explanations for the differences between male and female causes for offending. Pat Carlen (1992) argued, for example, that these were theoretically weak and represented a sort of 'bolt-on' to existing male criminology.

It was in response to the need for a feminist version of criminology, i.e. one that answered the concerns of women, that Carol Smart (1990) introduced the idea of a **transgressive criminology**. By this, Smart was suggesting that criminology itself as a discipline was tied to male questions and concerns and that it could never offer answers to feminist questions. Instead of trying to produce a feminist criminology by asking the question, 'What can feminism offer criminology?', feminists should be arguing, 'What can criminology offer feminists?' The answer to this question lay in looking at a whole range of activities (both legal and illegal) that actually harm women, and asking how these came about and how they could be changed. The term 'transgression', in this context then, meant to go beyond the boundaries of criminology. This did lead to feminists (and sympathetic male sociologists) looking more closely at things such as:

- the way women stayed in at night for fear of becoming victims
- domestic violence

Laidler and Hunt (2001)
The girls in the gang

Laidler and Hunt studied girl members of US gangs in the San Francisco Bay area. The research consisted of interviews with 141 gang members and ethnographic research over a period of 10 years. The researchers argue that gang membership is fragmented along gender lines, with female members of the gang having clear roles and responsibilities, as do the males. The 'homegirls' in the study face dilemmas similar to those faced by respectable girls, having to walk a narrow line between being attractive to males and valued for that, but also not engaging in sexual relationships with too many boys. Both males and females in the gang use informal methods of social control to ensure conformity.

Laidler and Hunt are suggesting therefore that, despite appearing deviant to the wider society, the majority of homegirls actually conform to gender roles.

Laidler, K.J. and Hunt, G. (2001) 'Accomplishing femininity among the girls in the gang', *British Journal of Criminology*, 41(4)

1 Identify the research method most closely associated with ethnographic research.

2 Explain how the findings of the study led the authors to the conclusion that 'the majority of homegirls actually conform to gender roles.'

- how women were treated by the law in issues of rape and harassment (where they form the overwhelming bulk of the victims).

Transgression is a good example of the postmodern influence in sociology, when the traditional boundaries of sociology and the categories used to classify issues are abandoned, and new, fresher ways of thinking are introduced.

Explaining male crime: male roles and masculinity

Smart's idea of transgression, linked to the growing importance of postmodern analysis, began to feed back into mainstream criminology. Some sociologists began to go beyond the traditional confines and to revisit the issue of why most crime is male crime.

Normative masculinity

The analysis of masculinity began with the Australian sociologist, Bob Connell (1995). He argued that there were a number of different forms of masculinity, which change over time – in particular, he identified the concept of hegemonic masculinity (see Topic 3, pp. 250–1). Although crime was not central to his analysis, the idea of multiple, constructed masculinities was taken up by Messerschmidt (1993).

Connell argues that a **'normative masculinity'** exists in society, highly valued by most men. Normative masculinity refers to the socially approved idea of what a 'real male' is. According to Messerschmidt, it 'defines masculinity through difference from and desire for women'. Normative masculinity is so prized that men struggle to live up to its expectations. Messerschmidt suggests then that masculinity is not something natural, but rather a state that males only achieve as 'an accomplishment', which involves being constantly worked at.

However, the construction of this masculinity takes place in different contexts and through different methods depending upon the particular male's access to power and resources. So, more powerful males will accomplish their masculinity in different ways and contexts from less powerful males. Messerschmidt gives examples of businessmen who can express their power over women through their control in the workplace, while those with no power at work may express their masculinity by using violence in the home or street. However, whichever way is used, both types of men are achieving their normative masculinity.

So, it is achieving masculinity that leads some men to commit crime – and in particular crime is committed by those less powerful in an attempt to be successful at masculinity (which involves material, social and sexual success).

The idea that masculinity is the actual basis of crime is reflected in the writings of a number of writers.

Katz: seductions of crime

A postmodern twist on the idea of masculinity is the work of Katz (1988), who argues that what most criminology has failed to do is to understand the role of pleasure in committing crime. This search for pleasure has to be placed within the context of masculinity, which stresses the importance of status, control over others and success.

Katz claims that crime is always explained with reference to background causes, but rarely attempts to look at the pleasure that is derived from the actual act of offending or 'transgression', as he calls it. Doing evil, he argues, is motivated by the quest for a 'moral self-transcendence' in the face of boredom. Different crimes provide different thrills, that can vary from the 'sneaky thrills' of shoplifting, to the 'righteous slaughter' of murder.

Katz argues that by understanding the emotional thrills that transgression provides, we can understand why males commit

synoptic link   sociological theory

Although male sociologists have largely ignored female offending, feminist writers from the various strands within feminism have all sought to include criminological analyses within their approaches.

Liberal feminism

This approach to feminism is based on the idea that by bringing women onto the agenda and by demonstrating how women have been ignored in research, there will be greater understanding of female deviance. In particular, new theories can be developed that will cover both males and females.

Radical feminism

Radical feminists argue that the only way to understand crime is to see it through a female perspective – and research should be based on the assumption that all men are prepared to commit crimes against women if given the chance. Women should construct their own unique approaches to explaining crime and deviance, and this should incorporate the threat from men.

Feminist perspectives on crime and deviance

Socialist feminism

This approach stresses that the position of men and women in general – and with reference to crime in particular – can only be understood by locating males and females within the context of societies divided by both sexism and by capitalism.

Postmodern feminism

The work of Smart (1990) and Cain (1986) is particularly important since they argue that the very concerns of criminology (burglary/street crime, etc.) are actually a reflection of male concerns, and that women should be looking beyond these to study how harm comes to women in the widest sense possible. Feminist criminology should not accept the (male) boundaries of criminology, but should look at the way women are harmed by a whole range of processes.

One of the most obvious points about crime is that the overwhelming majority of offenders are male. However, it wasn't really until the rise of feminist writings in the 1970s that sociologists began to look at the possible relationship with the values of being a 'real' male. Ideas about subculture began to be replaced with notions of how masculinity was created and the impact this had on how men, and particularly young men, behaved. Once the idea of masculinity emerged, sociologists realized that it could explain a lot about the behaviour of young men in general. One especially fruitful area of study was of the educational experiences of young males. Over the

past 20 years, there has been a huge shift in the comparative success rates of males and females at school, with girls having significantly better exam success than boys, and also exhibiting far less poor behaviour in the classroom. The reason for these differences in behaviour appears to be that the accepted notion of what a young male ought to be in society (or dominant hegemonic model of masculinity) contradicts the role required in the school of an obedient, hard-working pupil. Masculinity, as portrayed in the media, means being tough, possibly aggressive, sexually active and a person of action. None of this fits easily with the role of a school student.

crime. Katz gives the example of robbery, which is largely undertaken, he claims, for the chaos, thrill and potential danger inherent in the act. Furthermore, in virtually all robberies 'the offender discovers, fantasizes or manufactures an angle of moral superiority over the intended victim', such that the robber has 'succeeded in making a fool of his victim'. This idea of the thrill of crime has been used to explain the apparent irrational violence of football 'hooligans', and also the use of drugs and alcohol.

Katz's work is clearly influenced by the earlier work of Matza (1964) (see Topic 3), who has argued that constructing a male identity in contemporary society is difficult. Most youths are in a state of **drift** where they are unsure exactly who they are and what their place in society is. For most young males, this is a period of boredom and crisis. It is in this period of life that any event that unambiguously gives them a clear identity is welcomed, and it could equally be an identity of offender as much as employee. Committing offences provides a break from boredom, pleasure and a sense of being someone – for example, a gang member or a 'hard man'.

Lyng: edgework

A linked argument can be found in the work of Lyng (1990), who argues that young males search for pleasure through risk-taking. According to Lyng, the risk-taking can best be seen as

'edgework', by which he means that there is a thrill to be gained from acting in ways that are on the edge between security and danger.

This helps explain the attractiveness of car theft and 'joy riding', and of searching for violent confrontations with other groups of males. By engaging in this form of risk-taking, young men are in Messerschmidt's terms 'accomplishing masculinity', and also proving that they have control over their lives.

Masculinities in context

The work of Connell (via Messerschmidt) and the arguments of Katz and Lyng have been very influential in contemporary criminology. However, they have all been criticized for not slotting the notion of masculinities into a context. So, Winlow (2004) has asked questions about the conditions in which men demonstrate their aggressiveness, and why is that young, working-class males are more likely to be violent? The answer, he argues, lies in the changing nature of the economy in late modernity. For generations, working-class masculinity has been linked to manual employment in manufacturing industry. With the huge changes in the economy, most notably the decline in manual work and the increase in low-level, white-collar employment, a significant proportion of the male working-class population has been excluded from the possibilities of regular employment. According to Wilson (1996), this has resulted in the development of an urban underclass who manifest a range of violent and antisocial behaviours. The masculinity they exude, therefore, can only be understood within the context of the changing economic structure of Britain.

KEY TERMS

Drift – term used by Matza to describe a state where young men are unsure exactly who they are and what their place in society is.

Malestream – a term used to describe the fact that male ways of thinking have dominated criminology.

Normative masculinity – the socially approved idea of what a real male is. According to Messerschmidt, it 'defines masculinity

through difference from and desire for women'.

Sex-role theory – explanations based on the restricted roles women are claimed to have in society.

Transgression – feminist theorists use this term to suggest a need to 'break out' of the confines of traditional criminology.

Vicarious identification – when people obtain a thrill by putting themselves in the place of another person.

web.task

Go to the Home Office Research and Statistics Publications site. You will find a report on domestic violence, sexual assault and stalking at www.homeoffice.gov.uk/rds/pdfs04/hors276.pdf

What does this report tell you about the relationship between gender and these crimes?

Check your understanding

1 Why was it that criminology traditionally ignored female crime?

2 Give three examples of sex-role theory.

3 How is the idea of 'transgression' relevant to the debate about gender and crime?

4 In your own words, explain the term 'normative masculinity'. How does it help us to understand crime?

5 What is 'moral transcendence'?

6 Suggest three examples of 'edgework'.

7 What implication for the level of female crime is there as a result of the changing role of women in recent years?

research ideas

1 Devise a simple 'self-report' questionnaire (see Topic 6) with a maximum of ten questions. The offending behaviour or deviant acts should be fairly minor, but common (e.g. starting a fight, drinking alcohol under age).

2 Either working in groups or individually, divide your questionnaires into two sets. Give out one set of questionnaires to be completed anonymously. Use the other set with interview techniques to complete the questionnaire directly.

- Are there different results between the two methods?
- Are there any differences between males and females?

exploring gender issues and offending

Item A

Graham and Wells placed posters in three launderettes near their university in Ontario, Canada, offering $10 to young males who had been involved in bar fights to participate in a telephone interview. People who called were given an explanation of the study and assured that their responses would be confidential. All interviews were recorded. A total of 35 interviews were conducted – most were university students, with a small proportion of unemployed, and only 10 per cent actually in employment.

The authors wanted to find out the role of alcohol in aggression. What they discovered was that alcohol was not particularly important in leading to aggression in bars. They suggest that 'male honour, face-saving, group loyalty and fighting for fun were the key motivators. What emerged most strongly was the general acceptance, 'even positive endorsement' of aggression in bars as a normal part of male values.

Adapted from Graham, K. and Wells, S. (2003) '"Somebody's gonna get their head kicked in tonight!" Aggression among young males in bars: a question of values?', *British Journal of Criminology*, 43(3), p. 546

(a) Using material from **Item A**, identify and briefly explain **two** problems with the sampling method described. (8 marks)

This part of the question includes assessment of your understanding of the connections between Crime and Deviance and sociological methods.

(b) Examine ways in which women are socialized to conform, using material from **at least two** of the following areas: families and households; health; mass media; education; wealth, poverty and welfare; work and leisure; religion; power and politics; world sociology. (12 marks)

This part of the question includes assessment of your understanding of the connections between Crime and Deviance and other substantive topics you have studied.

(c) Assess sociological explanations of the different crime rates of men and women. (40 marks)

This part of the question includes assessment of your understanding of the connections between Crime and Deviance and sociological theory.

Occupational and corporate crime

gettingyouthinking

- In 1998, in Lanarkshire a local butcher failed to comply with hygiene regulations and to cooperate with local authority enforcement officials. As a result 450 people became ill, some very seriously, and 21 died.
- In 1999, in Glasgow, two students died in a fire in a house converted to small flats. The fire was started accidentally. The flats were not registered with the local authority and had not been inspected.

1 What, in your view, is the difference between an 'accident' which results in someone being harmed and a 'crime' which results in someone being harmed?

2 Should smoking be made illegal? Justify your view.

3 In your view, were the two incidents described above unfortunate 'accidents' or crimes?

4 Each year, small children die in Britain because of accidents resulting from playing with unsafe, cheap imitations of more expensive toys. Who is to blame? The children? The parents? The manufacturers? Or are these just unfortunate accidents?

What is meant by 'occupational crime' and 'corporate crime'?

The study of **occupational crime** and **corporate crime** developed from the original work of Sutherland (1940) in the 1940s. Sutherland used the term '**white-collar**' **crime** to refer to crime committed by people who worked in offices. However, Sutherland's work overlaps with the interests of Marxist writers who were interested in the 'crimes of the powerful'. Both approaches share the concern that traditional research into crime centres on such things as robbery and burglary, and in doing so focuses on working-class offenders. People committing offences such as fraud,

who tend to be at the other end of the class structure, tend to be ignored.

Although there has been general agreement with Sutherland's argument that crime committed by the powerful needed studying, there remains considerable debate between sociologists about exactly what should be studied under this term. Sutherland (1940) originally defined white-collar crime as 'crime committed by a person of respectability and high social status in the course of his occupation'.

The definition is unfortunately very vague and includes within it two, quite different activities: on the one hand, it means crimes against the organization for which the person works, and on the other, crimes for the benefit of the organization for which the person works or which they own

Occcupational and corporate offending: the problem of law

There is one more problem in the debate about what occupational/corporate crime actually is. Very often, when sociologists talk about white-collar or corporate crime, they may actually not be discussing actions that are illegal – that is, if the company or person is 'caught', no one is likely to go in front of a judge and face the possible personal risk of going to jail. Instead, the crime studied may actually be the breaking of supervisory codes (as in financial services) or technical standards (chemical content of consumer goods), or may refer to a whole range of actions that are, it could be argued, harmful and may even lead to death, but are not strictly speaking illegal – low safety standards at work, but that meet minimum legal criteria, for example. In fact, as Nelken (2002) points out, the debate about corporate crime is as much about corporate practices and sociologists' biases about what is morally wrong, as it is about breaking the law.

Some writers, such as Pearce and Tombs (1998), argue that corporate crime ought to extend to the manufacture of cigarettes or alcohol – both of which are linked to illness and death. Others point out that transnational companies that manufacture in poorer nations where safety standards are negligible, are engaging in human-rights violations and are therefore committing crime – even if they are acting in a perfectly legal way according to the laws of the country where they are manufacturing.

So, much of the debate about occupational or corporate 'crime' goes beyond the limits of the law and looks at actions that have harmful consequences – and, in doing so, takes us beyond the limits of conventional criminology, opening up debates about what the sociology of crime and deviance ought to study.

The distinctions between occupational and corporate crime

This has led to two confusing and overlapping traditions:

- Studies of *occupational crime* – How and why people steal from companies and the public in activities associated with their jobs; for example, the employee who claims false expenses from the company or who overcharges customers and keeps the additional amount.
- The study of *corporate crime* – Much more important as a field of study in sociology, this is crime by corporations or businesses that has a serious physical or economic impact on employees, consumers or the general public. Corporate crime is motivated by the desire to increase profits.

Corporate crime

The impact of corporate crime

Many sociological approaches – particularly that of the left realists – have pointed out the enormous costs of conventional crime to society, as well as the damage it does to the quality of people's lives. Those interested in studying corporate crime argue, however, that the costs of conventional crime are actually dwarfed by corporate crime. There are no contemporary calculations of the cost of corporate crime, but the figures used by Conklin (1977) 30 years ago in his study in the USA are still staggering today.

>> *The direct cost of business crime surpasses the cost of such conventional crimes as larceny, burglary, and auto-theft. (In 1977) the estimated loss from these three crimes was about $3 billion to $4 billion a year. This figure pales in significance when compared with an estimated annual loss of $40 billion from various white-collar crimes. Half that results from consumer fraud, illegal competition and deceptive practices.* >>

An example of this was the collapse of the US stock market (in particular, property and banking corporations) at the end of the 1980s in the USA. This was the result of financial mismanagement and sometimes downright fraud and has cost in the region of a trillion dollars. Yet, interestingly, this was largely covered by a US government 'loan' that has covered the deficit. In 1998, Enron, a huge US company, went bankrupt with debts of $31 billion. According to Reiman (2003):

>> *Enron hid the degree of indebtedness from investors by treating loans as revenue, hiding losses by creating new companies and then attributing losses to them and not Enron and of encouraging company employees to buy Enron shares while the executives apparently knew of its shaky condition and were busy selling off their own shares.* >>

The 'costs' of corporate crime are not just economic. Carson (1970) studied the loss of life in the exploration for oil in the North Sea resulting from the lack of concern by exploration companies about the safety issues of the workers. This was later tragically illustrated in 1988 by the loss of 168 lives when the Piper Alpha oil rig exploded. Similarly, corporate negligence and management failings have also been pointed to more recently in a series of rail crashes involving loss of life at Paddington, Potters Bar and Hatfield.

We pointed out earlier the way that corporate 'crime' can **transgress** the boundaries of crime through acts that may not actually be illegal, but are regarded by sociologists as morally reprehensible and often a violation of certain human rights.

According to Michalowski and Kramer (1987), modern transnational corporations can practise a policy of **law evasion**, for example setting up factories in countries that do not have pollution controls or adequate safety legislation, rather than producing in countries with stricter standards. They may sell goods to poorer countries when the goods have been declared unsafe in the more affluent countries (a fairly common procedure with pharmaceuticals). Box (1983) has claimed that multinationals dump products, plants and practices illegal in industrialized countries on to undeveloped or underdeveloped countries. They are able to do this because the poorer countries do not have the resources to control the large companies and also because officials are likely to accept bribes.

Corporate crime is, therefore, a major problem for society and actually cost economies more than conventional crimes. What is particularly interesting is just how little attention is paid to them and how sanctions against those engaged in this form of crime are relatively minor.

Obstacles organizations need to overcome to make profit, according to Box

Box suggests that there are a number of potential obstacles that organizations may have to overcome in order to achieve their goals:

- *The government* – This will impose laws to regulate production and commerce, for example on insider trading in investments, or pollution as a result of productive practices in manufacturing.
- *Employees* – They may not wish to work as hard or perform the sorts of tasks/run the risks the organization wants.
- *Consumers* – They might not wish to purchase certain products if they knew the full facts concerning their production, or might not be willing to pay the additional costs to make the product of good quality/safe. An example of this is the food industry that uses a wide range of food-adulterating practices and poor animal-husbandry to produce cheap food.
- *The public* – Pressure groups may want to influence consumers and the government to change or enforce legislation. The proposed regulations might harm the profits of the companies.

Box argues that all of these groups represent potential barriers to companies achieving their goals, and these barriers may have to be overcome, possibly in illegal ways.

Occupational crime

The impact of occupational crime

Theft by employees is a major source of crime in Britain – though whether the action of depriving an employer of goods, services or money is actually defined as theft is a real issue. Ditton (1977) and Mars (1982) have both studied theft by employees and found that in the range of industries they studied – from workers in the tourist industry to bakery delivery drivers – minor theft was regarded as a legitimate part of the job and redefined into a 'perk' or a 'fiddle'. Indeed, according to Mars, fiddling was part of the rewards of the job. For their part, according to Clarke (1990), management generally turned a blind eye to fiddles, accepting them as part of the total remuneration of the job and taking these into account in determining wage structures.

Fraud is a criminal offence covering a wide range of situations, but if we focus only on fraud by employees on employers, Levi (1987) found that in the late 1980s, 75 per cent of all frauds on financial institutions such as banks and building societies were by their own employees. Of 56 companies he surveyed, over 40 per cent had experienced fraud of over £50 000 by employees that year. However, employers were very reluctant to prosecute as they feared that by doing so, they could attract negative publicity.

Practices of occupational crime extend into the professions too. Functionalist writings on the reason for the existence of the professions (Parsons 1964) stress that the key difference between professionals and most other workers is the degree of trust placed in them by their clients/patients. According to Nelken (2002), however, there is a considerable body of evidence pointing to fraudulent claims made by doctors and dentists against insurance companies in the USA and, to a smaller extent, against the NHS in Britain.

288

Sociology A2 for AQA

synopticlink

The problem with studying any area of deviance is how to get information about the activities of those people involved. It is possible to ask questions about deviant and possibly illegal activity, but, understandably, the majority of people engaged in illegal acts are not too keen to provide the researcher with completely true answers! Studying crime at work, for example, illustrates this difficulty for sociologists in a very real way. It is well known that in many jobs people engage in minor acts of theft, which can be as minor as stealing pens or using the telephone for private calls. For many workers, these are not really regarded as acts of theft, but are perks of the job. Very often employers turn a blind eye to these activities, but if they are brought to their attention, then usually the employee is sacked.

Jason Ditton decided to study these minor perks or fiddles in a large bakery, using participant observational

sociological methods

methods. But the main issue he had to face was whether to be open with his co-workers or to engage in covert studies. He decided the best method in this case was to use covert methods. Covert methods have the advantage over overt methods in that the researcher has greater chance of actually studying deviant behaviour, and once in the group, there is no awareness by the group members of being researched, so they are more likely to act normally. There are recognized a number of problems, though, in using covert participant observation. These include the difficulty of making notes and the fact that the researcher, for obvious reasons, cannot conduct interviews/focus groups or give out questionnaires. However, above all else is the ethical issue that covert research does not get informed consent from the people being studied.

Explaining occupational and corporate crime

Sociologists have sought to incorporate occupational and corporate crime into existing theories – though with varying degrees of success. The approaches include:

- personality-based explanations
- differential association and subcultural theory
- emotion-based approaches
- labelling theory
- anomie
- Marxist explanations.

Personality-based explanations

Gross (1978) studied a range of individuals who had been successful in large companies. He found that they shared similar personality traits. They tended to be ambitious, to see their own success in terms of the company's success and, most relevant, that they had an 'undemanding moral code' (that we might term 'being unscrupulous'). According to Gross, the more successful they were, the less their sense of obligation to conform to wider social obligations. They accepted that personal and company success was more important than legal constraints. The difficulty with this kind of 'explanation', however, is then explaining why they are like this in the first place – it is rather like saying that criminals offend because they have an 'undemanding moral code'!

Differential association and subcultural theory

Sutherland (1940), who initiated the sociological discussion of white-collar crime, argued that his theory of differential association (see Topic 3) helped account for why business executives committed such enormous amounts of crime that benefited themselves and their organizations. Sutherland claimed that the culture of the organization might well justify committing illegal or dubious acts in order to achieve the organization's goals. Geis (1967), for example, examined the evidence given to congressional hearings into illegal price-fixing agreements of companies in the USA. He found that people taking up posts in organizations tended to find that price-fixing was an established practice and they would routinely become involved as part of the learning process of their jobs.

As early as 1952, Aubert studied how rationing procedures had been subverted during World War II by officials and members of food organizations, so that favouritism was shown to some groups and individuals (including themselves). Aubert (1952) found that these 'white-collar criminals' had an 'elaborate and widely accepted ideological rationalization for the offences'. In fact, criminal practices were quite normal. Evidence that such practices continue to this day comes from Braithwaite's (1984) study of the pharmaceutical industry, where bribing health inspectors was regarded as a perfectly normal part of business practice.

Emotion-based approaches

More recently, the interest in emotions and the meaning of masculinity has spilled over into explaining occupational and organizational crime. Often, when studying these forms of crime, the researcher is puzzled that people who earn huge incomes or who have enormous power, put themselves at risk either by seeking further personal gain, or more surprisingly perhaps, leading the company into illegal activity with limited personal benefits. According to Portnoy (1997), the answer could lie in the search for thrills and excitement. This is no different from the explanations offered for other forms of crime by writers such as Lyng and Katz (see Topic 8, pp. 283–4). Portnoy describes a world of excitement and thrill-seeking in the world of high finance where the excitement is as valued by the executives as are the financial benefits. In a similar manner, Punch (1996) argues that high finance is a world of 'power struggles, ideological debate, intense political rivalry, manipulation of information buffeted by moral ambiguity'. For these writers, then, crimes by companies and by individuals are explicable by thrill-seeking. Interestingly, this also links to ideas of masculinity, as the majority of people in senior positions are male, with high-risk 'macho' attitudes regarded positively by the culture of big business.

Labelling theory

According to Mars (1982), this approach provides the most appropriate avenue for understanding occupational crime and how employers respond to it. Employees build up expectations about what they deserve and what is an appropriate or 'fair' payment for the job; if they do not receive this, will engage in illegal practices to reach the 'fair' salary.

Mars, in his study of the catering industry (1982), explains theft by employees and sharp practice by restaurant owners by referring to the conflicting values of capitalism:

<< *There is only a blurred line between **entrepreneuriality** and flair on the one hand and sharp practice and fraud on the other.* >>

How this is labelled by the person and the company employing them will determine the outcome of the label – criminal, 'overstepping the mark' or simply 'sharp practice'. Nelken (2002) examined the workings of the English Family Practitioner Panels which examine the cases of NHS professionals accused of not having complied with their NHS contracts – in other words, accused of defrauding the NHS by overclaiming. His conclusion was that 'everything possible was done to avoid the impression that potentially criminal behaviour is at issue' – thus where 'misconduct' (theft) was proved, the NHS professional had income withheld, but nothing else. Nelken notes that on one occasion where the dentist involved admitted to 'fraud', the Panel 'pleaded with him to retract his admission' so that it would not pass on for criminal prosecution. Nelken therefore argues that crime committed by professionals is rarely defined as such.

On a broader scale, labelling theory can help explain corporate crime in a rather different way. Labelling theory argues that negative labels are applied to certain groups or organizations when other, more powerful groups are able to impose that label. According to Nelken (2002), much of corporate crime can be explained by this. Legislation making some forms of activity legal or illegal is 'fought over' by various interest groups and the resulting law will reflect the views and interests of the more powerful.

Anomie

Merton's anomie approach has also been applied to explain both occupational and corporate crime. Anomie theory states that every society has culturally approved goals and means to achieve these goals; if people are unable to obtain the goals by the culturally approved means, then they will develop alternatives. Box, who straddles a number of theoretical perspectives, used the idea of Merton's version of anomie (Topic 3) to help explain why organizations break the law. Box (1983) argues that if an organization is unable to achieve its goals using socially approved methods, then it may turn to other, possibly illegal, methods of achieving its goal of maximizing profit.

The idea of anomie was also developed in a wider way by Braithwaite (1984), who argued that corporate crime could be seen as: 'an illegitimate means of achieving any one of a wider range of organizational and personal goals when legitimate means are blocked.'

In his study of the pharmaceutical industry, he found that scientists were willing to fabricate their results in order to have their products adopted by their companies. The motivation for this was often not solely financial greed, but as often as not the desire for scientific prestige.

Similarly, in the high-pressure world of business, individuals who perceive themselves as failing may turn to various alternative modes of behaving, including occupational crime, according to Punch (1996).

However, Nelken (2002) is sceptical about the worth of anomie theory. He points out that anomie theory fails to explain why some individuals and companies choose illegal responses and others legal. Nelken suggests that until this is made clear, then the explanation is just too vague.

Marxist explanations

Perhaps the theoretical approach that has most enthusiastically adopted the study of corporate crime is the Marxist tradition. Corporate crime fits the critical criminological view that the real criminals are the rich and powerful. Critical criminologists argue that despite the fact that the powerful are able to use their dominance of society to avoid having the majority of their activities defined as illegal, they will still break the law where it conflicts with their interests. Furthermore, if they are actually caught, then they are less likely to be punished.

Swartz (1975) argues that as capitalism involves the maximization of corporate profits, then 'its normal functioning produces deaths and illnesses'. So, business crime is based upon the very values and legitimate practices of capitalism. Box (1983) has pointed out the success that the powerful have had in promoting the idea that corporate crime is less serious and less harmful than the range of normal street crimes, violence and burglary. Box describes this as a deliberate process of 'mystification' that has helped keep corporate crime as a minor object of study in criminology.

This theme was taken up by Frank Pearce (1976) who was interested in why there were so few prosecutions against corporations and senior business people. He concluded that they were so rare because otherwise there would be an undermining of the belief that the vast majority of crime is carried out by the working class. If the true pattern of crime came to be known by the bulk of the population, then it would create a crisis of legitimacy for the ruling class.

Slapper and Tombs (1999) claim that their research into the behaviour of large transnational companies in developing countries demonstrates the Marxist case that illegal and immoral practices are normal under capitalism. These companies routinely sell unsafe products, pay low wages and provide dangerous working conditions.

However, Carrabine et al. (2004) have criticized the Marxist position on corporate crime, by pointing out that the provision of poor working conditions, pollution of the environment and low pay are not restricted to capitalist societies. Until the collapse of the Soviet Union, some of the most dangerous and lowest paid work was under a communist regime. They point as well to the Chernobyl nuclear plant in the Ukraine which overheated, causing a large area of the country to be irradiated and caused a range of radiation-based diseases for generations to come. Nelken (2002) also points out that there are numerous laws controlling businesses in capitalist societies, when a simple Marxist perspective would suggest that the power available to the ruling class would limit such legislation to a minimum.

KEY TERMS

Corporate crime – crimes committed by companies against employees or the public.

Entrepreneuriality – qualities of people with original ideas for making money.

Law evasion – acting in such a way as to break the spirit of laws while technically conforming to them.

Occupational crime – crimes committed against a company by an employee.

Transgress – to cross over (conventional) boundaries; in criminology, it refers to legal acts that are harmful to others, but are not normally included in legal ideas of 'crime'.

White-collar crime – a term originally used by Sutherland for both occupational and corporate crime.

researchideas

- Interview some friends about their part-time work. Do petty pilfering and other minor fraud occur? How is it justified? Are they aware of any examples of illegal or irresponsible business practice in the organization itself? Emphasize the confidentiality of their responses.

Check your understanding

1. Explain the difference between corporate and occupational crime.

2. Which costs society more, white-collar crime or 'conventional' crime? Illustrate your answer with figures.

3. What three obstacles do companies have to overcome, according to Box?

4. How does this lead to corporate crime?

5. Explain how corporations can engage in law evasion.

6. Why are Marxists particularly interested in studying corporate crime?

7. Give two examples of occupational crime from the text.

web.tasks

1. Visit the Serious Fraud Squad website at www.sfo.gov.uk/publications.

   Go to the annual review for last year. What does this tell you about the number of cases of fraud under investigation and how many were actually prosecuted? In your view, what proportion of government resources is devoted to combating serious fraud?

2. Corporate Watch is a website packed with examples of corporate irresponsibility: www.corporatewatch.org

   Prepare a report on one or two examples.

exploring occupational and corporate crime

Item A

Reiman (2003) shows how the poor are arrested and charged out of all proportion to their numbers for the kinds of crimes poor people generally commit: burglary, robbery, assault and so forth. Yet when we look at the kinds of crimes poor people almost never have the opportunity to commit, such as antitrust violations (stock market fraud), industrial safety violations, embezzlement and serious tax evasion, the criminal justice system shows an increasingly benign and merciful state. The more likely it is for a particular form of crime to be committed by middle and upper-class people, the less likely it is that it will be treated as a criminal offence.

Carrabine, E., Iganski, P., Lee, M., Plummer, K. and South, N. (2004) *Criminology: A Sociological Introduction*, London: Routledge

(a) Identify and briefly explain two problems in using official crime statistics in the study of occupational and corporate crime. (8 marks)

This part of the question includes assessment of your understanding of the connections between Crime and Deviance and sociological methods.

(b) Examine the extent to which the study of two or more of the following areas can throw light on deviance in society: families and households; health; mass media; education; wealth, poverty and welfare; work and leisure. (12 marks)

This part of the question includes assessment of your understanding of the connections between Crime and Deviance and other substantive topic(s) you have studied.

(c) Using material from Item A and elsewhere, assess sociological explanations of white-collar and corporate crime. (8 marks)

This part of the question includes assessment of your understanding of the connections between Crime and Deviance and sociological methods.

Ethnicity and crime

gettingyouthinking

Racism 'rife in justice system'

One of the Home Office's own studies, published today, found that people from ethnic-minority communities were put off joining the police because they anticipated that they would be isolated and subjected to racism. Many also expected to face a level of hostility from their own communities if they joined the police. Members of Black and Asian groups sometimes themselves had negative attitudes towards ethnic-minority officers, the study found.

Vikram Dodd, *The Guardian*, Monday 20 March 2000

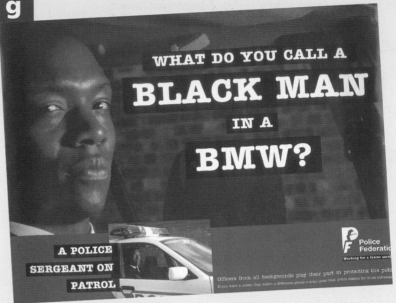

WHAT DO YOU CALL A **BLACK MAN** IN A **BMW?**

A POLICE SERGEANT ON PATROL

Police Federation

Working for a fairer service

Officers from all backgrounds play their part in protecting the public.

1 **What point is being made by the Police Federation poster above?**

2 **Why do you think this poster was thought necessary?**

3 **Why do you think that some members of ethnic-minority groups are 'put off' joining the police?**

4 **Why do you think that 'Black and Asian groups ... had negative attitudes towards ethnic minority officers'?**

A recurring theme in media reporting of street crime since the mid-1970s has been the disproportionate involvement of young males of African-Caribbean origin. It has partly been on this crime–race linkage that the police has justified the much greater levels of **stop and search** of young, Black males, than of White males.

Images of Asian criminality have, until recently, portrayed the Asian communities as generally more law-abiding than the majority population. However, after the attack on the World Trade Center in New York in 2001 and, more significantly, the bombings in 2005 on the London Underground, a new discourse has emerged regarding Muslim youths. The newer image is of them as being potentially dangerous – a threat to British culture.

Just discussing the relationship between criminality and race is itself a difficult task, and some sociologists argue that making the subject part of the A-level specifications actually helps perpetuate the link. After all, there are no discussions on 'White people and crime'!

Despite these reservations, sociologists have set out to examine the argument that there is a higher rate of crime by certain ethnic minorities, and the counterclaim that the criminal justice system is racist.

Offending, sentencing and punishment

Offending

There are three ways of gathering statistics on ethnicity and crime:

● official statistics
● victimization studies
● self-report studies.

Official statistics

According to Home Office statistics (Home Office 2005), about 9 per cent of people arrested were recorded as 'Black' and 5 per cent as 'Asian'. This means that relative to the arrest rates of the population as a whole, Black people were over three times more likely to be arrested than White people were. Asian people's rates were similar to those for White people.

Official statistics tell us the numbers of people arrested by the police. However, they are not necessarily a reflection of offending rates, but can be seen just as much as a comment on the actions of the police. If, as some sociologists argue, the

Waddington *et al.* (2004)

Race, the police, and stop & search

Waddington, Stenson and Don were concerned at the way it has become accepted that members of minority ethnic groups are unfairly stopped by the police. They therefore undertook research in Reading and Slough, two towns to the west of London. The researchers used a variety of methods. These included:

- direct non-participant observation of police officers, including watching CCTV footage
- detailed analysis of the official records of stop and search
- interviews with police officers about their stop and search activities.

The researchers argue that the evidence suggests that police officers do stop a proportionately high number of young members of ethnic minority groups (and of White groups), but that these figures are in direct proportion to their presence in the central city areas and their likelihood to be out at night. Those groups who are most likely to be out in the evening in high crime areas are most likely to be stopped and in these areas young people, and particularly young members of ethnic minority groups, are most likely to be out. They conclude that police stop and searches in the area they researched reflected the composition of people out on the streets, rather than any ethnic bias.

Waddington, P.A.J., Stenson, K. and Don, D. (2004) 'In proportion – race, and police stop and search', *British Journal of Criminology*, 44(6)

1 Comment on the range of methods used by the researchers. Are there any other groups that might have been interviewed?

2 Explain how the researchers reached their conclusion that 'police stop and searches in the area they researched reflected the composition of people out on the streets, rather than any ethnic bias'.

actions of some police officers are partly motivated by racism, then the arrest rates reflect this, rather than offending rates by ethnic-minority groups.

Victimization studies

Victim-based studies (such as the British Crime Survey) are gathered by asking victims of crime for their recollection of the ethnic identity of the offender. According to the British Crime Survey, the majority of crime is **intraracial**, with 88 per cent of White victims stating that White offenders were involved, 3 per cent claiming the offenders were Black, 1 per cent Asian and 5 per cent 'mixed'.

About 42 per cent of crimes against Black victims were identified as being committed by Black offenders and 19 per cent of crimes against Asians were by Asian offenders. The figures for White crimes against ethnic minorities are much higher – about 50 per cent, though this figure needs to be seen against the backdrop of 90 per cent of the population being classified as White.

Like official statistics, asking victims for a description of who committed the crimes is shot through with problems. For a start, only about 20 per cent of survey-recorded crimes are personal crimes (such as theft from the person), where the victims might actually see the offender. Bowling and Phillips (2002) argue that victims are influenced by (racial) stereotypes and 'culturally determined expectations' as to who commits crime. Certainly, research by Bowling (1999) indicates that where the offender is not known, White people are more likely to ascribe the crime to those of African-Caribbean origin.

Self-report studies

Self-report studies use an anonymous questionnaire to ask people what offences they have committed. Graham and Bowling's study (1995) of 14 to 25 year olds for the Home Office found that the self-reported offending rates were more or less the same for the White, Black and Asian respondents.

Sentencing

After arrest, those of African-Caribbean backgrounds are slightly more likely to be held in custody and to be charged with more serious offences than Whites. But they are more likely than average to plead, and to be found, not guilty. However, if found guilty, they are more likely to receive harsher sentences – in fact, those of African-Caribbean backgrounds have a 17 per cent higher chance of imprisonment than Whites.

Those of Asian origin are also more likely than average to plead not guilty, but more likely than average to be found guilty, but have an 18 per cent lesser chance of being imprisoned.

Sociologists are divided as to whether these statistics mean that members of ethnic minority groups are discriminated against. Bowling and Phillips (2002) summarize the 'patchy' knowledge of sociologists, by saying that the research indicates that both direct and indirect discrimination (types of charges laid, access to bail, etc.) against members of ethnic minority groups does exist.

In British prisons, the numbers of African and African-Caribbean prisoners is proportionately (that is, in terms of their proportion of the population as a whole) 7.8 times higher than would be expected, and is 0.77 times higher for those of Asian origin. In 1998, the rate of imprisonment per 100 000 of the general population was 1245 for Black people, 185 for Whites and 168 for Asians.

Policing and ethnic minority groups

We have already seen that there are considerable differences between the arrest rates for members of ethnic minority groups and those for Whites, with those of African-Caribbean origins having a four times higher rate of arrest than Whites. Sociologists are split between those who argue that this reflects real differences in levels of offending and those who argue that the higher arrest rates are due to the practices of the police.

A reflection of reality?

Sociologists all reject the idea that there is an association between 'race' and crime, in the sense that being a member of a particular ethnic group in itself has any importance in explaining crime. However, a number of writers (Mayhew *et al.* 1993) argue that most crime is performed by young males who come from poorer backgrounds. This being so, then there would be an overrepresentation of offenders from minority ethnic groups, quite simply because there is a higher proportion of young males in the ethnic-minority population than in the population as a whole. It is also a well-researched fact that minority ethnic groups overall are likely to have lower incomes and poorer housing conditions. These sociologists would accept that there is evidence of racist practices by certain police officers, but that the arrest rates largely reflect the true patterns of crime.

Phillips and Brown's (1998) study of ten police stations across Britain found that those of African-Caribbean origin accounted for a disproportionately high number of arrests. However, they found no evidence that they were treated any differently during the arrest process, with about 60 per cent of both Blacks and Whites and about 55 per cent of Asians eventually being charged.

Racist police practices?

A second group of sociologists see the higher arrest rates as evidence of police racism. Within this broad approach there are a number of different explanations.

Reflection of society approach

This approach, often adopted by the police, is that there are some individuals in the police who are racist, and once these 'bad apples' are rooted out, the police force will not exhibit racism. This approach was suggested by **Lord Scarman** (1981) in his inquiry into the inner-city riots of 1981. According to Scarman, the police reflect the wider society and therefore some racist recruits may join.

Canteen culture

The 'canteen (or working) culture' approach (see p. 243 and Key terms p. 244) argues that police officers have developed distinctive working values as a result of their job. Police officers have to face enormous pressures in dealing with the public: working long hours, facing potential danger, hostility from significant sections of the public and social isolation. The result is that they have developed a culture in response that helps them to deal with the pressures and gives them a sense of identity. The 'core characteristics' of the culture, according to Reiner (1992), include a thirst for action, cynicism, conservatism, suspicion, isolation from the public, macho values and racism.

Studies by Smith and Gray (1985), Holdaway (1983) who was himself a serving police officer at the time, and Graef (1989), all demonstrated racist views amongst police officers who, for example, held stereotypical views on the criminality of youths of African-Caribbean origin. Most importantly, it led them to stop and search these youths to a far greater extent than any other group. In fact, African-Caribbean people are six times more likely than Whites to be stopped and searched by the police.

Institutional racism

After the racist murder of a Black youth, Stephen Lawrence in 1993, and after very considerable pressure from his parents, the **Macpherson Inquiry** was set up to look at the circumstances of his death and the handling of the situation by the police. Sir William Macpherson concluded that the police were characterized by **institutional racism**. By this he meant that the police have 'procedures, practices and a culture that tend to exclude or to disadvantage non-White people' (cited in Bowling and Phillips 2002).

The key point about institutional racism is that it is not necessarily intentional on the part of any particular person in the organization, but that the normal, day-to-day activities of the organization are based upon racist ideas and practice. This means that police officers might not have to be racist in their personal values, but that in the course of their work they might make assumptions about young Black males and the likelihood of their offending that influence their (the police officers') attitudes and behaviour.

Theorizing race and criminality

Left realist approach

Lea and Young, leading writers in the left realist tradition, accept that there are racist practices by the police (1993). However, they argue that, despite this the statistics do bear out a higher crime rate for street robberies and associated 'personal' crimes by

The term 'moral panic' has moved from the confines of sociology into general use, so that every time there is media interest in a particular topic, it is described as a 'moral panic'. Even within sociology, the idea of moral panic has spread. Originally, it was used by labelling theorists interested in the effects of the media in labelling groups as deviant and troublemakers. Now, it is also used by Marxist-influenced writers, such as Stuart Hall, who has successfully integrated the concept into his analysis of how young Black youths come to be associated with high levels of crime. Weiner has taken a rather more cynical view of a moral panic and has suggested that there has been an antifeminist moral panic regarding the lower success rates of males in education. She argues that instead of there being a celebration of women finally overtaking males in the education system, the male-dominated media has

changed the message to a moral panic about the problem of male failure. Sociologists have identified moral panics over religion and its association with terrorism and with the collapse of the family.

However, some sociologists are now suggesting that because the term is now so widely used, its usefulness for sociological analysis has declined. Politicians, companies and even newspapers are fully aware of the potential of a moral panic and may seek to manipulate this. In Stanley Cohen's original study of mods and rockers, the media did not set out to create a moral panic; the 'panic' was identified by him as the unintentional outcome of media reporting. So moral panics have made a journey both within sociology and out into the wider public consciousness and, in doing so, the meaning and use of the term have changed.

youths of African-Caribbean origin. They explain this by suggesting that British society is racist and that young ethnic-minority males are economically and socially **marginalized**, with lesser chances of success than the majority population. Running alongside this is their sense of relative deprivation. According to Lea and Young, the result is the creation of subcultures, which can lead to higher levels of personal crime as a way of coping with marginalization and relative deprivation (see Topic 11 for a discussion of Realist criminologies).

Capitalism in crisis

A study by Hall et al. (1978) of street crime ('**mugging**') illustrates a particular kind of Marxist approach. According to Hall, the late 1970s were a period of crisis for British capitalism. The country was undergoing industrial unrest, there was a collapse in the economy and the political unrest in Northern Ireland was particularly intense. When capitalism is in crisis the normal methods of control of the population may be inadequate, and it is sometimes necessary to use force. However, using obvious repression needs some form of justification. It was in these circumstances that the newspapers, basing their reports on police briefings, highlighted a huge increase in 'mugging' (street robberies).

According to Hall, the focus on a relatively minor problem, caused by a group who were already viewed negatively, served the purpose of drawing attention away from the crisis and focusing blame on a scapegoat – young African-Caribbean males. This 'moral panic' (see Synoptic link above) then justified increased numbers of police on the streets, acting in a more repressive manner.

Hall's analysis has been criticized for not making any effort actually to research the motivations and thinking of young African-Caribbean males. What is more, the association between 'criminality and Black youth', made by the police and the media, has continued for over 25 years, and so it seems unlikely that this can be explained simply by a 'crisis of capitalism'.

Cultures of resistance

A third approach overlaps with the Marxist approach just outlined. According to this approach, linked with Scraton (1987) and Gordon (1988), policing, media coverage and political debates all centre around the issue of 'race' being a problem. Minority ethnic groups have been on the receiving end of discrimination since the first migrants arrived, leaving them in a significantly worse socioeconomic position than the White majority.

In response to this, **cultures of resistance** have emerged, in which crime is a form of organized resistance that has its origins in the **anticolonial** struggles. When young members of minority ethnic groups commit crimes, they are doing so as a political act, rather than as a criminal act.

There are a number of criticisms of this approach. Lea and Young (1993) have been particularly scathing, pointing out that the majority of crimes are actually 'intraracial', that is 'Black on Black'. This cannot therefore reflect a political struggle against the White majority. Second, they accuse writers such as Scraton of 'romanticizing' crime and criminals, and in doing so ignoring the very real harm that crime does to its victims.

Exclusion and alternative economies

This approach integrates the previous approaches and relates quite closely to the work of Cloward and Ohlin (1960) (see Topic 3). A good example of this sort of argument is provided by Philippe Bourgois' study (2002) of El Barrio, a deprived area in East Harlem, New York. Bourgois spent seven years living and researching the street life and economy of El Barrio, whose inhabitants were overwhelmingly Puerto Ricans, illegal Mexican immigrants and African-Americans.

Bourgois argues that the economic exclusion of these minority ethnic groups, combined with negative social attitudes towards them, has forced them to develop an 'alternative economy'. This involves a wide range of both marginally legal and clearly illegal activities, ranging from kerbside car-repair businesses to selling crack cocaine. Drug sales are by far the most lucrative employment: 'Cocaine and crack … have been the fastest growing – if not the only – equal-opportunity employers of men in Harlem'.

Running alongside this informal economy has developed a distinctive (sub)culture, which Bourgois calls 'inner-city street culture' – as he puts it:

≪ this 'street culture of resistance' is not a coherent, conscious universe of political opposition, but rather a spontaneous set of rebellious practices that in the long term have emerged as an oppositional style. ≫

This subculture causes great damage because the illegal trade in drugs eventually involves its participants in lifestyles of violence, substance abuse and '**internalized rage**'. Many of the small-scale dealers become addicted and drawn into violence to support their habit. Furthermore, their behaviour destroys families and the community. The result is a chaotic and violent 'community' where the search for dignity in a distinctive culture leads to a worsening of the situation.

Although this is an extreme lifestyle, even for the USA, elements of it can help us to understand issues of race and criminality in the UK. Exclusion and racism lead to both cultural and economic developments that involve illegal activities and the development of a culture that helps resolve the issues of lack of dignity in a racist society. But both the illegal activities and the resulting culture may lead to an involvement in crime.

Statistical artefact approach

The **statistical artefact** approach suggests that the higher levels of involvement of young males from an African-Caribbean background in crime is more a reflection of how the statistics are interpreted than of a genuinely higher level. Fitzgerald et al. (2003) researched ethnic-minority street crime in London, comparing crime rates against a wide range of socioeconomic and demographic data. They also interviewed a cross section of young, ethnic-minority offenders and their mothers, as well as running focus groups of 14 to 16 year olds in schools. The outcomes of the study were complex, but they throw light upon a number of the other explanations we have discussed so far:

- FitzGerald and colleagues found that street crime is related to levels of deprivation in an area, as well as to a lack of community cohesion, as measured by a rapid population turnover. This reflects crime levels in Britain as a whole, as we know amongst all ethnic groups that the higher the levels of deprivation in an area, the higher the levels of crime.
- They found that the high rates of ethnic-minority offending were directly linked to the numbers of young, ethnic-minority males. Once again, all statistics point to young males as the highest offending group in the population, whatever their ethnic background. As there are higher proportions of young, ethnic-minority males in the population as a whole, and in London in particular, then we would expect there to be higher rates of crime committed by ethnic-minority males – if only as a reflection of the high percentage they form of all young males.
- They found that there was a statistical link between higher crime levels and lone-parent families. African-Caribbean households are more likely to be headed by a lone parent, so there would be a statistical link here too.
- They found that there was a subculture which had developed amongst certain ethnic-minority children that provided justification for crime. This was very closely linked with school failure and alienation from school. However, similar views were held by White school-age students who were doing poorly at school or who were no longer attending. A disproportionate amount of all crime is performed by young, educationally disaffected children of all backgrounds.

In conclusion, therefore, Fitzgerald and colleagues suggest that there is no specific set of factors which motivate young, ethnic-minority offenders – they are exactly the same ones as motivate White offenders. However, the overrepresentation of young males from African-Caribbean backgrounds is partly the result of their sheer numbers in the age band in which most offending takes place.

KEY TERMS

Anticolonial struggles – historically, Black resistance to Western attempts to control and exploit Black people.

Cultures of resistance – the term used to suggest that ethnic-minority groups in Britain have developed a culture that resists the racist oppression of the majority society.

Institutional racism – racism that is built into the normal practices of an organization.

Internalized rage – term used by Bourgois to describe the anger and hurt caused by economic and social marginalization.

Intraracial – within a particular ethnic group.

Lord Scarman – in 1981 there were serious inner-city disturbances, particularly in Brixton in London. Lord Scarman led a government inquiry into the causes of these 'riots'.

Macpherson Inquiry – Sir William Macpherson led an inquiry into the events surrounding the murder of Stephen Lawrence (allegedly) by White racists, and the subsequent police investigation.

Marginalized – a sociological term referring to those who are pushed to the edge of society in cultural, status or economic terms.

Mugging – a term used to describe street robbery. It has no status as a specific crime in England and Wales.

Statistical artefact – the 'problem' emerges from the way that the statistics are collected and understood.

Stop and search – police officers have powers to stop and search those they 'reasonably' think may be about to, or have committed, a crime; this power has been used much more against ethnic-minority youths than White youths.

Check your understanding

1. What different interpretations are there concerning the arrest rates of members of ethnic minority groups?

2. What do we mean when we say that the majority of crime is 'intraracial'?

3. Identify any two problems with the statistics derived from 'victimization studies'.

4. What are self-report studies? Do they confirm the statistics derived from the arrest rates?

5. What two general explanations have sociologists put forward for the higher arrest rates of members of minority ethnic groups?

6. Explain the significance of the terms 'canteen culture' and 'institutional racism' in explaining the attitudes and behaviour of the police towards minority ethnic groups.

7. How do 'left realist sociologists' explain the relationship between ethnicity and crime?

8. What is the relationship between crises in capitalism and police action against 'muggers'?

9. What does the term 'culture of resistance' mean?

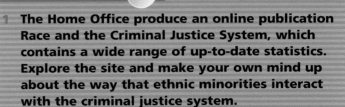

web.tasks

1. The Home Office produce an online publication Race and the Criminal Justice System, which contains a wide range of up-to-date statistics. Explore the site and make your own mind up about the way that ethnic minorities interact with the criminal justice system. www.homeoffice.gov.uk/rds/pdfs/s95race00.pdf

2. Look up the case of Anthony Walker who was murdered in Liverpool in July 2005. From you research on the internet, write a short article summarizing what happened – most importantly, the element of racism involved.

research idea

- Your local police force will have an ethnic minority liaison officer (or similar title). Ask them to come to your institution to talk about their work and, in particular, stop and search. Before they come, get into small groups and sort out a list of questions – ideally, you should then e-mail them to the officer to base their talk on.

exploring ethnicity and crime

Item A

The notion that increasing youth unemployment, coupled with a high young population in the Black community, and the effects of massive, well-documented, racial discrimination and the denial of legitimate opportunity, did not result in a rising rate of real offences is hardly credible... [This] real increase in crime is amplified as a result of police action and police prejudice.

Lea, J. and Young, J. (1993) *What is to be Done about Law and Order?* (revised edn), London: Pluto Press

(a) Using material from **Item A**, identify and briefly describe **two** problems in using official statistics to study ethnic-minority rates of offending. (8 marks)

This part of the question includes assessment of your understanding of the connections between Crime and Deviance and sociological methods.

(b) Examine some of the reasons why young males from minority ethnic backgrounds might be more likely than other groups to take part in criminal and deviant acts. In your answer use material from **at least two** of the following areas: families and households; health; mass media; education; wealth, welfare and poverty; work and leisure. (12 marks)

This part of the question includes assessment of your understanding of the connections between Crime and Deviance and other substantive topics you have studied.

(c) Assess the usefulness of Marxist approaches in explaining the causes and the extent of ethnic-minority offending in society. (40 marks)

This part of the question includes assessment of your understanding of the connections between Crime and Deviance and sociological theory.

Contemporary criminology: from realism to postmodernism

gettingyouthinking

People on large social-housing estates and in the inner cities are having their lives blighted by crime. Imagine you have just formed a new government and you have a choice. You are not sure, but you think the real causes of crime are probably poverty and deprivation. You can spend all your money tackling poverty and hope that it has an effect on crime in, say, 20 years or you can spend the money on more police officers, CCTV, better street lighting, and a whole range of other anti-crime measures. You are aware that these may lower the crime rate today, but do nothing to address the 'real' causes.

1 Do you think it is ever possible to eliminate crime? Explain your answer.

2 What would you do? (No, you cannot do both!) Give the reasons for your choice.

3 Are there problems with crime in the area where you live? What sorts of crime? What would be your ideal solution if you could do something about it today?

4 Do you feel 'at risk' of crime? If you do, what precautions do you routinely take?

5 Are there particular individuals or types of people you avoid? Why?

This topic brings us up to date with sociological theorizing on crime. Rather than seeing it as a topic completely isolated from other, earlier topics, it might be better to regard it as a topic of unfinished business! Throughout the book, but in the Theory and Methods unit in particular, we stress the importance of late-modern and postmodern ideas in contemporary sociology. These ideas are still working their way through sociology and are leading to new divisions and debates. In this topic, we refer back to earlier ideas and arguments from late-modernist and postmodernist thinkers and you should take the opportunity to go back and check on these earlier arguments.

The aim of this topic is to show the very different directions that contemporary sociology is taking in its approach to understanding crime. At the one extreme, we find the realist criminologies that have emerged from functionalism and Marxism. These have been 'tamed' in such a way that both are now very influential in government policy-making. The two approaches contain within them many of the themes and arguments we have examined during the course of this unit and have provided coherent explanations for crime and suggestions for tackling it.

At the other extreme, are the ideas drawn from late modernity and postmodernity which are critical of the way that

criminology has been drawn into the policy-making process. Indeed, much of the late-modernity perspective is an extended criticism of current policies.

Postmodern theorists go further in their criticisms of most sociological theorizing on crime. They suggest instead that the definitions of crime are simply social constructions in which criminologists have been very much involved in creating false notions of what crime is. They also suggest that the careful theorizing of crime promoted by most criminologists is based on the false belief that crime can be explained rationally; instead, they point to emotion and the irrational.

Realist criminology

In an earlier topic, we looked at criminal statistics. We learned that the victims of crime are, perhaps surprisingly, more likely to be the poor and the disadvantaged than the rich. Furthermore, the majority of crime occurs in in inner-city areas and in large social-housing developments, where there is real concern over the amount of crime – a concern which sociologists had previously simply missed. It was within this context of uncovering the true extent, victims and location of crime that two very different approaches developed:

- **right realism** – deriving from the **right-wing** theories of James Q. Wilson and emphasizing **'zero tolerance'**.
- **left realism** – deriving from the writings of Lea, Young and Matthews who emphasize the importance of tackling deprivation and of getting policing to respond to the needs of the local population.

Right realism

Right realism originated in the USA with the writings of James Q. Wilson. In 'Broken Windows' (Wilson and Kelling 1982), Wilson argued that crime flourishes in situations where social control breaks down. According to his analysis, in any community, a proportion of the population are likely to engage in 'incivilities', which might consist of such things as dropping litter, vandalism or rowdy behaviour. In most communities, this behaviour is prevented from going further by the comments and actions of other members of the local community. Effectively, the amount and extent of incivilities are held in check by the response of others. However, if the incivilities go unchecked, then the entire social order of the area breaks down and gradually there is a move to more frequent and more serious crime. The parallel which Wilson drew was with abandoned buildings; he asks whether anyone had ever seen just one window broken? The answer was, of course, that once one window was broken, then they all were.

Once crime is allowed to happen, it flourishes. Wilson was strongly influenced by the work of the American theorist Amitai Etzioni, and his theory of **communitarianism** (1993) – which stresses the fact that only local communities by their own efforts and local face-to-face relationships can solve social problems (see Topic 7).

The conclusion that Wilson drew was that the police should have a crucial role to play in restoring the balance of incivilities and helping to recreate community. He argued that most police officers engage in law enforcement – that is ensuring that the law is not broken and apprehending offenders if they have committed an offence. He argued that this did relatively little to reconstruct communities and prevent crime (after all only about 3 per cent of offences result in successful prosecutions). Police should instead be concentrating on order maintenance. By this he means using the law to ensure that the smaller incivilities – groups of rowdy youths, noisy parties, public drug use – are all crushed. According to him, this would help to create a different view of what was acceptable behaviour, and would make public areas feel safe again for the majority of people.

After a version of his ideas was adopted in New York, under the slogan 'zero tolerance', and there appeared to be a decline in crime, the term was adopted throughout America and to some extent in the UK as a description of a much harsher form of street policing.

Platt and Takagi (1977) criticize this approach for concentrating exclusively on working-class crimes and ignoring the crimes of the powerful. Furthermore, it ignores ideas of justice and law enforcement and advocates instead the maintenance of social order – even if it is at the expense of justice.

Left realism

Left realism developed primarily as a response to the increasing influence of right realism over the policymakers in Britain and America. In the USA, the main writer has been Elliot Currie, while in Britain, left realism is associated with Jock Young, John Lea and Roger Matthews.

Young was one of the founders of 'critical criminology' (see Topic 4) that introduced elements of interactionist theory into Marxism in order to provide a 'complete' theory of crime. However, Young became increasingly disenchanted with the Marxist approach that stressed that criminals should be seen as the victims of the capitalist system and that sociological analyses of crime should stress the criminality of the rich and powerful. This disillusionment was fuelled by a series of local victimization surveys (see Topic 5), e.g. in Islington and Merseyside, that showed that the real victims of crime were the poor and the powerless, and that these people viewed street crime and burglary as one of the main social problems they faced.

Young (1986) argued that it was the role of criminology to provide relevant and credible solutions for policymakers to limit the harm that crime was doing to the lives of the poorer sections of the community. This approach led to a bitter debate in sociology, with many influential left-wing criminologists attacking Young for selling out. (The implication of Young's new argument is that the role of sociologists is to help the government to combat crime. For Marxists, crime exists because of capitalism, and the government represents capitalism.) Young responded by labelling Marxist criminology as 'left idealism', meaning that it was great in theory, but had no practical solutions.

The left realist explanation of crime has three elements: relative deprivation, marginalization and subculture.

Relative deprivation

The concept of **relative deprivation** derives from the writings of Runciman (1966), who argued that political revolutions only occurred when the poor became aware of the sheer scale of the differences between themselves and the rich. Without this knowledge, they generally accepted their poverty and powerlessness. It is not, therefore, poverty that leads to revolution, but awareness of their relative poverty.

Applying this concept to crime, Lea and Young (1984) pointed out that poverty or unemployment do not directly cause crime, as, despite the high unemployment experienced in the economic depression in Britain from the late 1920s to the 1930s, crime rates were considerably lower than they were in the boom years of the 1980s. According to Lea and Young, the expectations of 1930s' youth were much lower than those of contemporary young people, who feel resentful at what they could actually earn compared with their aspirations.

Marginalization

Marginalization refers to the situation where certain groups in the population are more likely than others to suffer economic, social, and political deprivation. The first two of these elements of deprivation are fairly well known – young people living in inner cities and social-housing estates are likely to suffer from higher levels of deprivation than those from more affluent areas. The third element – political marginalization – refers to the fact that there is no way for them to influence decision-makers, and thus they feel powerless.

Subculture

This draws partially upon the Marxist subcultural approach (see Topic 4), but more heavily from the ideas of Robert Merton (see Topic 3). Subcultures develop amongst groups who suffer relative deprivation and marginalization. Specific sets of values, forms of dress and modes of behaviour develop that reflect the problems that their members face. However, whereas the Marxist subcultural writers seek to explain the styles of dress, and forms of language and behaviour as forms of 'resistance' to capitalism, Lea and Young do not see a direct, 'decodable' link.

For Lea and Young (1984), one crucial element of subcultures is that they are still located in the values of the wider society. Subcultures develop precisely because their members subscribe to the dominant values of society, but are blocked off (because of marginalization) from success. The outcome of subculture, marginalization and relative deprivation is street crime and burglary, committed largely by young males.

Criticisms of left realism

Marxist or 'critical criminologist' writers have attacked realism for ignoring the 'real' causes of crime that lie in the wider capitalist system and of ignoring the crimes of more powerful groups in society by simply concentrating on street crime.

Feminist and postmodernist criminologists, such as Pat Carlen (1992) and Henry and Milovanovich (1996), have argued that left realist criminology accepts the establishment's view of what crime is and so concentrates its attention on issues to do with street crime and burglary. They argue, instead, that one role of criminology ought to be exploring the way that society harms less powerful groups.

Overview of realism

Realist approaches to crime have actually been put into practice, in a modified form, by New Labour governments since the late 1990s. However, just as these were being accepted by decision-makers, a rather different view of society and the place of crime within it were emerging. Interestingly, the realist approaches are perfect examples of what the late-modern approaches argue is the main concern of modern society – risk. Both left and right realism emerged from the concerns about the high crime rates in the inner cities and large housing estates, where risk of crime was much higher. The theories and the policy options which emerged were directly informed by risk models. As we shall see in the next section, these ideas of risk are a construction of late-modern and postmodern societies.

Late modernity and crime

All sociology has been affected by the insights provided by the late-modernist and postmodernist perspectives, and criminology is no different. As outlined in Unit 4, Topic 2, late modernity refers to a number of changes in society which include:

- changes in the economy from production to service industry
- the growth of a global as opposed to national economies
- the decline in traditional social institutions such as social class and the family, and their replacement with greater emphasis on individual identity and aspirations
- the growth in importance of the mass media.

These changes provide the backdrop for a range of new theories and explanations for crime.

Actuarial approaches to crime

In earlier topics, we explored the development of notions of 'risk' as devised by Giddens (1999) and Beck, who suggested that late-modern society is characterized by the development in

synoptic link   poverty, wealth and welfare, religion

Left Realism's use of relative deprivation to help explain subculture is not a new idea, but was developed by Runciman in the 1950s to help explain political stability. Runciman argued that the actual amount of poverty and deprivation in a society is less important in bringing about radical social change than an *awareness* of being poor and deprived. Right-wing politicians often point out that people today are actually much better off than ever before in history, yet there is probably a greater sense of deprivation than ever before. This sense of relative deprivation has been explored by sociologists in a number of areas. A sense of relative deprivation fuels the motivation to commit crime: the media construct images of what success actually is and those who are

excluded from this feel that this exclusion is unfair. A similar idea was developed by Merton in the 1930s with his idea of 'anomie'. Relative deprivation has also been used by sociologists to explore the growth of religious communities. Where people feel unfairly excluded and relatively deprived, they may turn to religion both to explain their position and to gain solace and prestige. The growth in Pentecostal churches in Britain, attended largely by people of African and Caribbean origins, is one example of responses to relative deprivation. More recently, there has been a suggestion that interest in Islam by young British people of Pakistani origin is a response to their marginal and (relatively) deprived position in British society.

both personal and governmental spheres of a 'calculative attitude' towards risk. In criminology, too, writers such as O'Malley (1992) have developed similar ideas about the significance of ideas of risk to an understanding of crime. These writers suggest that in late-modern society, individuals and governments are less concerned about justice being done than they are about limiting risk to themselves. Although the difference between risk and justice does not seem very great, in fact, according to O'Malley, it is enormous. In societies where the concern is with justice, then when a crime is committed, the government will seek the person who is guilty, try and punish them.

In late modernity, where governments are concerned about risk, then an '**actuarial**' approach is taken. The term 'actuarial' is taken from insurance companies, who work out what the risks are for a particular problem and then base their charges on that – thus young males pay higher motor insurance premiums because they are the drivers most likely to be involved in accidents, even if individual young males are very good, careful drivers. Therefore, in late modernity, governments are not concerned with individual guilt or innocence, but with controlling the behaviour of potentially deviant groups. Through such reasoning, young people are now seen as a problem group, and a range of legal measures, such as Anti-Social Behaviour Orders (ASBOs), are brought in to control everyone – *before* any offence might be committed. Feeley and Simon (1992) called this the new penology, which they argue is 'less concerned with responsibility, fault, ... or diagnosis ... but with techniques to identify, manage and sort (people) by dangerousness'.

Actuarial theories do not explain crime, but they do provide a different way of understanding how societies respond to very high levels of crime. They suggest that as crime levels are so high, it is simply impossible to sustain the fiction (upon which criminology itself is based) that criminals are different from the mass of the population.

The criminology of the other

This idea of the lack of difference between the criminal and 'law-abiding', has been further explored by Garland (1996), who argues that in late modernity, crime levels are so high that there has been a cultural response. This response is to divide criminals into two types – the **criminology of the self** and the **criminology of the other**:

- The *criminology of the self* is based on the idea that these criminals are similar to the majority of the population – rational and self-seeking. Therefore, ordinary people must engage in sensible activities to limit the risk of violence or theft. Do not go in poorly lit streets, lock up your possessions and avoid confrontations.
- *Criminology of the other* refers to those on the borders of our understanding – child molesters, rapists and terrorists. These people are outsiders by whom we feel truly threatened and who should be excluded from normal standards of justice and punishment.

Young (1999), in his later writings, has taken up this theme and has moved away from left realism to explore the way in which societies in late modernity systematically exclude significant sectors of the population, labelling them as outsiders of whom we ought to be afraid. Referring in particular to US society, Young points out that there are currently almost 1.6 million people imprisoned, with a further 5.1 million under some form of judicial control – with the overwhelming majority coming from minority ethnic groups. Young also points out that Britain is steadily increasing its use of imprisonment, with more people in prison and on probation than ever before. Much of the writings of late-modernist writers on the subject of the role of crime and punishment shows similarities to the early work of Durkheim (see Topic 1).

Postmodernity and crime

Like late-modernist theorists, postmodernists have provided an entirely different way of looking at crime and, in some ways, these do not sit easily with more traditional explanations.

Postmodernism is based upon a rejection of the so-called grand narratives of science and structural sociological theories; postmodernists are particularly dismissive of Marxism and functionalism. Postmodern theorists agree with the analysis of social change which late-modernists describe, but provide a rather different analysis, one based upon the idea of fragmentation, difference and incoherence. One key element of this rejection of coherence involves resurrecting the importance of the irrational. This is very important, for most other forms of sociological theorizing have sought to explain the factors that could reasonably make someone offend, and so answers such as family upbringing, subcultural values, anomie and so on, were provided. Postmodernism breaks with this and takes us back to a whole range of emotions as precursors to crime.

Thrills

In Topic 8, we explored the work of Lyng and Katz, both of whom lie within this tradition, as well as the ideas of Connell and Messerschmidt. Lyng suggests that crime can be seen as a form of edgework, giving thrills by placing oneself on the edge of safety, but not stepping over. Katz wrote about the seductiveness of crime, whereby people are drawn into expressing their true feelings of rage and humiliation through what he calls 'righteous' acts, which can include violence and murder. Messerschmidt's work emphasizes the importance of maintaining the imagined role of masculinity.

However, a whole range of other emotion-based theories also exist. Levin and McDevitt (2002) have argued that much crime can be explained by thrill-seeking. Their reward for violence or theft is as much psychological as social, providing 'the joy of exhilaration and the thrill of making someone suffer'. However, Levin and McDevitt's argument fails to explain why this should provide thrills for some and not for the majority of people. Fenwick and Hayward (2000) provide this answer by suggesting that this thrill provides an escape from the dullness

Postmodernism rejects the traditional political and sociological explanations for the nature of society. Many of the original postmodernists were disillusioned, in particular, with Marxism and its claim to explain human society in rational, scientific terms. Their argument is that people are not governed entirely by rational, thoughtful processes and nor is society. Instead, people are motivated by complex and sometimes contradictory beliefs. Their actions, too, are contradictory and impulsive. Postmodernists argue that emotion, irrationality and confusion need to be incorporated into sociological theory. More fundamentally, they also argue that the search for an overall explanation for society is doomed because any explanation produced by sociologists will itself be a product of that society – sociology is socially produced. This critique of sociology from postmodernism has had a significant impact in sociological theory, but has not really had quite the impact that its originators expected. In fact, postmodernism has become incorporated into sociology as yet another competing perspective. Its analyses have been taken up by some sociologists and applied in particular to criminology, youth culture and the media, but it has been relatively underused in other areas.

of everyday routines. According to them, when a person commits a crime, they then have 'feelings of self-realization and self-expression', which 'bring them alive'.

Shame and self-esteem

Scheff *et al.* (1989) argue that notions of shame and self-esteem are very important, yet these emotions are rarely acknowledged in contemporary society. High self-esteem means that people usually feel proud of themselves, while low self-esteem reflects a feeling of shame about themselves. Scheff argues that shame is a fundamental concept that we are constantly monitoring by looking at ourselves as we imagine others see us. Scheff argues that when somebody who has low self-esteem (that is, feelings of shame) experiences what they consider to be a humbling situation, then they may explode into a 'rage', which is a defence against the threat to what little self-esteem they have. Anger and rage are, therefore, self-defence mechanisms. According to Scheff, this is why ideas of 'respect' and 'dissing' (disrespecting) people are so important for young males, particularly from minority ethnic groups. Two ethnographic studies of US life in urban ghettos in the USA powerfully illustrate Scheff's argument. Bourgois (2002) and Anderson (1999) both point out that a key feature of life in these deprived urban areas is the amount of respect that people seek to gain for themselves. Being respected has positive outcomes in terms of status in the eyes of others, which in turn provides social and economic benefits. However, respect has to be won, and in both studies this is generally obtained through the use of extreme violence when required, as well as appropriate dress and demeanour.

KEY TERMS

Actuarial – refers to the process of working out risk.

Communitarianism – an approach associated with the US writer Amitai Etzioni. He argues that government should encourage the rekindling of a sense of community. Local communities can then take over responsibilities for local problems.

Constitutive criminology – a postmodern term referring to the way that the idea of crime has been socially constructed.

Criminology of the other – the view that those who commit certain types of crime are non-human and evil.

Criminology of the self – the view that those who commit crime are essentially (flawed) people like ourselves.

Left realism – a Marxist-derived approach to criminology that argues that crime hurts the most vulnerable in society rather than the rich and powerful, and so more resources need to be spent on helping and protecting these poorer victims of crime.

Marginalization – refers to people living on the margins of society, in particular lacking any say over decision-making.

Relative deprivation – when the most deprived are put in a situation where they can compare their situation with others who are affluent, they become aware of their own relatively disadvantaged state and become discontented.

Right realism – approach to crime deriving from the right-wing theories of James Q. Wilson and emphasizing 'zero tolerance'.

Right-wing – approaches that reject the idea of state intervention in health, welfare and educational services, regarding private companies as more effective in providing services than the government.

Zero-tolerance – using the law to ensure that smaller incivilities (groups of rowdy youths, noisy parties, public drug use) are all crushed.

Check your understanding

1   Make a list of key similarities and differences between right and left realism.

2   How has the idea of communitarianism been applied to the fight against crime?

3   What do left realists believe are the causes of crime?

4   Explain the term 'relative deprivation'.

5   What do late-modern criminologists mean by 'risk'?

6   Explain the importance of shame and self-esteem for crime, according to postmodern theorists?

7   How do constitutive criminologists argue that crime is socially constructed?

Constitutive criminology

Perhaps the single most coherent attempt at a postmodern criminology has been provided by Henry and Milovanovic (1996), who argue that it is mistaken to seek causes of crime, as crime is just one way of thinking about certain acts – in other words, crime is a socially constructed concept. This argument may seem to take us back to the ideas of labelling theorists (Topic 5) and critical criminologists (Topic 4), but the crucial difference between the **constitutive criminology** and these approaches is that, while labelling and Marxist theories see the basis of law in differences in power, constitutive criminology sees instead 'drift, seduction, chaos, discourse' as reasons for law. Because of this, they argue that it is almost impossible to find a rational basis for criminal law and suggest instead that the basis of any future criminal law should be harm to others in any sense at all. They argue that two key groups who work to co-produce definitions of crime are criminologists and journalists:

- Criminologists are part of that process which separates one form of harm from others and calls it 'crime', by accepting the socially constructed notion of crime rather than challenging it
- The media are interested in only certain types and images of crime and thus their presentation of crime has become that which we regard as important crime.

web.tasks

1 Go to your local authority website and you should be able to find a section on 'community safety'. Alternatively, search for these words within the site. If this does not work, go to the Home Office website at www.homeoffice.gov.uk and then click on 'community safety'). Do the activities mentioned link with the ideas of 'realist' sociologists? If so, how?

2 Look up 'hate crimes' on the internet. There are a number of sites, one is www.hatecrime.org. How do these crimes relate to postmodernist ideas?

research idea

- Conduct a survey of local residents to find out their views about the best ways of reducing crime in your area. Do their ideas link to realist theories?

exploring realist criminologies

Item A

In the past there was a consensus stretching across a large section of informed opinion that the major cause of crime was impoverished social conditions. Antisocial conditions led to antisocial behaviour. Slums were demolished, educational standards improved, full employment advanced, and welfare spending increased: the highest affluence in the history of humanity achieved, yet crime increased.

Adapted from Young, J. (1997) 'Left Realist Criminology: Radical in its Analysis, Realist in its Policy', in *The Oxford Handbook of Criminology* (2nd edn), Oxford: Oxford University Press

(a) **Identify and briefly explain two advantages of using official crime statistics in the study of crime and deviance.** (8 marks)

This part of the question includes assessment of your understanding of the connections between Crime and Deviance and sociological methods.

(b) **Examine some of the ways in which the concept of relative deprivation can be linked to one or more of the following areas: education; wealth, welfare and poverty; work and leisure; power and politics; religion; world sociology.** (12 marks)

This part of the question includes assessment of your understanding of the connections between Crime and Deviance and other substantive topic(s) you have studied.

(c) **Using material from Item A and elsewhere, assess the usefulness of realist approaches to a sociological understanding of crime and deviance.** (40 marks)

This part of the question includes assessment of your understanding of the connections between Crime and Deviance and sociological theory.

Suicide

gettingyouthinking

Groups at increased risk of suicide

The following table lists the main groups at heightened risk of suicide, together with an estimate of the magnitude of their increased risk in comparison with the general population.

High risk group	Estimated magnitude of increased risk
Males compared to females	× 2–3
4 weeks following discharge from psychiatric hospital	× 100–200
People who have deliberately self-harmed in the past	× 10–30
Alcoholics	× 5–20
Drug misusers	× 10–20
Prisoners	× 9–10
Offenders serving non-custodial sentences	× 8–13
Doctors	× 2
Farmers	× 2
Unemployed	× 2–3
Divorced people	× 2–5
People on low incomes (social class IV/V)	× 4

Source: National Electronic Library for Health, 2001

1 **Look at the table above. Why do you think the groups mentioned are at particular risk of suicide?**

2 **Read through the extract on the right. Why do you think that suicides are at a 30-year low?**

3 **What possible explanations can you suggest as to why some places have higher suicide rates than others?**

THERE were 5755 adult suicides in the UK in 2003, the lowest number since 1973, according to data released today by the Office for National Statistics.

Suicide rates for men, which were rising through the 1970s and 1980s, have decreased steadily since 1998. The rate for 2003, 18.1 deaths per 100 000 population, was the lowest since 1978. Suicide rates for women, which fell steadily in the 1980s and early 1990s, have decreased only slightly since the mid-1990s. The rate for women remained around 5.8 deaths per 100 000 population in each of the years 2001 to 2003.

Suicide is much more for common for men than women. In 2003, men accounted for three-quarters of all suicides. This difference between the sexes widened in the 1970s and 1980s. In 1971, men accounted for slightly over half of all suicides (56 per cent). Across England and Wales, there were large regional differences in suicide rates for men in the period 2000–2003. The highest rates were in Wales, the North West and North East. The lowest rates were in the East of England, London and the South East. The regional pattern was less clear for women than for men, although rates were highest in the North West and lowest in the East of England.

Of the ten local authorities with the highest male suicide rates, six were in Wales, the North West and the North East. The highest rate for men was in Blackpool. At 39.1 deaths per 100 000 population this was over twice the average rate for England and Wales of 17.6. Some local authorities with the highest suicide rates for men were in regions with the lowest rates, such as Torbay and Brighton and Hove, in the South West and South East respectively.

The highest suicide rates for women in 2000–2003 were in the London Borough of Camden and Conwy in Wales, at 13.8 and 13.6 deaths per 100 000 population respectively, around two and a half times the England and Wales average of 5.5.

Source: Office for National Statistics, 'UK suicides reach 30-year low in 2003', www.statistics.gov.uk/pdfdir/suicide0305.pdf

You may have already developed some theories of your own as to why people commit suicide and why patterns of suicide exist. Suicide is, in many ways, the ultimate deviant act, as the act destroys the single most important element of society – the people in it. Yet suicide was relatively understudied by sociologists until the 1960s. This was because one major piece of work, by Durkheim in 1897, had so dominated sociological thought that it was believed there was little more to say. Yet,

when newer interpretations did come along, they carried with them some profound attacks on some of the pillars of theory and research upon which sociology had founded its very claim to be a social science.

So, in this topic, we study suicide not just because the subject matter is interesting for society, but also as a case study in how applying different theories and methods to the same problem can provide very different and contradictory explanations. In particular, we can see the deep divisions between the **positivists**, who believe in following the methods of the natural sciences wherever possible, and the **interpretive sociologists**, who prefer to explore the way society is constructed through people's interactions.

Suicide: a scientific approach

Durkheim's study of suicide

Durkheim (1897/1952) chose suicide as a subject of study, not just because it was interesting in itself, but in an attempt to prove that the (then) new subject of sociology could provide an explanation for an act that seemed to be the very opposite of what could be considered as 'social'. By proving that sociology had something useful to say in explaining suicide, Durkheim hoped to secure the status of sociology amongst the newly emerging sciences.

This attempt to locate sociology as a science, with its adherence to more social-scientific methods of research, is crucial in understanding how Durkheim tackled the issue. Durkheim's chosen method, now called '**multivariate analysis**', consisted of comparing the incidence of various social factors with the known incidence of a particular event – in this case suicide. He therefore studied the statistics of suicide that he collected from death certificates and other official documents and found that there were a number of clear patterns.

Over a period of 20 years, it could be seen that suicide rates were consistently different across countries and regions within countries, across different religions, and across the married and unmarried. These regularities immediately supported Durkheim's argument that there was a social explanation for suicide, for if suicide was an entirely individual matter, based on individual decisions, no such patterns should emerge.

To explain these patterns, Durkheim returned to the theme of shared values and **social cohesion**. According to him, people are naturally selfish and do not concern themselves with the problems faced by others, unless, that is, society can force them to do so. Society achieves this by finding ways of making people aware of their social bonds to others. The greater the level of **social integration**, the more harmonious a society. In fact, society achieves this form of social control by drawing people together on the basis of common values taught primarily through the family and reinforced by religion. (It is important to remember that religion was much more influential 120 years ago than it is today.)

Durkheim suggested that the individuals who feel most closely integrated into society are those with close family relationships. It follows that those without close family ties are the least bonded to society. We shall see the importance of this later.

Religion operated on a broader level, providing people with a moral underpinning for shared values. However, different religions do place varying amounts of stress on individual fulfilment. At one extreme, Protestant versions of Christianity give considerable importance to individual fulfilment, while religions such as Hinduism and Roman Catholicism stress the importance of the group, and consider the search for personal happiness relatively unimportant.

The outcome of the significance of the family and religion in different societies resulted in varying levels of social integration, with Protestant-based societies being less integrated and Catholic/Hindu ones being more integrated. Furthermore, individuals in society vary in their degree of social integration into society, depending upon their membership of family networks.

Durkheim's categorization of societies

It was Durkheim's hypothesis that suicide is directly related to the levels of social integration in a society or group within it. He placed societies into four categories, depending upon their levels of social integration.

Egoistic

In egoistic societies, individual rights, interests and welfare are heavily stressed and allegiance to the wider group is weak, with people being encouraged to look after themselves and those particularly close to them at the expense of the wider society. As a result, social bonds are weak and there is a low level of social integration. Egoistic societies are closely related to Protestantism, a strand of Christianity that stresses the

synopticlink **sociological theory and methods**

Taylor (1990) argues that Durkheim uses a 'realist' methodological approach in his study of suicide. Realists, like positivists, believe that scientific methods drawn from the natural sciences are appropriate for analysing society. Realists, such as Bhaskar (1998), argue that the physical sciences often have to use 'indicators' for things that are known to exist, but which are not directly observable in themselves, e.g. subatomic fields and 'quarks'. Instead, natural scientists must use some other indicator that is measurable and (theoretically) is an accurate representation of the unmeasurable concept. Sociologists have developed this idea in the study of society and argue that, although many things are not directly observable, they still exist; furthermore, there are indicators that can be used to measure them. The indicators that Durkheim uses are the official suicide rates.

responsibility of individuals to make their own decisions and to accept the consequences of doing so. Culturally, individual failure or unhappiness are viewed as acceptable grounds for people to take their own lives – **egoistic suicide**. This is typical of contemporary European and North American societies.

However, within this form of society, there are social institutions that counteract the wider egoistic values of society and provide a sense of belonging. These include the family and other forms of religion, such as Catholicism, that stress the importance of an individual's responsibility to the wider church. Durkheim also noted that in times of war or some other form of threat, societies draw together.

Durkheim concluded that there are likely to be relatively high rates of suicide in societies with low levels of social integration, but that, within those societies, people integrated in families or religious groups that provide greater levels of social integration are less likely to take their own lives. For example, married people are less likely to commit suicide than single people.

Altruistic

In altruistic societies, the welfare of individuals is viewed as far less important than that of the group. Individual choice or happiness is simply not a high priority. Durkheim therefore argued that there was insufficient motivation for members to commit suicide – with one exception. **Altruistic suicide** occurs when the individual is expected to commit suicide on behalf of the wider society – rather than in egoistic societies where the suicide takes place because of individual unhappiness. A contemporary example of altruistic suicide might be suicide bombers prepared to sacrifice themselves for their political or religious cause.

Anomic

Durkheim believed people are naturally selfish and will only look after their own interests unless society restricts their actions. According to Durkheim, societies develop cultural and social mechanisms that provide a clear framework of what is acceptable behaviour. However, if these restraints are weakened, for whatever reason, then some people may revert to their natural selfishness, whilst others may simply become bewildered. Social restraints on behaviour are most likely to weaken in periods of dramatic social change (for example, during an economic or political crisis). Durkheim, therefore, linked increases in suicide levels to periods of rapid social change – **anomic suicide**.

Fatalistic

This final form of suicide reflects the fact that in extremely oppressive societies, people may lose the will to live and prefer to die. Durkheim considered such **fatalistic suicide** a fairly uncommon occurrence, but it could be argued that it accounts for the very high levels of suicide in prisons, for example.

Internal criticisms of Durkheim

Durkheim's analysis of suicide was used for over 70 years as an excellent example of how to undertake positivistic sociological analysis. During that time, however, there was a degree of criticism of his approach from those who basically agreed with his approach. These criticisms are known as 'internal criticisms'.

- Durkheim's analysis depends upon the concept of social cohesion, for he argues that suicide rates vary with it. Yet, he never provides a clear, unambiguous definition of it, nor is there any obvious method of measuring it.
- He claimed that social integration was linked most closely to religion and family membership. But Durkheim provides no explanation of exactly how this can be verified or falsified. As we see in Unit 4, Topic 3, 'Sociology and science', a key element of science is the ability to carry out some form of research activity that can either prove or disprove a theory. Durkheim's methodology fails this test.
- Durkheim relied largely upon official statistics – yet official statistics are open to dispute – in particular, in Catholic-dominated countries and regions, suicide was regarded with great stigma and doctors were very reluctant to certify this as being the reason for death.

Interpretive criticisms of the scientific approach

However, a second group of writers have criticized Durkheim's analysis as fundamentally flawed. They argue that, rather than being an excellent example of sociological methodology, the research ought to be used as an example of why the use of traditional scientific methods in sociology is a mistake. These are known as 'interpretive criticisms'.

Interpretive approaches stress the way that society operates through people interacting on the basis of sharing meanings. Interpretive sociologists have paid great attention to exploring the way in that these meanings are constructed and how they influence individual behaviour. As we have pointed out elsewhere in the book, interpretive sociologists reject the idea that society can be studied with methods borrowed from the physical sciences – precisely the approach most favoured by Durkheim.

Two writers in this tradition, Douglas and Atkinson, have been particularly effective in their criticism of Durkheim's explanation.

Douglas – the meanings of suicide

Douglas (1967) argued that defining suicide simply by referring to the physical fact of killing oneself misses the central issue, which is that suicide has different meanings to those who take their own lives, and their motives vary too.

If this is the case, and we can only understand society by studying the meanings through which people understand and interpret the world, then suicide needs much greater exploration as to its meaning than Durkheim provided.

Douglas suggested that those who commit suicide may define their action in at least four ways:

- *Transforming the self* – A person commits suicide as a means of gaining release from the cares of the world.

- *Transforming oneself for others* – The suicide tells others how profound their feelings are on a particular issue.
- *Achieving fellow feeling* – The person is asking for help or sympathy; this includes 'suicide' attempts, in that the person hopes to be found.
- *Gaining revenge* – The person believes they have been forced into a position where they have to commit suicide.

So, there is no single act that can be termed 'suicide'. Since the meanings that individuals place upon their acts are so different, it is mistaken to categorize them as the same phenomenon. The only thing they have in common is death. The devastating conclusion, if this argument is accepted, is that Durkheim's statistical comparisons are worthless.

Atkinson – the social construction of suicide

Atkinson (1971) further developed this criticism that Durkheim failed to understand that categories such as 'suicide' are really socially constructed. In Britain, for example, before a death can be classified as suicide, a **coroner** must carry out an inquest and, on the basis of this, the death is classified as suicide or not. Atkinson argues that the official statistics therefore reflect coroners' decisions rather than any underlying 'reality'.

In order to make a decision, the coroner must piece together a series of 'clues' and then decide whether or not these point to suicide.

Atkinson suggests that the following clues are particularly important:

- *Suicide notes* – In about 30 per cent of suicides, a note is found, although more may have been written but the family have destroyed them because of the accusations contained in them.
- *Mode of death* – Some types of death are seen as more typical of suicide than others.
- *Location and circumstances of death* – Coroners believe that suicides are committed in places and circumstances where they will not be discovered and where the person is sure the outcome will be successful.
- *Life history and mental condition* – Coroners believe that suicide is often related to depression caused by significant events in the deceased's life. So coroners search for evidence of such events.

Integrating positivistic and interpretive approaches

The criticisms made by writers such as Douglas and Atkinson have generally been accepted by sociologists as a useful corrective to the more positivistic approach of Durkheim.

Taylor (1990), however, has suggested that both Durkheim and his critics have missed the significance of **parasuicides**, as in the majority of cases, people who attempt suicide do not die. Taylor points out that, when questioned, it seems most attempts at suicide are less a definite decision to finish with life and more of a gamble, in which people leave the

Singer Kurt Cobain, who committed suicide in 1994, leaving a long suicide note (see Webtask 3 on p. 309)

Jacobs (1967)
Suicide notes

Jacobs studied 112 suicide notes written by both adults and young people in Los Angeles who had committed suicide. The primary aim of the research had actually been to study suicide attempts by young people, but during the research process, Jacobs gained access to the notes of 'successful' suicides as well. On reading these, Jacobs was struck by just how sensible and rational the arguments put by the note-writers were. He then spent some time engaging in what he calls a phenomenological analysis of the notes – which involved thinking about the 'conscious deliberation that takes place before the individual is able to consider and execute the act of suicide'. Jacobs was able to categorize the notes into six clear groups, reflecting different reasons and intentions. For example, one group of people committed suicide because they were ill and no longer wanted to carry on; within these, there were people who asked for forgiveness for their act and those who did not. Jacobs' research does suggest a clarity and reasoned intent behind suicide – if one accepts that it is possible to put oneself (as he did) in the mind of the person committing suicide.

Jacobs, J. (1967) 'A phenomenological study of suicide notes', *Social Problems*, 15, pp. 60–72

1 Assess the extent to which the use of suicide notes provide a representative sample of those who take their own lives.

2 In what way does Jacobs' research challenge the idea that suicide is an irrational act?

outcome in the hands of fate. If they survive, then they were not meant to die; if they die, then that was what fate or God intended.

sociological theory and methods

The debate over suicide between different branches of sociology – in particular, between those who believe that statistics provide us with a reflection of reality and those sociologists who see statistics as simply a social construction – has implications for a wide range of sociological areas of study. These include such things as:

- religious belief and attendance
- the extent of aid to the developing nations

- voting patterns
- the existence of social class
- the extent of wealth and poverty.

Beyond this, the debate also reflects profoundly on theory and method. In theory, it illustrates the contribution of social-action theories to our understanding of everyday life; in methods, it is a perfect example of positivism versus constructionism as approaches to researching the social world.

Taylor suggests that parasuicide allows us to widen the discussion of suicide into one of 'risk-taking'. Developing the analysis of Durkheim further, he suggests that successful parasuicides could be categorized into 'ordeal' suicides, which can be related to a profound sense of anomie, and the more purposive suicides, similar to Durkheim's fatalism. Taylor also supports Durkheim's belief that suicide is more likely in individuals too detached from others in society (egoistic suicides) and those overattached (altruistic suicide).

The point of Taylor's argument is that it is possible to pull together the wider social factors that Durkheim emphasized with the sense of meaning that Douglas stressed. The two approaches are not necessarily exclusive. Indeed, much of contemporary sociology has been the search for ways of integrating the two traditions.

Check your understanding

1 **What do we mean by 'positivism'?**

2 **What do we mean by 'phenomenological' or 'subjectivist' approaches?**

3 **What approach to the study of suicide was used by Durkheim?**

4 **How is social integration linked to suicide?**

5 **Explain the term 'anomic suicide'.**

6 **Give any one 'internal criticism' of Durkheim's analysis of suicide.**

7 **Why is Douglas' criticism significant?**

8 **Give two examples of how coroners decide whether a death is suicide or not.**

9 **What does Taylor mean by 'parasuicide'? Why is the term important?**

focusonresearch

Suicide: case studies

Case 1

A man ingested barbiturates and went to sleep in his car, which was parked outside his estranged wife's house. A note he had written to her was pinned on his chest, indicating his expectation that she would notice him when she returned from her date with another man. This possibility of being rescued, however, was obliterated by a dense fog that descended around midnight.

Case 2

A woman had become depressed after her marriage of 15 years broke up and was being prescribed anti-depressants. One morning at work she began swallowing the tablets one by one. A colleague at work noticed what she was doing and reported it to a senior. The company doctor was called in and he summoned an ambulance. She was unconscious on arrival at hospital but survived, after intensive medical treatment. She later said that she was unsure about her intentions at the time she was taking the tablets.

1 Read the two cases above. What term is used by Taylor to describe this form of behaviour?

2 How do the cases illustrate the problem of treating official suicide statistics as 'social facts'?

KEY TERMS

Altruistic suicide – Durkheim's term for suicide in societies where people see their own happiness as unimportant.

Anomic suicide – Durkheim's term for suicide in societies where rapid change is occurring (see Unit 1, p. 4 for more discussion of 'anomie').

Coroners – officials who decide on cause of death.

Egoistic suicide – Durkheim's term for suicide in societies where people regard their individual happiness as very important.

Fatalistic suicide – Durkheim's term for suicide in extreme, usually oppressive, situations where people lose the will to live.

Interpretive sociologists – those whose approach to sociology stresses the need to study the way that society is based on socially constructed meanings.

Multivariate analysis – a method of gathering statistics from different societies and comparing the patterns to help explain social differences between the societies.

Parasuicide – a term used by Taylor for suicide attempts where the person is not certain whether they want to die or not, and 'gambles' with their life.

Positivism – belief that sociology should use the same approaches to research as the natural sciences such as physics.

Social cohesion – the extent to which a society is held together by shared culture and values.

Social integration – the extent to which people feel they 'belong' to a society or social group.

web.tasks

1 Go to the government's statistics site at www.statistics.gov.uk and search for 'suicide rates'. What patterns can you find? Which areas have the highest and lowest suicide rates? Suggest reasons for differences.

2 Search the worldwide web for suicide statistics (The National Library for Electronic Health is useful starting point). What statistics can you find? What is their source? What possible explanations are there for the patterns shown? How might they be interpreted by positivists and interpretive sociologists?

3 Kurt Cobain, lead singer and guitarist with the American rock band Nirvana, committed suicide in April 1994. Using any search engine, find his suicide note. Does the note give any indications of his motives? Try to analyse it using Durkheim's categories of suicide. How well do they work?

exploring suicide

Item A

Durkheim established correlations between suicides and other sets of social facts. He found that suicide rates were higher in predominantly Protestant countries than in Catholic ones. Jews had a low suicide rate, lower even than Roman Catholics.

Generally, married people were less prone to suicide than those who were single, although married women who remained childless for a number of years ended up with a high suicide rate. Durkheim also found that a low suicide rate was associated with political upheaval. War also reduced the suicide rate.

Adapted from Haralambos, M. and Holborn, M. (2004) *Sociology: Themes and Perspectives* (6th edn), London: Collins Education

(a) Identify and briefly explain **two** reasons why the suicide rates described in **Item A** might not be accurate. (8 marks)

This part of the question includes assessment of your understanding of the connections between Crime and Deviance and sociological methods.

(b) Examine some of the reasons why there might be 'correlations between suicides and other sets of social facts' (**Item A**). In your answer make use of material from **one or more** of the following areas: power and politics; religion; world sociology. (12 marks)

This part of the question includes assessment of your understanding of the connections between Crime and Deviance and other substantive topics you have studied.

(c) Assess the usefulness of interpretive approaches to the study of suicide. (40 marks)

This part of the question includes assessment of your understanding of the connections between Crime and Deviance and sociological theory.

SOCIOLOGISTS POINT OUT THAT STRATIFICATION AND DIFFERENTIATION lie at the heart of all our social experiences. This is the reason why this unit is a synoptic unit because our experience of social life, whether it be in the family, the educational system or at work, is largely shaped by factors such as our socioeconomic status, our gender, our age and our ethnicity. Our chances of going to university, getting a good job, owning our own home and enjoying a long life are all linked to our place in society. In other words, social inequality is a fact of life in modern capitalist societies.

Topic 1 explores the different ways in which different societies grade and rank their citizens, whether that is through religion and patriarchy (as in many developing countries) or according to occupation (as in the UK). This topic examines how occupation is used to produce social categories that we call 'social classes'.

Topic 2 examines sociological explanations for why most societies have stratification systems. In particular, it examines explanations for social-class systems.

Topic 3 explores the effect of social class upon our life-chances. For example, examination of health statistics allows us to say fairly confidently that if you come from an unskilled manual background in terms of your father's occupation, that you are less likely to live beyond 65 years compared with the child of a professional person. Topic 3, therefore, examines a range of outcomes that differ according to social class.

Most of us like to believe that the society we live in fairly rewards ability and intelligence. In other words, we believe that the UK is a meritocracy and that qualifications and hard work can propel us into jobs that are a distinct social improvement from those done by our parents. Topic 4 explores whether such social mobility is fact or fantasy.

Social commentators are very fond of announcing the death or decline of social class. They suggest that it no longer plays a significant role in our lives and that people today rarely see social class as an important facet of their identity. Topic 5 looks closely at the organization and social character of those broad groupings that we call social classes in order to ascertain the validity of these arguments.

It has long been argued by feminist sociologists that gender is just as important as social class in shaping division, inequality and identity. Topic 6 examines the extent of gender influence in areas such as education, work and health, and assesses how influential patriarchy actually is.

There has been some concern in recent years that, despite years of antidiscrimination legislation, racism is still very present in modern UK society. In a number of social fields, particularly education and employment, we can see that some ethnic-minority groups are experiencing inequality compared with the White population. Topic 7 investigates both the extent of, and explanations for, these differences in ethnic opportunity and outcome.

The young and the elderly have a great deal in common, although the former often do not recognize this! What unites their experience of the social world is that both groups have little status and experience prejudice and discrimination. Topic 8 investigates the concept of age divisions in order to identify their impact on teenagers and pensioners alike.

UNIT **6**

Stratification and differentiation

What is social stratification?

gettingyouthinking

Examine the photo on the right.

1 All these children enjoy equal access to education, but does this mean that they will enjoy similar lifestyles when adults?

2 What social factors may create barriers for them?

3 Look at the photographs below. What ways of measuring class do they indicate?

4 How do the photographs below relate to the criteria listed in the table?

5 Which of the criteria suggested in the table would you use to judge a person's social class and why?

When a random group of respondents were asked to identify the criteria they would use to assess a person's class, the results were as shown in the table on the right.

Adapted from Hadford, G. and Skipworth, M. (1994) *Class*, London: Bloomsbury, p.19

	%		%
Neighbourhood	36	How they talk	17
Job	31	What they wear	15
Pay	29	Parental background	13
Educational background	27	Use of leisure time	11
Wealth (assets such as property and material goods)	22	Political party support	11

It is generally believed that modern societies provide their citizens with the opportunities to better themselves. We all enjoy access to education and the chance to obtain formal qualifications; we all have access to a job market that offers decent incomes and promotion opportunities; we all enjoy the possibility of acquiring wealth. Or do we? The exercise above suggests that these opportunities may not exist for all social groups, or if they do, that some social groups have greater or easier access to these opportunities. In other words, inequalities between social groups are a fact of life in modern societies. The job of sociologists working in the field of stratification is to identify which social groups enjoy unfettered access to economic and social opportunities, and which are denied them, and why.

Differentiation and stratification

All societies **differentiate** between social groups – men and women, the young and the old, the working class and the middle class, and ethnic groups such as Whites, Asians and African-Caribbeans are often perceived to be socially different in some way. When these differences lead to greater status, power or privilege for some over others, the result is **social stratification**. This term – borrowed from geology – means the layering of society into strata, from which a hierarchy emerges reflecting different ranks in terms of social influence and advantage. The degree to which a society has a fixed hierarchy is determined by the degree of opportunity its members have to change their social position.

The sociological term for a person's social importance is **social status**. Status can be gained in two ways:

- **Ascribed status** is given at birth either through family (e.g. the Queen was 'born to rule') or through physical, religious or cultural factors (e.g. in some societies, women and girls are regarded as second-class citizens simply because they are female).
- **Achieved status** is the result of factors such as hard work, educational success, marriage, special talent or sheer good fortune (e.g. winning the lottery).

Societies that allow for and reward achievement are called **open societies**, whereas those that ascribe social position are known as **closed societies**. Politicians tend to see the degree of openness in society as a measure of the freedoms they have helped to create, but they often overemphasize the extent to which society is open. Modern Britain, for example, may have free education for all up to the age of 18 or 19, but, as we shall see in Topic 3, those who are rich enough to attend a top public school have significant advantages in life.

In reality, few societies are totally open or closed and each could be placed somewhere along a continuum (see Fig. 6.1). Traditional societies tend to be more closed because of the greater influence of religion and tradition, which means that people can play a limited range of roles and these tend to be fixed at birth. Modern societies, which seem more fluid and open, may actually experience significant levels of closure, in that some groups face social barriers and obstacles when attempting to improve themselves.

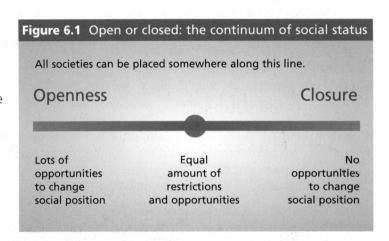

Figure 6.1 Open or closed: the continuum of social status

All societies can be placed somewhere along this line.

Openness — Closure

| Lots of opportunities to change social position | Equal amount of restrictions and opportunities | No opportunities to change social position |

Table 6.1 Examples of traditional societies based on ascribed status

	The caste system	The feudal estate system
Place and time	Although officially banned in India today, the Hindu **caste system** of stratification is still enormously influential.	The **feudal estate system** was found in medieval Europe.
Structure	There are four basic castes or layers, ranging from the Brahmins (religious leaders and nobles) at the top, to the Sudras (servants and unskilled manual workers) at the bottom. 'Untouchables' exist below the caste system and are responsible for the least desirable jobs, such as sewage collection.	The king owned all the land and, in return for an oath of loyalty and military support, he would allocate the land to barons who, in turn, would apportion parts of it to knights. The majority (95%) were peasants or serfs who had to work the knight's land and, in return, were offered protection and allowed to rent land.
Restrictions	People are born into castes and cannot move out of them during the course of their lives. There are strong religious controls over the behaviour of caste members – for example, you cannot marry a member of another caste, nor can you do certain jobs because these are assigned exclusively to certain castes.	Feudal societies, too, were mainly closed societies – people's positions were largely ascribed and it was rare for people to move up. Marriage between groups was rarely allowed and feudal barons even restricted the geographical movement of the peasants.
Possibility of social mobility	The system is based upon religious purity – the only way people can be promoted to a higher caste is by living a pure life and hoping that they will be reincarnated (reborn) as a member of a higher caste.	On rare occasions, exceptional acts of bravery could result in a gift of land.

Social class

Social class is the stratification system found in modern industrial societies such as Britain. **Social classes** are groups of people who share a similar economic position in terms of occupation, income and ownership of wealth. They are also likely to have similar levels of education, status and power. Class systems are different from previous systems in the following ways:

- They are not based on religion, law or race, but on economic factors such as occupation and wealth.
- There is no clear distinction between classes – it is difficult to say where the working class finishes and the middle class begins, for example.
- All members of society have equal rights irrespective of their social position.
- There are no legal restrictions on marriage between the classes.
- Social-class societies are open societies – you can move up or down the class structure through jobs, the acquisition of wealth or marriage.
- Such systems are usually **meritocratic** – that is, people are not born into ascribed roles. Individuals are encouraged to better themselves through achievement at school and in their jobs, by working hard and gaining promotion.

Just how meritocratic social-class societies really are, and the extent to which factors such as race, gender and age can affect access to opportunity, will be a key focus of this unit.

Measuring social class

Question 3 in the 'Getting you thinking' on p. 312 should have shown that measuring social class is not an easy exercise. People define social class in different ways and some even deny its existence altogether.

Why is there a need to measure class?

Various groups such as sociologists, advertisers and government agencies have vested interests in **operationalizing** the concept of social class in a consistent way for a number of reasons:

- Sociologists want to address class differences in all areas of social life in order to identify reasons why inequalities come about.
- Advertisers want to target particular social groups in order to maximize sales.
- Governments need to formulate social policies in order to address inequalities.

Each interest group has tended to operationalize the concept of social class in a different way. For example, governments and sociologists tend to approach social class as an objective reality that results in patterns of behaviour and inequality in areas such as health, life expectancy and education. Advertisers are more interested in how people subjectively interpret their class position, because this may affect their consumption patterns and their leisure pursuits.

Occupation as an indicator of social class

The single most objective measurable factor that corresponds best with the characteristics most often associated with class is occupation. It is something that the majority of the population has in common. It also governs other aspects of their life, such as income, housing and level of education. Occupation, therefore:

- governs a significant proportion of a person's life
- is a good indicator of income and wealth, and consequently lifestyle
- is a good indicator of similar skill and knowledge levels
- is an important influence on a person's sense of identity.

However, this still leaves out those who do not work, such as the extremely rich and the long-term unemployed. Objective measures using occupation have, however, enabled social class to be measured statistically. However, getting such measures right has proved to be more of a problem and the various occupational scales that have been constructed have all been criticized for failing to present a true picture of the class structure.

Scales of social class

The Registrar General's scale

This occupational scale was used by the government from 1911 until 2000 and involved the ranking of thousands of jobs into six classes based on the occupational skill of the head of household:

- Class I: Professional, e.g. accountants, doctors
- Class II: Lower managerial, professional and technical, e.g. teachers
- Class IIINM: Skilled non-manual, e.g. office workers
- Class IIIM: Skilled manual, e.g. electricians, plumbers
- Class IV: Semi-skilled manual, e.g. agricultural workers
- Class V: Unskilled manual, e.g. labourers, refuse collectors.

This scheme differentiated between middle-class occupations (non-manual jobs were allocated to classes I to IIINM) and working-class occupations (manual jobs were allocated to classes IIIM to V). The Registrar General's scheme has underpinned many important social surveys, particularly those focusing on class differences in educational achievement and life expectancy.

Criticisms of the Registrar General's scale

The Registrar General's scale was the main way in which class was measured in official statistics. Most sociological research conducted between 1960 and 2000 uses this classification system when differentiating between different classes. However, it does have disadvantages:

- Assessments of jobs were made by the Registrar General's own staff – Hence, there was a bias towards seeing non-manual occupations as having a higher status than manual occupations. However, as we shall see in later in this unit, Marxists argue that the working conditions of some white-collar workers, particular those found in workplaces such as call-centres, is remarkably similar to that of manual workers employed in factories.

- It failed to recognize those people who do not work – The unemployed were classified according to their last job. However, the increasing number of never-employed unemployed undermined this system.
- Feminists criticized the scale as sexist – The class of everyone in a household was defined by the job of the male head of household. Women were assigned to the class of their husbands (or their fathers, if unmarried).
- It glossed over the fact that workers allocated to the same class often had widely varying access to resources such as pay and promotion.
- It failed to distinguish between the employed and self-employed – This distinction is important because evidence shows that these groups do not share similar experiences. For example the **black economy** is much more accessible to the self-employed – they can avoid paying tax and VAT by working at a cheaper rate 'for cash', which cannot be traced through their accounts, or by not fully declaring all the work they do.

The Hope-Goldthorpe scale

Sociologists were often reluctant to use government-inspired scales as they lacked sufficient sociological emphasis. In order to study **social mobility** (see Topic 5), John Goldthorpe created a more sociologically relevant scale that has proved very popular with social researchers. Goldthorpe recognized the growth of middle-class occupations – and especially the self-employed – and based his classification on the concept of **market position**, i.e. income and economic **life-chances**, such as promotion prospects, sick pay and control of hours worked. He also took account of **work** or **employment relations**, i.e. whether people are employed or self-employed, and whether they are able to exercise authority over others. The Hope-Goldthorpe scale also acknowledged that both manual and non-manual groups may share similar experiences of work and, for this reason, Goldthorpe grouped some of these together in an **intermediate class**. Instead of the basic non-manual/manual divide used by the Registrar General's scale, Goldthorpe introduced the idea of three main social

divisions into which groups sharing similar market position and work relations could be placed: he referred to these as the **service class**, the intermediate class and the working class.

Goldthorpe's scale was first used in studies conducted in 1972, published in 1980. The scale more accurately reflected the nature of the British class system, but it was still based on the male head of household. He defended this position by claiming that, in most cases, the male worker still determines the market situation and lifestyle of a couple, i.e. the male is still the main breadwinner. However, many feminists remained unconvinced by this argument. They argued that scales based on the idea of a male 'head of household':

- overlook the significance of dual-career families, where the joint income of both partners can give the family an income and lifestyle of a higher class
- ignore situations where women are in a higher-grade occupation than their husbands
- overlook the significance of the increasing number of single working women and single working parents, who are classified according to the occupation of their ex-partners or fathers.

A feminist alternative: the Surrey Occupational Class Schema

This scale was developed by the feminist sociologists Arber, Dale and Gilbert (1986) in an attempt to overcome what they saw as the patriarchal bias inherent in the Hope-Goldthorpe scale. In this scheme, women are classified on the basis of their own occupations, whether they are married or not. The gendered nature of work in contemporary society, especially the growing service sector of the economy, is also taken into account. This is most evident in class 6 which is divided into 6a (sales and personal services – female dominated) and 6b (skilled manual – overwhelmingly male).

However, the inclusion of women in such occupational classifications does present some difficulties because women's relationship to employment is generally more varied than that of men. More women work part time or occupy jobs for short periods because of pregnancy and childcare. It is, therefore, difficult to know whether the class assigned provides a meaningful insight into their life experience as a whole or whether it merely reflects a short-term or temporary experience that has little impact on lifestyle and life-chances.

Table 6.2 The Hope-Goldthorpe Scale		
Service class	**Intermediate class**	**Working class**
1 Higher professionals High-grade administrators; managers of large companies and large proprietors	3 Routine non-manual (clerical and sales)	6 Skilled manual workers
	4 Small proprietors and self-employed artisans (craftspersons)	7 Semi-skilled and unskilled manual workers
2 Lower professionals Higher-grade technicians; supervisors of non-manual workers; administrators; small-business managers	5 Lower-grade technicians and supervisors of manual workers	Source: Goldthorpe, J.H. (1980) *Social Mobility and Class Structure*, Oxford: Clarendon Press

We can see from this topic that defining and measuring social class is a major problem for sociologists. This is because social class is an abstract social concept that needs to be operationalized. In other words, indicators of what identifies the social class of individuals must be identified. Most sociologists and civil servants faced with this problem have tended to use occupation and level of educational achievement as the indicator, although in their study of educational inequality, Boyland (cited in Gold 2003) also chose to use as his indicators receipt of free school meals alongside occupation. However, not all sociologists agree with these indicators. Goldthorpe actually acknowledges that a person's job is made up of a complex interplay of factors, while the NS-SEC (see below) focuses on a range of indicators related to work, such as authority over others, pay, autonomy over working practices and promotion potential. Finally, the debate about how to measure social class is complicated by the fact that people's subjective awareness of their class position and identity can differ from objective definitions. However, Pawson (1989) notes that, while people may be able to place themselves within class categories, these may not mean a great deal to them. Evans (1992) has demonstrated that people's attitudes towards inequality, for example, often have very little to do with their awareness of their class position.

Table 6.3 The Surrey Occupational Class Schema

1	Higher professional
2	Employers and managers
3	Lower professional
4	Secretarial and clerical
5	Supervisors, self-employed manual
6a	Sales and personal services
6b	Skilled manual
7	Semi-skilled
8	Unskilled

Source: Arber *et al.* (1986)

A new scale for the 21st century: the National Statistics Socio-Economic Classification (NS-SEC)

The NS-SEC scale, which essentially is a variation on the Hope-Goldthorpe scale, fully replaced the Registrar General's scale for government research and statistics and was used for the first time to classify data from the 2001 census (see Table 6.4).

Like the Hope-Goldthorpe scale, the NS-SEC is based on:

- **employment relations** – whether people are employers, self-employed, or employed and whether they exercise authority over others
- **market conditions** – salary scales, promotion prospects, sick pay, how much control people have over the hours they work, and so on.

Table 6.4 The National Statistics Socio-Economic Classification (NS-SEC)

	Occupational classification	% of working population	Examples
1	Higher managerial and professional	11.0	Company directors, senior civil servants, doctors, barristers, clergy, architects
2	Lower managerial and professional	23.5	Nurses, journalists, teachers, police officers, musicians
3	Intermediate	14.0	Secretaries, clerks, computer operators, driving instructors
4	Small employers and self-accountable workers	9.9	Taxi drivers, window cleaners, publicans, decorators
5	Lower supervisory, craft and related	9.8	Train drivers, plumbers, printers, TV engineers
6	Semi-routine	18.6	Traffic wardens, shop assistants, hairdressers, call-centre workers
7	Routine	12.7	Cleaners, couriers, road sweepers, labourers
8	Long-term unemployed or the never-worked		

Source: Rose, D. and Pevalin, D. (with K. O'Reilly) (2001) *The National Statistics Socio-economic Classification: Genesis and Overview*, London: ONS

Strengths of the NS-SEC

- It no longer divides workers exclusively along manual and non-manual lines. Some categories contain both manual and non-manual workers.
- The most significant difference between the Hope-Goldthorpe scale and the NS-SEC is the creation of Class 8, i.e. the long-term unemployed and never-employed unemployed. Some sociologists, most notably from New Right positions, have described this group of unemployed as an 'underclass'.
- Goldthorpe has finally acknowledged the feminist arguments and women are now recognized as a distinct group of wage-earners. They are no longer categorized according to the occupation of their husbands or fathers.

Potential weaknesses of the NS-SEC

- The scale is still based primarily on the objective criteria of occupation. This may differ from what people understand by the term 'social class' and their subjective interpretation of their own class position.
- Those who do not have to work because of access to great wealth are still not included.
- Some argue that the scale still obscures important differences in status and earning power, e.g. headteachers are in the same category as classroom teachers.
- Some critics have suggested that ethnicity and gender may be more important in bringing about social divisions and shaping identity.

Subjective measurements of social class

Social surveys suggest there is often a discrepancy between how objective measurements of social class classify jobs and how people who actually occupy those jobs interpret their social status or class position. For example, many teachers like to describe themselves as working-class despite their objective middle-class status. This is because many teachers have experienced upward mobility through educational qualifications from working-class origins and feel that their perspective on the world is still shaped by working-class values and experience. This subjective awareness of class position often conflicts with official objective interpretations.

More important, it is the subjective interpretation of class position that is responsible for the sharp boundary lines that exist between the social classes in the UK. In other words, there is some evidence (which will be explored in more detail in later sections) that those people who interpret themselves as 'working-class', 'middle-class' and 'upper-class' have very clear ideas about what characteristics people who 'belong' to their class should have. Moreover, they tend to have very strong views about the characteristics of other social classes. These subjective interpretations may have little or nothing in common with official and objective attempts to construct broad socioeconomic classifications

Savage, Bagnall & Longhurst (2001)
Class identities

Mike Savage and his colleagues carried out in-depth interviews with 178 people living in four sites in and around Manchester. They identified three groups of people in terms of subjective class identity:

- First, there was a small minority of their sample who strongly identified themselves as belonging to a specific class. These were often graduates who had the cultural confidence to express their class position in an articulate fashion.
- The second group was also well educated, but did not like to identify with a particular class position. Rather, this group tended either to reject the notion of social class, because they saw themselves as individuals rather than a product of their social-class background, or they preferred to debate the nature of social class rather than acknowledge their belonging to any particular group. Some felt happier differentiating themselves from other social classes rather than focusing on their own membership of a particular social class.
- The third group, which made up the majority of the respondents, actually identified with a social class, but did so in an ambivalent, defensive and uncommitted way. Some of this group prefaced their 'belonging' with remarks such as 'I suppose I'm …' or 'probably, I'm …'.

Savage and colleagues concluded that identification with the concepts of 'working-class' and 'middle-class' for this part of their sample was based on a simple desire to be seen as normal and ordinary, rather than any burning desire to be flagwavers for their class. They conclude that, in general, the notion of class identity was 'relatively muted'.

Savage, M., Bagnall, G. and Longhurst, B. (2001) 'Ordinary, ambivalent and defensive class identities in the North West of England', *Sociology*, 35(4),

1 Suggest reasons why Savage's research team used in-depth interviews in this study.

2 Explain how the findings of Savage and colleagues led them to conclude that class identity is 'relatively muted' (i.e. unclear, muffled).

based on employment. As Reay (1998, quoted in Bottero 2005) has noted:

>> *Class is a complicated mixture of the* **material**, *the* **discursive**, *psychological predispositions and sociological dispositions that quantitative work on class location and class identity cannot hope to capture … Now what is required are British-based ethnographic examinations of how class is 'lived' in gendered and raced ways to complement the macro versions that have monopolized our ways of envisaging social class for far too long.* >>
(p. 83)

Studies of subjective class identities confirm this observation. Marshall *et al.* (1988) found that 53 per cent of their sample saw themselves as 'working-class' despite the fact that the majority of their sample were in white-collar, non-manual jobs. However, Savage *et al.* (2001) are not convinced that identification with such class categories has any real meaning beyond the need to feel normal and ordinary. They argue that people identify with the term 'middle-class' because they see it as the least loaded of the terms offered to them by sociologists. In fact, Savage and colleagues argue that, by saying they are middle-class, people are actually saying they are typical, ordinary people, who are neither particularly well off nor particularly badly off. Bradley (1999) notes, too, that when people identify themselves as working-class, this does not involve a strong sense of group or collective loyalty or attachment to traditional working-class institutions such as trade unions. Again, it is more likely to indicate a claim to be an ordinary and typical working person. In other words, subjective interpretations of social class may have very little to do with the characteristics allocated to social class by objective official classifications.

Sociology A2 for AQA

Check your understanding

1. What is the difference between social differentiation and social stratification?

2. Why might those at the bottom of the caste system accept their lot?

3. What determined one's position in the hierarchy in the feudal estate system?

4. Why are most modern societies more open than most traditional societies?

5. Why is occupation considered to be the most defining characteristic for the measurement of social class?

6. What problems are created by using occupation as the key indicator of social class?

7. What were the strengths and weaknesses of each of the scales used before 2000?

8. How does the NS-SEC scale address the weaknesses of the other scales?

9. How might the NS-SEC scale still be said to be lacking?

research ideas

1. Imagine you are conducting sociological research on social class at a horse-racing track or a cricket match, using observation only – you are not allowed to distribute questionnaires or conduct interviews. What sorts of things might you listen or look out for that might give you clues as to a person's social class?

2. Undertake a piece of research using a structured interview to measure the class distribution of students on various school or college post-16 courses. Pilot it with a random sample of ten students across the institution. After each interview write down any issues that may affect the validity, representativeness or reliability of the evidence gathered. For example:

   - Did respondents understand the questions, answer truthfully or exaggerate aspects of lifestyle/income?
   - Did they find the questions too intrusive or personal? Were they confused by the terminology you used?
   - Identify the main problems you encountered in trying to operationalize social class.
   - Did you note any differences between people's subjective interpretations of their social class position and how the NS-SEC ranks them?
   - What, if any, conclusions can you draw from your findings?

web.tasks

1. Search the worldwide web to find out about the caste system in India. How did it work and how influential is it today? Does it have influence in the UK?

2. Use a careers service on the worldwide web such as www.prospects.ac.uk to compare occupations in different social classes. Find out about pay, working conditions and the skills and qualifications needed. Can these explain differences in their position on social-class scales?

Achieved status – the degree of social honour and prestige accorded to a person or group because of their achievements or other merits.

Ascribed status – the degree of social honour and prestige accorded a person or group because of their origin or inherited characteristics.

Black economy – illegal ways of increasing income.

Caste system – Hindu system of stratification, now officially banned in India but still influential.

Closed societies – societies with no social mobility or movement within or across each stratum.

Differentiation – perceived social differences between people, e.g. on lines of gender, age or race.

Discursive – up for discussion or debate.

Employment relations – see 'Work relations' below.

Feudal estate system – stratification system of medieval Europe.

Intermediate class – according to Goldthorpe, a lower grouping of the middle class containing those with the poorer work and market situations than the service class, e.g. clerical workers, small proprietors and lower-grade technicians.

Life-chances – opportunities for achieving things that provide a high quality of life, such as good housing, health and education.

Market position or conditions – income and economic life-chances, such as promotion prospects, sick pay, and control over hours worked and how work is done.

Material – physical, often economic, things such as money and consumer goods.

Meritocratic – rewarding hard work or talent, rather than inherited wealth or position.

Open societies – societies with a high degree of social mobility, where status is usually allocated on the basis of achievement and merit.

Operationalize – define something in such a way that it can be measured.

Service class – according to Goldthorpe, those with the highest work and market situations: the upper middle class, e.g. large proprietors as well as administrators, managers and professionals who service the economy.

Social class – hierarchically arranged groups in modern industrial societies based on similarities in status, wealth, income and occupation.

Social mobility – the movement of individuals up or down the social scale.

Social status – degree of social honour, prestige and importance accorded to a person or group.

Social stratification – the hierarchical layering of a society into distinct groups with different levels of wealth, status and power.

Work relations – whether people are employed or self-employed, and are able to exercise authority over others.

exploring what is social stratification?

Item A

Both the Registrar-General's and Goldthorpe's class schemes have been useful in highlighting class-based inequalities, such as those related to health and education, as well as reflecting class-based dimensions in voting patterns, political outlooks and general social attitudes. However, such schemes suffer from several significant limitations.

Occupational class schemes are difficult to apply to the economically inactive, such as the unemployed, students, pensioners and children. Such schemes are also unable to reflect the importance of property ownership and wealth to social class. Occupational titles alone are not sufficient indicators of a person's wealth and overall assets. The rapid economic transformations occurring in industrial societies have made the measurement of class even more problematic. New categories of occupations are emerging; there has been a general shift away from factory production towards service and knowledge work, and an enormous number of women have entered the workforce in recent decades. Occupational class schemes are not necessarily well suited to capturing the dynamic processes of class formation, mobility and change that are provoked by such social transformations.

Adapted from Giddens, A. (2001) *Sociology*, Cambridge: *Polity Press*, pp. 288–90

(a) Identify and briefly explain **two** 'class-based inequalities' that the Registrar-General's and Goldthorpe's class schemes might have highlighted (**Item A**). In your answer use material from one or more of the following areas: families and households; health; mass media; education; wealth, poverty and welfare; work and leisure. (8 marks)

This part of the question includes assessment of your understanding of the connections between Stratification and Differentiation and other substantive topic(s) you have studied.

(b) Using material from **Item A** and elsewhere, examine some of the problems involved in operationalizing the idea of social class. (12 marks)

This part of the question includes assessment of your understanding of the connections between Stratification and Differentiation and sociological methods.

(c) 'Scales of social class employed by sociologists in the last 30 years reflect patriarchal assumptions'. Assess the evidence for and against this view. (40 marks)

This part of the question includes assessment of the connections between Stratification and Differentiation and sociological theory.

Max Weber

Another classical theorist, Max Weber (1864–1920), disagreed with Marx's view on the inevitability of class conflict. Weber also rejected the Marxist emphasis on the economic dimension as the sole determinant of inequality. Weber (1947) saw 'class' (economic relationships) and 'status' (perceived social standing) as two separate but related sources of power that have overlapping effects on people's life-chances. He also recognized what he called '**party**' as a further dimension. By this, he meant the political influence or power an individual might exercise through membership of pressure groups, trade unions or other organized interest groups. However, he did see class as the most important of these three interlinking factors.

Like Marx, Weber saw classes as economic categories organized around property ownership, but argued that the concept should be extended to include 'occupational skill' because this created differences in life-chances (income, opportunities, lifestyles and general prospects) among those groups that did not own the means of production, namely the middle class and the working class. In other words, if we examine these two social classes, we will find status differences within them. For example, professionals are regarded more highly than white-collar workers, whilst skilled manual workers are regarded more highly than unskilled workers or the long-term unemployed. These differences in status lead directly to differences in life-chances for these groups.

The significance of status in inequality

People who occupy high occupational roles generally have high social status, but status can also derive from other sources of power such as gender, race and religion. Weber noted that status was also linked to consumption styles (how people spend their money). For example, some people derive status from conspicuous consumption – e.g. from being seen to buy expensive designer products. This idea has been taken further by postmodernists, who suggest that in the 21st century, consumption and style rather than social class will inform people's identity.

Weber defined social classes as clusters of occupations with similar life-chances and patterns of mobility (people's opportunities to move up or down the occupational ladder). On this basis, he identified four distinct social classes:

1   those privileged through property or education
2   the petty-bourgeoisie (the self-employed, managers)
3   white-collar workers and technicians (the lower middle class)
4   manual workers (the working class).

Weber's ideas have influenced the way in which social class is operationalized by sociologists such as Goldthorpe (1980a) and by the government through the recent NS-SEC scale – see Topic 1. The notion of market situation and work relations is based on the notion that status differences (and therefore, life-chances) exist between particular occupational groups.

Weber was sceptical about the possibility of the working class banding together for revolutionary purposes – i.e. becoming class conscious – because differences in statuses would always undermine the notion of common cause. Social classes were too internally differentiated, and this destabilized the idea of group identity and common action.

The concept of 'status groups' rather than social classes is central to Weber's theory of stratification. Weber noted that people make positive and negative judgements about other people's standing and esteem, and these can affect a person's life-chances. These judgements tend to focus on qualities which are shared by groups. Therefore, we might make judgements about people's education ('they are brilliant' or 'thick'; 'they went to university'), their religion ('they are extremists' or 'they treat women negatively'), their age ('they cannot cope with the responsibility'), their ethnicity ('they are all criminals'), their gender ('they are too emotional') and even their bodies ('they are too thin, too fat, ugly, beautiful'). Status groups, then, are those who share the same status position, as well as a common awareness of how they differ from other status groups. In other words, their identity is bound up with their exclusiveness as a group, and this will shape their lifestyle in terms of how they interact with others – for instance, they may only socialize with people like themselves.

Evaluation of Weber

Class, status and wealth

Marxists argue that Weber neglected the basic split between capitalists and workers, and argue that class and status are strongly linked – after all, the capitalist class has wealth, high status and political power. Weber recognized that these overlap, but suggested that a person can have wealth but little status – like a lottery winner, perhaps – or, conversely, high status but little wealth – such as a church minister. He suggested that it is very rare that high-status groups allow wealth alone to be sufficient grounds for entry into their status group. He noted that such groups may exclude wealthy individuals because they lack the 'right' breeding, schooling, manners, culture, etc. This practice of 'social closure' will be explored in more depth in later topics. Conversely, someone may be accepted as having high status by the wealthy, despite being relatively poor in comparison, such as the aristocrat who has fallen on hard times. Weber rightly points out that high status and political power can sometimes be achieved without great economic resources.

Party

Party or power plays a role in this too. Weber saw this third type of inequality as deriving from membership of any formal or informal association that sets out to achieve particular goals. Such associations might include political parties, trade unions, the freemasons, old boy networks and even sports clubs. Membership of these can influence the social status a person has in the community. For example, membership of the freemasons might increase a person's potential to make social and business contacts, and, therefore, their wealth, whilst many middle-class men may be keen to join the local golf club because of the prestige that such membership may confer on them.

Gate Gourmet supplies in-flight meals for airlines. Its workers went on strike in August 2005, disrupting British Airways flights. Many of its workers at Heathrow Airport are from ethnic minorities – in particular, the West London sikh community. Discuss the Gate Gourmet workers in terms of Weber's categories of class, status and party.

Gender and ethnicity

Weber's analysis helps explain why some groups may share economic circumstances but have more or less status than others, for example, due to gender or ethnic differences. Weber saw gender and ethnicity as status differences which have separate and distinct effects on life-chances compared with social class. In other words, the working class might have less status than the middle class, but working-class Black people and working-class women may have less status than working-class White men.

Status and identity

Savage *et al.* (2001) take issue with the importance of 'status' in terms of shaping people's identity or giving us insight into the nature of inequality. Savage notes that people rarely make status claims, and suggests that they are wary of 'appearing to demonstrate openly their cultural superiority'. In fact, Savage's research suggests that people are more concerned with stressing how ordinary or how mainstream they are. Very few social groups assert that they are a special case. However, Savage does acknowledge that Weber did note that as a general rule, class, status and party do go together. As Bottero (2005) notes:

<< *The rich tend to be powerful, the powerful to be wealthy, and access to high-status social circles tends to accompany both.* >> (p.41)

Conflict and stability

Bottero concludes that, unlike the Marxian theory of stratification, Weber provides an adaptable 'history-proof' model of stratification which may be more valid in analyzing the variety of stratification arrangements that exist. However, she notes that both Marx and Weber fail to explain why societies organized around conflict or difference are so stable, orderly and reasonably free of major conflict between the social groups who occupy them.

Interpretive sociology

Most of the accounts that we have examined – especially functionalism and Marxism – are structural theories. This type of stratification theory is often accused of over-determinism: reducing all human behaviour to a reaction to either social or economic structure, and presenting people as puppets of society, unable to exercise any choice over their destiny. Interpretivist sociologists suggest that the social actions of individuals are more important than the organization of society, – that is, its social structure. These sociologists argue that subjective meanings are important because they allow us to choose how to behave – for instance, we might decide that our ethnicity is more important to us than our social class and act accordingly.

Bottero, however, notes that this focus on **agency** or action assumes that social life is patternless. She argues that this ignores the constraints within which people must continue to live, in that structured social inequalities continue to set 'substantial limits on choice and agency for all and create situations in which some are more free to act than others' (p.56). She notes that Marx recognized the role of agency when he stated that 'men make their own history', but he also recognized that social structure shaped action when he said that 'they do not make it under circumstances chosen by themselves'.

Giddens and structuration

Giddens (1973) developed these ideas in his theory of structuration, in which he argued that individuals create structural forces, such as social class, by engaging in particular actions. For example, he noted that class advantages can be passed on to the younger generations through family interaction. He also noted that consensus about the status or standing of occupations, as well as our acceptance that some people have the authority to tell us what to do at work, creates a hierarchy of occupations and, therefore, a stratification system based on social class. In other words, we judge people by the type of house or area they live in, by the car they drive, by the clothes or logos they wear, by the consumer goods they buy. He argues that this consensus about consumption also contributes to stratification.

However, in 1990, Giddens decided social class was no longer as significant as it had been in the past. Rather, the major social division in society was between the employed and the unemployed or socially excluded. Social class no longer constrained the activities and lifestyle of a whole mass of people – it was now individuals who experienced constraints and opportunities. Moreover Giddens set himself on the postmodernist road when he argued that lifestyle and taste were now more significant than social class in the construction of identity.

Postmodernism

Postmodernists reject what they see as the **grand narratives** of the stratification theories discussed so far. They instead focus on the concepts of 'identity' and 'difference'. They argue that the increasing diversity and plurality found in postmodern social life has led to the break-up of collective social identity, and especially class identity. It is argued that the group categories of 'social class', 'ethnicity', and 'gender' no longer exist in an homogeneous form. Subjective individual identity is now more important than objective collective identity. Best (2005) argues that, for postmodernists, ' the problem of identity is one of avoiding a fixed identity and keeping one's options open, avoiding long-term commitments, consistency and devotion'.

Postmodernists, such as Waters (1995), argue that social class is in terminal decline as a source of identity and that consumption – how we spend our money – is now central in terms of how we organize our daily lives. As Best notes, 'we are all cast into the roles of consumers'. Increasing affluence and standards of living have led to individuals being faced with a variety of consumer choices about their lifestyle rather than being forced into particular forms of cultural behaviour by forces beyond their social control, such as social class. In particular, postmodernists argue that people now use a variety of influences, particularly those stemming from globalization, to construct personal identity. Waters, for example, suggests that as a result, postmodern stratification is about lifestyle choices, fragmented association (we never belong to or identify with one group for very long), being seduced into conspicuous consumption by advertising and constant change in terms of what we are supposed to be interested in, the choices available to us and how we are supposed to feel.

Topic 3 examines social class and its relationship to future life-chances and identity and, consequently, it is recommended that you use the evidence from that section to judge the validity of this postmodernist view of the influence of social class.

Sociology A2 for AQA

Check your understanding

1 Why is social stratification acceptable, according to Durkheim?

2 In what circumstances might stratification be dysfunctional to society, according to Durkheim?

3 Why, according to Davis and Moore, do some people deserve more rewards than others?

4 Why do functionalists like Davis and Moore see social stratification as good for society?

5 What, according to Marx, determines a person's social class?

6 What is false class consciousness and how does it aid stratification?

7 Marx is accused of being an economic reductionist – what does this mean?

8 What is the role of the superstructure with regard to stratification?

9 What three sources of inequality does Weber identify as important in modern societies?

10 How does the concept of status help explain gender and ethnic differences?

11 How do postmodernists view class identity?

research idea

Conduct a piece of research to discover young people's explanations of inequality. Design an interview schedule to assess the ways in which your sample explains inequality. Do they take a functionalist position and see inequality as beneficial, motivating and meritocratic? Alternatively, do they agree with Marxists that inequality is damaging, unfair and demotivating?

web.task

Go to one or more of the following sites and investigate in depth the writings on class of the classical sociologists:

- http://sosig.esrc.bris.ac.uk/Durkheim/Marx
- http://eddie.cso.viuc.edu/Durkheim/
- http://msomusik.mursuky.edu/~felwel/http/Weber/home.htm
- www.anu.edu.au/polsci/marx/marx.htm

KEY TERMS

Agency – social action.

Aspirations – ambitions.

Alienation – lack of fulfilment from work.

Bourgeoisie – the ruling class in capitalist society.

Capitalist societies – societies based on private ownership of the means of production, such as Britain and the USA.

Communism – system based on communal ownership of the means of production.

Class-for-itself – a social class that is conscious of its exploited position and wishes to change its situation.

Class-in-itself – a social group that shares similar experiences.

Cultural capital – attitudes, ways of thinking, knowledge, skills, etc., learnt in middle-class homes that give middle-class children advantages in education.

Determinist or reductionist – the view that phenomena can be explained with reference to one key factor.

Division of labour – the way the job system is organized.

Dysfunctions – the negative effects of social actions, institutions and structures.

False class consciousness – where the proletariat see the society in a way that suits the ruling class and so pose no threat to them.

Grand narratives – postmodernist term for big structural theories, such as functionalism and Marxism.

Ideological apparatuses – social institutions that benefit the ruling class by spreading the ideas that help maintain the system in their interests, e.g. the mass media, education system.

Ideology – set of beliefs underpinning any way of life or political structure. Used by Marxists and neo-Marxists to refer specifically to the way powerful groups justify their position.

Infrastructure – in a Marxist sense, the capitalist economic system that is characterized by class inequality.

Means of production – the material forces that enable things to be produced, e.g. factories, machinery and land.

Mode of production – economic base of society that constitutes the entire system involved in the production of goods.

Neo-Marxists – those who have adapted Marx's views.

Normative – accepted by all, taken for granted.

Party – term used by Weber to describe political influence.

Petit-bourgeoisie – term used by Marx to describe the small middle class sandwiched between the proletariat and bourgeoisie.

Polarization – at opposite ends of the spectrum.

Proletariat – the working class in capitalist societies.

Relations of production – the allocation of roles and responsibilities among those involved in production.

Superstructure – social institutions such as education, mass media, religion, which function to transmit ruling-class ideology.

Surplus value – term used by Marx to describe the profit created by the work of the proletariat but taken by capitalists.

Value consensus – moral agreement.

exploring theories of stratification

Item A

The Marxian analysis revolves around the concept of class, and Marx's great insight was to see the exploitation of the working class by the factory owners as the determining factor in social division. People's behaviour is determined by the class grouping in which they find themselves. Furthermore our ability to make perceptions of the world and act on the basis of those perceptions is class determined.

According to Marxian analysis, the state is viewed as an institution that helps to organize capitalist society in the best interests of the bourgeoisie. The legitimacy of the capitalist system is maintained by ideology; working-class people are victims of a false consciousness. In other words, working-class people are said to hold values, ideas and beliefs about the nature of inequality that are not in their own economic interests to hold. Working-class people have their ideas manipulated by the media, schools and religion, for example, and regard economic inequality as fair and just.

Adapted from Best, S. (2005) *Understanding Social Divisions*, London: Sage, p.14

(a) Identify and briefly explain **two** problems sociologists might face in researching whether 'working-class people are victims of false consciousness' (**Item A**). (8 marks)

This part of the question includes assessment of your understanding of the connections between Stratification and Differentiation and sociological methods.

(b) Using material from **Item A** and elsewhere, examine some of the ways in which 'working-class people have their ideas manipulated' (**Item A**). In your answer make use of material from any **two** of the following areas: families and households; health; mass media; education; wealth, poverty and welfare; work and leisure; religion; power and politics; world sociology. (12 marks)

This part of the question includes assessment of your understanding of the connections between Stratification and Differentiation and other substantive topic(s) you have studied.

(c) Assess the usefulness of functionalist approaches in explaining the social divisions brought about by stratification systems. (40 marks)

This part of the question includes assessment of the connections between Stratification and Differentiation and sociological theory.

Life-chances and social class

getting you thinking

GIVENCHY

1 Look at the photographs. How do they show that consumption and lifestyle may be becoming increasingly important as sources of identity?

2 How available are the lifestyle choices illustrated above to all social groups? Who may be denied access and why?

You may have concluded from the exercise above that the ground rules regarding the expected behaviour of different social classes are changing. You may also have concluded, however, that material factors still govern lifestyle choices and that these are class related. Some sociologists argue that class identity has come to depend not only on market situation but on differences and similarities in power and status, as well as **consumption** and lifestyle.

Does class still matter?

Savage (2000) argues that since 1979, when it suffered the first of four successive election defeats, the Labour party has deliberately avoided talking about class and has focused instead on the concept of '**social exclusion**'. Consequently, political debate has focused on the idea that groups such as the long-term unemployed, single mothers and the residents of socially deprived areas are somehow excluded from the benefits most of us take for granted. In response, social policy has been devised in the fields of education, training and welfare with the

concept of '**social inclusion**' in mind – that is, it has aimed to target these groups so that they can become part of mainstream society again. However, Savage argues that the concepts of 'social exclusion' and 'social inclusion' are deliberately 'bland and inoffensive' – they reflect the New Labour or **Blairite** view that social-class divisions are no longer important because we allegedly now live in a society 'where most social groups have been incorporated into a common social body, with shared values and interests'. Britain in the 21st century is perceived as a classless society, or if social class is to be acknowledged at all, a society in which the vast majority of us share in middle-class lifestyles and aspirations – as Tony Blair once said, 'we are all middle-class now'. Sociologists have also taken up this baton of classlessness. New Right sociologists such as Peter Saunders, as well as postmodernists such as Pakulski and Walters, have argued that social class is no longer important as a source of personal identity for people in the 21st century. These sociologists, despite their theoretical differences, have suggested that consumption patterns and '**cleavages**' are far more important than social class in shaping lifestyle and life-chances today.

Equality of outcome or equality of opportunity?

Another way to look at the relevance of social class today is to see a debate between those who argue for **equality of outcome** and those who argue for **equality of opportunity**.

The traditionalist view

Those sociologists and politicians who believe that equality of outcome should be the priority see class divisions and conflict as the key characteristics of British society; they believe that New Labour politicians have abandoned their commitment to equality and social justice for those exploited by the organization of capitalism, i.e. the working class. These 'traditionalists' believe that New Labour has betrayed its working-class roots because it has done nothing to redistribute wealth and income from rich to poor, nor to address the fundamental flaws that they see as inherent in the capitalist system. Rather, traditionalists accuse the government of tinkering with policies under the banner of social exclusion that raise the opportunities of groups such as the poor and single-parents without addressing what traditionalists see as the main cause of their inequality: the concentration of vast amounts of wealth in the hands of an obscenely rich few.

The new egalitarian view

Giddens and Diamond (2005), however, claim that the arguments of the traditionalists are both simplistic and misguided, especially in their insistence that equality of outcome and equality of opportunity are somehow vastly different objectives. As Giddens and Diamond argue: 'the promotion of equal opportunity in fact requires greater material equality: it is impossible for individuals to achieve their full potential if social and economic starting-points are grossly unequal' (p.101).

Giddens and Diamond argue that since 1997, New Labour's policies on social exclusion have significantly lowered levels of poverty, especially among children and the elderly, and have put a break on any further rises in income inequality, especially inequalities in disposable material resources. However, they accept that there is still a long way to go in reducing inequalities of opportunity. They note that 'the life chances of individuals today are still significantly influenced by the economic and social position of their parents' (p.104). However, Giddens and Diamond are reluctant to acknowledge the argument that 'economic and social position' has anything to do with social class.

Giddens and Diamond refer to themselves and others who subscribe to the equality of opportunity argument as the '**new egalitarians**'. They note that the 'new egalitarianism' stresses the following:

- Economic efficiency created by a dynamic, competitive and flexible capitalist economy is a necessary precondition for the future redistribution of wealth and income.

- Levelling-up through the provision of educational and training opportunities, tax breaks for the poor and minimum wage legislation rather than levelling-down by taxing the rich is more likely to equalize life-chances.
- There is some 'social exclusion at the top', however, which could be addressed in order to bring about a fairer society. This includes practices such as tax avoidance, tax evasion and irresponsible corporate behaviour.
- The large-scale entry of women into the labour force and the rise of mass consumerism have disrupted traditional patterns of class affiliation.
- Social and economic divisions today are more likely to be between groups such as dual-earner families and lone-parent households rather than between social classes.
- Tensions within society are likely to result from getting the balance right between ethnic and cultural diversity, and the need to incorporate and integrate newcomers into a unified national identity.

Giddens and Diamond, therefore, argue that the claim that social class lies at the heart of inequalities in capitalist societies is dated. Moreover, they strongly defend the use of the concept of social exclusion. They note that the term was invented by academic sociologists rather than New Labour in order to 'capture the range of deprivations' that make up the experience of poverty and prevent people from taking a full part in society. They note that government-sponsored studies have tended to use four indicators or measures of social exclusion:

- the number of people not in employment, education or training
- the number of those earning below 60 per cent of the average wage
- the number of those experiencing low levels of social interaction
- the number of those who believe that they live in an area characterized by high crime, vandalism or material dilapidation.

Such studies have concluded that less than 1 per cent of the UK's population is excluded on all four counts. Giddens and Diamond, therefore, conclude that **multiple deprivation** of this kind affects specific neighbourhoods rather than the working-class as a whole.

Segmented society

Will Hutton (1996) takes a similar new egalitarian line in his 30–30–40 thesis of economic inequality. He argues that society is now divided into segments (he avoids the use of the term 'social class'!) based on inequalities in income and wealth. He argues that the top 40 per cent comprises all those with secure jobs, the bottom 30 per cent comprises the disadvantaged – the unemployed and the poor – whilst the middle 30 per cent comprises the marginalized – those workers who are both insecure and low paid.

So, who is correct? The traditionalists or the new egalitarians? We need to examine the evidence in more detail before we can come to any firm conclusions.

Trends in income, wealth and poverty

A number of observations can be made about the distribution of income, wealth and poverty between 1945 and now.

Income

Between 1979 and 1997 (during an unbroken period of Conservative government), income inequality between the rich and poor in Britain widened until it was at its most unequal since records began at the end of the 19th century. No other Western industrialised country, apart from the USA, had experienced this level of inequality.

Average income rose by 36 per cent during this period, but the top 10 per cent of earners experienced a 62 per cent rise, whilst the poorest 10 per cent of earners experienced a 17 per cent decline. In 2000, those in the service class (professional, managerial and administrative employees) earned well above the average national wage, whereas every group of manual workers (skilled, semi-skilled and unskilled) earned well below the national average. In 2002/03, the richest 10 per cent of the population received 29 per cent of total disposable income (compared with 21 per cent in 1979), whilst the poorest 10 per cent received only 3 per cent (compared with 4 per cent in 1979).

Income inequality and market forces

Roberts (2001) notes that the most popular explanation for income inequality is market forces. It is argued that income inequalities have widened because skill requirements have been rising and workers with the right skills, most notably finance professionals working in the City of London, have benefited. New egalitarians, such as Giddens and Diamond, suggest that the economically successful often bring benefits to the wider society in terms of drive, initiative and creativity, and should not be penalized in the form of excessive taxes. However, Roberts notes that the facts do not support the market-forces view. He points out that pay rarely corresponds with labour shortages or surpluses. For example, he shows that universities today produce more graduates compared with 30 years ago and, logically, average graduate pay should have fallen. However, in practice, graduate pay has actually risen – pay differentials between graduates and non-graduate employees have widened. Roberts argues that only class theory can explain this, in that upper-middle-class occupations, such as company executives and senior managers, generally fix their own salaries. They also often supplement their salaries with other financial incentives, such as being given stock options, bonuses and profit-sharing deals, as they have overall day-to-day operational control over corporations and in some cases, actually own the majority of shares in the company. The reduction in tax rates for top earners from 83 per cent to 40 per cent in 1979 enormously benefited this group. Roberts notes that whilst some middle-class professionals can negotiate their salaries, the vast majority of lower-middle-class and working-class occupations either have to negotiate collectively as part of trade unions or they are told how much they will earn.

Corporate moral responsibility

In recent years there been some concern about the salaries of these so-called 'fat-cats'. It has been suggested that corporations should be more morally responsible in the context of a society in which poverty, deprivation and debt is a norm for many people. For example, in October 2005, Philip Green, the chief executive of Arcadia was criticized for being greedy in paying himself £1.4 billion in salary. Moreover, there are signs that society is increasingly unhappy because top executives are not only rewarded for success, but seemingly also for failure, in that many executives are paid off with 'golden goodbyes' often totalling hundreds of thousands of pounds.

Poverty

These arguments about corporate moral irresponsibility and executive greed become more acute when we consider that the Low Pay Unit estimated in 2000 that 45 per cent of British workers (overwhelmingly semi-skilled and unskilled workers) were earning less than two-thirds of the average wage. Furthermore, many low-paid workers are often caught in a **poverty trap**. This means they earn above the minimum level required to claim benefits, but the deduction of tax, etc., takes them below it. Similarly, many on benefits actually end up worse off if they take low-paid work because they are no longer eligible for state support.

Low pay has particularly impacted on levels of poverty. While levels of absolute poverty have fallen in the UK, especially since 1997, relative poverty has continued to rise steeply. As Savage notes, relative poverty in 1997 was twice the level it reached in the 1960s and three times what it had been in the late 1970s. Children have been particularly affected. Forty per cent of children are born into families in the bottom 30 per cent of income distribution. Treasury figures in March 1999 estimated that up to 25 per cent of children never escape from poverty and that deprivation is being passed down the generations by unemployment and underachievement in schools.

Wealth

The 20th century did see a gradual redistribution of wealth in the UK. In 1911, the most wealthy 1 per cent of the population held 69 per cent of all wealth, yet by 1993, this had dropped to 17 per cent. However, this redistribution did not extend down into the mass of society. Rather it was very narrow – the very wealthy top 1 per cent distributed some of its wealth to the wealthy top 10 per cent via trust funds in order to avoid paying taxes in the form of death duties. The result of this redistribution within the economic elite is that in 2000, the top 10 per cent owned 50 per cent of the nation's wealth and the wealth of the most affluent 200 individuals and families doubled. This polarization of wealth in the UK has also been encouraged by a soaring stock market (investments in stocks and shares) and property values, which as Savage notes 'have allowed those who were already wealthy to accumulate their wealth massively'.

The privatization of public utilities such as British Telecom and British Gas in the 1980s widened share ownership, so that by 1988, 21 per cent of people owned shares. However, the evidence suggests this was a short-term phenomenon as people who had never owned shares before sold their shares quickly as their value rose. Today, although about 17 per cent of all people own shares, the richest 1 per cent of the population still own 75 per cent of all privately owned shares. As Roberts notes:

>> *We are certainly not all capitalists now. In 1993, the least wealthy half of the population owned just 7 per cent of all personally-held wealth; around 30 per cent of adults do not own the dwellings in which they live; a half of all employees do not have significant occupational pensions. In fact, a half of the population has near-zero assets, and many are in debt when account is taken of outstanding mortgages, bank overdrafts, hire-purchase commitments, loans on credit cards, store cards and all the rest. It is only roughly a half of the population that has any significant share in the country's wealth.* >> (pp.178–9)

The fact that nearly half the population have a share in the country's wealth may sound impressive, but Roberts points out that most of these people will liquidate assets such as savings and pension funds in old age in order to safeguard the standard of living they have enjoyed in the latter half of their life. As Roberts notes, it is only the extremely wealthy who can expect to die with most of their wealth intact. A lot of wealth that people have is also tied up with property in which people live. Homeowners can make money out of their property but this is not the main reason most people buy their houses. Most people own one house, whilst the extremely wealthy may own several houses as well as land bought for its future investment value. Finally, Roberts notes that the proportion of the population with enough wealth that they do not have to work for others is still less than 1 per cent. This elite group employ others to work for them. On the other hand, the life-chances of the vast majority of the population depend on the kinds of jobs they can obtain. Roberts concludes:

>> *Despite the spread of wealth, this remains a clear class relationship and division. It is, in fact, the clearest of all class divisions, and it still splits the population into a tiny minority on the one side, and the great mass of the people on the other.* >> (p.180)

Health

Bottero (2005) claims that 'social inequalities are written on the body' and 'hierarchy makes you sick'. She notes that if illness was a chance occurrence, we could expect to see rates of **morbidity** (i.e. illness and disease) and **mortality** (i.e. death) randomly distributed across the population. However, it is clear from Department of Health statistics that the working class experience an overproportionate amount of illness. In general, health across the population has improved over the last 30 years but the rate of improvement has been much slower for the working class. Generally, the working class experience poorer mortality rates and morbidity rates than the middle classes. For example, 3500 more working-class babies would

synoptic link   education and health

This topic has outlined the statistical patterns and facts of class inequalities. You should be willing to explore those sociological theories and studies that focus on social class factors in their explanations of educational and health inequalities.

With regard to educational achievement, there are essentially four ideas worth exploring:

1 Cultural deprivation theory focuses on the deficiencies of working-class culture in terms of parental interest, child-rearing and language use. Such sociologists imply that middle-class family socialization better prepares children for success in education.
2 **Material deprivation** such as low income and fear of debt can also be an obstacle to working-class educational success.
3 Marxists blame the hidden curriculum, which they see as part of a middle-class dominated educational system, and the fact that the working-class through no fault of their own are denied access to the cultural capital required for educational success.
4 Marxist interpretivists such as Paul Willis argue that working-class kids choose to 'fail' at school because the middle-class goals of schools have little to do with their aspirations.

Similar class-based explanations exist for poor working-class health:

1 The New Right argue that cultural factors are to blame in that the working class choose to eat a less-healthy diet, exercise less and to smoke and drink excessively.
2 Material deprivationists argue that the working class cannot afford to indulge in behaviour that the middle class take for granted, such as membership of private gyms or taking-up sports such as tennis and golf.
3 The organization of health care across the country may be negatively affecting working-class health. There is evidence that middle-class patients have easier access to healthcare facilities of better quality, with shorter patient lists, and, in their relationship to their doctor, get more time and have their conditions better diagnosed, explained and treated.
4 Marxists argue that the working class are the victims of exploitative conditions in the workplace and society at large.

survive per year if the working-class infant mortality rate was reduced to middle-class levels. In other words, babies born to professional fathers have levels of infant mortality half that of babies born to unskilled manual fathers.

Class and death rates

If we examine death rates we can see that, between 1972 and 1997, death rates for professionals fell by 44 per cent, but fell by only 10 per cent for the unskilled. Bartley *et al.* (1996) note that men in Social Class I (using the old RG scale) had only two-thirds the chance of dying between 1986 and 1989 compared with the male population as a whole. However, unskilled manual workers (Social Class V using the old RG scale) were one-third more likely to die compared with the male population as a whole. In other words, despite the NHS providing free universal health care to all, men in Social Class V were twice as likely to die before men in Social Class I.

Bottero notes that:

<< *There is a strong socio-economic gradient to almost all patterns of disease and ill-health. The lower your socio-economic position, the greater your risk of low birthweight, infections, cancer, coronary heart disease, respiratory disease, stroke, accidents, nervous and mental illnesses.* >> (p.188)

Moreover, she points out that there are specific occupational hazards linked to particular manual jobs which increase the risk of accidental injury, exposure to toxic materials, pollution, etc. Poor people are more likely to live in areas in which there are more hazards, such as traffic and pollution, and fewer safe areas to play. Consequently, poor children are more likely to be run over and to suffer asthma.

The health gradient

Some studies have suggested that there exists a **health gradient**, in that at every level of the social hierarchy, there are health differences. Some writers, most notably Marmot *et al.* (1991), have suggested that social position may be to blame for these differences. They conducted a study on civil servants working in Whitehall, i.e. white-collar staff, and concluded that the cause of ill health was being lower in the hierarchy. Those low in the hierarchy had less social control over their working conditions, greater stress and greater feelings of low self-esteem. These psychosocial factors triggered off behaviour such as smoking and drinking, poor eating habits and inactivity. The net result of this combination of psychosocial and lifestyle factors was greater levels of depression, high blood pressure, increased susceptibility to infection and build-up of cholesterol. If we apply Marmot's findings to society in general, it may be the fact that working-class occupations are the lowest in the hierarchy that may be causing their disproportionate levels of morbidity and mortality.

Other sociologists, most notably Wilkinson (1996), argue that the health gradient is caused by income inequality. He argues that relative inequality affects health because it undermines **social cohesion** – the sense that we are all valued equally by society which affirms our sense of belonging to

society. Wilkinson argues that inequality disrupts social cohesion because it undermines self-esteem, dignity, trust and cooperation and increases feelings of insecurity, envy, hostility and inferiority, which lead to stress. As Wilkinson notes:

<< *To feel depressed, cheated, bitter, desperate, vulnerable, frightened, angry, worried about debts or job and housing insecurity; to feel devalued, useless, helpless, uncared for, hopeless, isolated, anxious and a failure; these feelings can dominate people's whole experience of life, colouring their experience of everything else. It is the chronic stress arising from feelings like these which does the damage. It is the social feelings which matter, not exposure to a supposedly toxic environment.* >> (p.215)

Wilkinson notes that egalitarian societies have a strong community life, in that strong social ties and networks exist in the wider society to support their members. In other words, members of these societies have access to '**social capital**' – social and psychological support from others in their community which helps them stay healthy. It is argued that in societies characterized by extreme income inequality, social capital in the form of these networks is less likely to exist and health inequalities continue to grow. We can see this particularly in residential areas in the UK characterized by high levels of council housing.

Housing

Government spending on health and education has increased by over 30 per cent since 1981, but the reverse is true of expenditure on public housing (the 5 million council houses managed by local authorities and the 800 000 managed by housing associations). Since the 1980s, the availability of such housing has actually fallen, for two reason:

● Many council houses were sold off to their tenants as a result of the Conservative government's '**Right to buy**' scheme, or were transferred to housing association control.
● Capital investment in new council housing has been so low that very few new homes have been built.

For example, in 1981, 32 per cent of the housing stock was made up of council housing, but this had fallen to 22 per cent by 2000. There has been a corresponding decline in the percentage of people renting private houses, flats, bedsits, etc. For example, in 1945, 62 per cent of the housing stock was privately rented, but this had fallen to 5 per cent by 2000. This public-housing shortage has led to both local authorities and housing associations allocating housing to those in greatest need. This has had the effect of concentrating socially deprived groups in particular areas, thus creating new class divisions locally and nationally. This tendency for lower-income households to be more concentrated in council housing is not new; the trend was clearly well-established before 1980. However, there was a degree of choice involved in where people wanted to live, giving residential areas a more comprehensive and socially cohesive feel. This choice no longer exists today.

Peter Saunders (1990)

A nation of homeowners

Saunders carried out a local household survey aimed at a sample of 500 respondents in three predominantly working-class towns; Burnley, Derby and Slough. People were interviewed using a questionnaire composed of both open and closed questions about the experience and meaning of home ownership in their daily lives. He found that 91 per cent of his sample expressed a preference for home ownership over council tenancy. He argued that home ownership was starting to change the character of wealth ownership in the UK – investment in housing was bringing capital gains to the 'middle mass' and benefiting future generations who were inheriting wealth because of their parents' ownership of property. Saunders, therefore, rejects the class traditionalist view that increased owner-occupancy has contributed to a polarization in inequality between social classes. However, his study does acknowledge a new division between the middle mass, who own their property, and a marginalized minority located on undesirable council estates, who experience multiple deprivations. Interestingly, he also discovered that 43 per cent of council tenants associated the home with family, love and children compared to only 33 per cent of home owners, and were twice as likely to view community as an important aspect of their daily lives.

Saunders, P. (1990) *A Nation of Homeowners*, London: Unwin Hyman.

1 In what sense, might Saunders qualify as a new egalitarian?

2 Saunders argues that council tenants should be able to buy their own homes at subsidised prices. Why?

3 In what way might Saunders' findings about community contradict the findings of Wilkinson?

Council estates and social capital

The trend towards home ownership in the UK has also contributed to the polarization of social classes in terms of areas in which people live. For example, in 1945 only 26 per cent of homes were privately owned, yet this figure was 76 per cent in 2000. This has led to an overconcentration of the poor on council estates. For example, in 1963, only 1 in 4 council tenants were made up of those on the lowest incomes, but this had increased to 1 in 2 by 2000, with less council housing stock to be distributed amongst them. For example, in 1979, there were 8 million council houses with 4 million tenants with low incomes. By 2000, there were only 5 million council houses with the same number of low-income tenants. Council estates, therefore, have large concentrations of people on income support, such as the unemployed, single mothers, the elderly, the low paid and asylum-seekers. According to the General Household Survey (2001), 51 per cent of single-parent families are council tenants compared to 15 per cent of the general population. In 2001, it was estimated that 45 per cent of tenants in publicly owned housing were on state benefits of one type or another. This trend has created less desirable residential areas and pockets of deprivation, with dysfunctional communities, failing schools and a disproportionate level of social problems such as crime. For example, it is estimated that 42 per cent of all burglaries happen to the homes of those belonging to the poor and single parents, the vast majority of whom are living on council estates.

Council estates are generally poorly resourced in terms of shops, recreational facilities, public transport and healthcare services such as GPs and hospitals. Very importantly, there is evidence of low social cohesion on these estates, and as a result, there may be high rates of depression, isolation, hostility and anxiety. Social capital in the form of supportive formal and informal social networks is also likely to be absent because of family breakdown, economic cutbacks in council services and a lack of community spirit fostered by people constantly moving in and out of the area, a high crime rate, fear of crime, antisocial behaviour and intensive policing.

Education

We can see distinct class differences in achievement in that working-class children perform much worse in education than all other social groups at all levels of the education system. For example, more working-class children leave school at the age of 16 with no qualifications than middle-class 16-year-olds, and while the number of working-class 18-year-olds entering university has increased, the number of middle-class undergraduates still far exceeds them. Connor and Dewson (2001) found that only one in five young people from working-class backgrounds participated in higher education. Moreover, as Savage and Egerton (1997) found, ability does not wipe out class advantage. For example, their study found that less than half of the 'high-ability' working-class boys in their study made it into the service class (compared with three-quarters of the 'high-ability' boys with service-class fathers). Furthermore, 65 per cent of their 'low-ability' service-class boys were able to avoid dropping down into manual work.

Cultural capital

The evidence suggests that middle-class children benefit from living in better areas (with better schools). This, of course, is assisted by the better incomes earned by their parents, which means they can afford to buy into areas which have schools with good league-table standings. Income increases educational choices, so, for instance, parents can choose to send their children to private schools or to hire personal tutors. The evidence overwhelmingly shows that children who attend the elite private schools in the UK (the public schools) have easier access to Oxbridge and the redbrick universities. Moreover the 'old school tie' network ensures important and valuable social contacts for years to come, particularly in the finance sector of the economy. Middle-class parents are also able to use their knowledge, expertise, contacts and greater confidence in expressing themselves and in dealing with fellow professionals, – their cultural capital – to ensure that their children are well served by the educational system.

Conclusions

The new egalitarians are undoubtedly correct in drawing our attention to the fact that a diversity of social groups, such as the long-term unemployed, single mothers and asylum-seekers, are socially excluded from mainstream society and so experience a range of social and economic deprivations. However, their reluctance to acknowledge the role of social class and its indicators (such as inequalities in income, wealth, housing, health and education) is incomprehensible given the weight of the evidence available. As Savage concludes:

>> *In recent years, whatever people's perceptions of their class might be, there is no doubting that class inequality has hardened. People's destinies are as strongly affected and perhaps more strongly affected, by their class background than they were in the mid-20th century.* >>

The evidence in this section also challenges the postmodernist view that social class has ceased to be the primary shaper of identity and that people exercise more choice about the type of people they want to be, especially in terms of lifestyle and consumption. Postmodernists and New Right thinkers, such as Saunders, neglect the fact that lifestyle choices and consumption depend on educational qualifications, the jobs we have and the income we earn. Unfortunately, members of the working class are less likely to qualify on all three counts for the postmodern lifestyle. Moreover, they are well aware that it is their social class more than any other social factor that is holding them back from making the sorts of choices that are taken for granted by social classes above them.

Check your understanding

1. **What groups are typically socially excluded according to the new egalitarians?**

2. **What is the main difference between traditionalists and new egalitarians?**

3. **What is the new egalitarian attitude towards the rich?**

4. **Why have income inequalities widened in the UK over the last thirty years?**

5. **What have been the main trends with regard to wealth redistribution in the UK over the past 30 years?**

6. **Give three statistical examples of health differences between classes.**

7. **What effect has the health gradient had on the social make up of some residential areas?**

8. **What evidence is there that council housing is becoming increasingly the domain of the socially deprived?**

9. **What problems do those living on council estates face?**

10. **How do educational inequalities support the view that social class may still be important?**

research ideas

Get an A to Z of your local area. Enlarge a residential area that you know to be a high-demand area. Similarly, enlarge an area in low demand. Annotate each as far as possible to highlight differences in facilities/resources. Conduct a survey of residents in each area to discover the level of services and facilities on offer there.

Compare and contrast the two areas to test the extent to which people in low-demand areas suffer a variety of social exclusions.

web.task

Go to the government statistics site at www.statistics.gov.uk.

Select Neighbourhood statistics. Choose your own postcode or the district or postcode where your school or college is situated. You will be able to investigate a variety of indicators of wealth and deprivation. How does your area compare with other parts of the region or with Britain as a whole?

KEY TERMS

Blairite – ideas uniquely associated with Tony Blair or New Labour.

Cleavage – a term used by Saunders to describe differences in the spending patterns of social groups.

Consumption – spending on goods and services.

Equality of opportunity – the idea that individuals should begin from the same starting point in terms of opportunities.

Equality of outcome – the idea that social groups should be able to achieve results on the basis of ability rather than wealth. Believers in equality of outcome suggest equality can never be achieved so long as inequalities in wealth and income continue to persist and be reproduced generation by generation.

Health gradient – the fact that the chances of dying or becoming ill progressively increase or decline the lower or higher you are on the occupational hierarchy.

Material deprivation – the lack of physical resources needed in order to lead a full and normal life.

Morbidity rate – reported ill health per 100 000 of population.

Mortality rate – number of deaths per 100 000 of population.

Multiple deprivation – the experience of a range of factors which inhibit life-chances, e.g. unemployment, single motherhood, residing in a high-crime area.

New egalitarians – a group of sociologists and politicians who believe that social-class divisions are in decline and that policies to socially include deprived groups are working.

Poverty trap – the fact that after taxation and national insurance contributions, the wages paid by some jobs fall below the official poverty line.

Right to buy initiative – a Conservative government scheme whereby councils were instructed to allow long-term council tenants to buy their rented homes at a fraction of their market value (typically half).

Social capital – social relationships that benefit people, e.g. in finding a job.

Social cohesion – the idea that people feel a sense of belonging to society because they feel valued and wanted.

Social exclusion – the fact that some people are excluded from what everyone else takes for granted usually because of poor educational, family or economic circumstances.

Social inclusion – being part of the mainstream because of the opportunities offered by government policies, e.g. training, education.

exploring life-chances and social class

Item A

In Wilkinson's view, the widening gap in income distribution creates resentment, social exclusion in terms of the poor and social isolation, where the more wealthy cut themselves off to protect their assets. Social cohesion is affected. People become isolated from their community. People are unable to cope with stress, which is reflected in poor health. Wilkinson argues that social factors such as the strength of social contacts, ties within communities, availability of social support and a sense of security are the main determinants of the relative health of a society. However, areas vary greatly in terms of safety, environmental conditions and the availability of services and public facilities. For example, deprived areas tend to have fewer basic services such as banks, food shops and post offices than do more desirable areas. Community spaces such as parks, sports grounds and libraries may also be limited. Yet people living in disadvantaged spaces are often dependent on local facilities as they lack the funds and transport that would allow them to use facilities and services provided sometimes more cheaply elsewhere.

Adapted from Giddens, A. (2001) *Sociology* (4th edn), Cambridge: Polity Press, pp.150

(a) Identify and briefly explain **two** problems in obtaining accurate figures about 'the widening gap in income distribution' **(Item A)**. (8 marks)

This part of the question includes assessment of your understanding of the connections between Stratification and Differentiation and sociological methods.

(b) Examine the extent to which social class influences people's lives in **two or more** of the following areas; families and households; health; mass media; education; wealth, poverty and welfare; work and leisure; religion; power and politics; world sociology. (12 marks)

This part of the question includes assessment of your understanding of the connections between Stratification and Differentiation and other substantive topic(s) you have studied.

(c) There is disagreement among sociologists about how greatly social class influences life-chances and lifestyles today.

Assess different sociological views, studies and evidence with regard to this statement. (40 marks)

This part of the question includes assessment of the connections between Stratification and Differentiation and sociological theory.

Changes in the class structure

gettingyouthinking

1 What do you think are the main differences between the people in the photographs above?

2 Which would you call 'posh' and why?

3 Why do you think Victoria Beckham was often referred to as 'Posh' when she performed with the Spice Girls?

4 With which social class do you most associate the Beckhams? Explain your answer.

5 What do the terms 'working class', 'middle class' and 'upper class' mean to you?

6 What factors other than class affect the way people are perceived today?

Your answers to the above questions may demonstrate that class is a difficult thing to define nowadays and that status is no longer a matter of being on the right side of the class divide. The old idea of the class structure was that it comprised a triangular shape, with numbers increasing towards the base, which was composed of a vast number of unskilled manual workers providing a strong industrial-based manufacturing sector. This model implied a strict hierarchy, with higher levels of income, status and power towards the top. Although this was never actually the true shape (because manufacturing jobs have never accounted for the majority of the workforce), there has been a dramatic shift in Britain's industrial structure with only about 18 per cent of the population working in manufacturing today. At the same time, numbers of those working in **tertiary** or **service-sector jobs** (those providing services such as transport, retailing, hotel work, cleaning, banking and insurance) have increased dramatically from 25 per cent to 75 per cent.

The upper class

It has been argued that the upper class (the extremely wealthy, property-owning elite who need not work in order to maintain their lifestyle), especially the aristocratic and traditional rich, have declined in wealth, power and influence over the course of the 20th century. In particular, it has been argued (Roberts 2001) that high death duties (now called 'inheritance tax') have resulted in a substantial number of upper-class families losing their family seats (the country houses where their family lived for generations) and experiencing downward social mobility. Some have even been forced to take up salaried employment in the service sector. In other words, it is argued that the upper class is in danger of being assimilated into the upper middle-class. So, how true are these assertions? A number of observations can be made on the basis of the evidence available.

Inherited wealth

The upper class is still very wealthy. We saw earlier how the top 1 per cent have got 'poorer', but only because they have made real efforts to avoid inheritance tax by transferring their wealth via trust funds to the top 5 per cent. Moreover, the top 1 per cent still own about one-third of the country's wealth.

The evidence suggests that we should talk about wealthy families rather than individuals. In this context, inheritance is very important. In general, individuals or families are wealthy because their fathers were also rich. Inheritance is responsible for most of the inequality in the distribution of wealth.

Positions of economic leadership

Scott (1982) argues that there now exists a unified propertied class which has actively used its wealth to maintain its privileged position at the top of the socio-economic structure. He argues that the core of the upper class – the richest 0.1 per cent

(between 25 000 and 50 000 people) – occupy positions of leadership in manufacturing, banking and finance. He suggests that this core is made up of three groups:

- entrepreneurial capitalists, who own (or mainly own) businesses founded by their family
- internal capitalists, the senior executives who head the bureaucracies that run the big companies
- finance capitalists, who usually own or run financial institutions such as merchant banks and firms of stockbrokers.

It can be argued that the traditional landed gentry, mainly aristocratic in character, has managed since the turn of the 20th century, through investment and marriage to the 'nouveau riche', to become an integral part of the three groups that make up the core of the modern upper class.

Networks and social closure

The upper class is also supported by networks that permeate throughout that class. These may be based on marriage or kinship. For example, there is a tendency for members of the upper class to marry other upper-class individuals. This obviously gives the class a unity based on marriage and kinship, and is instrumental in strengthening business and financial ties between families.

Membership of the upper class is strengthened by **social closure** – the ability to control mobility into upper-class circles. This is partly achieved by networking and being part of an 'in crowd'. Another major means of ensuring social closure is the emphasis on public-school education in generation after generation, especially at those schools seen as the 'great and good', such as Eton, Harrow, Winchester, Westminster, Charterhouse and Rugby. The large movement of such pupils into the elite universities of Oxford and Cambridge reinforces such students' belief in their 'difference' from the rest of society. The 'old-boy network', based very much on common schooling, results in self-recruitment to the upper class. This means that current members of the upper class are likely to be the offspring of wealthy individuals who attended the same schools and universities, as will their sons and daughters.

Scott notes evidence relating to interlocking directorships. He found that in 1976 eleven people had a total of 57 directorships in the top 250 companies and had many others in smaller companies. Such interlocking directorships provide a powerful network that cements connections between members of the upper class.

The 'Establishment'

Scott argues that the upper class's influence is not confined to business. There is overwhelming evidence that those in top positions in politics, the civil service, the church, the armed services and the professions come disproportionately from upper-class families. Scott refers to this group as the 'establishment' – a coherent and self-recruiting body of men with a similarity of outlook who are able to wield immense power. However, exactly how this group interacts and whether they do so for their own benefit is extremely difficult to prove.

Although the basis of the wealth of the upper class is no longer primarily land, this class still retains many of the characteristics it possessed 50 years ago, especially an emphasis on public-school education, thus helping to ensure that social closure continues unchallenged.

The middle classes in modern Britain

The expansion of the middle classes

In 1911, some 80 per cent of workers were in manual occupations. This number fell to 32.7 per cent in 1991 and is approximately 25 per cent today. Non-manual workers (traditionally seen as middle-class) have therefore fairly recently become the majority occupational group in the workforce. As Savage (1995) points out, there are now more university lecturers than coal miners in the UK.

Reasons for the expansion

The number of manual jobs in both primary and **secondary industries** has gone into decline since the 1970s. The decline has been caused by a range of factors, including new technology, the oil crisis and globalization (i.e. the same raw materials and goods can be produced more cheaply in developing countries). The tertiary or service sector of the economy that is focused around education, welfare, retail and finance has expanded hugely in the past 20 years. Mass secondary education and the expansion of both further and higher education have ensured the existence of a well-educated and qualified workforce. The service sector is made up of a mainly male professional workforce at its top end but, as a result of changes in women's social position, the bulk of workers in this sector are female.

The boundary problem

Studying the middle classes can be problematic because not all sociologists agree who should be included in this category. This is the so-called '**boundary problem**'. Traditionally, differentiating between the middle class and working class was thought to be a simple task involving distinguishing between white-collar, or non-manual, workers on the one hand and blue-collar, or manual, workers on the other. Generally, the former enjoyed better working conditions in terms of pay, holidays and promotion possibilities. Today, however, this distinction is not so clear cut. It is generally agreed that many **routine white-collar workers**, who are mainly women, especially those who work in call-centres, now have similar conditions of work and pay to manual workers and, therefore, cannot be seen as a higher class.

A fragmented middle class

The term 'middle class' covers a wide range of occupations, incomes, lifestyles and attitudes. Roberts et al. (1977) argued that the middle class was becoming fragmented into a number of different groups, each with a distinctive view of its place in the stratification system. They suggest that we should no longer talk of the middle class, but of the 'middle classes'. Savage et al. (1992) agrees that it is important to see that the middle class is now divided into strata, or '**class fractions**', such as higher and lower professionals, higher and middle managers, the petit bourgeoisie and routine white-collar workers.

Professionals

Savage et al. (1992) argue that higher and lower professionals mainly recruit internally – in other words, the sons and daughters of professionals are likely to end up as professionals themselves. The position of professional workers is based on the possession of educational qualifications. Professionals usually have to go through a long period of training – university plus professional examinations before they qualify. Savage argues that professionals possess both **economic capital** (a very good standard of living, savings, financial security) and **cultural capital** (seeing the worth of education and other cultural assets such as taste in high culture), which they pass on to their children. Moreover, they increasingly have social capital (belonging to networks that can influence decision-making by other professionals such as head teachers). Professionals also have strong occupational associations, such as the Law Society and the British Medical Association, that protect and actively pursue their interests (although the lower down the professional ladder, the weaker these associations/unions become). The result of such groups actively pursuing the interests of professionals is high rewards, status and job security.

Savage concludes that professionals are aware of their common interests and quite willing to take industrial action to protect those interests. In this sense, then, professionals have a greater sense of class identity than other middle-class groups. However, as the public sector has become increasingly privatized, many professionals are facing an increased threat of redundancy and reduced promotional opportunities as a result of de-layering (a reduction in the number of 'tiers' of management in an organization).

Managers

Savage and colleagues suggest that managers have assets based upon a particular skill within specific organizations. Such skills (unlike those of professionals) are not easily transferable to other companies or industries. Many managers have been upwardly mobile from the routine white-collar sector or the skilled working class. Often they lack qualifications such as degrees. They may even have worked their way up through an organization. Their social position, therefore, is likely to be the result of experience and reputation rather than qualifications. Savage notes that most managers do not belong to professional associations or trade unions. Consequently, they tend to be more individualistic in character and are less likely to identify a common collectivistic interest with their fellow managers – who are much more likely to be seen as competitors. Savage argues that managers actively encourage their children to pursue higher education because they can see the benefits of a professional career. However, managers, despite being well paid, are less likely to have the cultural capital possessed by professionals.

Savage argues that job security differentiates professionals from managers – managers are constantly under threat from recession, mergers and **downsizing**. Savage points out that it is middle managers such as bank managers whose jobs are under threat and who are more likely to be downwardly mobile.

However, higher managers, e.g. executives, are likely to be on spectacular salaries and to have share options worth millions. The Income Data Services showed that nearly half of all senior executives of Britain's 350 largest public companies made more than £1 million a year, with eight directors on packages of £5+ million (Cohen 2005). Adonis and Pollard (1998) claim that this 'superclass' of higher-salaried people (i.e. salariat) now makes up approximately 15 per cent of middle-class occupations. They note that it is mainly located in the South East of England, and employed mainly by banks that deal in currency speculation, stockbroker companies and the privatized utilities, many of which are based in the City of London. According to Adonis and Pollard, the lifestyle of this superclass revolves around nannies and servants, second homes, private education for their children, private health schemes, exotic foreign holidays and investment in modern art. The superclass tends to live on private urban estates patrolled by private security companies.

The self-employed

Between 1981 and 1991, the number of people **self-employed**, or '**petit-bourgeois**', has risen from 6.7 per cent of the workforce to over 10 per cent. Research by Fielding (1995) examined what the self-employed in 1981 were doing in 1991. He showed that two-thirds of his sample were a relatively stable and secure part of the workforce in that they remained self-employed over this ten-year period. However, the character of the self-employed has changed in some respects too. The number of managers who prefer to work for themselves (for example, as consultants) rose considerably in the 1980s, especially in the finance and computer industries. Some writers argue that many firms now prefer to contract services to outside consultants rather than employ people themselves. A large number of people, again mainly managers, have businesses 'on the side' whilst continuing to be employees.

Routine white-collar workers

Marxists such as Harry Braverman (1974) argue that routine white-collar workers are no longer middle class. Braverman argues that they have been subjected to a process of **proletarianization**. This means that they have lost the social and economic advantages that they enjoyed over manual workers, such as superior pay and working conditions. Braverman argues that in the past 20 years, employers have used technology, especially computers, to break down complex white-collar skills, such as book-keeping, into simplistic routine tasks. This process is known as '**de-skilling**' and is an attempt to increase output, maximize efficiency and reduce costs. Control over the work process has, therefore, been removed from many non-manual workers.

These developments have been accompanied by the parallel development of the feminization of the routine white-collar workforce (especially in the financial sector), because female workers are generally cheap to employ and are seen by employers as more adaptable and amenable to this type of work. Braverman concludes that de-skilling means that occupations that once were middle class are today in all respects indistinguishable from those of manual workers.

Marshall et al. (1988) challenged the idea of proletarianization. In a national random sample of female workers, they found that it was mainly manual workers who claimed that their work had been de-skilled. Over 90 per cent of non-manual workers felt that little had changed, and that they were as likely to identify themselves with the middle class as they were with the working class. Finally, they were more likely to vote Conservative than Labour. Marshall and colleagues therefore concluded that proletarianization among routine white-collar workers was not taking place.

New technology workers

In further contrast to Braverman however, Clark and Hoffman-Martinot (1998) highlight the growth of a technological elite of 'wired workers' – new professionals who are as productive through the use of technology as entire offices of routine non-manual workers, spending most of their days behind computers working in non-hierarchical settings. They enjoy considerable **autonomy**, are paid extremely well, often working flexibly, engaged in dynamic problem-solving activities. Such workers can be found in a wide range of new occupations regarded as part of the 'infotech sector' – jobs such as web designers, systems analysts, in e-commerce, software development, graphic design and financial consultancy. At the lower end of this sector, however, are growing numbers of casual workers who spend all day on the telephone in front of a VDU, often working in very poor conditions in call-centres.

The middle classes are, therefore, an important and vibrant part of the class structure. What was once the minority, perceived as a class apart from the working class in terms of income, lifestyle, status, and culture, has become a much larger, more heterogeneous (diverse) body.

The working class

Changes in class solidarity

Fulcher and Scott (1999) point out that until the late 20th century, the working class had a strong sense of their social-class position. Virtually all aspects of their lives, including gender roles, family life, political affiliation and leisure, were a product of their keen sense of working-class identity. Lockwood's (1966) research found that many workers, especially in industrial areas,

Simon Charlesworth

A phenomenology of working-class experience

Simon Charlesworth's study focuses on working-class people in Rotherham in Yorkshire, the town where he grew up. Charlesworth based his study on 43 unstructured, conversational interviews, though he clearly spoke to large numbers of people whom he knew socially. Many of the people to whom he spoke were male, but at least a third were female. Charlesworth finds class seeping into all aspects of life in Rotherham and the lives of the people are ones of suffering. The loss of a man's job, for instance, has a physical consequence because it can lead to fear and panic consequent on loss of earnings. Older people are

faced with the difficulties of learning to cope with a changing world, and even his younger respondents are often surprised by the behaviour of those even younger than themselves. One of the main points is that miserable economic conditions seem to cause people to feel both physically and psychologically unhealthy.

Many of the workers experience a lack of identity and a sense of being devalued because of the loss of status accompanying the lack of paid work. Others see no point in education or qualifications because even if they acquire them, they are not able to obtain decent work. There are further problems for those who do go to university or college in that they feel out of place and excluded from the culture because they are not fully part of it. The culture of the working-class lad demands that he be respected.

Changes in the social climate have left people without a sense of belonging to each other or of understanding how the world is developing. They have little sense of hope in the future and worry for their children. This has been one of the direst results of the years of Thatcherism and recent government policies that have not fully challenged the views of the New Right. He claims people feel rage and suffering; unemployment is destructive to people because it forces them into poverty. The culture that develops is one of having to make do, or to buy only what is necessary. It is marked by social and spiritual decay. Language is marked by heavy use of swearing and often friendship is displayed through a form of public insult.

Adapted from Blundell, J. and Griffiths, J. (2002) *Sociology since 1995*, Vol 2, Lewes: Connect Publications

1 Identify two criticisms that might be made of Charlesworth's methods as described in the passage above.

2 What factors have caused working-class culture in Rotherham to be marked by a 'social and spiritual decay'?

subscribed to a value system he called '**proletarian traditionalist**'. Such workers felt a strong sense of loyalty to each other because of shared community and work experience, and so were mutually supportive of each other. They had a keen sense of class solidarity and consciousness. They tended to see society, therefore, in terms of conflict, in terms of 'them versus us'.

Later research has claimed that this type of class identity is in decline because the service sector of the economy has grown more important as the traditional industrial and manufacturing sectors have gone into decline. Recession and unemployment have undermined traditional working-class communities and organizations such as trade unions. However, Cannadine (1998) argues that this idea – that once upon a time the working class subscribed to a collective class consciousness and an adversarial view of society – is exaggerated and the evidence lacking. He argues that the history of the working class suggests no clear

consistent pattern of class consciousness – collectivism only emerges at particular times and in particular contexts, and even then, is rarely universally shared.

Middle-class lifestyles?

In the 1960s, Zweig (1961) argued that a section of the working class – skilled manual workers – had adopted the economic and cultural lifestyle of the middle class. This argument became known as the '**embourgeoisement** thesis' because it insisted that skilled workers had become more like the middle class by supporting bourgeois values and the Conservative party as well as enjoying similar income levels.

This view was investigated in Goldthorpe and Lockwood's famous study of a car factory in Luton (1969). They found little evidence to support Zweig's assertion. Economically, whilst wages were comparable to those of members of the middle

Families and households

The concept of 'underclass' is a useful tool to use to construct synoptic links. The New Right see the growth of a criminal and antisocial underclass as fuelled by the rise in numbers of single teenage mothers, who are failing to control their delinquent children. Combined with the decline of marriage, and the growth of divorce and cohabitation, this group is seen as a threat to the stability of the nuclear family and social order.

Education

In terms of education, the underclass is also seen by the New Right as mainly responsible for problems such as poor classroom discipline, exclusion, truancy and poor levels of achievement in state schools in inner-city areas. It is argued that the poor attitude held by parents in the underclass towards education is more important than poverty or other forms of material deprivation in explaining educational underachievement.

Wealth, poverty and welfare

In the field of welfare and poverty, the New Right suggest that members of the underclass 'choose' to be poor and are happy to be dependent on welfare benefits.

Crime and deviance

Finally, the underclass are seen by the New Right as constituting a criminal class, in that, for them, the benefits of crime far outweigh the costs because they lack the normal range of controls that law-abiding people have in their lives.

---

classes, they did not enjoy the same working conditions or fringe benefits, such as expense accounts, company car, sick pay or company pensions. They had to work longer hours and had less chance of promotion. They did not readily mix with members of other classes, either inside or outside work, and 77 per cent of their sample voted Labour. Goldthorpe and Lockwood did, however, argue that there were signs of **convergence** between working-class and middle-class lifestyles, but concluded that, rather than an increase in the middle class, what had emerged was a new working class.

Privatization

Goldthorpe and Lockwood identified a new trend, the emergence of the 'privatized instrumentalist' worker who saw work as a means to an end rather than as a source of identity. These affluent workers were more home-centred than traditional working-class groups; they were also less likely to subscribe to the notion of working-class community and 'them-versus-us' attitudes. Fiona Devine (1992) undertook a second study of the Vauxhall plant at Luton, in which she argued that Goldthorpe and Lockwood's study may have exaggerated the degree of working-class privatization. She found that workers retained strong kinship and friendship links, and were critically aware of class inequalities such as the unequal distribution of wealth and income.

Although the concept of embourgeoisement is now rarely used, it is frequently argued that the working class have fragmented into at least two different layers:

- the traditional working class, typically situated in the north of England
- a new working class found in the newer manufacturing industries, mainly situated in the south who enjoy a relatively affluent lifestyle but still see themselves as working-class.

False consciousness?

Marxists reject the view that there is a fragmented working class. They argue that there is still a unified working class made up of manual workers – both Black and White, male and female, and routine white-collar workers. They would argue that the sorts of divisions discussed above are the product of ruling-class ideology, which attempts to divide and rule the working class. The fact that some groups do not see themselves as working class is dismissed by Marxists as false class-consciousness. They would argue that in relation to the means and social relations of production, all so-called 'class fractions' are objectively working class because they are alienated and exploited by the ruling class, whether they realize it or not.

Does class identity still exist?

Postmodernists argue that class identity has fragmented into numerous separate and individualized identities. Social identity is now more pluralistic and diverse. Pakulski and Waters (1996) argue that people now exercise more choice about what type of people they want to be. Gender, ethnicity, age, region and family role interact and impact with consumption and media images to construct postmodern culture and identity.

However, postmodern ideas may be exaggerated as recent surveys indicate that social class is still a significant source of identity for many (e.g. Marshall et al. 1988). Members of a range of classes are still aware of class differences and are happy to identify themselves using class categories. Savage, too, agrees that class identities continue to exist, but he argues that people only use them to indicate themselves as 'ordinary' or 'middling'. Class is rarely viewed as an issue by most people. According to Savage, class identities have declined in importance because of changes in the organization of the economy (for example, the decline of **primary industries** and factory work, the expansion of white-collar work as well as the rise of more insecure forms of manual and non-manual work), which Savage argues have dissolved class boundaries.

The underclass

The concept of the underclass has entered everyday speech to describe those living at the margins of society, largely reliant on state benefits to make ends meet. However, the concept is rejected by many sociologists due to its negative and sometimes politically charged connotations. Members of the political right, such as Charles Murray (1994) in the USA, have focused on the cultural 'deficiencies' of the so-called underclass, blaming them for their situation, and accusing them of relying on benefits and even manipulating their own circumstances to increase the amount that they can claim from the state. Sometimes, it is also argued, they supplement their income through petty crime, or compensate for deprivation through excessive drug and alcohol abuse. Murray has focused on a Black underclass which, he alleges, is to be found in most American cities. Similar points have been made about members of non-working groups in deprived areas of Britain (Dennis and Erdos 1993).

Check your understanding

1 **How has the structure of the upper class changed in the last 50 years?**

2 **What is the 'establishment'?**

3 **Why do some writers suggest that we should no longer talk of the middle class but of the 'middle classes'?**

4 **How do managers differ from professionals?**

5 **Why do Marxists see white-collar workers as experiencing proletarianization?**

6 **What was the 'embourgeoisement thesis' and how was it challenged?**

7 **How do Marxists challenge the view that the working class has fragmented?**

8 **What happened to class identity, according to postmodernists such as Pakulski and Waters?**

9 **What is an 'underclass'?**

10 **How does the New Right view of the underclass differ from the Marxist view?**

A matter of choice?

Many New Right commentators (such as Saunders 1995) suggest that a large number of the poor see 'poverty' as a choice, a way of life preferable to work. Young mothers are often cited as examples of this – for example, by having a second child in order to secure a flat that will be paid for by the state. Various studies such as those by Morris (1993) and Gallie (1994) have examined the extent to which the poor possess cultural differences that may account for their situation. They find that there is little evidence of an underclass culture and, if anything, find the most disadvantaged groups have greater commitment to the concept of work than many other groups.

Marxists are also sceptical about the existence of an underclass. They point out that capitalist economies produce large numbers of poorly skilled and insecure workers who are constantly at risk of falling into poverty because capitalism is an unstable and inconsistent economic system. Bottero (2005) notes:

<< *In highly unequal labour markets there is always someone at the bottom, but this does not mean that the lowest brick is any different from the other bricks in the pile. The underclass are simply elements of the working class who have been hit by adverse life-course events or economic recession.* >> (p.226)

Rather than blaming the cultural deficiencies of the poor, critics of the underclass thesis prefer to use the concept of social exclusion to explain poverty. Social exclusion can take many forms, the accumulated effects of which can lead to extreme poverty. Consider the current refugee 'crisis' concerning Eastern European immigrants to Britain: these people are excluded from gaining anything but casual low-paid work; they may be ineligible for state benefits; they have language barriers to contend with and may also be socially excluded due to xenophobic attitudes and racism.

It is perhaps understandable that social exclusion may build resentment that can lead to other social ills such as crime or increased suicide rates. Young (1999) suggests that crime rates may be reflecting the fact that a growing number of people do not feel valued or feel that they have little investment in the societies in which they live.

research ideas

1 Ask a sample of adults across a range of occupations how 'flexible' their work is. Ask them about their job security, the sort of tasks they do, their working hours, how much freedom they have, and so on.

2 Conduct a survey of your peers in casual part-time employment to find out the conditions of work they experience.

KEY TERMS

Autonomy – freedom to organize one's own workload.

Boundary problem – the constantly shifting nature of work makes it more difficult to draw boundaries between classes of workers.

Class fractions – subdivisions within particular mass groupings.

Convergence – coming together, e.g. of working-class and middle-class lifestyles.

Cultural capital – social advantages associated with the middle classes.

De-skilling – reducing the skill needed to do a job.

Downsizing – reducing the size of the permanent workforce.

Economic capital – money in shares (and so on) which generates more money.

Embourgeoisement – the idea that the working class is adopting the attitudes, lifestyle and economic situation of the middle classes.

Primary industries – those involved in extraction of raw materials, e.g. mining, agriculture, fishing.

Proletarianization – a tendency for lower-middle-class workers to become de-skilled and hence to share the market position of members of the working class.

Proletarian traditionalist – members of the working class with a strong sense of loyalty to each other because of shared community and work experience.

Routine white-collar workers – clerical staff involved in low-status, repetitive office work.

Secondary industries – those involved in producing products from raw materials.

Self-employed/petit-bourgeois – owners of small businesses.

Social closure – the process by which high-status groups exclude lower-status groups from joining their ranks.

Tertiary or service sector – jobs providing services such as transport, retailing, hotel work, cleaning, banking and insurance.

exploring changes in the class structure

Item A

There is a new working class employed typically in hypermarkets, restaurants and hotels and in other businesses connected with leisure, sport and tourism. Such work is usually mundane and low paid, low level, part-time and casual. However, because of their visibility to the client group such often young (attractive) people are required to supply aesthetic labour – looking right to boost the company's image and appearing human and interested in their commitment to customer satisfaction. Such work can be stressful and demeaning. There is more work in call centres, with security firms, in fast food outlets such as McDonalds and with contract cleaners. This new working class is fragmented. Their work is often part-time and insecure and likely to be at odd, variable hours.

Source: Roberts, K. (2001) *Class in Modern Britain*, Basingstoke: Palgrave

(a) Identify and briefly explain **two** reasons why researching the upper class might be more difficult than researching the middle and working classes. (8 marks)

This part of the question includes assessment of your understanding of the connections between Stratification and Differentiation and sociological methods.

(b) Using information from **Item A** and elsewhere, examine the idea that the working class is fragmented with regard to **at least two** of the following areas: education; wealth, poverty and welfare; work and leisure; family and households; health; religion; power and politics; world sociology. (12 marks)

This part of the question includes assessment of your understanding of the connections between Stratification and Differentiation and other substantive topic(s) you have studied.

(c) Assess the view that a classless society now exists in Britain. (40 marks)

This part of the question includes assessment of the connections between Stratification and Differentiation and sociological theory.

Social mobility

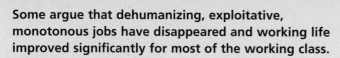

getting you thinking

Some argue that dehumanizing, exploitative, monotonous jobs have disappeared and working life improved significantly for most of the working class.

1 Look at the two photos of people doing different jobs. Are they evidence for or against the view expressed above? Explain your answer.

2 What does the extract tell us about increasing opportunities in Britain?

A north–south divide?
National statistics showing overall improvement may actually mask regional inequalities. The average household in Britain spent £359 per week in 1999/2000. However, a London household spent about £400, whereas in the North East it was £290.

Adapted from: Denscombe, M. (2001)
Sociology Update, Leicester: Olympus

The movement of individuals up or down the social scale is known as social mobility. We only need to look around us or to talk to older people to see that the population nowadays is generally more affluent and enjoys better working conditions – in other words, there appears to have been considerable upward social mobility. However, as the exercise above may have shown, the picture is far less simple once we start taking into account variations caused by factors such as region, ethnicity or gender. These difficulties have not prevented sociologists from attempting to measure social mobility and using their results to comment on the extent to which society is becoming more open or closed.

Types of social mobility

There are two main ways of looking at social mobility:

- **Intergenerational** mobility refers to movement between generations, e.g. a son moving further up the social scale than his father.
- **Intragenerational** mobility refers to the movement of an individual within their working life. An individual may start off as an office junior and work their way up to office manager, win the lottery or marry someone wealthy.

Problems of measuring social mobility

The use of occupation as an indicator of social class creates many problems (as discussed in Topic 1, p. 314). The earliest studies of social mobility used the Registrar General's scale which, as we have seen, considered an individual's social class solely in terms of the occupation of the male head of household. In fact, this indicator of class persisted well beyond the period for which it had any relevance at all, mainly because of the comparative nature of social mobility studies. How, after all, can you draw any conclusions about the nature of social movement if it is not possible to compare like with like?

Another key problem is that mobility studies focus on the working population and say nothing about the very rich and the very poor – important groups in society, both of whom are unlikely to work, albeit for different reasons. Most importantly, the gap between these two groups appears to be increasing.

Social mobility studies

The Oxford (Nuffield) Mobility Study (OMS) 1972

This large-scale study in 1972 led by John Goldthorpe (1980a) found high rates of what is known as **absolute mobility**. Absolute mobility refers to the overall numbers (in percentages) of individuals from specific origins reaching particular class destinations. The Oxford Mobility Study (OMS), using the Hope-Goldthorpe scale of measuring social class, compared sons with fathers in their sample and discovered much greater numbers of people from working-class origins being upwardly mobile into the service class compared with the 1950s and 1960s. Over two-thirds of the service class had started off either in the intermediate or working classes. For example, 16 per cent of working-class sons had risen into middle-class occupations by 1972, whilst 15 per cent of middle-class sons had experienced downward mobility into working-class jobs. Further data taken from the National Child Development Study (NCDS) in 1991 confirms these trends – according to its data, 26 per cent of working sons had experienced upward social mobility into middle-class jobs.

Why has absolute mobility increased?

Goldthorpe points out that an increase in absolute mobility is not necessarily the product of meritocracy or evidence that society has become open in terms of its opportunities. He suggests three reasons for this:

- There have been changes in the economy and, therefore, the occupational structure, i.e. the job market. The proportion of the working population in the service class (middle-class jobs with good pay and prospects) is increasing, while the intermediate class (lower white-collar jobs) and working class (manual work) are decreasing in size. For example, between 1901 and 1961, the proportion of working-class jobs as part of the working population declined from 75 per cent to 38 per cent, whilst the percentage of professionals and managers increased from 8 per cent to 34 per cent. In particular, the service class has more than doubled in numbers since the 1950s because of the expansion in government in areas such as the welfare state. This led to a greater demand for professionals and administrators in the fields of education, welfare and health.

Furthermore, the financial service sector, in particular, has expanded whilst heavy industry, which mainly employs manual workers, has gone into serious decline. These trends mean that the sons of those working in 1960 have significantly more chance of getting into the service class than their fathers.

- There have been differences in the fertility rate of social classes and consequently in the number of children being born. The fertility rate of the service class has been too low to cope with the growth of service-sector jobs. This sector therefore had no choice but to recruit from other social classes.

- Education has dramatically expanded since the Second World War. In particular, the introduction of free secondary education in 1944 and the expansion of higher education made recruitment into the service class easier because, for the first time, people from working-class backgrounds had access to educational qualifications.

The significance of relative mobility

On the face of it, it would appear that there has been a significant amount of social mobility across the generations. However, what such data masks is the relative chance that a person from a particular class has of moving upwards or downwards. This is known as **relative mobility**. By comparing the relative mobility chances of different generations, it is possible to determine whether the class structure has become more open. The data from the OMS suggests that there is little evidence of this. Rather, the OMS discovered that boys from the service class were four times more likely to obtain a service-class job than boys from the working class and twice as likely as boys from the intermediate class. The OMS dubbed this '**the 1–2–4 rule of relative hope**' and argued that, while there was more room at the top indicated by absolute mobility levels, there was little sign that this was accompanied by greater equality in opportunities for all social classes to get there.

The Scottish Mobility Study (SMS)

This study by Payne (1987) noted that the potential for social mobility was also dependent upon age and region. For example, the data noted that social mobility was more likely to occur in the south-east of England, especially London. Young people living in this region were more likely to enjoy both job and promotion opportunities that propelled them upwards compared with their parents. However, in contrast, people living in the North of England and Scotland, especially those belonging to an older age profile, were significantly less likely to experience job and promotion opportunities that would help them to escape the social class of their parents (see Table 6.6).

Such mobility patterns may lead to a growing heterogeneous (mixed) middle class, based largely in the south-east of England, underpinned by an increasingly homogeneous (similar) working class and underclass, located mainly in the north of England and Scotland. Some sociologists have suggested that members of the underclass, particularly young people, may grow resentful of their lack of opportunities and engage in disruptive behaviour, such as inner-city rioting, as a form of protest.

However, Payne is more optimistic and stresses that sociologists should be looking at mobility between jobs rather than between social classes. He argues that the emphasis on movement between broad class groupings detracts from the fact that there are still generally high rates of upward mobility, i.e. people from working-class origins are moving into middle-class jobs. In this sense, Payne argues that relative rates of mobility are less important than absolute rates.

The Essex University Mobility Study (EUMS)

This study by Marshall et al. (1988) largely confirmed the findings of the OMS. The EUMS found that someone starting in

Table 6.6 The Scottish Mobility Study's Findings

	Age	Location	Region
Associated with high mobility	Young	Urban	South of England
Associated with low mobility	Older	Rural	North and Scotland

the service class had a seven times greater chance of ending up in the service class than someone from a working-class background. Marshall argues that these relative rates tell us that we are still far from being an equal-life-chance society. Moreover, Marshall does not share Payne's optimism about absolute mobility; he argues that the data suggest that the expansion of service-class jobs has slowed down and will soon end, so blocking opportunities for those outside the service class.

Why have changes in absolute mobility not been accompanied by changes in relative mobility?

Politicians are fond of portraying the UK as a society in which people have the opportunities to better themselves, i.e. as a meritocratic society in which all social groups are treated fairly. However, as we have seen, data from the OMS and EUMS, in particular, contradict this view, indicating simply that the service sector has expanded, rather than that any revolution in equality has taken place. In fact, the OMS and EUMS go further and strongly suggest that equality is unlikely to occur in the near

synoptic link   sociological methods

Social mobility studies suffer a number of methodological problems that can undermine the reliability of their research tools and the validity of their findings:

- There has not been universal agreement on how to operationalize social class (see Topic 1) across all mobility studies. The earliest studies used the Registrar General's classification, which takes occupation as the primary indicator of social class. In the 1970s and 1980s, this was generally replaced by the Hope-Goldthorpe scale with its emphasis on market situation and employment conditions. However, this scale was particularly rejected by feminist sociologists because it classed women as economic appendages of either their husbands or fathers. To complicate matters further, this scale became the government's new classification –

the NS-SEC – in 2000, and included women on the basis of their jobs, independently from men. All these factors mean that comparative analysis of data from different mobility studies is extremely difficult.

- Such classifications very rarely keep up with contemporary developments. For example, employment conditions are constantly evolving and, as we see from the example of call-centres, occupations that might be classed as middle-class may have more in common with manual occupations in terms of job security, satisfaction and status.
- Some studies – notably, Saunders, and Savage and Egerton (see below) – have used the same data from the NCDS, but have interpreted this data in quite different ways. For example, Saunders sees such data as evidence that inequality is decreasing, whereas Savage and Egerton see the same data as evidence that inequality is still a major problem.

future because of the existence of class barriers and social closure that prevent bright working-class people, in particular, from getting ahead.

These views of the UK are not universally shared, however. The New Right sociologist, Peter Saunders claims the stress on relative mobility by Goldthorpe and Marshall indicates a deliberate desire by left-wing sociologists to obscure the fact that capitalism works reasonably well as a meritocratic system. He argues that absolute levels of mobility are more important than relative levels. A number of theories have evolved out of this debate.

Intelligence theory

Saunders (1995), using data from the NCDS, argues that there is a genetic base to social mobility. He suggests that people with middle-class jobs are generally brighter than those with working-class jobs. He claims that, like height and weight, there is a genetic base to most of the abilities and intelligence that people develop. Bright parents, therefore, have bright children. Saunders argues that the best predictor of where we end up in terms of occupations and social class is **innate** ability or merit, which he claims is twice as important as social-class background. He also suggests that middle-class parents are better at motivating their children. He further concludes that private schooling, cultural capital, material conditions in the home and parental contact with schools are only a minor influence on a child's future destination. Saunders concludes that 'in the end what matters most is whether you are bright, and whether you work hard' (p.72).

Saunders argues that absolute mobility is more important than relative mobility because it has had a profound effect on how people think about their social status and class position, and how they judge what is fair in modern society. In particular, Saunders argues that absolute mobility has had a profound effect upon people's attitudes towards the future – it has resulted in the working class becoming more aspirational and seeing upward mobility as a very real possibility for their children. Moreover, their experience of upward social mobility and the improvements in living standards that accompany it means that they have greater expectations about consumption than previous generations. Payne (1992) makes a similar point when he notes:

>> *Manual workers in this country now expect to own a car, and a television, to occupy a dwelling of several rooms in good physical condition, to take a holiday abroad, to have several sets of clothing. Such a lifestyle would in 1950 have been associated with the middle or upper classes, who made up about one quarter of society. In less than a single lifetime, manual workers have in consumption terms been upwardly mobile.>> (p.220)

Saunders argues that absolute mobility data is convincing evidence that capitalism has opened up new opportunities for advancement and brought fantastic benefits to the working class.

However, Saunders' methodology has come under sustained attack. Roberts (2001) is critical of Saunders' use of intelligence tests and argues that it is impossible to measure raw innate ability. He notes 'performance in intelligence tests, the construction of these tests, and what we mean by ability, are all socially contaminated' (p.219). Best (2005) notes that Saunders' sample was biased towards the middle class because he excluded part-time workers, housewives and the unemployed. Moreover, other research has clearly shown that some teachers often label working-class pupils negatively, thereby affecting their motivation. These classroom practices may lead to a self-fulfilling prophecy of low achievement. Apparent low ability and motivation may, therefore, be the product of class.

Savage (2000) argues that claims that middle-class children are brighter is an ideological myth. He states:

>> *It is quite plausible – indeed likely – that those who fill these (middle-class) jobs will be deemed to be 'brighter' than those who do not. However, in this case, 'brightness' does not cause mobility, it is simply the filter that distinguishes those who are upwardly mobile from those who are not.>> (p. 77)

Neo-Marxist theory

Marxists argue that inequalities in relative mobility reflect wider social-class inequalities that are a natural consequence of the exploitative social relations of production that exist under capitalism. They argue that the economically dominant classes are able to construct educational systems that reflect their cultural values. The educational environment benefits middle-class children because their home experience and upbringing have equipped them with the knowledge and skills (cultural capital) that fits the requirements of both the academic and the hidden curriculum. Working-class children, on the other hand, are disadvantaged because their knowledge, skills and experiences are often dismissed as unimportant by the educational system. Marxists, therefore, argue that the economic and social advantages enjoyed by middle-class children are responsible for their upward social mobility.

Marxists are interested in the ideological effects of social mobility. For example, they argue that the few working-class people who do achieve upward mobility are used to create the myth that capitalist societies are truly open and meritocratic. They also argue that sections of the lower middle class, particular white-collar workers working in call-centres, have experienced a decline in status, career prospects and relative income, and therefore, downward intragenerational mobility. Marxist sociologists argue that employment conditions in call-centres are not that dissimilar to the factory floor and assembly line. As Denscombe (1999) notes, such workers 'receive low pay and there is little opportunity for contact with other workers. There is little or no opportunity for creativity in their work, sticking as they do to a prepared script and having their calls monitored'. Marxists suggest that the very high level of staff turnover in these jobs indicates high levels of alienation.

Marxists note that, although reforms have widened the educational opportunities of working-class children and improved their attainment levels, it is the middle or service class that has taken most advantage of the expansion of educational opportunities in the UK, especially the expansion of higher education. For example, 80 per cent of middle-class children go into higher education, compared with less than 15 per cent of children from the unskilled working class. There is evidence, too, that because of cultural and social capital, people from middle-class origins are more likely to be promoted at work than those from working-class backgrounds. As Roberts comments:

<< Connections are useful – knowing people who will put in a word at the right time. Then there is the matter of having the right kind of accent, tastes and dress sense to be regarded as the right type of person.>> (p.217)

Savage and Egerton (1997), using the same NCDS data as Saunders, argue that people from working-class backgrounds need to have more intelligence and more qualifications to reach the same positions as their middle-class peers. They note that both the ruling class and the service class are able to find ways of preventing even their less 'able' sons from moving down the social ladder. They found that low-ability children with service-class fathers had much more chance of staying in the service class than ending up in other classes. Furthermore, 75 per cent of high-ability sons of service-class fathers ended up in the service class compared to 45 per cent of the high-ability sons of working class fathers. This disparity was even greater for working-class, high-ability girls who, it seems, had less than half the chance of their service-class counterparts of ending up in that class. Savage and Egerton concluded that working-class girls need to have higher levels of ability than working-class males if they are to progress into the service class.

Savage and Egerton argue that Saunders' focus on innate ability serves to justify inequality because the idea that some people are 'naturally' less intelligent hides the real cause of their inequality, i.e. their social-class position. However, neo-Marxist theory does not escape criticism. New Right sociologists have asked whether there really is such a match between what goes on in middle-class homes and the culture of education. If the system so benefits the economically dominant, why would some members of the middle class experience downward mobility?

Rational action theory

Goldthorpe (1996) argues that inequalities in relative levels of social mobility may be the result of the fact that people are '**rational actors**' who calculate the relative costs and benefits of trying to reach occupational destinations. However, Goldthorpe argues that these costs and benefits will differ in value depending on where in the socio-economic order a person starts. As Roberts (2001) notes:

<< Supporting a child through higher education will be a greater burden on a working-class family, relative to its resources, than for a middle-class family. A working-class child who achieves an intermediate-class position is likely to be regarded as successful, whereas a middle-class family will view this as a failure and might well do everything possible to secure a better outcome.>> (p.222)

focus on research

Geoff Payne & Judy Roberts (2002)
Male social mobility

Payne and Roberts used data from the 1987, 1992 and 1997 British Election Survey, in combination with OMS data from 1972 and 1983, to examine rates of absolute and relative mobility. In terms of absolute mobility, they found that the proportions of men being mobile between 1972 and 1997 had increased – for example, 55 per cent of men were in a different social class from the one in which they had been born. They also found that over half the men born into the manual class were upwardly mobile in 1992, compared with 39 per cent in 1972. In regard to relative rates of mobility, Payne and Roberts argued that the gates of equality opened quite wide between 1972 and 1992, in that a service-class child only had twice the odds of returning to the service class compared with a working-class child making it to the service class. This finding was obviously an improvement on the 1–2–4 rule of relative hope set out by the OMS in 1972. However, their 1997 data shows these gates closing again for two reasons: the service sector has stopped growing, i.e. there are fewer middle-class jobs to be upwardly mobile into, and the odds of working-class people making it into these jobs has increased again back to 1972 levels.

Adapted from Payne, G. and Roberts, J. (2002) 'Opening and closing the gates: recent developments in male social mobility in Britain', *Sociological Research Online*, 6(4), Feb 2002

1 What problems can you see in the methodology used by Payne and Roberts?

2 How might their data for 1972 to 1992 support that of Peter Saunders?

3 How might their 1997 data support the work of Savage or Marshall?

Evaluating theories of social mobility

Social mobility studies tend to work using fairly broad structural categories such as working class, intermediate class and service class. However, such studies often do not recognize that these categories are made up of occupations that have undergone profound changes in their conditions in recent years that may affect the status and job security of workers, and therefore, experience of mobility. For example, many middle-class jobs are no longer permanent. Rather, flexible working arrangements and contracts are becoming the norm, so that a white-collar worker or professional might job-share, work part-time, be a temporary worker (e.g. a supply teacher) or be on a fixed-term contract. Although Marxist theories have focused on call-centre employment, most mobility studies do not recognize the sometimes precarious nature of these new middle-class occupations. In many ways, it can be argued that such employment conditions reflect downward mobility as far as security and job satisfaction are concerned.

Women and social mobility studies

Feminist sociologists have long complained that women have been neglected in social-mobility studies. The major mobility studies have tended to compare sons' with fathers' occupations. There seem to be three reasons for this:

- Surveys that included women would involve larger samples and so would be more expensive and time-consuming.
- The focus on men in previous studies means it is easier to compare all-male samples.
- The nature of men's and women's work is different. For example, women are more likely to be employed part-time and many women are full-time housewives.

Goldthorpe (1980b) claimed that there was no need for any independent study of female mobility since most women take their class from their husband/father. He noted that whether a woman chooses to work or not largely depends upon her husband's performance as a breadwinner. He states that 'the status a woman derives from her man, or that she acquires herself, is more significant than the status she shares with other women'. However, Abbott (1990) disagrees with this view. She argues that there is a need to study female mobility because women's experience of work is different from that of men. Consequently, men and women experience different absolute-mobility rates. Abbott argues that the limited mobility prospects of women actually enhance men's opportunities. For example, if women find it difficult to enter the service class, men's chances of filling these jobs obviously improves.

Women's social mobility patterns

Studies of female mobility have come to several conclusions:

- There is considerable mobility from all social classes into lower white-collar work. However, this reflects the fact that most women who work are concentrated in this type of work. In contrast, few women experience downward social mobility into manual work, simply because few women are employed in this sector.
- The EUMS (which attempted to overcome sexism by using the term 'chief childhood supporter') found that women were much more likely to experience downward social mobility compared to their fathers. Even when their male and female samples had the same qualifications, the eventual destinations of women were less advantageous compared with men.
- Kay (1996) concluded that women were more likely to be downwardly mobile than men because of career interruptions such as pregnancy and childcare. Divorce and the likelihood of being head of a single-parent family also impede upward mobility.

However, recent studies of female social mobility, aspirations and educational performance indicate the probability of positive change. Roberts argues as follows:

<<Recent school-leaving cohorts have been the first waves of young women in modern times whose mothers worked for the greater part of their adult lives and during their daughters' (and sons') childhoods. These mothers (and fathers) have encouraged their daughters to aim for decent jobs – not to be left in the typing pools or at the supermarket check-outs.>>

Studies by Wilkinson (1994), and Roberts and Chadwick (1991) indicate what Wilkinson calls a '**genderquake**' in female attitudes. Females now regard future occupational careers as an important lifestyle choice. There has been a remarkable improvement in female educational performance in the last ten years in so far as females outperform males at all levels of the British educational system. The evidence suggests that if women postpone marriage and parenthood, or if they do have children, take maternity leave rather than give up work altogether, and invest in high-quality childcare, they are likely to be highly qualified, to be in middle-class jobs, and their career prospects are likely to remain more or less in line with those of men.

However, research does indicate class inequality in female patterns of social mobility. A study by the Economic and Social Research Council, *Twenty-Something in the 90s* (1997), looked at a group of 26-year-olds who were born in 1970. It confirmed that class of origin was still a major factor affecting mobility for both men and women. The study noted however, that middle-class women were just as likely as middle-class men to go to university and from there into well-paid jobs. Unskilled women were 30 times less likely to work full-time compared with professional women. In spite of this, the study found that women's career development opportunities are still influenced by discrimination from male employers, and by their primary responsibility for domestic work and childcare forcing them to downplay their careers.

Ethnic minority social mobility patterns

Roberts argues that all non-White minorities experience an 'ethnic penalty' with regard to social mobility, in that occupational and educational outcomes are lower and the risks of unemployment are higher compared with White people with similar qualifications. The only ethnic group that does not experience this ethnic penalty are Indians. The ethnic group which seems to experience the greatest inequality in terms of social mobility are African-Caribbeans. This group is most likely to underperform in education and is most likely to be unemployed.

Platt (2005) notes that many immigrants to the UK in the 1950s experienced downward mobility, in that well-qualified Asians were forced to take jobs in manual work. Platt conducted a study of second- and third-generation Asians and African-Caribbeans and compared job destinations with parents, who were often immigrants. She found that 35 per cent of her Indian sample and 22 per cent of her African-Caribbean sample had service-class jobs, compared with 38 per cent of her White control sample. However, like the OMS before her, she concludes that this is due to the expansion of the service class and contraction of the working class rather than any significant change in equal opportunities. She also noted that the children of African-Caribbeans employed in the service class were less likely than Indians to stay in that class. They were more likely than any other group to experience downward social mobility to the working class. Platt concludes that, in the face of institutional racism and economic deprivation, social class may be weak in protecting ethnic minority groups against the possibility of downward social mobility.

Conclusions

We can see that the children of the working class are experiencing greater opportunities than 50 years ago, but so are the children of the middle class. Working-class upward mobility probably has little to do with educational expansion, despite the fact that most educational social policy has been aimed at improving working-class opportunity. It has more to do with economic changes, especially the expansion in the service sector and decline in manual work. Moreover, there are signs that females are now beginning to experience improved social mobility. The signs, however, are not great for ethnic minorities. Whilst Indians are experiencing some upward mobility, most other groups, especially African-Caribbeans are stuck at the bottom of the socio-economic hierarchy.

Roberts (2001) points out that in the 21st century, middle-class occupations are still growing in number but more slowly compared with the 20th century. Absolute mobility, therefore, is still very positive. However, Roberts notes that, despite meritocratic education systems, most Western societies experience similar differences in relative mobility. He suggests that it is unlikely that these differences will ever disappear, despite government attempts to eradicate them. He concludes with the controversial suggestion that policy-makers only try to equalize opportunities because the ruling class 'need to be seen to be making all possible efforts to ensure that success is open to all the talents' (p.223) when, in reality, it is not.

Check your understanding

1 **Why do sociologists study social mobility?**

2 **What is the difference between absolute and relative mobility?**

3 **Why has absolute social mobility increased?**

4 **What is the 1–2–4 rule of relative hope?**

5 **According to the Scottish Mobility Study, how may the 'safety valve' function of social mobility be being undermined?**

6 **How does Saunders explain differences in relative mobility?**

7 **Why does Saunders think absolute mobility is more important than relative mobility?**

8 **What do absolute mobility levels tell us about capitalism according to Saunders?**

9 **How does Savage and Egerton's work challenge Saunders' claims?**

10 **Why have women been excluded from mobility studies for so long?**

11 **What are the main reasons for the patterns in women's mobility?**

12 **How does ethnic minority social mobility compare with social mobility in general?**

web.task

Go to the government statistical service website: www.statistics.gov.uk. Find out about low pay, the distribution of employment, regional variations in income and expenditure and gender differences in employment. What do they tell us about social mobility?

exploring social mobility

Item A

Those who start at the bottom can only rise. For the working class, social mobility will appear attractive. Start at the top and the only possible move is down; at this level social mobility is a threat. We have seen that there are wide inequalities in life-chances in Britain, but, despite this, working-class parents have reasonably good chances of seeing their children ascend. These statements are not contradictory, though they appear so at first. One is based on relative, and the other on absolute mobility rates. Both statements are true. Likewise the facts that, on the one hand, risks of demotion for those who start at the top are much lower than they would be in an equal life-chance society, but still sufficient to give the middle class realistic grounds for worry.

Downward mobility from the middle class is sufficiently common to be perceived as a very real threat. Middle-class parents will do almost anything to reduce the risks. They are keen to attend schools with good academic records, and at any sign of failure they are likely to provide private coaching or opt for full private education.

Adapted from Roberts, K. (2001) *Class in Modern Britain*, Basingstoke: Palgrave, pp. 201–2

(a) Using material from **Item A** and elsewhere, identify and briefly explain the meaning of absolute **and** relative mobility. (8 marks)

This part of the question includes assessment of the connections between Stratification and Differentiation and sociological theory.

(b) Examine the influence of upward and downward mobility on people's lives in **two or more** of the following areas: families and households; health; education; wealth, poverty and welfare; work and leisure; religion; power and politics; world sociology. (12 marks)

This part of the question includes assessment of your understanding of the connections between Stratification and Differentiation and other substantive topic(s) you have studied.

(c) 'Studies of social mobility are fundamentally flawed because their research methods are unreliable and consequently their findings lack validity.'

Assess the usefulness of sociological studies of social mobility in the light of this statement. (40 marks)

This part of the question includes assessment of your understanding of the connections between Stratification and Differentiation and sociological methods.

outcomes. Teachers, for example, may be committed to anti-racist education but schools still expel four times as many Black pupils as White.

One way of tackling institutional racism is to increase the numbers of ethnic-minority employees working within key institutions, especially in the higher positions. Also, close monitoring of inclusion and exclusion of ethnic-minority groups can highlight imbalances that can then be addressed through equal-opportunities strategies.

Ethnic minorities and life-chances: empirical evidence

Ethnic minorities are disadvantaged in many areas of social life. However, it is very important to be aware of the significant differences between the various minorities, and of the way inequalities also link with gender and class differences. For example, the majority of Muslim immigrants entered Britain at the bottom of the socio-economic ladder. Many (mostly Pakistanis and Bangladeshis) are still concentrated in semi-skilled and unskilled sectors of industry. These communities suffer from unemployment, poor working conditions, poverty, overcrowded housing, poor health, and low educational qualifications. The 2001 disturbances in Oldham, Burnley and Bradford highlighted how multiple social deprivation leads to deep disaffection, alienation and frustration. The areas most affected suffered from relatively high levels of youth unemployment, inadequate youth facilities, and a lack of strong civic identity or shared social values to unite the diverse local communities. Those communities remain strongly polarized along ethnic, cultural, religious and economic lines. A feeling of 'us' and 'them' developed between communities, enabling divisive racist organizations such as the British National Party (BNP) to exploit anti-Muslim feelings among many White people. However, a degree of social mobility exists within British Muslim communities. In the early 1990s, the proportion of Pakistanis in professional occupations already exceeded that for White people; successful business ventures in property, food, services and fashion have continued to expand. Many Pakistanis have moved to affluent suburbia. There is a high proportion of skilled Arab settlers employed in professional positions as engineers, professors, doctors and businesspeople. Currently, there are over 5000 Muslim millionaires in Britain.

synopticlink

health – education – wealth, poverty and welfare

Health

- Infant mortality is 100% higher among the children of African-Caribbean or Pakistani mothers than among children of White mothers.
- Pakistani and Bangladeshi people are five times more likely to be diagnosed with diabetes and 50% more likely to have coronary heart disease than White people.
- African-Caribbean women have 80% higher rates for diagnosed hypertension than Whites.
- 2000 fully qualified asylum-seeking and refugee doctors are either prohibited from working or are forced into unskilled work.

Education

- In 2002, 2000 asylum-seeking children did not receive formal education.
- Bangladeshi, Pakistani and Black pupils achieve less than other pupils at all stages of compulsory education. African-Caribbean children have equal, if not higher, ability than White children on entrance to school, but African-Caribbean boys do least well at school. In 2003, only 41% of Pakistani pupils, 37% of Black pupils, and 45% of Bangladeshi pupils achieved 5 or more GCSEs at grades A* to C, compared with 51% of White pupils and 65% of Indian pupils.
- African-Caribbean pupils are over four to six times more likely to be excluded than White pupils, and three times more likely to be excluded permanently. Many of those excluded are of higher or average ability, although the schools see them as underachieving.

- Over half of children from Traveller and Gypsy/Roma heritage and Asian Bangladeshi groups were eligible for free school meals (an indicator of low income). Children who were eligible for free school meals were far less likely to achieve the expected outcomes for Key Stages 1 to 4.

Public services

- 35% of Black people believe they will receive worse treatment than others from the police.
- About a third of Black people believe immigration services will treat them worse than they treat others.
- 28% identified prisons and courts as places where they could expect poorer treatment than other people.

Housing

- 70% of all people from ethnic minorities live in the 88 most deprived local authority districts, compared with 40% of the general population.
- Almost half of all people from ethnic-minority groups live in London, where they make up 28% of all residents.
- A fifth of the housing occupied by asylum seekers is unfit for human habitation.
- Some ethnic-minority groups are more likely to live in poor housing (English House Condition Survey 1996). 30% of Bangladeshi and 22% of Pakistani households live in overcrowded housing (all types of tenancy), reflecting a lack of larger housing and lower incomes (from the Survey of English Housing 1999 to 2002).

work and leisure – power and politics

Work

- One in eight people from ethnic-minority groups reported discrimination at a job interview.
- The number of employment tribunal claims under race discrimination was 3183 in 2001/02, almost double the number of cases in 1995. Statistics demonstrate that race discrimination cases remain the least likely to succeed of all tribunal cases and thus the percentage chance of success is very low indeed. Thus recent research indicates that only 16% of race discrimination cases win at tribunals. This figure is startlingly low, when one considers the level of apparent discrimination suffered by certain minorities at work.
- Those interviewed report being passed over for promotion, putting up with racist language, management only paying lip service to equal opportunities, and more subtle discrimination (TUC).
- Unemployment is considerably higher among ethnic-minority communities. In 2002, on average, 4.7% of White people of working age were unemployed, but among people from ethnic minorities it was nearly treble that at 14%. It was 16% for Pakistani people and 21% for Bangladeshi people.
- The disparity is even greater among the young, with 37% of Bangladeshis aged 16 to 24 and 35% of Pakistanis unemployed compared with 11% of White.
- An African-Caribbean graduate is more than twice as likely to be unemployed as a White graduate, while an African is seven times as likely.
- Ethnic-minority men are overrepresented in the service sector. The distribution industry (including restaurants and retail businesses) is the largest single source of service-sector jobs for men from ethnic-minority groups, employing 70 per cent of Bangladeshi and 58 per cent of Chinese men. In contrast, only 17 per cent of White and 19 per cent of Black men work in this industry (Labour Market trends 2000).

The legal system

- Racial harassment incidents are widespread and underreported — it is estimated that only 5% of incidents are reported to the police.
- Ethnic minorities are overrepresented throughout the criminal justice system from 'stop and search' to prison.
- Black people were eight times more likely to be stopped and searched than White people, and Asian people were almost three times more likely to be stopped and searched than White people.
- In a recent publication, *Race Equality in Prison*, the Commission for Racial Equality (CRE) found that for every 100 000 White people in Britain, 188 were in jail. For Black people, this figure was 1704. Black people are, therefore, over nine times more likely to be in prison than their White counterparts.
- People from ethnic minorities made up 18% of the male prison population and 24% of the female prison population, with Black people alone accounting for 12% of the male and 18% of the female prison population.
- 89% of young Black prisoners were sentenced for over 12 months compared to 75% of young White and 77% of Asian prisoners.

Sources: Commission for Racial Equality 2002; Home Office (2001) *Home Office Citizenship Survey: People, Families and Communities*, HORS 270; Trade Union Congress: *Black and Excluded* 2002, *Black and Underpaid* 2002, *Labour Research*, April 2002; Employment Tribunal Service 2001/02; DFES 2003.

Explanations of racism and racial inequality

Cultural explanations

Stereotypes associated with cultural racism probably originate in Britain's colonial past. People pick up these stereotypes today in the course of normal socialization. A great deal of prejudice is, therefore, the result of faulty stereotypes and a lack of accurate knowledge about the true nature of Black people. This is particularly so for those who live outside the inner city where most ethnic-minority people reside. However, The Chair of the Commission for Racial Equality Trevor Phillips, commented at the CRE Race in Media Awards 2005 that reality TV has done more for racial understanding than any other media creation in recent years. He said shows like Big Brother gave people a more varied view of what Asian and Black people could be like. So-called 'reality TV', he said, has given many British people a chance to encounter people from other ethnic groups they would never meet in their own everyday lives.

The host–immigrant model

A good example of an early sociological approach that stressed the importance of culture is the host–immigrant model (Patterson 1965), which shares many of the assumptions of functionalist sociology.

This theory depicted Britain as a basically stable, homogeneous and orderly society with a high degree of consensus over values and norms. This equilibrium was disturbed by the arrival of immigrant 'strangers' who subscribed to different sets of values. Patterson described the culture clash between West Indians (boisterous and noisy, and not in the habit of queuing at bus stops!) and the English hosts (who valued privacy, quiet and 'keeping oneself to oneself'). The host–immigrant model interpreted these clashes in terms of understandable fears and anxieties on the part of the host community. The hosts were not actually racist, just very unsure about how to act towards the newcomers. Their confusion sometimes spilled over into suspicion and resentment because the migrants competed with hosts for jobs and houses. For Patterson, the main problem was not so much racism or Black–White hostility, as cultural 'strangeness'. She was reasonably optimistic about the long-term prospects for racial harmony. She thought Britain's Black migrants would eventually move toward full cultural assimilation by shedding their 'old' ethnic values and taking on the values of the host society.

Criticisms

- The host–immigrant model focuses so much on culture that it tends to end up 'blaming the victim' or scapegoating them, by attributing the difficulties of ethnic groups to their 'strange' cultures.
- Racial hostility has not declined as predicted by Patterson. The basic structure of British society remains unchanged and the struggle over jobs, housing and money continues. This may create racial tension.
- Patterson underestimated the persistence and vitality of ethnic-minority cultures.

Today the goal of 'assimilation' has largely been abandoned by policymakers. Instead 'cultural pluralism' (where ethnic minorities retain their own cultures while adjusting to a society which accepts cultural diversity) is the norm.

Weberian explanations

Explanations based on the thinking of Max Weber (1864–1920) fall into three categories.

Status inequality

There is not only a class struggle for status, income and wealth, but there is also an ethnic struggle. However, status and power are in the hands of the majority-ethnic group, thereby making it difficult for ethnic-minority groups to compete equally for jobs, housing, etc. Ethnic minorities who do manual jobs are technically part of the working class, but are likely to face prejudice and discrimination from the White working class because they suffer from status inequality as well as class inequality. Even middle-class Asians doing professional jobs may experience status inequality in the form of prejudicial attitudes held by members of both the White middle and working classes.

Organization of the job market

Such prejudice and discrimination can be seen in the distribution of ethnic minorities in the labour force. The '**dual labour-market**' theory focuses on ethnic inequalities as well as gender inequalities in employment. There are two markets for labour:

- the primary sector, characterized by secure, well-paid jobs, with long-term promotion prospects dominated by White men

- the secondary sector consisting of low-paid, unskilled and insecure jobs.

Barron and Norris (1976) point out that women and Black people are more likely to be found in the secondary sector. They are less likely to gain primary-sector employment because employers may subscribe to racist beliefs about the unsuitability of Black people – and even practise discrimination against them, either by not employing them or by denying them responsibility and promotion.

Furthermore, the legal and political framework supporting Black people is weak. Trade unions are generally White-dominated and have been accused of favouring White workers and being less interested in protecting the rights of Black workers. The Race Relations Act 1976 (which was supposed to protect Black people from discriminatory practices) was generally thought to be feeble. However, the recent amendment to the Race Relations Act which came into force in 2001, increases the need for greater clarity concerning the meaning and status of race. Building on the Macpherson report into the murder of Stephen Lawrence, it extends coverage of the Race Relations Act 1976 to the functions of public authorities in general – not just the police. It also 'places a general duty on public authorities to work towards the elimination of unlawful discrimination and promote equality of opportunity and good relations between persons of different racial groups'. With this amendment, the Race Relations Act has a much wider impact – seeking to ensure that racial discrimination is outlawed throughout the public sector and placing a duty on all public bodies and authorities to promote good race relations. It is too early, though, to say whether this amendment has had any real impact.

Underclass

Rex and Tomlinson (1979) argue that ethnic-minority experience of both class and status inequality can lead to poverty, which is made more severe by racism. Consequently, a Black underclass may be created of people who are marginalized and feel alienated and frustrated. Sometimes, if young Blacks feel they are being harassed by the police and socially excluded, these feelings may erupt in the form of inner-city riots.

In criticism, there is considerable overlap between the White and Black population in terms of poverty and unemployment, but the constant threat of racism does suggest some sort of break with the interests of the White working class. In addition, the concept of status inequality does help to explain the apparent divisions between the White and Black working class.

Marxist explanations

Marxists argue that Black people are part of the exploited working class and it is this, rather than any lack of status due to ethnicity, that determines their fate in capitalist society. Racial conflicts are usually the symptoms of some deeper underlying class problem.

Marxists suggest that racism and racial inequality are deliberately encouraged by the capitalist class for three ideological reasons:

Tariq Modood *et al.* (1997)
Ethnic minorities in Britain

The fourth major survey of ethnic minorities in Britain, carried out in 1997 by the independent Policy Studies Institute, together with survey specialists SCPR, showed that ethnic-minority groups should no longer all be seen to be in the same position. The differences between minority groups are as important as the Black–White divide. The study also suggested that some groups can no longer be considered economically disadvantaged.

Ethnic Minorities in Britain: Diversity and Disadvantage is still the largest study of ethnic minorities ever carried out in Britain. It was based on detailed interviews with 5196 people of Caribbean, South Asian and Chinese origin, while 2867 White people were also surveyed to provide a comparison.

The study extended the scope of race-relations research by investigating several issues in new ways. Among its key findings:

● Ethnic variations in health can be explained by socio-economic circumstances rather than biological or cultural factors.
● Racial prejudice, discrimination and harassment were still problems which concern all minority groups, and a quarter of a million people suffer harassment every year.
● Distinct cultural practices are giving way among the British-born to more culturally mixed lifestyles; younger generations have a more assertive attitude to their ethnic identity, certainly compared with their grandparents, who typically arrived with a desire to fit in, even if that meant suppressing their own traditions.
● Of those born in Britain, half of Caribbean men and a third of Caribbean women have a White partner. Getting on for half of 'Caribbean' children have one White parent.

Modood, T., Berthoud, R., Lakey, J., Nazroo, J., Smith, P., Virdee, S. and Beishon, S. (1997) *Ethnic Minorities in Britain: Diversity and Disadvantage*, London: Policy Studies Institute

365

Unit 6 Stratification and differentiation

1 How do the findings support the view that ethnic-minority groups are not to blame for the inequalities that they experience?

2 What evidence is there both from the report and elsewhere that the 'melting pot' idea of racial harmony (see Getting You Thinking, p. 360) has some validity?

● *Legitimization* – Racism helps justify low pay and poor working conditions because Black workers are seen as second-class citizens. Capitalist employers benefit from the cheap labour of ethnic minorities.
● *Divide and rule* – If Black and White workers unite, then they are in a stronger position to campaign for better wages and conditions. Marxists such as Castles and Kosack (1973) argue that employers prefer them to be divided by racism so they can be played off against one another. Employers may use the Black workforce as a '**reserve army of labour**' to prevent White workers from demanding higher wages.
● *Scapegoating* – When a society is troubled by severe social and economic problems, then widespread frustration and aggression can arise. Instead of directing this anger at the capitalist class, Whites are sometimes tempted to pick on relatively vulnerable groups. They use Black people as scapegoats and it may be Blacks who are blamed for

unemployment and housing shortages. Scapegoating is in the interests of the richer and more powerful groups because it protects them from direct criticism and reduces pressures for radical change.

Miles (1989) argues that the class position of Black people is complicated by the fact that they are treated as socially and culturally different. They become the victims of racist ideologies which prevent their full social inclusion. Miles argues that ethnic minorities are members of '**racialized class fractions**'. Whilst most Black people are members of the working class, they also recognize the importance of their ethnicity. Whilst members of the White working class may stress the importance of ethnicity through prejudice and discrimination, Black people may react by stressing their ethnicity in actions such as campaigning for recognition of their need to observe particular religious or cultural traditions.

Miles acknowledges that some ethnic minorities may become part of the middle classes and see their interests lying with capitalism. Furthermore, their ethnicity may be a crucial influence in their business practices and financial success. However, the fact of their ethnicity probably makes it impossible for them to be fully accepted by the White middle class.

Recent approaches

It would be a mistake to think that all Black people 'lose out'. Owen and Green (1992) cite Indians and Chinese as two ethnic groups that have made significant economic progress in the British labour market since the 1980s. Recent figures indicate that their average earnings are indeed similar to those of White workers. More generally, evidence suggests that increasing numbers from the ethnic minorities are entering the ranks of the professional middle class. Sociologists are also starting to notice the growth of 'Black businesses' and the spread of self-employment among ethnic minority groups. Even though groups such as Indians are moving into white-collar work, it is quite possible that Whites fill the higher status positions within this sector.

However, some sociologists have questioned whether self-employment is really a privileged sector of the economy. Minorities may be forced into setting up their own businesses because racial discrimination prevents them from getting employment. Sometimes, these businesses are precarious ventures in extremely competitive markets, offering small returns for long hours and with the owners only managing to survive because they are able to draw upon cheap family labour.

Postmodernist approaches

Postmodernists, such as Modood (1992), reject the notions of Weberian and Marxist sociology that seek to generalize and offer blanket explanations for ethnic groups as a whole. They stress difference and diversity among ethnic groups and focus on identity. They argue that the globalization of culture has led to national cultural identities being eroded. British culture is not immune, and all ethnicities, including White, have begun to 'pick and mix', producing an array of new **hybrid identities**. Racial difference becomes a matter of choice and racial disadvantage is impossible to discuss as ethnic identity is not fixed.

The extent and impact of racism will differ from person to person as identities are chosen and interact. Postmodernists argue that once identity is better understood, targeted ethnic disadvantage can be addressed. Once we know that Jamaican boys not born in Britain in a particular area are more likely to drop out of school, for example, then something meaningful could be done to address this problem.

While postmodern ideas are illuminating, they can be accused of neglecting social and economic factors that impact on life-chances.

Check your understanding

1 How can it be argued that the term 'race' has more explanatory value than the term 'ethnicity'?

2 Where does racial prejudice come from? Give examples to back up your arguments.

3 Explain why members of organizations deemed 'institutionally racist' may not necessarily be racist individuals.

4 How can institutional racism be tackled?

5 What is wrong with early functionalist explanations of ethnic inequality?

6 Why has assimilation been abandoned by policymakers?

7 Briefly summarize three Weberian accounts of ethnic inequality in the workplace.

8 How do Marxists argue that racism benefits capitalism?

9 Why do postmodernists reject Weberian and Marxist explanations of ethnic inequality?

KEY TERMS

Cultural attitudes/prejudice – a style of thinking that relies heavily on stereotypes that are usually factually incorrect, exaggerated and distorted.

Dual labour-market theory – the view that two labour markets exist: the first has secure, well-paid jobs with good promotion prospects, while the second has jobs with little security and low pay; vulnerable groups such as women, the young, elderly and ethnic minorities are concentrated in this second sector.

Ethnicity – cultural heritage shared by members of a particular group.

Hybrid identities – new identities created by ethnic mixing.

Institutional racism – where the sum total of an organization's way of operating has racist outcomes.

Race – variation of physical appearance, skin colour and so on between populations that confers differences in power and status.

Racialized class fractions – term used by Miles to describe splits in the working class along racial lines.

Racism – systematic exclusion of races or ethnic groups from full participation in society.

Reserve army of labour – Marxist concept used to describe an easily exploitable pool of workers drawn from vulnerable groups such as women, ethnic minorities and the old and young.

1 Carry out a piece of research to explore local people's knowledge of ethnic differences. Do they understand the distinctions between the various Asian groups? Do they understand the significance of particular festivals? Do they know of prophets or holy books? Can they point on a world map outline to the countries of origin of the various groups?

2 Assess the extent to which an organization such as your school or college might be deemed to be institutionally racist. Look at the distribution of ethnic groups on the various courses. Try to acquire statistics on exclusions, achievement rates and progression. What problems might you encounter in your research and how might you overcome them?

1 Go to the guardianunlimited website at www.guardianunlimited.co.uk. Search the archive by typing in 'race equality'. Read the articles highlighting a range of issues from institutional racism, social policy reform to rural racism and racial harassment.

2 The website of the Commission for Racial Equality, at www.cre.org.uk, contains a range of research findings and factsheets. Select one or two and write summaries.

exploring ethnicity and stratification

Item A

The 'immigrant–host' model is a functionalist approach to ethnic and race relations. It assumes that immigrants are entering a society that is based on a set of shared values. The need for value consensus means that a group with different values and beliefs is likely to be seen as both strange and inferior. If this group is also physically distinct from the host community, then racial inequality develops. Although functionalists accept the need for *social* inequality, they see *racial* inequality as dysfunctional, since it prevents talented individuals from minority groups achieving their full

potential and society is less efficient as a result. Similarly, racial conflict disrupts the smooth functioning of the social system. However, functionalists are optimistic that minorities will be gradually integrated into a shared value system and that this, along with measures to guarantee equal opportunity, will result in an end to racial conflict and inequality.
In criticism of the immigrant–host model, it can be argued that, first, the model makes no reference to the time scale over which full assimilation might take place.
Second, it assumes that assimilation

is a desirable aim of race relations, and hence assumes that the host culture is superior. Third, it does not accept that racism is a force that divides groups, maintaining that 'race relations' issues arise from a temporary lack of accommodation and assimilation, and not from something more fundamental in human nature. Finally, Marxists do not accept this model, as they see racial conflict as deriving from economic oppression and do not accept the fundamental functionalist premises behind the immigrant–host model.

(a) With reference to **Item A**, examine **two** major criticisms of the functionalist view of race and ethnicity. (8 marks)

This part of the question includes assessment of the connections between Stratification and Differentiation and sociological theory.

(b) Identify and briefly explain **two** problems that sociologists face in defining and measuring ethnicity. (12 marks)

This part of the question includes assessment of your understanding of the connections between Stratification and Differentiation and sociological methods.

(c) 'Society continues to be ethnically divided.'

Assess the sociological arguments and evidence for this view with reference to material drawn from one or more of the following areas: families and households; health; education; wealth, poverty and welfare; work and leisure; religion, power and politics and world sociology. (40 marks)

This part of the question includes assessment of your understanding of the connections between Stratification and Differentiation and other substantive topic(s) you have studied.

Age and stratification

gettingyouthinking

Read through the points on the right and then answer the following questions:

1 Suggest reasons for the patterns of inequality shown above.

2 What may the implications of these patterns be for the future stability of British society? (Consider the family, carers and carer support, social security and taxation, intergenerational conflict.)

3 Substitute gender, race or sexuality for age. Under these new circumstances, do you think that such prejudices and discrimination would be acceptable?

- Why are magistrates or jurors not allowed to serve past the age of 70?

- Why are people over 65 who find it difficult to get around not eligible for help with travel – while those who are disabled but below 65 are?

- Why are nearly a third of jobseekers between 50 and state pension age unable to find paid work?

- In 2002/03, 69 per cent of pensioner households depended on state benefits for at least half of their income, compared with a figure of 30 per cent of all households.

- According to a recent report commissioned for Age Concern (2005), people from 55 onwards were nearly twice as likely to have experienced age prejudice than any other form of discrimination.

- In 2002/03, of pensioners mainly dependent on state pensions and living alone:

  - 88 per cent had central heating, compared with 93 per cent of all households

  - 16 per cent had a car, compared with 77 per cent of all households.

  - 14 per cent had a mobile phone, compared with 84 per cent of all households

  - 74 per cent had a washing machine, compared with 96 per cent of all households.

- Despite the increasing number of over 55s in the population as a whole, and their potentially greater engagement as readers, listeners and, according to Hanley (2002), as viewers of television (the over 65s averaging over 36 hours per week), 46 per cent of fictional portrayals show them as grumpy, interfering, lonely, stubborn and sexless.

Sources: *Pensioners' incomes series 2002/3*, DWP Pensions Analysts Division, 2004; *Family spending: a report on the 2002–03 Expenditure and Food Survey*, National Statistics © Crown Copyright 2004

Age cultures: a natural or social creation?

Ageing is a physical and natural process that happens to everyone and has always happened. However, childhood, youth, adulthood and old age are also associated with different behaviour, lifestyles and social position. Different societies – and even the same societies over different historical periods – have divided ageing into different periods. These periods have then had different meanings attached to them. For example, old age, now seen as a period of dependence, was once viewed as a time of wisdom. In fact, the very term used in tribal, more ancient societies to connote those in old age – 'Elder' – carried with it positive connotations of dignity and authority. Compare that with the modern term for the old – 'Elderly' – with its connotations of disability and dependency. In contrast, the typical image of youth is characterized by two overlapping images of enjoyment and bad behaviour.

These age categories, or **age strata**, are not 'natural' but created by society. That is, they are **social constructions**. The consequences of such constructions, as the above exercise shows, are that members of different age groups will face differing degrees of social status, inclusion, marginalization or inequality. Ageism, for example, is a common experience for older people, not just in terms of social institutions, such as employment, but also in terms of attitudes. Consider, for example, the range of negative phrases applied to the elderly ranging from the patronizing ('old dears') to the insulting ('old gits').

The elderly

Bradley (1996) refers to age as the neglected dimension of inequality – for example, the elderly are one of the most significant groups that comprise the poor. Whilst the experience of the elderly in tribal society gives them status and influence, in Britain many of the elderly are seen as lacking the ability to contribute meaningfully to modern society, which is perceived as having 'passed them by'. There are, however, no objective bases for seeing those in old age in negative terms. Such perceptions of age groups are socially constructed. Nonetheless, these ascribed characteristics serve to exclude many elderly people from full involvement in society.

Age also combines with other social characteristics such as class, gender and ethnicity in causing unequal outcomes. For example, the differing pension rights accorded to male and female employees affect their standard of living after retirement. Oppenheim and Harker (1996) found that whilst 73 per cent of male employees receive company pensions, this only applies to 68 per cent of female full-time employees and to only 31 per cent of the many female part-time workers.

Third agers

For the more wealthy, the later years of life are increasingly being seen as a time of great opportunity and even celebration. It is a time for reflecting on the accomplishments of a full life, but it also allows people to continue growing, learning and exploring. The years when people are free from parenting responsibilities and work are often referred to as the 'Third Age'. (The first age being childhood, and the second, working age). During this period, which is now longer than ever before, individuals are free to lead active independent lives – travelling, pursuing further education or developing new skills.

For those in 'comfortable retirement', a host of products and services are being offered that recognize their consumer power and increasing **consumerism**. This is enhanced by the growing phenomenon of early retirement. Laczko and Phillipson (1991) point out that in 1965, 90 per cent of men between 60 and 65, were working whereas this had fallen to 60 per cent by 1990 – and the trend seems to be continuing among the higher earners, who have the luxury of planned retirement. However, how long it can continue is another question – one we will consider next.

Milne *et al.* (1999)
Grey power

A study of elderly people in Britain (Milne *et al.* 1999) found evidence of two distinct 'worlds'. In one world, composed of people in the early years of retirement who live in a shared household with an occupational pension, there is a reasonably comfortable lifestyle. In the second world, made up of those over 80 who live alone with few savings, people can suffer acute poverty.

The former grouping, comprising relatively affluent older people, is much sought after by manufacturers all over the industrialized world, where the term 'grey power' is sometimes used to refer to the consumption habits and patterns of those over 65. Of course, the term cannot be applied to all older people. First, social-class differences continue into retirement. Lifestyle and taste differences, and the impact of different occupations as well as different forms of housing tenure, persist. Second, ill health is also gendered, with men more likely to experience it at an earlier age. The jobs people did also affect their income in old age; ex-professional and managerial workers have more income than ex-manual workers. Finally, older men have generally higher incomes than older women.

Adapted from Abercrombie, N. and Warde, A. (2000) *Contemporary British Society* (3rd edn), Cambridge: Polity Press

1 **Why is it that the term grey power 'cannot be applied to all older people'?**

2 **What might be the circumstances which lead to an older person belonging to either of the 'worlds' described above?**

YES – YOU'VE ENJOYED STUDYING A2-LEVEL SOCIOLOGY. Yes – the issues you've covered have been interesting. Yes – you've learned a lot about society today. Yes – you feel more confident in discussions about social issues. But, in the end, you know that your feelings about the course will probably depend on how well you get on in the exam board assessments that measure the standard of your work. Even if you did very well at AS, how can you be certain that you will display your knowledge in the way expected by the examiner? Will they be able to read your writing? Will they understand what you are trying to say? Well, practise writing so that anyone can read it, using a black pen or biro, and writing that is large enough to be read by the average person. If in doubt, ask friends and family if they can read it. Then practise writing under pressure for about an hour and a quarter, and then go back and read what you have written. Can you understand what you were trying to say? If you can, the chances are the examiner will understand as well. They have had some practice at this!

Your performance in the AQA A-level course will be judged either totally by exams or through a combination of exams and coursework. Either way, you need to be completely confident about the organization of the exams: how long they last, how the questions are phrased, and what knowledge and skills are being tested. You also need to be aware of the nature of the coursework task, how it is broken down and how marks are allocated.

This unit guides you through both AQA exams and AQA coursework. It provides essential information about the content and assessment of the course, including some really useful tips for both exams and coursework. After working through this unit, you should feel a lot more confident about the way your performance will be judged and be in a good position to get full value for all the work you've put in to your A-level Sociology course. Remember that the examiner and moderators are there to ensure that you get the grade your work deserves. They mark what is written on the paper, but they can cope with the odd spelling mistake, or slip of the pen. As long as they are confident about what you meant, they can and will award you the marks. The questions have been carefully designed to be as clear as possible, and to allow students to display their knowledge to the best of their ability. If you deserve full marks, then you will be given full marks. After you have read this unit, you should feel you know what you need to do to get the mark you deserve.

Preparing for the A2 exam

Preparing for the A2 exam

What will I study?

Aim/rationale of the course

The AQA specification at A2 builds on the knowledge and skills of the AS-level. It offers you the opportunity to acquire deeper knowledge and understanding of key aspects of sociological thought, a sound introduction to sociological research methods, and the opportunity to study in depth a number of different areas of social life.

The A2 course allows choice of topic areas within Units 4 and 6 and the choice of a written examination or a coursework project for Unit 5. It also ensures a thorough coverage of sociological perspectives and of the two 'core themes':

● Socialisation, culture and identity
● Social differentiation, power and stratification.

These 'core themes' are required elements of any A2-level sociology specification.

The knowledge and skills acquired in this course should enable you to take a more informed and critical look at many aspects of society and how they relate to people's lives. At the same time, the course should help you to develop and practise the skills of informed debate and critical analysis. The skills acquired in a sociology course can be of lifelong benefit.

Modules of study and Units of assessment

The AQA A2 course is divided into three 'Modules of study', which lay out what you should know (see Table 7.1 below). (They are numbered 4 to 6, because the AS-level covers

Table 7.1 Modules of study and Units of assessment

Module of study	Topics	Unit of assessment	Forms of assessment
4	● Power and politics ● Religion ● World sociology	4	Written examination of 1 hour 30 minutes: short data-response section with two questions and one essay from a choice of two per topic area
5	● Theory and methods	5	**Either**: written examination of 1 hour 30 minutes with one compulsory data-response section **Or**: coursework project carrying out your own research.
6	● Crime and deviance ● Stratification and differentiation	6	Written examination of 1 hour 30 minutes: one data-response section with two questions and an essay (no choice) per topic area

Modules 1 to 3.) When you enter for an examination, the module becomes a 'Unit of assessment':

- Module 4 contains three topic areas, and each topic area forms the basis of a question in the written examination Unit of assessment.
- Module 5 covers only one area of study, namely 'Theories and methods', and you are given a choice regarding how this unit is assessed.
- Module 6 is the synoptic module, which will test your knowledge and understanding of the links between all the sections of the course that you have studied. The two topic areas which form the basis of synoptic assessment are 'Crime and deviance' and 'Stratification and differentiation', and there will be a question on each of these in the Unit of assessment/exam paper. You will answer a question on one of these topics only. The questions on this paper will require you to show an informed and critical knowledge and understanding of your chosen synoptic topic and its links with sociological theory, sociological methods, and the other topic areas you have studied over the two years of the course.

How will I be assessed?

Skills

The skills you will acquire and develop in your A2 course are tested in the examination by two 'Assessment Objectives': AO1 counts for 40 per cent and AO2 counts for 60 per cent of the available marks.

Assessment Objective 1 (AO1): Knowledge and understanding

This requires you to demonstrate your knowledge and understanding of the chosen topic area that forms the basis of the assessment. It covers knowledge and understanding of relevant sociological theories and perspectives, concepts, studies and social policies. You should also be able to make reference to relevant issues and events. Also included in AO1 is the skill of 'Communication'. While this is not assessed separately, and therefore does not carry a particular mark weighting, it is an important skill, as poor communication will prevent you from showing the examiner what you mean.

Assessment Objective 2 (AO2): Identification, analysis, interpretation and evaluation

This range of skills together accounts for 60 per cent of the available marks. To demonstrate them successfully, you will need to be able to *identify* correctly perspectives, reasons, examples, criticisms, etc., as required by the particular question.

The skill of *interpretation* covers your ability to work out and respond to what the question is requiring you to do, and to interpret different types of evidence, including research studies and statistical data, by discussing what they can tell us.

Table 7.2 Weighting given to AS units at A-level

Unit of Assessment	A-level weighting
Unit 4	15% of the total A-level marks
Unit 5	15% of the total A-level marks
Unit 6	20% of the total A-level marks

Good *analysis* is shown by presenting an informed, detailed and accurate discussion of a particular theory, perspective, study or event, and also by the ability to present your arguments and evidence in a clear and logical manner.

Evaluation refers to your ability to recognise and discuss the strengths and weaknesses of theories and perspectives, studies, sociological methods and data presented in a variety of forms.

Units of assessment/exams

The basic structure of the Units of assessment is shown in Table 7.1, and the question structure is discussed in more detail in the next section. The weighting given to each of the three A2 units is shown in Table 7.2 above, where you will see the percentage of the marks allocated to each unit in terms of the full A-level.

Coursework

The A2 Coursework is offered in Unit 5 as an alternative to the written examination. It takes the form of an actual research project in the second year of the course. Further details of the A2 coursework are given in the 'How do I do well in the coursework?' section below.

How can I do well in the written examinations?

Question style and structure

A2 questions vary from paper to paper, but all include a 'data-response' section. In Units 4 and 6, this usually consists of *one* piece of data (labelled as an 'Item') and contains two questions, but in Unit 5, the data-response question usually consists of *two* pieces of data ('Items') and contains four questions.

The Items at A2-level are there to prompt your thoughts and point you in the right direction when answering the questions in that section. They may also prompt ideas that you can use in the essay question, but this is more likely to be a happy accident rather than a result of careful design.

Each question is marked out of 60, and it might be helpful to think of the 60 marks being allocated in two distinct groups, one of 20 marks (data-response question) and one of 40 marks (essay). It follows that if you have 90 minutes for the whole paper, you should spend about 30 minutes on the data-response question and about 60 minutes on the essay. Don't forget to leave yourself time to read the Item(s), plan your answers and read through your work at the end.

In the data-response section for Units 4 and 6, the questions will carry 8 and 12 marks, whilst in Unit 5, the question marks will combine to make a total of 20 marks. These questions and the essays are likely to include the following words: 'identify', 'explain', 'examine', 'assess' and/or 'evaluate'.

- *Identify* – Name whatever you have been asked for, e.g. in answer to the question 'identify a system of social stratification', you could refer to the caste system or the class system.
- *Explain* – Pick out distinguishing features of a named phenomenon and say why they are important, e.g the role of religious beliefs in the caste system.
- *Examine* – Look at the advantages and disadvantages of a theory, or look at the evidence for and against a statement or theory.
- *Assess* – Look at all sides, or all theories that relate to the topic and come to a conclusion.
- *Evaluate* – Similar to assess, look at all sides and weigh up the evidence for and against them all, and come to a conclusion.

Some tips for doing well in written exams are listed in the panel on the right.

How can I do well in the coursework task?

Requirement

You are expected to carry out a piece of sociological research that relates to one of the areas of the specification. Normally, you will do this after you have finished your AS-level. You may use either primary or secondary data-collection methods to complete your task. There is overall word limit of 3500 words. You may either carry out the proposal you submitted for AS or you may start afresh: the choice is yours.

The marks are awarded both for AO1 skills (24 out of the 60 marks) and for AO2 (36 out of the 60 marks), and the coursework should be laid out in the agreed format of

- Rationale/hypothesis or aim
- Context
- Methodology
- Evidence
- Evaluation.

In addition, you should include a contents page, a bibliography and a photocopied page from your research diary.

Table 7.3 opposite shows you in outline what you have to do.

Exam tips

- Throughout A2, there is more emphasis on the AO2 skills than there was at AS, so the examiner is looking at how you use the knowledge and how you analyse and evaluate it. Although some description will be necessary, do not spend too long on this as your use of that evidence is more important than demonstrating the detail. You can assume that the examiner has also read the study to which you are referring.

- Read both the Item/s and the whole question very carefully before you begin to answer. The Item/s will contain information that is essential, helpful, or both, and reading the whole question will give you an understanding of which aspects of the topic have been covered. If you find you are trying to use the same material twice, make sure you have fully understood the questions as the examiner strives to prevent duplication of material.

- Keep an eye on the time, it is very important that you allow sufficient time for each section, but do not spend too long on the first part since the essay carries two-thirds of the marks.

- Plan all the sections of your answer before you start to write. As you are answering the first part you will probably remember points to put into your essay.

- In all your answers, refer to appropriate theories, perspectives, studies and evidence to support and inform your response. Where possible, bring in examples of recent or current events or social policies to illustrate the points you are making. Make quite sure that you have given sufficient demonstration of the AO2 skills, particularly analysis and evaluation.

- Finally – make sure that you answer the question that the examiner has set, rather than the one that you wished for! This is a serious point – many candidates fail to achieve marks because they have not kept to the focus of the question. No question is likely to ask you simply to 'Write everything you know about …', and yet this is what some students do. However, it is better to write something than to sit there doing nothing. Leaving a blank means you cannot score any marks, but if you write something, it could be correct enough or relevant enough to pick up some marks.

Approaching the coursework

Before you start, be sure to:

- read a copy of the ethical guidelines
- read the mark scheme
- check the areas covered by the specification.

Table 7.3 Requirements of coursework

Section and Assessment Objective covered	Outline requirements	Recommended number of words	Total marks for that section
AO1 Context	An outline of sociological sources, either theoretical or empirical, or both, and relevant sociological concepts that form the context and background to your study.	700–750	12
AO1 Method	**Primary-based research**: an account of the single research method chosen for the collection of data, saying why you think it is appropriate to test/explore your hypothesis or aim, and a recognition of associated problems, practical, theoretical and ethical.	700–750	12
	Secondary-based research: an account of the methodology used by the author(s) of the data, reasons for that choice and a recognition of associated problems, both with the research under discussion and in using secondary methods		
AO2 Evidence and how you carried out your research	How you did your research and presented the evidence you found, especially relating these findings both to your hypothesis/aim and the context pieces you chose to use.	1100–1200	18
AO2 Rationale	A hypothesis/aim, objectives, where appropriate, and reasons for choosing this topic.	100–150	
Evaluation and conclusions	An evaluation of the methods used (either your own or those of the secondary authors), conclusions about the findings and recommendations for further research	700–800	
	Total	**3500**	**60**

Note: You must try to make sure the total does not exceed 3500 words, so you need to be aware that If you write 750 words for each of the AO1 skills, you will only have 2000 words left for the AO2 sections.

Ethical guidelines

The most important of these concern:

1   the wellbeing of those who take part in the research
2   people's right to privacy
3   anonymity and confidentiality
4   not bringing sociology into disrepute.

You should consider all these issues before even choosing your topic. For example, people might be psychologically harmed if you remind them of parts of their lives that were painful, so avoid such topics as child deaths, personal misfortune, how they feel about disasters, and so on.

Always ensure that those you talk to are not identifiable. Anonymity can be gained by changing people's names, or assigning a number or letter in place of a name. If you research your own school or college, disguise it by calling it 'X college' and describe your town by saying 'a medium-sized Midlands town' for somewhere like Northampton, or a 'southern coastal resort' for Brighton, or 'a long-established university city' for Cambridge [or Oxford]. Try not to do research that would make splash headlines in the Sunday tabloids – that is bringing sociology into disrepute. 'Girl student in stripper shock' is not desirable – so no participant observation studies of the local lap-dancing club.

Mark scheme

This is not an official secret – your teacher should provide you with a copy, so look at what it suggests you need to do in order to get top marks. Always look at the top band and aim to cover those criteria. Even if you don't quite achieve them all, you should get some of them.

Specification

Make sure that the area you want to look at is covered by the specification. If it isn't, don't do it. Also, remember that if you were to discover something criminal, then you (and your teacher and moderator) would be committing a crime if you did not inform those in authority, so avoid asking questions about underage drinking, drug-taking or any similar activity.

Doing the research: tips

On the following page is a list of tips to bear in mind when doing your research.

Doing the research: tips

- Do keep a diary and note in it any ideas, such as what you think you plan to do, who you might ask, when you change your mind and so on. Jot things down in note form – especially when things start to go wrong – and note how you try to put them right. This will help you write the evaluation section, and you should include a photocopy of one page with your coursework.

- Make sure that your research has a clear sociological focus. One way of doing this is to keep clearly within the topic areas of the sociology specification.

- Keep the hypothesis or aim very simple/limited. This will make it easier to carry it out and keep to the word limit.

- Make the hypothesis/aim very specific. Rather than saying 'I aim to discover why boys fail at GCSE compared with girls' be more precise – for example: 'attitudes to school cause different rates of success at GCSE between boys and girls of the same social class', which is a much more focused topic.

- Keep referring back to your hypothesis or aim – all the other sections should show a clear link to this.

- Make sure that you spend time choosing appropriate pieces of context and show how and why these provide an appropriate background for the proposed research. Remember you have very few words, so be brief in your summary of any findings.

- Having chosen your context pieces, keep linking them in to the rest of the piece, refer to them when designing your research, and show how they were proved or refuted by your research in your evidence and evaluation sections.

- Choose only one research method to collect your data.

- Make sure the research method chosen is appropriate to your research aim. If you need a large sample to get statistics, do not think about using unstructured interviews.

- If your method involves asking questions, make sure you use all the information you collect. Have a reason for every question you ask. If, for example, you ask for people's ages, use this information to group their answers according to their age to see if it had an effect on their response. If you don't use the information, the moderator will think 'Why did they bother to ask the question?'

- Choose your sample carefully, explaining how it will be representative. Also, explain where you are going to find these people.

- Don't forget to do a pilot study. It is usually appropriate to do so, and don't forget to explain how it altered your research method.

- Remember to give clear reasons for all your choices and decisions. Include the practical, theoretical and ethical aspects of your choices and decisions.

- Allow sufficient time to carry out your research – it always takes longer than you expect. Make sure that you are aware of, and meet, the set deadline.

- When writing up the evidence, keep referring your findings to the material in your context. If you are not going to refer back to it, ask yourself why you included it in the first place.

- Don't be afraid to change things – you can put new things in the context after you have done the research if they are helpful to what you are wanting to say.

- Remember, the moderator wasn't around when you were discussing things with your tutor/teacher, so they can only mark what you have put on the paper. *You* may understand what it all means, but will anybody else? You could always ask a critical friend to read it and ask you questions about anything they don't understand. If they can't understand what you did, or why you did it, then probably the moderator won't either.

- Stick to the word limit.

Finally, good luck with all you choose to do.

Abbott, P. (1990) 'A re-examination of "Three theses re-examined"', in Payne, G. (ed) *The Social Mobility of Women,* London: Routledge

Abbott, P. and Wallace, C. (1997) *An Introduction to Sociology: Feminist Perspectives,* London: Routledge

Abercrombie, N. and Warde, A. (2000) *Contemporary British Society* (3rd edn), Cambridge: Polity Press

Abercrombie, N., Hill, S. and Turner, B.S. (1980) *The Dominant Ideology Thesis,* London: Allen and Unwin

Adamson, P. (1986) 'The rich, the poor, the pregnant', *New Internationalist,* 270

Adler, I. (1975) *Sisters in Crime,* New York: McGraw-Hill

Adonis, A. and Pollard, S. (1998) *A Class Act: the Myth of Britain's Classless Society,* Harmondsworth: Penguin

Adorno, T.W. (1991) *The Culture Industry: Selected Essays on Mass Culture,* London: Routledge

Age Concern (2005) *How Ageist is Britain?,* available at www.ageconcern.org.uk

Ahmed, L. (1992) *Women and Gender in Islam: Historical Roots of a Modern Debate,* New Haven and London: Yale University Press

Akers, R.L. (1967) 'Problems in the sociology of deviance: social definitions and behaviour', *Social Forces* 46 (4)

Alexander, J. (1985) *Neo-Functionalism,* London: Sage

Alibhai-Brown, Y. (2005) quoted in *Africans on Africa: Colonialism,* www.news.bbc.co.uk

Allen, T. and Thomas, A. (2001) *Poverty and Development in the 21st Century,* Oxford: Oxford University Press

Althusser, L. (1969) *For Marx,* Harmondsworth: Penguin

Althusser, L. (1971) *Lenin and Philosophy and Other Essays,* London: New Left Books

Anderson, E. (1999) *Code of the Streets: Decency, Violence and the Moral Code of the Inner City,* New York: W.W. Norton

Anderson, S., Kinsey, R., Loader, I. and Smith, C. (1994) *Young People, Crime and Policing in Edinburgh,* Aldershot: Avebury

Anthias, F. (2001) 'The concept of social division and theorising social stratification: looking at ethnicity and class', *Sociology,* 35(4), pp.835–54

Arber, A., Dale, S. and Gilbert, N. (1986) 'The limitations of existing social class classification of women' in A. Jacoby (ed.) *The Measurement of Social Class,* Guildford: Social Research Association

Armstrong, K. (1993) *The End of Silence: Women and the Priesthood,* London: Fourth Estate

Aron, R. (1967) 'Social class, political class, ruling class' in R. Bendix and S.M. Lipset *Main Currents in Sociological Thought,* Vols 1 and 2, Harmondsworth: Penguin

Atkinson, J.M. (1971) 'Social reactions to suicide: the role of coroners' definitions', in S. Cohen (ed.) *Images of Deviance,* Harmondsworth: Penguin

Aubert, V. (1952) 'White collar crime and social structure', *American Journal of Sociology,* 58

Bachrach, P. and Baratz, M.S. (1970) *Power and Poverty: Theory and Practice,* Oxford: Oxford University Press

Badawi, L. (1994) 'Islam' in J. Holm, and J. Bowker (eds), (1994) *Women in Religion,* London: Pinter

Bainbridge, W.S. (1978) *Satan's Power.* Berkley: University of California Press

Bakan, J. (2004) *Corporation: The Pathological Pursuit of Profit and Power,* London: Constable and Robinson

Baldwin, J. and Bottoms, A.E. (1976) *The Urban Criminal,* London: Tavistock

Baran, P. (1957) *The Political Economy of Growth,* New York: Monthly Review Press

Barber, B.R. and Schulz, A. (eds) (1995) *Jihad vs McWorld,* New York: Ballantyne Books

Barker E. (1984) *The Making of a Moonie,* Oxford: Blackwell

Barker, P. (1982) *The Other Britain: a New Society Collection,* London: Routledge & Kegan Paul

Barron, R.G. and Norris, G.M. (1976) 'Sexual divisions and the dual labour market', in D.J. Barker and S. Allen (eds) *Dependence and Exploration in Work and Marriage,* London: Longman

Bartkey, S.C. (1992) 'Reevaluating French feminism', in N. Fraser and S.C. Bartkey (eds) *Critical Essays in Difference, Agency and Culture,* Bloomington: Indiana University Press

Bartley, M., Carpenter, L., Dunnell, K. and Fitzpatrick, R. (1996) 'Measuring inequalities in health: an analysis of mortality patterns using two social classifications', *Sociology of Health and Illness,* 18(4) p.455–74.

Baudrillard, J. (1980) *For a Critique of the Political Economy of the Sign,* New York: Telos Press

Baudrillard, J. (1994) *The Illusion of the End,* Cambridge: Polity Press

Baudrillard, J. (1998) *Selected Writings* (M. Poster ed.), Cambridge: Polity Press

Bauer, P.T. (1982) *Equality, the Third World, and Economic Delusion,* London: Routledge

Bauman, Z. (1978) *Hermeneutics and Social Sciences: Approaches to Understanding,* London: Hutchinson

Bauman, Z. (1983) 'Industrialism, consumerism and power', *Theory, Culture and Society,* 1(3)

Bauman, Z. (1990) *Thinking Sociologically,* Oxford: Blackwell

Bauman, Z. (1992) *Intimations of Postmodernity,* London: Routledge

Bauman, Z. (1997) *Postmodernity and Its Discontents,* Cambridge: Polity Press

Bauman, Z. (2000) 'Sociological enlightenment – For whom, about what?', *Theory, Culture and Society,* 17(2), pp. 71–82

Beck, U. (1992) *Risk Society: Towards a New Modernity,* London: Sage

Beck, U. (1999) *World Risk Society,* Cambridge: Polity Press

Becker, H. (1950) *Through Values to Social Interpretation: Essays on Social Contexts, Actions, Types and Prospects,* California: Duke University Press

Becker, H. (1963) *The Outsiders: Studies in the Sociology of Deviance* New York: Free Press

Becker, H. (1970) 'Whose side are we on?', in H. Becker, *Sociological Work,* New Brunswick: Transaction Books

Beckford, J.A. (1985) *Cult Controversies,* London: Routledge

Bellah, R. (1970) 'Civil religion in America', in *Beyond Belief: Essays in Religion in a Post-traditional World',* New York: Harper & Row

Benston, M. (1972) 'The political economy of women's liberation' in N. Glazer-Mahlbin and H.Y. Wahrer (eds) (1972) *Women in a Man-made World,* Chicago: Rand MacNally

Berger, A.L. (1997) *Children of Job: American Second Generation Witnesses to the Holocaust,* New York: New York State University Press

Berger, P. (1967) *The Sacred Canopy: Elements of a Sociological Theory of Religion,* New York: Anchor Books

Berger, P. (1973) *The Social Reality of Religion,* Harmondsworth: Penguin

Bergesen, A. (1990) 'Turning world-system theory on its head', in M. Featherstone (ed.) *Global Culture: Rationalism, Globalisation and Modernity,* London: Sage

Bernard, J. (1976) *The Future of Marriage,* Harmondsworth: Penguin

Bernasco, W. and Nieuwbeerta, P. (2005) 'How do residential burglars select target areas? A new approach to the analysis of criminal location choice', *British Journal of Criminology,* 45(3)

Best, S. (2005) *Understanding Social Divisions,* London: Sage

Bhaskar, R. (1986) *Scientific Realism and Human Emancipation,* London: Verso

Bhaskar, R. (1998) *The Possibility of Naturalism: A Philosophical Critique of the Contemporary Human Sciences* (3rd edn), New York and London: Routledge

Bhavani, K. (2000) *Feminism and Race,* Oxford: Oxford University Press

Bhopal, R., Phillimore, P. and Kohli, H.S. (1991) 'Inappropriate use of the term "Asian": an obstacle to ethnicity and health research', *Journal of Public Health Medicine,* 13, pp.244–6

Billig, M., Condor, S., Edwards, D., Gane, M., Middleton, D. and Radley, A.R.(1988) *Ideological Dilemmas,* London: Sage Publications.

Bird, J. (1999) *Investigating Religion,* London: HarperCollins

Black, M. (2002) *The No-Nonsense Guide to International Development,* London: Verso

Blackman, S. (1995) *Youth: Positions and Oppositions, Style, Sexuality and Schooling,* Aldershot: Avebury

Blackshaw T. and Long, J. (2005) 'What's the big idea? A critical exploration of the concept of social capital and its incorporation into leisure policy discourse', *Leisure Studies,* 24(3), pp. 239–58

Blumer, H. (1962) 'Society as symbolic interaction', in N. Rose (ed.) *Symbolic Interactionism,* Englewood Hills, NJ: Prentice-Hall

Bocock, B.J. (1986) *Hegemony,* London: Tavistock

Bonger, W. (1916) *Criminality and Economic Conditions,* Chicago: Little Brown

Boserup, E. (1970) *Women's Role in Economic Development,* London: Earthscan

Bottero, W. (2005) *Stratification: Social Division and Inequality,* London: Routledge

Bourgois, P. (1995, 2002 [2nd edn]) *In Search of Respect,* Cambridge: Cambridge University Press

Bowling, B. (1999) *Violent Racism: Victimisation, Policing and Social Context* (revised edn), Oxford: Oxford University Press

Bowling, B. and Phillips, C. (2002) *Racism, Crime and Justice,* Harlow: Pearson

Box, S. (1981) *Deviance, Reality and Society* (2nd edn), Eastbourne: Holt Rheinhart Wilson

Box, S. (1983/1993) *Crime, Power and Mystification,* London: Tavistock

Bradley, H. (1996) *Fractured Identities: Changing Patterns of Inequality,* Cambridge: Polity Press

Bradley, H. (1999) *Gender and Power in the Workplace,* Basingstoke, Macmillan

Braithwaite, J. (1984) *Corporate Crime in the Pharmaceutical Industry,* London: Routledge

Brake, M. (1980) *The Sociology of Youth and Youth Subcultures,* London: Routledge

Brantingham, P.J. and Brantingham, P.L. (1984) *Patterns of Crime,* New York: Macmillan

Brantingham, P.J. and Brantingham, P.L. (1991) *Environmental Criminology* (revised edn), Prospect Heights: Waveland Press

Braverman, H. (1974) *Labour and Monopoly Capitalism,* New York: Monthly Press

Brenner, M., Brown, J. and Canter, M. (1985) *The Research Interview: Uses and Approaches,* London: Academic Press

Brierley, P. (ed.) (1979, 1989, 1999, 2000, 2001) *Christian Research Association, UK Christian Handbook, Religious Trends* 1979, 1989, 1999, 2000, 2001, London: HarperCollins

British Youth Lifestyles Survey (2000) Home Office Research Study 209

Brooks, A. (1997) *Postfeminisms: Feminisms, Cultural Theory and Cultural Forms,* London: Routledge

Brown, C.G. (2001) *The Death of Christian Britain: Understanding Secularization 1800–2000,* London: Routledge

Bruce, S. (1995) *Religion in Modern Britain,* Oxford: Oxford University Press

Bruce, S. (1996) *Religion in the Modern World: From Cathedrals to Cults*, Oxford: Oxford University Press

Bruce, S. (2001) 'The social process of secularisation' in R.K. Fenn (2004) *The Blackwell Companion to the Sociology of Religion*, Oxford: Blackwell

Bruce, S. (2002) *God is Dead: Secularization in the West*, Oxford: Blackwell

Bryman, A. (2004) *Social Research Methods* (2nd edn), Oxford: Oxford University Press

Bryman, A. and Burgess, A. (1994) *Analysing Qualitative Data*, London: Routledge

Bulman, J. (2003) 'Patterns of pay: results of the 2002 New Earnings Survey', *Labour Market Trends*, London: HMSO

Burchill, J. (2001), *The Guardian,* Saturday 18 August

Burkey, S. (1993) *People First*, London: Zed Books

Butler, C. (1995) 'Religion and gender: young Muslim women in Britain', *Sociology Review*, 4(3), Oxford: Philip Allan

Butler, D. and Kavanagh, D. (1985) *The British General Election of 1983*, London: Macmillan

Butler, D. and Rose, R. (1960) *The British General Election of 1959*, London: Frank Cass

Butler, D. and Stokes, D. (1971) *Political Change in Britain*, London: Macmillan

Cain, M. (1986) 'Realism, feminism, methodology and law', *International Journal of the Sociology of Law*, 14

Campbell, B. (1985) *Wigan Pier Re-visited*, London: Virago Press Ltd

Campbell, B. (1993) *Goliath: Britain's Dangerous Places*, London: Methuen

Cannadine, D. (1998) *Class in Britain*, London: Yale University Press

Caplan, L. (ed.) (1987) *Studies in Religious Fundamentalism*, London: Macmillan

Caplow, T. (1954) *The Sociology of Work*, New York: McGraw-Hill

Cardoso, F.H. (1972) 'Dependency and development in Latin America', *New Left Review*, 74, July/Aug

Carlen, P. (1988) *Women, Crime and Poverty*, Milton Keynes: Open University Press

Carlen, P. (1992) 'Criminal women and criminal justice: the limits to and potential of feminist and left realist perspectives', in R. Matthews and J. Young (eds) *Issues in Realist Criminology*, London: Sage

Carmen, R. (1996) *Autonomous Development: Humanising the Landscape*, London: Zed Books

Carnell, B. (2000) Article titled 'Paul Ehrlich' dated 17 May 2000 downloaded from www.overpopulation.com

Carrabine, E., Iganski, P., Lee, M., Plummer, K. and South, N. (2004) *Criminology: A Sociological Introduction*, London: Routledge

Carson, W.G. (1970) 'White collar crime and the enforcement of factory legislation', *British Journal of Criminology*, 10

Cassen, R. (1986) *Does Aid Work? Report of the Independent Consultants' Study of Aid-Effectiveness.* Oxford: Oxford University Press

Castles, S. and Kosack, G.C. (1973) *Immigrant Workers and Class Structure in Western Europe*, Oxford: OUP

Chambliss, W.J. (1975) 'Towards a political economy of crime', *Theory and Society*, Vol. 2 pp.149–170

Charlesworth, S. (2000) *A Phenomenology of Working-Class Experience*, Cambridge: Cambridge University Press

Chase-Dunn, C. (1975) 'The effects of international economic dependence on development and inequality: a cross national study', *American Sociological Review*, 40, December

Chrispin, J. and Jegede, F. (2000) *Population, Resources and Development*, London: HarperCollins

Clark, T.N. and Hoffman-Martinot, V. (eds) (1998) *The New Political Culture*, Boulder CO: Westview

Clarke, M. (1990) *Business Crime: Its Nature and Control*, Bristol: Policy Press

Clarke, R.V.G. (1995) 'Situational crime prevention', in M. Tonry and D. Farrington (eds) *Building a Safer Society*, Chicago: University of Chicago

Clegg, S.R. (1989) *Frameworks of Power*, London: Sage

Clinard, M.B. (1974) *The Sociology of Deviant Behavior*, New York: Holt, Reinhart & Winston

Cloward, R. and Ohlin, L. (1960) *Delinquency and Opportunity*, London: Collier Macmillan

Cochrane, A. and Pain, K. (2000) 'A globalising society' in D. Held (ed.) *A Globalising World: Culture, Economics and Politics*, London: Routledge

Cohen, A. (1955) *Delinquent Boys*, New York: The Free Press

Cohen, L.E. and Felson, M. (1979) 'Social change and crime rate trends: a routine activities approach', *American Sociological Review*, 44

Cohen, N. (2005) 'Capital punishment', *The Observer*, 6 November

Cohen, R. and Kennedy, P. (2000) *Global Sociology*, Basingstoke: Macmillan

Cohen, R. and Rai, S. (eds) (2000) *Global Social Movements*, Athlone: Continuum International Publishing Group

Cohen, S. (1972, 1980 [2nd edn]) *Folk Devils and Moral Panics*, London: Paladin

Cohen, S. (1985) *Visions of Social Control*, Cambridge: Polity Press

Cohen, S. (2002) 'Moral panics as cultural politics (New introduction)', in *Folk Devils and Moral Panics: The Creation of the Mods and Rockers* (3rd edn), London: Routledge

Collins, H. and Pinch, T. (1998) *The Golem: What You Should Know About Science* (2nd edition) Cambridge: Cambridge University Press

Collinson, M. (1995) *Police, Drugs and Community*, London: Free Association Books

Collison, M. (1996) 'In search of the high life', *British Journal of Criminology*, 36(3), pp.428–44

Colman, A. and Gorman, L. (1982) 'Conservatism, dogmatism and authoritarianism amongst British police officers', *Sociology* 16(1)

Commission For Africa (2005) *Our Common Interest*, London: Penguin

Conklin, J.E. (1977) *Illegal but not Criminal: Business Crime in America*, Englewood Cliffs, NJ: Prentice Hall

Connell, R.W. (1995) *Masculinities*, Cambridge: Polity Press

Connor H. and Dewson S., with Tyers C., Eccles J., Regan J. and Aston J. (2001) *Social Class and Higher Education: Issues Affecting Decisions on Participation by Lower Social Class Groups*, DfEE Research Report RR267

Coussins, J. (1976) *The Equality Report*, NCCL Rights for Women Unit: London

Coxall, B. (1981) *Parties and Pressure Groups*, Harlow: Longman

Craib, I. (1992) *Anthony Giddens*, London: Routledge

Crewe, I. (1984) 'The electorate: partisan de-alignment ten years on' in H. Berrington (ed.) *Change in British Politics*, London: Frank Cass

Croall, H. (2001) *Understanding White-collar Crime*, Milton Keynes: Open University Press

Crook, S., Pakulski, J. and Waters, M. (1992) *Postmodernisation: Change in Advanced Society*, London: Sage

Cross, M. (1979) *Urbanisation and Urban Growth in the Caribbean*, Cambridge: Cambridge University Press cited in M. O'Donnell (1983) *New Introductory Reader in Sociology*, London: Nelson Harrap

Cuff, E.C., Sharrock W.W. and Francis, D.W. (1990) *Perspectives in Sociology*, London: Routledge

Dahl, R. (1961) *Who Governs: Democracy and Power in an American City*, New Haven: Yale University Press

Dalton, K. (1964) *The Pre-menstrual Syndrome and Progesterone Therapy*, London: Heinemann Medical

Daly, M. (1973) *Beyond God the Father*, Boston, MA: Beacon Press

Daly, M. (1978) *Gyn/Ecology: The Meta-ethics of Radical Feminism*, Boston, MA: Beacon Press

Darlington, Y. and Scott, D. (2002) *Qualitative Research in Practice: Stories from the Field*, Milton Keynes: Open University Press

Davidman, L. (1991) *Religion in a Rootless World: Women turn to Orthodox Judaism*, Berkeley: University of California Press

Davie, G. (1994) *Religion in Britain 1945–1990, Believing Without Belonging*, Oxford: Blackwell

Davie, G. (1995) 'Competing fundamentalisms', *Sociology Review*, 4(4), Oxford: Philip Allan

Davis, K. and Moore, W.E. (1955) 'Some principles of stratification', in Bendix, R. and Lipset, S.M. (eds) *Class, Status and Power* (2nd edn 1967), London: Routledge & Kegan Paul

Davis, M. (1990) *City of Quartz*, London: Verso

de Beauvoir, S. (1953) *The Second Sex*, London: Jonathan Cape

Delamont, S. (2001) *Changing Women: Unchanged Men: Sociological Perspectives on Gender in a Post-Industrial Society*, Buckingham: Open University Press

Delphy, C. (1977) *The Main Enemy*, London: Women's Research & Resources Centre

Dennis, N. (1993) *Rising Crime and the Dismembered Family*, London: IEA Health And Welfare Unit

Dennis, N. and Erdos, G. (1993) *Families without Fatherhood*, London: IEA

Denscombe, M. (1999) *Sociology Update*, Leicester: Olympus Books

Denscombe, M. (2001) 'Uncertain identities and health-risking behaviour: the case of young people and smoking in late modernity', *British Journal of Sociology*, 52, March

Devine, F. (1992) *Affluent Workers Revisited*, Edinburgh University Press: Edinburgh

Diani, M. (1992) 'The concept of social movement', *Sociological Review*, 40, pp. 1-25

Digby, B., *et al.* (2001) *Global Challenges*, Oxford: Heinemann

Ditton, J. (1977) *Part-time Crime: An Ethnography of Fiddling and Pilferage*, Basingstoke: Macmillan

Douglas, J.D. (1967) *The Social Meaning of Suicide*, Princeton, N.J: Princeton University Press

Downes, D. (1966) *The Delinquent Solution*, London: Routledge

Drury, B. (1991) 'Sikh girls and the maintenance of an ethnic culture', *New Community*, 17(3), pp. 387–99

Durkheim, E. (1897/1952) *Suicide: A Study in Sociology*, London: Routledge Kegan Paul

Durkheim, E. (1912/1961) *The Elementary Forms of Religious Life*, London: Allen & Unwin

Durkheim, E. (1960, originally 1893) *The Division of Labour in Society*, Glencoe: Free Press

Durkheim, E. (1982) *The Rules of Sociological Method* (ed. S. Lukes), London: Macmillan

Duverger, M. (1972) *Party Politics and Pressure Groups*, London: Nelson

Economic and Social Research Council (1997) *Twenty-Something in the 90s: Getting on, Getting by, Getting Nowhere*, Research Briefing, Swindon: ESRC

Edwards, C. (1992) 'Industrialisation in South Korea', in T. Hewitt, H. Johnson and D. Wield (eds) *Industrialisation and Development*, Oxford: Oxford University Press

Ehrlich, P. (1968) *The Population Bomb*, New York: Ballantyne

El Sadaawi, N. (1980) *The Hidden Face of Eve: Women in the Arab World*, London: Zed Books

Elkington, J. (1999) *Cannibals With Forks: The Triple Bottom Line of 21st Century Businesses*, Oxford Capestone

Elliot, A. (2002) 'Beck's sociology of risk: a critical assessment', *Sociology*, 36(2), pp. 293–315

Ellwood, W. (2001) *The No-Nonsense Guide to Globalisation*, London: Verso

Elson, D. and Pearson, R. (1981) 'The subordination of women and the internationalisation of factory production', in K. Young *et al.* (eds) *Of Marriage and the Market: Women's Subordination in International Perspective*, London: CSE Books

EOC (2005a) *Sex and Power: Who Runs Britain?*, Manchester: Equal Opportunities Commission

EOC (2005b) *Facts about Women and Men in Great Britain*, Manchester: Equal Opportunities Commission

Erixon, F. (2005) *Why Aid Does Not Work*, www.news.bbc.co.uk

Escobar, A. (1995) *Encountering Development: The Making and Unmaking of the Third World*, Princeton: Princeton University Press

Esteva, G. (1992) 'Development' in W. Sachs (ed.) *The Development Dictionary: A Guide for Knowledge and Power*, London: Zed Books

Esteva, G. and Austin, J.E. (1987) *Food Policy in Mexico: the Search for Self-Sufficiency*, Ithaca: Cornell University Press

Etzioni, A. (1993) *The Spirit of Community*, New York: Crown Publishers

Evans, G. (1992) 'Is Britain a class-divided society? A re-analysis and extension of Marshall *et al.*'s study of class consciousness', *Sociology*, 26(2), pp.233–58

Evans, P. (1979) *Dependent Development: The Alliance of Multinational, State and Local Capital in Brazil*, Princeton: Princeton University Press

Fahmy, E. (2004) *Encouraging Young People's Political Participation In The UK*, London: Routledge,

Faludi, S. (1992) *The Undeclared War against Women*, London: Chatto & Windus

Farrington, D.P. and Painter, K.A. (2004) *Gender Differences in Offending: Implications for risk focussed prevention*, Home Office Online Report 09/04 www.homeoffice.gov.uk/rds/onlinepubs1.html

Farrington, D.P. and West, D.J. (1990) 'The Cambridge Study in Delinquent Development: a long-term follow-up of 411 London males', in H.J. Kerner and G. Kaiser (eds) *Criminality; Personality, Behaviour and Life History*, Berlin: Springer-Verlag

Feeley, M. and Simon, J. (1992) 'The new penology', *Criminology*, 30(4)

Fenn, R.K. (ed.) (2004) 'Feminism and the sociology of religion: from gender blindness to gendered difference', in *The Blackwell Companion the Sociology of Religion*, London: Blackwell

Fenwick, M. and Hayward, K.J. (2000) 'Youth Crime, Excitement and Consumer Culture' in J. Pickford (ed.) *Youth Justice: Theory and Practice*, London: Cavendish

Ferrell, J. (1999) 'Cultural criminology', *Annual Review of Sociology*, 25(1)

Festinger, L., Riecken, H., and Schachter, S. (1956) *When Prophecy Fails*, Minneapolis: University of Minnesota Press

Feyerabend, P. (1975) *Against Method*, London: New Left Review Editions

Fielding, A. (1995) 'Migration and middle-class formation in England and Wales' in T. Butler and M. Savage (eds) (1995) *Social Change and the Middle Class*, London: UCL

Firestone, S. (1971/2) *The Dialectic of Sex*, London: Cape

Fitzgerald, M., Stockdale, J. and Hale, C. (2003) *Young People's Involvement in Street Crime*, London: Youth Justice Board

Forster, N. (1994) 'The analysis of company documentation' in C. Cassell and G. Symon (eds) *Qualitative Methods in Organizational Research*, London: Sage

Foster, J. (1995) 'Informal Social Control and Community Crime Prevention, *British Journal of Criminology*, 35

Foster, J., Newburn, T. and Souhami, A. (2005) *Assessing the Impact of the Stephen Lawrence Inquiry*, Home Office Research Study 294, London: Home Office Research, Development and Statistics Directorate

Foster-Carter, A. (1985) *The Sociology of Development*, Ormskirk: Causeway Press

Foster-Carter, A. (1993) 'Development', in Haralamabos, M. (ed.) *Developments in Sociology*, Vol 9, Ormskirk: Causeway Press

Foucault, M. (1963/1975) *The Birth of the Clinic*, New York: Vintage Books

Foucault, M. (1977) *Discipline and Punish*, London: Allen Lane

Foucault, M. (1980) *Power/Knowledge: Selected Interviews and Other Writings 1972–77* (ed. C. Gordon), Brighton: Harvester Press

Frank, A.G. (1971) *The Sociology and Development and the Underdevelopment of Sociology*, London: Pluto Press

Frobel, F., Heinrichs, J. and Kreye, O. (1980) *The New International Division of Labour*, Cambridge: Cambridge University Press

Fulcher, J. and Scott, J. (1999) *Sociology*, Oxford: Oxford University Press

Furlong, A. and Cartmel, F. (1997) *Young People and Social Change*, Buckingham: Open University Press

Galeano, E. (1992) *Open Veins of Latin America*, New York: Monthly Press Review

Gallie, D. (1994) 'Are the unemployed an underclass: some evidence from the Social Change and Economic Life Initiative', *Sociology*, 28

Garfinkel, H. (1967) *Studies in Ethnomethodology*, Englewood Hills, NJ: Prentice-Hall

Garland, D. (1996) 'The limits of the sovereign state: strategies of crime control in contemporary society', *British Journal of Criminology*, 36(4), pp.445–71

Garland, D. (2001) *Punishment and Control*, Oxford: Oxford University Press

Geis, G. (1967) 'The heavy electrical equipment anti-trust cases of 1961', in M.B. Clinard and R. Quinney (eds) *Criminal Behaviour Systems*, New York: Holt, Rhinehart & Winston

General Household Survey (2001), London: ONS, HMSO

George, S. (1993) 'The debt boomerang', *New Internationalist*, 243, May

Gereffi, G. (1994) 'Rethinking development theory: insights from East Asia and Latin America', in A. Douglas-Kincaid and A. Portes (eds) *Comparative National Development: Society and Economy in the New Global Order*, North Carolina: University of North Carolina Press

Giddens, A. (1973) *The Class Structure of the Advanced Societies*, London: Hutchinson

Giddens, A. (1976) *The New Rules of Sociological Methods*, London: Hutchinson

Giddens, A. (1984) *The Constitution of Society: Outline of the Theory of Structuration*, Cambridge: Polity Press

Giddens, A. (1991) *Modernity and Self-Identity*, Cambridge: Polity Press

Giddens, A. (1999) *A Runaway World? The BBC Reith Lectures*, London: BBC Radio 4, BBC Education

Giddens, A. (2001) *Sociology* (4th edn), Cambridge: Polity Press

Giddens, A. and Diamond, P. (2005) *The New Egalitarianism*, Cambridge: Polity

Giddens, A. and Pierson, C. (1998) *Conversations with Anthony Giddens: Making Sense of Modernity*, Cambridge: Polity Press

Gilroy, P. (1982) 'Steppin' out of Babylon: race, class and autonomy, in *The Empire Strikes Back: Race and Racism in Britain*, London: CCCS/Hutchinson

Ginn, J., *et al.* (1996) 'Feminist fallacies: a reply to Hakim on women's employment', *British Journal of Sociology*, 47

Glaser, B.G. and Strauss, A. (1965/7) *Awareness of Dying*, Chicago: Aldine

Glasgow University Media Group (1985) *War and Peace News*, Milton Keynes: Open University Press

Glasner, P. (1977) *The Sociology of Secularisation*, London: Routledge & Kegan Paul

Glass, D.V. (1954) *Social Mobility in Britain*, London: RKP

Glock, C.Y. and Stark, R. (1969) 'Dimensions in religious commitment', in R. Robertson (ed.) (1969) *The Sociology of Religion*, Harmondsworth: Penguin

Goffman, E. (1968) *Asylums*, Harmondsworth: Penguin

Gold, K. (2003) 'Poverty is an excuse', *Times Educational Supplement*, 7 March

Gold, R. (1958) 'Roles in sociological field investigation', *Social Forces*, 36, pp.217–23.

Goldthorpe, J. (1975) *The Sociology of the Third World*, Cambridge: Cambridge University Press

Goldthorpe, J. (1980a) *Social Mobility and the Class Structure in Modern Britain*, Oxford: Clarendon Press

Goldthorpe, J. (1980b) 'Women and class analysis: in defence of the conventional view', *Sociology*, 17(4)

Goldthorpe, J. (1983) 'Women and class analysis: in defence of the conventional view', *Sociology*, 14

Goldthorpe, J. (1996) 'Class analysis and the reorientation of class theory', *British Journal of Sociology*, 47(3), pp.481–505

Goldthorpe, J. and Lockwood, D. (1969) *The Affluent Worker in the Class Structure* (3 vols), Cambridge: Cambridge University Press

Goodwin, J. and O'Connor, H. (2005) 'Exploring complex transitions: looking back at the golden age of from school to work', *Sociology*, 39(2), pp. 201–20

Gordon, P. (1988) 'Black people and the criminal law: rhetoric and reality', *International Journal of the Sociology of Law*, 16

Gouldner, A.W. (1968) 'The sociologist as partisan: sociology and the welfare state', *The American Sociologist*, May

Graef, R. (1989) *Talking Blues: The Police in Their Own Words* London: Collins Harvill

Graef, R. (1989) *Talking Blues: The Police in Their Own Words,* London: Collins Harvill

Graham, J. and Bowling, B. (1995) *Young People and Crime*, Home Office Research Study 145, London: Home Office

Gramsci, A. (1971) *Selections from the Prison Notebooks*, London: Lawrence and Wishart

Grant, W. (1999) *Pressure Groups and British Politics*, Basingstoke: Palgrave

Greeley, A. (1972) *Unsecular Man*, New York: Schocken Books, Inc

Greeley, A. (1992) *Sociology and Religion: A Collection of Readings*, New York: HarperCollins Publishers

Grimshaw, D. and Rubery, G. (2001) *The Gender Pay Gap: A Research Review*, Manchester: Equal Opportunities Commission

Gross, E. (1978) 'Organisations as criminal actors', in J. Braithwaite and P. Wilson (eds) *Two Faces of Deviance: Crimes of the Powerless and the Powerful*, Brisbane: University of Queensland Press

Gross, R.M. (1994) 'Buddhism' in J. Holm, and J. Bowker (eds), (1994) *Women in Religion*, London: Pinter

Habermas, J. (1979) *Communication and the Evolution of Society*, London: Heinemann

Hadden, J. and Bromley, D. (1993) *Religion and the Social Order: The Handbook on Cults and Sects in America*, Greenwich, CT: JAI Press

Haddon, J.K. and Long, T.E. (eds) (1993) *Religion and Religiosity in America*, New York: Crossroad Publishing Company

Hagan, J. (1987) *Modern Criminology: Crime, Criminal Behaviour and its Control*, New York: McGraw-Hill

Hakim, C. (1979) *Occupational Segregation*, Department of Employment Research Paper no. 9, London: HMSO

Hakim, C. (2000) *Work–Lifestyle Choices in the 21st Century*, Oxford: Oxford University Press

Halevy, E. (1927) *A History of the English People in 1815*, London: Unwin

Hall, S. (1985) 'Religious ideologies and social movements in Jamaica', in R. Bocock and K. Thompson (eds) *Religion and Ideology*, Manchester: Manchester University Press

Hall, S. and Jacques, M. (1983) *The Politics of Thatcherism*, London: Lawrence & Wishart

Hall, S. and Jefferson, T. (1976) *Resistance through Rituals*, London: Hutchinson

Hall, S., Critcher, C., Jefferson ,T., Clarke, J. and Roberts, B. (1978) *Policing the Crisis: The State and Law and Order*, London: Macmillan

Hallsworth, S. (1994) 'Understanding New Social Movements', *Sociology Review*, 4(1), Oxford: Philip Allen

Hamilton, M. (2001) *The Sociology of Religion* (2nd edn) London: Routledge

Hammersley, M. (1992) 'By what criteria should ethnographic research be judged?', in M. Hammersley, *What's Wrong with Ethnography?*, London: Routledge

Hancock, G. (1989) *Lords of Poverty*, New York: Atlantic Monthly Press

Hanley, P. (2002) *The Numbers Game: Older People and the Media*, ITC Research Publication

Hanson, E. (1997) *Decadence and Catholicism*, Cambridge, Mass: Harvard University Press

Haralambos, M. (ed.) (1985) 'The sociology of development', *Sociology: New Directions*, Ormskirk: Causeway Press

Harding, S. (1986) *The Science Question in Feminism*, Milton Keynes: Open University Press

References

Harding, S. (1987) *Feminism and Methodology*, Bloomington, IN & Buckingham: Indiana University Press & Open University Press

Harper, D. (1978) 'At home on the rails: ethics in a photographic research project', *Qualitative Sociology*, 1, pp. 66–77

Harper, P., Pollak, M., Mooney, J., Whelan, E. and Young, J. (1986) *The Islington Crime Survey*, London Borough of Islington

Harris, G. (1989) *The Sociology of Development*, London: Longman

Harrison, P. (1990) *Inside the Third World: The Anatomy of Poverty* (2nd edn), Harmondsworth: Penguin

Hart, N. (1994) *New Left Review*, November, 1/208

Hartnett, O. (1990) 'The sex role system', in P. Mayes *Gender*, Longman: London

Harvey, D. (1990) *The Condition of Modernity*, Blackwell: Oxford

Hayek, F.A. (1944/1986) *The Road to Serfdom*, London: Routledge

Hayter, T. (1981) *The Creation of World Poverty* (2nd edn), London: Pluto Press

Heath, A. (1991) Understanding Political Change: The British Voter, 1964–87, Oxford: Butterworth Heinemann

Heath, A. and C. Payne (1999) *Twentieth Century Trend in Social Mobility in Britain*, University of Oxford Centre for Research into Elections and Social Trends, Working Paper No. 70

Heelas, P. (1996) *The New Age Movement*, Cambridge: Polity Press

Heelas, P., Woodhead, W., Seel, B., Tusting, K. and Szerszynski, B. (2004) *The Spiritual Revolution: Why Religion Is Giving Way to Spirituality*, Oxford: Blackwell

Heidensohn, F. (1989, 1996 [2nd edn]) *Women and Crime*, London: Macmillan

Heidensohn, F. (2002) 'Gender and crime', in M. Maguire, R. Morgan and R. Reinder, *The Oxford Handbook of Criminology* (3rd edn), Oxford: Oxford University Press

Held, D. (ed.) (2000) *A Globalising World: Culture, Economics*, Politics, London: Routledge

Held, D. and McGrew, A. (2002) *Globalization and Anti-Globalization*, Cambridge: Polity Press

Henry, S. and Milovanovic, D. (1996) *Constitutive Criminology: Beyond Postmodernism*, London: Sage

Herberg, W. (1960) *Protestant – Catholic – Jew* (revised edn), New York: Anchor Books

Hetherington, K. (1998) *Expressions of Identity: Space, Performance, Politics*, London: Sage

Hirschi, T. (1969) *Causes of Delinquency*, Berkeley, CA: University of California Press

Hirst, P.Q. (1975) 'Radical deviancy theory and Marxism: a reply to Taylor, Walton and Young', in E. Taylor, P. Walton and J. Young (eds) *Critical Criminology*, London: Routledge

Hobbs, D. (1988) *Doing the Business, Entrepreneurship, the Working Class and Detectives in the East End of London*, Oxford: Oxford University Press

Hobbs, D., Lister, S., Hadfield, P. and Winlow, S. (2000) 'Receiving shadows: governance and liminality in the night-time economy', *British Journal of Sociology*, 51(4) pp.682–700

Holdaway, S. (1983) *Inside the British Police*, Oxford: Blackwell

Holden, A. (2002) *Jehovah's Witnesses: Portrait of a Contemporary Religious Movement*, London/New York: Routledge

Holm, J. and Bowker, J. (eds) (1994) *Women in Religion*, London: Pinter

Home Office (1998) *British Crime Survey*, Research and Statistics Directorate of the Home Office

Hood, R. and Joyce, K. (1999) 'Three generations: oral testimony of crime and social change in London's East End', *British Journal of Criminology*, 39(1), pp.136–60

Hoogvelt, A. (2001) *Globalisation and the Post Colonial World* (2nd edn), Basingstoke: Palgrave

Hook, S. (1990) *Convictions*, New York: Prometheus Books

Horkheimer, M. (1974) *Eclipse of Reason*, New York: Oxford University Press

Hoselitz, B. (1964) *Sociological Aspects of Economic Growth*, Chicago: Chicago Free Press

Howell, J.M. and Frost P.J. (1989) 'A Laboratory Study of Charismatic Leadership', *Organizational Behavior and Human Decision Processes*, 43, pp.243–69

Hunt, J. (2004a) 'Aid and development', in D. Kingsbury, J. Remenyi, J. McKay and J. Hunt (eds) *Key Issues in Development*, Basingstoke: Palgrave

Hunt, J. (2004b) 'Gender and development', in D. Kingsbury, J. Remenyi, J. McKay and J. Hunt (eds) *Key Issues in Development*, Basingstoke: Palgrave

Hunter, J.D. (1987) *Evangelism: The Coming Generation*, Chicago: University of Chicago Press

Huntington, S.P. (1993) 'The clash of civilisations', *Foreign Affairs*, 72

Hutton, W. (1996) *The State We're In*, London: Vantage

Inglehart, R. and Baker, W. (2000) 'Modernisation, Cultural Change and the Persistence of Traditional Values', *American Sociological Review*, 65(1), February, pp.19–21

Inkeles, A. (1969) 'Making modern men: on the causes and consequences of individual change in six developing countries', *American Journal of Sociology*, 75

Inland Revenue (2004) Distribution of Personal Wealth – www.hmrc.gov.uk/stats/personal_wealth/menu.htm

Jackson, B. (1978) 'Killing time: life in the Arkansas penitentiary', *Qualitative Sociology*, 1 pp. 21–32

Jessop, B. (2002) *The Future of the Capitalist State*, Cambridge: Polity Press

Jewkes, Y. (2005) 'Creating a stir? Prisons, popular media and the power to reform', in P. Mason (ed.) *Captured by the Media: Prison Discourse in Media Culture*, Cullompton: Willan

Johal S. (1998) 'Brimful of Brasia', *Sociology Review*, 8(1), Oxford: Philip Allan

Jones, T., Maclean, B. and Young, J. (1995) *The Second Islington Crime Survey*, London Borough of Islington

Joseph Rowntree Foundation (1995) *Income and Wealth: Report of the JRF Inquiry Group*, York: JRF

Katz, J. (1988) *Seductions of Crime: Moral and Sensual Attractions in Doing Evil*, New York: Basic Books

Kaur-Singh, K. (1994) 'Sikhism' in J. Holm, and J. Bowker (eds), (1994) *Women in Religion*, London: Pinter

Kautsky, K. (1953) *Foundations of Christianity*, New York: Russell

Kay, T. (1996) 'Women's work and women's work': implications of women's changing employment patterns', *Leisure Studies*, 15, pp.49–64

Kenyatta, M.L. and Tai, R.H. (1999) *Critical Ethnicity: Countering the Waves of Identity Politics*, Oxford: Rowman and Littlefield

Kepel, G. (1994) *The Revenge of God: The Resurgence of Islam, Christianity and Judaism in the Modern World*, Cambridge: Polity Press

Kilby, P. (2001) quoted in D. Kingsbury, J. Remenyi, J. McKay and J. Hunt (eds) *Key Issues in Development*, Basingstoke: Palgrave

Kingsbury, D., Remenyi, J., McKay, J. and Hunt, J. (eds) (2004) *Key Issues in Development*, Basingstoke: Palgrave

Kitsuse, J. (1962) 'Societal reaction to deviant behaviour', *Social Problems*, (9) Winter

Klein, N. (2001) *No Logo*, London: Flamingo

Korten, D. (1995) 'Steps towards people-centered development: vision and strategies', in N. Heyzer, J.V. Ricker and A.B. Quizon (eds) *Government–NGO Relations in Asia: Prospects and Challenges for People-centred development*, Basingstoke: Palgrave

Kuhn, T.S. (1962/1970) *The Structure of Scientific Revolutions* (2nd edn), Chicago: University of Chicago Press

Laczko, F. and Phillipson, C. (1991) *Changing Work and Retirement: Social Policy and the Older Worker*, Open University Press: Milton Keynes

Lakatos, I. (1970) 'Falsification and the methodology of scientific research programmes', in I. Lakatos and A. Musgrave (eds) *Criticism and the Growth of Knowledge*, Cambridge: Cambridge University Press

Landes, D. (1998) *The Wealth and Poverty of Nations*, London: Little Brown and Company

Langone, M.D. and Martin, P. (1993) 'Deprogramming, exit counselling, and ethics: clarifying the confusion', *Cult Observer*, 10(4)

Lappe, F. and Collins, J. (1977) *Food First*, Boston: Houghton Miflin

Laumann, E.O., Gagnon, J.H., Michael, R.T. and Michaels, S. (1995) *The Social Organization of Sexuality: Sexual Practices in the United States*, Chicago: University of Chicago Press

Lea, J. and Young, J. (1984) *What is to be Done about Law and Order?*, Harmondsworth: Penguin

Lea, J. and Young, J. (1993) *What is to be Done about Law and Order?* (revised edn), London: Pluto Press

Leach, E. (1988) *Culture and Communication*, Cambridge: Cambridge University Press

Lee-Treweek, G. (2000) 'The insight of emotional danger: research experiences in a home for the elderly', in G. Lee-Treweek and S. Lingogle (eds) *Danger in the Field: Risk and Ethics in Social Research*, London: Routledge

Lemert, E. (1967/1972) *Human Deviance, Social Problems and Social Control*, Englewood Cliffs, NJ: Prentice-Hall

Lenin (1965) *Collected Works*, Vol. 10, Moscow: Progress Publishers

Leonard, M. (1992) 'Women and Development', *Sociology Review*, September

Lerner, D. (1958) *The Passing of Traditional Society*, Glencoe: Free Press

Levi, M. (1987) *Regulating Fraud*, London: Tavistock

Levin, J. and McDevitt, J. (2002) *Hate Crimes Revisited*, Boulder, CO: Westview Press

Levine, E. (1980) 'Deprogramming without tears', *Society*, 17 (March), pp.34–8

Liazos, A. (1972) 'The poverty of the sociology of deviance: nuts, sluts and perverts', *Social Problems* 20

Lockwood, D. (1966) 'Sources of variation in working-class images of society', *Sociological Review*, 14

Luhman, N. (1995) *Social Systems*, Stanford: Stanford University Press

Lukes, S. (1974) *Power: A Radical View*, London: Macmillan

Lukes, S. (1986) 'Domination by economic power and authority' in S. Lukes (ed.) *Power*, Oxford: Blackwell

Lyng, S. (1990) 'Edgework: a social psychological analysis of voluntary risk-taking', *American Journal of Sociology*, 95(4), pp.851–6

Lyon, D. (2000) *Jesus in Disneyland: Religion in Postmodern Times*, Cambridge: Polity Press

Lyotard, J.-F. (1984) *The Post-Modern Condition: A Report on Knowledge*, Manchester: University of Manchester Press

Mac an Ghaill, M. (1988) *Young, Gifted and Black*, Milton Keynes: Open University Press

Mac an Ghaill, M. (1992) 'Coming of age in 80s England: reconceptualising black students' educational experience', in D. Gill, B. Mayor and M. Blair (eds) *Racism and Education: Structures and Strategies*, London: Sage

Mac an Ghaill, M. (1994) *The Making of Men: Masculinities, Sexualities and Schooling*, Milton Keynes: Open University Press

Mac An Ghaill, M. (ed.) (1996) *Understanding Masculinities: Social Relations and Cultural Arenas*, Buckingham: Open University Press

Macdonald, K. and Tipton, C. (1993) 'Using documents', in N. Gilbert (ed.) *Researching Social Life*, London: Sage

McDowell, L. (1992) 'Gender divisions in a post-Fordist era', in L. McDowell and R. Pringle (eds) *Defining Women*, Cambridge: Polity Press

MacGuire, M.B. (1981) *Religion: The Social Context*, California: Wadsworth Publishing

Mack, J. and Lansley, S. (1985) *Poor Britain*, London: Allen & Unwin

McKay, H. (2000) 'The globalisation of culture', in D.Held (2000) *A Globalising World? Culture, Economics, Politics*, London: Routledge

McKay, J. (2004) 'Reassessing development theory: "modernization" and beyond', in D. Kingsbury, J.

Remenyi, J. McKay and J. Hunt (eds) *Key Issues in Development*, Basingstoke: Palgrave

McKee, L. and Bell, C. (1985) 'Marital and family relations in times of male unemployment', in B. Roberts, R. Finnegan and D. Gallie (eds) *New Approaches to Economic Life*, Manchester: Manchester University Press

McKenzie, R.T. and Silver, A. (1968) 'The working class Tory in England' in P. Worsley *Angels in Marble*, London: Heinemann

McKie, L., Bowlby, S. and Gregory, S. (2004) 'Starting well: gender, care and health in the family context', *Sociology*, 38(3), pp. 593–611

Madriz, M. (2000) 'Focus groups in feminist research' in N.K. Denzin and Y.S. Lincoln (eds) *Handbook of Qualitative Research* (2nd edn), Thousand Oaks, CA: Sage

Maduro, O. (1982) Religion and Social Conflicts, New York: Orbis Books

Maffesoli, M. (1996) *The Time of the Tribes,* London: Sage

Maguire, M. (2002) 'Crime statistics: the data explosion and its implications', in M. Maguire, R. Morgan and R. Reiner (eds) *The Oxford Handbook of Criminology* (3rd edn), Oxford: Oxford University Press

Maguire, M., Morgan, R. and Reiner, R. (eds) (1997) *The Oxford Handbook of Criminology* (2nd edn), Oxford: Oxford University Press

Malinowski, B. (1954) *Magic, Science and Religion and Other Essays*, New York: Anchor Books

Malinowski, B. (1982) *Magic, Science and Religion and Other Essays,* London: Souvenir Press

Mamdani, M. (1996) *Citizen and Subject: Contemporary Africa and the Legacy of Late Colonialism*, Princeton: Princeton University Press

Mann, M. (1986) *The Sources of Social Power*, Vol. 1, Cambridge: Cambridge University Press

Mannheim, K. (1960) *Ideology and Utopia*, London: Routledge

Marcuse, H. (1964/1991) *One Dimensional Man: Studies in the Ideology of Advanced Industrial Societies*, London: Routledge

Marmot, M.G., Smith, G.D., Stansfeld, S., Patel, C., North, F., Head, J., White, I., Brunner, E. and Feeney A. (1991) 'Health inequalities among British civil servants: the Whitehall II study, *The Lancet*, 337, pp.1387-93.

Mars, G. (1982) *Cheats at Work: an Anthropology of Workplace Crime*, London: George Allen & Unwin

Marshall, G. (1982) *In Search of the Spirit of Capitalism: Max Weber and the Protestant Ethic Thesis*, London: Hutchison

Marshall, G. (1987) 'What is happening to the working class?', *Social Studies Review*, January

Marshall, G., Newby. H., Rose, D. and Vogler, C. (1988) *Social Class In Modern Britain*, London, Hutchinson

Martin, D. (1978) *A General Theory of Secularisation*, Blackwell: Oxford

Marx, K. (1844) *Selected Writings* (2000 edn), Oxford: Oxford University Press

Marx, K. (1867/1973) *Capital: A Critique of Political Economy*, Harmondsworth: Penguin

Marx, K. and Engels, F. (1848/2002) *Manifesto of the Communist Party*, North Charleston, SC: BookSurge

Marx, K. and Engels, F. (1957) *On Religion*, Moscow: Progress Publishers

Marx, K. and Engels, F. (1975) 'On the history of early Christianity', in *Collected Works of Karl Marx and Frederick Engels,* Vol. 27, Moscow: Progress Publishers

Matthews, R. and Young, J. (eds) (1992) *Issues in Realist Criminology*, London: Sage

Matza, D. (1964) *Delinquency and Drift*, New York: Wiley

May, T. (2001) *Social Research: Issues, Methods and Process*, Buckingham: Open University Press

Mayhew, H. (1851) *London Labour and the London Poor* (republished 1985), Harmondsworth: Penguin

Mayhew, P., Aye Maung, N. and Mirrlees-Black, C. (1993) *The 1992 British Crime Survey*, Home Office Research Study 111, London: Home Office

Maynard, M. and Purvis, J. (eds) (1994) *Researching Women's Lives from a Feminist Perspective*, London: Taylor & Francis

Mead, G.H. (1934) *Mind, Self and Society* (ed. C. Morris) Chicago: University of Chicago

Melucci, A. (1989) *Nomads of the Present*, London: Hutchinson

Merton, R. (1938) 'Social structure and anomie', *American Sociological Review*, 3

Merton, R. (1957) *Social Theory and Social Structure*, New York: The Free Press

Merton, R.K. (1938) 'Social structure and anomie', *American Sociological Review* 3

Merton, R.K. (1938/1968) *Social Theory and Social Structure*, New York: The Free Press

Messerschmidt, J. (1993) *Masculinities and Crime*, Lanham, MD: Rowman & Littlefield

Metcalf, H., Modood, T. and Virdee, S. (1996) *Asian Self-Employment*, London: Policy Studies Institute

Michalowski, R. and Kramer, R. (1987) 'The space between laws: the problem of corporate crime in a transnational context', *Social Problems*, 34

Miles, R. (1989) *Racism*, London: Routledge

Miliband, R. (1970) *The State in Capitalist Society*, London: Quartet

Millen, D. (1997) 'Some methodological and epistemological issues raised by doing feminist research on non-feminist women', *Sociological Research Online* www.socresonline.org.uk/socresonline/2/3/3.html

Miller, A.S. and Hoffman, J.P. (1995), 'Risk and religion: an explanation of gender differences in religiosity', *Journal for the Scientific Study of Religion* 34, pp. 63–75

Miller, W.B. (1962) 'Lower class culture as a generating milieu of gang delinquency', in M.E. Wolfgang, L. Savitz and N. Johnston (eds) *The Sociology of Crime and Delinquency*, New York: Wiley

Millett, K. (1970) *Sexual Politics*, New York: Doubleday

Mills, C.W. (1959) *The Sociological Imagination*, Oxford: Oxford University Press

Milne, A., Hatzidimitradou, E. and Harding, T. (1999) *Later Lifestyles: A survey by Help the Aged and* Yours *Magazine*, London: Help the Aged

Modood, T. (1992) *Not Easy Being British: Colour, Culture and Citizenship*, Runnymede Trust and Trentham Books

Modood, T., Beishon, S. and Virdee, S. (1994) *Changing Ethnic Identities*, London: Policy Studies Institute

Mohanty, C. (1997) 'Under western eyes: feminist scholarship and colonial discourse', in, N. Visuanathan, L. Duggan, L. Nisonoff and N.Wiergersma (eds), *The Women, Gender and Development Reader*, London: Zed Books

Molyneux, M. (1981) 'Women in socialist societies: problems of theory and practice', in K.Young *et al.* (eds) *Of Marriage and the Market: Women's Subordination in International Perspective*, London: CSE Books

Monaghan, L. (1999) 'Creating "the perfect body": a variable project', *Body and Society*, 5(2-3), pp.267–90

Monaghan, L. (2005) 'Get ready to duck: bouncers and the realities of ethnographic research on violent groups', *British Journal of Criminology*, 41, pp. 536–48

Moore, M. (2001) *Stupid White Men*, London: Penguin

Moore, M. (2003) *Dude, Where's My Country?,* London: Penguin

Moore, S. and Scourfield, P. (2005) Eliminating the visible: exploring community response to anti-social behaviour', *Crime Prevention and Community Safety*, 7(3)

Moores, M. (1998) 'Sociologists in white coats', *Sociology Review*, 7(3)

Morgan, I. (1999) *Power and Politics*, London: Hodder & Stoughton

Morley, D. (1980) *The Nationwide Audience*, London: BFI

Morris, L. (1993) *Dangerous Classes: The Underclass and Social Citizenship*, London: Routledge

Morris, T.P. (1957) *The Criminal Area: A study in Social Ecology*, London: Routledge

Mosca, G. (1939) *The Ruling Class*, New York: McGraw Hill

Mouzelis, N. (1995) *Sociological Theory: What Went Wrong?*, London: Routledge

Murray, C. (1990) *The Emerging British Underclass*, London: Institute of Economic Affairs, Health and Welfare Unit

Murray, C. (1994) *The Crisis Deepens*, London: IEA

Myrdal, G. (1968) *Asian Drama: An enquiry into the Poverty of Nations*, New York: The Twentieth Century Fund

Need, N. and Evans, G. (2001) 'Analysing Patterns of Religious Participation in Post-communist Eastern Europe', *British Journal of Sociology*, 52(2)

Nelken, D. (2002) 'White collar crime', in M. Maguire, R. Morgan and R. Reiner, *The Oxford Handbook of Criminology* (3rd edn), Oxford: Oxford University Press

Nelson, G.K. (1986) 'Religion' in M. Haralambos (ed.) *Developments in Sociology*, Vol. 2, Ormskirk: Causeway Press

New Internationalist (1986) 'Fly Me to the Moon', Issue 169

Newton, K. (1969) 'A Critique of the Pluralist Model', *Acta Sociologica,* 12

Niebuhr, H.R. (1929) *The Social Sources of Denominationalism*, New York: The World Publishing Company

Nightingale, C. (1993) *On the Edge*, New York: Basic Books

O'Connell Davidson, J. and Layder, D. (1994) *Methods, Sex and Madness*, London: Routledge

O'Malley, P. (1992) 'Risk, power and crime prevention', *Economy and Society*, 21(3), pp.242–75

Oakley, A. (1974) *Housewife*, London: Allen Lane

Oakley, A. (1981) 'Interviewing women: a contradiction in terms', in H. Roberts (ed.) *Doing Feminist Research*, London: Routledge

Oakley, A. (1998) 'Gender, methodology and people's ways of knowing: some problems with feminism and the paradigm debate in social science', *Sociology*, 32, pp. 707–31

Olsen, W. and Walby, S. (2004) *Modelling Gender Pay Gaps*, Manchester: Equal Opportunities Commission

ONS (2004) *Labour Force Survey Spring 2004*, Office for National Statistics

Oppenheim, C. and Harker, L. (1996) *Poverty: The Facts* (3rd edn), London: CPAG

O'Toole, R. (1984) *Religion: Classic Sociological Approaches*, Toronto: McGraw Hill

Owen, D.W. and Green, A.E. (1992) 'Labour market experience and occupational change amongst ethnic groups in Great Britain', *New Community*, 19, pp.7–29

Pakulski, J. and Waters, M. (1996) *The Death of Class*, London: Sage

Pareto, V. (1935) *The Mind and Society*, New York: Dover

Parker, H. (1974 [1st edn], 1992 [2nd edn]) *View from the Boys*, Aldershot: Ashgate

Parker, H., Aldridge, J. and Measham, F. (1998) *Illegal Leisure: the Normalization of Adolescent Recreational Drug Use*, London, Routledge

Parkin, F. (1972) *Class Inequality and Political Order*, St. Albans: Paladin

Parsons, T. (1937) *The Structure of Social Action*, New York: McGraw-Hill

Parsons, T. (1951/52) *The Social System*, New York: Free Press

Parsons, T. (1963) 'On the concept of political power', *Proceedings of the American Philosophical Society*, 107

Parsons, T. (1964) 'Evolutionary universals in society', *American Sociological Review*, 29 June

Parsons, T. (1964) *Essays in Social Theory*, New York: The Free Press

Parsons, T. (1965) 'Religious perspectives in sociology and social psychology', in W.A. Lessa and E.Z. Vogt (1965) *Reader in Comparative Religion: An Anthropological Approach* (2nd edn), New York: Harper & Row

Parsons, T. (1977) *The Evolution of Societies* (ed. J. Toby), Englewood Cliffs, NJ: Prentice-Hall

Patterson, S. (1965) *Dark Strangers*, Harmondsworth: Penguin

Pawson, R. (1989) *A Measure For Measures*, London: Routledge

Payne, G. (1987) *Economy and Opportunity*, Basingstoke: Macmillan

Payne, G. (1992) 'Competing views of contemporary social mobility and social divisions' in R. Burrows and C. Marsh (eds) *Consumption and Class,* Basingstoke: Macmillan

Peace, M. (2005) quoted on www.sociologystuff.com

Pearce, F. (1976) *Crimes of the Powerful*, London: Pluto Press

Pearce, F. and Tombs, S. (1998) *Toxic Capitalism: Corporate Crime and the Chemical Industry*, Aldershot: Ashgate

Pearson, R. (2001) 'Rethinking gender matters in development' in T. Allen and A. Thomas (2001) *Poverty and Development in the 21st Century*, Oxford: Oxford University Press

Pew Global Attitudes Project (2002) www.pewglobal.org

Phillips, C. and Brown, D. (1998) *Entry into the Criminal Justice System: A Survey of Police Arrests and their Outcomes*, Home Office Research Study 185, London: Home Office

Phillips, K. (2004) *American Dynasty; Aristocracy, Fortune and the Politics of Deceit in the House of Bush*, London: Penguin

Phillipson, C. (1982) *Capitalism and the Construction of Old Age*, Basingstoke: Macmillan

Philo, G. and Miller, D. (2000) *Market Killing: What the Free Market Does and What Social Scientists Can Do About It,* Harlow: Longman

Pilcher, J. and Whelehan, I. (2004) *50 Key Concepts in Gender Studies*, London: Sage

Platt, L. (2005) 'The intergenerational social mobility of minority ethnic groups', *BSA Publications*, Volume 39(3), pp.445–61

Platt, T. and Takagi, P. (1977) 'Intellectuals for law and order; a critique of the new realists', *Crime and Social Justice*, 8, pp.1–16

Plummer, K. (2000) *Documents of Life*, Thousand Oaks, CA: Sage

Popper, K. (1959) *The Logic of Scientific Discovery*, London: Hutchinson

Porritt, J. (1985) *Seeing Green: The Politics of Ecology*, Oxford: Blackwell

Portes, A. (1998) 'Social capital: its origins and applications in modern sociology', *Annual Review of Sociology* (24), pp.1–24

Poulantzas, N. (1973) *Political Power and Social Classes*, London: New Left Books

Pryce K. (1979) *Endless Pressure*, Harmondsworth: Penguin

Punch, K.F. (1998) *Introduction to Social Research*, London: Sage

Punch, M. (1994) 'Politics and ethics in qualitative research', in N.K. Denzin and Y.S. Lincoln (eds) *Handbook of Qualitative Research*, Thousand Oaks, CA: Sage

Punch, M. (1996) *Dirty Business: Exploring Corporate Misconduct*, London: Sage

Putnam, R. (2000) *Bowling Alone: The collapse and revival of American community*, New York: Simon Schuster

Ramazanoglu, C. (1992) 'On feminist methodology: male reason versus feminist empowerment', *Sociology*, 26(2), pp.213–18

Ransom, D. (1996) 'The Poverty of Aid', *New Internationalist*, 285

Rathje, W.L. and Murphy, C. (2002, originally 1992) *Rubbish! The Archaeology of Garbage*, Phoenix: University of Arizona Press

Reay, D. (1998) 'Rethinking social class: qualitative perspectives on gender and social class', *Sociology*, 32(2), pp.259–75

Redhead, S. (ed.) (1993) *Rave off: Politics and Deviance in Contemporary Youth Culture*, Aldershot: Avebury

Rees, W. (1996) quoted in M. Wackernagel and W. Rees, *Our Ecological Footprint: Reducing Human Impact On Human Health*, Gabriola Island, BC: New Society Publishers

Reiman, J. (2003) *The Rich Get Richer and the Poor Get Poorer: Ideology, Class and Criminal Justice*, Harlow: Allyn & Bacon / Pearson Longman

Reiner, R. (1992) *The Politics of the Police,* Hemel Hempstead: Wheatsheaf

Reiner, R. (1997) 'Policy on police', in M. Maguire, R. Morgan, R. Reiner (eds) *The Oxford Handbook of Criminology* (2nd edn), Oxford: Oxford University Press

Reinharz, S. (1992) *Feminist Methods in Sociological Research*, New York: Oxford University Press

Reiss, A.J. (1961) 'The social integration of queers and peers', *Social Problems*, 9(2), p.102–20

Remenyi, J. (2004) 'What is development', in D. Kingsbury, J. Remenyi, J. McKay and J. Hunt (eds) *Key Issues in Development*, Basingstoke: Palgrave

Rex, J. and Tomlinson, S. (1979) *Colonial Immigrants in a British City*, London: Routledge & Kegan Paul

Ritzer, G. (1993) *The McDonaldisation of Society*, Thousand Oaks, California: Pine Forge Press

Robbins, T. (1988) *Cults, Converts, and Charisma*, London: Sage

Roberts, B. (1978) *Cities of Peasants: The Political Economy of Urbanisation in the Third World*, London, Edward Arnold

Roberts, K. (1977) *The Fragmentary Class Structure*, London: Heinemann

Roberts, K. (2001) *Class in Modern Britain,* Basingstoke: Palgrave

Roberts, K. and Chadwick, C. (1991) *Transitions into the Labour Market: The New Routes of the 1980s*, Youth Cohort Series 16, Research and Development Series 65, Sheffield: Employment Department

Roberts, K., Cook, F.G., Clark, S.C. and Semeonoff, E. (1977) *The Fragmentary Class Structure*, London: Heinemann

Robertson, R. (1992) *Globalisation: Social Theory and Global Culture*, London: Sage

Rock, P. (1988) 'The present state of British criminology' in *The British Journal of Criminology*, 28(2)

Room, G. (1995) *Beyond the Threshold: The measurement and analysis of social exclusion*, Bristol: The Policy Press

Rorty, R. (1980) *Philosophy and the Mirror of Nature,* Oxford: Blackwell

Rosenthal, R. and Jacobson, L. (1968) *Pygmalion in the Classroom*, New York: Holt, Rinehart & Winston

Rostow, W.W. (1971) *The Stages of Economic Growth*, Cambridge: Cambridge University Press

Rowntree, B.S. (1901) *Poverty: A Study of Town Life*, London: Macmillan

Runciman, W. (1966) *Relative Deprivation and Social Justice*, London: Routledge

Rusche, G. and Kircheimer, O. (1939) *Punishment and Social Structure*, New York: Columbia University Press

Sachdev, S. and Wilkinson, F. (1998) *Low Pay and the Minimum Wage*, Institute of Employment Rights

Sachs, J. (2005) *Why Aid Does Work*, www.news.bbc.co.uk

Sachs, W. (1992) 'Where all the world's a stooge', *The Guardian*, 29 May

Sahlins, M. (1997) 'The original affluent society' in M. Rahnema and V. Bawtree (eds) (1997) *The Post Development Reader*, London: Zed Books

Said, E. (2003) *Orientalism: Western Conceptions of the Orient*, Harmondsworth: Penguin

Sampson, R.J., Raudenbusch, S.W. and Earls, F. (1997) 'Neighbourhoods and violent crime: a multi-level study of collective efficacy', *Science*, 277, pp.918–24

Sankara, T. (1988) *Thomas Sankara Speaks: The Burkina Faso Revolution 1983–1987*, New York: Pathfinder Press

Sarap, M. (1993) *An Introductory Guide to Post-structuralism and Postmodernism*, Hemel Hempstead: Harvester Wheatsheaf

Saunders, P. (1979) *Urban Politics*, Harmondsworth: Penguin

Saunders, P. (1990) *Social Class and Stratification*, London: Routledge

Saunders, P. (1995) *Capitalism – A Social Audit*, Buckingham: Open University Press

Saunders, P. (1996) *Unequal but Fair? A Study of Class Barriers in Britain*, London: Institute of Economic Affairs

Savage, M. (1995) 'The middle classes in modern Britain', *Sociology Review*, 5(2), Oxford: Philip Allan

Savage, M. (2000) *Class Analysis and Social Transformation*, Buckingham: Open University Press

Savage, M. and Egerton, M. (1997) 'Social mobility, individual ability and the inheritance of class inequality', *Sociology*, 31(4)

Savage, M., Bagnall, G. and Longhurst, B. (2001) 'Ordinary, ambivalent and defensive class identities in the North West of England', *Sociology*, 35(4), pp.875–92

Savage, M., Barlow, J., Dickens, P. and Fielding, I. (1992) *Prosperity, Bureaucracy and Culture: Middle-class Formation in Contemporary Britain*, London: Routledge

Sayer, A. (1992) *Method in Social Science: A Realist Approach* (2nd edn), London: Routledge

Scarman, Lord (1981) *The Scarman Report*, Harmondsworth: Penguin

Scheff, T.J., Retzinger, S.M. and Ryan, M.T. (1989) 'Crime, violence and self-esteem: review and proposals', in A. Mecca, N.J. Smelser and J Vaasconcellos (eds) *The Social Importance of Self-Esteem*, Berkeley: University of California

Schutz, A. (1972) *The Phenomenology of the Social World*, London: Heinemann

Schwartz, H. and Jacobs, J. (1979) *Qualitative Sociology: A Method to the Madness*, London: Collier-Macmillan

Scott MacEwen, A. (1994) 'Gender segregation and the SCELI research' in Scott MacEwen, A. (ed.) *Gender Segregation and Social Change*, Oxford: Oxford University Press

Scott, A. (1990) *Ideology and The New Social Movements*, London: Unwin Hyman

Scott, J. (1982) *The Upper Classes: Poverty and Privilege in Britain*, London: Macmillan

Scott, J. (1991) *Who Rules Britain?,* Cambridge: Polity Press

Scraton, P. (1985) *The State of the Police*, London: Pluto

Scraton, P. (1987) *Law, Order and the Authoritarian State: Readings in Critical Criminology*, Milton Keynes: Open University Press

Scraton, P. (1997) 'Whose "childhood"? What "crisis"?', in P. Scraton (ed.) *'Childhood' in 'Crisis'?*, London: UCL Press

Scraton, P. (2002) 'Defining "power" and challenging "knowledge": critical analysis and resistance in the UK', in K. Carrington and R. Hogg (eds) *Critical Criminology: Issues, debates, challenges*, Cullompton: Willan Publishing

Scraton, P. and Chadwick, K. (1982) 'The theoretical and political priorities of critical criminology', in G. Mars, *Cheats at Work, an Anthropology of Workplace Crime*, London: Allen & Unwin

Select Committee on Home Affairs (1999) *Examination of Witnesses*, (Questions 1060–1079) Wednesday, March 10 1999, Sir Paul Condon QPM, Mr Denis O'Connor QPM and Commander Richard Cullen

Sen, A. (1987) *Hunger and Entitlements*, Helsinki: World Institute for Development Economics Research

Shapin, S. (1995) 'Here and everywhere: sociology of scientific knowledge', *Annual Review of Sociology*, 21

Sharpe, S. (1994) *Just Like a Girl: How Girls Learn to be Women – From the Seventies to the Nineties,* Harmondsworth: Penguin

Sharrock, W., Hughes, J. and Martin, P. (2003) *Understanding Modern Sociology*, London: Sage

Shaw, C.R. and McKay, H.D. (1931) *Social Factors in Juvenile Delinquency*, Washington, DC: Government Printing Office

Shaw, C.R. and McKay, H.D. (1942) *Juvenile Delinquency and Urban Areas,* Chicago: University of Chicago Press

Shearing, C. and Stenning, P. (1983) 'Private security: implications for social control', *Social Problems*, 30(5), pp.493–506

Shiner, L. (1967) 'The concept of secularization in empirical research', *Journal for the Scientific Study of Religion*, 6, pp.207–20

Shiva, V. (1989) *Staying Alive: Women, Ecology and Development*, London: Zed Books

Simon, R.J. and Nadell, P.S. (1995) 'In the same voice or is it different? Gender and the clergy', *Sociology of Religion*, 56(1)

Skeggs, B. (1997) *Formations of Class and Gender*, London: Sage

Skeggs, B. (2001) 'Feminist ethnography', in P. Atkinson, A. Coffey, S. Delamont, J. Lofland and L. Lofland (eds) *Handbook of Ethnography*, London: Sage

Sklair, L. (2004) *Globalization: Capitalism and its Alternatives*, Oxford: Oxford University Press

Skogan, W.G. (1990) *Disorder and Decline: Crime and the Spiral of Decay in American Neighbourhoods*, New York: Free Press

Skolnick, J. (1966) *Justice without Trial*, New York: Wiley

Slapper, G. and Tombs, S. (1999) *Corporate Crime*, Harlow: Longman

Smart, C. (1990) 'Feminist approaches to criminology; or postmodern woman meets atavistic man', in L. Gelsthorpe and A. Morris (eds) *Feminist Perspectives in Criminology*, Milton Keynes: Open University Press

Smith, D. (1973) 'Women's perspective as a radical critique of sociology', *Sociological Inquiry*, 44

Smith, D. J. and Gray, J. (1985) *People and Police in London*, London: Gower

Spender, D. (1985) *Man Made Language*, London: Routledge

Spybey, T. (1998) 'Globalisation or imperialism', *Sociology Review*, Feb

Stark, R. and Bainbridge, W. (1985) *The Future of Religion: Secularisation, Revival and Cult Formation*, Berkeley: California University Press

Steinem, G. (1995) 'Words and Change', *Ms Magazine*, Sept/Oct

Steven, P. (2004) *The No-Nonsense Guide to Global Media*, London: Verso

Stinchcombe, A. (1963) 'Institutions of privacy in the determination of police administration', *American Journal of Sociology*, 69

Storr, M. (2002) 'Sociology and social movements: theories, analyses and ethical dilemmas', in P. Hamilton and K. Thompson (eds) *The Uses of Sociology*, Oxford: The Open University/Blackwell

Sutherland, E.H. (1940) 'White-collar criminality', *American Sociological Review*, 5, pp.1–12

Sutherland, E.M. and Cressey, D. (1966) *Principles of Criminology* (revised edn), Chicago: University of Chicago Press

Sutton, R.I. (1992) 'Feelings about a Disneyland visit: photography and the reconstruction of bygone emotions', *Journal of Management Enquiry*, 1, pp. 278–87

Swartz, J. (1975) 'Silent killers at work', *Crime and Social Justice*, 3, pp.15–20

Sykes, G.M. and Matza, D. (1962) 'Techniques of neutralization – a theory of delinquency', in M.E. Wolfgang *et al.* (eds) *The Sociology of Crime and Delinquency*, New York: Wiley

Tarling, R. (1988) *Police Work and Manpower Allocation*, Paper 47, London: Home Office

Taylor, I. (1999) *Crime in Context: A Critical Criminology of Market Societies*, Cambridge: Polity Press

Taylor, J., Walton, P. and Young, J. (1973) *The New Criminology*, London: Routledge

Taylor, S. (1990) 'Beyond Durkheim: sociology and suicide', *Social Studies Review*, November

Taylor-Gooby, P. (with Vic George) (1996) *Welfare Policy: Squaring the Welfare Circle*, Basingstoke: Macmillan

Thomas, W.I. and Znaniecki, F. (1918) *The Polish Peasant in Europe and America*, Chicago: University of Chicago Press

Thompson, D. (1996) *The End of Time: Faith and Fear in the Shadow of the Millennium*, London: Sinclair Stevenson

Thompson, G.F. (2000) 'Where do MNCs conduct their business activity and what are the consequences for national systems' in S. Quack, G. Morgan and R. Whitely (eds) *National Capitalisms, Global Competition and Economic Performance*, Amsterdam: John Benjamins

Thompson, I. (1986) *Sociology in Focus*: Religion. Harlow: Longman

Thornton, S. (1995) *Club Cultures: Music, media and subcultural capital*, Cambridge: Polity Press

Thrasher, F. (1927) *The Gang*, Chicago: University of Chicago Press

Timmons Roberts, J. and Hite, A. (2000) from *Modernisation to Globalization*, Oxford: Blackwell

Tizard, B. and Hughes, M. (1991) 'Reflections on young people learning', in G. Walford (ed.) *Doing Educational Research*, London: Routledge

Tonnies, F. (1957, originally 1887) *Community and Society: Gemeinschaft und Gesellschaft*, translated and edited by Charles P. Loomis, Detroit: The Michigan State University Press

Touraine, A. (1982) *The Voice and The Eye*, Cambridge: Cambridge University Press

Townsend, P. (1979) *Poverty in the United Kingdom*, Harmondsworth: Penguin

Troeltsch, E. (1931/1976) *The Social Teachings of the Christian Churches*, Chicago: University of Chicago Press

Turner, B. (1983) *Religion and Social Theory*, London: Sage

Turner, B.S. (1994) 'From regulation to risk', in B.S. Turner (ed.) *Orientalism, Postmodernism and Globalism*, London: Routledge

Urry, J. (1990) *The Tourist Gaze*, London: Sage

Valier, C. (2001) *Theories of Crime and Delinquency*, Harlow: Longman

Van der Gaag, N. (2004) *The No-Nonsense Guide to Women's Rights*, London: Verso

Vincent, J. (1995) *Inequality and Old Age*, London: UCL Press

Waddington, P.A.J., Stenson, K. and Don, D. (2004) 'In proportion – race, and police stop and search', *British Journal of Criminology*, 44(6)

Walby, S. (1986) *Patriarchy at Work*, Cambridge: Polity Press

Walby, S. (1990) *Theorizing Patriarchy*, Oxford: Blackwell

Walby, S. (1997) *Gender Transformations*, London: Routledge

Wallace, W. (1971) *The Logic of Science in Sociology*, Chicago: Aldine-Atherton

Wallerstein, E. (1979) *The Rise and Future Demise of the World Capitalist System: Concepts for Comparative Analysis from the Capitalist World-economy*, Cambridge: Cambridge University Press

Wallis, R. (1984) *The Elementary Forms of New Religious Life*, London: Routledge

Warner, R.S. (1993) 'Work in progress toward a new paradigm for the sociological study of religion in the United States', *American Journal of Sociology*, 98(5), pp.1044–93

Waters, M. (1995) *The Death of Class*, London: Sage

Watson, H. (1994) 'Women and the veil: personal responses to global process', in A. Ahmed and H. Donnan (eds) *Islam, Globalisation and Postmodernity*, London: Routledge

Webb, E., Campbell, D., Schwartz, R. and Sechrest, L. (1981) *Nonreactive Measures in the Social Sciences* (2nd edn), Boston: Houghton Mifflin

Weber, M. (1905/1958) *The Protestant Ethic and the Spirit of Capitalism*, London: Unwin

Weber, M. (1920/1963) *The Sociology of Religion*, Boston, MA: Beacon Press

Weber, M. (1947) *The Theory of Social and Economic Organisation*, New York: Free Press

West, C. and Zimmerman, D.H. (1991) 'Doing gender' in J. Larber and S.A. Farrell (eds) *The Social Construction of Gender*, London: Sage, pp.13–37

Westergaard, J. (1995) *Who Gets What: The hardening of class inequality in the late 20th century*, Cambridge: Polity Press

Westergaard, J. (1996) 'Class in Britain since 1979; facts, theories and ideologies', in D. Lee and B. Turner (eds) *Conflicts about Class: Debating Inequality in Later Industrialisation*, Harlow: Longman

Westwood, S. (1999) 'Representing gender', *Sociology Review*, September

Westwood, S. (2002) *Power and the Social*, London: Routledge

White, C. (2004) *The Middle Mind: Why Consumer Culture is Turning Us Into The Living Dead*, London: Penguin

Whyte, W.F. (1943) *Street Corner Society: The Social Structure of an Italian Slum*, Chicago: University of Chicago Press

Wilkins, L. (1964) *Social Deviance: Social Policy, Action and Research*, London: Tavistock

Wilkinson, H. (1994) *No Turning Back: Generations and the Genderquake*, London: Demos 1994

Wilkinson, H. and Mulgan, G. (1997) 'Freedom's children and the rise of generational politics' in G. Mulgan (ed.) *Life After Politics: New Thinking for the Twenty-first Century*, London: Fontana

Wilkinson, R. (1996) *Unhealthy Societies: The Afflictions of Inequality*, Routledge: London

Wilkinson, S. (1999) 'Focus groups: a feminist method', *Psychology of Women Quarterly*, 23, pp.221–44

Wikstrom, P.H. (1991) *Urban Crime, Criminals and Victims: the Swedish Experience in an Anglo-American Comparative Perspective*, New York: Springer-Verlag

Williams, W.M. (1956) *The Sociology of an English Village: Gosforth*, London: Routledge & Kegan Paul

Willis, P. (1977) *Learning to Labour: How Working-class Kids get Working-class Jobs*, Farnborough: Saxon House

Willott, S.A. and Griffin, C.E. (1996) 'Men, masculinity and the challenge of long-term unemployment', in M. Mac An Ghaill (ed.) (1996) *Understanding Masculinities: Social Relations and Cultural Arenas*, Buckingham: Open University Press

Wilson, B. (1982) *Religion in Sociological Perspective*, Oxford: Oxford University Press

Wilson, B.R. (1966) *Religion in a Secular Society*, London: B.A. Watts

Wilson, J.Q. and Kelling, G. (1982) 'Broken windows', *Atlantic Monthly*, March

Wilson, W.J. (1996) *When Work Disappears: The World of the New Urban Poor*, New York: Albert Knopf

Winlow, S. (2004) 'Masculinities and crime', *Criminal Justice Matters*, 55(18)

Woodhead, L. (2004) 'Feminism and the sociology of religion: from gender blindness to gendered difference', in R.K. Fenn (ed) *The Blackwell Companion to the Sociology of Religion*, London: Blackwell

Woodhead, L. and Heelas, P. (2000) *Religion in Modern Times: An Interpretive Anthology*, Oxford: Blackwell

Wright Mills, C. (1956) *The Power Elite*, Oxford: Oxford University Press

Young, J. (1971) *The Drug Takers*, London: Paladin

Young, J. (1986) 'The failure of criminology: the need for a radical realism', in J. Young and R. Mathews (eds) *Confronting Crime*, London: Sage

Young, J. (1999) *The Exclusive Society: Social Exclusion, Crime and Difference in Late Modernity*, London: Sage

Zweig, E. (1961) *The Worker in an Affluent Society*, London: Heinemann